# OXFORD COMMENTARIES ON INTERNATIONAL LAW

General Editors: *Professor Philip Alston*, Professor of International Law at New York University, and *Professor Vaughan Lowe*, Chichele Professor of Public International Law in the University of Oxford and Fellow of All Souls College, Oxford.

# Commentaries on Arms Control Treaties

## VOLUME I

# Commentaries on Arms Control Treaties

## VOLUME I

*The Convention on the Prohibition of the Use,*
*Stockpiling, Production, and Transfer of*
*Anti-Personnel Mines and on their Destruction*

STUART MASLEN

OXFORD

UNIVERSITY PRESS

# OXFORD

UNIVERSITY PRESS

Great Clarendon Street, Oxford OX2 6DP

Oxford University Press is a department of the University of Oxford.
It furthers the University's objective of excellence in research, scholarship,
and education by publishing worldwide in

Oxford   New York

Auckland   Bangkok   Buenos Aires   Cape Town   Chennai
Dar es Salaam   Delhi   Hong Kong   Istanbul   Karachi   Kolkata
Kuala Lumpur   Madrid   Melbourne   Mexico City   Mumbai   Nairobi
São Paulo   Shanghai   Taipei   Tokyo   Toronto

Oxford is a registered trade mark of Oxford University Press
in the UK and in certain other countries

Published in the United States
by Oxford University Press Inc., New York

British Library Cataloguing in Publication Data
Data available

Library of Congress Cataloging in Publication Data
Data available

ISBN 0-19-926977-7

1  3  5  7  9  10  8  6  4  2

Typeset by Newgen Imaging Systems (P) Ltd., Chennai, India
Printed in Great Britain
on acid-free paper by
Biddles Ltd., Guildford and King's Lynn

# *Preface*

## Background

On 18 September 1997, 89 States gathered in Oslo at a specially convened diplomatic conference[1] adopted a new instrument of international law, the Convention on the Prohibition of the Use, Stockpiling, Production and Transfer of Anti-Personnel Mines and on their Destruction. The Anti-Personnel Mine Ban Convention, as it is hereinafter referred to for the sake of brevity,[2] is, for a number of reasons, a remarkable achievement, not only for the States that negotiated it, but also for the International Campaign to Ban Landmines, a network of more than 1,000 non-governmental organizations (NGOs) worldwide, and the International Committee of the Red Cross (ICRC), both of which campaigned effectively for a total prohibition on anti-personnel mines.[3]

Indeed, such was the momentum that had been achieved by the summer of 1997, that rather than weakening the draft treaty that had been submitted to it as often occurs in these situations, the Oslo Diplomatic Conference strengthened the text in a number of ways, not least by requiring comprehensive clearance of emplaced anti-personnel mines within an initial deadline of 10 years[4] and promoting the provision of assistance to all mine victims.[5] The level of consultation and cooperation between States, NGOs, and the ICRC in the elaboration of the Convention is probably unprecedented in international law. It may be some time before its like is seen again.

The global campaign for the adoption of the Convention was swiftly followed by a determined push for its swift entry into force. More than 120 States had signed the Convention before the end of 1997, and the necessary level of ratifications or accessions (40) was secured by September 1998, with the result that the Anti-Personnel Mine Ban Convention entered into force as

---

[1] The Diplomatic Conference on an International Total Ban on Anti-Personnel Land Mines, held in Oslo, Norway, on 1–18 September 1997. It is hereinafter referred to as the Oslo Diplomatic Conference.

[2] The abbreviated form of the title used here is currently employed by the United Nations but has no formal legal status.

[3] Others, of course, played an important role in promoting the adoption of the Convention, not least the Secretary-General of the United Nations, and UN bodies such as the Office of the UN High Commissioner for Refugees (UNHCR) and the United Nations Children's Fund (UNICEF).

[4] See below the commentary on Article 5.  [5] See below the commentary on Article 6(3).

binding international law on 1 March 1999. By 2003, more than two-thirds of the world's States had become parties to it.[6]

Even many States outside the purview of the Convention—a number of major military powers have yet to accede to it—have endorsed the concept of a total prohibition of anti-personnel mines and some have destroyed part of their stockpiles of anti-personnel mines. Globally, production of anti-personnel mines appears to have slowed significantly, and trade has reduced to a trickle. A new humanitarian norm has been created that may one day become custom applicable to all.

## The Aim and Layout of the Commentary

A commentary is defined as: 'An expository treatise; a series of comments or annotations on a text'.[7] It is hoped that given the international attention paid to landmines,[8] and the Anti-Personnel Mine Ban Convention in particular, this 'expository treatise' will be not only well-founded in fact and law but also useful and usable. If, further, the commentary comes to be considered as authoritative, this will be thanks to the many experts who have willingly and generously contributed their time and their insights to its development. Where there are errors or omissions, however, these remain the author's sole responsibility.

The introduction to the commentary discusses the development and use of anti-personnel mines and their perceived military utility, and provides a historical overview of the legal regulation of the weapons and the negotiation of the Anti-Personnel Mine Ban Convention.

The commentary on the Convention itself addresses first its title and preamble and then, separately but in chronological order, each of its articles, with the respective commentary broken down into sub-paragraphs, where relevant. All paragraphs are numbered and accordingly cross-references, as well as the index at the end of the book, refer to paragraph, rather than page, numbering. In discussing the interpretation of a provision, the commentary follows the schematic hierarchy laid down in Article 31 of the 1969 Vienna Convention on the Law of Treaties, as discussed below.

The bibliography for the commentary is followed by the appendixes. The first appendix contains key provisions of international treaty law from the 1969

---

[6] Although States outside the Convention contain a majority of stockpiled anti-personnel mines as well as the world's population.

[7] *The Shorter Oxford English Dictionary*, 5th edn. on CD-ROM (Oxford: Oxford University Press).

[8] The term 'landmines' encompasses all mines, including anti-tank or anti-vehicle mines, although it is sometimes used loosely to refer only to anti-personnel mines.

Vienna Convention; subsequent appendixes include documentation relating to the Anti-Personnel Mine Ban Convention itself, including relevant United Nations General Assembly resolutions, various drafts of the Convention, and the proposals tabled formally at the Oslo Diplomatic Conference.

## The Principles of International Treaty Interpretation

The commentary bases its interpretation of the Convention on the basic principles of treaty law,[9] notably the 1969 Vienna Convention on the Law of Treaties.[10] General principles and methods for treaty interpretation are embodied in Articles 31 and 32 of the 1969 Vienna Convention.[11] The International Court of Justice (ICJ) has expressly affirmed that these provisions, which set out, respectively, the general rule and supplementary means of treaty interpretation, reflect customary law. Thus, 'a treaty must be interpreted in good faith in accordance with the ordinary meaning to be given to its terms in their context and in the light of its object and purpose. Interpretation must be based above all upon the text of the treaty. As a supplementary measure recourse may be had to means of interpretation such as the preparatory work of the treaty and the circumstances of its conclusion.'[12] By virtue of Article 31(3), any subsequent agreement or practice[13] relating to the treaty together with any relevant rules of international law must be considered together with the context.

S.M.

February 2004

---

[9] For a more detailed discussion of international treaty law see generally Aust, A., *Modern Treaty Law and Practice* (Cambridge: Cambridge University Press, 2000); de la Guardia, E., *Derecho de los tratados internacionales* (Buenos Aires: Abaco de Rodolfo Depalma, 1997); McNair, A., *Law of Treaties*, 2nd edn. (Oxford: Clarendon Press, 1961); Reuter, P., *Introduction au droit des traités*, 3rd edn. (Geneva: Publications de l'Institut Universitaire des Hautes Etudes Internationales—Genève 1995); and Sinclair, I., *The Vienna Convention on the Law of Treaties*, 2nd edn. (Manchester: Manchester University Press, 1984). [10] Hereinafter, referred to as the 1969 Vienna Convention.

[11] See Appendix 1 for the text of the relevant articles.

[12] *Territorial Dispute (Libyan Arab Jamahariya/Chad)* case, *ICJ Reports*, 1994, pp. 21–2.

[13] The International Law Commission has included, in a non-exhaustive list, the following acts as forms that State practice may take: 'treaties, decisions of international and national courts, national legislation, diplomatic correspondence, opinions of national legal advisers and the practice of international organisations'. Other categories could be policy statements, official manuals on legal questions, such as manuals of military law, executive decisions and practices, comments by governments on draft treaties produced by the International Law Commission, press releases, and resolutions relating to legal questions in the United Nations General Assembly. See Harris, D. J., *Cases and Materials on International Law*, 5th edn. (London: Sweet & Maxwell, 1998), 25–6, citing also Brownlie. As far as anti-personnel mines are concerned, State practice also includes instructions to armed forces and their behaviour with respect to the weapons.

# Donation of Royalties to Mine Victim Assistance

All the royalties from this book are being donated to *Standing Tall Australia* on behalf of mine survivors and other persons with disabilities. *Standing Tall Australia* (also known by its acronym, STAIRRSS) is an Australian non-governmental organization that provides financial and technical support to local organizations working in mine-affected countries and regions to promote the rehabilitation and socio-economic reintegration of all persons with disabilities into their communities.

For further information on *Standing Tall Australia* please contact the organization at the following address:

PO Box 98
Toowong
Queensland 4066
Australia

Tel: +61 7 3369 7735
Fax: +61 7 3367 1779
Email: bailey@icbl.org

# *Acknowledgements*

The success of the project to prepare a commentary of the Convention is owed first and foremost to the Canadian Department for Foreign Affairs and International Trade (DFAIT), which has supported it from the outset, both administratively and financially. The author would therefore like to express his thanks to Dr Dan Livermore, his successor as Canadian Ambassador for Mine Action, Ross Hynes, Shannon Smith, and all the members of DFAIT's Mine Action Team. Their continuous support does not of course mean that DFAIT necessarily endorses the views expressed herein. Research assistance for the project was carried out by Daniel Rietiker; his help is gratefully acknowledged. The author would also like to thank Professor Guy Goodwin-Gill and Jack Glattbach for their support to this project.

Many individuals have submitted information, answered questions, or commented on earlier drafts of the commentary, though this in no way reflects their agreement with the contents of this work. These include: David Atwood, Peter Balmer, Kerry Brinkert, Professor Lucius Caflisch, Deborah Chatsis, Dr Robin Coupland, Thomas Desch, Louise Doswald-Beck, Ambassador Michel Duclos, Paul Ellis, Brigadier-General Ed Fitch, Dr Juan Manuel Gómez-Robledo, Steve Goose, Peter Goosen, Mark Gwozdecky, Ambassador Thomas Hajnoczi, Dirk Roland Haupt, Danielle Haven, Peter Herby, Paul van den Ijssel, Lieutenant-Colonel Mike Kelly, Lieutenant-Commander Guy Killaby, Lieutenant-Colonel Jean LaPointe, Ambassador Steffen Kongstad, Robert Lawson, Ambassador Jean Lint, Bennie Lombard, Ralph Lysyshyn, Lieutenant-Colonel (ret.) John MacBride, Darach Macfhionnbhairr, Tom Markram, Eric Newsom, Gro Nystuen, Dr Bertie Ramcharan, Robert Sherman, Johanne Dorais-Slakmon, Dr Walter Schmid, Jacob Selebi, Don Sinclair, Jill Sinclair, Dr Cornelio Sommaruga, Alexander Verbeek, Susan Walker, and Captain T. G. Whiting. In addition, a number of individuals providing information for this commentary have requested anonymity; that the author is unable to thank them publicly in no way diminishes his gratitude to them.

# Contents

# Table of Cases

# Table of Treaties and UN Resolutions

## TREATIES

# GENERAL ASSEMBLY RESOLUTIONS

*See Appendix 2 for copies of selected General Assembly resolutions*

# INTRODUCTION

## The Development and Use of Anti-Personnel Mines

### The Origin of the Anti-Personnel Mine

0.1 The exact origin of the anti-personnel mine is the subject of debate. A 1998 publication, *The History of Landmines*, argues that modern landmines 'trace their lineage from non-explosive predecessors such as the spikes and stakes that were employed by ancient armies.'[1] Similarly, it is claimed that: 'The concept of mine warfare has been around for a very long time. More than 2,000 years ago, the Romans used the caltrop to stop enemy cavalry. Outnumbered forces have always turned to any means, from mines to poisoned water to scorched earth, to mitigate the advantage of superior forces.'[2] According to another commentator:

In the Middle Ages, the so-called 'mine' was a common feature of medieval siege warfare . . . The besieger removed as much earth as he could carry away from beneath some exposed corner of the fortifications, and shored up the hole with beams. He then filled the space between the beams with straw and brushwood, and set fire to it. When the supports were consumed, the wall crumbled downwards into the hole, and a breach was produced . . . Over time, gunpowder and explosives took the place of fire, but the essentially medieval technique was retained, and was used as recently as the First World War.[3]

0.2 The first-known explosive mine can be dated back to at least the eighteenth century, when a German military historian referred to the use of a *fladdermine* (literally, a flying mine). This consisted of a ceramic container with glass and metal fragments embedded in the clay containing two pounds of gunpowder, buried at a shallow depth in the glacis of a fortress and activated by the pressure of a footstep or disturbance of a low-strung wire.[4] Yet in April 2001, archaeologists in northern China reported the discovery of more than 20 ancient 'landmines' dating back more than 600 years.[5]

---

[1] Croll, M., *The History of Landmines* (Barnsley: Leo Cooper, 1998), p. ix; see also 1–8.

[2] Epstein, A., 'Mine Warfare', in United States Department of State, *Hidden Killers: The Global Problem with Uncleared Landmines: A Report on International Demining* (Washington: Bureau of Political-Military Affairs, Department of State Publication 10098, July 1993), 11.

[3] Cornish, P., *Anti-Personnel Mines, Controlling the Plague of 'Butterflies'* (London: Royal Institute for International Affairs, 1994), 18, citing Oman, C., *The Art of War in the Middle Ages, Volume One: 378–1278AD* (London: Greenhill, 1991), 133.

[4] Freiherr von Flemming, *The Perfect German Soldier*, 1726, cited by Croll, *The History of Landmines*, 10; see Kreuzfeld, U., in Dupuy, T. N. (ed.), *The International Military and Defence Encyclopaedia*, iv (London: Brassey's, 1993), 1757–8.

[5] '600-Year-Old Mines Unearthed in Inner Mongolia', *Xinhua Press Agency* (Hohhot, Mongolia, 11 Apr. 2001).

## The American Civil War

**0.3** It is claimed that a Russian engineer designed an anti-personnel fragmentation mine in 1855.[6] But modern explosive landmines, or 'torpedoes' as they were initially termed, are more often said to be the invention of the American Civil War.[7] In the spring of 1862, when commanding a garrison of 2,500 men at Yorktown, Virginia, Gabriel Rains, a Brigadier-General in the Confederate Army, ordered his troops to prepare artillery shells so that they could be exploded by pulling tripwires or by being stepped on. The first casualties of these early anti-personnel mines were reported on 4 May 1862; even some of the Confederate troops deemed the devices 'barbaric' and Rains's commanding officer forbade their further use, declaring them neither a 'proper nor effective method of war'.[8] Yet, despite concerns on both sides, use of the weapons continued and in 1864 at Fort McAllister, near Savannah, mines killed 12 men and wounded 80 others during the Union assault. It was following this battle that the commander of the Union Army, General William T. Sherman uttered his now famous dictum that the use of mines 'was not war, but murder'.[9]

## The 1914–1918 and 1939–1945 Wars

**0.4** Anti-personnel mines were not widely deployed on the battlefields of Europe during the 1914–18 war.[10] Tripwire-activated mines were reportedly laced within wire entanglements early in the war but they were often as dangerous to the side that had laid them as they were to the enemy and this use was quickly phased out.[11] However, a number of anti-personnel mines and booby-traps were laid in abandoned positions in anticipation of an enemy advance. These weapons were adapted from artillery shells, with specially designed fuses screwed into the bottom of the shell.[12]

---

[6] Association of Military-Political and Military-Historic Research 'The Position of Russia as Regards the Problem of Use of Anti-Personnel Mines Considering the Conferences in Brussels and Oslo' (Moscow, 1997), 5. It is further asserted that 'Russian troops used shrapnel mines . . . very similar to their modern successors' when defending Port Arthur in 1905 (ibid.).

[7] See generally Perry, M. F., *Infernal Machines: The Story of Confederate Submarine and Mine Warfare* (Baton Rouge, La.: Louisiana State University Press, 1985).

[8] Croll, *The History of Landmines*, 16.    [9] ibid. 18.

[10] Although, under Article 8 of the Armistice Agreement of 11 November 1918, Germany was required to hand over plans showing where any mines had been laid.

[11] School of Military Engineering, *The Work of the Royal Engineers in the European War 1914–19*, (Chatham: SME, 1924), 257.    [12] Croll, *The History of Landmines*, 26; see also 27–8.

**0.5** In contrast, in the 1939–1945 war anti-personnel and anti-tank mines were both used on a huge scale.[13] According to the United States (US) Defense Intelligence Agency, more than 300 million anti-tank mines were used during the war, including 220 million by the Soviet Union.[14] Landmines were a key factor during the battles at El Alamein[15] and Kursk,[16] among others.[17] Chinese records of their Japanese occupation place great stress on the role played by 'mines' in their resistance against the Japanese.[18] It is claimed that one German anti-personnel mine, the *Schrapnellmine 35* or S mine as it was later called, 'was probably the most feared device encountered by Allied troops in the war'.[19] Following the end of the war, demobilized soldiers introduced the term 'minefield' into everyday parlance, meaning a situation beset with problems.[20]

## The Post-1945 Period

**0.6** Anti-personnel mines were used widely in the wars in Korea and Vietnam, with landmines accounting for slightly less than 5 per cent of US troop casualties in Korea.[21] The Vietnam war saw the first widespread use of remotely delivered

---

[13] According to Rae McGrath, the first widespread use of anti-personnel mines on their own (distinct from anti-tank mines) was probably in the war between Finland and Russia. McGrath, R., *Landmine and Unexploded Ordnance: A Resource Book* (London: Pluto Press, 2000), 4.

[14] US Defense Intelligence Agency and US Army Foreign Science and Technology Center, 'Landmine Warfare: Trends and Projections (U)', DST-1160S-019-92 (Washington, Dec. 1992), sec. 2-1.

[15] For details of the use of mines in North Africa see for instance Ceva, L., 'The Influence of Mines and Minefields in the North African Campaign of 1940–1943', Paper presented to the Symposium on Material Remnants of the Second World War on Libyan Soil (Geneva, 28 Apr.–1 May 1981); Vines, A., 'The Crisis of Anti-Personnel Mines', in Cameron, M. A., Lawson, R. J., and Tomlin, B. W. (eds.), *To Walk Without Fear: The Global Movement to Ban Landmines* (Toronto: Oxford University Press, 1998), 119.

[16] See generally Healy, M., *Kursk 1943: The Tide Turns in the East* (London: Osprey Military, 1997).

[17] According to Croll, by the end of the war, the Germans had manufactured 16 different types of anti-tank mine, 10 different types of anti-personnel mine, and used many different types of improvised devices and captured mines. This included the development and incorporation of anti-handling devices, and the first use of an aerially delivered scatterable anti-personnel mine. Towards the end of the war, the Germans experimented with magnetic-influence, vibration-sensitive, radio-controlled and frequency-induction fuses.

[18] Although in most cases the term is incorrectly applied; the devices used by the Chinese resistance were more often booby-traps than landmines.

[19] Sloan, Lieutenant-Colonel C. E. E., *Mine Warfare on Land* (London: Brassey's, 1986), 36.

[20] Croll, *The History of Landmines*, 53.

[21] ibid. 97. As a result of experiences during the Korean war, in particular following human-wave attacks against United Nations positions, the United States developed the M18 Claymore directional fragmentation mine. When detonated, either by tripwire or by electric command wire, hundreds of steel ball bearings are expelled in a 60-degree arc; the lethal radius is around 50 metres.

or 'scatterable' mines by US forces seeking to stop the flow of men and material from North to South Vietnam through Laos and Cambodia.[22] Based on its experiences in Vietnam, the USA committed considerable resources to the development of anti-personnel mines that would self-destruct within a pre-set time (usually 4–48 hours).[23] It also developed landmines that could serve as chemical weapons, each mine containing a quantity of VX nerve gas.[24]

**0.7** Yet, while mine technology advanced rapidly, the typical use of landmines involved the manual emplacement of 'long-duration'[25] anti-personnel mines in internal armed conflicts by both government armed forces and armed opposition groups.[26] In Angola, Cambodia, Ethiopia, Mozambique, Nicaragua, Iraq, Somalia, Sudan, and many other war-torn nations, anti-personnel mines were widely used as part of military strategy or simply to terrorize civilians or control their movements. Proliferation was fuelled by low cost and ready availability, with average prices ranging from US$3–15 per mine.[27] And as the Soviet Union collapsed, bitter conflicts in the Caucasus and the former Yugoslavia, which included some of the world's leading landmine producers, saw widespread and often indiscriminate use of anti-personnel mines.

[22] Aerially delivered anti-personnel mines had a number of obvious advantages over their manually emplaced counterparts: they could be deployed rapidly, required little logistic support, and could be laid deep within enemy-held territory, causing disruption in troop movements and supply lines, all with minimal risk to the aircrews. But at the same time, they represented a substantial danger to advances by friendly forces unless equipped with an effective self-destructing or self-neutralizing mechanism. It is reported that between 1966 and 1968, the US Department of Defense procured more than 114 million anti-personnel mines for use in the Vietnam war. Cornish, *Anti-Personnel Mines*, 7.

[23] Following the difficulties encountered in clearing mines left over from the battles in North Africa in the 1939–45 war, a British report entitled 'Engineer Lessons from the North African Campaign' recommended the design of a new form of mine capable of 'self-destroying after a certain period to avoid the need for lifting'. Croll, *The History of Landmines*, 65.

[24] On 30 November 2000, the Department of Defense reported the successful destruction on Johnston Atoll in the Pacific of more than 13,000 landmines filled with VX gas. 'Chemical Weapons Destruction Complete on Johnston Atoll', Press Release No. 715-00, Office of the Assistant Secretary of Defense (Public Affairs) (Washington, 30 Nov. 2000).

[25] That is, mines not equipped with self-destruct or self-neutralization devices or a self-deactivation feature. Such mines are sometimes referred to as 'dumb' or 'persistent' mines. A self-destruct mechanism is, as the name suggests, an automatically functioning timing device incorporated into the mine that causes it to explode after a pre-set period of time; self-neutralization, on the other hand, uses an automatically functioning timing device to render the mine inert. Self-deactivation is not a device, but rather a process by which an essential component of the mine, usually the battery, exhausts itself in a predictable time.

[26] Although the increasingly widespread use of anti-personnel mines was not limited to armed forces and groups, for by the 1990s, civilians in many countries were laying mines for their own purposes.

[27] See e.g. UN Department for Humanitarian Affairs, 'Fact Sheet on Manufacturing and Trade' (New York, 1996). Hi-tech mines are, however, considerably more expensive.

## Current and Future Landmine Technology

**0.8** Landmines continue to develop in sophistication. Already in 1992, a US defense agency study had found that:

A massive infusion of technology in the 1970s and 1980s has drastically altered land-mine holdings the world over. The widespread introduction of scatterable landmines allows a much more dynamic and responsive placement of minefields. Improved fuzes can employ pressure and contact, and also magnetic, infrared, seismic/acoustic, command-detonated,[28] anti-disturbance, and anti-mine detector[29] technologies. Advances have also been made in landmine warhead designs, giving landmines more than sufficient lethality in smaller packages. As awesome and effective as landmines have become, the outlook is even more overwhelming. Micro-electronics are enabling the technical capabilities of landmines to be expanded. Brilliant sensors with target discrimination, two-way communication between the minefield and the employer, and mobile landmines are futuristic, but are actually in development.[30]

**0.9** It has also been asserted that, in the future, 'the role of the mine will be expanded to such an extent that its original form will be scarcely recognisable. No longer will the victim have to activate the mine physically; the mine will sense its target at considerable range—tank, helicopter, possibly even jet air-craft and satellite—and deploy a lethal warhead.'[31]

## The Military Utility of Anti-Personnel Mines

### Anti-Personnel Mines and Military Doctrine

*Introduction*

**0.10** Anti-personnel mines clearly have military utility.[32] Thus, a 1997 South African defence review suggested that 'anyone doubting the effectiveness of . . . an anti-personnel minefield, should try it sometime'.[33] Similarly,

---

[28] Command detonation in fact renders a device not a mine, since one of the key characteristics of a mine under international law is its victim activation.

[29] This has since been prohibited by international law, under Amended Protocol II to the Convention on Certain Conventional Weapons.

[30] US Defense Intelligence Agency and US Army Foreign Science and Technology Center, 'Landmine Warfare—Trends and Projections (U)', A Defense S&T Intelligence Study, DST-1160S-019-92 (Washington, Dec. 1992), p. xvii.                    [31] Croll, *The History of Landmines*, 143.

[32] As a Canadian defence research paper has noted: 'The fact that millions of anti-personnel mines are in the ground today attests to the military utility of landmines'. Roy, R. L., 'Tactical Impact of Removing Antipersonnel Landmines', Research Note RN 0005, Department of National Defence (Kingston, Canada, Nov. 2000), p. iii.

[33] Department of Defense, Landmines in the Department of Defense, South African National Defence Forces, Logistical Division, 20 May 1997, cited in International Campaign to Ban Landmines,

an independent study of the military utility of anti-personnel mines conducted in the mid-1990s records that 'it is extremely difficult to counter the claim that anti-tank mines and anti-personnel mines have a military utility'.[34] Further, it has been said that:

Landmines are subtle and much misunderstood weapons. Traditionally they are a means of transforming the terrain to the defender's advantage, rather than providing a definitive barrier. They can inflict casualties but need to be covered by fire. They shape the attacker's posture, but do not define the outcome of battle. They provide economies in defence while imposing attrition on the attacker. They are laid without relish and contemplated with fear. They are simple to lay but remarkably difficult to remove. They are not activated unless an attacker advances but they do not recognise ceasefires. The employment of mines is complex and synergistic.[35]

**0.11** Indeed, mine warfare has been an element in military doctrine in many of the world's armed forces, especially at the operational[36] and tactical[37] level, for several decades.[38] Thus, for example, concerned by moves towards the national and international prohibition of anti-personnel mines, leading members of the US military wrote to the chairman of the Armed Services Committee in July 1997, declaring that:

Landmines are a 'combat multiplier' for US land forces, especially since the dramatic reduction of the force structure. Self-destructing landmines greatly enhance the ability to shape the battlefield, protect unit flanks, and maximize the effects of other weapons

---

*Landmine Monitor Report 1999: Toward a Mine-Free World* (Washington: Human Rights Watch, Apr. 1999), 783.

[34] Smith, Dr C. (ed.), *The Military Utility of Landmines . . . ?*, North–South Defence and Security Programme, Centre for Defence Studies, King's College, University of London (June 1996), 98.

[35] See Croll, *The History of Landmines*, p. x; see also *Anti-Personnel Landmines—Friend or Foe?* (Geneva: International Committee of the Red Cross, Mar. 1996), 37–8 and 40–1.

[36] 'The level of war at which campaigns and major operations are planned, conducted, and sustained to accomplish strategic objectives within theatres or areas of operations', US Department of Defense, Joint Chiefs of Staff, *Dictionary of Military Terms* (London: Greenhill Books, 1999), 278.

[37] 'The level of war at which battles and engagements are planned and executed to accomplish military objectives assigned to tactical units or task forces', ibid. 374.

[38] Thus, for instance, an Australian government document from 1993 stated that: 'Anti-Personnel mines represent a significant tactical capability that has had a well-established place in . . . Australian Defence Force plans for the conduct of military operations. Finding alternatives will involve a costly research and development effort. As alternative technology does not exist and is some years away, the ADF for this period could face an increased risk of casualties, especially if deployed overseas, and a potentially reduced capacity for coalition operations in certain circumstances.' Department of Foreign Affairs and Trade, Conventional and Nuclear Disarmament Section, International Security Division, 'National Interest Analysis: Convention on the Prohibition of the Use, Stockpiling, Production and Transfer of Anti-Personnel Mines and on their Destruction', tabled on 26 May 1998, available at: www.austlii.edu.au/au/other/dfat/nia/1998/1998019n.html.

systems. Self-destructing landmines are particularly important to the protection of early entry and light forces, which must be prepared to fight outnumbered during the initial stages of a deployment.[39]

## *The Operational Use of Anti-Personnel Mines*

**0.12** The situation most usually cited as the justification for the continued possession and use of anti-personnel mines is the case of those countries that, by reason of geography, are forced to defend long borders against potential aggressors. Thus, for example, in the 1991–2 Gulf war, the Iraqis laid several million mines to impede the coalition advance, most in well-organized fields that were often fenced. In accordance with standard military doctrine, the minefields were covered with fire and the overall defence was developed in considerable depth, although they were probably not sufficiently wide.[40] In fact, the minefields were breached by Coalition forces in only about two hours.[41]

**0.13** Other experiences cast doubt on the effectiveness of barrier minefields. In 1988, South Africa scrapped plans to build a 30 km-long minefield along Namibia's northern border, in part because it determined that such a barrier would only delay any potential invasion by around half an hour.[42] Further, a study of the use of anti-personnel mines in conflicts in southern Africa found 'few, if any, examples where anti-personnel mines have provided significant or lasting military advantages. In Mozambique, during the 1977–92 war Renamo quickly breached government minefields. In Angola, government mine belts around the main towns did not stop UNITA from capturing several of them. In the 1960s and 1970s, saboteurs simply shovelled their way across the minefield protecting the Kariba power station in Rhodesia, did their damage and left.'[43] According to a Royal Engineer who served during the Falklands conflict: 'minefields should not be too big a hindrance to the advance. Mines are

---

[39] Letter from the US Joint Chiefs of Staff to the Chairman of the Senate Armed Services Committee, 10 July 1997.                                    [40] Croll, *The History of Landmines*, 118.

[41] US Army, Office of the Chief of Staff, *Certain Victory: United States Army in the Gulf War*, Desert Storm Study Project (US Army, 1993), 232, cited in *Anti-Personnel Landmines—Friend or Foe?*, 41. Croll alleges that barrier minefields still have a role to play in defence arguing that 'mines, even in Kuwait, added to the strain of war—additional fear was created, movement was inhibited, and extra matériel, training and coordination were required. Although ultimately peripheral to the Gulf war, barrier minefields were the only means of enhancing defence available to the Iraqis' (Croll, *The History of Landmines*, 121). It has been remarked that the mining of beaches by the Iraqi forces did prevent an amphibious assault by US Marines. Gard, R., 'The Military Utility of Anti-Personnel Mines', in Cameron *et al.*, *To Walk without Fear*, 142.

[42] *Still Killing: Landmines in Southern Africa*, Human Rights Watch (USA, 1997), 110. Vines, A., 'The Crisis of Anti-Personnel Mines', in Cameron *et al.*, *To Walk without Fear*, 127.

[43] *Anti-Personnel Landmines—Friend or Foe?*, 30.

terrifying things but their aim is to demoralise rather than hinder . . . You need thousands of them to stop an advance.'[44] Thus, the long-term effectiveness of a large permanent barrier minefield is dubious against a competent adversary.

### The Tactical Use of Anti-Personnel Mines

0.14 When used as a temporary barrier or fixing device, landmines have a unique psychological impact. When crossing a field made hazardous by conventional means such as artillery or automatic-weapons fire, soldiers feel pressured to advance as rapidly as possible, in order to minimize their exposure time. But when crossing a minefield, exposure time is of little relevance. The hazard lies in taking the next step, regardless of whether that step is slow or fast. Thus, mines create a unique psychological pressure on the advancing troops to not take another step—that is, to freeze in place. According to a South African landmine expert, tactical uses of anti-personnel mines include: surveillance/early warning; delaying/canalizing enemy forces on foot; delaying/canalizing mobile/mechanized enemy forces (protection of anti-tank mines/minefields); protection of bases and installations; and demoralizing the enemy and overloading his support systems.[45] Similarly, in 1998, the Director of Military Engineering of the Canadian armed forces set out seven principal functions for anti-personnel mines: to provide early warning; to protect anti-tank mines; to delay or canalize enemy forces; to provide economy of force in close terrain; to inflict casualties on enemy personnel; to deny use of terrain; and to provide close protection of defenders.[46]

## Assessments of the Effectiveness of Anti-Personnel Mines

0.15 A number of studies, especially in the 1990s, have reviewed the specific effectiveness of anti-personnel mines (as opposed to other landmines or landmines in general). In 1994, the Office of the US Secretary of Defense commissioned an independent research organization, the Institute for Defense Analyses (IDA), to conduct a study of the military utility of anti-personnel mines in high-intensity mechanized warfare. Robert Gard, a retired US army

---

[44] Cited in McManners, Captain H., *Falklands Commando* (London: William Kimber, 1984), 220.

[45] Rossouw, Colonel A. J., 'Rethinking Military Doctrine: Making War without Anti-Personnel Landmines', unpublished paper, undated, 4.

[46] Colonel (now Brigadier-General) E. Fitch, Presentation to the ICRC Seminar on the Humanitarian Impact and Military Utility of Anti-Personnel Mines (Budapest, 26–8 March 1998). See also Hewish, M., and Pengelley, R., 'In Search of a Successor to the Anti-Personnel Landmine, Non-lethal Weapons, Precision Weapons and Close Surveillance', *Jane's International Defense Review* (Mar. 1998), 30; Faulkner, F., 'Anti-Personnel Landmines: A Necessary Evil?' *International Relations*, 13/4 (Apr. 1997), 42–5.

general supporting a comprehensive prohibition of anti-personnel mines, concedes that 'one can support different positions by citing various sections of the IDA study', but affirms that the study's principal conclusion is that anti-personnel mines have only a 'quite modest' utility.[47] 'While anti-personnel mines are judged to be useful in static defensive situations, the study concludes that they are of marginal utility in a defence that also employs tactical offensive operations . . . The study determined that the use of anti-personnel mines by both sides during US offensive operations would probably yield a "*negative* net military utility" for US forces.'[48]

0.16 A subsequent study was requested by the Chairman of the US Joint Chiefs of Staff, General Shalikashvili, and conducted in April 1996 by an independent non-profit organization, the Dupuy Institute.[49] Following additional analysis, the President of the Institute, a recently retired US Major General, wrote a memorandum to General Shalikashvili on 2 January 1997 in which he concluded that 'our historical research, when coupled with probable future engagements, indicates that a total ban on this [anti-personnel] type of mine, if eventually adhered to by most nations, will only benefit U.S. ground forces in the long run'. On the basis of the study, it was recommended 'that the United States support a total ban on anti-personnel mines'.[50]

0.17 Humanitarian organizations have also commissioned research into the military utility of anti-personnel mines. In March 1996, the International Committee of the Red Cross (ICRC) published a study of the military use and effectiveness of anti-personnel mines entitled *Anti-Personnel Landmines—Friend or Foe?*[51] The study looked at the use of anti-personnel mines in 26 conflicts since 1940 and found that few instances could be cited where use had been consistent with international law and that, even when used on a massive scale, anti-personnel mines had at best a marginal tactical value under certain specific but demanding conditions. The study conclusions, which were drafted by ten military experts from eight countries, declare *inter alia*, that 'the limited military utility of anti-personnel mines is far outweighed by the appalling humanitarian consequences of their use in actual conflicts. On this basis, their

[47] Gard, 'The Military Utility of Anti-Personnel Mines', 140.

[48] ibid. 140–1 (emphasis in original), citing Institute for Defense Analyses, 'The Military Utility of Landmines: Implications for Arms Control', Doc. D–1559 (Washington, June 1994), p. iv.

[49] Dupuy Institute, 'Military Consequences of Landmine Restrictions' (Washington, Apr. 1996). See Gard, 'The Military Utility of Anti-Personnel Mines', 141.

[50] Krawciv, N., 'Banning of Antipersonnel Mines', Memorandum (2 Jan. 1997), cited in Gard, 'The Military Utility of Anti-Personnel Mines', 141.

[51] *Anti-Personnel Landmines—Friend or Foe?*

prohibition and elimination should be pursued as a matter of utmost urgency by governments and the entire international community.'[52]

0.18 Anti-personnel mines have been widely used in internal armed conflicts, typically in violation of international law and legal norms. Thus, 'if anti-personnel mines have a debatable utility when used in tandem with anti-tank mines, they really come into their own when used in low intensity conflicts. In Afghanistan, Viet Nam, Sri Lanka, El Salvador and throughout Africa the anti-personnel mine had a devastating impact upon both soldiers and civilians mixed up in low intensity conflicts. Anti-personnel mines laid by irregular forces can be very valuable as a way of affecting morale and terrorising civilians in the battle for hearts and minds.'[53] The use of landmines by the African National Congress (ANC) during its struggle against the apartheid regime in South Africa was specifically criticized by the Truth and Reconciliation Commission for being indiscriminate in its effects.[54]

0.19 It has been remarked that although anti-personnel mines are low cost their effectiveness is also low while their humanitarian cost is high.[55] This applies particularly to long-duration mines. None the less, debate as to the present and future utility of anti-personnel mines will probably persist as a number of States outside the Convention remain convinced by their military utility.[56]

---

[52] See Maresca, L., and Maslen, S. (eds.), *The Banning of Anti-Personnel Landmines: The Work of the International Committee of the Red Cross 1955–1999* (Cambridge: Cambridge University Press, 2000), 415ff.          [53] Smith, *The Military Utility of Landmines . . . ?*, 101.

[54] See e.g. 'Apartheid Indictment finds Fault on all Sides', CNN (Pretoria, 29 Oct. 1998), available at: www.cnn.com/WORLD/africa/9810/29/truth.commission.03/. The ANC responded with a claim that 'It was out of this consideration to minimise the loss of civilian lives that the ANC discontinued the use of land mines, after it made an assessment that this form of warfare was, according to its own principled humanitarian norms, leading to an unacceptable loss of civilian lives'. Submission of the African National Congress to the Truth and Reconciliation Commission in Reply to the Section 30 (2) of Act 34 of 1996 on the TRC 'Findings on the African National Congress' (Oct. 1998).

[55] Fitch, Presentation to the ICRC Seminar. Colonel (now Brigadier-General) Fitch noted, however, that anti-tank mines have the reverse relationship to anti-personnel mines: high military utility and low humanitarian effect.

[56] The 1992 US defense agency study referred to above found that: 'New technologies boost the effectiveness of landmines, simplify laying minefields, and lower logistical burdens . . . Even with relatively costly new technologies, landmines are an affordable weapon for the entire range of military organisations, from terrorist groups to large, well-equipped armies. Landmines reduce the number of military personnel needed to defend a given area. They are ideal autonomous harassment devices. Landmine warfare will continue to be a significant element in armed conflicts at all levels of intensity well into the foreseeable future. Landmines remain a problem beyond the end of an armed conflict.' US Defense Intelligence Agency and US Army Foreign Science and Technology Center, *Landmine Warfare—Trends and Projections (U)*, sec. 5-1. Similarly, Mike Croll suggests that: 'Technological, economic and social factors combine to ensure that not only will mines be used in the future, but that they will be used in increasing numbers . . . The ability of mines rapidly to deny land and destroy the enemy with limited manpower in a cost-effective manner will be critical to defensive success.' Croll, *The History of Landmines*, 143.

The North Atlantic Treaty Organization (NATO), for instance, is said to continue actively to study the utility of anti-personnel mines.[57] On 30 September 2002, the US General Accounting Office (GAO), the investigative arm of Congress, published a study entitled 'Military Operations: Information on US Use of Land Mines in the Persian Gulf War'. The study found that concerns about landmines, including fear of fratricide and loss of battlefield mobility, led to the reluctance of some US commanders to use mines in areas that US and allied forces might have to traverse. Six per cent of total US casualties (killed and injured) in the Gulf war were the result of mines.[58]

**0.20** In tandem with ongoing study of the utility of landmines is the search for more humane alternatives to anti-personnel mines. In 1994, the United Nations (UN) General Assembly adopted resolution 49/75D, which encouraged 'further international efforts to seek solutions to the problems caused by anti-personnel land-mines, with a view to their eventual elimination'.[59] The sixth preambular paragraph to the resolution recognized 'that States can move most effectively towards the goal of the eventual elimination of anti-personnel land-mines as viable and humane alternatives are developed'.

**0.21** There are a number of doctrinal and weapons alternatives to using anti-personnel mines in combat,[60] although it is widely agreed by military experts that no other single weapon or tactic can fulfil as successfully the military tasks performed by anti-personnel mines.[61] Thus, for example, the United Kingdom

---

[57] Thus, in 2001, the US Commission on Engineering and Technical Systems (CETS) reported that 'several countries are participating in a North Atlantic Treaty Organization (NATO) study on the consequences of the [anti-personnel mine] ban and possible technological alternatives that do not have the negative effects of [anti-personnel mines]'. CETS (Commission on Engineering and Technical Systems), *Alternative Technologies to Replace Antipersonnel Landmines* (Washington: National Academies Press, 2001), 115 (Appendix F).

[58] General Accounting Office, 'Military Operations: Information on U.S. Use of Land Mines in the Persian Gulf War', Report No. GAO-02-1003 (Washington, 30 Sept. 2002), available at: www. access.gpo.gov/su_docs/aces/aces160.shtml.

[59] Operative paragraph 6, UN General Assembly resolution 49/75D, adopted by consensus on 15 Dec. 1994.

[60] For a review of some of the alternatives available or being developed see generally Roussouw, 'Rethinking Military Doctrine'; Roy, 'Tactical Impact of Removing Antipersonnel Landmines', Gard Jr., R. G., 'Alternatives to Anti-Personnel Mines', Vietnam Veterans Monograph Series, 1/1 (Washington, spring 1999), and esp. 22–3.

[61] According to Brigadier-General Ed Fitch, the utility of the anti-personnel mine can be reduced to two fundamental military tasks: area defence (through surveillance and early warning) and the infliction of casualties (and therefore the protection of anti-tank mines). No other single weapon can achieve these two activities, although there are a plethora of surveillance devices that will alert defenders to the presence of the enemy without their knowledge. Interview with the author in Ottawa, 19 Aug. 2002. See also Sage, Lieutenant-Colonel J., 'Anti-Personnel Mines, their Military Utility and Humanitarian Considerations', *Journal of the Royal Military College of Science* (UK, July 1995).

(UK) Ministry of Defence believes that in renouncing anti-personnel mines it has lost an operational capability, but it has accepted to do so because of the humanitarian imperative.[62] According to a Canadian military research adviser: 'Specific attempts to completely replace the anti-personnel mine have proven extremely difficult and costly to implement'.[63]

**0.22** The use of 'Claymore-type' directional fragmentation devices, lawful under the Anti-Personnel Mine Ban Convention when command detonated, 'may provide a cost-effective and legitimate solution to the replacement of anti-personnel mines'.[64] Indeed, a number of States Parties to the Convention have already selected these devices as alternatives.[65] Other weapons and tactics include the better use of early warning and surveillance techniques and equipment, such as the 'anti-personnel obstacles system' under development by the Japan Defense Agency.[66] However, the effectiveness of these concepts is, so far, unproven.

**0.23** Starting in its financial year 1999, and following its decision not to join initially the Anti-Personnel Mine Ban Convention, the USA has been actively engaged in pursuing research into alternatives to anti-personnel mines. This pursuit has followed three tracks: Track 1 focusing on a replacement for so-called 'dumb' mines, the NSD-A (Non-Self-Destructing antipersonnel mine Alternative); Track 2 aiming to develop a Self-Healing Minefield; and Track 3 looking at an alternative to the USA's mixed systems.[67] The future of the research programme is likely to be determined by the decisions taken by the landmine policy review announced by the Bush administration in June 2001, but not yet completed.

**0.24** In sum, a Canadian research adviser concluded that:

There are several existing and many potential systems that can perform most of the functions of anti-personnel mines. Continuous unattended electronic or electro-optical sensors can improve the detection from hidden approaches and data links can

---

[62] Information provided by Peter Balmer, UK Ministry of Defence (London, 3 June 2002).

[63] Roy, 'Tactical Impact of Removing Antipersonnel Landmines', p. iii.    [64] ibid.

[65] Both Austria and Norway, for instance, opted to rely on these weapons, with the Dutch military deciding to use them to protect observation posts and installations and to deploy anti-tank mines, including scatterable mines, to provide obstacles. Smith, *The Military Utility of Landmines . . . ?*, 99. Using JANUS war game scenarios, Canada found that a field of remotely detonated Claymores up to 500 m ahead of the defended position and/or using 40 mm Automatic Grenade Launchers, along with wire obstacles, provide a capability that compensates for the loss of anti-personnel mines against a mass assault. Roy, 'Tactical Impact of Removing Antipersonnel Landmines', p. iii. Australia was said to be developing a similar system to the command-detonated Claymore. CETS, *Alternative Technologies to Replace Antipersonnel Landmines*, 115 (appendix F).    [66] ibid.

[67] See International Campaign to Ban Landmines, *Landmine Monitor Report 2002: Toward a Mine-Free World* (Washington: Human Rights Watch, Aug. 2002), 703.

trigger immediate response by long-range direct and indirect fire weapons, achieving both greater effectiveness and far fewer indiscriminate casualties than anti-personnel mines. Improved barbed-wire entanglements covered by coordinated use of Automated Grenade Launchers, Claymores, machine guns and aimed fires can provide close protection, exert an equivalent deterrence effect on enemy troops and help delay hand-breaching by dismounted troops. However, there is the possibility of greater ammunition consumption levels, increased unit footprint, and greater manpower and logistics requirements that result from these anti-personnel mine alternatives.[68]

There is also the possibility of greater friendly force losses, and greater post-combat risk to civilians due to the large amounts of unexploded ordnance that would result from using much larger numbers of less efficient instant-acting munitions to replace anti-personnel mines.

## A Historical Overview of the Legal Regulation of Anti-Personnel Mines

### Historical Background

**0.25**  Despite widespread use of anti-personnel mines in the 1939–45 war, the 1949 Geneva Conventions only addressed issues of mine clearance, prohibiting expressly the forcible use of prisoners of war for such purposes.[69] In 1955, the ICRC published a set of *Draft Rules for the Protection of the Civilian Population from the Dangers of Indiscriminate Warfare*.[70] The rules provided *inter alia* that:

The use of so-called delay-action projectiles is only authorized when their effects are limited to the objective itself.

Weapons capable of causing serious damage shall, so far as possible, be equipped with a safety device which renders them harmless when they can no longer be directed with precision against a military objective.[71]

---

[68]  Roy, 'Tactical Impact of Removing Antipersonnel Landmines', p. iv.

[69]  Thus, Article 52 of the Geneva Convention Relative to the Treatment of Prisoners of War (Geneva Convention III) provides in part that: 'Unless he be a volunteer, no prisoner of war may be employed on labour which is of an unhealthy or dangerous nature . . . The removal of mines or similar devices shall be considered as dangerous labour.' It is otherwise asserted, however, that the use of prisoners of war for such activities was already implicitly prohibited under the 1929 Geneva Convention. See Pictet, J. S. (ed.), *Commentary, III Geneva Convention Relative to the Treatment of Prisoners of War* (Geneva: International Committee of the Red Cross, 1960), 277–8.

[70]  *Draft Rules for the Protection of the Civilian Population from the Dangers of Indiscriminate Warfare* (Geneva: ICRC, June 1955), 86–7.          [71]  Articles 10(4) and 11, respectively.

**0.26**  But States were reluctant to transform the draft rules into binding international law and the issue dropped down the international agenda until the 1968 International Conference for Human Rights, which adopted a resolution calling for a study of 'the need for additional humanitarian international conventions or for possible revision of existing Conventions to ensure the better protection of civilians, prisoners and combatants in all armed conflicts and the prohibition and limitation of the use of certain methods and means of warfare'.[72] Most of the attention, however, focused on napalm, which was being extensively deployed by the USA in Vietnam.[73]

**0.27**  In the mid-1970s, a series of three meetings convened by the ICRC to discuss a variety of conventional weapons,[74] identified landmines (in general) as a means of warfare deserving particular legal regulation. At the last of these meetings, held in Lugano, Switzerland, in 1976, France, the Netherlands, and the UK introduced a written proposal for the regulation of landmines and booby-traps. The proposal contained draft provisions requiring that records of minefields containing more than 20 mines be made public upon the cessation of hostilities, that remotely delivered mines should either be equipped with a neutralizing mechanism or the area in which they were delivered be marked, and that the civilian population be ensured of a minimum level of protection against the impact of mines.[75]

## The Negotiation of the 1980 Convention on Certain Conventional Weapons and Protocol II

**0.28**  It had been hoped that the use of certain conventional weapons would be specifically restricted by the Protocol Additional to the Geneva Conventions of 12 August 1949, and Relating to the Protection of Victims of International

---

[72]  Operative Paragraph 1, Resolution XXIII, 'Human rights in armed conflicts' of 12 May 1968 of the International Conference on Human Rights, Tehran, 22 Apr. to 13 May 1968, UN Doc. A/CONF.32/41.

[73]  See Shaw, M., 'The United Nations Convention on Prohibitions or Restrictions on the Use of Certain Conventional Weapons, 1981', *Review of International Studies,* 9/2 (1983), 110.

[74]  Participants considered the possible legal regulation of a number of categories of weapons, including incendiary weapons, small calibre projectiles, blast and fragmentation weapons, and delayed action and treacherous weapons.

[75]  Working Paper submitted by the Experts of France, the Netherlands and the UK, 'Land Mines and Booby-Traps and Proposals for the Regulation of Their Use', Annex A2 (COLU/203) in ICRC, *Report on the Conference of Government Experts on the Use of Certain Conventional Weapons. Second Session (Lugano, 28 January–26 February 1976)* (Geneva: ICRC, 1976), 167–71. See Rogers, Lieutenant-Colonel A. P. V., 'A Commentary on the Protocol on Prohibitions or Restrictions on the Use of Mines, Booby-Traps and Other Devices', *Military Law and Law of War Review,* 26 (1987), 187.

Armed Conflicts (Protocol I)[76] and Protocol Additional to the Geneva Conventions of 12 August 1949, and Relating to the Protection of Victims of Non-International Armed Conflicts (Protocol II).[77] But final agreement on the regulation of three categories of conventional weapons—fragments not detectable by X-ray; landmines and booby-traps; and incendiary weapons—remained elusive, and on 9 June 1977 the Diplomatic Conference that adopted the two protocols[78] decided to recommend to the UN General Assembly that a separate conference be convened under UN auspices to negotiate a distinct legal instrument.[79]

**0.29** Subsequently, and in accordance with successive General Assembly resolutions,[80] preparatory conferences involving some 85 States were held in August–September 1978 and March–April 1979. The United Nations Conference on Prohibitions or Restrictions of Use of Certain Conventional Weapons which may be Deemed to be Excessively Injurious or to have Indiscriminate Effects met for two sessions in Geneva: from 10 to 28 September 1979,[81] and from 15 September to 10 October 1980.[82] Although controls on the use of landmines, especially remotely delivered mines, were discussed at length, the most controversial issue continued to be the regulation of incendiary weapons, particularly napalm. A last-minute compromise enabled the adoption of the Convention on Certain Conventional Weapons (CCW),[83]

---

[76] Hereinafter, 1977 Additional Protocol I.      [77] Hereinafter, 1977 Additional Protocol II.

[78] The Diplomatic Conference on the Reaffirmation and Development of International Humanitarian Law Applicable in Armed Conflicts was convened by the Swiss government between 1974 and 1977. See e.g. Roberts, A. and Guelff, R., *Documents on the Laws of War*, 3rd edn. (Oxford: Clarendon Press, 2001), 419.

[79] A number of delegations had pushed hard for the establishment of a permanent international weaponry review committee under 1977 Additional Protocol I, but this proposal too, was voted down, albeit only by a narrow margin. Fenrick, W. J., 'The Conventional Weapons Convention: A Modest but Useful Treaty', *International Review of the Red Cross*, no. 279 (Nov.–Dec. 1990), 501.

[80] UN General Assembly Resolutions 32/152 of 19 Dec. 1977 and 33/70 of 14 Dec. 1978. Resolution 32/152, which was adopted by 115 votes to 0, with 21 abstentions, including, once again, France, the UK, the USA and the USSR, called for a UN Conference to be convened in 1979 with a preparatory conference to precede it 'with a view to reaching agreements on prohibitions or restrictions on the use of specific conventional weapons'.

[81] For a brief report on the first session of the conference see Szasz, P., 'The Conference on Excessively Injurious or Indiscriminate Weapons', *American Journal of International Law*, 74 (Jan. 1980), 212–15.

[82] See UN, 'Summary of Negotiations Leading to the Conclusion of the Convention on Prohibitions or Restrictions on the Use of Certain Conventional Weapons which may be Deemed to be Excessively Injurious or to have Indiscriminate Effects and of Subsequent Developments related to the Convention', UN Doc. CCW/CONF.I/GE/5 (6 May 1994), 5–18.

[83] The Convention on Prohibitions or Restrictions on the Use of Certain Conventional Weapons which may be Deemed to be Excessively Injurious or to have Indiscriminate Effects entered into force on 2 December 1983 in accordance with its Article 5.

and three annexed Protocols: Protocol on Non-Detectable Fragments (Protocol I); Protocol on Prohibitions or Restrictions on the Use of Mines, Booby-Traps and Other Devices (Protocol II); and Protocol on Prohibitions or Restrictions on the Use of Incendiary Weapons (Protocol III).

**0.30**  The structure of the Convention was an unusual one, comprising a *chapeau* Convention of ten Articles, to which were annexed the three Protocols. The idea, intended to allow flexibility in the future regulation of weapons, came from Mexico. At the end of the second preparatory conference, it had put forward an 'Outline of a General Treaty' whereby a series of optional protocol agreements would be annexed to an 'umbrella' agreement.[84] Following negotiations with a number of Western States, at the first session of the Conference proper, the Dutch and UK delegations jointly tabled a draft treaty reflecting this approach.[85]

**0.31**  In adhering to the Convention, States were obliged to accept at least two of the three annexed Protocols.[86] There had been concern that because of the relative redundancy of CCW Protocol I, which banned the use of a weapon no one believed in existence or even under development,[87] governments would be tempted to ratify just this Protocol so as to become party to the Convention.[88]

## The Negotiation of Amended Protocol II to the CCW

**0.32**  International reaction to the new instruments was subdued and few States chose to adhere to them. Most of the attention concentrated on the continuing, if restricted, legality of the use of incendiary weapons, or the need to address the use of fuel-air explosives.[89] As the decade drew towards a close, however, there were signs that the indiscriminate use of landmines was increasing, despite the adoption of Protocol II. Anti-personnel mines had become a significant, particular threat to life and limb in war-torn States, such as Afghanistan, Angola, and Cambodia. War surgeons working for the ICRC, for instance, found themselves confronted with large numbers of traumatic amputations

---

[84]  See e.g. Roach, 'Certain Conventional Weapons Convention', 13.      [85]  ibid.

[86]  Article 4(3), CCW. According to Levie, the USA had even proposed that adherence to *all* annexed Protocols should be mandatory. See Levie, H. S., 'Prohibitions and Restrictions on the Use of Conventional Weapons', *St John's Law Review*, 68 (summer 1994), 651–2.

[87]  'Any weapon the primary effect of which is to injure by fragments which in the human body escape detection by X-rays.' Many weapons, of course, have such secondary effects.

[88]  See e.g. Fenrick, W. J., 'The Law of Armed Conflict: The CUSHIE Weapons Treaty' *Canadian Defence Quarterly*, 11 (1981), 27; Fenrick, 'The Conventional Weapons Convention', 501.

[89]  See e.g. Wulff, T., *Barriers Against Weapons: Development of Weapons and Restrictions on their Use* (Stockholm: Swedish Red Cross, 1984), 51.

resulting from individuals stepping on blast anti-personnel mines.[90] This presented a specific challenge in how to close the stumps without provoking an infection; medical literature gave little guidance[91] and Western doctors were not skilled in mine injuries.

**0.33** In September 1991, Asia Watch, a division of Human Rights Watch, and Physicians for Human Rights jointly published *The Coward's War: Landmines in Cambodia*, a seminal work in the burgeoning non-governmental response to the mine threat.[92] At the same time, the two organizations called for a total ban on landmines.[93] Two months later, the Vietnam Veterans of America Foundation, based in Washington DC, and Medico International, based in Frankfurt, discussed a joint advocacy campaign to bring together non-governmental organizations (NGOs) in a coordinated effort to ban landmines.[94] In October 1992, the six NGOs that would form the steering committee of the future International Campaign to Ban Landmines—Handicap International, Human Rights Watch, Medico International, Mines Advisory Group, Physicians for Human Rights, and the Vietnam Veterans of America Foundation—sat down together in New York to plan a coordinated NGO campaign.

**0.34** On 9 February 1993, having previously expressed its desire, upon signature of the CCW, to seek to strengthen the provisions in the Convention relating to verification of compliance, France formally submitted a request to the Secretary-General of the UN to convene a Review Conference of the Convention, in accordance with its Article 8.[95] On 16 December 1993, the UN General Assembly formally welcomed the request, encouraged the establishment of a

---

[90] Coupland, R. M., 'Technical Aspects of War Wound Excision', *British Journal of Surgery*, 76 (July 1989), 663–7. Dr Robin Coupland was seconded by the British Red Cross Society to the International Committee of the Red Cross. In 1989, as a result of his experiences with Afghan and Cambodian war victims, he wrote a paper for the *British Journal of Surgery*, which discussed the appropriate treatment of mine injuries, notably through complete excision of foreign material and delayed primary closure of the wounds.

[91] Thus, in December 1991, in an edition of the *British Medical Journal*, Dr Coupland and Dr Adriaan Korver described the results of a study of 757 patients with anti-personnel mine injuries, noting that 'surprisingly little attention' had been paid to the subject in the medical literature. Coupland, R. M., and Korver, A., 'Injuries from Antipersonnel Mines: The Experience of the International Committee of the Red Cross', *British Medical Journal*, 303 (14 Dec. 1991), 1509–12.

[92] The Americas Watch division of Human Rights Watch had already in 1986 published a report on landmines in El Salvador and Nicaragua. It did not, however, call for a ban on the weapons at that time.

[93] See 'ICBL ban chronology', available at: www.icbl.org. Although not specified, it appears that this applied to all landmines, not merely anti-personnel mines.          [94] ibid.

[95] In February 1993, Handicap International passed on to the French Ministry of Foreign Affairs a letter from US Senator Patrick Leahy to the organization in which he encouraged it to persuade the French government to call for a review conference of the CCW. See Chabasse, P., 'The French Campaign', in Cameron *et al.*, *To Walk without Fear*, 61–2.

group of governmental experts to prepare the review conference, and called upon 'the maximum number of States' to attend.[96] Six days later, States Parties requested the Secretary-General to set up a group of governmental experts to consider among other things 'as a matter of priority' concrete proposals for amendments to Protocol II, and especially:

- strengthening restrictions on the use of anti-personnel mines and, in particular, those without neutralizing and self-destruction mechanisms;
- considering the establishment of a verification system for provisions of this Protocol;
- studying opportunities for broadening the scope of this Protocol to cover armed conflicts that are not of an international character.[97]

**0.35** The ICRC began to become more actively involved in the mines issue at the legal and political level, largely as a result of prompting from its recently created Medical Division. In April 1993, the organization convened the so-called Montreux Symposium, bringing together lawyers, mine clearance experts, surgeons, and campaigners to discuss the many facets of the landmine problem. NGOs had already issued a call for an outright ban on anti-personnel mines.[98] At the Symposium, however, the ICRC's policy was to call only for the incorporation of self-destruct mechanisms in anti-personnel mines[99] as a way to tackle what it would come to term the 'epidemic of mine injuries'.[100] The Symposium spurred a number of initiatives, notably the study of the socio-economic impact of landmines, conducted by the Vietnam Veterans of America Foundation,[101] and research by Human Rights Watch into global production and trade in the weapons.[102]

**0.36** At the beginning of 1994, the ICRC convened a meeting of military experts to discuss the military utility of anti-personnel mines. Although opinions were divided, it was acknowledged that anti-personnel mines could be harmful to one's own soldiers, but there was a general belief in their military utility and a marked reluctance to renounce their use before an alternative was available.

---

[96] UN General Assembly Resolution 48/79, operative paras. 5–7.

[97] See UN Doc. CCW/CONF.I/GE/4, 2–3.

[98] The NGO 'joint call to ban antipersonnel landmines', issued by the six NGOs making up the steering committee of the ICBL in October 1992, sought 'an international ban on the use, production, stockpiling and sale, transfer or export of antipersonnel mines'.

[99] Although ICRC President Sommaruga was believed to already personally favour a ban.

[100] See e.g. *The Worldwide Epidemic of Landmine Injuries: The ICRC's Health Oriented Approach* (Geneva: ICRC, 1995).

[101] Roberts, S. and Williams, J., *After the Guns Fall Silent: The Enduring Legacy of Landmines* (Washington: Vietnam Veterans of America Foundation, 1995).

[102] See e.g. Human Rights Watch and Physicians for Human Rights, *Landmines: A Deadly Legacy* (New York: Human Rights Watch, Oct. 1993).

**0.37** In accordance with General Assembly Resolution 48/79, the ICRC had been invited to participate as an observer in the Group of Governmental Experts convened to prepare the first Review Conference of the CCW. Just prior to the Group's first meeting, the ICRC called a press conference in Geneva to enable its President to set out the organization's position on the issues to be covered. Following considerable internal debate within the institution, on 24 February 1994, ICRC President, Cornelio Sommaruga, declared that 'from a humanitarian point of view', a 'worldwide ban on anti-personnel mines' was 'the only truly effective solution'.[103]

**0.38** Subsequently, certain UN bodies began to support the campaign against landmines, sometimes to the obvious irritation of certain States. The Office of the United Nations High Commissioner for Refugees (UNHCR), the United Nations Children's Fund, and the Secretary-General himself, all called for a total ban on anti-personnel mines. On 10 July 1994, the Chairman's Statement of the Group of seven meeting in Naples included a paragraph, which, *inter alia*, stated that the G7 assigned 'priority to the problems of anti-personnel landmines, including efforts to curb their indiscriminate use, halt their export, assist in their clearance worldwide'.[104] In September 1994, at the UN General Assembly, the US President, William Jefferson Clinton, called for the 'eventual elimination' of anti-personnel mines.[105] This call was endorsed in Resolution 49/75D, adopted without a vote on 15 December 1994.

**0.39** Yet, despite this bold call, progress in the review process of the Convention was slow and difficult,[106] largely because of the practice of taking all decisions by consensus.[107] In total, four meetings of the group of governmental

---

[103] See e.g. Maresca and Maslen, *The Banning of Anti-Personnel Landmines,* 264–5.

[104] Para. 7, Chairman's Statement, Naples G7 Summit (10 July 1994).

[105] The Assembly had already adopted a resolution the previous year by consensus, calling for a moratorium on the export of anti-personnel mines. This followed domestic legislation enacted by the United States in 1993, the Landmine Moratorium Act, which imposed a one-year ban on the sale, export, and transfer abroad of landmines. National Defense Authorization Act for Fiscal Year 1993, Pub. L. No. 102-484, sect. 1365.

[106] Major issues were whether non-detectable mines should be banned, whether both self-destruction and self-deactivation should be required, and what the duration and reliability requirements for self-destruction and self-deactivation should be. China initially insisted that it could accept a required limit on duration or a required minimum reliability, but not both—a position which would have rendered the restrictions meaningless. The final issue to be resolved was the length of the transition period to be permitted; the Western group favoured the shortest possible period, while China in particular held out for the longest possible period.

[107] In fact, the Preparatory Conference to the 1979–80 UN Weapons Conference had itself failed to reach agreement on the rules for decision-making. According to one expert: 'Decisions were reached on the basis of an unofficial, and undefined, consensus', although he notes that a number of delegations repeatedly asserted that voting would be possible. See Fenrick, W.J., 'The Conventional Weapons Convention: A Modest but Useful Treaty', *International Review of the Red Cross,* no. 279 (Nov.–Dec. 1990),

experts were necessary to prepare the Review Conference, which proved unable to report before the end of 1994 as had been hoped because of the problems in reaching agreement.[108] The first session of the Review Conference—originally intended to be its only session—was held in Vienna on 25 September to 13 October 1995.[109] As agreement on amendments to Protocol II proved impossible to achieve,[110] the Conference decided to continue its work at resumed sessions in Geneva on 15–19 January 1996 and on 22 April to 3 May 1996.[111] Finally, on 3 May 1996, after last-minute negotiations with Pakistan,[112] States Parties to the Convention adopted by consensus Amended Protocol II.[113] In accordance with its *chapeau* Article 2,[114] the Protocol entered into force on 3 December 1998, after 20 States had notified the depositary of their consent to be bound by it.

## The Negotiation of the Anti-Personnel Mine Ban Convention

### Background

**0.40**　Reaction by many States to the adoption of Amended Protocol II was quite negative,[115] as its provisions were widely considered to be overly complex

---

501; Fenrick, W. J., 'New Developments in the Law concerning the Use of Conventional Weapons in Armed Conflict', *Canadian Yearbook of International Law*, 19, 19 (1981), 238 n. 36. It is otherwise asserted that the US delegation believed that the relevant language in Article 8 of the CCW ('shall be adopted . . . in the same manner as this Convention and the annexed Protocols') meant by consensus 'and only by consensus'. Roach, 'Certain Conventional Weapons Convention', 43.

[108]　The group met from 28 Feb.–4 Mar. 1994, from 16–27 May 1994, from 8–19 Aug. 1994, and from 9–20 Jan. 1995. Altogether, 33 States Parties and 33 States non-parties to the Convention participated in the work of the Group. In addition to the ICRC, the UN was subsequently invited to attend the group of governmental experts as an observer. NGOs, however, were excluded, with China effectively imposing a veto on their participation.

[109]　Altogether representatives of 44 States Parties and 40 States non-parties to the Convention participated in the first session of the Review Conference.

[110]　Although the Review Conference successfully agreed to adopt Protocol IV banning the use of blinding laser weapons.

[111]　UN General Assembly Resolution 50/74, adopted on 12 Dec. 1995, called upon States Parties to 'intensify their efforts in order to conclude negotiations on a strengthened Protocol II'.

[112]　Pakistan opposed the extension of the scope of the protocol to cover internal armed conflicts on the basis that it encroached on its national sovereignty.

[113]　Protocol on Prohibitions or Restrictions on the Use of Mines, Booby-Traps and Other Devices as Amended on 3 May 1996 (Protocol II as amended on 3 May 1996), hereinafter, Amended Protocol II. The two versions of the Protocol continue to co-exist even though Protocol II as amended has formally entered into force and it remains open to States to ratify the 1980 Protocol, or the Amended Protocol II, or even both. See further Roberts, A. and Guelff, R.. *Documents on the Laws of War*, 3rd edn. (Oxford: Clarendon Press, 2001), 518.

[114]　See UN Doc. CCW/CONF.I/16 (Part I), 32.

[115]　Although China, the Russian Federation, and the USA have made positive statements about the Protocol on a number of occasions. In addition, the Swedish Ministry of Foreign Affairs declared

and insufficiently stringent to deal with the extent of the humanitarian crisis. The Protocol banned the use (and transfer) of 'undetectable' anti-personnel mines,[116] and remotely delivered anti-personnel mines that did not self-destruct and self-deactivate to a stated standard,[117] but allowed States to opt for a nine-year period of deferral from its entry into force to fully comply with each of the two prohibitions on use.[118] It further required that anti-personnel mines not equipped with self-destruction and self-deactivation features be laid in marked and protected areas,[119] but included an exception to that requirement (not to the requirement applied to remotely delivered anti-personnel mines) for certain situations, including where direct enemy military action made it impossible to comply,[120] and again allowed for a nine-year period of deferral as long as the use of non-compliant mines was 'to the extent feasible' minimized and such mines at least self-deactivated within 120 days.[121]

0.41 The ICRC called the restrictions on the use of anti-personnel mines 'woefully inadequate' and indicated that the Protocol alone was 'unlikely to significantly reduce the level of civilian landmine casualties'.[122] The then Secretary-General of the United Nations, Boutros Boutros-Ghali, said he was

the agreement a significant diplomatic success for Sweden. (The Review Conference had been presided over by the Swedish Ambassador, Johan Molander.) 'La Suède se félicite sur l'accord sur les mines antipersonnel', *Agence France Presse* (Stockholm, 3 May 1996).

[116] According to Article 4 of Amended Protocol II and Article 2(a) of the Technical Annex, all anti-personnel mines produced after 1 January 1997 should 'incorporate in their construction a material or device that enables the mine to be detected by commonly-available technical mine detection equipment and provides a response signal equivalent to a signal from 8 grams or more of iron in a single coherent mass'. According to Article 2(b) of the Technical Annex, a similar requirement was made with respect to mines produced before 1 January 1997, with the exception that as an alternative to incorporation, such a material or device could be attached prior to emplacement 'in a manner not easily removable'.

[117] At least 90 per cent of all 'activated' remotely delivered anti-personnel mines must automatically detonate within 30 days of emplacement and after 120 days the back-up self-deactivating mechanism must have ensured that no more than 1 in 1,000 of the mines originally laid is capable of functioning as a mine. Article 5 of Amended Protocol II and Article 3(a) of the Technical Annex.

[118] Article 2(c) of the Technical Annex.

[119] Under Article 5 of Amended Protocol II, all anti-personnel mines that are not equipped with both self-destructing and self-deactivating mechanisms to the same effectiveness as for remotely delivered anti-personnel mines, must be 'placed within a perimeter-marked area which is monitored by military personnel and protected by fencing or other means, to ensure the effective exclusion of civilians from the area. The marking must be of a distinct and durable character and must at least be visible to a person who is about to enter the perimeter-marked area.'

[120] Under Article 5(3) of Amended Protocol II, a party to a conflict is 'relieved from further compliance' with the obligation to mark, fence, and monitor 'only if such compliance is not feasible due to forcible loss of control of the area as a result of enemy military action, including situations where direct enemy military action makes it impossible to comply'.

[121] Article 3(b) and (c) of the Technical Annex.

[122] Statement of Eric Roethlisberger, Vice-President of the ICRC, to the closing session of the First Review Conference of the 1980 Convention on Certain Conventional Weapons (3 May 1996). See Maresca and Maslen, *The Banning of Anti-Personnel Landmines*, 445–6.

'deeply disappointed' by the failure to agree a ban.[123] Jody Williams, the Coordinator of the International Campaign to Ban Landmines (ICBL), declared that the agreement was a 'humanitarian failure'.[124] Even Ambassador Jahan Molander, the President of the Review Conference, would later remark that,

the cumbersome diplomatic process, based on universality and consensus, set in motion a chain reaction that was difficult to foresee. It created the focal point for the international efforts to ban landmines. The haggling over seemingly unimportant details and procedure in comfortable Geneva, on [the] one hand, and the nameless suffering of children, women and men torn to pieces by the hidden killers in the rice paddies of Cambodia, the valleys of Afghanistan or the fields of Angola, on the other—this contrast was too stark, too brutal not to bring home the message to millions around the globe that anti-personnel mines represent an evil that must be stopped.[125]

0.42  Indeed, it had been clear even from the early discussions in the Group of Governmental Experts that amendments to the Protocol were unlikely to be far-reaching and to include an outright ban on anti-personnel mines. These difficulties led to greater unilateral activities towards a prohibition on anti-personnel mines. The ICBL, which had been sceptical from the outset at the likelihood of achieving a prohibition under UN auspices with decision-making by consensus, had been growing in size and influence with national campaigns in dozens of countries, and conferences and meetings on the issue that were bringing together several hundred participants, not only from NGOs but also representatives of States and international organizations.[126]

0.43  In March 1995, Belgium became the first country in the world to adopt national legislation outlawing anti-personnel mines, including components, parts and technology. Other governments, in Europe and beyond, were being pushed and cajoled one by one into supporting, at least publicly, an international ban on production, stockpiling, transfer, and use of anti-personnel mines. States could not persuasively argue that they were pursuing a realistic solution to the problem as it was widely believed that the Protocol would be complex, difficult to implement, and largely ineffective. Thus, by May 1996, more than 40 States, many of which were party to the CCW, had publicly expressed their support for a total international prohibition on anti-personnel

---

123  See Williams, F., 'UN Fails to Agree Outright Ban on Landmines', *Financial Times* (4 May 1996).
124  See Agence France Presse wire release, *AFP-DL82* (3 May 1996).
125  Molander, J., 'Foreword', to Maresca and Maslen, *The Banning of Anti-Personnel Landmines*, p. xxiii.
126  In June 1995, the Cambodian Campaign to Ban Landmines and the NGO Forum on Cambodia hosted a three-day international conference on landmines attended by more than 400 people from 42 countries, representing NGOs, governments, the UN, demining organizations and landmine victims. See www.icbl.org.

mines, 25 States had renounced the use of anti-personnel mines by their own forces and 11 were destroying their stockpiles of the weapon.[127] In addition, Werner Ehrlich of the Austrian Ministry of Foreign Affairs had taken the initiative, informally, to draft the text of a treaty banning anti-personnel mines.[128]

0.44 In Canada, diplomats—and the military[129]—engaged in the review process had identified landmines as an issue that was deserving of further work. In the spring of 1996, after having consulted with the ICRC and the ICBL and subsequently with sympathetic governments,[130] Jill Sinclair, the Director of the Non-Proliferation, Arms Control, and Disarmament Division (IDA) at the Department of Foreign Affairs and International Trade (DFAIT), sought and obtained approval to propose a 'think-in' of States which had endorsed the objective of an international ban on the use, production, transfer, and stockpiling of anti-personnel mines. Initially, a small, informal meeting was foreseen with a view to discussing strategy on how to push the issue forward.[131] On 3 May 1996, at the closing session of the Review Conference, Canadian Ambassador Mark Moher announced that Canada would host a meeting of pro-ban States in the summer. The announcement was followed by a press conference.[132]

---

[127] See for instance Maresca and Maslen, *The Banning of Anti-Personnel Landmines,* pp. 460–1. The level of support for a total ban that had been achieved by the time of the 1996 Ottawa Conference was largely responsible for convincing the then Canadian Foreign Minister, Lloyd Axworthy, and his staff that the necessary 'critical mass' could result in the successful fast-track negotiation of a treaty prohibiting anti-personnel mines. See below the section dealing with the 1996 Ottawa Conference.

[128] The 'first draft' of the Convention on the Prohibition of Anti-Personnel Mines, dated April 1996. Ehrlich reportedly drafted the text in his hotel room in Geneva during frustration at the review process.

[129] Ed Fitch became Director of Military Engineering in the Canadian army in December 1995, reporting to the Deputy Military Chief of Staff. Within two months of his appointment it became clear that landmines were going to be an issue that could not be avoided. Previously, the Canadian armed forces had taken the view that they were 'not part of the problem' but in the experiences at UNPROFOR in Bosnia and Herzegovina and then SFOR they saw at first hand what mines could do. Discussion with Brigadier-General E. S. Fitch, Assistant Chief of the Land Staff, Canadian National Defence Headquarters (Ottawa, 15 Aug. 2001).

[130] An initial lunch meeting with ICBL and eight supportive governments had been convened by Pax Christi Netherlands in January 1996. The meeting, which identified the need to coalesce pro-ban States, led to a memorandum being sent by the Canadian delegation to their Minister for Foreign Affairs regarding a possible Canadian initiative. The idea for a conference was subsequently discussed during a dinner meeting of 14 States at the offices of the Quaker United Nations Office in Geneva on 22 April 1996. States present were: Afghanistan, Australia, Austria, Belgium, Canada, Denmark, Germany, the Holy See, Ireland, the Netherlands, New Zealand, Norway, Peru, and Sweden. The reaction to the idea from all parties was positive. Then at the beginning of May 1996, Canada convened a second informal meeting with 'pro-ban' States and NGOs at the Palais des Nations in Geneva.

[131] Discussion with Ralph Lysyshyn, 14 Aug. 2001.

[132] Other countries, even those supporting an international prohibition, were unclear about Canada's agenda, discussing privately whether it was merely an attempt to appease public opinion or a serious initiative, and if the latter, what its underlying strategy was.

**0.45** Yet, as the months went by and the scope of the meeting and its intended participation grew apace, there was a fear that a number of States would attend with a view to blocking progress towards the objective of a total prohibition of anti-personnel mines. For this reason, DFAIT decided to set criteria whereby each State wishing to come would have to decide whether it came as a full participant or merely an observer, depending on whether it specifically endorsed the objective of a total ban. A proposed conference declaration was circulated in advance of the meeting not for comment but to help States make up their mind.[133]

**0.46** Internal discussions were also engaged in the host country, Canada, with DFAIT using the conference as an opportunity to improve Canada's own position towards anti-personnel mines.[134] After intensive internal discussions between ministries, the Department of National Defense agreed that it would eliminate its stockpile of anti-personnel mines in the context of a global agreement to prohibit the weapons and, for the purposes of the Conference, they undertook to destroy half of Canada's anti-personnel mine stockpiles.[135] The announcement was made on 2 October 1996.

**0.47** In Geneva, meanwhile, discussions on the text of a possible anti-personnel mine ban treaty were already being held between interested governments, NGOs, and the ICRC. David Atwood, Associate Representative at the Quaker UN Office in Geneva, convened regular strategy meetings. On 7 July 1996, he circulated a note to selected NGOs, UNICEF, UNIDIR, and representatives of Austria, Canada, and Switzerland, reporting on a small meeting held at his offices on 26 June. Attached to this note was the draft treaty text prepared by Werner Ehrlich.[136] The draft,[137] which comprises 11 articles, provided for a complete prohibition of the employment, production, transfer, and stockpiling of anti-personnel mines, required destruction of stockpiles within one year of entry into force, and clearance of laid anti-personnel mines within five years. It represents the essence of what would subsequently be elaborated into the first Austrian draft text of the Anti-Personnel Mine Ban Convention.

---

[133] On the other hand, concerns were also expressed by certain States about non-governmental participation, especially of a number of vociferous individuals and NGOs from the ICBL.

[134] Discussion with Ralph Lysyshyn, former Director-General, International Security Division, DFAIT, 14 Aug. 2001.

[135] Discussions with Mark Gwozdecky and Jill Sinclair, DFAIT, Ottawa, 14 Aug. 2001.

[136] Jozef Goldblat, a leading academic authority on disarmament, had also offered to draft a treaty banning anti-personnel mines.          [137] See Appendix 4 for the draft treaty texts.

## The 'Ottawa Process'

### *The 1996 Ottawa Conference*

**0.48**  The International Strategy Conference: Towards a Global Ban on Anti-Personnel Mines (the 1996 Ottawa Conference), was held in the Canadian capital on 3–5 October 1996. During the Conference, the Chair, Ralph Lysyshyn, the then Director-General of DFAIT's International Security Division, sensed that there was sufficient momentum to initiate fast-track negotiations for an international agreement prohibiting anti-personnel mines. Aware that such a process would be costly, on the morning of 4 October, he telephoned the Assistant Deputy Minister for Foreign Affairs to propose that Canada launch negotiations and asked for two million Canadian dollars to support the initiative. The same afternoon, he received confirmation that the money would be available. A meeting was then held with the Minister of Foreign Affairs, Lloyd Axworthy, to discuss the idea of a total ban treaty. Warning was given of the consequences of unilaterally calling for the negotiation of a ban: there was a significant risk of failure,[138] and friendly countries and other allies were likely to be antagonized.

**0.49**  Despite the concerns, Lloyd Axworthy decided to call for the negotiation and signature of a treaty by the end of 1997 in his closing address to the Ottawa Conference. The Secretary-General of the UN was informed in advance and sent a message of support. Jody Williams, the ICBL Coordinator, and Cornelio Sommaruga, the President of the ICRC, were both primed and on hand to give verbal expressions of support before the conference was abruptly closed. To other States, the announcement came as not only a surprise,[139] but also a shock. The head of the US delegation had enquired of Ralph Lysyshyn on the morning of 5 October whether there was any reason for him to postpone his flight home before the end of the Conference and was told that there was none. Australia and France were particularly angered by Canada's unilateralism; even close allies had not been told in advance. Other countries believed that 'something could be done', but they were not clear how fast. A number, at least, understood that, if well managed, the process could become a bandwagon with many governments feeling unable or unwilling to stay outside.

**0.50**  Thus, the Anti-Personnel Mine Ban Convention was negotiated outside the UN,[140] an implicit recognition of the international community's failure

---

[138]  In the memorandum to the Minister, 100 signatory States were felt to be the threshold for credibility. Discussion with Robert Lawson, DFAIT, Ottawa, 15 Aug. 2001.

[139]  Diplomats closely involved in the process believe that surprise was critical to prevent certain States blocking the initiative before it had got off the ground.

[140]  Other multilateral treaties have also been negotiated outside the UN, such as the Organization for Security and Cooperation in Europe, the Conventional Forces in Europe (CFE) agreement, the

to act as one in response to a humanitarian emergency. The Conference had successfully set the stage for coordinated action on landmines with a strong declaration and detailed Chairman's Agenda for Action on Anti-Personnel Mines.[141] The Ottawa Process mirrored the more traditional mechanism for negotiating an international humanitarian law agreement—typically a single State would offer to convene a Diplomatic Conference—but was an anathema to many of the diplomats engaged in consensus-based disarmament negotiations.[142] This fast-track negotiation of the Anti-Personnel Mine Ban Convention became known as the Ottawa Process.

0.51 A 'core group' of friendly States was quickly assembled, bringing together, initially, Austria, Belgium, Canada, Ireland, Mexico, Netherlands, Norway, the Philippines, South Africa, and Switzerland.[143] There was an obvious need for dedicated countries[144] and some semblance of geographical distribution, although the weight was heavily European.[145] In February 1997, after the Expert Meeting on the Text of a Convention to Ban Anti-Personnel

---

Seabed Treaty and the Antarctica Treaty, though many were Cold War constructs. International trade law agreements, such as the General Agreement on Trade and Tariffs, and the agreement to establish the World Trade Organization, were also negotiated outside UN auspices.

[141] The Conference declaration, for instance, included a call for 'a commitment to work together to ensure: the earliest possible conclusion of a legally-binding international agreement to ban anti-personnel mines; progressive reductions in new deployments of anti-personnel mines with the urgent objective of halting all new deployments of anti-personnel mines; support for an UNGA 51 resolution calling upon member states, inter alia, to implement national moratoria, bans or other restrictions, particularly on the operational use and transfer of anti-personnel mines at the earliest possible date; regional and sub-regional activities in support of a global ban on anti-personnel mines; and, a follow-on conference hosted by Belgium in June 1997 to review the progress of the international community in achieving a global ban on anti-personnel mines.'
   The Chairman's Agenda listed actions to be taken, broken down into global action, regional action, and land mine clearance, mine awareness and victim assistance. See Appendix 3 for a copy of the Conference Declaration and Chairman's Agenda.

[142] According to two international lawyers, disarmament 'is the traditional term for the elimination, as well as the limitation or reduction (through negotiation of an international agreement) of the means by which nations wage war'. It is increasingly regarded as a subset of 'arms control'. Matthews, R. J. and McCormack, T. L. H., 'The Influence of Humanitarian Principles in the Negotiation of Arms Control Treaties', *International Review of the Red Cross*, 81, 834 (1999), 333–4.

[143] The precise membership of the core group is the subject of some debate. This list is the one claimed by the Canadians most closely involved in the Ottawa process. See Lawson, R. J *et al.*, 'The Ottawa Process and the International Movement to ban Anti-Personnel Mines', Cameron *et al.*, *To Walk without Fear*, 167.

[144] There appeared to be intense loyalty to the Core Group among its original members—a loyalty that would be severely tested towards the end of the Oslo Diplomatic Conference. See below paragraph 0.89.

[145] Within the European Union (EU), Canada was fortunate that a very sympathetic ally, Ireland, held the EU presidency. This prevented a common position in favour of putting negotiations into the Conference on Disarmament. Subsequently, changes in governments in France and the UK were, in the words of one diplomat, 'tremendously significant', as they led to both States joining the Ottawa Process.

Mines (the Vienna Conference), Germany would join the group, thereby accentuating this bias.[146]

## The First Draft of the Convention

0.52  The Austrian delegation to the Ottawa Strategy Conference already had a first draft of an anti-personnel mine ban convention with them, but although they referred to it in their remarks, they did not circulate it formally.[147] The initial draft prepared by Ehrlich was revised following input from his colleagues and a second draft dated 30 September 1996 had been elaborated.[148] The draft was significantly more detailed than his initial draft, with a small number of annotations to the text. Article 3 on prohibitions already reflected the approach taken in the 1993 Chemical Weapons Convention and Article 7 on verification provided for challenge inspections 'in the case of serious doubts about compliance'. Forty ratifications were set as the threshold for entry into force, with a view to rebutting 'the argument of lack of universality'. No reservations were allowed. The draft, with only minor alterations but now entitled the Austrian draft text, was sent out worldwide in November 1996.[149]

0.53  At the end of 1996, Werner Ehrlich left his post in the Disarmament Department of the Ministry of Foreign Affairs to become Austrian Ambassador to Iran. He was replaced as 'drafter' by his former superior, Thomas Hajnoczi, who had headed the Disarmament Division at the Austrian Ministry of Foreign Affairs since January 1996. He was assisted throughout the process by an international lawyer 'seconded' from the Ministry of Defence, Thomas Desch, Head of the International Legal Division, and Hans Hamberger, also from the Ministry of Defence.[150] Dr Desch had a good grounding in international humanitarian law, which balanced the more disarmament-oriented bent of Ambassador Hajnoczi.

0.54  Disquieted by rumours of a watered-down approach to a treaty to attract wider support, especially from the USA, Thomas Hajnoczi contacted Jill Sinclair at the beginning of 1997 to suggest that they 'stick as long as possible to the concept of a comprehensive total ban. As a first line in the search of

---

[146]  The Netherlands claims credit for serving as the intermediary between the Core Group and Germany.

[147]  Discussions with Mark Gwozdecky and Jill Sinclair, DFAIT, Ottawa, 14 Aug. 2001.

[148]  The provisions were largely adapted from those contained in the 1993 Chemical Weapons Convention and Amended Protocol II to the CCW. See Appendix 4 for a copy of the draft text by Dr Ehrlich.

[149]  The Chairman's Agenda of the 1996 Ottawa Conference formally asked Austria to circulate a first draft of a treaty prohibiting anti-personnel mines to a follow-up meeting to be held in Brussels. See Appendix 3 for a copy of the Chairman's Agenda.

[150]  The Ministry of Defence was solidly behind a ban treaty as it had already renounced anti-personnel mines so was keen to bring other States—and their militaries—on board.

compromise transitional periods could be prolonged.'[151] Indeed, Canada did make a number of attempts during the autumn of 1996 to bring the USA on board (as well as to reconcile relations with allies such as Australia, France and Japan). For instance, it was suggested that a *chapeau* Convention could be adopted with four annexed Protocols, each dealing with a distinct prohibition (production, stockpiling, transfer, and use). This would respect the principle of a total prohibition, while allowing States to choose how far they would go in meeting that objective.[152] The USA rebuffed the idea, however,[153] believing that they could steer the issue and any negotiations into the Conference on Disarmament (CD), where it would be subject to the consensus rule—a 'slow-track' approach to a total prohibition, as it was characterized by the ICBL.[154]

0.55 Belgium also prepared a draft treaty text in both English and French. Although it appears to have had little direct influence on the Austrian drafts, Austria was keen to include Belgium as much as possible in the process because of the role it could play within the EU. The ICBL draft treaty text,[155] which was promoted actively with governments in New York towards the end of 1996, had a much greater impact on subsequent draft treaty texts. The ICBL draft contained 19 draft articles and a proposed fact-finding annex, and much of its desired language would subsequently be reflected in the text of the Convention as adopted.

## The UN General Assembly

0.56 By 1996, the UN General Assembly had already adopted a number of resolutions relating to anti-personnel mines. A call for a moratorium on the export of anti-personnel mines was contained in the first operative paragraph

---

[151] Fax from Thomas Hajnoczi to Jill Sinclair, 7 Jan. 1997. There was concern even among potential signatories about the feasibility of a total prohibition. Germany, for instance, saw three options: a draft with the possibility of exceptions, a *chapeau* Convention with annexed Protocols, or a phased approach starting with transfers.

[152] Other members of the Core Group were concerned about the four protocol approach, which remained an option until the success of the 1997 Vienna Conference. Pressure was brought to bear on Canada by a number of core group members that their support could be withdrawn if they were not satisfied with the process and the likely outcome. Eric Newsom, the head of the US delegation at the Oslo Diplomatic Conference, raised the idea during the Conference to allow the USA to adhere to the treaty but by then it was too late.

[153] It is claimed by one source that the USA did not genuinely engage with Canada on the issue until June 1997 when a delegation came to Ottawa for a briefing.

[154] Indeed, right to the end of the process, Canadian diplomats were concerned that the CD would be given the negotiating role, which would effectively have ended serious prospects for an early agreement. In particular, DFAIT was concerned to contest any language suggesting equivalence as they fought to establish the legitimacy of the Ottawa Process.

[155] Convention on the Prohibition of the Development, Production, Stockpiling, Transfer and Use of Anti-Personnel Mines and on their Destruction, Proposal by the International Campaign to Ban Landmines, ICBL, 20 Dec. 1996.

of Resolution 48/75K, adopted without a vote on 16 December 1993.[156] On 12 December 1995, the Assembly adopted, also without a vote, Resolution 50/70O, which included a call for 'further immediate international efforts to seek solutions to the problems caused by anti-personnel landmines, with a view to the eventual elimination of anti-personnel landmines'.[157] The resolution had been proposed by the USA and was co-sponsored by 110 States.[158]

**0.57** At the Assembly in 1996, the USA initially touted a resolution referring to a total ban on anti-personnel mines, but Canada felt that the initial draft was not sufficiently strong and began to circulate its own prospective text. On the basis that the USA would not refer to the CD in the resolution,[159] agreement was reached to merge the two texts into a single draft that would be introduced by the USA.[160] Resolution 51/45S, which attracted 115 co-sponsors, was adopted on 10 December 1996 by 155 votes to nil with 10 abstentions.[161] Its first operative paragraph urged States 'to pursue vigorously an effective, legally binding international agreement to ban the use, stockpiling, production and transfer of anti-personnel landmines with a view to completing the negotiation as soon as possible'.[162]

## The 1997 Vienna Conference

**0.58** A whirlwind series of conferences followed in the first half of 1997. The first, in Vienna on 12–14 February 1997,[163] was a formal follow-up to

---

[156]  See para. 0.20. See Appendix 2 for copies of relevant UN General Assembly resolutions.

[157]  Operative para. 6.

[158]  In 1994, the General Assembly had already established as a goal of the international community the eventual elimination of anti-personnel mines. UN General Assembly Resolution 49/75D, adopted on 15 Dec. 1994.

[159]  On 6 February 1997, Canada made the following declaration before the CD: 'In our view, USE is the problem and it is the USE of anti-personnel mines which must be urgently addressed . . . In conclusion, Mr President, let us make two points: if it is the will of this body to pursue the issue of anti-personnel mines, we will not oppose it; but we will strongly oppose any initiative which does not reinforce or complement the ongoing work of the Ottawa Process or which delays unduly the establishment of the urgently needed norm against anti-personnel mines.'

[160]  Tomlin, B. W., 'On a Fast Track to a Ban: The Canadian Policy Process', in Cameron *et al.*, *To Walk without Fear*, 197. This was despite strong pressure from France and the United Kingdom (UK).

[161]  Those abstaining were: Belarus, China, Cuba, the Democratic People's Republic of Korea, Israel, Pakistan, the Republic of Korea, the Russian Federation, Syria, and Turkey. A Canadian academic, David Lenarcic, refers to an unsourced remark by China that the vote on the resolution was a 'beauty and popularity contest'. Lenarcic, D. A., *Knight-Errant? Canada and the Crusade to Ban Anti-Personnel Land Mines*, Contemporary Affairs No. 2 (Toronto, Canada: Irwin Publishing, 1998), 28.

[162]  See also paras. 0.101 and 0.119 below.

[163]  Originally, it had been planned to hold two meetings in Vienna, with the second envisaged for May 1997 intended to address specific concerns, such as how verification measures would be included in the treaty. This second meeting was not deemed necessary, as it was agreed in Vienna that Germany could host a meeting on verification in April of the same year.

Lloyd Axworthy's call for the fast-track negotiation of a total ban treaty.[164] The Expert Meeting on the Text of a Convention to Ban Anti-Personnel Mines (the 1997 Vienna Conference) provided States with an initial opportunity to comment directly on Austria's first draft of the Convention, which had been circulated the previous November.[165] Austria had expected representatives of around 90 governments to attend—in fact 111 turned up.[166] In addition, the room chosen to host the meeting was long and narrow—and full—creating a strong impression on the participants that the process was serious, and with momentum behind it.[167]

**0.59** The Conference was chaired by Ambassador Thomas Hajnoczi now the person primarily responsible for the draft treaty text. He had already received written comments on the draft Austrian text from more than a dozen governments in advance of the meeting, but it was felt that bilateral comments made in a multilateral forum would give legitimacy to the draft[168] as well as helping Austria to decide how to revise the text.[169] NGOs, which were working on an almost daily basis with the members of the Core Group, were allowed to attend the plenary sessions, and the UN and the ICRC were invited to participate in the closed meetings.[170]

---

[164] The Conference had to compete with a proposed French project for an EU seminar on anti-personnel mines, planned, coincidentally, to be held in Paris on 10–11 Feb. 1997.

[165] See paras. 0.52 to 0.54 above.

[166] The attention of the international media had focused strongly on anti-personnel mines in January 1997 when Diana, Princess of Wales, on a visit to Angola as a guest of the British Red Cross, had called publicly for an international ban on anti-personnel mines in defiance of instructions from the British Foreign and Commonwealth Office. A junior minister would famously describe her as a 'loose cannon', thereby drawing further public attention to the issue. It is not known, however, if this had any bearing on the level of participation.

[167] According to one commentator, based on the results of the Vienna Conference, Canada thought that 50–60 signatories were likely, Belgium was more conservative, predicting around 40–50. Short, N., 'International Efforts to Ban Landmines: The Vienna Conference', Briefing Notes, Centre for European Security and Disarmament (Brussels, 4 Mar. 1997). Austria, at least, saw the success of the meeting as the effective end of the CD as a credible threat to the Ottawa Process. Information provided by Thomas Hajnoczi, Austrian Ambassador to Norway, Oslo, 24 Oct. 2001.

[168] Thus, Japan, one of a number of States that were at best lukewarm *vis-à-vis* the Ottawa Process, had more than 20 questions on the text. This represented a welcome engagement in the process, notwithstanding any of its oral or written caveats. There were unconfirmed reports of parallel meetings with key States opposed to the Ottawa Process convened to discuss how to kill it. One of the alleged members, Germany, decided to 'change sides' and as a 'reward' Germany was brought into the Core Group, a fact not to every other member's liking. Their participation was important to Austria because of the strength of the Franco-German alliance within the EU. As a further quid pro quo, Germany was also invited to organize a meeting as part of the Ottawa Process. Germany believed, as did France and the UK, that verification was essential to the credibility of a total ban treaty.

[169] The ICBL circulated an annotated review of the Austrian draft treaty text.

[170] Core Group members were instructed to intervene as much as possible in the debates and to be supportive. South Africa spoke first and Belgium, in particular, was very talkative. Very few governments

## *The Mobilization of Southern Africa*

**0.60** On 25–8 February 1997, following the 1997 Vienna Conference, the ICBL convened its Fourth International Non-governmental Organization Conference on Landmines, 'Toward a Mine-Free Southern Africa', in Maputo, Mozambique. The conference, which brought together more than 450 participants from 60 countries, stressed the need for regional organizations, such as the Organization of African Unity (OAU) and the Southern Africa Development Community (SADC), to follow the lead of South Africa and Mozambique, which announced a unilateral ban on landmines the week before and during the conference. The conference's final declaration also called upon the international community to increase resources for mine clearance and assistance to survivors, especially in those countries and regions that had banned landmines.[171]

**0.61** Within the context of the Conference, the ICRC brought together twelve National Societies from southern Africa 'to discuss their role in moving the region forward towards a total ban on anti-personnel mines'.[172] The National Societies issued a strong declaration calling upon their governments to support the Ottawa Process, to prohibit anti-personnel mines at national level, and to work together to establish an anti-personnel mine-free zone in the region.[173] Indeed, as a result of the work of South Africa, the OAU, the ICBL, and the ICRC, at the Oslo Diplomatic Conference, southern African States would prove to be key to the achievement of a total ban without exceptions.

## *The Second Draft of the Convention*

**0.62** Based on comments received at the 1997 Vienna Conference, Austria prepared a second 'tentative' draft of its treaty text on 7 March 1997 and circulated it to the Core Group. The draft was reviewed by the Core Group on 12 and 13 February 1997 and the Second Austrian Draft was completed on 14 March 1997.[174] This text differed quite significantly from the first draft, with the removal of the article on the scope of application, a major change to the definition of an anti-personnel mine and the consequent inclusion of a definition of an anti-handling device, as well as the addition of definitions of 'transfer' and 'minefield'. The key prohibitions were recast as 'general obligations' in the style of the 1993 Chemical Weapons Convention and moved up to the beginning of

spoke out against a ban, demonstrating that international opinion was turning away from the legitimacy of anti-personnel mines as a means of warfare.

[171]  Indeed, support for mine clearance and victim assistance was seen by a number of countries as a quid pro quo for bringing southern nations on board.

[172]  Maresca and Maslen, *The Banning of Anti-Personnel Landmines*, 509.

[173]  ibid. 509–11.        [174]  See Appendix 4.

the treaty;[175] and an undertaking to destroy anti-personnel mines was added to the provision.

0.63 The deadline for the destruction of stockpiled anti-personnel mines was extended from one to three years, and an obligation to destroy emplaced anti-personnel mines, now limited to those laid within minefields, extended to ten years. Other emplaced mines were to be destroyed but no time limit was prescribed. The draft provision on grave breaches, included in the previous draft, was removed. New articles were added on the settlement of disputes, review conferences, and meetings of the States Parties. A footnote was added to the effect that the draft provisions on verification, which were unchanged from those in the first Austrian draft, would be reviewed following a conference dedicated to the issue, to be held in Bonn in April 1997.

## The 1997 Bonn Conference

0.64 Thus, the International Expert Meeting on Possible Verification Measures to Ban Anti-Personnel Landmines, the second formal follow-up gathering to the 1996 Ottawa Conference, was held in Bonn on 24–5 April 1997. In advance of the meeting, Germany circulated an 'Options Paper for a possible verification scheme for a convention to ban anti-personnel landmines', which implied a desire to see significant and intrusive verification measures common in disarmament treaties.[176] Within the Core Group, Canada presented proposals for more cooperative compliance. Although there was little initial enthusiasm from Core Group members, the spirit of the concept can be seen reflected in the text, especially in the first paragraph of Article 8 of the Anti-Personnel Mine Ban Convention.

0.65 A total of 121 States were represented at the meeting, and views were divided, as they had been at the 1997 Vienna Conference, between States who believed that detailed verification was essential to ensure that any agreement was effective, and others that argued, as did the ICRC, that the proposed agreement was essentially humanitarian in character and stressing the overriding importance of a clear norm prohibiting anti-personnel mines.[177] Diplomats intimately involved in the negotiation of the Convention noted afterwards that:

While some progress was achieved, no convergence of minds was in sight. Having dodged this controversial issue in the second version, the final Austrian draft had to

---

[175] See below the commentary on Article 1.

[176] Yet, even Germany understood that there were limits to the extent of verification that would be acceptable and achievable, especially given the tight deadlines of the process.

[177] The ICBL had changed the position it had held during the negotiation of Amended Protocol II. It now maintained that extensive verification was not crucial to the treaty and should not be used as a pretext to weaken the scope of a total ban.

find a viable middle ground. After numerous consultations, Austria presented a compromise solution that did not satisfy any side fully, but was conceptually acceptable for everyone.[178]

**0.66** As noted above, the Second Draft of the Convention did not include a provision on grave breaches, a potentially significant tool for the implementation of international humanitarian law. At the Bonn Conference, the ICRC had circulated an informal draft article on national implementation measures. Central to this draft was a proposal for a provision laying down modified compulsory jurisdiction for all nationals of a State Party to the Convention 'alleged to have used, or to have ordered the use of, anti-personnel mines' in violation of the Convention.[179]

Opinions on the success of the Bonn Conference are extremely mixed. Certainly, disagreements were brought into sharper focus, with Mexico at one end of the spectrum refusing all manner of verification, and Germany at the other demanding sophisticated disarmament verification measures, with the rest of the Core Group supporting shades in between.[180]

*The Third Draft of the Convention*

**0.67** Austria circulated its Third Austrian Draft on 28 April 1997 to the Core Group and then, after revision, especially concerning compliance issues, issued the text on 14 May 1997. In other respects, most of the changes from the Second Austrian Draft were small; the most significant was the inclusion of a provision in the article dealing with duration and withdrawal prohibiting an effective withdrawal where the State in question was involved in an armed conflict at the conclusion of the notice period. This provision would be keenly contested during the Oslo Diplomatic Conference.

**0.68** The period that followed the publication of the third draft text saw two members of the UN Security Council join the Ottawa Process, in both instances shortly after a change of national government. By the end of April 1997, France, which had previously been an ardent supporter of the role of the

---

[178] Hajnoczi, T., Desch, T., and Chatsis, D., 'The Ban Treaty', in Cameron *et al.*, *To Walk without Fear*, 301. Ambassador Molander of Sweden, on the other hand, complained subsequently that the Anti-Personnel Mine Ban Convention 'contains provisions on verification which make an unusual combination of total intrusiveness in principle and considerable weakness in practice'. Molander, J., 'Foreword' to Maresca and Maslen, *The Banning of Anti-Personnel Landmines*, p. xxv.

[179] See further below paras. 8.8 and 9.9 of the Commentary.

[180] Norway, for instance, had already expressed its view at the 1997 Vienna Conference that it did not see that a legally binding ban on anti-personnel mines needed any traditional verification instruments and agreed with the 'widespread view' that complete verifiability was 'neither feasible, nor necessary, nor desirable'.

CD in tackling the mines issue,[181] knew the Ottawa Process was irreversible and was planning how to join without losing face diplomatically.[182] In 'exchange' for its participation, the French Ministry of Foreign Affairs sought a reference to the role of the CD in the preamble stressing the complementarity of the two fora, and the deletion of the draft article prohibiting reservations.

0.69 In the UK, on 21 May 1997, the newly installed Labour government announced that it was joining the process, imposing an operational moratorium on the use of anti-personnel mines and that it would ensure the destruction of UK stockpiles by 2005. The Ministry of Defence announced that to make up for the operational shortfall it would improve battlefield surveillance, and use air-blast mortar systems, which would be operational by 2005.[183]

0.70 A few days later, the Organization of African Unity (OAU) organized a major conference in Kempton Park, near Johannesburg, in cooperation with the government of South Africa. The First Continental Conference of African Experts on Landmines, Landmine Free Africa: The OAU and the Legacy of Anti-Personnel Mines, took place on 19–21 May 1997. The conference attracted significant participation from African nations and proved to be a further catalyst for the significant role that Africa played in the adoption of the Convention.

0.71 On 23–5 May 1997, in Stockholm, three Swedish NGOs[184] organized a Seminar on Anti-Personnel Mines and Strategy Workshop for countries of the Baltic and Eastern Europe Region. Many of these States were reluctant to embrace the Ottawa Process and stressed their support for a primary role for the CD in any negotiations.

0.72 There was also a conference on anti-personnel mines for Central Asian States held in Ashgabat, the capital of Turkmenistan. In a letter to his Canadian counterpart, Lloyd Axworthy, proposing the conference, the Turkmen Foreign

---

181 See for instance the letter on behalf of the French President, signed by Françoise Delattre, of 31 December 1996 in response to a letter from ICBL Coordinator, Jody Williams: 'Afin de mobiliser la communauté internationale dans son ensemble, la France a proposé que soit négocié dans le cadre de la Conférence du Désarmement, un accord international juridiquement contraignant et vérifiable sur l'interdiction totale et générale des mines anti-personnel'. The communication noted, however, the important contribution that the Ottawa Process could make and promised that France would continue to participate in the most positive manner. In January 1997, French Ambassador Joëlle Bourgeois declared that: 'France preferred an efficient treaty, even if the result took time, to a hastily concluded but useless agreement'. See 'Disarmament Conference hears Further Calls for Bans on Landmines and Fissile Materials, Establishment of Negotiating Committee on Nuclear Disarmament', UN Press release DCF/283 (Geneva, 23 Jan. 1997).

182 For one view of the evolution of French policy on landmines, see Chabasse, P., 'The French Campaign', in Cameron *et al.*, *To Walk without Fear*, 60–7.

183 'Forces will have to Destroy all Landmines', *The Times* (22 May 1997).

184 Swedish United Nations Association, Christian Council of Sweden and Rädda Barnen (Swedish Save the Children).

Minister, Boris Shikhmuradov, announced his country's support for a ban on anti-personnel mines and the Ottawa Process. The conference itself, A Global Ban on Anti-Personnel Mines: Central Asia Regional Conference, which took place on 10–12 June 1997, demonstrated the difficulties of attracting adherence to a future ban treaty in the region. Pakistan proved particularly reluctant to endorse a total ban on anti-personnel mines and demanded a redraft of the conference declaration to reflect its position.

### The 1997 Brussels Conference

**0.73** One of the factors in the Canadian decision in October 1996 to seek unilaterally a treaty prohibiting anti-personnel mines was the knowledge that Belgium had already offered to host a follow-up conference[185] and there was concern that it might itself launch such an initiative.[186] The International Conference for a Global Ban on Anti-Personnel Mines, held in Brussels in June 1997, proved essential to the Ottawa Process as it provided a clear selection process for the forthcoming diplomatic conference, and formally identified the Third Austrian Draft as the basis for its negotiations.[187] Austria did not want too much discussion of its draft text prior to the Diplomatic Conference, but saw input from the conference as valuable as it helped to confirm where the main sticking points would be.

**0.74** The conference itself suffered from a number of organizational hiccups, although none was of sufficient gravity to seriously undermine the process. Ambassador André Mernier was called in at a late stage to oversee its organization and most of the sessions were chaired by the Belgian Foreign Minister, Eric Derycke. A number of States joined the Ottawa Process during the conference: Angola, Bosnia and Herzegovina, Brazil, the Czech Republic, Hungary, and Slovakia. Argentina would join shortly afterwards.

**0.75** The USA attended the conference in some force and summoned delegations to its hotel for bilateral discussions, ostensibly for a briefing on why the USA could not support the process, but was believed also to sound out possible support for its position were it to join.[188] The USA would forcefully

---

[185] Belgium formally announced its intention to host such a meeting on 3 October 1996 at the 1996 Ottawa Conference. It hoped subsequently that the conference would be the negotiating forum for the treaty but Canada and others felt that it would be too soon.

[186] Tomlin, B. W., 'On a Fast Track to a Ban: The Canadian Policy Process', in Cameron *et al.*, *To Walk without Fear*, 203. Indeed, the Belgians were said to be furious at the initiative by Lloyd Axworthy.

[187] The 1997 Brussels Conference was also notable for the call by the ICBL for a ban treaty with 'no exceptions, no reservations, and no loopholes'. This became a mantra repeated until the adoption of the Convention in Oslo.

[188] According to a May 1997 policy paper the USA was 'committed to ending the carnage and devastation caused by APL. The comprehensive USA APL policy directs the United States to seek an

reject allegations of attempted sabotage made by NGOs.[139] The US case, however, was not well formulated. It primarily consisted of a comparison of the defence of South Korea including both anti-personnel and anti-tank mines, as against defence with no mines at all. Since the Convention being prepared did not propose to ban anti-tank mines, the US presentation seemed unpersuasive and irrelevant. During the Brussels Conference, the CD appointed a Special Coordinator on Landmines tasked with exploring the possibility of future negotiations in the Conference on landmines.[190]

**0.76** The primary document emanating from the conference was the Brussels Declaration. Ninety-seven of the 156 States attending the Brussels Conference signed the 'Brussels Declaration', which affirmed that the essential elements of a treaty to ban anti-personnel mines were: a comprehensive ban on the use, stockpiling, production, and transfer of anti-personnel mines; the destruction of all stockpiled and cleared anti-personnel mines; and international cooperation and assistance in the area of mine clearance in affected countries. The Brussels Declaration also referred to the convening of the diplomatic conference to adopt the treaty and confirmed that the third Austrian draft would be the basis of negotiations at the conference.

**0.77** In addition to forwarding the Austrian draft text to the Oslo Diplomatic Conference, States supporting the Brussels Declaration also reaffirmed the goal set by the Canadian Foreign Minister of signing the treaty in Ottawa before the end of 1997. At the close of the conference, Canada announced that the treaty signing conference would be held in Ottawa on 2–4 December 1997:

Last October I invited the international community to return to Ottawa before the end of 1997 with the goal of signing a treaty banning anti-personnel mines. It is now clear that

international agreement to ban the use, stockpiling, production and transfer of APL, with a view to completing the negotiations as soon as possible . . . In calling for an international agreement, the policy acknowledges current U.S. reliance on APL to deter aggression against, or if necessary, successfully defend U.S. interests on the Korean peninsula. In light of the current reliance, the USA policy states that any international agreement will need to protect and preserve the right of the United States to use APL on the Korean peninsula until APL alternatives become available or the risk of aggression has been removed. Moreover, the policy states that until such time as an international agreement takes effect, the United States will reserve the right to use self-destructing/self-deactivating APL in military hostilities in Korea—and elsewhere if necessary—to safeguard American lives and hasten an end to fighting.' Report to the Secretary of Defense on the Status of DOD's Implementation of the US Policy on Anti-Personnel Landmines, Office of the Under Secretary of Defense for Policy (May 1997), 2, 3.

[189] Pinon, B., 'Les Etats Unis accusés de vouloir "saboter" la Conférence de Bruxelles', *Agence France Presse* (Brussels, 26 June 1997).

[190] 'Un "coordonnateur" pour les négociations sur les mines anti-personnel', *Agence France Presse* (Geneva, 26 June 1997). By this point, however, the CD was only a minor distraction and no longer posed a realistic threat to the Ottawa Process.

we will reach this goal. In Ottawa, from December 2 to 4, we will be able to establish a new global norm against these terrible weapons.[191]

0.78  Surprisingly, the Brussels Declaration did not include a reference to the importance of international support for assistance to mine victims.[192] Despite extensive discussions between South African and Belgian diplomats, the Belgian Foreign Minister refused to add any new language to address this. This upset African governments in general, and South Africa in particular, which refused to sign the Declaration as a result, deciding merely to associate itself with it.[193] Also notable by its absence was an absolute duty to clear emplaced mines, the requirement seemingly being only to destroy 'cleared' anti-personnel mines.

0.79  Of obvious importance to the outcome of the negotiations would be the rules of procedure to be followed at the Oslo Diplomatic Conference. A first draft of the rules was prepared by Gro Nystuen, a legal adviser at the Norwegian Ministry of Foreign Affairs; the draft drew on an extensive range of sources.[194] The Norwegians first consulted on its draft with South Africa, particularly Jacob Selebi, who had already been approached to preside over the Diplomatic Conference, then Canada[195] and finally Austria. The revised draft was formally presented to States at the closing session of the Brussels Conference.

0.80  There were two key issues to be resolved within the Rules of Procedure: the method of adoption of the treaty, and participation in the Diplomatic

---

[191] 'Axworthy Announces Dates for Landmine Treaty Conference', News Release, Canadian Embassy (Brussels, 27 June 1997).

[192] A joint statement by 12 landmine survivors present in Brussels called on governments to: 're-read the current draft of the treaty and consider how it appears to us landmine survivors. There is virtually nothing in it to urge governments to take responsibility for the victims. Yet people are bleeding and dying even as we speak. To this day, the real needs of mine-affected communities are not being addressed. Survivors remain an afterthought. Their numbers grow each day, but without your help they have little hope of ever receiving proper medical attention or rehabilitation.' White, J. and Rutherford, K., 'The Role of the Landmine Survivors Network', in Cameron, *et al.*, *To Walk without Fear*, 111.

[193] This was particularly embarrassing for the process as Ambassador Jacob Selebi of South Africa was due to chair the Oslo Diplomatic Conference.

[194] The United Nations Standard Rules of Procedure (the most recent version of which was from 1994), the rules of procedure used for the adoption of the Convention on the Law of the Sea, the 1977 Additional Protocols to the 1949 Geneva Conventions, the Functional Committees of the United Nations Economic and Social Council (ECOSOC), the Convention against Torture, the Joint Convention on the Safety of Spent Fuel Management and on the Safety of Radioactive Waste Management, and the rules of procedure used in the United Nations General Assembly and during the International Conference on the Protection of War Victims.

[195] Particular assistance was provided by Philippe Kirsch and Deborah Chatsis from DFAIT's Legal Division.

Conference. With respect to the latter, voting rights were accorded only to States that had adhered to the Brussels Declaration, either by signing or associating themselves with it. The ICBL was allowed to participate as a full observer, despite concerns from a number of States.

0.81 The method of adoption of the treaty was of critical importance. According to Article 9(2) of the 1969 Vienna Convention on the Law of Treaties: 'The adoption of the text of a treaty at an international conference takes place by the vote of two-thirds of the States present and voting, unless by the same majority they shall decide to apply a different rule'. The CD takes all decisions by consensus; by tradition, the CCW has done the same.[196] On the other hand, the UN General Assembly requires a two-thirds majority for substantive issues, whereas ECOSOC Functional Committees only require a simple majority.

0.82 The draft rules put forward for the Oslo Diplomatic Conference provided for a two-thirds majority for any substantive decisions—thus any changes to the Third Austrian Draft required the support of two-thirds of the States participating in the Diplomatic Conference, a significant threshold. Indeed, the barrier would prove critical to the failure of the USA to secure the text of a treaty to which it felt it could adhere.

*Between Brussels and Oslo*

0.83 In the interval between the Brussels Conference and the Oslo Diplomatic Conference, there were two events of significance. The first was a regional seminar of military experts, 'Anti-Personnel Mines: What Future for Asia?', organized by the ICRC and hosted by the Philippines in Manila. It was 'generally agreed that a total ban on anti-personnel mines was a necessary objective', although three participants were unwilling to sign the Manila Declaration.[197]

0.84 The second event of note was the decision by the USA to join the Ottawa Process,[198] two weeks before the opening of the Diplomatic

---

[196] See para. 0.39 above.

[197] Maresca and Maslen, *The Banning of Anti-Personnel Landmines*, 562.

[198] The question of whether to attend the coming Oslo Conference was a subject of intense and protracted debate within the US government. On the one hand, the Department of Defense insisted that it needed continued access to the benefits of persistent anti-personnel mines in Korea, and of self-destructing self-deactivating anti-personnel mines anywhere its forces were sent. On the other hand, the State Department and the National Security Council staff were unwilling to accept the political consequences of refusal to join in the anti-personnel mines ban, and believed the Ottawa Core Group would go to extreme lengths to bring the USA into the treaty. Additionally, the close relationship between President Clinton and Senator Patrick Leahy on a variety of issues made the Administration still more reluctant to break with the Ottawa Process. Finally, the National Security Council staff, in coordination with General Joseph Ralston, the Deputy Chairman of the Joint Chiefs of Staff, devised

Conference.[199] Shortly afterwards, the US Secretary of State, Madeleine Albright, sent a letter to key foreign ministers in which she laid down five conditions for the USA's eventual signature of the treaty:[200]

- a geographical exception for the use of mines in South Korea;
- a change in the definition of anti-personnel mines to allow the USA to continue to use its mixed anti-tank and anti-personnel 'munitions' systems;[201]
- a transition period, either through entry into force requiring 60 countries, including all five permanent members of the Security Council and at least 75 per cent of historic producers and users of anti-personnel mines, or an optional nine-year deferral period for compliance with certain provisions;
- a strengthening of the verification regime; and
- a clause permitting a party to withdraw when its supreme national interests were threatened.

## *The 1997 Oslo Diplomatic Conference*

**0.85**  Norway had gone to the 1996 Ottawa Conference with the offer to host a short follow-up meeting. In early March 1997, Jill Sinclair, from DFAIT's Disarmament Division, asked her Norwegian counterpart, Steffen Kongstad, if Norway would be willing to host the formal negotiating forum for

what they hoped would be a successful compromise: all US self-destructing anti-personnel mines would be repackaged together with anti-tank mines into 'mixed munitions', as was already the case with other existing systems, such as Gator, Volcano, and the MOPMS. The USA would then propose changing the definitions of anti-personnel mines under the Convention so that the anti-personnel mines in mixed munitions would be considered to be anti-handling devices rather than mines. The Arms Control and Disarmament Agency (ACDA) pointed out that this contradicted the CCW Amended Mines Protocol under which the anti-personnel mines in mixed munitions were clearly defined to be anti-personnel mines. Further, ACDA saw an irreconcilable conflict between the US military's requirement to use anti-personnel mines and the Ottawa Group's determination to ban them, and predicted that other key States in the process would not accept continued use of anti-personnel mines simply because they were renamed. ACDA therefore recommended that the USA make clear from the outset that it could not join the new Convention, and attend the Oslo Conference as a friendly observer, offering its services to help with drafting, verification, and so on, while not attempting to alter the terms of the treaty. But the final decision was made by NSC staff.

[199] The White House announced on 18 August 1997 that the USA would be a full participant in the negotiations at the Oslo Diplomatic Conference. See for instance 'United States to Join Ottawa Process', Statement by the Press Secretary (Martha's Vineyard, Mass., 18 Sept. 1997).

[200] The decision by the USA immediately stimulated concerns about the ability of Canada to withstand pressure from its southern neighbour. In the words of one Core Group member: 'When an elephant sneezes, the surrounding land feels an earthquake'.

[201] According to an unnamed delegate at the Oslo Diplomatic Conference, the idea of redefining anti-personnel mines as something else 'was nutty as the proverbial fruitcake. It would be like painting the label "DOG" on the side of a cow and expecting it to therefore bark.'

the Convention. This posed a number of problems, not least the cost, organization (given the short time), and logistics (finding an appropriate venue). There was also an impending general election that would occur during the diplomatic conference itself.

**0.86** The Norwegian Ministry of Foreign Affairs initially intimated a willingness to offer a two-week session and not more. On 27 March 1997, Lloyd Axworthy sent a formal request to Bjørn Tore Godal, the Norwegian Foreign Minister, asking Norway to host two rounds of negotiations: one session during the first two weeks of September and a second session during the last week of September and the first week of October 1997. It was ultimately agreed that the Conference would be held in one three-week session.[202]

**0.87** The Diplomatic Conference on an International Total Ban on Anti-Personnel Land Mines (the Oslo Diplomatic Conference), convened by Norway, opened on 1 September 1997, and was chaired by Jacob Selebi, South African Ambassador to the CD in Geneva.[203] At the opening of the Oslo Diplomatic Conference, delegates observed a minute's silence in memory of the Princess of Wales, who had died in a car crash in Paris the weekend before.[204] Once Selebi had been formally elected President of the Conference, he outlined his plans for the negotiations—a series of working groups coordinated by 'Friends of the Chair',[205] in parallel where necessary, no square brackets around text under discussion, and all negotiations to be concluded by 17 September allowing time for the text to be checked in all languages. He then

---

[202] Although only conjecture, it is probable that if two sessions of the diplomatic conference had been held, some of the provisions in the Convention would have been significantly weakened.

[203] On 4 April 1997, Canadian and Norwegian Permanent Representatives to the UN in Geneva met with Ambassador Selebi and asked him to chair the conference. He had previously served as chair of the Preparatory Commission for the Comprehensive Test Ban Treaty Organization and had been instrumental in promoting expansion in the Conference in Disarmament in 1996.

[204] The issue of whether the Princess's death altered the negotiations in any way remains disputed. An unnamed member of the US delegation was reported as having stated that he did not know a single country that had changed its position because of Diana. Bonner, R., 'How a Group of Outsiders Moved Nations to Ban Landmines', *New York Times* (20 Sept. 1997). Steve Goose, the head of the ICBL delegation to the Oslo Diplomatic Conference, remarked that the tragedy did not shift the negotiating process or positions of governments in Oslo, though he suggested that the increased media attention might have made it 'that much more difficult for governments to seriously consider any changes that would affect the integrity of the mine ban treaty'. Goose, S. D., 'The Ottawa Process and the 1997 Mine Ban Treaty', *Yearbook of International Humanitarian Law*, i (The Hague: Asser Press, 1998), 278. There is, however, a strong suspicion that it prevented the UK from offering stronger support to the USA during the negotiations.

[205] There were five Friends of the Chair: for definitions, Austria; for mine clearance, Ireland; for international cooperation, Brazil; for compliance, Canada; and for the preamble, Mexico. All except Brazil had been Core Group members from the outset of the Ottawa Process. No African or Asian delegation had been chosen.

proposed the draft rules of procedure for adoption by the conference. The most significant provision was Rule 35, which stated that: 'Decisions of the Conference on all matters of substance shall be taken by a two-thirds majority of the representatives present and voting'.[206] Only France intervened, stressing the importance of making every effort to achieve consensus. The rules of procedure were then duly adopted by consensus, in accordance with tradition at international conferences.[207]

**0.88** For a variety of reasons, including the subsequent death of the person responsible, Norway proved unable to produce a diplomatic record of the Diplomatic Conference. Tape recordings of the final session exist and it is likely that somewhere in the Ministry of Foreign Affairs' archives lie tapes of the plenary meetings[208] and meetings of the 'Committee of the Whole',[209] but Norway has been unable to locate them. This represents an obstacle to the interpretation of certain articles, and one which has been exploited by opponents of the Ottawa Process as evidence of its lack of seriousness.

**0.89** Even if located, however, the tapes would not be able to shed light on the negotiations in the meetings of the Friends of the Chair or any of the informal discussions that characterize any multilateral negotiation. These discussions multiplied as the USA became increasingly frustrated at its inability to make headway on its five demands. By the end of the second week, most of the other outstanding issues in the Convention had been resolved amicably. In Washington DC at least, US officials still believed that it would be able to secure sufficient support for amendments that would allow it to accept the Convention.[210] It therefore sought a suspension of a day to continue discussions with

---

[206] Draft Rules of Procedure, Diplomatic Conference on a Convention on the Prohibition of the Use, Stockpiling, Production and Transfer of Anti-Personnel Mines and on Their Destruction, APL/CRP.2 (Oslo, 1 Sept. 1997).

[207] See e.g. Aust, *Modern Treaty Law and Practice*, 67.

[208] A total of six plenary meetings were held during the Diplomatic Conference. See APL/CRP.5 of 18 Sept. 1997.

[209] The Committee of the Whole was a meeting of all the participants held to discuss general or particular issues of concern. Most of the detailed negotiations were undertaken in meetings of Friends of the Chair.

[210] According to the head of the Canadian delegation, the USA entered the Diplomatic Conference in Oslo believing that they could steer the negotiations towards an outcome that they could live with. But their interagency bargaining had already been carried to a conclusion in Washington, and so their final negotiating position scarcely varied in substance from their initial one. In its final proposal, the United States sought a nine-year deferral period for compliance for ending the use of anti-personnel mines globally, an exemption for its mixed munition systems, and the possibility of withdrawal during an armed conflict. Discussion with Ralph Lysyshyn, 14 Aug. 2001. Canadian diplomats have implied, probably correctly, that had the US negotiators been able to isolate the period of deferral from the definition of anti-personnel mines, their chances of success would have improved significantly. Lawson, R. *et al.*, 'The Ottawa Process and the International Movement to Ban Anti-Personnel Mines', in Cameron *et al.*, *To Walk without Fear*, 178.

other delegations, as well as to consult further with Washington.[211] As President Selebi required a new proposal to justify an extension, the USA asked Canada to introduce one. Under instructions from the Canadian Prime Minister and Foreign Minister, both of whom were keen to have US support for the Convention, the Canadian delegation drafted an amendment and handed it in to the Secretariat in order to give the USA more time to consider its position. This gesture, and the lobbying that accompanied it, both in Oslo and in capitals, earned the Canadian delegation considerable opprobrium from the NGOs and from many other delegations. It is clear, however, that Canada was not the only State participating in the Diplomatic Conference willing to make significant compromises to secure US support for the treaty.

0.90 The USA requested and obtained from the Plenary a 24-hour suspension of the negotiations. With the Core Group having been battered by US pressure,[212] it looked to some as if the USA might obtain at least some of the demands it had been pushing for. But on 18 September 1997, the US delegation announced to the plenary that it was withdrawing its proposals as it had been unable to garner the necessary support for them.[213] After confirmation that Japan would not pursue one of its own proposed amendments, the Convention was formally adopted to a round of enthusiastic applause from States and NGOs alike.[214]

## The 1997 Ottawa Conference

0.91 In accordance with its Article 15, the Convention was opened for signature in Ottawa on 3–4 December 1997 at a formal treaty signing conference.[215] A total of 121 States signed the Convention at the Conference,[216] an

---

[211] See for instance 'US Wins more Time for Landmines Pact', *Financial Times* (17 Sept. 1997); Bonner, R., 'New US Terms on Mine Ban are Called Unacceptable', *New York Times* (16 Sept. 1997).

[212] Views differ as to which countries remained determined not to accept the US proposals. Belgium, Ireland, and Norway are often cited as those that held firm with South Africa. What is certain is that the South African delegation felt isolated in the final few days of the conference, although President Nelson Mandela gave unequivocal support to them when under pressure from the US President and they were confident that they could count on the support of other African delegations to block undesirable amendments if the issue were to come to a vote.

[213] In justifying the US rejection of the treaty, President Clinton declared that 'there is a line I simply cannot cross and that line is the safety and security of our men and women in uniform'. See e.g. Gertz, B., 'Clinton Resisted Pressure to Join ban on Landmines', *Washington Times* (20 Sept. 1997).

[214] The initiative had ultimately succeeded for a number of reasons: initially, the lack of support from the five permanent members of the UN Security Council had actually increased its credibility among a number of States from the South, although subsequently French and UK support was to prove significant.

[215] In accordance with Article 15, signature of the Convention was possible until its entry into force, which took place on 1 March 1999.

[216] Kenya signed the Convention on 5 December 1997. In total, 150 governments attended the 1997 Ottawa Conference. See e.g. Canadian Department of Foreign Affairs and International Trade, 'A Global Ban on Landmines', Fact Sheet, undated but 1997.

achievement described by Canadian Prime Minister Jean Chrétien, as 'without precedent or parallel in either international disarmament or international humanitarian law'.[217]

**0.92** Many States praised Canada's role in launching the Ottawa Process and at the end of the 1997 Ottawa Conference a 67-page report, Agenda for Mine Action, detailed pledges of more than US$500 million to the mine effort over a five-year period. The same month, by Resolution 52/38A, the UN General Assembly welcomed the conclusion of the Convention at Oslo and requested the Secretary-General to render the necessary assistance and provide such services as might be necessary to fulfil the tasks entrusted to him.[218]

## The Role of the Conference on Disarmament

**0.93** The principal threat to the success of the Ottawa Process came from the international body for disarmament negotiations, the Conference on Disarmament (CD).[219] Predictably, a number of States had turned to the CD on the basis of its success in negotiating the text of the 1993 Chemical Weapons Convention.[220] On 17 January 1997, the White House declared that,

when the Conference on Disarmament opens its 1997 session on Monday, the United States will seek to initiate negotiations on a worldwide treaty banning the use, production, stockpiling and transfer of anti-personnel landmines. After extensive consultations with many countries, the President believes that the Conference on Disarmament offers the most practical and effective forum for achieving our aim of a ban that is global. Both the Comprehensive Test Ban Treaty and the Chemical Weapons Convention were

---

[217] See Lawson *et al.*, 'The Ottawa Process and the International Movement to Ban Anti-Personnel Mines', 181.

[218] Resolution 52/38A of 9 December 1997 was adopted by 142 votes to nil with 18 abstentions. The abstentions were: Azerbaijan, China, Cuba, Egypt, India, Iran, Israel, Kazakhstan, Mongolia, Morocco, Myanmar, Pakistan, the Republic of Korea, the Russian Federation, Syria, Tajikistan, Turkey, and the USA. Of these, only Tajikistan and Turkey were States Parties to the Convention as of 1 March 2004.

[219] See e.g. Tomlin, 'On a Fast Track to a Ban: The Canadian Policy Process', 202. See also Goose, S., 'Anti-Personnel Mines and the Conference on Disarmament', ICBL (Washington, Feb. 1999). It should, however, be noted that when the Belgian Foreign Minister first raised the possibility of an anti-personnel mine ban treaty in July 1995 he suggested entrusting the Conference on Disarmament 'with the preliminary studies of such a Convention'. Speech of Belgian Foreign Minister Eric Derycke, Chairman of the International Meeting on Demining (Geneva, 6 July 1995).

[220] Though the difference in context was startling. The use, or at least the first use, of chemical weapons in warfare had been prohibited for decades by the time the CD was entrusted with the task of negotiating their total prohibition. In stark contrast, only the use of certain, limited types of anti-personnel mines had been prohibited by international agreement (Amended Protocol II), and even these were subject to an optional nine-year deferral period for compliance.

successfully negotiated in the Conference on Disarmament . . At the same time, the United States welcomes efforts outside that forum, including the free-standing process initiated by Canada, that can help provide momentum to our common goal.[221]

This was a big disappointment to a number of States and particularly the ICBL, which had lobbied hard for the USA to support actively the Ottawa Process.

**0.94** On 30 January 1997, the UK introduced a proposed mandate for an ad hoc committee on a ban on anti-personnel landmines within the CD,[222] but this was not accepted.[223] Then in March 1997, the Netherlands, prompted by other EU countries,[224] suggested a draft mandate on anti-personnel mines for the Conference.[225] Meanwhile, within the CD itself aside from those proposing that the Conference be seized of the issue, opinions among other members were split between those who did not want a ban to be discussed at any cost and those, for instance Mexico, who wanted the CD to concentrate on other

---

[221] 'United States Announces Next Step on Anti-Personnel Landmines', Statement by the Press Secretary, Office of the Press Secretary, The White House (Washington 17 Jan. 1997).

[222] Doc. CD/1443 of 30 January 1997, available at: www.unog.ch/disarm/curdoc/1443.pdf.

[223] On 6 March 1997, Mexico stated before the CD that: 'To sum up, as we stated in the First Committee of the General Assembly of the United Nations, we are not convinced that this is an appropriate forum in which to complete as soon as possible negotiations on an agreement to ban the use, stockpiling, production and transfer of anti-personnel landmines. The Conference on Disarmament must give the highest priority to negotiations on nuclear disarmament and should not embark on exercises which duplicate efforts that are being successfully pursued in other forums and which would divert us from the responsibilities which the international community has entrusted to us.' See CD/PV.758 of 6 Mar. 1997. On 15 May 1997, Hungary and Japan made another, similarly unsuccessful attempt to create an ad hoc committee on anti-personnel mines. Doc. CD/1455 of 15 May 1997, available at: www.unog.ch/disarm/curdoc/1455.htm.

[224] Until the late spring of 1997, France and the UK had been ardent supporters of a common EU position in favour of negotiating a ban on anti-personnel mines in the Conference on Disarmament and abandoning the Ottawa Process. This was blocked by other EU States, notably Ireland Finland, which did not support the principle of an immediate ban, sought unsuccessfully to make an alliance with France on the issue. See for instance Mannion, J., 'US Wants Talks on Landmine Ban held in Geneva', *Agence France Presse* (Washington, 17 Jan. 1997); UN Information Service, 'Disarmament Conference Hears Further Calls for Bans on Landmines and Fissile Materials, Establishment of Negotiating Committee on Nuclear Disarmament', Press release DCF/283 (Geneva, 23 Jan. 1997); 'Britain Calls for Ban on Landmine Exports', *Financial Times* (31 Jan. 1997).

[225] The Dutch proposed the following language: 'The Conference on Disarmament decides to establish an ad hoc committee under item (x) of its agenda to negotiate, for conclusion at the earliest possible date, an effective legally binding international agreement to ban worldwide the use, stockpiling, production and transfer of anti-personnel landmines . . . In order to carry forward this negotiating mandate effectively, the Conference directs the ad hoc committee to make provisions for speedy and continuous negotiations, and to establish the necessary working groups. These working groups could cover the separate components of a total ban on anti-personnel landmines, while the ad hoc committee should, at the same time, preserve the comprehensive nature of the total ban.' 'Draft Elements for a mandate for an ad hoc committee in the Conference on Disarmament on a total ban on Anti-Personnel Landmines.'

issues, particularly nuclear disarmament.[226] As a result, the proposal for an ad hoc committee was not accepted.

**0.95**  On 26 June 1997, agreement was reached to appoint a Special Coordinator for Anti-Personnel Landmines,[227] Australian Ambassador John Campbell, although this was only made possible by the discreet departure of the Syrian Representative from the room while the decision was taken.[228] The task of the Special Coordinator was to try to find an agreed mandate that could form the basis for discussions. On 14 August 1997, the Special Coordinator declared that there was little point in the CD taking any decisions on a possible mandate until the outcome of the Ottawa Process was known in December 1997.[229] None the less, at the UN General Assembly, a resolution entitled 'Contributions towards banning anti-personnel mines' invited the CD 'to intensify its efforts on the issue of anti-personnel landmines'.[230]

**0.96**  In 1998, the USA again sought to initiate negotiations in the CD, this time opting to call for an agreement to ban transfers of anti-personnel mines as opposed to a comprehensive ban of the weapons. As in 1997, however, the only progress made was in the appointment of a Special Coordinator (once more, Australian Ambassador John Campbell) to examine the possibility of further action. Attempts to secure agreement on the creation of an ad hoc committee to negotiate on mines were again unsuccessful. With the success of the Anti-Personnel Mine Ban Convention[231] (and current deadlock in the CD), proposals to initiate negotiations in the CD on landmines appear infeasible for the foreseeable future. Indeed, the USA has pursued greater restrictions on anti-vehicle mines within the context of the CCW rather than the CD; a mandate was agreed by States Parties to the CCW for negotiations which led, in November 2003, to the adoption of a Protocol V on explosive remnants of war.[232]

---

[226] Mexico saw the attempt by the USA to address landmines in the CD as a pretext to avoid discussion of comprehensive nuclear disarmament.

[227] A formal proposal to appoint a Special Coordinator was jointly tabled on 27 March 1997 by Chile, Finland, and Poland. CD/1452 of 27 Mar. 1997, available at: www.unog.ch/disarm/curdoc/1452.pdf.

[228] All decisions in the Conference on Disarmament are taken by consensus.

[229] 'Disarmament Conference Hears Statements on Anti-Personnel Landmines Nuclear Disarmament and Fissile Material Cut-off', UN Press release DCF/311 (Geneva, 15 Aug. 1997).

[230] UN General Assembly resolution 52/38H of 9 December 1997, adopted by 147 votes to nil with 15 abstentions (Benin, Botswana, Cuba, Eritrea, Indonesia, Kenya, Malawi, Mexico, Mozambique, Namibia, the Philippines, South Africa, Togo, Zambia, and Zimbabwe). In the First Committee Eritrea and South Africa had initially opposed the adoption of the resolution, which was passed with 121 votes in favour and 19 abstentions.

[231] See the following section, 'Key Developments since the Adoption of the Convention'.

[232] See UN Doc. CCW/NSP/2002/CRP.1 of 12 Dec. 2002.

## Key Developments since the Adoption of the Convention

**0.97**  While the CD has remained static, the Anti-Personnel Mine Ban Convention has proved dynamic.[233] Since its entry into force on 1 March 1999, it has attracted widespread support, with 141 States having ratified or acceded to it[234] and 9 signatories[235] as of 1 December 2003. Following a decision at the First Meeting of States Parties in 1999,[236] intersessional Standing Committees meetings have been organized regularly to support universality and implementation of the Convention as well as broader mine action activities.[237] Standing Committees address the general status and operation of the Convention, as well as efforts to carry out programmes of mine awareness, mine clearance, stockpile destruction, and victim assistance. At the Third Meeting of States Parties in 2001,[238] States Parties agreed to establish an Implementation Support Unit; this is hosted by the Geneva International Centre for Humanitarian Demining (GICHD).[239]

---

[233] See e.g. *A Guide to Mine Action* (Geneva: GICHD, July 2003).

[234] Afghanistan, Albania, Algeria, Andorra, Angola, Antigua and Barbuda, Argentina, Australia, Austria, Bahamas, Bangladesh, Barbados, Belarus, Belgium, Belize, Benin, Bolivia, Bosnia and Herzegovina, Botswana, Brazil, Bulgaria, Burkina Faso, Burundi, Cambodia, Cameroon, Canada, Cape Verde, Central African Republic, Chad, Chile, Colombia, the Comoros, the Republic of the Congo, Costa Rica, Côte d'Ivoire, Croatia, Cyprus, the Czech Republic, the Democratic Republic of the Congo, Denmark, Djibouti, Dominica, the Dominican Republic, Ecuador, El Salvador, Equatorial Guinea, Eritrea, Fiji, the Former Yugoslav Republic of Macedonia, France, Gabon, The Gambia, Germany, Ghana, Greece, Grenada, Guatemala, Guinea, Guinea-Bissau, Guyana, Holy See, Honduras, Hungary, Iceland, Ireland, Italy, Jamaica, Japan, Jordan, Kenya, Kiribati, Lesotho, Liberia, Liechtenstein, Lithuania, Luxembourg, Madagascar, the Maldives, Malaysia, Malawi, Mali, Malta, Mauritania, Mauritius, Mexico, the Republic of Moldova, Monaco, Mozambique, Nauru, Namibia, the Netherlands, New Zealand, Nicaragua, Niger, Nigeria, Niue, Norway, Panama, Paraguay, Peru, the Philippines, Portugal, Qatar, Romania, Rwanda, Saint Kitts and Nevis, Saint Lucia, Saint Vincent and the Grenadines, Samoa, San Marino, São Tomé e Principe, Senegal, Serbia and Montenegro, the Seychelles, Sierra Leone, Slovakia, Slovenia, Solomon Islands, South Africa, Spain, Sudan, Surinam, Swaziland, Sweden, Switzerland, Tajikistan, Tanzania, Thailand, Timor Leste, Togo, Trinidad and Tobago, Tunisia, Turkmenistan, Uganda, the UK, Uruguay, Venezuela, Yemen, Zambia, and Zimbabwe. A State becomes party to the Convention on the first day of the sixth month after it deposits its instrument of ratification or accession. See further the commentary on Article 17.

[235] Brunei Darussalam, the Cook Islands, Ethiopia, Haiti, Indonesia, Marshall Islands, Poland, Ukraine, and Vanuatu.

[236] See the Final Report of the First Meeting of States Parties, UN Doc. APLC/MSP.1/1999/1 of 20 May 1999.

[237] It is said that a number of key governments were aware from the outset that a strong follow-up mechanism would be needed to ensure the effective implementation of the Convention. See for instance Lawson *et al.*, 'The Ottawa Process'.

[238] See Paragraph 31 of the Final Report of the Second Meeting of States Parties, UN Doc. APLC/MSP.3/2001/1 of 10 Jan. 2002, p. 7.

[239] According to the GICHD, the Implementation Support Unit 'provides independent professional advice and support to the Presidents of Meetings of the States Parties, the Co-Chairs of the

**0.98** In a 2003 publication, *A Guide to Mine Action*, the GICHD stresses the ongoing 'spirit of partnership established by the Ottawa Process between governments, the UN, the ICRC and NGOs' and notes that:

> The cooperative approach of the States Parties has gone beyond their formal agreements to establish various implementation mechanisms as a third category of mechanisms has emerged to assist in implementing the Convention. These are mechanisms that have emerged on an informal basis. For example, to promote widespread international participation in the work of the Convention, a group of States Parties has established a delegate Sponsorship Programme. On the basis of voluntary contributions from a group of donors, this programme has ensured that more than 200 delegates each year are provided with financial support thereby ensuring that all States Parties—even those with limited means—can have their voices heard in discussions concerning the fulfilment of their responsibilities to implement the Convention . . . Other informal mechanisms that have emerged include Contact Groups—voluntary associations of States Parties and non-State partners which meet regularly to discuss matters of common interest. For example, since 2000 contact groups have been established to consider cooperative means to promote the universal acceptance of the Convention, the exchange of information in accordance with the Convention's reporting requirements and the mobilization of resources.[240]

Standing Committees and individual States Parties. It disseminates a range of information on the Convention to the States Parties and all other interested actors. In addition, on the basis of its mandate, the Implementation Support Unit has established and maintains a documentation resource facility.' See *A Guide to Mine Action*, ch. 4.

[240] See *A Guide to Mine Action*, ch. 4.

# COMMENTARY

## The Title and Preamble of the Convention

## The Title of the Convention

The Convention on the Prohibition of the Use, Stockpiling, Production and Transfer of Anti-Personnel Mines and on their Destruction.

### Introduction

**0.99** The title of the Convention on the Prohibition of the Use, Stockpiling, Production and Transfer of Anti-Personnel Mines and on their Destruction (the Anti-Personnel Mine Ban Convention)[1] betrays its mixed heritage of disarmament[2] and humanitarian law. It recalls in particular the title of the Convention on the Prohibition of the Development, Production, Stockpiling, and Use of Chemical Weapons and on their Destruction (the 1993 Chemical Weapons Convention), from which a number of the provisions have been adapted or taken verbatim.[3]

## The Formal Title of the Convention

**0.100**  In contrast to the 1993 Chemical Weapons Convention, and to the 1972 Convention on the Prohibition of the Development, Production and Stockpiling of Bacteriological (Biological) and Toxin Weapons and on their Destruction,[4] the order of the prohibited activities in the title of the Anti-Personnel Mine Ban Convention is not alphabetical. In accordance with the traditional focus of international humanitarian law, special emphasis is put on the prohibition on the *use* of anti-personnel mines so as to highlight the cause of the humanitarian problem.[5]

**0.101**  The formal title as ultimately adopted first appeared in the Second Austrian Draft of 14 March 1997, following comments by Mexico[6] and Portugal at the 1997 Vienna Conference that the title should contain a reference to the destruction of anti-personnel mines.[7] It follows exactly the order

---

[1]  As already noted in the Preface above, this title has no formal legal status. For a discussion of the varied nomenclature of the Convention see below para. 0.102.

[2]  According to two international lawyers, disarmament 'is the traditional term for the elimination, as well as the limitation or reduction (through negotiation of an international agreement) of the means by which nations wage war'. It is increasingly regarded as a subset of 'arms control'. Matthews and McCormack, 'The Influence of Humanitarian Principles in the Negotiation of Arms Control Treaties', 333–4.

[3]  The text of the Convention can be found in *International Legal Materials*, 31 (1993), 800ff.

[4]  Hereinafter referred to as the 1972 Biological Weapons Convention.

[5]  This does not explain, though, why 'stockpiling' follows 'use' rather than, in alphabetical terms, 'production'. It is also perhaps surprising that 'development' is not contained in the list of prohibited activities in the title of the Convention, as it is in the 1993 Chemical Weapons Convention, despite the prohibition on the development of anti-personnel mines contained in Article 1(1)(b) of the Anti-Personnel Mine Ban Convention. This is explained by the desire to follow the order and content of UN General Assembly Resolution 51/45S.

[6]  Mexico also had in mind the 1968 Treaty for the Prohibition of Nuclear Weapons in Latin America, otherwise known as the Treaty of Tlatelolco. Information provided to the author by Dr Juan Manuel Gomez-Robledo, Geneva, 3 June 2002.

[7]  The First Austrian Draft was entitled the Convention on the Prohibition of Anti-Personnel Mines—unchanged from the title proposed by Werner Ehrlich of the Austrian Ministry of Foreign Affairs in his first informal draft of April 1996. See para. 0.47 above. The ICBL draft text was entitled the Convention on the Prohibition of the Development, Production, Stockpiling, Transfer and Use of Anti-Personnel Mines and on their Destruction, Proposal by the International Campaign to Ban Landmines, ICBL, 20 Dec. 1996.

contained in UN General Assembly Resolution 51/45S of 10 December 1996, which urged all States 'to pursue vigorously an effective, legally binding international agreement to ban the use, stockpiling, production and transfer of anti-personnel mines'.[8]

## The Informal Title of the Convention

**0.102** For the purposes of brevity, the author has chosen to employ the nomenclature currently favoured by the UN secretariat, the Anti-Personnel Mine Ban Convention, although the treaty is also known informally as the Convention on the Prohibition of Anti-Personnel Mines, the Ottawa Convention,[9] the Ottawa treaty,[10] the Mine Ban Convention,[11] or the Mine Ban Treaty.[12]

# The Preamble

Preamble

The States Parties,

*Determined* to put an end to the suffering and casualties caused by anti-personnel mines, that kill or maim hundreds of people every week, mostly innocent and defenceless civilians and especially children, obstruct economic development and reconstruction, inhibit the repatriation of refugees and internally displaced persons, and have other severe consequences for years after emplacement,

*Believing* it necessary to do their utmost to contribute in an efficient and coordinated manner to face the challenge of removing anti-personnel mines placed throughout the world, and to assure their destruction,

*Wishing* to do their utmost in providing assistance for the care and rehabilitation, including the social and economic reintegration of mine victims,

---

[8] For details of the voting on the resolution see para. 0.57 and accompanying footnotes.
[9] See e.g. Aust, *Modern Treaty Law and Practice*, 23.
[10] e.g. by the International Committee of the Red Cross. See e.g. *Banning Anti-Personnel Mines: The Ottawa Treaty Explained* (Geneva: ICRC, 1998). [11] e.g. by Norway.
[12] The term is used by the International Campaign to Ban Landmines (ICBL), and a number of States, including South Africa. The surprising absence of any reference to Ottawa in the title can be explained, in part at least, by disappointment at the behaviour of Canada towards the end of the Oslo Diplomatic Conference. See above para. 0.89 and below para. 15.5. The term has also been used in the past by the Geneva International Centre for Humanitarian Demining (GICHD), which hosts the intersessional Standing Committee meetings and the Implementation Support Unit of the Convention.

*Recognizing* that a total ban of anti-personnel mines would also be an important confidence-building measure,

*Welcoming* the adoption of the Protocol on Prohibitions or Restrictions on the Use of Mines, Booby-Traps and Other Devices, as amended on 3 May 1996, annexed to the Convention on Prohibitions or Restrictions on the Use of Certain Conventional Weapons Which May Be Deemed to Be Excessively Injurious or to Have Indiscriminate Effects, and calling for the early ratification of this Protocol by all States which have not yet done so,

*Welcoming* also United Nations General Assembly Resolution 51/45 S of 10 December 1996 urging all States to pursue vigorously an effective, legally-binding international agreement to ban the use, stockpiling, production and transfer of anti-personnel landmines,

*Welcoming* furthermore the measures taken over the past years, both unilaterally and multilaterally, aiming at prohibiting, restricting or suspending the use, stockpiling, production and transfer of anti-personnel mines,

*Stressing* the role of public conscience in furthering the principles of humanity as evidenced by the call for a total ban of anti-personnel mines and recognizing the efforts to that end undertaken by the International Red Cross and Red Crescent Movement, the International Campaign to Ban Landmines and numerous other non-governmental organizations around the world,

*Recalling* the Ottawa Declaration of 5 October 1996 and the Brussels Declaration of 27 June 1997 urging the international community to negotiate an international and legally binding agreement prohibiting the use, stockpiling, production and transfer of anti-personnel mines,

*Emphasizing* the desirability of attracting the adherence of all States to this Convention, and determined to work strenuously towards the promotion of its universalization in all relevant fora including, inter alia, the United Nations, the Conference on Disarmament, regional organizations, and groupings, and review conferences of the Convention on Prohibitions or Restrictions on the Use of Certain Conventional Weapons Which May Be Deemed to Be Excessively Injurious or to Have Indiscriminate Effects,

*Basing* themselves on the principle of international humanitarian law that the right of the parties to an armed conflict to choose methods or means of warfare is not unlimited, on the principle that prohibits the employment in armed conflicts of weapons, projectiles and materials and methods of warfare of a nature to cause superfluous injury or unnecessary suffering and on the principle that a distinction must be made between civilians and combatants,

Have agreed as follows:

## Introduction

**0.103** The preamble of an international treaty typically sets out the background and purpose of the treaty although there is no legal requirement that it do so,[13] nor even that a preamble be included.[14] According to Article 31(2) of the 1969 Vienna Convention on the Law of Treaties, the preamble forms part of the 'context' of a treaty and is therefore significant for its interpretation.[15] Strictly speaking, however, the preamble is not legally binding on the States Parties.

**0.104** None of the draft texts that preceded the adoption of the Anti-Personnel Mine Ban Convention, including the text that served initially as the basis of negotiations at the Oslo Diplomatic Conference, contained a proposed preamble. On the first day of the Diplomatic Conference, Norway tabled a proposal for the preamble,[16] and the following day, France put forward a more detailed proposal.[17] The only other formal proposal for a preambular paragraph was made by Slovenia.[18] In addition, in advance of the Oslo Diplomatic Conference, Colombia,[19] the Philippines, the ICBL, and the Landmine Survivors Network, an NGO based in the USA focusing on mine victims [20] had circulated informally proposed preambular language.

**0.105** During the Oslo Diplomatic Conference, Mexico served as the 'Friend of the Chair' for the preamble. Following difficult negotiations, the final text was only agreed towards the end of the Conference, largely as a result of disagreement with France as to how the role of the Conference on Disarmament (CD) would be reflected in the preamble. The second principal bone of contention was the wish of Colombia that the Convention should refer expressly to the obligations on armed opposition groups. The debate on Colombia's proposal resulted in the introduction of the final introductory paragraph in the preamble on the principles of international (humanitarian) law.[21]

---

[13] See e.g. Aust, *Modern Treaty Law and Practice*, 336–7.

[14] Thus e.g. the four Geneva Conventions of 12 Aug. 1949 do not contain a preamble, but merely cite the conditions of their adoption.     [15] See Appendix 1 for the full text of the provision.

[16] See APL/CW.3 of 1 Sept. 1997.     [17] APL/CW.22 of 2 Sept. 1997.

[18] 'Understanding anti-personnel mines as a primarily defence weapon, their total prohibition is to be observed as an important confidence building measure'. APL/CW.28 of 2 Sept. 1997.

[19] See paras. 0.132 and 1.11 below.

[20] For a review of the use of the terms 'victim' and 'survivor' see e.g. *The Role of Mine Action in Victim Assistance* (Geneva: GICHD, 2001).     [21] See para. 0.132 below.

## The 'States Parties'

> The States Parties,

**0.106** The term 'States Parties' is used in the 1969 Vienna Convention on the Law of Treaties, and generally in multilateral treaties concluded within or under the auspices of the UN. It is, for instance, used in the 1993 Chemical Weapons Convention and other disarmament treaties.

**0.107** Early draft texts of the Anti-Personnel Mine Ban Convention used the term 'High Contracting Parties', following the nomenclature employed in the 1980 Convention on Certain Conventional Weapons (CCW).[22] The Second Austrian Draft of 14 March 1997 replaced this with 'States Parties' following objections by a number of States,[23] and this remained unchanged through to the Convention as adopted.

## Ending the Impact of Anti-Personnel Mines

> *Determined* to put an end to the suffering and casualties caused by anti-personnel mines, that kill or maim hundreds of people every week, mostly innocent and defenceless civilians and especially children, obstruct economic development and reconstruction, inhibit the repatriation of refugees and internally displaced persons, and have other severe consequences for years after emplacement,

**0.108** The first preambular paragraph sets out the object and purpose of the Convention: to put an end to the human, social, and economic impact of anti-personnel mines. Although it does not refer specifically to the use of anti-personnel mines as the cause of that impact, this is implicit.[24] The paragraph does not include a specific estimate of the numbers of casualties inflicted by anti-personnel mines, referring instead to 'hundreds' of people being killed or maimed each week.[25]

---

[22] See Appendix 4.

[23] Several reasons have been advanced for these objections. A number of States believed that they were negotiating an agreement primarily of disarmament and felt that the term 'High Contracting Parties' belonged to the domain of international humanitarian law. Others were concerned that the absence of a specific reference to States might open up a difficult discussion of the applicability of the Convention to armed opposition groups, and lead to a corresponding call for a separate provision dealing with its scope.

[24] See in paras. 1.16 to 1.30 below the commentary on Article 1(1)(a) for a discussion of the definition of the term 'use' for the purposes of the Anti-Personnel Mine Ban Convention.

[25] Although there is evidence that the number of new anti-personnel mine victims has generally been falling, this claim may still be true. Thus, according to Landmine Monitor, the monitoring arm of the ICBL: 'While acknowledging that it is impossible to arrive at an exact figure of casualties, it is likely that the number of new landmine casualties is between 15,000 and 20,000 per year'. ICBL,

## The Need for Mine Clearance

*Believing* it necessary to do their utmost to contribute in an efficient and coordinated manner to face the challenge of removing anti-personnel mines placed throughout the world, and to assure their destruction,

**0.109**  In seeking to achieve its object and purpose—to protect life and limb from anti-personnel mines and to remove a long-term obstacle to social and economic development—it is evident that although a prohibition on new use of anti-personnel mines would prevent the situation from deteriorating, it would not in and of itself reduce the impact of anti-personnel mines significantly. Accordingly, the second preambular paragraph refers to the 'challenge of removing anti-personnel mines placed throughout the world, and to assure their destruction'.

**0.110**  Article 5 of the Convention requires the clearance of all anti-personnel mines in mined areas under the jurisdiction or control of each State Party.[26] Article 6 supports *inter alia* the implementation of the obligation to clear mines through international cooperation and assistance.[27]

## Assistance to Mine Victims

*Wishing* to do their utmost in providing assistance for the care and rehabilitation, including the social and economic reintegration of mine victims,

**0.111**  As mentioned in the Introduction,[28] the absence of a reference to the need for victim assistance in the Brussels Declaration led to a diplomatic row between Belgium and South Africa during the International Conference for a Global Ban on Anti-Personnel Mines in June 1997 (the Brussels Conference). Subsequently, in the negotiation of what would become Article 6 of the Convention,[29] there was considerable discussion of whether to include language supported by many States, especially from Africa, calling for assistance for the 'social and economic reintegration' of mine victims. A number of donor governments were said to be concerned about the financial ramifications of such obligations. Germany, in particular, was vocal in opposing the inclusion of the

---

*Landmine Monitor Report 2002*, 40; see also ICBL, *Landmine Monitor Report 2001: Toward a Mine-Free World* (Washington: Human Rights Watch, Sept. 2001), 37. The figures seemingly refer to *all* landmine victims, not merely those killed or injured by anti-personnel mines, and may also include victims of unexploded ordnance.

[26]  See below the commentary on Article 5, especially on Article 5(1).
[27]  See below the commentary on Article 6(1), (2), (4), and (6)–(8).
[28]  See para. 0.78 above.       [29]  See paras. 6.5 and 6.8–6.10 below.

phrase 'social and economic reintegration' although, ultimately, it was included in both Article 6 and the preamble.

0.112  Arguably, the Convention does not impose an absolute legal obligation upon States Parties to assist mine victims, even their own nationals. Prior to the Oslo Diplomatic Conference, the International Committee of the Red Cross proposed that States Parties accept a clear obligation to assist landmine victims and to provide mine awareness programmes, suggesting its inclusion either within the general obligations in Article 1,[30] or, later, in a watered-down form, to be made a separate article.[31]

0.113  The preambular paragraph refers to mine victims in general, which indicates a wish to assist the victims of any landmines, even though the primary motivation for the negotiation of the Convention had been the specific impact of anti-personnel mines.[32] This approach is maintained in the body of the Convention, particularly Article 6(3).

## A Total Ban as a Confidence-Building Measure

*Recognizing* that a total ban of anti-personnel mines would also be an important confidence-building measure,

0.114  This paragraph was amended from a proposal by Slovenia during the Oslo Diplomatic Conference.[33] 'Confidence building', which normally means measures short of actual disarmament, such as transparency and exchange of information, is part and parcel of the disarmament lexicon, though it was also introduced into the preamble of the CCW, perhaps as an indirect consequence of the disarmament background of many of the government negotiators.[34]

---

[30]  'Each State Party undertakes to provide for the care and rehabilitation of landmine victims and for mine-awareness programs in accordance with the provisions of this Convention.' 'Comments of the International Committee of the Red Cross on the Third Austrian Draft (13/5/97) of the Convention on the Prohibition of Anti-personnel Mines', reproduced in Maresca and Maslen, *The Banning of Anti-Personnel Landmines*, 548.

[31]  'Each State Party undertakes to provide, as far as it is able, for the care and rehabilitation of landmine victims and for mine awareness programs in areas under its jurisdiction and control.'

[32]  Although most landmine victims are killed or injured by anti-personnel mines, the impact of anti-vehicle mines on civilians should not be underestimated. See e.g. ICRC, 'Anti-Vehicle Mines: Effects on Humanitarian Assistance and Civilian Populations', UN doc. CCW/GGE/II/WP.9 of 12 July 2002.            [33]  APL/CW.28 of 2 Sept. 1997. See para. 0.104 above.

[34]  Thus, a broader paragraph was included in the preamble to the CCW: '*Desiring* to contribute to international détente, the ending of the arms race and the building of confidence among States, and hence to the realization of the aspiration of all peoples to live in peace.' One commentator notes that the chief negotiators in the conference that adopted the 1980 Convention were arms control and disarmament specialists, most of whom had not been involved in the drafting of the 1977 Additional Protocols. He adds that the 'mixed lineage' of the Convention is well illustrated in its preamble, which

## The Relationship to Amended Protocol II

*Welcoming* the adoption of the Protocol on Prohibitions or Restrictions on the Use of Mines, Booby-Traps and Other Devices, as amended on 3 May 1996, annexed to the Convention on Prohibitions or Restrictions on the Use of Certain Conventional Weapons Which May Be Deemed to Be Excessively Injurious or to Have Indiscriminate Effects, and calling for the early ratification of this Protocol by all States which have not yet done so,

**0.115** This paragraph, which calls for the early ratification of Amended Protocol II 'by all States which have not yet done so',[35] was amended from one contained in the French proposal for the preamble.[36] The language appears more akin to a UN General Assembly resolution than a preambular paragraph in an international treaty. On 1 December 2003, 62 States had ratified both the Anti-Personnel Mine Ban Convention and Amended Protocol II (a total of 74 States had consented to be bound by Amended Protocol II);[37] and seven States were bound only by 1980 Protocol II.[38]

**0.116** The preambular paragraph does, however, beg the question—what is the relationship of the Convention to Amended Protocol II? The former prohibits all use and, except for certain limited circumstances, transfer of anti-personnel mines, whereas the latter permits use and transfer of certain anti-personnel mines under certain circumstances.

**0.117** The preambular language suggests that the two instruments should be seen as complementary. The Anti-Personnel Mine Ban Convention specifically requires that each States Party perimeter mark all areas under its jurisdiction or control, at least to the standards set out in Amended Protocol II.[39] Further, the subject-matter of Amended Protocol II is broader than that of the

combines four paragraphs on the principles of international humanitarian law followed by five paragraphs referring to wider issues of disarmament. Roach, 'Certain Conventional Weapons Convention', 14.

[35] There is no reference to the Protocol on Prohibitions or Restrictions on the Use of Mines, Booby-Traps and Other Devices (1980 Protocol II), although it remains open to States to consent to be bound by that Protocol.

[36] '*Welcoming* also the adoption, on May 3rd 1996, of the revised Protocol 2 to the Convention on prohibitions or restrictions on the use of certain conventional weapons which may be deemed to be excessively injurious or to have indiscriminate effects, and calling for the early ratification of this protocol by all countries who have not yet done so.' See APL/CW.22.

[37] The following States are parties to Amended Protocol II, but not to the Anti-Personnel Mine Ban Convention: China, Estonia, Finland, India, Israel, the Republic of Korea, Latvia, Morocco, Pakistan, Poland, Ukraine, and the USA, although Poland and Ukraine are signatories to the Convention.

[38] Cuba, Georgia, the Lao Democratic People's Republic, Mongolia, Poland, the Russian Federation, and Uzbekistan. As already noted, Poland is a signatory to the Anti-Personnel Mine Ban Convention.

[39] Article 5(2). See below the commentary on this provision, especially para. 5.29.

Anti-Personnel Mine Ban Convention[40] as, in addition to governing anti-personnel mines, the former also regulates all anti-vehicle mines, booby-traps, and other devices.[41]

**0.118** Thus, the International Committee of the Red Cross (ICRC) encourages States to adhere to Amended Protocol II annexed to the 1980 CCW[42] as well as to the Anti-Personnel Mine Ban Convention on the grounds that: 'In addition to regulating weapons that are not covered by the . . . [Anti-Personnel Mine Ban Convention], the Protocol enables a State to invoke its provisions, such as that requiring a party which uses mines to remove them at the end of the hostilities'.[43] In addition, in accordance with Amended Protocol II, if the forces of a party to a conflict gain control of an area in which anti-personnel mines other than remotely delivered mines have been laid, 'such forces shall, to the maximum extent feasible, maintain and, if necessary, establish the protections required by this Article [Article 5] until such weapons have been cleared'.[44]

## UN General Assembly Resolution 51/45S

> *Welcoming* also United Nations General Assembly Resolution 51/45 S of 10 December 1996 urging all States to pursue vigorously an effective, legally-binding international agreement to ban the use, stockpiling, production and transfer of anti-personnel landmines,

**0.119** Resolution 51/45S, introduced into the UN General Assembly by the USA, urged States to 'pursue vigorously an effective, legally binding international agreement to ban the use, stockpiling, production and transfer of anti-personnel landmines with a view to completing the negotiation as soon as

---

[40] On this basis, Article 30 of the 1969 Vienna Convention, which deals with the application of successive treaties relating to the same subject-matter, is not directly relevant to the two treaties.

[41] According to Article 5(2) of Amended Protocol II: ' "Other devices" means manually-emplaced munitions and devices including improvised explosive devices designed to kill, injure or damage and which are actuated manually, by remote control or automatically after a lapse of time'. Directional fragmentation devices, such as the Claymore type, fall within this definition when used in command detonation mode (when otherwise triggered by tripwire they are anti-personnel mines for the purposes of the Anti-Personnel Mine Ban Convention).

[42] In addition, the ICRC does not recommend that States which have consented to be bound by 1980 Protocol II denounce the Protocol.

[43] ICRC Fact Sheet on the Convention on the Prohibition of Anti-Personnel Mines and on their Destruction (Geneva: ICRC, 2000), 2. Article 10(1) and (2) of Amended Protocol II provides that: '1. Without delay after the cessation of active hostilities, all minefields, mined areas, mines, booby-traps and other devices shall be cleared, removed, destroyed or maintained in accordance with Article 3 and paragraph 2 of Article 5 of this Protocol . . . 2. High Contracting Parties and parties to a conflict bear such responsibility with respect to minefields, mined areas, mines, booby-traps and other devices in areas under their control.'          [44] Article 5(4), Amended Protocol II.

possible'.[45] Despite efforts, especially by France, to refer to the Conference on Disarmament as the forum within which negotiations were to take place, the resolution ultimately did not specify where the agreement was to be negotiated. The preambular paragraph in the Anti-Personnel Mine Ban Convention does not, however, expressly link the 'Ottawa Process' or the Convention to the resolution.

## Unilateral and Multilateral Measures

*Welcoming* furthermore the measures taken over the past years, both unilaterally and multilaterally, aiming at prohibiting, restricting or suspending the use, stockpiling, production and transfer of anti-personnel mines,

0.120 The preambular paragraph welcoming the unilateral and multilateral measures 'aiming at prohibiting, restricting or suspending the use, stockpiling, production and transfer of anti-personnel mines' was slightly amended from a French proposal. Following the adoption of UN General Assembly Resolution 48/75K in 1993,[46] most landmine-producing States, including those that did not support a total prohibition of the weapons, had declared a limited or comprehensive moratorium on the export of anti-personnel mines.

0.121 In March 1995, Belgium had become the first country in the world to adopt national legislation comprehensively outlawing anti-personnel mines, including components, parts, and technology. On 4 December 1996, Switzerland adopted a Federal Law on War Material that prohibited the development, manufacture, acquisition, transfer, import, or stockpiling of anti-personnel mines. In Austria, a Federal Law entered into force on 1 January 1997 prohibiting the production, acquisition, transfer, and use of anti-personnel mines. In Sweden, a major defence bill, which also entered into force on 1 January 1997, prohibited the use of anti-personnel mines and required that all stockpile destruction be completed by 2001.

0.122 By 17 March 1997, the ICRC had recorded that 53 States had unilaterally supported a global ban on the production, stockpiling, transfer, and use of anti-personnel mines,[47] 21 States had renounced future use of anti-personnel mines by their own forces, and a further seven States had suspended such use. In addition, 15 States had begun destroying their own stockpiles.[48]

---

[45] The resolution was adopted on 10 Dec. 1996 by 155 votes to nil with 10 abstentions (Belarus, China, Cuba, the Democratic Republic of Korea, Israel, Pakistan, the Republic of Korea, the Russian Federation, Syria, and Turkey). See para. 0.57 above.    [46] See para. 0.56 above.

[47] Of these, only Laos and the USA have not yet adhered to the Anti-Personnel Mine Ban Convention.

[48] ICRC, 'Progress towards a Ban on Anti-Personnel Landmines: Measures by Countries and Organizations' (Geneva: ICRC, 17 Jan. 1997).

Cajoled and encouraged by the ICBL and the ICRC, a critical mass of pro-ban States had formed in little more than four years.

## The Campaign for a Total Ban on Anti-Personnel Mines

> *Stressing* the role of public conscience in furthering the principles of humanity as evidenced by the call for a total ban of anti-personnel mines and recognizing the efforts to that end undertaken by the International Red Cross and Red Crescent Movement, the International Campaign to Ban Landmines and numerous other non-governmental organizations around the world,

**0.123** The first clause of this preambular paragraph recalls the language of the so-called Martens clause, named after the Russian jurist Fedor Fedorovitch Martens who was instrumental in drafting it and ensuring its adoption.[49] The clause first appeared in the Preamble to 1899 Hague Convention IV as a means to resolve a dispute at the 1899 Peace Conference on the status of civilians who took up arms against an occupying force.[50] It was subsequently included in the clause on denunciation common to the four 1949 Geneva Conventions of 12 August 1949[51] and then as Article 1(2) of 1977 Additional Protocol I, with only slight amendments.[52] A variation of the clause is included in the preamble to the 1980 CCW.[53]

---

[49] For background on the adoption of the clause see e.g. Pustogarov, V., 'Fyodor Fyodorovich Martens (1845–1909): A Humanist of Modern Times', *International Review of the Red Cross*, no. 312 (Geneva: May–June 1996), 300–14; and Best, G., *Humanity in Warfare* (New York: Columbia University Press, 1980), 163–6.

[50] Although its inclusion (unchanged) in the Preamble to 1907 Hague Convention IV is more often cited in the literature. The paragraph reads as follows: 'Until a more complete code of the laws of war has been issued, the high contracting Parties deem it expedient to declare that, in cases not included in the Regulations adopted by them, the inhabitants and the belligerents remain under the protection and the rule of the principles of the law of nations, as they result from the usages established among civilised peoples, from the laws of humanity, and the dictates of the public conscience'. See Best, *Humanity in Warfare*, 164; Ticehurst, R., 'The Martens Clause and the Laws of Armed Conflict', *International Review of the Red Cross*, no. 317 (Geneva: Mar.–Apr. 1997), 125ff.

[51] e.g. Article 63 of the Geneva Convention for the Amelioration of the Condition of the Wounded and Sick in Armed Forces in the Field of 12 Aug. 1949 states among other things that: 'The denunciation shall have effect only in respect of the denouncing Power. It shall in no way impair the obligations which the Parties to the conflict shall remain bound to fulfil by virtue of the principles of the law of nations, as they result from the usages established among civilized peoples, from the laws of humanity and the dictates of the public conscience.'

[52] 'In cases not covered by this Protocol or by any other international agreements, civilians and combatants remain under the protection and authority of the principles of international law derived from established custom, from the principles of humanity and from the dictates of public conscience.'

[53] '*Confirming* their determination that in cases not covered by this Convention and its annexed Protocols, the civilian population and the combatants shall at all times remain under the protection and authority of the principles of international law derived from established custom, from the principles of humanity and from the dictates of public conscience.'

**0.124** Opinions differ as to the legal implications of the Martens clause.[54] It could be argued, for instance, that the adoption of the prohibition on the use of gas as a means of warfare in 1925 and the taboo against napalm and nuclear weapons are to be largely ascribed to public outrage. In 1996, the International Court of Justice declared in its *Nuclear Weapons Advisory Opinion*—though without providing any evidence—that the Martens clause had 'proved to be an effective means of addressing the rapid evolution of military technology'.[55]

**0.125** The specific recognition of the campaigning work of the International Red Cross and Red Crescent Movement and the ICBL is probably unique in an international treaty.[56] Both were instrumental in mobilizing public opinion and thereby political will in support of a total ban on anti-personnel mines. For its part, the ICBL worked on a daily basis with Core Group governments, and in December 1997, the Campaign was awarded the Nobel Peace Prize jointly with its Coordinator, Jody Williams.

**0.126** Notable by its absence is a reference to the work of the UN in promoting the adoption of the Convention,[57] even though two successive Secretaries-General—Boutros Boutros-Ghali and Kofi Annan—had adopted clear public positions in favour of the total prohibition of anti-personnel mines, and a number of UN bodies, particularly UNICEF and its national committees, had campaigned actively in favour of the prohibition of anti-personnel mines. On 3 September 1997 in his address to the Oslo Diplomatic Conference, the Secretary-General of the UN, Kofi Annan, committed the organization to support the implementation of the future Convention and reminded delegates that 'the very first peace-keeper to sacrifice his life in the cause of the United Nations was killed by a landmine in the Middle East'.[58]

## The Ottawa and Brussels Declarations

*Recalling* the Ottawa Declaration of 5 October 1996 and the Brussels Declaration of 27 June 1997 urging the international community to negotiate an international and legally binding agreement prohibiting the use, stockpiling, production and transfer of anti-personnel mines,

---

[54] See e.g. Greenwood, C., 'Humanitarian Law and Laws of War', Centennial of the First International Peace Conference, Preliminary Report (June 1998), 28.

[55] Nuclear Weapons Advisory Opinion, para. 78, *ICJ Reports*, 1996.

[56] Especially since the ICBL did not at that stage possess a legal personality, being a loose coalition of independent NGOs that endorsed a common set of objectives: the 'Joint Call'.

[57] Even though, as already noted, the Convention was negotiated outside UN auspices. See para. 0.50.

[58] Statement of the Secretary-General of the UN to the Diplomatic Conference on an International Total Ban on Anti-Personnel Land Mines (Oslo, 3 Sept. 1997).

**0.127**  The Ottawa Declaration, the document emanating from the 1996 Ottawa Conference, was the seminal text of the Ottawa Process.[59] According to the Declaration:

States represented at the Ottawa Conference, the 'Ottawa Group', have agreed to enhance cooperation and coordination of efforts on the basis of . . . a recognition that the extreme humanitarian and socio-economic costs associated with the use of anti-personnel mines require urgent action on the part of the international community to ban and eliminate this type of weapon.

**0.128**  The Brussels Declaration was the formal text adopted at the Brussels Conference in June 1997. Adherence to the Declaration, through 'signature' or association with its general principles, was a prerequisite for full participation in the Oslo Diplomatic Conference, and accordingly voting rights in the negotiations.[60] In recalling UN General Assembly Resolution 51/45S,[61] it affirmed that the 'essential elements' of the treaty should include: 'A comprehensive ban on the use, stockpiling, production and transfer of anti-personnel mines; the destruction of stockpiled and removed anti-personnel mines,[62] and international cooperation and assistance in the field of mine clearance in affected States'.[63]

## Universality of the Anti-Personnel Mine Ban Convention

*Emphasizing* the desirability of attracting the adherence of all States to this Convention, and determined to work strenuously towards the promotion of its universalization in all relevant fora including, inter alia, the United Nations, the Conference on Disarmament, regional organizations, and groupings, and review conferences of the Convention on Prohibitions or Restrictions on the Use of Certain Conventional Weapons Which May Be Deemed to Be Excessively Injurious or to Have Indiscriminate Effects,

**0.129**  In spite of a seemingly straightforward call for adherence to the Anti-Personnel Mine Ban Convention, and the promotion of its universalization 'in all relevant fora', this paragraph was probably the hardest of all the preambular paragraphs to agree on.[64] France was especially determined[65] that a future role

---

[59] The Ottawa Declaration is contained in Appendix 3.          [60] See para. 0.56 above.

[61] See paras. 0.57 and 0.119 above.

[62] i.e. not a duty to clear emplaced anti-personnel mines.

[63] As discussed in paragraph 0.78 above, the absence of a specific reference in the Brussels Declaration to assistance to mine victims was the subject of an animated dispute at the Brussels Conference. It resulted *inter alia* in South Africa associating itself with the Brussels Declaration rather than actually signing it.

[64] See para. 0.105 above.

[65] According to one source this was primarily a face-saving gesture for France, which had previously remained outside the Ottawa Process advocating a leading role for the Conference on Disarmament in negotiating any new text on landmines.

of the Conference on Disarmament in the elimination of anti-personnel mines be explicitly recognized[66] and had included a paragraph to that effect in its proposal for the preamble introduced at the Oslo Diplomatic Conference.[67] Less contentious were the references to the United Nations and the Review Conferences of the CCW.[68]

**0.130** Many regional 'organizations' and 'groupings' played an important role in supporting the adoption of a treaty prohibiting anti-personnel mines and would therefore naturally promote the universalization of the Anti-Personnel Mine Ban Convention. Thus, for example in January 1997, the ICRC recorded support for a global ban on anti-personnel mines from the following regional entities: the Parliamentary Assembly of the Council of Europe; the Council of the European Union; the Organization of African Unity (OAU); the Organization of the Islamic Conference (OCI); the Organization of American States (OAS); the Central American Parliament; and the Union of African Parliaments.[69]

## The Principles of International Humanitarian Law

> *Basing* themselves on the principle of international humanitarian law that the right of the parties to an armed conflict to choose methods or means of warfare is not unlimited, on the principle that prohibits the employment in armed conflicts of weapons, projectiles and materials and methods of warfare of a nature to cause superfluous injury or unnecessary suffering and on the principle that a distinction must be made between civilians and combatants,

### Introduction

**0.131** Although the Anti-Personnel Mine Ban Convention is typically regarded as a hybrid of disarmament and humanitarian law, the final preambular paragraph is a clear expression of its fundamental humanitarian law

---

[66] Even though no preambular paragraphs had been included in the three Austrian draft treaty texts, in April 1997, as it prepared to join formally the Ottawa Process, France had suggested the following preambular paragraph: 'Reconnaissant le rôle éminent cui incombe à la Conférence du Désarmement' ('Recognising the leading role of the Conference on Disarmament'). Proposal contained in a facsimile transmission from the French Ministry of Foreign Affairs to the Canadian Department of Foreign Affairs and International Trade, Paris, 24 Apr. 1997.

[67] 'Recognising the complementary efforts undertaken in the Conference on disarmament towards achieving a worldwide solution for the total and definitive elimination of anti-personnel mines.' See above para. 0.104.

[68] The Second Review Conference of the Convention took place in Geneva in December 2001 and a third Review Conference is scheduled to be convened no later than 2006.

[69] ICRC, 'Progress towards a Ban on Anti-Personnel Landmines'.

underpinnings and origins.[70] It represents an amalgamation of two preambular paragraphs to the 1980 Convention on Certain Conventional Weapons (CCW).[71]

**0.132** As already noted,[72] the preambular paragraph was drafted in response to the call from Colombia[73] that the Convention specifically regulate the activities of armed opposition groups as well as States. Thus, the reference to 'parties to an armed conflict' covers both States and armed non-governmental actors. Indeed, its inclusion in the preamble to the Anti-Personnel Mine Ban Convention has sometimes been cited as evidence of the applicability of the obligations of the Convention not only to States Parties, but also to entities other than States engaged in an armed struggle within the territory of States Parties. This argument is not persuasive. Given the clear nature of the undertakings, notably in Article 1, there is general agreement that the Convention is not directly applicable to such armed opposition groups,[74] other than under national legislation adopted in accordance with Article 9 of the Convention.

### The Right to Choose Methods or Means of Warfare is not Unlimited

**0.133** According to 1977 Additional Protocol I: 'In any armed conflict, the right of the parties to the conflict to choose methods or means of warfare is not unlimited'.[75] This rather awkwardly phrased rule means simply that a party to a conflict, whether a State or an armed opposition group, is not free to use any weapon it wishes, nor in a manner of its own choosing; restraint is therefore

---

[70]  A number of those most closely involved in drafting the Anti-Personnel Mine Ban Convention wrote afterwards that it was 'firmly rooted in international humanitarian law' but that it also contained 'important elements of disarmament law'. Hajnoczi, T., Desch, T., and Chatsis, D., 'The Ban Treaty', in Cameron *et al., To Walk without Fear*, 296. See further, below, the commentary on Article 1. In the view of another authority, the Convention could be described as a disarmament law treaty with a humanitarian, rather than a military or security purpose. See *A Guide to Mine Action*, ch. 5.

[71]  'Further recalling the general principle of the protection of the civilian population against the effects of hostilities', and 'Basing themselves on the principle of international law that the right of the parties to an armed conflict to choose methods or means of warfare is not unlimited, on the principle that prohibits the employment in armed conflicts of weapons, projectiles and materials and methods of warfare of a nature to cause superfluous injury or unnecessary suffering'.

[72]  See para. 0.105 above.          [73]  See e.g. APL/CW.46.

[74]  In contrast to disarmament law treaties, purported legal applicability to all 'parties to the conflict', not just States, is no stranger to international humanitarian law. Yet, suggestions made during the 1997 Vienna Conference and the Oslo Diplomatic Conference that the Convention should seek to bind armed opposition groups were not accepted. Reasons for this decision included a fear of complicating negotiations and deterring adherence. See paras. 1.4 and 1.9–1.12 below.

[75]  Article 35(1), 1977 Additional Protocol I. The term 'means of warfare' refers to weaponry; 'methods of warfare' are tactics and the manner of use of weaponry. See for instance Verri, P., *Dictionary of the International Law of Armed Conflict* (Geneva: ICRC, 1992), 126.

imposed by both customary and conventional law. The rule itself is widely regarded as being a rule of customary international law applicable to all States.[76]

## Superfluous Injury and Unnecessary Suffering

**0.134** The prohibition of the use of weapons inflicting superfluous injury or unnecessary suffering (*maux superflus*) dates back to the nineteenth century[77] and possibly before.[78] Its most recent codification is to be found in 1977 Additional Protocol I, wherein it is prohibited 'to employ weapons, projectiles and material and methods of warfare of a nature to cause superfluous injury or unnecessary suffering'.[79]

**0.135** It is generally agreed that the prohibition forms part of customary law. According to the International Court of Justice in 1996:

The cardinal principles contained in the texts constituting the fabric of humanitarian law are the following . . . According to the second principle, it is prohibited to cause unnecessary suffering to combatants: it is accordingly prohibited to use weapons causing them such harm or uselessly aggravating their suffering.[80]

However, no consensus can be found in the relevant literature as to the precise ambit of the prohibition, nor how it is to be applied to specific

[76] Thus, in the Nuclear Weapons Advisory Opinion, the International Court of Justice (ICJ) referred to the many humanitarian law instruments and stated that: 'All this shows that the conduct of military operations is governed by a body of legal prescriptions. This is so because "the right of belligerents to adopt means of injuring the enemy is not unlimited", as stated in Article 22 of the 1907 Hague Regulations relating to the laws and customs of war on land.' Nuclear Weapons Advisory Opinion, *ICJ Reports*, 1996, para. 77.

[77] In the 1868 St Petersburg Declaration, which outlawed the use of explosive projectiles under 400 grams in weight, States accepted that 'the only legitimate object which States should endeavour to accomplish during war is to weaken the military forces of the enemy,' and that 'this object would be exceeded by the employment of arms which uselessly aggravate the sufferings of disabled men, or render their death inevitable.'

[78] Oeter, S., 'Methods and Means of Combat', in Fleck, D. (ed.), *The Handbook of Humanitarian Law in Armed Conflicts* (New York: Oxford University Press, 1995), 113. Thus, in Ancient India the Book of Manu had declared unlawful arrows with hooked spikes, which after entering human flesh would be difficult to remove. See Singh, N., 'Armed conflicts and humanitarian laws of ancient India', in Swinarski, C. (ed.), *Studies and Essays on International Humanitarian Law and Red Cross Principles* (Geneva/The Hague: ICRC/Martinus Nijhoff, 1984), 532.

[79] Article 35(2), 1977 Additional Protocol I.

[80] *Nuclear Weapons Advisory Opinion*, para. 78. 1977 Additional Protocol I included both concepts: *unnecessary suffering* and *superfluous injury*, the latter of which is felt to better render the French 'maux superflus' with its notion of a more objective criterion than *suffering* capable of being measured. It is generally accepted that this combined rendition of the term has entered the realm of customary international law, although the *Nuclear Weapons Advisory Opinion* only refers specifically to 'unnecessary suffering'.

weapons.[81] According to a number of States, the principle of superfluous injury or unnecessary suffering embodies the purpose of the principles of military necessity and humanity, requiring a finding that the suffering or destruction caused by the use of a given weapon is 'plainly excessive or disproportionate to the military advantage reasonably expected to be gained from its use' for the weapon to be deemed unlawful.[82]

**0.136** 1977 Additional Protocol I requires that parties to the Protocol determine whether the use of a 'new weapon, means of method of warfare' would be unlawful according to the protocol or to another rule of international law.[83] Through its SIrUS Project,[84] the ICRC has sought to develop a set of medical data that can be used in judging whether any given weapon might be of a nature to cause superfluous injury or unnecessary suffering.[85] In 1996, the then ICRC President, Dr Cornelio Sommaruga, questioned publicly whether blast anti-personnel mines were not of such a nature:

If a person steps on a buried anti-personnel mine, his or her foot or leg is blown off. The force of the blast drives earth, grass, the vaporized mine case and portions of the victim's shoe and foot upwards into the tissues of the other leg, buttocks, genitals, arms and sometimes the eyes. With those mines which have a larger volume of explosive, death may be inevitable. If the wounded person gets to hospital and if the hospital has the necessary facilities and expertise (both of which are rare in mine affected countries) he or she will require several operations, will stay in hospital four weeks at least and will require a safe blood transfusion. Awaiting the survivor is permanent and severe disability with all the social, psychological and economic implications of being an amputee. Mines are designed to produce these effects. Likewise, fragmentation mines,

---

[81] According to one authority, 'the prohibition of *maux superflus* is characterised by a particularly complex mixture of very definite prohibitions of certain specific categories of arms on [the] one hand, and a rather abstract prohibition of means of warfare which cause unnecessary sufferings on the other; the relationship between these two sets of rules is far from clear. How far the definite prohibitions are only specific expressions or materialisations of the general prohibitory provision, and to what extent they are, to the contrary, constitutive developments of a merely political programme envisaged in Article 23(e) [of the] Hague Regulations, is a question which still needs careful consideration'. Oeter, 'Methods and Means of Combat', 114.

[82] See e.g. Robblee Jr., Captain P.A., 'The Legitimacy of Modern Conventional Weaponry,' *The Military Law and Law of War Review*, 26/4 (1977), 415; Oeter, 'Methods and Means of Combat', 114.

[83] Article 36, 1977 Additional Protocol I.

[84] See e.g. Daoust, I., 'ICRC Expert Meeting on Legal Reviews of Weapons and the SIrUS Project', *International Review of the Red Cross*, no. 842 (Geneva: ICRC, 30 June 2001), 539–42.

[85] It remarks for instance, that: 'The concept of superfluous injury or unnecessary suffering, its objective effect on the victim (severity of the injury, intensity of the suffering), and its relation to military necessity (rendering the enemy *hors de combat*) are not interpreted in a consistent and generally accepted manner. This concept continues to be the basis on which judgement is formed, but debates have shown its relative and imprecise character.' *ICRC Commentary on the 1977 Additional Protocols*, 409–10.

which can propel hundreds of metal fragments into a person at waist height, are designed to inflict very severe wounds. 'Very severe' means tearing the person apart, or, for the one who triggers the mine, death . . . Would not most people, including soldiers, describe the effects of mines described above as superfluous and excessive to the military need?[86]

**0.137** Similarly, in its suggestion for preambular language to the Convention, the ICBL put forward the following proposal: '*Recognizing* that international law prohibits the use of weapons that are of an indiscriminate nature or that cause superfluous injury or unnecessary suffering, and recognizing that anti-personnel mines are of such a nature'.[87] As has been seen, this proposal was not included in the preamble.[88]

## The Principle of Distinction

**0.138** The principle of distinction—the duty to 'distinguish' between military targets and civilians and civilian objects and to attack only military objectives—is central to the protection afforded to civilians by international humanitarian law.[89] In the application of the principle to weapons, it is now well established that customary international law prohibits the use of indiscriminate weapons, both in international and in internal armed conflict,[90] that is, weapons that are incapable of being targeted against military objectives. According to the Nuclear Weapons Advisory Opinion: 'States must never make civilians the object of attack and must consequently never use weapons that are incapable of distinguishing between civilian and military targets'.[91]

---

[86] Sommaruga, C., 'Does the Nature of Mine Injuries also Justify a Total Ban?' in UN, *Landmines*, 1.4 (Sept. 1996), 11.

[87] ICBL Comments on the Third Austrian Draft of 13 May 1997.

[88] Presumably on the basis that it would accuse non-party States using anti-personnel mines of violating international law, while accepting that States Parties that had used the weapons in the past had previously employed an unlawful weapon.

[89] According to Article 48(2) of 1977 Additional Protocol I: 'In order to ensure respect for and protection of the civilian population and civilian objects, the Parties to the conflict shall at all times distinguish between the civilian population and combatants and civilian objects and military objectives and accordingly shall direct their operations only against military objectives'.

[90] Although efforts to include general prohibitions on the use of weapons in 1977 Additional Protocol II were unsuccessful, the *Tadić Case* before the Appeals Chamber of the International Tribunal for the Prosecution of Persons Responsible for Serious Violations of International Humanitarian Law Committed in the Territory of Former Yugoslavia since 1991, clearly identified the protection of civilians against hostilities, in particular from indiscriminate attacks, as a customary rule governing internal armed conflict. *Prosecutor* v. *Tadić, Case No. IT-94-1-AR72*, Appeal on Jurisdiction, 2 Oct. 1995 (hereinafter the *Tadić Case*), 67–8, para. 127; see also Meron, T., 'The Continuing Role of Custom in the Formation of International Humanitarian Law', Editorial Comment in *The American Journal of International Law*, 90/238 (Apr. 1996), 242.

[91] Nuclear Weapons Advisory Opinion, para. 78, *ICJ Reports*, 1996.

**0.139** The prohibition on inherently indiscriminate weapons has been codified in Article 51(4) of 1977 Additional Protocol I, which provides that: 'Indiscriminate attacks are prohibited. Indiscriminate attacks are . . . (b) those which employ a method or means of combat which cannot be directed at a specific military objective'.[92] According to a commentary on the provision published by the ICRC, the weapons covered are 'primarily long-range missiles which cannot be aimed exactly at the objective. The V2 rockets used at the end of the Second World War are an example of this'.[93] There has been continual debate, resuscitated by the campaign against landmines,[94] as to whether the prohibition includes weapons that are typically used indiscriminately or only weapons that are inherently indiscriminate.[95] In this regard, the Rome Statute for the International Criminal Court sets the threshold high, providing for the Court's jurisdiction over the use, in international armed conflicts only, of,

weapons, projectiles and material and methods of warfare . . . which are inherently indiscriminate in violation of the international law of armed conflict, provided that such weapons, projectiles and material and methods of warfare are the subject of a comprehensive prohibition and are included in an annex to this Statute, by an amendment in accordance with the relevant provisions set forth in articles 121 and 123.[96]

---

[92] The USA considers that the prohibition on indiscriminate attacks is already part of customary law applicable to all weapons. Nash, M., 'Contemporary Practice of the United States Relating to International Law', *American Journal of International Law*, 91 (Apr. 1997), 336. A violation of Article 51 that results in civilian deaths or serious injuries is treated as a grave breach subject to compulsory universal jurisdiction.

[93] Sandoz, Y., Swinarski, C., and Zimmerman, B. (eds.), *Commentary on the Additional Protocols of 8 June 1977 to the Geneva Conventions of 12 August 1949* (Geneva: ICRC/Martinus Nijhoff, 1987), 621.

[94] According to the ICBL, landmines are weapons with indiscriminate effects whose use should already be prohibited under customary law. See e.g. Human Rights Watch and Physicians for Human Rights, *Landmines, A Deadly Legacy*, especially ch. 8.

[95] See e.g. International Committee of the Red Cross, *Report on the Conference of Government Experts on the Use of Certain Conventional Weapons (Lucerne, 24 September–18 October 1974)* (Geneva: ICRC, 1975), para. 31. See Kalshoven, F., 'The Conference of Government Experts on the Use of Certain Conventional Weapons, Lucerne, 24 September to 18 October 1974', *Netherlands Yearbook of International Law*, vi (1975), 91–2.

[96] Article 8(2)(b)(xx), 1998 Rome Statute of the International Criminal Court. See e.g. Roberts and Guelff, *Documents on the Laws of War*, 678. See also, in relation to the International Criminal Court, the commentary on Article 9, especially in paras. 9.13–9.14 below.

# Article 1. General Obligations

Article 1—General obligations

1. Each State Party undertakes never under any circumstances:

(a) To use anti-personnel mines;

(b) To develop, produce, otherwise acquire, stockpile, retain or transfer to anyone, directly or indirectly, anti-personnel mines;

(c) To assist, encourage or induce, in any way, anyone to engage in any activity prohibited to a State Party under this Convention.

2. Each State Party undertakes to destroy or ensure the destruction of all anti-personnel mines in accordance with the provisions of this Convention.

# Introduction

**1.1**  Article 1 contains the core provisions—termed general obligations—of the Anti-Personnel Mine Ban Convention. Each State Party undertakes 'never under any circumstances' to use, or, directly or indirectly, to develop, produce, otherwise acquire, stockpile, retain, or transfer anti-personnel mines.[1] Similarly, each State Party undertakes never under any circumstances to assist, encourage, or induce anyone to engage in such activities. In accordance with Articles 3 and 4 of the Convention,[2] each State Party undertakes to destroy or ensure the destruction of all anti-personnel mines that it owns or possesses, or that are under its jurisdiction or control, except a minimum quantity retained for permitted, humanitarian purposes.

**1.2**  The general obligations contained in paragraph 1, which are adapted from Article I (General obligations) of the 1993 Chemical Weapons Convention, are, in keeping with that Convention, phrased positively rather than in terms of prohibitions. Similarly, although the undertakings appear to be both comprehensive and absolute, they are implicitly subject to the remaining provisions of the Convention. In the case of the Anti-Personnel Mine Ban Convention, Articles 2, 3, and 4, dealing with definitions, exceptions, and the destruction of stockpiled anti-personnel mines, respectively, are particularly relevant.[3]

---

[1] Anti-personnel mines are defined in Article 2(1)–(3) of the Convention. See below paras. 2.12–2.60.                                     [2] See below the commentary on these articles.

[3] A proposal by South Africa, repeated by Estonia, at the Vienna Experts Meeting on 12–14 February 1997 to preface the general obligations with the phrase 'subject to the provisions of Article . . .' was not retained in Article 1, although the idea was incorporated into Article 3(1) itself. At the Oslo Diplomatic Conference, Canada pointed out that the phrase 'never under any circumstances' was employed in the 1993 Chemical Weapons Convention, which itself contained certain exceptions.

**1.3** Prior to the Oslo Diplomatic Conference, the ICRC had proposed a third paragraph to the Article, which was not accepted, whereby: 'Each State Party undertakes to provide for the care and rehabilitation of landmine victims and for mine awareness programs in accordance with the provisions of this Convention'.[4] Part of the proposal was, however, incorporated into Article 6(3) of the Convention.[5]

## Paragraph 1

1. Each State Party undertakes never under any circumstances:

(a) To use anti-personnel mines;

(b) To develop, produce, otherwise acquire, stockpile, retain or transfer to anyone, directly or indirectly, anti-personnel mines;

(c) To assist, encourage or induce, in any way, anyone to engage in any activity prohibited to a State Party under this Convention.

## The Scope of the Obligations

### The Comprehensive Nature of the Obligations

**1.4** The Anti-Personnel Mine Ban Convention does not contain a separate article setting out its scope of application. This is in accord with disarmament law treaties, and contrasts with most instruments of international humanitarian law, which apply primarily in situations of armed conflict.[6] Given the Convention's disarmament and other obligations,[7] which are not linked to any ongoing armed conflict, a separate article setting out the scope was not

---

[4] 'Comments of the International Committee of the Red Cross on the Third Austran Draft (13/5/97) of the Convention on the Prohibition of Anti-personnel Mines', reproduced in Maresca and Maslen, *The Banning of Anti-Personnel Landmines*, 548–9. Similar language had also been suggested by the Landmine Survivors Network, a US-based NGO, which delivered a statement to the Brussels Conference calling for preambular language in the treaty 'recalling the human suffering inflicted by mines and the urgent needs of mine-affected communities'. It also sought the inclusion of a provision in the draft article on international cooperation and assistance whereby: 'Each State Party in a position to do so shall provide assistance for the rehabilitation of mine victims'. Landmine Survivors Network, 'Landmine Survivors Call on Governments to Address the Plight of Mine Victims Worldwide', Statement to the Brussels Conference (Brussels, 26 June 1997), p. 1. See also para. 0.78 above.

[5] See below the commentary on this provision in paras. 6.8–6.9 and 6.19–6.31.

[6] Though note that Article 1 common to the four Geneva Conventions of 1949 refers to applicability 'in addition to those provisions which apply in peacetime'.

[7] For example, to clear mined areas containing emplaced anti-personnel mines, or to provide assistance and cooperation to other States Parties in implementing the Convention. See below the commentary on Articles 5 and 6.

deemed necessary, and it was felt that any attempt to include one might impede negotiations and could have the unintended effect of limiting the Convention's application.[8]

1.5 The First Austrian Draft of the Convention on the Prohibition of Anti-Personnel Mines had included a separate scope provision whereby: 'This Convention shall apply in all circumstances including armed conflict and times of peace'.[9] The draft provision was removed in the Second Austrian Draft and was not reinstated despite proposals by a number of States.[10] That said, the phrase 'never under any circumstances', which is taken from the 1993 Chemical Weapons Convention,[11] serves to clarify the breadth and extent of the core obligations under the Anti-Personnel Mine Ban Convention, and seemingly

[8] Considerable difficulties were encountered in negotiating the scope of Amended Protocol II. Only after very lengthy and involved discussions was it possible to agree to extend the scope of the Protocol beyond the application of the Convention on Certain Conventional Weapons, which was limited to armed conflicts of an international character, including armed conflicts 'in which peoples are fighting against colonial domination and alien occupation and against racist regimes in the exercise of their right of self-determination'. Thus, Amended Protocol II applies also to situations referred to in Article 3 common to the Geneva Conventions of 12 August 1949 (armed conflict not of an international character occurring in the territory of one of the High Contracting Parties) but not to 'situations of internal disturbances and tensions, such as riots, isolated and sporadic acts of violence and other acts of a similar nature, as not being armed conflicts'. See Article 1(2)–1(6), Amended Protocol II. At the adoption of Amended Protocol II, Belgium read out a statement supported by several other delegations whereby certain provisions of the Protocol also applied in peacetime. The USA subsequently gave examples of such provisions: the provisions regarding the recording, marking, monitoring, and protection of areas containing mines and the provisions of Articles 8, 13, and 14. See the UN summary records of the statement contained in UN doc. CCW/CONF.I/SR.14 of 6 June 1996, p. 4.

[9] Article 1 of the First Austrian Draft. See Appendix 4 for a copy of the text.

[10] France, for instance, proposed in writing that the Convention 'be made applicable in situations covered by Article 2 common to the 1949 Geneva Conventions, situations of peace, armed conflicts not of an international character and situations of internal disturbances and tensions'. (Proposal contained in a facsimile transmission from the French Ministry of Foreign Affairs, Paris, 24 Apr. 1997.) At the Oslo Diplomatic Conference, Colombia proposed the following article: 'Nothing in this Convention shall be invoked as in any way limiting or detracting from the obligations assumed by any State Party under all applicable norms of International Humanitarian Law. In particular, this Convention shall apply to situations and to parties mentioned in article 3 common to the Geneva Conventions of 12 August 1949 and its additional Protocols of 1977'. APL/CW.46 of 3 Sept. 1997. See paras. 0.105 and 0.132 above.

[11] In a commentary on the 1993 Chemical Weapons Convention, it is stated that the wording 'emphasizes the comprehensive and totally binding character of the prohibitions . . . This relates to the geographical scope of these prohibitions: They have a universal dimension, which means they extend to all activities of State Parties everywhere. The wording excludes any justification for such activity, whether for self-defence in the case of attack with those weapons or in other exceptional circumstances. [footnote omitted] The wording covers all intents and purposes for such activities, independent of the character of the armed conflict, whether . . . an international or non-international one, whether the parties involved had recognized themselves or whether or not it is a civil strife.' Krutzsch, W. and Trapp, R., *A Commentary on the Chemical Weapons Convention* (Dordrecht: Martinus Nijhoff, 1994), 12–13.

leaves no room for exception in either its geographical[12] or substantive application.[13] Indeed, it is hard to conceive of a formulation that could be broader and more unequivocal than the one used in the Convention.

1.6 In accordance with Article 31(1) of the 1969 Vienna Convention: 'A treaty shall be interpreted in good faith in accordance with the ordinary meaning to be given to the terms of the treaty in their context and in the light of its object and purpose'.[14] In addition to the ordinary meaning to be given to the term 'never under any circumstances', the title of the Convention and its preamble provide evidence for the unambiguous and unequivocal nature of the obligation.[15]

1.7 A broad interpretation of the term 'never under any circumstances' is also confirmed if one has recourse to the preparatory work of the treaty and the circumstances of its conclusion, in accordance with Article 32 of the 1969 Vienna Convention.[16] During the negotiation of the Convention, both prior to and during the Oslo Diplomatic Conference, a number of States, including Poland, Spain, Sweden, and Turkey, sought to replace 'never' with 'not' in recognition of exceptions that a number of States were seeking, notably to the prohibition on use of anti-personnel mines. This change was not accepted because of the general desire not to allow exceptions to the comprehensive nature of the prohibitions.

1.8 The Convention therefore applies in all situations, including peacetime, any armed conflict, and situations of internal disturbances and tensions, such as riots, isolated and sporadic acts of violence. A State Party may not

[12] See further below the commentary on Article 19, which addresses the (non)-admissibility of reservations.

[13] Article 3, which is entitled exceptions, allows a State to retain or transfer a limited amount of anti-personnel mines, is intended to support one of the broader aims of the Convention—the clearance of emplaced anti-personnel mines as required by Article 1(2) and Article 5—and should not be seen as in any way undermining the general obligations contained in Article 1(1).

[14] See further below Appendix 1 for the key texts on treaty interpretation contained in the 1969 Vienna Convention on the Law of Treaties.

[15] This interpretation has been further evidenced by the contents of the Maputo Declaration, adopted by States Parties on 7 May 1999 at the First Meeting of the States Parties, which included a recognition 'that the enduring value of this unique international instrument rests in fully realizing the obligations and the promise contained within the Convention: to ensure no new use; to eradicate stocks; to cease development, production and transfers; to clear mined areas and thus free the land from its deadly bondage; and to assist the victims to reclaim their lives and to prevent new victims'. Point 4, Maputo Declaration, Part II to the Final Report of the First Meeting of the States Parties to the Convention on the Prohibition of the Use, Stockpiling, Production and Transfer of Anti Personnel Mines and on their Destruction, adopted by States Parties on 7 May 1999, UN Doc. APLC/MSP.1/1999/1 of 20 May 1999.

[16] Article 32 allows recourse 'to supplementary means of interpretation, including the preparatory work of the treaty and the circumstances of its conclusion', *inter alia* 'in order to confirm the meaning resulting from the application of Article 31 . . .'.

violate its undertakings in self-defence, against aggression or terrorism, whether the threat to its security comes from within its territory or from abroad. Thus, an attempt by Angola, when a treaty signatory, to justify continued use of anti-personnel mines on the basis that the Convention should implicitly allow an exception to the core obligations amid an ongoing armed conflict was firmly opposed by the States Parties.[17]

## The Application of the Obligations to Armed Opposition Groups

**1.9** The obligations are addressed to States Parties, and do not seek to bind entities other than States directly,[18] as have a number of international humanitarian law treaties.[19] Thus, for instance, Article 3 common to the 1949 Geneva Conventions provides that each party to an armed conflict not of an international character occurring in the territory of one of the High Contracting Parties is bound to apply, as a minimum, a set of basic humanitarian obligations listed in the article.

**1.10** None of the Austrian draft treaty texts contained a provision seeking to apply all or some of the articles to armed opposition groups. This was a deliberate decision by the drafters, who hoped to avoid unnecessary legal and political difficulties in order to concentrate on the disarmament obligations of States Parties. In its comments on the First Austrian Draft, the ICBL put forward, unsuccessfully, a proposal to apply the Convention to each party to an armed conflict:

[17] The Maputo Declaration referred to above included the following statement: 'In this spirit, we voice our outrage at the unabated use of anti personnel mines in conflicts around the world. To those few signatories who continue to use these weapons, this is a violation of the object and purpose of the Convention that you solemnly signed. We call upon you to respect and implement your commitments.' Point 11, Maputo Declaration, See Appendix 6 for a copy of the Maputo Declaration. Angola has since become a State Party to the Convention and appears to have ended all use of anti-personnel mines.

[18] In this work, they are usually referred to as armed opposition groups, although generally the term Non State Actors or Non State Entities is also often used.

[19] The legal applicability of international law to third parties (i.e. in this case, armed opposition groups) has been hotly debated for many years both within and outside the realms of international humanitarian law. In an analysis of the status of rebels under 1977 Additional Protocol II, one leading authority refers to the 'more widespread opinion that Article 3 . . . is able to confer rights and impose obligations on insurgents because, as a consequence of the State's ratification, the treaty becomes part of domestic law and therefore obliges all citizens, including rebels'. Cassese, A., 'The Status of Rebels under the 1977 Geneva Protocol on Non-international Armed Conflicts', *International and Comparative Law Quarterly*, 30 (Apr. 1981), 424. Cassese asserts that this is a misconception of the relationship between international and domestic law since what is at stake is not whether rebels are subjects of domestic law, but their legal standing in international law. But the argument is also used that if the leadership of the insurgents exercise effective authority, they are bound by the very fact that they claim to represent the country, or part of the country. Pictet, J. (ed.), *Commentary to the I Geneva Convention* (Geneva: ICRC, 1952), 51.

In the case of an armed conflict involving one of the States Parties to this Convention, each party to the conflict shall be bound to apply the Convention. In peacetime, this Convention shall apply to each State Party to the Convention and all persons and entities operating on the territory or under the control or jurisdiction of a State Party to the Convention.[20]

**1.11** Although there was sympathy with the need to constrain the activities of armed opposition groups in the Anti-Personnel Mine Ban Convention, care was taken not to risk limiting the scope of State Party obligations or to delay negotiations.[21] Thus, Colombia's suggestion to specifically regulate parties to a conflict other than States was resisted.[22] None the less, the 'members' of, or participants in, armed opposition groups are regulated indirectly, through the obligation upon States Parties in Article 9 to 'take all appropriate legal, administrative and other measures, including the imposition of penal sanctions, to prevent and suppress any activity prohibited to a State Party under this Convention undertaken by persons or on territory under its jurisdiction or control'.[23]

**1.12** In addition, the undertaking in Article 1(1)(c) 'never under any circumstances' to 'assist, encourage or induce, in any way, anyone to engage in any activity prohibited to a State Party under this Convention' clearly prohibits States Parties from providing anti-personnel mines not only to other States but also to any non-State entities or training them in the use of the weapons.[24]

## The Prohibition of Use

### Introduction

**1.13** Each State Party 'undertakes never under any circumstances . . . to use anti-personnel mines'. This obligation is separated out from the other general obligations, as it is in the 1993 Chemical Weapons Convention, but, in

---

[20] The ICBL adds a footnote to the proposed provision, which states that: 'The Convention should cover both States and non-state entities involved in the same conflict . . . as well as entities operating under the control of a State Party'. 'ICBL comments and proposed redrafting to the First Austrian Draft' (7 Feb. 1997). In fact, the drafting of the proposed provision would also have the apparent intent to bind non-party States to the obligations of the Convention if any were involved in an armed conflict with a State Party. This would seem to violate Article 34 of the 1969 Vienna Convention, which provides that: 'A treaty does not create either obligations or rights for a third State without its consent'.      [21] See para 1.4 above.

[22] See para. 0.132 above.      [23] See the commentary on Article 9 below.

[24] See also paragraph 1.52 below. Amended Protocol II had already prohibited the transfer of any landmines to 'any recipient other than a State or a State agency authorised to receive such transfers'. See Article 8(1)(b), Amended Protocol II.

contrast to that instrument, is placed first to stress its importance.[25] Indeed, the prohibition on the use of anti-personnel mines can be seen as the core of the Convention,[26] and for a number of States was the main stumbling block to adherence, given the comprehensive nature of the undertaking.

1.14 One such State was Spain, which, at the Oslo Diplomatic Conference, formally proposed an exception to the prohibition on use entitled Proposal for a Temporary Arrangement:

Notwithstanding the general obligations under Article 1 and the exceptions under Articles 3 and 17, a State Party, under exceptional circumstances for its National Security, may resort to the use of antipersonnel mines in accordance with the International Laws of armed conflict and in full compliance with the amended Protocol II on landmines.

The use of antipersonnel mines would never be authorised in conflicts amongst States Parties to this Convention.

This is a temporary arrangement which will cease to apply when the Meeting of States Parties so decides.[27]

It was not until the final day of the negotiations that the proposal was withdrawn and Spain declared its readiness to sign the Convention.

1.15 Also at the Conference, the USA, with the oral support of Australia, Ecuador, Japan, Poland, Spain, and Venezuela, tabled a proposal for a geographical exception to be included in Article 3 allowing the continued use of anti-personnel mines on the Korean peninsula.[28] In presenting its draft text for inclusion as an exception in Article 3, the USA claimed that the situation was 'unique' and that its acceptance by the other delegations was 'fundamental' to US support for the treaty.[29] The USA was also supported by the Republic of Korea, which, attending the Diplomatic Conference as an observer, declared

---

[25] According to Article 1(1) of the 1993 Chemical Weapons Convention: 'Each State Party undertakes never under any circumstances: (a) To develop, produce, otherwise acquire, stockpile or retain chemical weapons, or transfer, directly or indirectly, chemical weapons to anyone; (b) To use chemical weapons . . .'.

[26] Thus, in February 1997, Canada declared before the CD that: 'In our view, USE is the problem and it is the USE of anti-personnel mines which must be urgently addressed'. Statement of the Canadian Ambassador to the Conference on Disarmament (Geneva, 6 Feb. 1997) (emphasis in original).

[27] Doc. APL/CW.7 of 1 Sept. 1997. The ICBL reported that Spain had stockpiles of antipersonnel mines, which it intended to use in the event of an attack on Ceuta and Melilla—towns in Morocco under Spanish jurisdiction. See ICBL, *Landmine Monitor Report 1999*, 654.

[28] See paras. 3.8–3.9 below.

[29] A journalist for the *Washington Post* reported that in Korea, 'military officials painted a scenario, with visual aids, of allied carnage that would occur if one million North Korean troops, unimpeded by mines, overran the Demilitarised Zone on the way to Seoul some 27 miles away'. Priest, D., 'Mine Decision Boosts Clinton–Military Relations', *Washington Post* (21 Sept. 1997), p. A22.

that mines were needed to deter North Korean aggression[30] and to serve as a defensive barrier.[31] The South Korean representative claimed, apparently incorrectly, that mines laid near the Demilitarised Zone (DMZ) had not caused civilian casualties.[32] After lengthy discussions, the US proposal failed to gain acceptance from the Conference.

## The Definition of Use

### Introduction

**1.16** The Convention does not define what constitutes use of anti-personnel mines, although the USA formally proposed a definition at the Oslo Diplomatic Conference.[33] Although use certainly encompasses new emplacement of anti-personnel mines, it must also be considered whether tactical reliance on previously laid anti-personnel mines, the maintenance of existing minefields containing anti-personnel mines, or the maintenance of protection of minefields containing anti-personnel mines also fall within the scope of the term.

### New Emplacement of Anti-Personnel Mines

**1.17** New emplacement of anti-personnel mines by a State Party, including its armed forces operating abroad, would *typically* (see the following paragraph) violate the undertaking never under any circumstances to use anti-personnel mines. In addition, a failure to sanction a private individual or company operating within the jurisdiction of a State Party that emplaced anti-personnel mines could also result in international legal responsibility being imputed to the State.[34]

**1.18** Article 3 allows a State Party to retain or transfer a number of anti-personnel mines for the development of and training in mine detection, mine

---

[30] In an obvious piece of mischief-making, the North Korean Ambassador to the Russian Federation opposed the US calls for a geographical exemption for Korea, declaring that: 'The position of the DPRK is that no region should be excluded from the zone of application of such a Convention'. 'North Korea against Landmine Ban Exclusion', *Reuters* (Moscow, 14 Sept. 1997).

[31] Not all military strategists were convinced by the overriding need for anti-personnel mines. In an editorial in *The Times* on 12 Sept. 1997, it was pointed out that 'if any North-Korean assault were armour-led, it would be accompanied by mechanised mine-clearing devices against which anti-personnel mines are of no effect. And in more difficult terrain the North Koreans would use "human-wave" tactics in which mine casualties would simply be disregarded.' The editorial further mentioned that 'Western strategists are already looking at alternatives to mines. Spy satellites and drones could monitor frontiers, and air-blast bombs could be as deadly a deterrent to aggression.'

[32] A claim that subsequently seemed to be contradicted by a report from the South Korean Defence Ministry, which on 2 October 1997 declared that at least 35 people had been killed and 43 injured by landmines on the southern approaches to the DMZ in the preceding five years. Although the Defence Ministry did not disclose the number of civilians, the opposition legislator who had requested the report claimed that 29 of the victims were civilians, including some children. See 'Border Landmines kill 35 South Koreans: Minister', *Agence France Presse* (2 Oct. 1997).

[33] See para. 1.25 below.     [34] See below the commentary on Article 9 of the Convention.

clearance or mine destruction techniques. Use is not, explicitly at least, a lawful exception, even though live mines could be said to be 'used' when they are employed for the purposes of training in mine detection and clearance. On the other hand, the terms 'development' and 'training' both imply the need for simulation (although whether live, fused mines are required for either might be debated).[35] Furthermore, in its comments on the Second Austrian Draft of 14 March 1997, New Zealand had suggested that 'use' for the stated purposes be included as an exception in Article 3,[36] but this proposal was not retained. This could further indicate that the emplacement of anti-personnel mines for permitted purposes is not to be deemed 'use'.

*Tactical Reliance on Previously Laid Anti-Personnel Mines*

**1.19** During the Oslo Diplomatic Conference, the USA asked whether an army that moved into an area where mines are emplaced and which then uses them for protection would violate the prohibition on use.[37] In accordance with Article 31 of the 1969 Vienna Convention: 'A treaty shall be interpreted in good faith in accordance with the ordinary meaning to be given to the terms of the treaty in their context and in the light of its object and purpose'.[38] To 'use' something is 'to take, hold or deploy' it 'as a means of accomplishing a purpose or achieving a result'.[39] This suggests that the ordinary meaning of the term is not *necessarily* a single act, as is the emplacement of an anti-personnel mine, but can be something that takes place over a period of time.

**1.20** The context for the Anti-Personnel Mine Ban Convention is the prohibition of a weapon that by design has longevity and long-term effects. Similarly, the object and purpose of the Convention, as evidenced by its title and preamble, is to address the humanitarian impact of anti-personnel mines—by ending the 'use' of anti-personnel mines as well as production, transfer, and

---

[35] Canada, for instance, has reported that Canadian Forces Base Suffield, Alberta, contains two mined areas (with mines that have been defused) for research and development of mine clearance equipment and procedures. See Canada's Article 7 Report for the period 16 Feb. 2001–1 Mar. 2002, submitted on 24 Apr. 2002, Form C. Further, Canada's *Anti-Personnel Mines Convention Act*, which entered into force on 1 Mar. 1999, allows the acquisition, possession, transfer, or placement of no more than the minimum number of anti-personnel mines deemed necessary for the development of and training in mine detection, mine clearance, or mine destruction techniques. Ibid., Form A. See also paras. 3.18–3.20 below.

[36] Note Verbale from New Zealand Ministry of Foreign Affairs to the Austrian Embassy, Wellington, 18 Apr. 1997.

[37] Oral remarks, Meeting of the Friend of the Chair for Article 2, Oslo Diplomatic Conference, 4 Sept. 1997.

[38] See Appendix 1 for the key texts on treaty interpretation, as contained in the 1969 Vienna Convention on the Law of Treaties.

[39] Pearsall, J. (ed.), *The New Oxford Dictionary of English* (Oxford: Clarendon Press, 1998), 2038.

stockpiling, encouraging comprehensive mine clearance 'as soon as possible' and promoting victim assistance.[40] It is both the short and long-term impact of anti-personnel mines that resulted in its adoption: not only the hundreds of casualties each week ('mostly innocent and defenceless civilians and especially children'), but also the longer-term impact on economic development and reconstruction and the repatriation of refugees and internally displaced persons, and 'other severe consequences for years after emplacement'.[41]

1.21 The use of a weapon is typically an act: pulling a trigger or dropping a bomb, for example. But in the case of anti-personnel mines, a time-lag is built into the design of the weapons—they are constructed to be victim-activated, whether they are emplaced for long-term border or infrastructure protection, or shorter-term area denial or the protection of military personnel. Indeed, the distinction to be drawn between the term 'use' and 'emplacement' is significant. Emplacement is ordinarily defined as the 'process or state of setting something in place or being set in place'[42]—a much narrower concept than 'use'. Thus, the reference in the first preambular paragraph to anti-personnel mines having 'other severe consequences for years after emplacement' suggests that the terms 'use' and 'emplacement' are not synonyms in the context of the Convention.

1.22 Yet, States Parties are not to be expected to ask their soldiers to act as if minefields did not exist, if for no other reason than their own protection. Moreover, the consequences for a soldier of 'using' anti-personnel mines laid by others are potentially very severe with heavy penal sanctions. How could a court be asked to rule on whether a soldier merely protected himself or whether he 'used' the minefield?[43] The answer may lie in a close nexus between the mined area and the behaviour of the armed forces. Where anti-personnel mines are laid by for the benefit of a State Party and their presence is actively incorporated into the State Party's operational or tactical planning, that State can be said to use anti-personnel mines. Thus, the UK has stated that British forces are instructed that they may not seek benefit from anti-personnel mines laid by allies not bound to the Convention.[44]

---

[40] See above paras. 0.108–0.113 for commentary on the first three preambular paragraphs.

[41] First preambular paragraph to the Convention; see above para. 0.108.

[42] Pearsall, *The New Oxford Dictionary of English*, 605.

[43] Of course, if anti-personnel mines are laid by an ally not party to the Convention at the behest of the armed forces of the State Party, the responsibility of that State Party and the individual soldiers responsible would be engaged in accordance with Article 1(1)(c) below. See paras. 1.63–1.65 below.

[44] In a statement to the intersessional Standing Committee on the General Status and Operation of the Convention, the UK declared that its forces 'should not seek to derive direct military benefits from the deployment of [anti-personnel mines] in combined operations. It is not, however, always

**1.23**  The UK was already confronted with the issue in the context of joint operations in the Balkans, as reported in the *Landmine Monitor Report 2001*:

On 17 May 2000 the Ministry of Defence stated in a Parliamentary Written Answer that 'U.K. armed forces were involved in 15 joint operations involving the use of antipersonnel landmines over the last three years, primarily involving operations in the Balkans. However, in no instances were U.K. armed forces responsible for their use.'[45] This was subsequently clarified as referring to mines 'not laid at that time by our operation partners or the U.K. Armed Forces but [mines that] were a remnant of war, or previous actions, in the area of operations. As such the 15 operations did not involve the laying of anti-personnel landmines, but their existence in the areas in which operations took place means that their presence was a factor in those operations.'[46]

The Norwegian Ministry of Defence has stated its view that Norway can participate in joint operations with States which are not party to the Anti-Personnel Mine Ban Convention, and in such cases may take advantage of cover from already mined areas, but cannot strengthen or renew the mining of these areas.[47]

**1.24**  There is otherwise little State practice to draw on in seeking to confirm the meaning adduced, though what practice does exist seems largely to support an interpretation broader than simply the act of emplacement.[48] Portugal, for example, has stated that it 'understands that it may participate in joint operations with armed forces which use antipersonnel mines, but it won't gain any benefit from such use. A guarantee that Portugal will not benefit, in such case, would be assured at the operational level'.[49] Upon ratification of the Convention, Australia declared its understanding that,[50] 'in relation to Article 1(a), the term "use" means the actual physical emplacement of anti-personnel

---

possible to say in advance that military benefit will not arise where this results from an act that is not deliberate or pre-planned'. 'United Kingdom intervention on Article 1', Statement to the Standing Committee on the General Status and Operation of the Convention (Geneva, 16 May 2003), available at: www.gichd.ch. The UK believes that any interpretation of obligations under the Convention must take into account the military realities of the battlefield. Information provided by Peter Balmer, UK Ministry of Defence in email of 5 June 2003.

[45]  *Hansard*, 17 May 2000, col. 161W.

[46]  Letter dated 18 Oct. 2000 from John Spellar MP, Minister of State for the Armed Forces, to Dr Jenny Tonge MP, cited in ICBL, *Landmine Monitor Report 2001*, 814.

[47]  Letter from Ministry of Defense, 9 Apr. 2001, cited in ibid. 753–4.

[48]  Article 31(3) of the 1969 Vienna Convention provides that there shall be taken into account 'any subsequent practice in the application of the treaty which establishes the agreement of the parties regarding its interpretation'. See Appendix 1 for the full text of the provision.

[49]  Letter from the Ministry of Defense (4 Jan. 2001); letter from the Ministry of Foreign Affairs (9 Jan. 2001), cited in ICBL, *Landmine Monitor Report 2001*, 763.

[50]  For a discussion of the value of interpretive declarations, see below the commentary on Article 19.

mines and does not include receiving an indirect or incidental benefit from anti-personnel mines laid by another State or person'.[51] It is not prohibited to 'indirectly' use anti-personnel mines under Article 1(1)(a), but neither this nor the Australian declaration appears to exclude responsibility where there is actual physical emplacement of anti-personnel mines by a non-party State and a State Party receives a *direct* benefit from the mines. This position is supported by the prohibition on active planning for the use of anti-personnel mines, in accordance with Article 1(1)(c).[52]

**1.25** Article 32 of the 1969 Vienna Convention provides *inter alia* that: 'Recourse may be had to supplementary means of interpretation, including the preparatory work of the treaty and the circumstances of its conclusion, in order to confirm the meaning resulting from the application of article 31'. At the Oslo Diplomatic Conference, the USA tabled a proposed definition of use to be included in Article 2 as new paragraph 6 whereby: ' "Use" means the act of emplacement'.[53] Canada objected on the basis that use is a wider concept, including 'gaining benefits' from existing minefields. Sweden proposed orally that 'use means the act of emplacing mines or maintaining minefields already laid. The temporary control of the minefield laid by another State does not imply use'. The ICRC suggested that use be defined as 'the act of emplacement by any means whatsoever or taking military advantage of a minefield which it would have been feasible to remove'. This proposal was supported by Belgium.

**1.26** After the Friend of the Chair requested that proposals be submitted in writing, Sweden withdrew its proposal and the ICRC offered not to pursue its proposed amendment if the USA decided not to pursue its proposed definition. (The USA formally withdrew the proposal the following morning in the meeting of the Friend of the Chair.) The discussion ended with the Friend of the Chair[54] noting that use was 'very difficult to define'.[55]

**1.27** In sum, the emplacement of anti-personnel mines by a State Party, other than in accordance with the provisions of Article 3,[56] violates the undertaking contained in Article 1(1)(a) never under any circumstances to use anti-personnel mines. Similarly, it is asserted that a State Party is prohibited from taking operational or tactical advantage from anti-personnel mines that

[51] Canada's implementing legislation does not expressly define use although it provides that 'no person shall (a) place an anti-personnel mine under, on or near the ground or other surface area with the intent to cause the explosion of the anti-personnel mine by the presence, proximity or contact of a person'. Bill C-22, Clause 6(1).                    [52] See paras. 1.60–1.61 below.

[53] Doc. APL/CW.9 of 1 Sept. 1997.        [54] Ambassador Thomas Hajnoczi of Austria.

[55] Discussion in the meeting of the Friend of the Chair for Article 2, Oslo Diplomatic Conference, 4 Sept. 1997.

[56] See below the commentary on Article 3, especially commentary para. 3.21.

have been laid for its benefit or where it was in a position to choose not to take the benefit, for example where it could reasonably be expected to clear and destroy the emplaced mines in accordance with the provisions of Article 5 of the Convention.[57]

*Maintenance of Minefields Containing Anti-Personnel Mines*

1.28 The 'maintenance' of anti-personnel mines within an existing minefield, also referred to as 'replenishing' or 'refurbishing' a minefield, is a clear violation of Article 1(1)(a).[58] This falls within the prohibition on the physical emplacement of new anti-personnel mines, which is at the heart of the undertaking never to use anti-personnel mines, and does not appear to be contested. Thus, for example, according to the Canadian Department of National Defence: 'Operationally, Canadian soldiers are allowed to assume responsibility for an area in which anti-personnel mines have been laid . . . They are restricted to monitoring the minefield and maintaining the markings, but will not conduct maintenance of the mines within the field'.[59]

1.29 Further, in a document issued to the armed forces by the Office of the Judge Advocate General in 2001, it is stated that: 'If [in such a situation] self-neutralising/self-destructing anti-personnel mines have been used, Canada will not seek their replacement once they expire. If the anti-personnel mines are not self-destructing or self-neutralising Canada will only monitor the minefield and maintain the markings, but will not conduct the maintenance thereof'.[60]

*Maintenance of the Protection of Minefields Containing Anti-Personnel Mines*

1.30 On the other hand, the maintenance of fencing and marking signs around existing minefields would not be considered a use of anti-personnel mines as these activities are intended to prevent civilian deaths and injuries— the object and purpose of the Convention as a whole. Indeed, Article 5(2) of the Anti-Personnel Mine Ban Convention requires that States Parties maintain or put in place a set of measures to protect the civilian population from mined areas containing anti-personnel mines:

Each State Party shall make every effort to identify all areas under its jurisdiction or control in which anti-personnel mines are known or suspected to be emplaced and shall ensure as soon as possible that all anti-personnel mines in mined areas under its

---

   [57] See below the commentary on Article 5, especially on para. 1 of the Article.
   [58] Maintenance should be clearly distinguished from the 'monitoring' of a minefield, as discussed in paras. 1.30ff below.
   [59] Canadian Department of National Defence, 'The Canadian Forces and Anti-Personnel Landmines', Department of National Defence (Ottawa, 13 Feb. 2002).
   [60] Office of the Judge Advocate General, 'The Law of Armed Conflict at the Operational and Tactical Level', Department of National Defence (Canada, 21 Mar. 2001), 5.10.

jurisdiction or control are perimeter-marked, monitored and protected by fencing or other means, to ensure the effective exclusion of civilians, until all anti-personnel mines contained therein have been destroyed. The marking shall at least be to the standards set out in the Protocol on Prohibitions or Restrictions on the Use of Mines, Booby-Traps and Other Devices, as amended on 3 May 1996, annexed to the Convention on Prohibitions or Restrictions on the Use of Certain Conventional Weapons Which May Be Deemed to Be Excessively Injurious or to Have Indiscriminate Effects.[61]

## The Prohibition on Development

1.31 Under Article 1(1)(b) of the Anti-Personnel Mine Ban Convention, States Parties undertake never under any circumstances to develop, directly or indirectly, anti-personnel mines, although the term is not defined in the Convention.[62] To develop something is to cause it to come into existence or operation.[63] This concept demands more than the collation of information inherent to the research phase and would probably prohibit the preparation of plans for production or the testing of prototypes or other activities intended to lead to the production of new types of anti-personnel mines. The provision in Article 1(1)(b) of the Convention is adapted from the general obligations of the 1993 Chemical Weapons Convention. A commentary on the 1993 Chemical Weapons Convention claims that, ' "develop" is by virtue of its purpose, the preparation of the production of chemical weapons as distinct from permitted research. This prohibited objective might also materialize and become obvious through specific equipment used and methods applied'.[64]

1.32 The undertaking in the Anti-Personnel Mine Ban Convention is, however, broader in ambit than the one in the 1993 Chemical Weapons Convention, as the prohibition includes indirect development.[65] This would seemingly cover development of anti-personnel mines by offshore corporations or

[61] See paras. 5.27 to 5.30 below for the commentary on this provision.

[62] In its comments on the Second Austrian Draft, dated 9 May 1997, Japan had suggested that definitions of the terms in Article 1, including 'develop' be included in the Convention. Prior to the Oslo Diplomatic Conference, the Philippines had informally put forward the following definition in the Core Group, but did not table it during the Conference: ' "Develop" means to engage in research and development activities for the purpose of producing or improving anti-personnel mines'.

[63] See e.g. Brown, L. (ed.), *The New Shorter Oxford English Dictionary* (Oxford: Clarendon Press, 1993), 654.

[64] Krutzsch and Trapp, *A Commentary on the Chemical Weapons Convention*, 13.

[65] Article I(1)(a) of the 1993 Chemical Weapons Convention provides that: 'Each State Party undertakes never under any circumstances to develop, produce, otherwise acquire, stockpile or retain chemical weapons, or transfer, directly or indirectly, chemical weapons to anyone'. Thus, the prohibition is limited to direct or indirect transfer and not the preceding activities in the clause.

companies providing funding for research and development (R&D) in non-party States, seeking to avoid the reach of national legislation within the jurisdiction. A State Party may not commission, provide funding, or issue licences for such activities, and, in accordance with Article 9 of the Convention, should ensure that it has taken all appropriate measures to prevent or suppress the development of anti-personnel mines by persons or on territory under its jurisdiction or control.[66] There is no prohibition, however, on developing components that *could* be used in anti-personnel mines, such as batteries, in the absence of intent to develop anti-personnel mines or foreknowledge that they will be so used.[67]

**1.33**  Care must be taken when developing mines other than anti-personnel mines to ensure that the undertaking in Article 1(1)(b) is not being breached. In accordance with 1977 Additional Protocol I, parties to the Protocol must determine whether in 'the study, development, acquisition or adoption of a new weapon, means or method of warfare' its employment 'would, in some or all circumstances, be prohibited by [the] Protocol or by any other rule of international law applicable to the High Contracting Party'.[68]

## The Prohibition on Production

**1.34**  Under Article 1(1)(b) of the Anti-Personnel Mine Ban Convention, States Parties undertake never under any circumstances to produce, directly or indirectly, anti-personnel mines, although the term is not defined.[69] Similar to the prohibition on development, the prohibition on the production of anti-personnel mines encompasses indirect as well as direct production, which would encompass the licensing of foreign companies to produce anti-personnel mines or components intended to be employed in anti-personnel mines.

---

[66]  This includes both natural and legal persons, i.e. an individual could not hide behind the veil of a corporation to conduct unlawful activity. See below the commentary on Article 9 of the Convention.

[67]  Cf. the 1993 Convention on the Prohibition of Chemical Weapons, which allows research for purposes not specifically prohibited by its provisions. See Krutzsch and Trapp, *A Commentary on the Chemical Weapons Convention*, 13.

[68]  Article 36, 1977 Additional Protocol I. See Sandoz *et al.*, *Commentary on the Additional Protocols*, 425.

[69]  To produce something is to compose, make, or bring it into existence by mental or physical labour. Brown, *The New Shorter Oxford English Dictionary*, ii. 2367. In its comments on the Second Austrian Draft, dated 9 May 1997, Japan had likewise suggested that the term 'produce' be included in the Convention and that it be made clear that this 'refers to the manufacture of complete devices of anti-personnel mines and does not include the manufacture of parts of them'. Prior to the Oslo Diplomatic Conference, the Philippines had informally circulated the following definition within the Core Group, but did not table it during the Conference: ' "Produce" means to manufacture or process certain materials that would result in the existence and availability of anti-personnel mines'.

**1.35** As already noted,[70] care must be taken in the production of other munitions, especially mines other than anti-personnel mines, to ensure that this undertaking is not being breached. The definition of anti-personnel mine for the purposes of the Anti-Personnel Mine Ban Convention is contained in Article 2.[71]

## The Prohibition on Acquisition

**1.36** The undertaking never under any circumstances to 'otherwise acquire,'[72] directly or indirectly, anti-personnel mines' overlaps with the undertakings never to retain or transfer the weapons.[73] It is intended to ensure that a State Party may not obtain or keep any anti-personnel mines that it may have, beyond those lawfully retained under the exceptions set out in Article 3.[74]

**1.37** The inclusion of the word 'otherwise' is intended to cover all methods of obtaining anti-personnel mines, other than production. Thus, in addition to prohibiting the import of anti-personnel mines,[75] which is also covered by the term transfer as discussed below, the provision applies to anti-personnel mines received as a gift, captured from another State or armed opposition groups, discovered in ammunition storage areas,[76] or confiscated from ordinary civilians and which are not destroyed, or retained in accordance with Article 3.[77]

---

[70] In para. 1.33.  [71] See below the commentary on Article 2.1) and 2(3).

[72] The term 'acquire' is not defined in the Convention, although in its comments on the Second Austrian Draft, dated 9 May 1997, Japan had suggested that definitions of the terms in Article 1, including 'otherwise acquire' be included. Prior to the Oslo Diplomatic Conference, the Philippines had informally put forward the following definition in the Core Group, but did not table it during the Conference: ' "Acquire" means to procure anti-personnel mines by any means including buying, importation, transfer or production'. An ordinary definition of the term is 'to come into possession of', which appears suitably broad. Brown, *The New Shorter Oxford English Dictionary*, i. 20.

[73] Transfer includes import as well as export. See paras. 1.40 and 2.61 below.

[74] See, below, the commentary on Article 3.

[75] Of course, apart from the minimum number absolutely necessary for the development of and training in mine detection, mine clearance, or mine destruction techniques.

[76] A number of States Parties have had to revise their declarations under Article 7 of the number of stockpiled anti-personnel mines they own or possess or which are under their jurisdiction or control following discoveries of additional stockpiles. See para. 4.35 below.

[77] Possession and use of anti-personnel mines by civilians is not uncommon in a number of countries. In Cambodia, for instance, they have been used to protect homes and livestock, for fishing, even to settle local disputes. See e.g. Davies, P., 'Mines and Unexploded Ordnance in Cambodia and Laos: Understanding the Costs', in Kumar, K. (ed.), *Rebuilding Societies after Civil War: Critical Roles for International Assistance* (Boulder, Colo.: Lynne Rienner, 1997), 243. In Colombia and the Casamance region of Senegal, anti-personnel mines are allegedly used to protect illegal drug plantations. ICBL, *Landmine Monitor Report 1999*, 299; ICBL, *Landmine Monitor Report 2000*, 98. And in Georgia, landmines are reportedly used to uproot trees! ICBL, *Landmine Monitor Report 2000*, 794.

## The Prohibition on Stockpiling and Retention

**1.38** State Parties undertake never under any circumstances to stockpile or retain,[78] directly or indirectly, anti-personnel mines. This prohibits not only maintaining stocks or quantities of anti-personnel mines but also adding new mines to existing stocks, apart from in accordance with the exception in Article 3.

**1.39** To fulfil the undertaking, a State Party must respect the provisions of Article 1(2) and Article 4—to destroy or ensure the destruction of all anti-personnel mines under its jurisdiction or control, or which it owns or possesses, within four years of the Convention's entry into force for that State. It must also destroy any anti-personnel mines that may come into its possession (beyond those used for Article 3 purposes) once stockpile destruction has been completed.

## The Prohibition on Transfer

**1.40** States Parties undertake never under any circumstances to transfer, directly or indirectly, anti-personnel mines to anyone. It is therefore unlawful for a State Party to transfer anti-personnel mines not only to another State, but also to any individual or group of individuals, and any company or corporation. The only exception to the prohibition is for the transfer of an unlimited number of anti-personnel mines for the purposes of destruction,[79] or of the minimum number absolutely necessary, for the development of and training in mine detection, mine clearance, or mine destruction techniques.[80] Transfer includes both import and export, and whether or not any payment or fee is involved.

---

[78] The terms to 'stockpile or retain' are not defined in the Convention, although in its comments on the Second Austrian Draft, dated 9 May 1997, Japan had suggested that definitions of the terms in Article 1, including 'stockpile' and 'retain' be included. They further asked what the difference was between the two terms and suggested that if there was none, that only one should be used. Prior to the Oslo Diplomatic Conference, the Philippines had informally put forward the following definitions in the Core Group, but did not table them during the Conference: ' "Stockpile" means to collect and place in warehouses or ordnance centers for safekeeping and maintenance in a state of readiness for transport to any area or for immediate use'; and ' "Retain" means to keep within a State Party's jurisdiction or control'. An ordinary definition of the verb to 'stockpile' is 'to accumulate a stockpile of', with the noun stockpile in turn being defined as 'an accumulated reserve of goods, materials, munitions, weapons, etc. available for use during a shortage, emergency, etc.'. To 'retain' is a more general term meaning to 'keep hold or possession of; continue to have, keep or possess'. Brown, *The New Shorter Oxford English Dictionary*, ii. 3068, 2571.

[79] See below the commentary on Article 3(2).

[80] See below the commentary on Article 3(1).

**1.41** Transfer is defined in Article 2(4) as follows:[81] '"Transfer" involves, in addition to the physical movement of anti-personnel mines into or from national territory, the transfer of title to and control over the mines, but does not involve the transfer of territory containing emplaced anti-personnel mines'. Thus, in accordance with the definition, the transfer of territory containing emplaced anti-personnel mines is not prohibited. In other respects, however, the definition is potentially ambiguous, depending on whether the second and third clauses are considered to be cumulative requirements or merely alternatives.[82] If they are cumulative, to constitute transfer there must be *not only* 'the physical movement of anti-personnel mines into or from national territory' *but also* 'the transfer of title to and control over the mines'. Mere physical movement is deemed 'transit'. A broader view is that transfer is *either* 'the physical movement of anti-personnel mines into or from national territory' *or* (without the need for any physical movement) 'the transfer of title to and control over the mines'.

**1.42** The ordinary definition of the transitive verb 'to transfer'[83] includes both of the main elements of the definition in Article 2(4). The most common meaning of the term is to 'move, take, or convey from one place . . . to another; . . . transport; give or hand over from one to another'.[84] The secondary meaning of the term is to 'convey or make over (title, right, or property) by deed or legal process'.[85] Thus, it could be asserted that the definition in Article 2(4) is so phrased because it is not only the most common meaning of the term (physical transport of something) that is intended, but to ensure that transfer also encompasses the secondary meaning (conveyance of title, without the need for any movement). This is supported by the words 'directly or indirectly' in the prohibition on transfer, which enlarges the definition.

**1.43** Further evidence that the broader interpretation of the term is the correct one is to be found in Article 3(2), which states that the transfer of anti-personnel mines for the purposes of destruction is permitted. In transporting anti-personnel mines for the purposes of destruction within or from its national territory, a State Party would typically retain title over the mines (to prevent

---

[81] The definition, which is taken almost verbatim from Article 2(15) of Amended Protocol II to the CCW (the reference is made specific to anti-personnel mines), was first included in the Second Austrian Draft of 14 Mar. 1997, and was unchanged throughout the negotiating process. No suggested amendments were presented during the Oslo Diplomatic Conference, although in the meeting of the Friends of the Chair on 5 Sept. 1997, the USA orally reserved the right to propose amendments to the draft definition.

[82] In its comments on the Second Austrian Draft of 14 Mar. 1997, dated 9 May 1997, Japan had specifically asked for clarification of the meaning of the phrase 'in addition to'.

[83] A transitive verb is one that takes an object; in this case, it is anti-personnel mines.

[84] Brown, *The New Shorter Oxford English Dictionary*, ii. 3368.     [85] ibid.

them becoming the lawful property of the receiving State or company to do with as they wished) until their destruction. If a narrow interpretation of transfer is adopted, this exception would seem unnecessary.

1.44 None the less, State Party practice on the issue is far from uniform, although many States have interpreted the provision broadly. Denmark, for instance, has stated that:

In accordance with Article 1 of the Ottawa Convention, Denmark cannot transfer to anyone, directly or indirectly, anti-personnel mines or allow anyone to do so on Danish territory. According to Article 3, physical movement (transfer) of anti-personnel mines are [*sic*] permitted if the purpose is the development of and training in mine detection, mine clearance, mine destruction techniques or if the purpose is destruction of anti-personnel mines.[86]

This view is shared by France, Slovakia,[87] and South Africa.[88] Italy has stated that it cannot be involved in activities which are not compatible with the Anti-Personnel Mine Ban Convention, and transit of anti-personnel mines is only allowed for the purpose of their destruction.[89]

1.45 Similarly, although not explicit in its interpretation of the definition in Article 2(4), Australia appears to concur with an understanding of the phrase 'in addition to' as indicating alternative rather than cumulative requirements. In its national implementing legislation, it is stated that: 'A person is guilty of an offence if: . . . (e) the person physically moves an anti-personnel mine; or (f) the person transfers ownership or control of an anti-personnel mine, whether directly or indirectly, to another person'.[90]

1.46 Germany has likewise adopted a broader view of the term. In May 2002, it declared that:

Another question that has been raised with respect to Article 1 concerns the issue of stockpiling and transit of foreign antipersonnel mines. The relevant provisions of the German War Weapons Control Act clearly stipulate that it is prohibited to manufacture, acquire, import, export or transfer anti-personnel mines . . . Germany is therefore not of the opinion that transit of anti-personnel mines is permitted under the Ottawa Treaty except under the provisions of Article 3 . . .[91]

---

[86] Cited in ICBL, *Landmine Monitor Report 1999*, 582.      [87] ibid. 713.

[88] Oral remarks to the intersessional Standing Committee Meeting on General Status and Operation of the Convention (Geneva, 10 Jan. 2000).

[89] Oral remarks to the Standing Committee on General Status and Operation of the Convention (Geneva, 11 May 2001).

[90] Section 7(1), Part 2, Anti-Personnel Mine Convention Act 1998.

[91] Statement of Germany to the Standing Committee on the General Operation and Status of the Convention (Geneva, 27 May 2002).

**1.47** Without initially giving the legal justification for its position,[92] the UK has determined that transit of anti-personnel mines by a non-party State would be 'contrary to the United Kingdom's obligations under the Ottawa Convention'.[93] Similarly, Brazil has stated that it will never allow transiting of anti-personnel mines across its territory.[94] Further, although the specific rationale is not made explicit, national implementing legislation in Belgium, New Zealand,[95] and Spain[96] prohibits the transit of another State's anti-personnel mine stockpiles across the national territory.[97] Thus, for example, according to New Zealand's Minister for Foreign Affairs:

Under the Anti-Personnel Mines Prohibition Act 1998, 'transfer' is defined as including both importation into, and exportation from, New Zealand. Under the Customs Excise Act 1996, importation and exportation are defined in terms of entry to or exit from New Zealand territory, including New Zealand territorial waters. Therefore, any transit of anti-personnel mines through New Zealand territory would constitute a transfer, and would be prohibited under [section] 7(1)(d) of the Anti-Personnel Mines Prohibition Act.

**1.48** A number of States do not, however, accept that transit is unlawful under the Convention. Thus, for example, Norway deems anti-personnel mines that are moved through or transferred into the country only as a Norwegian 'concern' if the transfer happens both physically and in terms of property rights: 'Norway will not oppose the transit of [U.S.] mines over Norwegian territory . . . since transit is not prohibited by the Ottawa Convention . . . The [U.S.] will be able to transport mines both in and out of the storages in Norway during this four-year period'.[98]

**1.49** Similarly, Canada's instructions to its armed forces in 1998,[99] as repeated in a document issued by the Department of National Defence in February 2002, state that:

---

[92] It appears that it considers this to be 'assistance' under Article 1(1)(c) of the Convention.

[93] Statement on behalf of the Secretary of State for Foreign and Commonwealth Affairs to Parliament (26 Mar. 2002). See *Hansard*, col. 812W.

[94] Statement by Brazil on Issues concerning Article 1 (General Obligations) of the Mine Ban Convention to the intersessional Standing Committee on General Status and Operation of the Convention (1 Feb. 2002).

[95] Letter from Phil Goff, Minister of Foreign Affairs and Trade, 13 Apr. 2000, cited in ICBL, *Landmine Monitor Report 2000*, 417–18.

[96] Though, curiously, Spain does not appear to agree that transfer as prohibited by the Convention includes transit. See ICBL, *Landmine Monitor Report 2000*, 723.

[97] See Ayllón, L., 'España insiste a EE. UU. para que destruya sus minas antipersonal', *ABC* (2 Nov. 1998), 23.

[98] Letter from Knut Vollbaeck, Norwegian Minister of Foreign Affairs, to US Secretary of State, Madeleine Albright (20 May 1998).

[99] Chief of the Defence Staff, 'Anti-Personnel Mines—Restrictions on Canadian Forces Personnel' (11 Aug. 1998).

The Convention does not prohibit the transit of anti-personnel mines, which is defined as the movement of anti-personnel mines within a State, or from a State, to its forces abroad. Canada, however, discourages the use of Canadian territory, equipment or personnel for the purpose of transit of anti-personnel mines.[100]

1.50  The preponderance of State practice appears to favour a broad interpretation of the term 'transfer'. Yet, even if a narrower interpretation were to be accepted by the States Parties, the transit of anti-personnel mines[101] may still be unlawful in accordance with the undertaking in Article 1(1)(c) of the Convention never under any circumstances to assist in any way anyone to engage in any activity prohibited to a State Party in accordance with the provisions of the Convention.[102] The UK, for instance, holds the view that 'permitting transit [of anti-personnel mines] across UK territory would amount to assistance under the terms of Article 1'.[103] Similarly, in its interpretation of the provision, the ICRC has stated that, 'permitting the transit of anti-personnel mines through the territory of a State Party would undermine the object and purpose of the [Convention] . . . and contradict its prohibition on assisting anyone in the stockpiling and use of anti-personnel mines . . . The ICRC believes that permitting or assisting the transit of anti-personnel mines through the territory of a State Party, by provision of transport, infrastructure or other means, constitutes assistance in the stockpiling of anti-personnel mines and is prohibited.'[104]

## The Prohibition on Assisting, Encouraging, or Inducing Prohibited Activities

### Introduction

1.51  In accordance with Article 1(1)(c) of the Convention, each State Party undertakes never under any circumstances to assist, encourage, or induce, in any way, anyone to engage in any activity prohibited to a State Party under this

---

[100] Canadian Department of National Defence, 'The Canadian Forces and Anti-Personnel Landmines'.

[101] Transit is not defined in the Convention, but is ordinarily defined as 'the action of passing across or through'. Ibid. 3370.          [102] See, further, below the commentary on this provision.

[103] 'United Kingdom intervention on Article 1', Statement to the Standing Committee on the General Status and Operation of the Convention (Geneva, 16 May 2003), available at: www.gichd.ch.

[104] 'International Committee of the Red Cross, Annex to Landmine Monitor, March 1999', in ICBL, *Landmine Monitor Report 1999*, 1005–6.

Convention. This provision, which was one of the most straightforward to draft, being taken verbatim from Article I(1)(d) of the 1993 Chemical Weapons Convention, has been probably the hardest to interpret and apply in the case of the Anti-Personnel Mine Ban Convention. It was first included in the Second Austrian Draft of 14 March 1997, also as Article 1(1)(c), and was unchanged through to the final text adopted at the Oslo Diplomatic Conference.

1.52 The ambit of the undertaking is certainly wide: as is the case in the 1993 Chemical Weapons Convention, it 'prohibits any action which contributes to prohibited activities'.[105] Indeed, in responding to a question by the USA as to the full reach of Article 1(1)(c) during a discussion of the provision at the Oslo Diplomatic Conference, Austria referred to the 1993 Convention and stated that it enlarged the obligation accepted by States Parties.[106] Further, 'as . . . indicated by the word "anyone", the accomplice of the prohibited assistance may not only be a State, irrespective of whether it is a Party to the Convention or not, but also an organization, an enterprise, a person or a group of persons,[107] irrespective of citizenship'.[108]

1.53 Controversy, however, has surrounded the meaning of the terms 'assist', 'encourage', and 'induce', none of which is defined either in the Anti-Personnel Mine Ban Convention, or in the 1993 Chemical Weapons Convention.[109] Yet, they may have far-reaching consequences for the legality of joint operations including one or more State Parties and one or more non-party States, or of operations by a non-party State taking place on the territory of a State Party. Also to be considered in the context of this provision are the legality of the transit of anti-personnel mines in, from, or through the territory of a State Party;[110] of stockpiling of anti-personnel mines belonging

---

[105] See Krutzsch and Trapp, *A Commentary on the Chemical Weapons Convention*, 15.

[106] Plenary discussion, Oslo Diplomatic Conference (8 Sept. 1997). The USA asked that Austria's statement be included as part of the negotiating record.

[107] Including, of course, armed opposition groups. See also paras. 0.9–0.12 above.

[108] Krutzsch and Trapp, *A Commentary on the Chemical Weapons Convention*, 15. The authors note that similar provisions are found in a number of other disarmament and arms control agreements, including the 1972 Biological Weapons Convention.

[109] A commentary on the corresponding provision in the 1993 Chemical Weapons Convention, however, states that assistance 'can be given by material or intellectual support . . . but also financial resources, technological-scientific know-how or provision of specialised personnel, military instructors, etc. to anybody who is resolved to commit such prohibited activity or by support in the concealment of such activities'. The prohibition on 'encouraging or inducing' means 'contributing to the emergence of resolve of anybody to commit a prohibited activity by instigating, promising assistance, etc.'. Krutzsch and Trapp, *A Commentary on the Chemical Weapons Convention*, 17.

[110] See also above para. 1.40–1.50.

to a non-party State on the territory of a State Party; and the transfer of components for use in anti-personnel mines.

## The Definition of 'Assist'

**1.54**  To 'assist' is ordinarily defined as to 'help . . . a person in necessity; an action, process or result; support, further, promote'.[111] Each State Party undertakes never under any circumstances to assist in any way, anyone to engage in any activity prohibited to a State Party under the Convention. The assistance is therefore not linked only to the use of anti-personnel mines, but covers also the development, production, acquisition, stockpiling, retention, or transfer of the weapons.[112] The inclusion of the term 'in any way' demonstrates that the assistance may be provided directly or indirectly.

**1.55**  Upon ratification of the Convention, Australia entered an understanding of the definition of the term 'assist' in the context of the provision in question, declaring that: 'In Article 1(c) Australia will interpret the word "assist" to mean the actual and direct physical participation in any activity prohibited by the Convention but does not include permissible indirect support such as the provision of security for the personnel of a State not party to the Convention engaging in such activities . . .'. In a statement to an intersessional Standing Committee meeting in May 2002, Zimbabwe set out a similarly restricted interpretation of the term:

Our troops will therefore not in any way be directly or otherwise be involved in any activity banned by the Convention wherever they are operating. We therefore in our view, believe that the term *assist* should be interpreted, relating directly to the activity in question and should not be applied liberally or given too wide a definition . . . Active participation also means actively participating in the carrying, laying and training in the use, manufacture, distribution, encouraging or inducing someone in the use of [anti-personnel mines]. It is therefore our humble submission that the terms assist and active participation in the context of Article 1 mean knowingly and intentionally participating directly or rendering assistance on the use, transfer and/or production of [anti-personnel] mines.[113]

Given the clarity of language contained in Article 1(1)(c)—'to assist, encourage or induce, *in any way*'[114]—it is not clear how these interpretations

---

[111]  Brown, *The New Shorter Oxford English Dictionary*, 132.

[112]  A number of State Party statements on the legal consequences of Article 1(1)(c) have focused only on the prohibition of assistance to a non-party State *using* anti-personnel mines.

[113]  Statement by Zimbabwe on Issues concerning Article 1 (General Obligations) of the Anti-Personnel Mine Ban Convention to the Standing Committee on the General Status and Operation of the Convention (Geneva, 31 May 2002), available at: www.gichd.ch.      [114]  Emphasis in original.

can be legally sustained. Reservations are prohibited by Article 19 of the Anti-Personnel Mine Ban Convention.[115]

**1.56** Indeed, a number of other States have followed a broader interpretation of the term. The UK, for instance, has declared that it holds a broad interpretation of assistance under the terms of Article 1 of the Convention: 'Unacceptable activities include: planning with others for the use of anti-personnel mines (APM); training others for the use of APM; agreeing Rules of Engagement permitting the use of APM; agreeing operational plans permitting the use of APM in combined operations; requests to non-States Parties to use APM; and providing security or transport for APM. Furthermore, it is not acceptable for UK forces to accept orders that amount to assistance in the use of APM.'[116] Brazil goes even further, having stated its view that 'Article 1 of the Convention clearly bans joint operations with non-States Parties that may involve the use of anti-personnel mines. Even if the States Parties involved in such operations do not participate directly and actively in the laying of anti-personnel mines, the operations should be considered illegal if the use of land-mines by a non-State Party is of direct military benefit to those States Parties. In the absence of such a broad interpretation of the term "assist", Article 1 would contain a serious and unfortunate loophole. All States Parties should commit strictly to observe the provisions of Article 1, which would include giving the term "assist" as broad an interpretation as possible'.[117]

**1.57** For the purposes of its guidance to personnel in the armed forces, Australia has usefully broken down potential assistance into three categories: logistics, security, and planning.[118] Relevant logistical support might include, for example, fuelling or refuelling an aircraft or a lorry containing anti-personnel

---

[115] The 1969 Vienna Convention defines a reservation as a 'unilateral statement, however phrased or named, made by a State, when signing, ratifying, accepting, approving or acceding to a treaty, whereby it purports to exclude or to modify the legal effect of certain provisions of the treaty in their application to that State'. Article 2(1)(d), 1969 Vienna Convention. See, further, below the commentary on Article 19, including a discussion of the status of interpretive declarations.

[116] 'United Kingdom intervention on Article 1', Statement to the Standing Committee on the General Status and Operation of the Convention (Geneva, 16 May 2003), available at: www.gichd.ch.

[117] Statement by Brazil on Issues concerning Article 1 (General Obligations) of the Anti-Personnel Mine Ban Convention to the Standing Committee on General Status and Operation of the Convention (Geneva, 1 Feb. 2002). See also Brazil's statement on this issue at the Standing Committee on General Status and Operation of the Convention (7 Feb. 2003), available at: www.gichd.ch.

[118] Email to the author by Lieutenant-Colonel Mike Kelly, Australian Defence Force (Geneva, 3 June 2002). A fourth category, relating to financing, might usefully be added. Thus, for instance, Norway's Petroleum Fund withdrew its investment in the company, Singapore Technologies Engineering, which produces anti-personnel mines because it was considered to be potentially a violation of Article 1(1)(c). Statement of Norway to the Standing Committee on General Status and Operation of the Convention (1 Feb. 2002).

mines, or providing medical assistance to a soldier engaged in laying anti-personnel mines. Security could involve providing protection to soldiers laying anti-personnel mines or to aircraft on a mission to deploy anti-personnel mines. Planning would typically cover joint planning exercises in which the use of anti-personnel mines is discussed.

**1.58** A State Party that provides logistical support to anyone, including non-party States and armed opposition groups, to assist them to engage specifically in a prohibited activity seemingly contributes to the commission of that prohibited activity. Under this interpretation, which appears to be widely accepted by States Parties, in the examples given above, the provision of medical assistance to a soldier engaged in laying anti-personnel mines would fall outside the reach of the term 'assist', whereas fuelling vehicles to transport anti-personnel mines, loading trucks with anti-personnel mines, or providing trucks or drivers to move anti-personnel mines would be captured by the prohibition. Thus, a State Party could provide logistical support to a non-party State that, in general, uses anti-personnel mines as long as it did not furnish such support for any *specific* operation involving anti-personnel mines. Equally, a State Party running a logistics centre could maintain trucks that were later used for prohibited activities unless it knew that the trucks would be so used.

**1.59** A similar situation exists with respect to the provision of security. A State Party may generally offer protection for a non-party State that uses anti-personnel mines as long as it does not provide such protection for any *specific* operation involving anti-personnel mines. As set out above,[119] this does not appear to be the position as understood by Australia, which has declared that the term assist 'does not include permissible indirect support such as the provision of security for the personnel of a State not party to the Convention engaging in such activities'.

**1.60** In terms of planning, it is clearly a violation of Article 1(1)(c) of the Convention for armed forces personnel of a State Party to engage actively in planning for the use of anti-personnel mines. As long as the personnel take no active part—verbally or non-verbally—in any discussions among personnel of non-party States concerning the use of anti-personnel mine, they should not be required to leave the room, as they will need to know where mines are being emplaced for their own contingent's security. Yet, if they remain and a proposal is made by a non-party State to lay mines for the State Party's benefit, what should they do? Will silence not be taken as acquiescence or even encouragement?

---

[119] See para. 1.55.

**1.61** In giving instructions to its armed forces, Canada's Office of the Judge Advocate General has stated that: 'When engaged in pre-conflict or combined operations with foreign forces, Canada will not agree to operational plans which authorize the use by the combined force of anti-personnel mines. While Canadians may participate in operational planning as members of a multinational staff they may not participate in planning for the use of anti-personnel mines. This would not prevent a State that is not a signatory or party to the APM Convention from participating in a multinational force or planning for the use of anti-personnel mines by its own forces for strictly national purposes. However, CF personnel will not be involved in any such planning'.[120]

**1.62** In a combat situation, however, it is clear that respecting the letter of the Convention as well as its spirit will be extremely challenging where a non-party State is operating in a coalition with States Parties and is using anti-personnel mines. As an Australian military lawyer has pointed out:

You cannot begin to imagine how difficult this Treaty is to manage in coalition operations, particularly in relation to the many personnel mixed with U.S. units and performing coalition staff functions . . . For example, the military command of one country which shared our view that re-fuelling airframes fitted with anti-personnel mine systems would be in breach has come to the conclusion that it is operationally impossible to follow through on this and has gone back to their government to get the policy changed. They have found that is not possible to interrogate every aircraft and then make alternative arrangements with the pace of activity. This also applies to the provision of fighter escort. We are also concerned about situations where our ground elements may call for Close Air Support and then find the support that is delivered features anti-personnel mines. My call on this is that this would not be in breach of the treaty as the ground elements cannot be expected to attempt to ascertain what form Close Air Support will take and if it is delivered without being asked for then they would not be in breach.[121]

As of writing this commentary, there is no hard evidence that the USA has used anti-personnel mines, either in the conflict in Afghanistan or in Iraq. This has seemingly helped to avoid some difficult decisions for its coalition partners.

## The Definition of 'Encourage'

**1.63** To 'encourage' is ordinarily defined as to 'urge, incite; recommend, advise' and to 'stimulate (a person, personal activity) by help, reward, etc.' and to 'promote or assist (an activity or situation)'.[122] Each State Party undertakes never

---

[120] Office of the Judge Advocate General, 'The Law of Armed Conflict', sect. 5.10.

[121] Personal email communication from Lieutenant-Colonel Mike Kelly, Australian Defence Force (Geneva, 5 Feb. 2003). [122] Brown, *The New Shorter Oxford English Dictionary*, i. 814.

under any circumstances to encourage in any way, anyone to engage in any activity prohibited to a State Party under the Convention. As with assistance, the encouragement is therefore not linked only to the use of anti-personnel mines, but covers also the development, production, acquisition, stockpiling, retention, or transfer of the weapons. The inclusion of the term 'in any way' demonstrates that the encouragement may be provided directly or indirectly.

**1.64** Upon ratification of the Convention, Australia entered an under-standing of the definition of the term 'encourage' in the context of Article 1(1)(c): 'In Article 1(c) Australia will interpret the word . . . "encourage" to mean the actual request for the commission of any activity prohibited by the Convention'. The requirement for an 'actual request' appears to be an unnecessarily restrictive interpretation of the term encourage, as encouragement may be formulated other than through an 'actual request'. For instance, the Chief of the Canadian Defence Staff issued an instruction to the armed forces in 1998 that stated that 'the Canadian Forces may not request, even indirectly, the use of anti-personnel mines by others'.[123]

**1.65** In September 2001, Sweden issued a memorandum on its interpretation of Article 1(1)(c) of the Convention, which included the following assertion: 'Article 1(c) [*sic*] ought not to be interpreted so that any kind of participation in a joint military operation with a non-party would be considered as an encouragement to activities under the Ottawa Convention'.[124] This is clearly correct as there is no nexus between mere participation in such an operation and any specific instance of prohibited activity.

## The Definition of 'Induce'

**1.66** To 'induce' something is ordinarily defined as to 'lead, persuade, influence (a person) to do something'.[125] Each State Party undertakes never under any circumstances to encourage in any way, anyone to engage in any activity prohibited to a State Party under the Convention. As with the other two terms, the inducement is therefore not linked only to the use of anti-personnel mines, but covers also the development, production, acquisition, stockpiling, retention, or transfer of the weapons. The inclusion of the term 'in any way' demonstrates that the inducement may be provided directly or indirectly.

**1.67** Upon ratification of the Convention, Australia entered an understanding of the definition of the term 'induce' in the context of Article 1(1)(c): 'In Article 1(c)

---

[123] Chief of the Defence Staff, 'Anti-Personnel Mines', annex A, para. 3(a).

[124] 'Swedish Position on the Significance of Article 1(c) of the Ottawa Convention as regards Participation in International Peace Operations', Memorandum, Ministry of Foreign Affairs (1 Sept. 2001).          [125] Brown, *The New Shorter Oxford English Dictionary*, 1354.

Australia will interpret the word . . . "induce" to mean the active engagement in the offering of threats or incentives to obtain the commission of any activity prohibited by the Convention'. Again, its interpretation seems overly narrow, with the introduction of a requirement that threats or incentives be offered to obtain the commission of any activity prohibited by the Convention.

## *Interoperability*

**1.68** Interoperability[126] is a major issue within military alliances. Prior to the Oslo Diplomatic Conference, the Canadian Department of National Defence (DND) had raised the issue of North Atlantic Treaty Organization (NATO) interoperability in the context of Article 1(1)(c), asking for a clarification in the Convention.[127] A number of discussions were held within NATO, but mainly at a junior level. In addition, the USA had entertained bilateral negotiations with some of its NATO partners on the issue.

**1.69** During the Oslo Diplomatic Conference, Canada chaired an informal meeting of NATO countries on how to proceed.[128] At that stage, however, the USA did not appear to want to engage actively on the issue. As it became clear that the USA would not become a party to the Convention in the near future, Canada and a number of other concerned States decided to clarify their positions, through an interpretive declaration at the time of the deposit of the instrument of ratification.[129] Thus, upon ratification of the Convention Canada declared that,

in the context of operations, exercises or other military activity sanctioned by the United Nations or otherwise conducted in accordance with international law, the mere participation by the Canadian Forces, or individual Canadians, in operations, exercises or other military activity conducted in combination with the armed forces of States not party to the Convention which engage in activity prohibited under the Convention would not, by itself, be considered to be assistance, encouragement or inducement in accordance with the meaning of those terms in article 1, paragraph 1 (c).

---

[126] The US Department of Defense defines interoperability as 'the ability of systems, units or forces to provide services to and accept services from other systems, units, or forces and to use the services so exchanged to enable them to operate effectively together'. US Department of Defense, Joint Chiefs of Staff, *Dictionary of Military Terms*, 198.

[127] DND had advocated internally for a specific exception for joint operations to be included in Article 3 of the Convention, but this idea was not retained. Discussion with Brigadier-General E. S. Fitch, Assistant Chief of the Land Staff, Canadian National Defence Headquarters (Ottawa, 15 Aug. 2001).

[128] Although not a member of NATO, Austria was invited to participate in the discussions.

[129] Discussions with Jill Sinclair and Mark Gwozdecky, Canadian Department of Foreign Affairs and International Trade (Ottawa, 14 Aug. 2001).

**1.70** Similar declarations were subsequently made on ratification by Australia,[130] the Czech Republic, and the United Kingdom.[131] It has been claimed that Spain wished to make a similar declaration, but backed down in the face of public pressure.[132] The Norwegian government has made a declaration to Parliament whereby it subscribes to the declaration of understanding submitted by Canada 'in order to avoid any doubts concerning future Norwegian participation in various military exercises or operations'.[133]

**1.71** These understandings appear to be in accord with the terms of the Convention since the 'mere participation' or 'participation . . . by itself' in operations, exercises, or other military activity conducted in combination with the armed forces of States not party to the Convention which engage in activity prohibited under the Convention is not an act that *per se* assists, encourages, or induces anyone to commit prohibited activities. What is critical is the nexus between the actions of a State Party and specific prohibited activities. Thus, these are not to be considered reservations,[134] which are prohibited by Article 19 of the Anti-Personnel Mine Ban Convention.[135]

**1.72** The problems of joint operations involving both States Parties and non-party States are not, though, limited to NATO. The ICBL has 'consistently raised concerns about the possible participation of States Parties in joint

---

[130] 'It is the understanding of the Government of Australia that, in the context of operations, exercises or other military activity authorised by the United Nations or otherwise conducted in accordance with international law, the participation by the Australian Defence Force, or individual Australian citizens or residents, in such operations, exercises or other military activity, conducted in combination with the armed forces of States not party to the Convention which engage in activity prohibited under that Convention would not, by itself, be considered to be in violation of the Convention.'

[131] 'It is the understanding of the Government of the United Kingdom that the mere participation in the planning or execution of operations, exercises or other military activity by the United Kingdom's Armed Forces, or individual United Kingdom nationals, conducted in combination with the armed forces of States not party to the [said Convention], which engage in activity prohibited under that Convention, is not, by itself, assistance, encouragement or inducement for the purposes of Article 1, paragraph (c) of the Convention.'

[132] Letter from Raul Romeva included in 'News from Afghan and Spanish campaigns', email from Liz Bernstein, ICBL Coordinator (7 Oct. 1998).

[133] Unofficial translation from Norwegian: 'En slik klargjøring er viktig for å unngå at det skapes tvil vedørrende framtidig norsk deltakelse I ulike militære øvelser eller operasjoner'. White Paper No. 73 (1997–8), The Government's proposal to Parliament regarding acceptance of ratification of the Convention on the Prohibition of the Use, Stockpiling, Production and Transfer of Anti-Personnel Mines and on their Destruction, signed in Ottawa on 3 Dec. 1997.

[134] The 1969 Vienna Convention defines a reservation as a 'unilateral statement, however phrased or named, made by a State, when signing, ratifying, accepting, approving or acceding to a treaty, whereby it purports to exclude or to modify the legal effect of certain provisions of the treaty in their application to that State'.

[135] See below the commentary on Article 19, including a discussion of the status of interpretive declarations.

military operations with non-States Parties that retain the right to use anti-personnel mines . . . Though often discussed in terms of potential US use of antipersonnel mines in NATO operations, this is by no means a problem limited to the NATO alliance'.[136] According to the ICBL:

There are increasingly serious questions regarding the position of Tajikistan, a State Party, toward the use of antipersonnel mines by Russian forces stationed in Tajikistan. In addition, it appears that a number of States in Africa have engaged in military operations with (or in support of) armed forces that may be using antipersonnel mines. This would include Namibia (with Angola against UNITA before the peace agreement in April 2002), as well as Rwanda and Zimbabwe with various forces in the DR Congo. Namibia and Zimbabwe have denied any involvement by their forces in emplacing antipersonnel mines while engaged in joint operations.[137]

## Operations Involving Anti-Personnel Mines on the Territory of a State Party

**1.73** In fact, Tajikistan does not appear to be involved in joint operations with the Russian forces stationed on its territory,[138] although it may have acquiesced or even consented to the use of anti-personnel mines by these forces.[139] Russian forces are stationed along Tajikistan's border with Afghanistan. The situation may therefore be more accurately described as an operation involving anti-personnel mines on the territory of a State Party. If the Tajik government has indeed acquiesced or consented to use of anti-personnel mines, then it has induced or encouraged that use, which is a violation of Article 1(1)(c). If, on the other hand, Russian forces have laid anti-personnel mines without its consent, this would fall within Tajikistan's obligations under Article 9: to 'take all appropriate legal, administrative and other measures, including the imposition of penal sanctions, to prevent and suppress any activity prohibited to a State Party under this Convention undertaken by persons or on territory under its jurisdiction or control'.

## The Transit of Anti-Personnel Mines

**1.74** The legality of the transfer and transit of anti-personnel mines, including the definitions of the two terms, is discussed above.[140] As already

---

[136] ICBL, *Landmine Monitor Report 2002*, 17.    [137] ibid.

[138] Although there are reports that 80 per cent of the troops (not the officer corps) are Tajik citizens and that 10 per cent of the funding for the border troops is provided by Tajikistan. Nivat, A., 'Tadjikistan: la sale frontière', *Le Nouvel observateur* (TéléCinéObs) (26 Dec. 2002), 54–5.

[139] According to information received by ICBL, a senior official in the Russian Federal Border Service confirmed to Landmine Monitor in December 2001 that Russian troops had laid anti-personnel mines inside Tajikistan with the full knowledge and consent of the Tajik government and in accordance with a military cooperation agreement signed in 1993. ICBL, *Landmine Monitor Report 2002*, 473–4.    [140] See paras. 1.40–1.50 above.

noted, the ICRC has declared that, 'permitting the transit of anti-personnel mines through the territory of a State Party would undermine the object and purpose of the [Convention] . . . and contradict its prohibition on assisting anyone in the stockpiling and use of anti-personnel mines . . . The ICRC believes that permitting or assisting the transit of anti-personnel mines through the territory of a State Party, by provision of transport infrastructure or other means, constitutes assistance in the stockpiling of anti-personnel mines and is prohibited'.[141] Indeed, the prohibition is wide—to assist *in any way*—and therefore providing airspace or allowing movement by road of anti-personnel mines would seem to breach the provision.

### The Stockpiling of Foreign Anti-Personnel Mines

**1.75**  In accordance with Articles 1 and 4, each State Party undertakes never under any circumstances to stockpile anti-personnel mines or to assist, encourage, or induce anyone in any way to do so. Offering one's territory to a non-party State or providing storage facilities for anti-personnel mines clearly violates the prohibition on assistance, encouragement, or inducement to stockpile anti-personnel mines. However, a distinction should be made between 'permitting' and 'assisting'. Although the term 'permit' was initially included in the First Austrian Draft of the Convention, it was removed in the subsequent draft and does not appear in the text of Article 1(1)(c) as adopted.[142]

**1.76**  Thus, although it is generally unlawful for foreign stockpiles to be present on the territory of a State Party, strictly speaking it would appear that foreign stockpiles are permissible in the exceptional cases where they do not fall under either the State Party's jurisdiction or its control, and as long as the State Party is not assisting in any way in the stockpiling. This is seemingly the position of the ICBL, which has stated that: 'The ICBL believes that it would violate the spirit of the Mine Ban Treaty for a State Party to permit any government or entity to stockpile antipersonnel mines on its territory, and would violate the letter of the treaty if those stocks are under the jurisdiction or control of the State Party'.[143]

### Components of Anti-Personnel Mines

**1.77**  There is no explicit prohibition on the production or transfer of components of anti-personnel mines contained in the Anti-Personnel Mine Ban

---

[141] 'International Committee of the Red Cross, Annex to Landmine Monitor, March 1999', ICBL, *Landmine Monitor Report 1999*, 1005–6.

[142] Following remarks by Ecuador and Japan at the 1997 Vienna Experts Meeting, the word 'permit' in Article 1(1)(c) was removed, as it was perceived to be covered by the requirement to implement the Convention under Article 9, for instance through domestic legislation.

[143] ICBL, *Landmine Monitor Report 2002*, 21.

Convention. That said, however, the prohibition on assisting anyone in any way to engage in a prohibited activity has legal consequences for components in certain circumstances. Thus, as the ICRC has pointed out:

The treaty itself does not explicitly refer to the component parts of [anti-personnel] mines. Nonetheless, knowingly manufacturing, transferring or selling components intended to be used to assemble [anti-personnel] mines would violate the prohibition on assisting in the production of [anti-personnel] mines. The national laws passed by a number of States classify [anti-personnel] mine components as prohibited objects.[144]

Similarly, according to the ICBL, 'transfer of components destined for use in antipersonnel mines would not only violate the spirit of the Mine Ban Treaty, but would also run counter to Article 1.1(c), which prohibits a State Party from assisting anyone to engage in a prohibited activity'.[145]

1.78 Further, the undertaking in Article 1(1)(b) never under any circumstances to produce or transfer anti-personnel mines 'directly or indirectly' would also encompass the production or sale of components intended for the production of, adaptation to, or inclusion in, an anti-personnel mine. The Czech Republic is one of the few States Parties to the Convention that has expressly prohibited under its criminal law the 'development, production, transfer, storage or stockpiling of anti-personnel mines *or their components*' as well as the 'exercise and transfer of patent rights for the production of anti-personnel mines *or their components*'.[146]

## Concluding Remarks

1.79 According to the Final Report of 2001–2 of the Standing Committee on the General Status and Operation of the Convention:

It was recalled that interest existed over recent years to hold further discussions of understandings of the word 'assist' in Article 1(c) of the Convention. In this context, States Parties were invited to share information on how, in operational terms, Article 1 is being implemented. Some States Parties took advantage of this opportunity to inform the Standing Committee on their application of the Article, particularly in instances wherein they may be participating in joint operations with States not Parties to the Convention. It was noted that an increasing number of national views was bringing greater clarity to this matter . . . [147]

---

[144] 'Implementing the Ottawa Treaty: National Legislation', *Information Paper* (Geneva: ICRC, Apr. 1999), 2.  [145] ICBL, *Landmine Monitor Report 2001*, 605.
[146] See Act of 18 Nov. 1999 on the prohibition of the use, stockpiling, production, and transfer of anti-personnel mines and on their destruction, Part 1, Sect. 1, available at: www.icrc.org/IHL-NAT.NSF.
[147] Final Report, 2001–2002, Standing Committee on the General Status and Operation of the Convention, Doc. APLC/MSP.4/2002/SC.4/1 of 19 July 2002, p. 4, available at: www.gichd.ch.

Yet, optimism notwithstanding, the interpretation of the provision clearly remains controversial. New Zealand and the United Kingdom are among the few States Parties that have specifically criminalized assisting, encouraging, or inducing a prohibited activity under its national implementing legislation.[148] Most have not.

# Paragraph 2

2. Each State Party undertakes to destroy or ensure the destruction of all anti-personnel mines in accordance with the provisions of this Convention.

## The General Obligation to Destroy All Anti-Personnel Mines

1.80 This provision sets out the general obligation on a State Party to destroy or ensure the destruction of all emplaced anti-personnel mines in mined areas under its jurisdiction or control or stockpiled anti-personnel mines it owns or possesses or which are under its jurisdiction or control.[149] The extent of the obligations is set out in Articles 3, 4, and 5 of the Convention. The phrase 'ensure the destruction of' was proposed by Sweden during the Oslo Diplomatic Conference to make it explicit that a State Party might wish to arrange for another State or a private company to destroy the mines elsewhere. Under Article 3, transfer of anti-personnel mines for the purpose of destruction is specifically authorized.[150]

1.81 Neither 'destroy' nor 'destruction' is defined in the Convention. In standard usage, to destroy something is to 'put an end to' its 'existence . . . by damaging or attacking it'.[151] Similarly, 'destruction' is 'the action or process of causing so much damage to something that it no longer exists or cannot be repaired'.[152] It is clear that a variety of different methods of destruction are lawful, as Article 7(1)(f) requires reporting on the 'status of programs for the

---

[148] Section 7, Part II, Anti-Personnel Mines Prohibition Act 1998, available at: www.icrc.org/IHL-NAT.NSF.

[149] The inclusion as a general obligation of the undertaking to destroy anti-personnel mines followed comments by Hungary at the Vienna Experts Meeting. In this respect, it follows the logic of the 1993 Chemical Weapons Convention, which includes within the general obligations the undertaking to destroy chemical weapons it owns or possesses or that it has abandoned on the territory of another State Party in accordance with the provisions of the Convention. Article I(2) and (3), 1993 Chemical Weapons Convention.

[150] Thus, the words 'ensure the destruction' anticipate the exception in Article 3(2) to the general prohibition on transfer whereby: 'The transfer of anti-personnel mines for the purpose of destruction is permitted'. See below the commentary on this provision.

[151] Pearsall, *The New Oxford Dictionary of English*, 502.

[152] ibid.

destruction of anti-personnel mines in accordance with Articles 4 and 5, including details of the methods which will be used in destruction'. Physical destruction techniques available range from the relatively simple open burning and open detonation (OBOD) techniques to highly sophisticated industrial processes. The decision to opt for any particular technique is likely to be based on cost, safety, and environmental considerations.[153] State practice has included dismantling as well as physical destruction of the mine or its components.[154]

**1.82** The International Mine Action Standards (IMAS), published by the United Nations, include a specific standard for anti-personnel mine stockpile destruction.[155] According to the IMAS, there were traditionally five options for the logistic disposal of ammunition and explosives; however, in the case of anti-personnel mines four of these options are banned by international treaty. The Anti-Personnel Mine Ban Convention does not permit the sale, gift, or increased use in training of anti-personnel mines, and the Convention for the Prevention of Marine Pollution by Dumping from Ships and Aircraft (the Oslo Convention) has outlawed deep sea dumping.[156] Therefore, the international community is now left with destruction 'as the only available option for the disposal of anti-personnel mines'.[157]

**1.83** Directional fragmentation 'mines' (i.e. Claymore-type devices fitted with tripwires) are covered by Article 2 of the Convention and are therefore not only prohibited but also legally subject to the requirements for destruction under Article 4.[158] States Parties have tended to implement this requirement by reconfiguring the devices by removing and sometimes destroying the fusing but leaving the devices themselves intact. The UK has reconfigured its Claymore-type mines, which is said to involve more than simply removing the tripwire.[159]

**1.84** Further, mines ostensibly categorized as anti-tank or anti-vehicle mines, but which fall under the definition of anti-personnel mine in Article 2 of the Convention because of the fusing system they contain, should, in accordance

---

[153] *A Guide to Mine Action.*

[154] One could even argue that dismantling is to be preferred given the requirement in Article 7(1)(f) for details of the 'environmental standards to be observed'. The detonation of large numbers of certain anti-personnel mines may have toxic side-effects as noxious chemicals are released into the atmosphere. See e.g. the experiences of the Ukraine, reported in ICBL, *Landmine Monitor Report 2000*, 786–7.

[155] IMAS 11.10, 2nd edn. (1 Jan. 2003), available at: www.mineactionstandards.org.

[156] Convention for the Prevention of Marine Pollution by Dumping from Ships and Aircraft, adopted in Oslo on 15 Feb. 1972.                    [157] IMAS 11.10, 2nd edn. (1 Jan. 2003), 5.

[158] See below the commentary on Article 2(1) and Article 4.

[159] Information provided by Peter Balmer, UK Ministry of Defence (Geneva, 3 June 2002).

with Article 1(2) and Article 4, be destroyed. In such cases, however, a number of States Parties have simply removed or altered the fusing mechanism, rather than destroy the mine itself.

## Other Proposals

1.85  Prior to the Oslo Diplomatic Conference, the Côte d'Ivoire had put forward a proposal to include in the paragraph a requirement to destroy 'all production facilities of such [i.e. anti-personnel] mines'. This was not accepted for two reasons: first, it did not allow for the conversion of production facilities,[160] and second, it did not take account of the fact that a facility might produce multiple products, the others being lawful, and it was not necessary or appropriate to destroy the entire facility as a result of the requirements of the Convention, simply to desist from the production of anti-personnel mines.

1.86  Also prior to the Conference, the Philippines, a member of the Core Group, had put forward a proposal to include in the paragraph a requirement 'to engage in international cooperation and assistance', giving centre stage to the obligations developed in Article 6. It was dissuaded by other Core Group members from formally proposing the amendment during the Conference.

---

[160]  See below the commentary on Article 7(1)(e), which requires that a report be submitted on 'the status of programmes for the conversion or decommissioning of anti-personnel mine production facilities'.

# Article 2. Definitions

Article 2—Definitions

1. 'Anti-personnel mine' means a mine designed to be exploded by the presence, proximity or contact of a person and that will incapacitate, injure or kill one or more persons. Mines designed to be detonated by the presence, proximity or contact of a vehicle as opposed to a person, that are equipped with anti-handling devices, are not considered anti-personnel mines as a result of being so equipped.

2. 'Mine' means a munition designed to be placed under, on or near the ground or other surface area and to be exploded by the presence, proximity or contact of a person or a vehicle.

3. 'Anti-handling device' means a device intended to protect a mine and which is part of, linked to, attached to or placed under the mine and which activates when an attempt is made to tamper with or otherwise intentionally disturb the mine.

4. 'Transfer' involves, in addition to the physical movement of anti-personnel mines into or from national territory, the transfer of title to and control over the mines, but does not involve the transfer of territory containing emplaced anti-personnel mines.

5. 'Mined area' means an area which is dangerous due to the presence or suspected presence of mines.

# Introduction

## Overview

**2.1** Article 2 sets out a number of definitions for the purpose of the Convention:[1] anti-personnel mine, mine, anti-handling device, transfer, and mined area. These were taken, and in certain instances adapted, from the definitions contained in Amended Protocol II. Three of these terms—'anti-personnel mine', 'anti-handling device', and 'transfer'[2]—are subject to differing interpretations among States Parties to the Anti-Personnel Mine Ban Convention.

**2.2** During the negotiation of the Convention, a number of other definitions were either requested or proposed, formally or informally. These include the verbs, 'use',[3] 'produce', 'stockpile', 'retain', 'otherwise acquire', 'assist', 'encourage', and 'induce'. None of these terms is defined in the Convention as adopted. At the Oslo Diplomatic Conference, Australia proposed, unsuccessfully, a definition of 'designed',[4] a term found in the definition of both 'anti-personnel mine' and 'mine', and crucial to understanding its scope. In addition, an international non-governmental organization (NGO), the Landmine Survivors Network, called for 'mine victim' to be defined in the Convention.

---

[1] At the Oslo Diplomatic Conference, Japan had proposed specifying at the beginning of Article 2, that the definitions were '[f]or the purposes of this Convention', but this was felt by other delegations, notably Cameroon and Norway, to be unnecessary. See APL/CW.48 of 3 Sept. 1997, included in Appendix 5.

[2] See the commentary on the definition of the term 'transfer' in Article 1(1)(b) in paras. 1.40–1.50 above.                               [3] See para. 1.16 above.

[4] ' "Designed" means both the manufacturer's technical specifications and any intentional modification, adaptation or improvisation of any other munition or explosives so as to operate as a mine.' APL/CW.2 of 1 Sept. 1997. The proposal was discussed in the meeting of the Friends of the Chair on 4 Sept. 1997. Canada objected to its inclusion on the basis that it was assigning a special meaning to a normal English word, which might 'cause problems'.

**2.3** A number of other terms would have merited clarification, including 'anti-vehicle mine',[5] 'assist', 'destruction' and 'destroy', 'in a position to do so', 'jurisdiction', and 'control'.[6] It is probable, however, that drafting acceptable definitions would have been impractical in the circumstances.

## The Negotiation of the Article

**2.4** The definition of an anti-personnel mine is clearly central to the Anti-Personnel Mine Ban Convention.[7] Indeed, in his first informal draft text of April 1996, Werner Ehrlich included a definition only of anti-personnel mines. This he did indirectly, by reference to Amended Protocol II to the 1980 Convention on Certain Conventional Weapons (CCW):

Article 1

Scope of application

This Convention shall apply to anti-personnel mines as defined in paragraph 3 of article 2 of Protocol II of the CCW-Convention as amended on 3 May 1996 . . .

The definition in Article 2(3), which had been one of the most controversial issues of the various negotiations in the context of Amended Protocol II, reads as follows: ' "Anti-Personnel mine" means a mine primarily designed to be exploded by the presence, proximity or contact of a person and that will incapacitate, injure or kill one or more persons'.

**2.5** At the fourth and final meeting of the Group of Governmental Experts convened to prepare the First Review Conference of the CCW, Germany,[8] with the support of the USA and others, had proposed the insertion of the word 'primarily' in the draft definition, ostensibly to protect anti-vehicle mines equipped with anti-handling devices. Both the International Campaign to Ban Landmines (ICBL) and the International Committee of the Red Cross (ICRC) criticized severely the inclusion of the word as narrowing the definition of an anti-personnel mine. Indeed, 'primarily', which is the adverb of the adjective 'primary', ordinarily means (*inter alia*) 'a thing which is first in order, rank or

---

[5] Although a definition may well have been 'mines, other than anti-personnel mines', which would hardly have resolved the debate as to the precise ambit of the definition of an anti-personnel mine.

[6] See below the commentary on Articles 4 and 5 with regard to the destruction of anti-personnel mine stockpiles and anti-personnel mines in mined areas, respectively.

[7] Thus, in its 1994 report to the Review Conference, the ICRC, hoping for agreement to prohibit the use of anti-personnel mines, had already warned of the importance of a careful definition to ensure that responsibilities were not evaded. ICRC, 'Report of the ICRC for the Review Conference of the 1980 UN Convention on Certain Conventional Weapons', *International Review of the Red Cross* (Geneva: ICRC, Mar.–Apr. 1994), 137.

[8] It has also been suggested that the original suggestion came from Israel.

importance'.[9] This suggests that in the case of anti-vehicle or anti-tank mines, 'secondary' design features, such as impact on personnel, are thereby excluded.

**2.6** Following the criticism, which continued throughout the Review Conference, upon the adoption of Amended Protocol II, Germany delivered an interpretive statement on behalf of 17 other States[10] that 'primarily' was included to ensure that 'mines designed to be detonated by the presence, proximity or contact of a vehicle as opposed to a person, that are equipped with anti-handling devices, are not considered anti-personnel mines as a result of being so equipped'.[11] The statement did not address the situation of anti-vehicle mines that would also be detonated by a person. The ICRC, however, was concerned that the term 'primarily' would also exclude what it termed 'dual use' mines or munitions and declared its opinion that an anti-personnel mine 'must continue to be understood as any mine which is "designed to be exploded or detonated by the presence, proximity or contact of a person" . . . whatever other functions the munition may also have'.[12]

**2.7** Notwithstanding the controversy, however, the First Austrian Draft of October 1996 contained the same definition of anti-personnel mine as the one in Amended Protocol II. It also included a definition of 'mine', which was slightly amended from the one in the Protocol:[13]

Article 2
Definitions

1. 'Anti-personnel mine' means a mine primarily designed to be exploded by the presence, proximity, or contact of a person and that will incapacitate, injure or kill one or more persons.

2. 'Mine' means a munition designed to be placed under, on or near the ground or other surface area and to be exploded by the presence, proximity or contact of a person or a vehicle.[14]

---

[9] *The Shorter Oxford English Dictionary.*

[10] Australia, Bulgaria, Canada, Czech Republic, Denmark, France, Greece, Hungary, Ireland, Italy, Latvia, Netherlands, Norway, Poland, Romania, South Africa, the UK, and the USA. See UN Doc. CCW/CONF.I/SR.14 of 6 June 1996, pp. 3–4, available at: disarmament.un.org/ccw/ccwmeetings.html.

[11] Upon their declarations of consent to be bound by Amended Protocol II this position was confirmed by the following States: Austria, Canada, Denmark, Finland, France, Germany, Greece, Ireland, Italy, the Netherlands, South Africa, Sweden, and Switzerland.

[12] Herby, P., 'Third Session of the Review Conference of States Parties to the 1980 United Nations Convention on Certain Conventional Weapons (CCW). Geneva, 22 April–3 May 1996', *International Review of the Red Cross*, no. 312 (May–June 1996), 366.

[13] According to Article 2(1) of Amended Protocol II: 'Mine' means a munition placed under, on, or near the ground or other surface area and designed to be exploded by the presence, proximity, or contact of a person or a vehicle.

[14] Similar definitions were also included in the Belgian Draft Text of October 1996.

**2.8** At the 1997 Vienna Conference that discussed the text of the First Austrian Draft,[15] many States that intervened in the discussion of the definition of an anti-personnel mine proposed its retention as set out in Amended Protocol II,[16] although a number declared that they were (also) willing to accept a definition without the word 'primarily'.[17] The ICBL and the ICRC argued vigorously for the word's deletion and the ICRC circulated an informal paper indicating mines that were already being reclassified to avoid being termed anti-personnel mines.[18] With regard to other definitions, several States called for the inclusion of a definition of transfer based on the one included in Amended Protocol II.[19] Australia and Croatia requested a definition of 'booby-trap', an issue that remains controversial.[20] Sri Lanka also called for a definition of 'stockpiles'.

**2.9** Despite the number of States that had expressed their support for retaining the definition of an anti-personnel mine in Amended Protocol II, the definition in the Second Austrian Draft was amended, with the word 'primarily' deleted.[21] An explicit exception was included for anti-vehicle mines equipped with anti-handling devices, in accordance with the declaration by Germany, on behalf of 17 other States, at the adoption of Amended Protocol II.[22] This in turn demanded a definition of an anti-handling device; this was taken directly from Amended Protocol II.[23] In addition, definitions of 'mine', 'minefield', and 'transfer' were added to the draft article.

Article 2

Definitions

1. 'Anti-personnel mine' means a mine designed to be exploded by the presence, proximity or contact of a person and that will incapacitate, injure or kill one or more

---

[15] See paras. 0.57–0.58 above.

[16] Australia, Belgium, Canada, Cuba, Honduras (on behalf of Central American States), Hungary, Ireland, Mexico, Norway, Poland, South Africa, Sweden, and Switzerland. Norway and Switzerland were said to be against changing the definition because it risked slowing the process of negotiating the Convention. Short, N., 'International Efforts to Ban Landmines: The Vienna Conference', Briefing Notes, Centre for European Security and Disarmament (Brussels, 4 Mar. 1997).

[17] Canada, Mexico, and St Lucia (on behalf of the CARICOM States).

[18] And thereby evading the imposition of additional restrictions, such as detectability, and self-destruction and self-deactivation mechanisms.

[19] Canada, France, Hungary, Japan, Mexico, the Netherlands, and Japan.

[20] See, below, paras. 2.38–2.41 for a discussion of the legality of booby-traps under the Anti-Personnel Mine Ban Convention.

[21] According to Thomas Hajnoczi, who was responsible for the text within the Austrian Ministry of Foreign Affairs, the Core Group recognized that the existing definition might be abused, although not all members were in favour of changing it. He therefore preferred to remove the word 'primarily' on the basis that it could always be put back if it were felt necessary. Discussion with Ambassador Hajnoczi in Oslo, 24 Oct. 2001.                                           [22] See para. 2.6 above.

[23] Article 2(14), 1996 Amended Protocol II.

persons. Mines designed to be detonated by the presence, proximity or contact of a vehicle as opposed to a person, that are equipped with anti-handling devices, are not considered anti-personnel mines as a result of being so equipped.

2.   'Mine' means a munition designed to be placed under, on or near the ground or other surface area and to be exploded by the presence, proximity or contact of a person or a vehicle.

3.   'Anti-handling device' means a device intended to protect a mine and which is part of, linked to, attached to or placed under the mine and which activates when an attempt is made to tamper with the mine.

4.   'Transfer' involves, in addition to the physical movement of anti-personnel mines into or from national territory, the transfer of title to and control over the mines, but does not involve the transfer of territory containing emplaced anti-personnel mines.

5.   'Minefield' is a defined area in which mines have been emplaced.

**2.10** In its comments on the Second Austrian Draft, France suggested reintroducing 'primarily' into the definition,[24] but the Third Austrian Draft maintained the draft Article 2 on definitions unchanged. During the 1997 Bonn Conference,[25] a number of States, notably France, Germany, the UK, and the USA, had privately expressed concern that the definition was too wide, and might encompass other weapons that do not cause a similarly severe humanitarian problem to anti-personnel mines, especially anti-vehicle mines.

**2.11** At the Oslo Diplomatic Conference, the draft article was one of the most hotly contested. A total of eight proposals were formally tabled in relation to the various definitions. Where relevant, these are addressed individually in the commentary on the respective paragraphs below. In addition, a more general proposal, submitted by Japan, sought explicitly to restrict all of the definitions to the present Convention, as set out below:[26]

Article 2

*For the purposes of this Convention,*

1.   'Anti-personnel mine' means . . .

This proposal was not accepted by the Conference, as being superfluous, and was withdrawn at the meeting of the Friend of the Chair for Article 2, chaired by Austria, on 5 September 1997.

---

[24] Fax from French Ministry of Foreign Affairs (Paris, 24 Apr. 1997).
[25] See paras. 0.64–0.66 above for details of the 1997 Bonn Conference.
[26] APL/CW.48 of 3 Sept. 1997.

# Paragraph 1

1. 'Anti-personnel mine' means a mine designed to be exploded by the presence, proximity or contact of a person and that will incapacitate, injure or kill one or more persons. Mines designed to be detonated by the presence, proximity or contact of a vehicle as opposed to a person, that are equipped with anti-handling devices, are not considered anti-personnel mines as a result of being so equipped.

## The Elements of an Anti-Personnel Mine

**2.12** According to the definition in the Convention, there are a number of elements, all of which must be present, if any given device is to be considered an anti-personnel mine. It must be a *mine*; it must be *designed* to be *exploded* by the *presence, proximity, or contact of a person*; and its effects must be such that it will *incapacitate, injure, or kill one or more persons*. In addition, mines designed to be detonated by the presence, proximity or contact of a vehicle, and which are equipped with anti-handling devices, are not thereby considered anti-personnel mines.

### *A mine . . .*

**2.13** First, the device must be considered a mine in accordance with Article 2(2) of the Convention.[27] Thus, it must be 'a munition designed to be placed under, on or near the ground or other surface area and to be exploded by the presence, proximity or contact of a person or a vehicle'. The term 'munition' is not defined in the Convention, but used here is a military technical term synonymous with ammunition. It is usefully defined by the USA as follows: 'A complete device charged with explosives, propellants, pyrotechnics, initiating composition, or nuclear, biological or chemical material for use in military operations, including demolitions'.[28]

### *. . . designed*

**2.14** Second, the mine must be *designed* to be 'exploded by the presence, proximity or contact of a person'. The notion of 'design', which is contained in the definition of both mine and anti-personnel mine, but which is not defined in the Convention, has proved problematic. In ordinary usage, something that is designed is 'planned' or 'intended', or 'fashioned according to a design'.[29]

---

[27] The definition of 'mine' is generally uncontroversial, being drawn directly and with only minor amendment, from the one included in Article 2(1), Amended Protocol II.

[28] US Department of Defense, Joint Chiefs of Staff, *Dictionary of Military Terms*, 256.

[29] See for instance Brown, *The New Shorter Oxford English Dictionary*, i. 646.

This is clearly both a general and a broad definition, far broader than, for example, the word 'manufactured'. Moreover, there is no temporal restriction inherent in the definition. Thus, it seemingly encompasses not only the original manufacture of a mine, but also its modification, adaptation, and improvisation, including in the field.

2.15 Such a wide interpretation, in accordance with ordinary usage, is supported by reference to the *travaux préparatoires* in accordance with Article 32 of the 1969 Vienna Convention. On 5 September 1997, at a meeting of the Friend of the Chair for Article 2, Australia proposed that new language be included in Article 1(1)(b) whereby States Parties would undertake never under any circumstances: 'To configure or adapt any mine or any other munitions, or improvise any other explosive devices, for use as anti-personnel mines'. Belgium, supported by Denmark and Germany, stated that the language was not necessary as the treaty text as it stood already covered these weapons. As a consequence, Australia withdrew its proposal, and on 8 September stated its interpretation that, *inter alia*, bounding mines were captured by the definition in Article 2(1), as were anti-vehicle mines functioning as anti-personnel mines, anti-vehicle mines operating as anti-personnel mines,[30] and munitions improvised to operate as anti-personnel mines.[31] No delegation objected to this interpretation.[32]

2.16 More broadly, however, the definition of 'designed' has been problematic with respect to the assessment of the requisite 'plan', 'design', or 'intent'. In particular, is it the stated intent of the 'designer' or the actual functioning of his or her 'design' that will determine whether or not a given mine or munition falls within the definitions in Article 2(1) and (2)?

2.17 States Parties views on this issue appear to differ. According to the UK, for example, 'it is the design of the mine that is the key. We believe that the definition of what constitutes an anti-personnel mine in the Ottawa Convention does not turn on any unintended effects that mine might have when deployed. We do not agree with those who argue for an effects based definition'.[33]

---

[30] The distinction, if indeed there is one, between anti-vehicle mines functioning as anti-personnel mines, and those 'operating' as anti-personnel mines is not clear.

[31] The Australian implementing legislation for the Convention provides that '*anti-personnel mine* means a mine that: (a) is designed, altered or intended so as . . .'. Anti-Personnel Mine Convention Act 1998, No. 126, 1998, Section 4, p. 3, original emphasis.

[32] Further evidence for the interpretation is drawn from the negotiation of the term 'mine' under Amended Protocol II, from which the definition in the Anti-Personnel Mine Ban Convention is drawn. The USA, for example, has declared that the definition applies 'whether a munition is designed for this purpose in the factory or adapted for this purpose in the field'. Nash, 'Contemporary Practice of the United States Relating to International Law', 331.

[33] Statement by the United Kingdom on Article 2 of the Convention on the Prohibition of the Use, Stockpiling, Production and Transfer of Anti-Personnel Mines and on Their Destruction, Standing Committee on the General Status and Operation of the Convention (Geneva, 30 May 2002).

The UK statement has been supported orally by France, which declared that it had 'nothing to add to the United Kingdom statement, nor to take away'.[34]

**2.18** Those who argue for a function-based definition include the Netherlands and Norway. During the Third Meeting of States Parties, in Managua, in September 2001, the Netherlands 're-emphasised' its position that any device that functions like an anti-personnel mine is considered to be an anti-personnel mine and is banned by the treaty.[35] Similarly, the head of the Norwegian delegation, Ambassador Kongstad, declared that: 'During the Oslo negotiations in 1997, there was agreement on an effect oriented definition of APMs . . . it does not matter how a weapon is labelled or defined. As long as it de facto functions as an APM, it falls within the scope of Article 2 . . . What counts is the humanitarian impact'.[36]

**2.19** In May 2002, at the Standing Committee on the General Status and Operation of the Convention, Austria declared that: 'In our view, the definition of APMs is straightforward. It is a mine which is designed to be exploded by the presence, proximity or contact of a person . . . In this respect, we completely agree with the argument put forward by the ICRC in its Working Paper of January 2002, that any mine—regardless of how it is labelled—is banned by the Convention "if the design is such that it would detonate by the presence, proximity or contact of a person" '.[37]

**2.20** Thus, where, based on the design of the mine, a person travelling on foot under normal circumstances[38] will typically[39] trigger it, that munition is captured by the scope of the definition in Article 2(1) and is therefore prohibited as being an anti-personnel mine.

**2.21** Evidence for this interpretation is to be found in the *travaux préparatoires*. In the First Austrian Draft of the Convention of October 1996,

[34] Landmine Monitor notes, reported in ICBL, *Landmine Monitor Report 2002*, 263.

[35] ibid. 366.      [36] ibid. 388.

[37] In May 2003, at the intersessional Standing Committee meeting of the General Status and Operation of the Convention, the ICRC stated that it 'continues to insist, based on the negotiating history, the object and purpose of the Convention and the basic rules of treaty interpretation, that any mine which is likely to be detonated by the presence, proximity or contact of a person is an anti-personnel mine prohibited by this Convention'. Statement to the intersessional Standing Committee meeting of the General Status and Operation of the Convention (Geneva, 16 May 2003), available at: www.gichd.ch. This is a somewhat narrower definition than it has previously advocated. It had previously suggested that it would be enough that a mine be *capable* of detonation by a person: 'it is . . . the view of the ICRC that *any* mine with a fusing mechanism capable of being detonated by the presence, proximity or contact of a person would be prohibited by the Convention'. Statement of the International Committee of the Red Cross on Article 2 of the Convention to the Third Meeting of States Parties (Managua, 20 Sept. 2001), 1.

[38] Thus, for example, this would not apply to a person jumping down onto a mine from considerable height or walking around with a large quantity of metal in his or her pockets.

[39] This is a high threshold, much higher than 'may trigger', and higher also than 'is likely to'.

the definition of an anti-personnel mine reproduces the one contained in 1996 Amended Protocol II without amendment: ' "Anti-personnel mine" means a mine primarily designed to be exploded by the presence, proximity, or contact of a person and that will incapacitate, injure or kill one or more persons'.[40]

2.22 A great deal of attention focused on the inclusion of the word 'primarily', which had originally been proposed by Germany during the negotiation of the Amended Protocol.[41] The term was put forward to reduce the scope of the definition of an anti-personnel mine under the Protocol, as a number of requirements, including the need for self-destruction and self-deactivation, or maintenance within marked and monitored minefields, were made applicable only to anti-personnel mines.[42] Thus, at the Third Meeting of States Parties, Norway stated that: 'By omitting that term it was made clear that the definition in the Mine Ban Convention would cover a wider scope of mines, not just those primarily designed to be [anti-personnel] mines, but those functioning as [anti-personnel] mines'.[43]

### . . . to be exploded

2.23 The third element in an anti-personnel mine is that the mine must be designed to be *exploded* by the presence, proximity, or contact of a person. Thus, it is not sufficient that it be designed to be triggered, armed, or fused, it must also be designed so that an explosion results.[44] To explode something is ordinarily to cause it to expand, burst, or shatter with extreme violence and noise.[45] Thus, the mere emission, without an accompanying explosion, of a gas, chemical, or liquid from a pre-formed tube or hole in a device would not appear to be caught within the definition (notwithstanding the illegality of the weapon under other rules of international law).[46] Similarly, a discharge of electricity would not be sufficient for a weapon to be considered, legally, as a

---

[40] Article 2(1), First Austrian Draft.    [41] See para. 2.5 above.

[42] In the original Protocol II, adopted in 1980, obligations were imposed on all landmines without distinction.

[43] Statement of Norway to the Third Meeting of States Parties, Managua, Sept. 2001. A similar statement was made by the Netherlands.

[44] At the Oslo Diplomatic Conference, Australia had argued that the word 'triggered' would be more appropriate than 'exploded', as the latter expression might exclude bounding mines, which, when triggered, leap into the air to a height of around one metre before exploding. This argument was not accepted by the Conference, and it is understood that bounding anti-personnel mines are indeed covered by the Anti-Personnel Mine Ban Convention and therefore prohibited.

[45] Brown, *The New Shorter Oxford English Dictionary*, 888.

[46] An explosion requires that the shock wave travel more rapidly than the speed of sound within the medium of the explosive.

mine.[47] Equally, a spear could be implanted vertically in the ground, with a strong spring underneath it and a trigger mechanism on top, so that the foot-fall of a victim would cause the victim to be impaled. This would not be a mine, and would be compliant with the Convention.

### . . . by the presence, proximity, or contact of a person

2.24 The fourth element is that, to be considered an anti-personnel mine, the mine must be designed to be exploded by the presence, proximity, or con-tact of a person. Thus, for instance, munitions designed to be exploded by the pressure of an ordinary footfall, or the triggering of a tripwire, breakwire, or tilt rod by a person, even the presence or proximity of body heat, would satisfy this requirement. The fact that it is also designed to be exploded by the presence, proximity, or contact of a vehicle is irrelevant. 'Contact' is not defined in the Convention, but in ordinary usage is the 'state or condition of touching; an instance of touching',[48] which suggests that actual disturbance of the mine is not required.

### . . . and that will incapacitate, injure, or kill one or more persons

2.25 The fifth element in an anti-personnel mine is that the effect of the explosion of the mine must be to incapacitate, injure, or kill one or more per-sons. Thus, in contrast to the example in paragraph 2.23 above, a mine that is designed to be exploded by the presence, proximity, or contact of a person *and* which contains an incapacitating gas, chemical, or liquid, or which discharges a significant quantity of electricity, is certainly captured by the definition.[49]

2.26 The final part of the paragraph of Article 2(1) excludes from the definition of anti-personnel mine '[m]ines designed to be detonated by the pres-ence, proximity or contact of a vehicle as opposed to a person, that are equipped with anti-handling devices'. This demonstrates that they would otherwise fall within the scope of the definition.[50]

2.27 In conclusion, within the context of the Anti-Personnel Mine Ban Convention, it is clear that all weapons that contain the five foregoing ele-ments, save those explicitly excluded in accordance with Article 2(1) and (3), are to be considered anti-personnel mines. Thus, no exception is made for

[47] Thus, for example, there was a press report in April 2003 that an American company had devel-oped a 'non-lethal' landmine that disables intruders with a 50,000 volt shock. The Pentagon was said to be interested. ' "Safe" Landmine', *The Times* (24 Apr. 2003), 11. [48] ibid. 491.

[49] For example, in the Introduction above, reference is made to the USA's earlier development of landmines that could serve as chemical weapons, each mine containing a quantity of VX nerve gas. See para. 0.6 above.

[50] The legality of these mines under the Convention is discussed in paras. 2.53–2.54 below.

anti-personnel mines that self-destruct, self-neutralize, or self-deactivate—all are captured and therefore prohibited.

## The Application of the Definition to Selected Weapons and Ordnance

**2.28** The following paragraphs discuss the legality of a number of weapons and weapon systems that might be deemed to fall within the definition in the Convention. These are, respectively, mixed munitions, directional fragmentation devices (or charges), improvised mines, improvised explosive devices (IEDs), booby-traps, unexploded ordnance (UXO), and mines with sensitive fuses. The following section considers anti-vehicle mines equipped with anti-handling devices.

### Mixed Munitions

**2.29** A thorny discussion at the Oslo Diplomatic Conference concerned the legality of so-called mixed munitions. These are projectiles or canisters containing both anti-vehicle and anti-personnel mines; some cluster bombs, for example, contain mines as their submunition payload. The USA, which pushed strongly for such weapons systems to be excluded from the ambit of the Convention, has three primary systems,[51] and has been considering manufacturing a fourth.[52] It sought, ultimately without success, to persuade other States that the anti-personnel mines contained in its mixed systems were in fact anti-handling devices. At the Diplomatic Conference, the USA put forward a number of proposals, the first of which, issued on 1 September 1997, reads as follows:

Likewise, mines that are integral submunitions in a munition that is designed for other than anti-personnel purposes (e.g., anti-tank, anti-vehicle, or runway denial) are not considered to be anti-personnel mines, provided that all such mines have self-destruction and self-deactivation features in compliance with paragraph 3(a) of the Technical Annex to the Protocol on Prohibitions or Restrictions on the Use of Mines, Booby-Traps and Other Devices as Amended on 3 May 1996, whether or not such mines are remotely-delivered.[53]

**2.30** A redrafted proposal, issued at the Conference the following week, sought instead to amend the definition of anti-handling device to exclude a 'submunition' intended to protect a mine other than an anti-personnel mine.[54]

---

[51] Gator, Volcano, and MOPMS. See ICBL, *Landmine Monitor Report 1999*, 318 ff.

[52] RADAM. Ibid. See also ICBL, *Landmine Monitor Report 2002*, 763.

[53] APL/CW.9 of 1 Sept. 1997. It was intended that the provision be included in a separate subparagraph following the second sentence of Article 2(1).

[54] APL/CW.9/Rev.1 of 8 Sept. 1997.

Subsequently, the delegation at the Oslo Diplomatic Conference called for a device intended to protect an anti-tank mine and placed 'near' the mine to be treated as an anti-handling device.[55] This proposed reclassification was again resisted by the Conference, and it is generally understood that mixed munitions containing anti-personnel mines are prohibited by the Convention.[56] Thus, for example, the Netherlands has destroyed its stockpile of 272 CBU-89 Gator mines, which it had described as 'non-Ottawa Convention compliant'.[57]

## Directional Fragmentation Devices

**2.31** Directional fragmentation devices or charges,[58] of which the Claymore is the best-known type, are typically triggered either by remote control or by tripwire. They remain outside the purview of the present Convention when equipped to function through command detonation because they are not 'designed . . . to be exploded by the presence, proximity or contact of a person or a vehicle' and do not therefore fall within the definition of a mine.[59] When equipped to function through tripwire activation, on the other hand, they are anti-personnel mines and accordingly prohibited. This appears to be uncontroversial.[60]

**2.32** A number of States have either prohibited the use and distribution of the tripwire fuse for such devices in order to prevent their use as anti-personnel mines,[61] reconfigured the munitions,[62] or destroyed the tripwires. Thus, for

---

[55] See the verbatim report of a News Briefing on the issue by Kenneth Bacon of the US Department of Defense given on 16 Sept. 1997, www.defenselink.mil.

[56] See the definition of an anti-handling device in Article 2(3).

[57] 'Cluster Bomb Units 89 "GATOR" are non-Ottawa Convention compliant because they contain APMs. Until recently, it was the policy of the Netherlands to have all APMs in these systems replaced by ATMs. Since March 1996 and until this adaptation was completed, these systems were not available to support any operation. Recently, however, the Minister of Defence has announced that all GATOR systems will be dismantled and destroyed. This decision was communicated to parliament in a letter dated Sept. 8, 1999. The destruction of the 272 GATOR systems will be completed within the time frame the Convention stipulates. For the Netherlands the deadline is October 1, 2003'. Article 7 report, submitted on 7 Jan. 2000, for the period 1 Mar.–31 Dec. 1999, Form B. The destruction has since been completed. [58] Norway e.g. calls them 'sector charges'.

[59] These weapons are termed 'other devices' under 1996 Amended Protocol II. According to Article 2(5) of the Protocol, these are '. . . manually-emplaced munitions and devices including improvised explosive devices designed to kill, injure or damage and which are actuated manually, by remote control or automatically after a lapse of time'.

[60] Thus, for instance, at the conclusion of the Oslo Diplomatic Conference, Australia reiterated its understanding that command-detonated fragmentation munitions were not covered by the Convention. Upon deposit of its instrument of ratification, it again put on record this understanding.

[61] The UK, for instance, has withdrawn all tripwire mechanisms for Claymore-type devices and instructed soldiers that use in tripwire mode is illegal. ICBL, *Landmine Monitor Report 2000*, 750–1.

[62] Thus, Norway's Claymore-type anti-personnel mines were rebuilt for command detonation by a Swedish company between 1998 and 2000. ICBL, *Landmine Monitor Report 2000*, 700. Similar changes have been made by Switzerland to its Claymores.

example, Canada reported to Mines Action Canada that Canadian Forces were deployed to Afghanistan with the 'C19 Command Detonated Defensive Weapon' and explained that 'the C19 inventory . . . is designed to be placed on the ground, aimed and controlled by a soldier who assesses the situation and makes a deliberate decision as to detonation. The Canadian Forces does not have, nor would be permitted to have, tripwire or victim-activating accessories for the C19 Command Detonated Defensive Weapons. All Canadian Forces in Afghanistan are instructed to act in accordance with the provisions of the Ottawa Convention'.[63]

### Improvised Anti-Personnel Mines

**2.33** It is quite straightforward to improvise an anti-personnel mine. It is sufficient to take an ordinary hand grenade and attach a wire to it such that when the wire is snapped by the movement of a person, the pin is removed and the grenade detonates. Thus, the munition becomes a *de facto* and *de iure* fragmentation anti-personnel mine as it is thereby 'a mine designed to be exploded by the presence, proximity or contact of a person'.

**2.34** At the meeting of the Friend of the Chair on Article 2 on 5 September 1997, Australia proposed a new Article 1(1)(b) whereby States Parties would undertake never under any circumstances: 'To configure or adapt any mine or other munitions, or improvise any other explosive devices, for use as anti-personnel mines'. Delegations agreed that the situation that Australia wished to see covered was already covered by the existing language of the Austrian draft. On this basis, Australia agreed not to pursue the proposed amendment.[64]

**2.35** Accordingly, although hand grenades are normally lawful, their improvisation as anti-personnel mines is prohibited in accordance with the definitions in Articles 2(1) and 2(2) of the Convention. This applies to other munitions similarly adapted or improvised that meet the requisite criteria under these definitions.

### Improvised Explosive Devices

**2.36** Although no formal definition currently exists under international law,[65] improvised explosive devices (IEDs) have been deployed in a number of conflicts, especially by armed opposition groups. The US Department of

---

[63] See ICBL, *Landmine Monitor Report 2002*, 155.    [64] See para. 2.15 above.

[65] Article 2(5) of 1996 Amended Protocol II refers to IEDs in its definition of 'other devices' but does not otherwise define them: ' "Other devices" means manually-emplaced munitions and devices including improvised explosive devices designed to kill, injure or damage and which are actuated manually, by remote control or automatically after a lapse of time'.

Defense defines an improvised explosive device as: 'A device placed or fabricated in an improvised manner incorporating destructive, lethal, noxious, pyrotechnic, or incendiary chemicals and designed to destroy, incapacitate, harass, or distract. It may incorporate military stores, but is normally devised from non-military components'.[66]

2.37 Thus, IEDs are devices containing explosives, sometimes crudely constructed or adapted from other munitions, that are used in conflict, often by entities other than States. Improvised explosive devices are clearly munitions, but if, as sometimes occurs, they are detonated by remote control, they do not fall within the definition as they are not 'exploded by the presence, proximity or contact of a person'. Where they are victim-actuated, on the other hand, they are covered by the definition in Article 2(1) in the same way as improvised anti-personnel mines, and are therefore prohibited.

*Booby-traps*

2.38 A booby-trap is not defined in the Anti-Personnel Mine Ban Convention,[67] but is elsewhere defined as 'any device or material which is designed, constructed or adapted to kill or injure and which functions unexpectedly when a person disturbs or approaches an apparently harmless object or performs an apparently safe act'.[68] Thus, according to this definition, a booby-trap does not necessarily contain explosive material—sharpened sticks placed at the bottom of a hidden pit would fall within its ambit—but, necessarily, outside the purview of this Convention, as not being mines under Article 2(2).

2.39 Yet, as one commentator has pointed out, 'the difference between mines and booby-traps has never been adequately defined and sometimes the distinction becomes unclear'.[69] Thus, in ratifying 1996 Amended Protocol II, the United States declared its understanding that under the Protocol a trip-wired hand-grenade should be considered a 'booby-trap' under Article 2(4) of the Protocol and not a mine or anti-personnel mine. This is despite the prior assertion by a lawyer at the Department of State that the definition of a mine

---

[66] US Department of Defense, Joint Chiefs of Staff, *Dictionary of Military Terms*, 183. Similarly, the United Nations (UN) has informally defined it as incorporating 'destructive, lethal, noxious, pyrotechnic or incendiary chemicals, designed to destroy, incapacitate, distract or harass; is normally devised from non-military components; the category includes also booby-traps, which are IEDs with a special purpose'. UN, *Humanitarian Demining, Terminology Bulletin No. 349*, ST/CS/SER.F/349, UN, New York, 1997, p. 70, no. 583.

[67] Australia and Croatia had requested, unsuccessfully, at the 1997 Vienna Conference that one be included. See para. 2.8 above.          [68] Article 2(2), 1980 Protocol II.

[69] King, C., 'Legislation and the Landmine', *Jane's Intelligence Review*, Special Report No. 16 (UK, Nov. 1997), 18.

under Amended Protocol II applies 'whether a munition is designed for this purpose in the factory or adapted for this purpose in the field'.[70]

**2.40** At the Oslo Diplomatic Conference, the ICRC raised the issue of whether booby-traps were to be covered by its provisions. Canada, Germany, and the UK declared that these were already adequately covered by 1996 Amended Protocol II. Upon the adoption of the Convention, Australia declared its understanding that booby-traps were not covered by the Convention, but this understanding was challenged by Mexico in so far as the booby-trap falls within the definition of an anti-personnel mine in the Convention. Indeed, prima facie, victim-actuated explosive booby-traps[71] that are designed to be detonated by the presence, proximity, or contact of a person would appear to be covered by the language of Article 2(1) and 2(2). For although non-explosive booby-traps are not covered by Article 2(1) and (2) of the Convention, if the device is a munition designed to be detonated by the presence, proximity, or contact of a person, then it is both covered and prohibited. Moreover, a mine used in a booby-trap in conjunction with other material is still a mine.

**2.41** In terms of State practice, Canada has since declared to its armed forces that: 'Explosive booby-traps are not to be employed or to be used as a substitute for anti-personnel mines'.[72] Further, in South Africa's national implementing legislation, which, as of writing, was awaiting the signature of the President to be enacted, it is provided that anti-personnel mines includes 'any other mine or device which performs in a manner consistent with an anti-personnel mine as defined in the Convention'.[73]

*Unexploded Ordnance*

**2.42** According to Article 2(2) of CCW Protocol V on Explosive Remnants of War, adopted in November 2003, unexploded ordnance (UXO) means 'explosive ordnance that has been primed, fused, armed, or otherwise prepared for use and used in an armed conflict. It may have been fired, dropped, launched or projected and should have exploded but failed to do so.' Article 2(1) of

---

[70]  Nash, 'Contemporary Practice of the United States Relating to International Law', 331.

[71]  Thus, for example, in January 2003, the Colombian press reported that government troops had deactivated an explosive football containing 4 kilograms of 'R1' explosive. 'Desactivan explosive en balón', *El Tiempo* (9 Jan. 2003), 17.

[72]  Office of the Judge Advocate General, 'The Law of Armed Conflict', p. 5.9, point 10.

[73]  Anti-Personnel Mine Prohibition Bill, B44B-2002, Definitions. In a number of other respects, however, the legislation goes beyond the strict terms of the Convention so its evidential value for a broad interpretation of this provision must be seen in that light.

the Protocol explains that UXO covers 'conventional munitions containing explosives, with the exception of mines, booby traps and other devices' as defined in Amended Protocol II.

2.43 As set out above, an anti-personnel mine is defined as a mine 'designed to be exploded by the presence, proximity or contact of a person' and in turn, a mine is defined as a 'munition designed to be placed under, on or near the ground'. Accordingly, items of ordnance that have been fired but which, through malfunction, have failed to detonate upon impact are not a 'munition designed to be placed under, on or near the ground and to be exploded by the presence, proximity or contact of a person'.

## *Mines with Sensitive Fuses*

2.44 The understanding of the term 'designed'[74] has been crucial to the ongoing debate among States Parties as to whether mines that are, ostensibly, *anti-vehicle*, but which incorporate fuses that are typically detonated by a person as well as a vehicle, are covered by the Anti-Personnel Mine Ban Convention and therefore prohibited.[75] These refer, in particular, to mines triggered by tilt rods, breakwires, or tripwires. Thus, for instance, in the context of the Group of Governmental Experts on mines other than anti-personnel mines of the Convention on Certain Conventional Weapons (CCW), the UK has declared that these are not 'acceptable' methods of detonating mines other than anti-personnel mines. Similarly, a 'synopsis' prepared by Germany for the Group of Governmental Experts, based on consultation with other States Parties to the CCW, reports that these 'three fuses seem unable to be designed in such a way that an individual cannot initiate the mine and are therefore not a recommended method of detonation'.[76] Following the failure of States Parties to pursue efforts within the framework of the Convention to agree on 'best practices' in relation to mines with sensitive fuses, as suggested by the ICRC,[77] the ICBL has called upon States Parties to 'be prepared at the 2004 Review Conference to state explicitly that mines or other munitions fitted with these sensitive fuzes are prohibited'.[78]

[74] See paras. 2.14 to 2.22 above.
[75] For a further discussion of anti-vehicle mines with sensitive fuses see e.g. Gravett, R., 'Report on the Technical Expert Meeting on Anti-Vehicle Mines with Sensitive Fuzes or with Sensitive Anti-Handling Devices, Hosted by the ICRC in Geneva, 13–14 March 2001' (Apr. 2001).
[76] 'Sensitive Fuses for Anti-Vehicle Mines, Overview of Fuses, Sensors and Recommendations for Best Practice', UN doc. CCW/GGE/V/WG.2/WP.2 of 13 June 2003, p. 1.
[77] See Statement to the Standing Committee on the General Status and Operation of the Convention (Geneva, 16 May 2003), 1–2, available at: www.gichc.ch.  [78] ibid.

**2.45** Certainly, the Convention does not generally encompass anti-vehicle mines. In accordance with Article 31 of the 1969 Vienna Convention, however, treaty provisions must be interpreted in good faith. This certainly precludes a State Party from simply reclassifying its stockpile of anti-personnel mines as anti-vehicle mines,[79] or developing or producing new mines described as anti-vehicle but which are 'designed to be exploded by the presence, proximity or contact of a person'.

**2.46** In accordance with Article 32 of the 1969 Vienna Convention, recourse may be had to the preparatory work of the treaty in order to confirm the meaning discerned. A number of, largely Western, States had expressed concern during the negotiation of the Convention that it should not apply to anti-vehicle mines.[80] Norway, for instance, was concerned prior to the Oslo Diplomatic Conference that the definition as it stood would encompass all anti-vehicle mines and accordingly it put forward a proposed amendment to the second sentence of the definition of anti-personnel mine: 'Mines designed to be detonated by the presence, proximity or contact of a vehicle as opposed to a person, including those which are equipped with anti-handling devices, are not considered anti-personnel mines'.[81] Such an amendment might conceivably have narrowed the scope of the definition to exclude anti-vehicle mines with sensitive fuses, but Norway decided not to push it vigorously and it was not included by the Diplomatic Conference in the treaty as adopted. Further, at the Diplomatic Conference itself, Australia put forward a proposal to exclude, *inter alia*, dual purpose mines,[82] but this was rejected by the Conference. Thus, at the end of the Conference, Australia formally stated its view that anti-tank mines configured as anti-personnel mines were covered by Article 2(1) and therefore prohibited. This understanding was not challenged by any delegation at the Conference.

**2.47** The UK, however, declared to the intersessional Standing Committees in May 2003 that it 'does not accept that certain so-called sensitive fuses for anti-vehicle or anti-tank mines are banned by the Convention . . . Differences

---

[79] Thus, with respect to Amended Protocol II, at the 1997 Vienna Conference, the ICRC produced an informal 'Information Paper on Dual-Use Munitions', which illustrated the attempted reclassification of anti-personnel mines that had already been occurring as a direct or indirect result of the word 'primarily'. One example given was of an Italian-made mine described as a directional fragmentation *anti-personnel* mine in *Jane's Military Vehicles and Logistics*, 1994–1995, but in August 1995 was described in a *Jane's Special Report* entitled *Trends in Landmine Warfare* as a directional *anti-vehicle* mine despite the fact that the actuating load needed to detonate the mine was between only 3–6 kilograms.

[80] See para. 2.10 above. According to a French official, for instance, it was not France's 'political' intention to cover anti-vehicle mines. Information provided by Thomas Wagner, Permanent Mission of France to the United Nations in Geneva, 24 Apr. 2002.          [81] APL/CW.4 of 1 Sept. 1997.

[82] APL/CW.2 of 1 Sept. 1997.

on detailed interpretation of treaties is a normal situation. We have worked closely on our legal interpretation of the definition, as we did at the Oslo conference, and are confident in our interpretation. If we are to move forward on fuses, we need to look at the substantive humanitarian issues and not get bogged down in a fruitless search for an elusive consensus'.[83]

2.48  In accordance with Article 31 of the 1969 Vienna Convention, subsequent State Practice shall be taken into account when determining the correct interpretation of the treaty. At the Third Meeting of States Parties, France, Germany, Japan, and the UK expressed the view that anti-vehicle mines should be considered in the context of the 1980 CCW and not the Anti-Personnel Mine Ban Convention.[84] Denmark has stated that it shares the view expressed by the UK that the treaty does not cover anti-vehicle mines that may function as anti-personnel mines.[85] Subsequently, however, at the Fourth Meeting of States Parties in September 2002, Germany, which had previously supported the position of France and the UK, declared that:

The Convention clearly defines what is to be considered an anti-personnel mine, and provides for anti-handling devices. A mine fitted with a fuze—not the anti-handling device—of which the construction on purpose is designed to include the actuation also by a person, should be considered an anti-personnel mine and banned under the Convention, regardless of an attached label possibly calling it an anti-vehicle mine, and of the respective amount of explosives going with it. We should reach a common understanding to this end. This does not affect the anti-handling devices which activate when an attempt is made to tamper with or otherwise intentionally disturb the mine.[86]

2.49  Moreover, State practice is otherwise divergent from this position, suggesting in particular that any mine that will typically be detonated by a person under normal circumstances is deemed an anti-personnel mine for the purposes of the present Convention.[87] Thus, for instance, the French Ministry of Defense is studying ways to replace the breakwire system on two of its

---

[83] 'United Kingdom intervention on Article 2', Statement to the Standing Committee on the General Status and Operation of the Convention (Geneva, 16 May 2003), available at: www.gichd.ch.

[84] Human Rights Watch, 'Antivehicle Mines with Sensitive Fuzes or Antihandling Devices', Memorandum for Delegates to the Fifth Meeting of the Intersessional Standing Committee on the General Status and Operation of the 1997 Mine Ban Treaty, Human Rights Watch (Washington, 1 Feb. 2002), 3.

[85] Oral remarks by Denmark to the Standing Committee on the General Status and Operation of the Convention (Geneva, 31 May 2002), reported in ICBL, *Landmine Monitor Report 2002*, 226–7.

[86] Statement by the Permanent Representative of Germany to the Conference on Disarmament, Ambassador Volker Heinsberg, to the Fourth Meeting of States Parties to the Convention on the Prohibition of the Use, Stockpiling, Production and Transfer of Anti-Personnel Mines and on their Destruction (Geneva, 17 Sept. 2002), 2.

[87] According to the ICBL, 'Several States Parties have destroyed or dismantled mines with tripwire and tilt rods because they considered them banned by the treaty. Our perception is that there is near

anti-vehicle mines, which could reportedly be broken by the contact of a child,[88] so as to discriminate between vehicles and people.[89] It is reported that the German armed forces have replaced the detonator of one anti-vehicle mine to avoid unintentional triggering because the old, corroded detonators caused the pressure fuse to set off the mine below the standard pressure of 180 kilograms. Significant funds have also been requested to replace a fuse on another mine to avoid unintentional activation of the mine.[90]

**2.50** The UK has reported in Parliament that 'all U.K. weapons systems have been checked for compliance with the Mine Ban treaty. There are no weapons or munitions in the U.K. inventory which fall under the Ottawa definition of an anti-personnel mine'.[91] The L27 Anti-Tank Mine, which was initiated by a breakwire fuse, was withdrawn from service in 1997, ostensibly because it was 'obsolete and no longer required for service use'.[92] In 2000, Hungary declared that it would destroy its stockpiles of its UKA-63 anti-vehicle mine, which is equipped with a tilt rod fuse, and reported that it had already destroyed half its inventory.[93]

**2.51** In 2001, Switzerland responded to criticism of its Panzerabwehrmine 88 by declaring that: 'The electronic of the fuze is programmed that only certain categories of vehicle can actuate the mine. The mine is optimised to military, heavy vehicles'.[94] In March 2002, the Slovakian Ministry of Defence 'stated that an inventory has been made of anti-vehicle mines in stock and under development to identify which may be considered prohibited or permissible by the [Anti-Personnel Mine Ban Convention], and will consider any measures necessary to prevent anti-vehicle mines with anti-handling devices or sensitive fuzes from functioning as anti-personnel mines'.[95]

**2.52** In conclusion, therefore, although anti-vehicle mines are generally excluded from the ambit of the Convention, mines that are ordinarily detonated by civilians under normal circumstances are to be considered anti-personnel mines, whatever their categorization by governments, as being 'designed to be exploded by the presence, proximity or contact of a person'.

---

unanimity among States Parties that tripwires, break-wires, tilt rod fuzes and low-pressure fuzes should not be used'. Statement to the Standing Committee on the General Status and Operation of the Convention (Geneva, 16 May 2003), 1–2, available at: www.gichd.ch/pdf/mbc/SC_may03/speeches_gs/ICBL_Art2.pdf.

[88] See Commission nationale pour l'élimination des mines antipersonnel, *Rapport 2000*, CNEMA (Paris, 2001), 17.                    [89] ibid. See also ICBL, *Landmine Monitor Report 2002*, 264.

[90] ICBL, *Landmine Monitor Report 2002*, 274.          [91] *Hansard*, 19 Oct. 1999, col. 420.

[92] ibid., 17 Mar. 2000.          [93] ICBL, *Landmine Monitor Report 2002*, 298.

[94] ibid. 467–8.          [95] ibid. 436.

## Anti-Vehicle Mines Equipped with Anti-Handling Devices

2.53 One of the main military functions of anti-personnel mines is to protect anti-vehicle mines from being removed or deactivated safely, by making the task dangerous for enemy sappers. A number of States have incorporated anti-handling (otherwise known as anti-lift) devices on their anti-vehicle mines, thus obviating the need for anti-personnel mines to serve that protective function. The USA, however, has argued that anti-handling devices are too easy to defeat thereby 'increasing blue losses in the absence of protective sub-munitions'.[96] Thus, at the Oslo Diplomatic Conference, the USA called on a number of occasions, though ultimately without success, for a change in the proposed definitions such that the anti-personnel mines in its mixed munition systems would be reclassified as anti-handling devices.[97] After considerable discussion, their proposals were not accepted by the Conference.

2.54 Although there is no evidence that anti-handling devices integral to anti-vehicle mines have, to date, resulted in significant civilian casualties, considerable attention has been paid to the scope of this exception, in particular to the definition of an anti-handling device.[98] On a straightforward reading of the ordinary meaning of the terms of paragraph 3, a device (which can, in theory, itself be an anti-personnel mine) that is attached to the mine in some form and which activates when an attempt is made to tamper with or otherwise intentionally disturb the mine (as opposed to the device) is to be considered an anti-handling device for the purposes of the present Convention.[99] The scope of the definition of an anti-handling device is considered further in the commentary on Article 2(3) below.

# Paragraph 2

2. 'Mine' means a munition designed to be placed under, on or near the ground or other surface area and to be exploded by the presence, proximity or contact of a person or a vehicle.

---

[96] US presentation during a technical discussion on anti-handling devices at the Oslo Diplomatic Conference, 3 Sept. 1997.

[97] One of the last US proposals at the Conference defined an anti-handling device as 'a device intended to protect a mine and which is part of, linked to, attached to, or placed under *or near* the mine and which activates when an attempt is made to tamper with or otherwise intentionally disturb the mine'.

[98] For a brief discussion of anti-vehicle mines equipped with anti-handling devices see e.g. Gravett, 'Report on the Technical Expert Meeting', 12–14.

[99] In fact, the text is poorly drafted. To ensure that the definition of an anti-handling device is narrowly construed (therefore providing greater humanitarian protection) the word 'only' should have been inserted such that the paragraph would have read as follows: ' "Anti-handling device" means a device intended to protect a mine and which is part of, linked to, attached to or placed under the mine and which activates only when an attempt is made to tamper with or otherwise intentionally disturb the mine'.

**2.55** A definition of 'mine' was first included in the Second Austrian Draft of 14 March 1997 and it was ultimately adopted without change.[100] The definition is slightly different from the one contained in 1996 Amended Protocol II;[101] it was amended at the suggestion of Austria, which was concerned that if 'designed' were not placed before 'to be placed under, on or near the ground or other surface area' the definition would apply only to those munitions emplaced and not to any lying in stockpiles.[102]

**2.56** At the Oslo Diplomatic Conference, it was proposed by Japan and the Netherlands to reorder the first two paragraphs of Article 2, such that the definition of anti-personnel mine would follow the definition of mine. This idea had previously been supported by members of the Core Group as being more logical. However, at the meeting of the Friend of the Chair on Article 2 on 5 September 1997, delegations agreed to retain the order in the definitions existing in the Austrian draft.

## Paragraph 3

3. 'Anti-handling device' means a device intended to protect a mine and which is part of, linked to, attached to or placed under the mine and which activates when an attempt is made to tamper with or otherwise intentionally disturb the mine.

**2.57** As noted in paragraph 2.54 above, on a straightforward reading of the ordinary meaning of the terms of paragraph 3, a device (which could itself be an anti-personnel mine, even if such use would be unlawful) that is attached to the mine in some form and which activates when an attempt is made to tamper with or otherwise intentionally disturb the mine (as opposed to the device) is to be considered an anti-handling device for the purposes of the present Convention.[103]

**2.58** To tamper with something is 'to interfere with (something) in order to cause damage or make unauthorised alterations'.[104] The words 'or otherwise

---

[100] At the Oslo Diplomatic Conference, Australia proposed to amend the definition of 'mine' as follows: ' "Mine" means a munition designed to be placed under, on, near or suspended above the ground or other surface area and to be triggered automatically and solely by the presence, proximity or contact of a person or a vehicle'. APL/CW.2 of 1 Sept. 1997. The intent was to clarify that directional fragmentation devices did not fall within the purview of the Convention.

[101] ' "Mine" means a munition placed under, on or near the ground or other surface area and designed to be exploded by the presence, proximity or contact of a person or a vehicle.' Article 2(1), 1996 Amended Protocol II.

[102] Although other members of the Core Group were not convinced of the need to amend the definition, they had no substantive objections.   [103] See especially footnote 99 above.

[104] Pearsall, *The New Oxford Dictionary of English*, 1893.

intentionally disturb' require that the mine be at least physically impacted and, arguably, that the disturbance be of some significance. The Third Austrian Draft of 13 May 1997, which served as the basis for negotiations at the Oslo Diplomatic Conference, had provided a definition as follows: 'Anti-handling device' means a device intended to protect a mine and which is part of, linked to, attached to or placed under the mine and which activates when an attempt is made to tamper with the mine.

2.59 At the Conference, the UK proposed that the final clause of the sentence be amended as follows: 'and which activates when an attempt is made to tamper with *or otherwise disturb* the mine'.[105] This resulted in concern that the use of extremely sensitive anti-handling devices would lead to future civilian casualties. A number of delegations, including Austria, Canada, and Norway, referred to what became known as the 'doctrine of the innocent act', whereby an anti-handling device would not be considered as such if it could be triggered by the innocent act of a passer-by. To incorporate this doctrine in the definition, Norway proposed to amend the UK proposal by including the word 'intentionally' as follows: ' "Anti-handling device" means a device intended to protect a mine and which is part of, linked to, attached to or placed under the mine and which activates when an attempt is made to tamper with or otherwise intentionally disturb the mine'.

2.60 After debate,[106] the text was adopted as above in the Convention. According to the UK Ministry of Defence, however, the word 'intentionally' has no legal force because a mine cannot tell whether an act was intentional or otherwise.[107]

# Paragraph 4

4. 'Transfer' involves, in addition to the physical movement of anti-personnel mines into or from national territory, the transfer of title to and control over the mines, but does not involve the transfer of territory containing emplaced anti-personnel mines.

---

[105] APL/CW.32 of 2 Sept. 1997, emphasis in original.

[106] For a general review of the negotiation of Article 2(3), see Goose, S., 'The Diplomatic History Regarding Anti-Vehicle Mines with Anti-Handling Devices', Attachment 3 to Human Rights Watch Memorandum for Delegates: Anti-Vehicle Mines with Sensitive Fuzes or Anti-Handling Devices (1 Feb. 2002), 17.

[107] Discussion with Peter Balmer and Paul Ellis, Proliferation and Arms Control Secretariat, United Kingdom Ministry of Defence (London, 30 Oct. 2001).

**2.61** As discussed in the commentary on Article 1(1)(b) and Article 3, although State practice is divergent, transfer appears to be either the physical movement of anti-personnel mines into or from national territory, or the transfer of title to and control over the mines. Transfer includes importation and exportation, gift and sale, but, as per the definition in paragraph 4, it does not cover the transfer of territory containing emplaced anti-personnel mines.

# Paragraph 5

5. 'Mined area' means an area which is dangerous due to the presence or suspected presence of mines.

**2.62** Until the Oslo Diplomatic Conference, the draft Convention contained a definition of minefield rather than mined area. The definition, and the concept, which were taken from Amended Protocol II,[108] proved problematic as the draft sought to distinguish between minefields and other areas containing mines, with different obligations depending on how a given area was classified. There was a concern that any reference to an area being marked, monitored, and recorded would simply provide States with a loophole to avoid the obligation to clear a minefield merely by claiming that the anti-personnel mines contained in the area were not recorded or could not be located.[109]

**2.63** Amended Protocol II also contained a definition of mined area as an 'area which is dangerous due to the presence of mines'.[110] The US Department of Defense defines a mined area as 'an area declared dangerous due to the presence or suspected presence of mines'.[111] It was decided at the Oslo Diplomatic Conference to merge draft Articles 5 and 6 to create a single obligation to clear all emplaced anti-Personnel mines. Thus, the definition as adopted in the Anti-Personnel Mine Ban Convention of a mined area is broad: 'an area which is dangerous[112] due to the presence or suspected presence of mines'.

**2.64** Article 5(1) requires that all anti-personnel mines in mined areas under the jurisdiction or control of a State Party be destroyed within 10 years of entry into force of the Convention, unless a request for an extension is granted in accordance with Article 5(5) and, where relevant, 5(6).

---

[108] Article 2(8), Amended Protocol II.

[109] Moreover, the definition that had been taken from Amended Protocol II was not necessarily appropriate for the Anti-Personnel Mine Ban Convention, as in the Convention it was intended to govern the obligation to clear anti-personnel mines, whereas in the Protocol it was more relevant to the emplacement of landmines.                          [110] Article 2(8), Amended Protocol II.

[111] US Department of Defense, Joint Chiefs of Staff, *Dictionary of Military Terms*, 247.

[112] Mexico complained that the term 'dangerous' was subjective, but did not pursue its concern.

# Article 3.  Exceptions

Article 3—Exceptions

1. Notwithstanding the general obligations under Article 1, the retention or transfer of a number of anti-personnel mines for the development of and training in mine detection, mine clearance, or mine destruction techniques is permitted. The amount of such mines shall not exceed the minimum number absolutely necessary for the above-mentioned purposes.
2. The transfer of anti-personnel mines for the purpose of destruction is permitted.

## Introduction

3.1 The exceptions laid down in Article 3 are intended to assist the implementation of the Convention and its humanitarian objectives,[1] particularly to clear emplaced anti-personnel mines and to destroy stockpiles of the weapons.[2] Provisions with this, or a similar, intent were included in subsequent drafts throughout the negotiations, though in the earliest texts, the article focused on facilitating only clearance and not stockpile destruction.

3.2 Article 4 of the First Austrian Draft of October 1996 stipulated that: 'The acquisition and retention of small amounts of anti-personnel mines is not prohibited if they are exclusively used for the development and the teaching of mine detection, mine clearance, or mine destruction techniques and if the

---

[1] And thus did not fall foul of the ICBL's rallying cry prior to, and during, the Oslo Diplomatic Conference of 'No exceptions, no reservations, no loopholes!'.

[2] The apparent inconsistency between this article and the undertaking in Article 1 'never under any circumstances' to retain or transfer anti-personnel mines, is discussed below in paras 3.10–3.11. See also Short, 'International Efforts to Ban Landmines'.

responsible institutions, the amount and the types are registered with the Depositary of this Convention'. At the 1997 Vienna Conference,[3] Australia, Poland, and the International Committee of the Red Cross (ICRC) called for clarification of what constituted 'small amounts'; a proposal was put forward for 2,000 to be set as a maximum quantity.[4] Poland asked whether the term 'acquisition' included the right to produce anti-personnel mines, and requested clarification of the procedure to be followed in registration with the Depositary. The Republic of Korea, presaging one of the main negotiating issues at the Oslo Diplomatic Conference, suggested that an exception be included to the general obligations permitting the use of anti-personnel mines in self-defence.

3.3  The Second Austrian Draft of 14 March 1997 clarified that continued production was not permissible, with States Parties able only to 'retain or transfer' a number of anti-personnel mines. It did not put a figure on the maximum amount that could lawfully be retained or transferred but specified that it 'shall not exceed that absolutely necessary'.[5] In addition, new subparagraphs, respectively, specifically allowed transfer for the purposes of destruction, and required that the types and quantities were to be registered annually with the Depositary. No wider exception to the general obligations, though, was included.[6]

3.4  In its comments on the Second Austrian Draft, Brazil made a proposal for another exception 'that would facilitate acceptance of the Convention by Brazil and many other countries that have particular concerns regarding their borders or other areas of strategic importance, thus helping us to achieve the universality and effectiveness this Convention should have from its inception'.[7] Brazil's proposal centred on the following language:

In addition to the exceptions referred to in paragraphs 1 and 2, a State Party may retain a number of anti-personnel mines that could be laid within appropriately fenced,

---

[3]  See paras. 0.57–0.58 above.

[4]  Short, 'International Efforts to Ban Landmines'. As noted below, the issue of a specific number would again be discussed—both during the Diplomatic Conference and subsequently in the context of the implementation of the Convention, especially in the Meetings of the States Parties and the intersessional meetings. See generally, below, the commentary on Article 11.

[5]  This adopts the approach taken in the 1993 Chemical Weapons Convention, whereby the definition of chemical weapons included '[t]oxic weapons and their precursors, except where intended for purposes not prohibited under this Convention, as long as the types and quantities are consistent with such purposes'. Article II(1)(a), 1993 Chemical Weapons Convention.

[6]  Thus, Article 3 of the draft provided as follows: '1. Notwithstanding the general obligations under Article 1, a State Party may retain or transfer a number of anti-personnel mines necessary for the development and teaching of mine detection, mine clearance, or mine destruction techniques. The number of such mines shall not exceed that absolutely necessary for the above-mentioned purposes. 2. The transfer of anti-personnel mines for the purpose of destruction is permitted. 3. The types and quantities of anti-personnel mines referred to in paragraphs 1 and 2 shall be registered annually with the Depositary of this Convention.'

[7]  Fax dated 8 May 1997 from Ambassador Ivan Cannabrava, Brazilian Ministry of External Relations.

marked and monitored minefields, only in exceptional, emergency circumstances and for a limited period, with the exclusive purpose of protecting its armed forces within clearly specified areas of strategic interest.

Brazil also indicated its intention to propose the creation of a dedicated programme of research and development in mine clearance technology within the framework of the United Nations.[8]

**3.5** However, no substantive changes were made to the respective provision in the Third Austrian Draft of 14 May 1997,[9] although the subparagraph on 'registration' was moved to draft Article 8 on transparency measures, where all reporting obligations were consolidated into one article.[10]

Article 3

Exceptions

1. Notwithstanding the general obligations under Article 1, a State Party may retain or transfer a number of anti-personnel mines necessary for the development and teaching of mine detection, mine clearance, or mine destruction techniques. The number of such mines shall not exceed that absolutely necessary for the above-mentioned purposes.

2. The transfer of anti-personnel mines for the purpose of destruction is permitted.

**3.6** Prior to the Oslo Diplomatic Conference the Canadian Department of National Defense had reportedly been seeking to include in Article 3 an explicit exception to the undertaking in Article 1(1)(c) for 'mere participation' in a multi-national force in which a non-party State intended to use anti-personnel mines. However, it decided not to table a proposal, preferring instead to include an interpretive declaration upon its ratification of the Convention.[11] In addition, Germany had put forward language to the Core Group aiming to set an upper limit on the number of anti-personnel mines that could be retained or transferred, whereby it would 'not exceed the number of one per cent of a State Party's combatant forces or 3,000 pieces, whichever is higher'. In addition to questions from the UK about how to identify the armed forces, Mexico was concerned that if a specific ceiling was set, this would require a sophisticated verification regime.

**3.7** Thus, at the Conference itself, there was renewed discussion of the merits of setting an upper limit for quantities that could lawfully be retained or transferred for the purposes of development and teaching of mine detection,

---

[8] ibid.

[9] As discussed in the commentary on Article 1(1)(a) above, in its comments on the Second Austrian Draft, New Zealand had suggested that 'use' be specifically included in Article 3 for the stated purposes, but this suggestion was not retained. See above para. 1.18.

[10] See below the commentary on Article 7.

[11] See above the commentary on Article 1(1)(c) in para. 1.69.

mine clearance, or mine destruction techniques.[12] A number of delegations, including Côte d'Ivoire, the Czech Republic, and Slovakia, with strong support from the International Campaign to Ban Landmines (ICBL),[13] were in favour of including a specific limit to the number of anti-personnel mines,[14] but their efforts were not successful. This issue is discussed further below.

**3.8** Most of the attention, though, focused on a proposal by the USA to amend Article 3 to include a geographical exception for the Korean peninsula to the general prohibitions on anti-personnel mines: 'The general obligations under Article 1 shall not apply to activities in support of a United Nations command or its successor, by a State Party participating in that command, where a military armistice agreement had been concluded by a United Nations command'.[15] As part of its proposal, the USA also proposed changes to three other articles of the draft Convention, dealing, respectively, with the review conference, amendments to the Convention, and entry into force, to accommodate an amendment process.[16] In sum, the proposed exception would have allowed continued maintenance of minefields along the Demilitarized Zone that separates the Democratic People's Republic of Korea in the north from the Republic of Korea in the south, as well as refurbishment of the minefields and, in particular, new emplacement of anti-personnel mines.

**3.9** The USA received support from Ecuador, Japan, Poland, Spain, and Venezuela as full participants at the Diplomatic Conference, and, as might be expected, strong support from the Republic of Korea, attending as an Observer. Opposition to the inclusion of such an exception came from Austria, Belgium, Bosnia and Herzegovina, Burkina Faso, Cameroon, Canada, Colombia, Croatia, Denmark, El Salvador, France, Guinea, Holy See, Italy, Mexico, the Netherlands, Norway, Papua New Guinea, the Philippines, Slovenia, South Africa, Sudan, Sweden, Tanzania, Zimbabwe, and the ICBL and the ICRC, although a number of States indicated that some transitional period or period of deferral of compliance could be envisaged.[17] Colombia and France pointed

---

[12]   Clearly, there was no question of setting an upper limit for the number of mines that could be transferred for the purposes of destruction.

[13]   The ICBL was particularly concerned about the reported intention of Italy to retain a total of 100,000 mines for training purposes. One of its delegates, Sayed Aqa, an Afghan deminer, pointed out that in several years of mine clearance his organization had used only a few hundred mines for training and he called on delegates to set a similar limit in the Convention. Italy subsequently decided it would retain only 10,000 mines at most, a figure that has since been further reduced. See ICBL, *Landmine Monitor Report 1999*, 728–9; see also Goose, 'The Ottawa Process and the 1997 Mine Ban Treaty', 282.     [14]   The figure of 3,000 was typically suggested as a stipulated maximum.

[15]   APL/CW.8 of 1 Sept. 1997.     [16]   ibid.

[17]   Australia, Belgium, Canada, Germany, Italy, and the Philippines.

out that a solution might be found through the period of time allowed for clearance of emplaced anti-personnel mines. But based on the discussions, the Conference President, Jacob Selebi, declared that 'a significant, if not overwhelming, number of States' would have considerable problems should an exception or exceptions be included in the Convention.

# Paragraph 1

1. Notwithstanding the general obligations under Article 1, the retention or transfer of a number of anti-personnel mines for the development of and training in mine detection, mine clearance, or mine destruction techniques is permitted. The amount of such mines shall not exceed the minimum number absolutely necessary for the above-mentioned purposes.

## Compatibility with Article 1

**3.10** There is an apparent incongruity between, on the one hand, the exceptions set out in Article 3 and, on the other, the undertaking in Article 1 'never under any circumstances' to commit certain stipulated acts, as clarified by the duty in Article 4 upon each State Party to destroy all stockpiled mines it owns or possesses or which are under its jurisdiction or control. With a view to reconciling this dissonance, at the 1997 Vienna Conference, South Africa had proposed that the general obligations in Article 1 be prefaced with the phrase 'subject to the provisions of Article [3]'. Although this proposal was not retained, the idea was incorporated into Article 3(1) itself by the use of the language, 'Notwithstanding the general obligations under Article 1'.

**3.11** The question of the relationship between the two provisions was again raised at the Oslo Diplomatic Conference within the context of a debate as to whether the word 'never' in Article 1 should be changed to 'not'. In response, Canada pointed out that the phrase 'never under any circumstances' was employed in the 1993 Chemical Weapons Convention, which itself contained certain exceptions. In fact, given that the objective of Article 3 is to advance the humanitarian aims of the Convention, it falls squarely within its object and purpose and accordingly the legal interrelationship is not problematic.

## Permitted Activities

**3.12** States Parties are permitted to retain or transfer a number of anti-personnel mines for certain, specified purposes. There is, of course, no requirement to do so, and as discussed below, many States Parties, including some that previously held stockpiles of the weapon, have chosen not to retain any anti-personnel mines. This does not, however, preclude such a State Party from subsequently acquiring a number of anti-personnel mines.[18]

3.13 The use of the term 'retention' allows a State Party, for a permitted purpose, not only to maintain a small quantity of anti-personnel mines from its former stockpiles, but also to keep weapons that otherwise come into its possession, for example through general or specific amnesties for private citizens holding anti-personnel mines, mine clearance operations, or captures or discoveries of ammunition caches or stockpiles. Thus, Landmine Monitor has reported that 'it appears that each year, as [the Cambodian Mine Action Centre] discovers new mines in stockpiles or removes them from the ground, it transfers a certain quantity to its Training Centre, which it consumes shortly thereafter'.[19]

3.14 As discussed above,[20] the term 'transfer' includes both import and export and Article 3 imposes no temporal restriction: a State Party may therefore continue to transfer anti-personnel mines for the permitted purposes for the duration of the Convention.[21] There is no restriction on the recipient or supplier, so a State Party is free to transfer to and from a signatory or non-signatory State[22] as well as another State Party, as long as it meets the other relevant criteria. Thus, for example, Canada has reported receiving small quantities of mines from the USA and the Federal Republic of Yugoslavia (now Serbia and Montenegro), neither of which is a signatory or party to the Convention.[23]

3.15 Furthermore, the article as ultimately adopted is not phrased in terms of a right accorded only to State Parties,[24] suggesting that its scope might have relevance also for signatory States. As discussed below in the commentary on Article 15, under international treaty law signatory States are obliged to refrain

---

[18] Thus, for example, national legislation in Burkina Faso, which possesses no stockpiles of the weapon allows the authorities to 'retain and transfer anti-personnel mines for training in detection, demining and destruction', with the number being limited to no more than 500 mines. Decree No. 2001-180/PRES/PM/SECU of 2 May 2001, cited in ICBL, *Landmine Monitor Report 2002*, 136. Similarly, the Norwegian Ministry of Defence has expressly reserved the right to import anti-personnel mines for permitted purposes, though the option to do so would still exist in the absence of any such declaration.                                             [19] ICBL, *Landmine Monitor Report 2002*, 139.

[20] See paras. 1.40 ff.        [21] See below the commentary on Article 20(1).

[22] Thus, for example, on 2 January 2002, the US Embassy in Quito facilitated the transfer of 1,644 anti-personnel mines to the US Navy Explosive Ordnance Disposal Technology Division in Maryland, where the US will use them for research purposes. Article 7 Report submitted on 31 May 2002 for the period Apr. 2001–Mar. 2002, Form D. All Article 7 reports are available on the website of the UN Department for Disarmament Affairs at: disarmament.un.org/MineBan.nsf.

[23] Article 7 Report submitted on 24 Apr. 2002 for the period 16 Feb. 2001–1 Mar. 2002, Form D. See ICBL, *Landmine Monitor Report 2002*, 154. Serbia and Montenegro has since acceded to the Convention.

[24] See above the content of Article 3 in the Third Austrian Draft.

from any actions that might frustrate the object and purpose of a treaty in anticipation of ratification.[25] It could also be argued that a signatory State that transferred its stocks of anti-personnel mines abroad would contravene this principle of international treaty law if it were seeking to avoid the obligation to destroy stockpiles laid down in Article 4, rather than on the basis of one of the purposes explicitly permitted by Article 3(1).

3.16 Further, in accordance with the provisions of the paragraph, it is not lawful to continue to produce anti-personnel mines for the permitted purposes. At the Oslo Diplomatic Conference, Japan had declared that it might need to carry out 'limited' production of anti-personnel mines within the context of the provision. The Netherlands, however, stated that there were sufficient stockpiles of anti-personnel mines worldwide, and export and import were allowed for the relevant purposes, so new production would not be necessary. Japan did not pursue its suggested amendment.

3.17 There is no specific exception allowing use of anti-personnel mines for the permitted purposes. As already discussed, it appears that the emplacement of anti-personnel mines for the development of and training in mine detection, mine clearance, or mine destruction techniques is not generally to be considered 'use' for the purposes of the Convention.[26]

## The Use of Live and Dummy Mines

3.18 A number of States Parties have not retained live mines for training. Albania, for instance, has concluded that 'there are no justifiable reasons for the retention of [anti-personnel mines] for training or any other purpose'.[27] New Zealand has stated that: 'No live [anti-personnel mines] are retained for operational or training purposes . . . All mines being retained are either practice or inert and contain no explosives'.[28] Similarly, the ICBL has questioned the need for live mines for training (as opposed to testing), and has called on States Parties to 'continue to evaluate the necessity for this exception'.[29]

3.19 Yet, in accordance with the provision in Article 3(1), however, it is clearly lawful for States Parties to retain live mines. Canada has reported that it 'retains live anti-personnel mines to study the effect of blast on equipment, to

[25] Article 18, 1969 Vienna Convention.
[26] For a discussion of the definition of use for the purposes of the Convention and specifically its implication for this Article see paras. 1.16–1.30 above.
[27] Article 7 Report submitted on 3 Apr. 2002 for calendar year 2001, Section 4.1.
[28] Letter from Brigadier C. W. Lilley, Deputy Chief of General Staff, NZ Defence Force to Neil Mander, Convenor CALM (23 Feb. 1999), cited in ICBL, *Landmine Monitor Report 1999*, 372.
[29] See ICBL, *Landmine Monitor Report 2002*, 12.

train soldiers on procedures to defuse live anti-personnel mines and to demonstrate the effect of landmines'.[30] According to Guinea-Bissau, 'you cannot have an Engineering Unit without having real mines; you cannot have military forces which have never seen real mines'.[31] Furthermore, in the case of testing, it is hard to see how, for example, mechanical demining equipment can be effectively trialled without using live mines as machines need to demonstrate that they can both detonate live mines successfully and withstand the blast.

3.20  The use of so-called 'dummy' or 'inert' anti-personnel mines does not come within the ambit of the Convention, as these devices fall outside the definition of an anti-personnel mine laid down in Article 2(1) of the Convention. Thus, a State Party is not limited in the number of these devices that it may retain or transfer. Argentina, for example, has reported its intention to empty 12,025 anti-personnel mines of their explosive content to make them inert, and considers that, once this has been done, these 'exercise mines' should be considered as 'destroyed'.[32] Similarly, Italy has declared that the 8,000 retained anti-personnel mines that it has reported 'should probably be more correctly assessed to a lower level', on the basis that 2,500 units are components that should not be counted as mines.[33]

## Permitted Purposes

3.21  Although the permitted purposes for the retention or transfer of a number of anti-personnel mines are explicit in Article 3(1)—development of and training in mine detection, mine clearance, or mine destruction techniques—the precise nature of the activities involved is neither defined nor explained. Mine detection and clearance seemingly covers countermine measures and minefield breaching (i.e. military activities), as well as humanitarian demining (thus, a humanitarian activity).[34] Thus, for example, Canada has reported expending retained anti-personnel mines 'for research and development in countermine and

---

[30]   Article 7 Report submitted on 24 Apr. 2002 for the period 16 Feb. 2001–1 Mar. 2002. See ICBL, *Landmine Monitor Report 2002*, 154.

[31]   Remarks by the Director of the National Mine Action Centre, cited in ICBL, *Landmine Monitor Report 2002*, 286.                    [32]  See ICBL, *Landmine Monitor Report 2002*, 79.

[33]   ibid. 307. For details of other similar State practice, see also pp. 337, 372, 390, and 509.

[34]   Humanitarian demining (or just demining, the terms are used interchangeably) is defined in the International Mine Action Standards (IMAS) as 'activities which lead to the removal of mine and UXO hazards, including technical survey, mapping, clearance, marking, post-clearance documentation, community mine action liaison and the handover of cleared land. Demining may be carried out by different types of organizations, such as NGOs, commercial companies, national mine action teams or military units. Demining may be emergency-based or developmental.' Definition 3.40, IMAS 04.10, available at: www.mineactionstandards.org.

humanitarian demining procedures and equipment for the training of Canadian forces personnel'.[35] On the other hand, emplacement of anti-personnel mines during military training exercises or operations other than for the permitted purposes of training in mine detection, mine clearance, or mine destruction techniques, would not be lawful under Article 3(1) and would constitute use for the purposes of the Convention.

3.22   There is no obligation upon States Parties to include in their Article 7 reports or otherwise reveal the intended purpose or actual use of retained mines although the Standing Committee on the General Status and Operation of the Convention has taken note of the ICBL's suggestion that they do so.[36] Thus, in its final report for the Fourth Meeting of States Parties in 2002, the Standing Committee 'recalled that the President's Action Programme of the [Third Meeting of States Parties] stated that "to further clarify the reasons why mines are retained for training and development under Article 3 and, in particular, to reaffirm the common understanding as regards the amount of mines that can be retained in a manner consistent with Article 3, the Co-Chairs . . . will continue to ensure that this topic is raised during future meetings of the Standing Committee" '.[37]

3.23   The ICBL 'believes that it is important to have complete transparency on [anti-personnel] mines retained for training, and strongly supports' the recommendation. It further notes that 'Belgium, Canada, and Sweden have commendably provided substantial detail on the anticipated purpose and then actual use of their retained mines in their Article 7 reports submitted in 2002'.[38] Thus, Sweden reported in 2003 that: 'During 2002 the Armed Forces used a total of 1002 mines for these purposes; 908 mines for training purposes and 94 mines for development of mine clearance equipment'.[39] France has reported verbally that retained anti-personnel mines 'were destroyed in accordance with the provisions governing training and testing of equipment'.[40] Moldova has stated that some of its retained mine types will be expended for 'instruction and training' and the remainder will be used 'as tactical mines and

---

[35]   Article 7 Report submitted on 24 Apr. 2002 for the period 16 Feb. 2001–1 Mar. 2002, Form D. See ICBL, *Landmine Monitor Report 2002*, 154.

[36]   Report of the Standing Committee on the General Status and Operation, of the Convention to the Third Meeting of States Parties, Annex III to the Final Report of the Third Meeting of the States Parties to the Convention on the Prohibition of the Use, Stockpiling, Production and Transfer of Anti-Personnel Mines and on their Destruction, Doc. APLC/MSP.3/2001/1 of 10 Jan. 2002, p. 40.

[37]   Final Report, 2001–2002, Standing Committee on the General Status and Operation of the Convention, Doc. APLC/MSP.4/2002/SC.4/1 of 19 July 2002, p. 5, available at: www.gichd.ch.

[38]   ICBL, *Landmine Monitor Report 2002*, 12.

[39]   Article 7 Report, submitted on 30 Apr. 2003 for calendar year 2002, Form D.

[40]   Cited in ibid. 263.

for training'.[41] It is to be assumed that the reference to tactical mines refers to countermine training and does not imply their operational use, which is clearly unlawful under the Convention.

## The Maximum Number to be Retained

**3.24** The Convention does not specify a maximum number of anti-personnel mines that may lawfully be retained or transferred, despite various proposals for it to do so,[42] only that it 'shall not exceed the minimum number absolutely necessary'.[43] Further, there is no restriction on how many of the permitted number, even phrased as a percentage, may be allocated to each of the permitted purposes.

**3.25** As a result of concern that Article 3 could be used as a loophole to retain substantial quantities of anti-personnel mines, following a request for clarification from the ICBL, upon the adoption of the Convention, Germany was first among a number of States at the Oslo Diplomatic Conference to declare that they would retain only a few hundred or at most a few thousand mines for training purposes. It had previously declared in the plenary on 11 September 1997 its understanding that States Parties could not retain tens of thousands of anti-personnel mines under this provision.

**3.26** Four years later, the Standing Committee on General Status and Operation of the Convention reported to the Third Meeting of States Parties, held in Managua in September 2001, that:

> It was noted that 34 States Parties have reported in their Article 7 reports that they retained anti-personnel mines for training and development purposes. It was reiterated that the understanding of the Oslo negotiators was that the numbers of retained anti-personnel mines should be the 'minimum number absolutely necessary and should be calculated in hundreds or thousands, and not in tens of thousands'.[44]

The Meeting adopted a final report in which it was stated that: 'States Parties endorsed, and expressed satisfaction with, the work of the Standing Committees, warmly welcoming the reports of the Standing Committees, as contained in Annex III. The Meeting was in general agreement with the recommendations

---

[41]   Article 7 report, submitted on 8 Apr. 2002 for calendar year 2001, Form D.

[42]   See above paras. 3.2 and 3.6.

[43]   Compare Article II(1)(a), 1993 Chemical Weapons Convention, which incorporates a similar exception into the definition itself of chemical weapons: 'Toxic weapons and their precursors, except where intended for purposes not prohibited under this Convention, as long as the types and quantities are consistent with such purposes'.

[44]   Report of the Standing Committee on the General Status and Operation of the Convention to the Third Meeting of States Parties, 40.

made by the Standing Committees and urged States Parties and all other relevant parties, where appropriate, to act with urgency on these recommendations.' Although not a formal acceptance of the findings of the Standing Committee, no delegation opposed their inclusion in the final report. Japan had previously objected strongly to the formulation but did not do so when the report was presented to the Meeting.

3.27 State practice has largely followed the 'understanding of the Oslo negotiators', with most of the States Parties that elected to retain anti-personnel mines announcing the intention to retain between 1,000 and 5,000.[45] Only two States have so far reported an intention to retain more than 20,000 anti-personnel mines, and one of these subsequently reduced the amount far below that threshold. Thus, Chile initially declared in its Article 7 report in 2002 that it would retain 28,647 out of a total stockpile of 211,076 anti-personnel mines.[46] It subsequently reduced the amount to be retained to 6,245 mines.[47] On the other hand, the decision of Turkmenistan to retain nearly 70,000 anti-personnel mines appears to violate the provisions of Article 3. In March 2003, the Foreign Ministry of Turkmenistan reported to the UN that it had completed its stockpile destruction obligations by the end of the previous month but that it would retain 69,200 anti-personnel mines for research and training.[48]

3.28 Of the other States Parties retaining more than 10,000 anti-personnel mines, Brazil is retaining 16,545 (down from a previous total of 18,000), Sweden 16,015,[49] Bangladesh 15,000,[50] and Japan currently 10,767 (having already consumed 3,777 anti-personnel mines in 1999–2001 of its original retention of 15,000).[51] For its part, Japan has stated that it needs the mines to 'conduct training by exploding actual mines, as part of the educational training process' of its Self Defence Forces, 'aimed at safe and appropriate mine detection

---

[45] For details, see e.g. Human Rights Watch, 'Mines Retained for Training and Development', Landmine Monitor Fact Sheet (Geneva, 7 Feb. 2003), available at: www.icbl.org.

[46] Article 7 Report, submitted on 5 Sept. 2002 for the period 9 Mar.–5 Sept. 2002, Forms B and D.

[47] Article 7 Report, submitted on 30 Apr. 2003 for the period 6 Sept. 2002–30 Apr. 2003, Form D.

[48] Meeting report of the intersessional Standing Committee on Stockpile Destruction, 15 May 2003, p. 2, available at: www.gichd.org.

[49] Article 7 Report, submitted on 30 Apr. 2003 for calendar year 2002, Form D. The report notes, however, that: 'During 2003 it will be further examined how the amount of mines should be reduced'. According to Landmine Monitor, the Swedish Ministry of Defence tasked its armed forces to analyse the consequences if Sweden decided to retain only 5,000 anti-personnel mines. The armed forces concluded that this would require the purchase of mines from abroad to carry out planned activities, and considered the alternative of foreign mines to be difficult and expensive. ICBL, *Landmine Monitor Report 2002*, 461.

[50] Article 7 Report, submitted on 28 Aug. 2002 for the period 5 Mar. 2001–10 Mar. 2002, Form D.

[51] Article 7 Report, submitted on 24 Apr. 2002 for calendar year 2001, Form D.

and mine clearance' as well as to 'examine the performance of hardware of mine detection and clearance'.[52]

**3.29** One State Party, Zambia, initially reported its intention to retain its entire original stockpile of anti-personnel mines for training purposes.[53] It is hard to see how this could be compatible with the requirement in Article 3(1) that the 'amount of such mines shall not exceed the minimum number absolutely necessary' for the permitted purposes, unless it could be demonstrated that the stockpile was not originally maintained for possible military use. In accordance with one of the fundamental rules of treaty law, a State Party must interpret and apply an international treaty in good faith.[54] Zambia subsequently declared that it would destroy some of its retained mines upon handover of a number of demined areas to the affected communities.[55] Lithuania, a treaty signatory, voluntarily submitted an Article 7 report indicating that it, too, intended to retain its entire stockpile of 8,091 anti-personnel mines under the provisions of Article 3.[56] It has since ratified the Convention, but it is not known, as of writing, whether it has revised this intention.

**3.30** There is no requirement that mines be consumed as part of the process of training and research; indeed, in many instances they will be emplaced and then recovered without damage or destruction. The testing of mechanical demining equipment, however, typically leads to the destruction of a quantity of landmines. A number of States Parties have elected to report on the quantities of mines destroyed. Annual consumption by States Parties ranges from nil to more than 1,000 anti-personnel mines.[57]

**3.31** On the other hand, more than 50 States Parties are not currently retaining any anti-personnel mines (although most of these had none in stockpiles before adherence to the Convention). In addition, as of writing, more than 20 States Parties had yet to declare whether they intended to retain anti-personnel mines in accordance with the provisions in Article 3(1).

---

[52]   Letter to the Japanese Campaign to Ban Landmines. See ICBL, *Landmine Monitor Report 2002*, 314.

[53]   Article 7 Report, submitted on 31 Aug. 2001 for the period 1 Apr.–31 Aug. 2001, Form D. Furthermore, at the Second Meeting of States Parties, held in Geneva in 2000, Zambia's Deputy Foreign Minister declared that his country believed that 'the surest way of preventing the use of landmines lies in their total destruction. Stockpiling of anti-personnel mines under the guise of training is a loophole that could be capitalised on to justify the retention of large numbers of these weapons'. Statement of Deputy Minister of Foreign Affairs of the Republic of Zambia to the Second Meeting of States Parties (Geneva, 12 Sept. 2000).

[54]   On this point, see below the commentary on Article 4 in para. 4.16.

[55]   Statement of Zambia to the intersessional Standing Committee on Mine Clearance, Mine Risk Education and Mine Action Technologies (Geneva, 5 Feb. 2003), available at: www.gichd.ch.

[56]   Article 7 Report, submitted on 2 July 2002 for calendar year 2001, Form D.

[57]   See generally Human Rights Watch, 'Mines Retained for Training and Development', available at: www.icbl.org.

**3.32** Moreover, State practice has been generally to reduce the number of anti-personnel mines retained for permitted purposes. Thus, for example, in May 2003 the UK remarked that on ratification of the Convention, it 'found it difficult to estimate the minimum number of mines needed for the purposes permitted under Article 3. In the event, we decided to retain some 5,000 mines. Despite the fact that the UK is active in the areas of research specified in Article 3, we have found that our initial estimate of requirement is more than we need. We are therefore planning to reduce our holding significantly in the near future'.[58] Indeed, the ICBL notes that after it 'repeatedly raised this issue, 11 States Parties have decided to significantly decrease the number of mines kept, including Argentina, Australia, Bulgaria, Croatia, Denmark, Slovakia, Slovenia, Spain, and Thailand. Six of these States Parties had intended to keep 10,000 mines or more, but decided to greatly reduce that number; for example, Croatia went from 17,500 to 7,000 and Thailand went from 15,600 to 5,000'.[59] The significant reduction by Chile in the number of mines it is planning to retain has already been referred to. An exception to the general trend is the Former Yugoslav Republic of Macedonia, which reported its intention to retain 4,000 anti-personnel mines, a major increase on the previously announced quantity of 50.[60]

## Paragraph 2

2. The transfer of anti-personnel mines for the purpose of destruction is permitted.

**3.33** States Parties are entitled to entrust responsibility for the destruction[61] of its stockpiles of anti-personnel mines to others, in accordance with the possibility set out in Article 1(2) to 'ensure the destruction' of anti-personnel mines. States Parties that have taken advantage of this possibility include Denmark, Italy, and the Netherlands[62] (all three transferred anti-personnel mines to Germany) and Mauritania.[63] As already noted, there is no limit to the number that can be transferred for destruction.

---

[58] 'United Kingdom intervention on Article 3', Statement to the Standing Committee on the General Status and Operation of the Convention (Geneva, 16 May 2003), available at: www.gichd.ch.

[59] ICBL, *Landmine Monitor Report 2002*, 11.    [60] ibid. 331.

[61] As already noted, 'destruction' is not defined in the Convention. but its ambit is presumably wide, the main issue being that the mines are rendered effectively unusable. See above paras. 1.80–1.81.

[62] Statement by the Netherlands on the destruction of stockpiled anti-personnel mines to the intersessional Standing Committee on Stockpile Destruction (Geneva, 6 Feb. 2003).

[63] In 2002, Mauritania reported the transfer of 8,084 anti-personnel mines for destruction. Article 7 Report, submitted on 12 June 2002 for the period 1 June 2001–1 June 2002, Form D.

# Article 4.  Destruction of Stockpiled Anti-Personnel Mines

Article 4—Destruction of stockpiled anti-personnel mines

Except as provided for in Article 3, each State Party undertakes to destroy or ensure the destruction of all stockpiled anti-personnel mines it owns or possesses, or that are under its jurisdiction or control, as soon as possible but not later than four years after the entry into force of this Convention for that State Party.

## Introduction

**4.1**  Article 4 sets out the disarmament obligation to destroy all stockpiled anti-personnel mines that a State Party owns or possesses, or that are under its jurisdiction or control. Each State Party has an obligation to destroy or ensure the destruction of its stockpiles as soon as possible but not later than four years after the date on which it became a party to the Convention. In accordance with its Article 17, the Anti-Personnel Mine Ban Convention entered into force on 1 March 1999. Thus, all 45 States that adhered formally to the Convention before the end of September 1998 were due to have completed stockpile destruction by 1 March 2003.[1]

---

[1] Andorra, Austria, Bahamas, Belgium, Belize, Benin, Bolivia, Bosnia and Herzegovina, Bulgaria, Burkina Faso, Canada, Croatia, Denmark, Djibouti, Equatorial Guinea, Fiji, the Former Yugoslav Republic of Macedonia, France, Germany, Grenada, Holy See, Honduras, Hungary, Ireland, Jamaica,

## The Negotiation of the Article

**4.2** A similar obligation was contained in each of the drafts leading to the adoption of the Anti-Personnel Mine Ban Convention, beginning with the one prepared by Werner Ehrlich of the Austrian Ministry of Foreign Affairs in April 1996. Article 5 of his draft provided that each State Party had one year to destroy its anti-personnel mine stockpiles, but granted the possibility of an extension of one year to States requiring it to fulfil the obligation. Although the language was amended,[2] the essence of the proposal was maintained in the first Austrian Draft which provided that:

Article 5

Destruction of stocks

1. Each High Contracting Party undertakes to destroy stockpiles of anti-personnel mines it owns or possesses, or that are located in any place under its jurisdiction or control, within one year and anti-personnel mines already employed within five years of the individual entry into force of this Convention for the High Contracting Party.

2. If a High Contracting Party cannot comply with this obligation in time, it may declare this when depositing its instrument of ratification, acceptance, approval or accession and defer such destruction, in addition to the periods mentioned in paragraph one, for one year in the case of stockpiles and for two years in the case of employed anti-personnel mines, if all relevant data are notified with the Depositary.

**4.3** Other draft treaty texts had suggested longer periods for the completion of stockpile destruction. The ICBL proposed that States be given two years and Belgium suggested that the deadline be three years.[3] At the 1997 Vienna Conference, Canada and Colombia agreed that it was realistic to set a specific deadline for the destruction of stockpiles, though Croatia and Belgium called for the time limits for destruction to be extended—to two and three years, respectively. In addition, Croatia and Moldova[4] both proposed that States be made responsible for destroying anti-personnel mine stockpiles abandoned on the territory of a State Party in an approach similar to that contained in the 1993 Chemical Weapons Convention.[5]

Japan, Malawi, Mali, Mauritius, Mexico, Mozambique, Namibia, Niue, Norway, Peru, Samoa, San Marino, Senegal, South Africa, Switzerland, Trinidad and Tobago, Turkmenistan, the United Kingdom, Yemen, and Zimbabwe.

[2] The language employed in the defining the scope of the obligation was taken directly from the 1993 Chemical Weapons Convention. See below para. 4.18.

[3] See the draft treaty texts contained in Appendix 4.

[4] The Russian Federation is said to have abandoned significant stockpiles on the territory of the Republic of Moldova. See e.g. ICBL, *Landmine Monitor Report 2002*, 349.

[5] Article I(3), 1993 Chemical Weapons Convention.

**4.4** Following a suggestion by Brazil at the 1997 Vienna Conference, the Second Austrian Draft separated into two distinct articles the obligation to destroy stockpiled anti-personnel mines from the obligation to clear and destroy emplaced anti-personnel mines. The nature of the obligation was narrowed such that it covered only those stocks under the jurisdiction or control of a State Party, rather than those 'located in any place' under its jurisdiction or control.[6] In addition, Article 4 of the Draft extended the deadline to three years for the destruction of stockpiles.

**4.5** The text of the draft provision was unchanged in the Third Austrian Draft, and therefore the draft Convention that served as the basis for negotiations at the Oslo Diplomatic Conference. At the Conference, a number of proposals were put forward to amend the text. Recognizing that it might not be in a position to adhere to the Convention, the USA unsuccessfully proposed an amendment intended to protect NATO stockpiles in such an eventuality.[7]

Article 4
Destruction of stockpiled anti-personnel mines

Each State Party undertakes to destroy all stocked anti-personnel mines it owns or possesses, or that are under its jurisdiction or control, as soon as possible but not later than three years after the entry into force of this Convention for that State Party.

**These provisions apply to anti-personnel mines that are owned or possessed by natural or legal persons on the territory of the State Party. These provisions do not apply to anti-personnel mines that are owned or possessed by a State not Party to this Convention, provided that such mines are not also owned or possessed by the State Party.**

**4.6** Japan proposed adding an introductory phrase to the draft Article, such that it would read: 'Without prejudice to the rules and practices of international law, each State Party'.[8] The intent of this phrase is unclear. It also proposed an Article 6bis, which reads as follows: 'Each State Party, during the destruction of anti-personnel mines, shall assign the highest priority to ensuring the safety of the people and to protecting the environment. Each State Party shall destroy anti-personnel mines in accordance with its national standards for safety and emissions'.[9]

Neither of these two proposals was accepted by the Conference, although an amendment was made to the provisions on transparency measures such that Article 7(1)(f) of the Convention requires that States Parties report on the 'status of programs for the destruction of anti-personnel mines . . ., including

[6] See below para. 4.21.    [7] APL/CW.10 of 1 Sept. 1997.
[8] APL/CW.18 of 2 Sept. 1997.    [9] APL/CW.19 of 2 Sept. 1997.

details of the . . . applicable safety and environmental standards to be observed'.[10]

4.7 With regard to the time allowed for stockpile destruction, Sweden had already signalled its intention prior to the Conference to propose an extension of the deadline to five years. At the Conference, a number of States called for the time limit to be increased.[11] After an exchange of views in the plenary on 11 September,[12] it was agreed that the limit would be increased to four years, and the article was agreed and adopted on this basis. Sweden proposed including the phrase 'or ensure the destruction of', in order to reflect the fact that not all States Parties would be able, or would wish, to carry out the destruction themselves.

## The Relationship to Other Articles of the Convention

4.8 The obligation to destroy stockpiles of anti-personnel mines must be considered in the context of Articles 1, 3, 6, and 7. Under Article 1(2), 'Each State Party undertakes to destroy or ensure the destruction of all anti-personnel mines in accordance with the provisions of this Convention'. Article 4 clarifies the scope of that undertaking.

4.9 Article 3 allows each State Party to retain 'a number of anti-personnel mines for the development of and training in mine detection, mine clearance, or mine destruction techniques', as long as the number does 'not exceed the minimum number absolutely necessary'. Article 4 begins by clarifying that 'Except as provided for in Article 3', indicating that retention is a broader concept than stockpiling.

4.10 It was generally understood that a number of States would need assistance—technical, financial, and material—in order to complete their stockpile destruction within a specific deadline. Thus, as discussed below, Article 6(5) provides that: 'Each State Party in a position to do so shall provide assistance for the destruction of stockpiled anti-personnel mines'.

4.11 It is clear that a variety of different methods of destruction are lawful, as Article 7(1)(f) requires reporting on the 'status of programs for the destruction

---

[10] See, below, the commentary on Article 7(1).

[11] Brazil, Chile, Croatia, Ecuador, Italy, Mexico. Finland, an Observer at the Conference, suggested that no deadline be set, as stockpiles were 'no danger to civilians'.

[12] In response, South Africa pointed out that the time necessary for the Convention to enter into force would result in a five-year period. Austria noted that it took one second to blow up anti-personnel mines, and, as an alternative, it was relatively cheap to destroy mines in a machine and to retain the explosives.

of anti-personnel mines in accordance with Articles 4 and 5, including details of the methods which will be used in destruction'. This issue is discussed further below.

## The Obligation on States Parties

**4.12** The obligation to destroy stockpiles is imposed only on States Parties. For those States that agreed to apply provisionally Article 1(1) of the Convention in accordance with Article 18, this does not require that they initiate stockpile destruction prior to entry into force, but would surely preclude importing new anti-personnel mines to add to the existing stockpiles before they became parties. Similarly, under international treaty law, a signatory State is obliged to refrain from acts that would frustrate the object and purpose of the treaty, but this would only render unlawful new stockpiling of the weapons.[13]

## The Obligation to Destroy or Ensure the Destruction of Stockpiles

**4.13** Recalling the language in Article 1(2) of the Convention, each State Party undertakes to 'destroy or ensure the destruction of' its anti-personnel mine stockpiles. Thus, States Parties may either destroy the stockpile themselves or, in accordance with Article 3(2), transfer them to another State (not necessarily a party) or to a private company for destruction.

**4.14** The Convention does not define either 'destroy' or 'destruction'.[14] Typically, States may use the open burning and open detonation method. Thus, the Republic of Moldova favours the 'electric' method of destruction,[15] which involves use of an electric wire to initiate explosives placed on the stockpiles to

---

[13] Article 18, 1969 Vienna Convention. See also below the commentary on Article 15.

[14] Compare with the 1993 Chemical Weapons Convention, which defines the destruction of chemical weapons as 'a process by which chemicals are converted in an essentially irreversible way to a form unsuitable for the production of chemical weapons, and which in an irreversible manner renders munitions and other devices unusable as such'. Each State Party may 'determine how it shall destroy chemical weapons, except that the following processes shall not be used: dumping in any body of water, land burial or open-pit burning. It shall destroy chemical weapons only at specifically designated and appropriately designed and equipped facilities'. Paras. 12–13, Verification Annex, Part IV (A), 1993 Chemical Weapons Convention. See Kellman, B. and Tanzman, E. A., *Manual for National Implementation of the Chemical Weapons Convention*, 2nd edn. (Chicago: International Criminal Justice and Weapons Control Center, Feb. 1998), 20.

[15] See ICBL, *Landmine Monitor Report 2002*, 349.

be destroyed.[16] Yet, as discussed in the commentary on Article 1(2) above, reference to the object and purpose of the Convention supports a broad interpretation of the two terms as its humanitarian aims are equally well served by dismantling and/or recycling, as by detonation.[17] Thus, for example, in Albania's stockpile destruction programme, supported by the North Atlantic Treaty Organization (NATO):

The project costs were offset by recycling of ferrous metals (1,100 tons, from which KM Poliçan is making manhole covers and Kurum International is making steel reinforcing rods) and of TNT explosives (192 tons, converted into about 2,000 tons of ammonite explosive for construction use). The programme is reported to have been completed at below the projected cost of U.S.$790,000 (approximately 45 U.S. cents per mine).[18]

4.15 A particular problem arises with respect to the destruction of PFM scatterable mines, produced by the former Soviet Union, and held in large numbers in stockpiles in a number of countries that are due to become parties to the Convention in the foreseeable future, such as Ukraine (currently a signatory), or which have joined recently, such as Belarus. These contain liquid explosive and result in a number of 'demilitarization hazards'.[19] Likely approaches to safe destruction are contained chamber detonation with an integrated pollution control system, or cementation and destruction.

## The Weapons to be Destroyed

4.16 The obligation upon States Parties is to destroy *all* stockpiled anti-personnel mines. Thus, as mentioned above,[20] it is difficult legally to sustain any State Party's decision to keep the whole of its original stockpile, ostensibly for training and research in accordance with Article 3. In accordance with customary international law, a treaty is to be interpreted and applied in good faith.[21]

4.17 The definition of an anti-personnel mine contained in Article 2(1) to 2(3) determines which weapons are to be destroyed under Article 4. Although

---

[16] A safety fuse may also be employed to initiate detonation.

[17] One State suggested during the Oslo Diplomatic Conference changing the word 'destruction' to 'disposal'.                                    [18] ICBL, *Landmine Monitor Report 2002*, 52.

[19] These include explosive degradation and toxic products of combustion and detonation. In addition, removal of the mine from the dispenser starts the arming process, and additional pressure of 3.4 mm displacement on the mine body will then arm and fire the fuse. There is no in-built neutralization mechanism. See Wilkinson, A., 'Evaluating Destruction Techniques for PFM APM' (Geneva: GICHD, Dec. 2000), available at: www.gichd.ch.                                    [20] See para. 3.29.

[21] See Appendix 1 for key provisions relating to treaty interpretation.

a number of States Parties have destroyed directional fragmentation mines or anti-vehicle mines with 'sensitive' fuses,[22] no explicit objections have been raised to reconfiguring the weapons, for example by removing or replacing the tripwires or offending fuses such that the mine is not 'designed to be exploded by the presence, proximity or contact of a person'.

## The Scope of the Obligation

**4.18**  The undertaking accepted by each State Party is to destroy or ensure the destruction of 'all stockpiled anti-personnel mines it owns or possesses, or that are under its jurisdiction or control'. The language employed in defining the scope of the obligation was taken directly from the 1993 Chemical Weapons Convention. Article 1(2) of the Convention provides that: 'Each State Party undertakes to destroy chemical weapons it owns or possesses, or that are located in any place under its jurisdiction or control, in accordance with the provisions of this Convention'.

**4.19**  There is little dispute as to the application of the obligation to anti-personnel mines that are owned or possessed by a State Party. The notions of owning and possessing clearly overlap, although legally, ownership refers more to the fact of having lawful title over the weapons ('to be the proprietor of'),[23] whereas possession focuses more on physical holding, as in the well-known epigram, 'Possession is nine-tenths of the law'.[24] Thus, a State Party has four years and six months from the date of the deposit of its instrument of ratification, acceptance, approval, or accession to complete the destruction of anti-personnel mines it owns or possesses.

**4.20**  On the other hand, the phrase 'jurisdiction or control' is more problematic. Its use in the 1993 Chemical Weapons Convention was intended to be as broad as possible, given the objective of ridding the world of an entire category of weapon of mass destruction. According to a commentary on the Convention, it 'compels States Parties to use jurisdiction with regard to natural and legal persons on its territory, in other places under the jurisdiction outside the territory and on vessels flying its flag or on aircraft registered under the national law, to implement the destruction obligation. The same goes for places under the control of a State Party, that means places over which the State Party exercises

---

[22]  The Philippines, for instance, destroyed its entire stockpile of 2,460 Claymore mines in July 1998. See ICBL, *Landmine Monitor Report 2002*, 413.

[23]  Brown, *The New Shorter Oxford English Dictionary*, ii. 2059.

[24]  Possession is defined as 'visible power or control over a thing, especially land, which is similar to but may exist apart from lawful ownership'. Ibid. 2301.

factual power or authority, in particular occupied territories. Such places may belong to another State but have an extraterritorial status, or belong to the international parts of the globe. In cases in which the legal status of a place is disputed, for instance in an occupied territory, the State Party actually exercising the control is addressed by this provision'.[25]

4.21 Yet, there is an important distinction between the phrase as employed in the 1993 Chemical Weapons Convention and the one included in the Anti-Personnel Mine Ban Convention. That is, in the former it refers to chemical weapons that are located in any place under the jurisdiction or control of a State Party, whereas in the latter, jurisdiction or control must be over the anti-personnel mine stockpiles themselves. This change was made in the Second Austrian Draft, reportedly at the suggestion of a number of Core Group members, with the specific intention that any liability resulting from the possession or use of anti-personnel mines by non-party States holding stockpiles on the territory of a State Party would be covered by relevant Status of Forces Agreements.

4.22 The definition of 'jurisdiction' in the context of the Convention is not wholly clear.[26] It is ordinarily defined as: 'Exercise of judicial authority, or of the functions of a judge or legal tribunal; power of administering law or justice. Also, power or authority in general; administration, control'.[27] In a case before the European Court of Human Rights, decided on 12 December 2001, the Court was asked to consider *inter alia* the meaning of the words 'within their jurisdiction', contained in Article 1 of the European Convention on Human Rights. The judgment of the Court included the following finding:

As to the 'ordinary meaning' of the relevant term in Article 1 of the Convention, the Court is satisfied that, from the standpoint of public international law, the jurisdictional competence of a State is primarily territorial. While international law does not exclude a State's exercise of jurisdiction extra-territorially, the suggested bases of such jurisdiction (including nationality, flag, diplomatic and consular relations, effect, protection, passive personality and universality) are, as a general rule, defined and limited by the sovereign territorial rights of the other relevant States.[28]

The respondent governments in the case had suggested that the meaning of 'jurisdiction' should be interpreted 'in accordance with the ordinary and

---

[25] Krutzsch and Trapp, *A Commentary on the Chemical Weapons Convention*, 16–17.
[26] Notwithstanding remarks to the Oslo Diplomatic Conference by Austria, which stated that 'jurisdiction or control' was a well-established concept under international law with a common understanding. [27] Brown, *The New Shorter Oxford English Dictionary*, i. 1465.
[28] *Bankovic* et al. v. *Belgium* et al., European Court of Human Rights, Application No. 52207/99, para. 59, available at: www.hudoc.echr.coe.int.

well-established meaning of that term in public international law. The exercise of "jurisdiction" therefore involves the assertion or exercise of legal authority, actual or purported, over persons owing some form of allegiance to that State or who have been brought within that State's control. They also suggest that the term "jurisdiction" generally entails some form of structured relationship normally existing over a period of time'.[29]

4.23  Thus, in a narrower legal understanding, jurisdiction refers to the lawful power to move and enforce rules;[30] a broader understanding would encompass not only the judicial power of a State, but the full machinery of government, including legislative and executive power.[31] In accordance with Article 31 of the 1969 Vienna Convention, the term jurisdiction has to be interpreted in the context with the other terms of the treaty and in the light of the treaty's object and purpose. Such interpretation would lead to the conclusion that the term jurisdiction has to be interpreted in its broad sense. Article 4 of the Anti-Personnel Mine Ban Convention is not restricted to regulating the exercise of 'criminal and disciplinary jurisdiction', as is, for example, Article VII of the 1951 NATO Status of Forces Agreement (SOFA), but defines the ambit and scope of the obligation to destroy or ensure the destruction of anti-personnel mines in the broadest possible sense.[32] This result is further corroborated by the object and purpose of the Anti-Personnel Mine Ban Convention which is, among other things, to do the 'utmost to contribute in an efficient and coordinated manner to face the challenge of removing anti-personnel mines placed throughout the world, and to assure their destruction'.[33]

4.24  In practice, the 'sending' State has typically reserved jurisdiction over foreign military bases, including weapons stored within them, with sovereignty retained by the 'receiving' State.[34] Reference can usefully be made to the American–Cuban Treaty of 1903 concerning the Guatanamo Naval Base whereby the USA recognized 'the continuance of the ultimate sovereignty of

---

[29] *Bankovic* et al. v. *Belgium* et al., European Court of Human Rights, Application No. 52207/99, para. 59, available at: www.hudoc.echr.coe.int, para. 36.

[30] See e.g. Oxman, B. H., 'Jurisdiction of States', in *Encyclopaedia of Public International Law*, iii, (Amsterdam: Elsevier, 1997), 55.

[31] O'Connell, D. P., *International Law*, 2nd edn. vol. ii (London: Steven & Sons, 1970), 600–1; see also Beale J.H., 'The Jurisdiction of a Sovereign State', *Harvard Law Review*, 36 (1923), 241.

[32] Thus, under Articles 1 and 4, respectively, each State Party undertakes never under any circumstances to stockpile anti-personnel mines and to destroy all anti-personnel mines it owns or possesses, or that are under its jurisdiction or control.

[33] Second preambular paragraph of the Convention; see above the commentary on this paragraph in paras. 0.107–0.108.

[34] In its comments on the Second Austrian Draft, Japan, for example, asked for clarification of the meanings of 'jurisdiction' and 'control' with respect to Articles 4 and 5 (then 4–6) and 'in particular, the applicability of these terms to the facilities of foreign military forces stationed in a country and

the Republic of Cuba' while the USA 'shall exercise complete jurisdiction and control over and within said areas'.[35] In 1934, Cuba's Supreme Court concluded that 'the territory of the Naval Station is for all legal effects regarded as foreign'.[36]

4.25  With respect to the Anti-Personnel Mine Ban Convention, State practice is mixed depending on the individual circumstances of the State Party. For example, Norway had both jurisdiction *and* control over stockpiles of US anti-personnel mines held on its territory on behalf of NATO. It informed the USA that the mines would have to be removed by 1 March 2003—Norway's deadline for stockpile destruction—having become a State Party on 1 March 1999.[37] In accordance with the provisions of Article 4, Norway ought rather to have destroyed the mines. Moreover, their removal was not permitted by the Convention, as they were not being transferred for the purposes of destruction. Thus far, however, no State Party has raised any objection.

4.26  At the other end of the spectrum, Germany,[38] Japan,[39] and the UK have stated that they have neither jurisdiction nor control over anti-personnel mines stockpiled by the USA on their territory. In May 2001, the UK stated that: 'We wish to affirm that U.S. stocks do not fall under our national jurisdiction or control and we do not therefore have any obligations under Article 4 . . . in respect of them. We have fully complied with our obligations in respects of stocks that were under our jurisdiction or control'.[40]

---

foreign diplomatic establishments . . . .' Comments on the Second Austrian Draft from the Japanese Ministry of Foreign Affairs, dated 9 May 1997.

[35]  Whiteman, M., *Digest of International Law*, ii. 1216–17, cited by Suy, E., 'Reflexions sur la distinction entre la Souveraineté et la compétence territorial', in *Internationale Festschrift für Alfred Verdross zum 80. Geburtstag* (Munich/Salzburg: Wilhelm Fink Verlag, 1971), 457.          [36]  ibid.

[37]  Letter from Norwegian Minister of Foreign Affairs, Knut Vollebaeck, to US Secretary of State, Madeleine Albright (20 May 1998). See also Capece, C. M., 'The Ottawa Treaty and its Impact on U.S. Military Policy and Planning', *Brookings Journal of International Law*, 25/1 (1999), 191–3.

[38]  In a case decided by the German Constitutional Court in 1983, with respect to the placing by the USA of Pershing II and Cruise Missiles on German territory it was decided that: 'In any event, not absolutely every effect of the conduct of a foreign State related to the Federal Republic's own previous conduct may be attributed to the responsibility of the Federal Republic . . . If the Federal Republic is prevented on legal and practical grounds from influencing by control of apparently decisive circumstances a course of events leading to intervention in a constitutionally protected legal value, the effect of this course of events cannot be constitutionally attributed to it as a result of its own conduct . . . The danger by which appellants see themselves threatened cannot be attributed to German sovereign power under the given circumstances. The circumstances which appear to be an essential requirement for the occurrence of this danger are removed from a decisive exercise of influence to the Federal Republic'. 'Pershing II and Cruise Missile . . . Decision 1', BVerfGE 66, 39, 2 BvR 1150/83 *et al.*, available at: www.ucl.ac.uk.          [39]  See e.g. ICBL, *Landmine Monitor Report 2002*, 313.

[40]  United Kingdom Permanent Representation to the Conference on Disarmament, 'APL Mine Stockpiles and their Destruction: A Progress Report: Landmine Monitor Fact Sheet' (11 May 2001), cited in ICBL, *Landmine Monitor Report 2002*, 22.

**4.27**   A further problem, however, arises where a State has jurisdiction over stockpiles of anti-personnel mines located on its territory but is not in control of them because of the existence and activities of one or more armed opposition groups. This issue was raised by the UK at the meeting of the Core Group in August 1997 and again at the Oslo Diplomatic Conference.[41] In accordance with Article 4, there is a prima-facie legal obligation to destroy or ensure the destruction of the stockpiles held by such entities or on territory within their control, despite the practical challenges to implementation.[42] Such is the situation in Georgia, for example, with respect to the breakaway Abkhaz republic, and this has been one of the key reasons advanced for Georgia's decision not to adhere to the Convention as it is unable to fulfil the resultant obligations.[43] A number of States Parties—Colombia, for example—are faced with similar problems.

**4.28**   According to the 1969 Vienna Convention: 'Unless a different intention appears from the treaty or is otherwise established, a treaty is binding upon each party in respect of its entire territory'. Ordinarily, States may expressly exclude a part of their territory from the scope of an international treaty, however, this is tantamount to a reservation,[44] which is prohibited by Article 19 of the Anti-Personnel Mine Ban Convention.[45]

**4.29**   Instead, reference should again be made to the fundamental principle of treaty law—to interpret and apply an international treaty in good faith. The principle of '*pacta sunt servanda*' is enunciated in Article 26 of the 1969 Vienna Convention: 'A State is bound to carry out in good faith the obligations which it has assumed by a treaty'. A State that is unable, for reasons beyond its control, to implement certain obligations, can legitimately claim to be acting in good faith as long as it does not exploit an internal armed conflict in order to avoid implementing all of its obligations. It should also give further evidence of good faith, for example, by implementing domestic measures in accordance with Article 9 of the Convention to make it a criminal offence to use, stockpile, transfer or produce anti-personnel mines, and in situations where it captures

---

[41]   For a brief background to the constitution of the Core Group, see above para. 0.51.

[42]   Yet, similar obligations are contained in the 1972 Biological Weapons Convention and the 1993 Chemical Weapons Convention.

[43]   In its comments on the Second Austrian Draft, New Zealand had enquired whether the term 'jurisdiction or control' included so-called non-State actors. Note Verbale from New Zealand Ministry of Foreign Affairs addressed to Austrian Embassy (Wellington, 18 Apr. 1997).

[44]   Article 2(1)(d), 1969 Vienna Convention, defines a reservation as a 'unilateral statement, however phrased or named, made by a State, when signing, ratifying, accepting, approving or acceding to a treaty, whereby it purports to exclude or to modify the legal effect of certain provisions of the treaty in their application to that State'.          [45]   See, further, below the commentary on this provision.

anti-personnel mines from armed opposition groups it must destroy them as soon as possible.

4.30  A final issue with respect to the reach of the phrase jurisdiction or control is where a State Party gains control of an area outside its national territory on which stockpiles of anti-personnel mines are located. Should it then destroy these stockpiles in accordance with the provisions of Article 4? Control is ordinarily defined as 'the act or power of directing or regulating; command, regulating influence'.[46] At the Oslo Diplomatic Conference, it was stated that this was a legal term with a common understanding.

4.31  According to an Australian interpretative statement made upon ratification, the phrase *jurisdiction or control* 'is intended to mean within the sovereign territory of a State Party or over which it exercises legal responsibility by virtue of a United Nations mandate or arrangement with another State and the ownership or physical possession of anti-personnel mines'.[47]

4.32  Thus, physical possession of the weapons may be sufficient to invoke the obligations under Article 4. Moreover, the provision does not refer to 'long-term' control. One obvious case to consider is that of Afghanistan. It has been reported by Landmine Monitor, for instance, that French troops participating in the international peacekeeping force destroyed 70,000 anti-personnel mines stored near Kabul airport in February 2002.[48] It is not known whether this action was in any way connected with France's understanding of its obligations under the Anti-Personnel Mine Ban Convention. Similar issues may arise for the UK and other States Parties to the Convention whose forces are, as of writing, occupying Iraq.

4.33  It can be argued that where a State Party is acting under the command of an international organization, such as the UN or NATO, 'control' for the purposes of Article 4 cannot be directly imputed to the State. But the mandate for the mission will have to be carefully scrutinized in each case, as the task of stockpile destruction may be incorporated within it.

## The Deadline for Completion of Stockpile Destruction

4.34  Each State Party undertakes to destroy stockpiles 'as soon as possible but not later than four years after the entry into force of this Convention for that State Party' (i.e. four years and six months after formally adhering to the

---

[46] Brown, *The New Shorter Oxford English Dictionary*, i. 499.

[47] This declaration applies also to the use of the phrase in Article 7(1)(b) and (c) relating to reporting obligations.          [48] ICBL, *Landmine Monitor Report 2002*, 10.

Convention). In applying that provision in good faith, as required by international treaty law, a State should develop destruction plans and initiate destruction early within the allotted time period and should not wait for the deadline to loom large. Although each party's destruction programme is dependent on national resources and capacity, Australia, for instance, destroyed its entire known stockpile of 128,161 anti-personnel mines in five days in September and October 1999,[49] only three months after it became party to the Convention.

**4.35** A number of States Parties have discovered additional stocks of anti-personnel mines,[50] sometimes after ostensibly completing the destruction of stockpiles.[51] In a number of cases, mines are 'stockpiled' by civilians.[52] How does this affect the deadline laid down in Article 4? As long as a State Party has not sought to conceal stockpiles, it is to be assumed that they should destroy any new anti-personnel mines located in stocks or caches 'as soon as possible'. They should also include full details in their next Article 7 report. Given initial good faith on the part of the State Party, the identification of very significant new stocks of anti-personnel mines should normally be considered unlikely.

**4.36** In Bosnia and Herzegovina, for instance, the Stabilization Force (SFOR) has been collecting landmines and other explosive munitions for the purpose of destruction in what it terms 'Operation Harvest'. Since Operation Harvest began in 1998, close to 9 million rounds of ammunition, nearly 110,000 hand grenades, 27,000 small arms, 28,000 mines, and over 24,000 kg of explosives have been collected. Destruction of all explosive devices is carried out by SFOR.[53]

## Progress in Stockpile Destruction

**4.37** According to Ambassador Jean Lint, the President of the Fourth Meeting of States Parties, by 1 March 2003, States Parties to the Convention had destroyed some 30 million anti-personnel mines and 44 of the first

---

[49] ICBL, *Landmine Monitor Report 2002*, 83.

[50] e.g. Argentina. See ICBL, *Landmine Monitor Report 2002*, 78.

[51] e.g. Bosnia and Herzegovina, Cambodia, Croatia, and Nicaragua. See ICBL, *Landmine Monitor Report 2002*, 115–16, 137, 138–9, 211.

[52] Thus, for example, Landmine Monitor reports that in Nicaragua a resident of the town of San Fernando kept a stock of anti-personnel mines to trade for materials or for money, as he had heard that the army was paying for them (ibid. 375).

[53] NATO/SFOR Press Briefing (12 Dec. 2002), available at: www.nato.int/sfor/trans/2002/t021212a.htm.

45 States Parties would meet the deadline for stockpile destruction.[54] 'To date, a total of 55 States parties either have completed the destruction of stockpiles of anti-personnel mines or are in the process of doing so. Some States have destroyed incredible numbers of mines, including Italy, which recently completed destruction of over 7.1 million mines and Japan, which destroyed almost 1 million mines'.[55] Many States Parties began with nil stocks of anti-personnel mines even before the negotiation of the Anti-Personnel Mine Ban Convention, so had no action to take under Article 4. A small number had destroyed their stockpiles before entry into force, including Austria, which completed destruction in 1996,[56] and Germany, which completed destruction in December 1997.[57]

4.38 According to Landmine Monitor, in August 2002, a total of 41 States Parties accounted for some 6 million anti-personnel mines, although it noted that the figure would fluctuate with progress in destruction programmes and new parties to the Convention. The first deadline for stockpile destruction elapsed on 1 March 2003, with specific concerns about compliance expressed only with regard to Turkmenistan.

4.39 Thus, Turkmenistan stated in its first Article 7 report in October 2001 that there remained 761,782 anti-personnel mines from an initial stockpile of 1.17 million. It also declared, however, that: 'It will take approximately eight years to destroy all of the stocks of anti-personnel mines. Therefore, Turkmenistan is requesting an extension of the time allowed for the destruction of the whole arsenal of anti-personnel mines to the year 2010'.[58] Subsequently, the Co-chairs of the Standing Committee on Stockpile Destruction were in contact with Turkmenistan, which indicated that it planned to meet the deadline set down by Article 4 of the Convention and that it had only about 250,000 mines left to destroy.[59] It subsequently reported successful completion of stockpile destruction, but stated its intention to retain nearly 70,000 anti-personnel mines for training and research in accordance with Article 3 of the Convention.[60]

[54] UN Information Service, 'Anti-Personnel Mine Treaty's Fourth Anniversary Coincides with First Deadline: Almost 30 Million Mines Destroyed', Press release DC/2854 (27 Feb. 2003).

[55] ibid.    [56] Article 7 report, submitted on 29 July 1999 for the period 1 Mar.–30 Apr. 1999.

[57] Auswärtiges Amt, Referat Öffentlichkeitsarbeit (Ministry of Foreign Affairs, Division of Public Relations), June 1998, p. 57, cited in ICBL, *Landmine Monitor Report 1999*, 621.

[58] Article 7 report, dated 1 Oct. 2001, but submitted on 14 Nov. 2001 for the period to 1 Oct. 2001, Forms B–D.

[59] Standing Committee on Stockpile Destruction, 'Update on Implementation of Article 4' (30 May 2002), available at: www.gichd.ch. See ICBL, *Landmine Monitor Report 2002*, 499–500.

[60] See above commentary para. 3.27.

# Article 5.  Destruction of Anti-Personnel Mines in Mined Areas

Article 5—Destruction of anti-personnel mines in mined areas

1. Each State Party undertakes to destroy or ensure the destruction of all anti-personnel mines in mined areas under its jurisdiction or control, as soon as possible but not later than ten years after the entry into force of this Convention for that State Party.

2. Each State Party shall make every effort to identify all areas under its jurisdiction or control in which anti-personnel mines are known or suspected to be emplaced and shall ensure as soon as possible that all anti-personnel mines in mined areas under its jurisdiction or control are perimeter-marked, monitored and protected by fencing or other means, to ensure the effective exclusion of civilians, until all anti-personnel mines contained therein have been destroyed. The marking shall at least be to the standards set out in the Protocol on Prohibitions or Restrictions on the Use of Mines, Booby-Traps and Other Devices, as amended on 3 May 1996, annexed to the Convention on Prohibitions or Restrictions on the Use of Certain Conventional Weapons Which May Be Deemed to Be Excessively Injurious or to Have Indiscriminate Effects.

3. If a State Party believes that it will be unable to destroy or ensure the destruction of all anti-personnel mines referred to in paragraph 1 within that time period, it may submit a request to a Meeting of the States Parties or a Review Conference for an extension of the deadline for completing the destruction of such anti-personnel mines, for a period of up to ten years.

4.  Each request shall contain:

(a)  The duration of the proposed extension;

(b)  A detailed explanation of the reasons for the proposed extension, including:

  (i)  The preparation and status of work conducted under national demining programs;

  (ii)  The financial and technical means available to the State Party for the destruction of all the anti-personnel mines; and

  (iii)  Circumstances which impede the ability of the State Party to destroy all the anti-personnel mines in mined areas;

(c)  The humanitarian, social, economic, and environmental implications of the extension; and

(d) Any other information relevant to the request for the proposed extension.

5. The Meeting of the States Parties or the Review Conference shall, taking into consideration the factors contained in paragraph 4, assess the request and decide by a majority of votes of States Parties present and voting whether to grant the request for an extension period.

6. Such an extension may be renewed upon the submission of a new request in accordance with paragraphs 3, 4 and 5 of this Article. In requesting a further extension period a State Party shall submit relevant additional information on what has been undertaken in the previous extension period pursuant to this Article.

# Introduction

## An Overview of Article 5

**5.1** Under Article 5, each State Party undertakes to destroy all emplaced anti-personnel mines located in mined areas under its jurisdiction or control within 10 years of the Convention's entry into force for it. This is consistent with the humanitarian objectives of the Convention, as expressed in the second preambular paragraph, but is a remarkable achievement, particularly given the extent of contamination in certain States and the resultant financial obligations on both donors and affected States.

**5.2** A number of States had taken the view that it would be unrealistic to clear all emplaced mines within a specified time-frame. The International Committee of the Red Cross (ICRC) pointed out, however, that technology might advance such that clearance would become much simpler and cheaper than is currently the case. The Convention ultimately did not distinguish between an obligation to clear anti-personnel mines emplaced in minefields and those lying outside such areas ('mined areas'), although, as seen below, several of the draft treaty texts did so, including the one before negotiators at the Oslo Diplomatic Conference.

5.3  To reflect the realities of mine clearance, however, which is painstaking and costly, the article affords the possibility for affected States Parties to obtain one or more extension periods of up to 10 years each, subject to the agreement, and review, of the other States Parties. There is no requirement that a State Party clear anti-personnel mines that it has itself laid on the territory of another State, although it may already be responsible for them under the provisions of 1996 Amended Protocol II if it is bound by the Protocol.[1]

## The Negotiation of Article 5

5.4  The first informal draft text by Werner Ehrlich of April 1996 had proposed a deadline of five years for the clearance of all emplaced anti-personnel mines, with an option to defer compliance for a further two years as long as the location of minefields was reported to the Depositary. The obligations were reiterated, though in an amended form, in the First Austrian Draft of October 1996, as follows:

Article 5

Destruction of stocks

1.  Each High Contracting Party undertakes to destroy stockpiles of anti-personnel mines it owns or possesses, or that are located in any place under its jurisdiction or control, within one year and anti-personnel mines already employed within five years of the individual entry into force of this Convention for the High Contracting Party.

2.  If a High Contracting Party cannot comply with this obligation in time, it may declare this when depositing its instrument of ratification, acceptance, approval or accession and defer such destruction, in addition to the periods mentioned in paragraph one, for one year in the case of stockpiles and for two years in the case of employed anti-personnel mines, if all relevant data are notified with the Depositary.

5.5  The International Campaign to Ban Landmines (ICBL) proposed that affected States Parties undertake to clear and destroy anti-personnel mines 'on

---

[1] Australia, Brazil, and Colombia proposed that mines emplaced by another State should be cleared by that State, following the relevant provisions contained in Amended Protocol II. Under the Protocol, each party to a conflict is 'responsible' for all mines employed by it and must clear all mines, mined areas, and minefields in areas under its control 'without delay after the cessation of active hostilities' or to comply with the obligations to mark, fence, and monitor a minefield containing long-lived anti-personnel mines. Furthermore, a party that has used mines in an area over which it no longer has, or has never had, control is obliged to provide technical and material assistance to the party now in control (to the extent that this is permitted by that party). Articles 3 and 10, 1996 Amended Protocol II. See below commentary on para. 5.7.

its territory or in places under its jurisdiction or control', but did not include a deadline for doing so.[2] In contrast, the Belgian draft text did not specify a requirement for a State Party to clear emplaced mines, merely to communicate the location of minefields under their control and the intention of the State Party about their removal.[3] Indeed, in comments on the First Austrian Draft at the 1997 Vienna Conference, Australia, Canada, Colombia, and Turkey all expressed the view that it was either unrealistic or unfeasible (or both) to set a time limit for the destruction of emplaced anti-personnel mines.

**5.6** Other States, however, such as Belgium, Croatia, and Sweden, preferred to keep the obligation, and there were calls by Afghanistan, Brazil, Canada, Honduras, Mexico, and the ICRC for the inclusion of a separate article on assistance for demining to assist in the implementation of the provision.[4] In addition, Belgium, Canada, Mexico, and Norway proposed the insertion of a new article dealing with known, existing minefields. Mexico suggested a requirement to monitor such minefields until such time as they are cleared.

**5.7** Australia, Brazil, and Colombia proposed that mines emplaced by another State should be cleared by that State, in accordance with the relevant provisions contained in Amended Protocol II. Under the Protocol, each party to a conflict is 'responsible' for all mines employed by it,[5] and must clear all mines, mined areas, and minefields in areas under its control 'without delay after the cessation of active hostilities' or comply with the obligations to mark, fence, and monitor a minefield containing long-lived anti-personnel mines.[6] Furthermore, a party that has used mines in an area over which it no longer has, or has never had, control is obliged to provide technical and material assistance to the party now in control (to the extent that this is permitted by that party).[7]

---

[2] Article 5(1), ICBL Proposal for a Convention on the Prohibition on the Development, Production, Stockpiling, Transfer and Use of Anti-Personnel Mines and on their Destruction. It also suggested that the party laying mines in areas controlled by another State be required to provide technical and material assistance necessary to remove and destroy the mines. Ibid., Article 5(2).

[3] 'Article 6. Existing antipersonnel minefields. States Parties will communicate to the Depository of the Convention the geographical location as well as the amount of APL mines in the existing antipersonnel minefields under their control. This communication is made annually from the date of deposit of their instrument of ratification or accession to the present Convention. This communication will also include the intention of the State Party concerned, about the removal of these minefields. This article concerns only the minefields which already exist before the deposit of the instrument of ratification or accession to the present Convention by the State Party concerned; it cannot be interpreted as detracting from the general prohibition imposed by article 3'.

[4] In this regard, it was felt that the relevant provisions included in Article 11 of Amended Protocol II would not be appropriate in this context, which was seeking to achieve broader humanitarian objectives.

[5] Article 3(2).     [6] Article 10(1) and (2). See also Articles 3(2) and 5.     [7] Article 10(3).

**5.8** Taking into account the comments made at the 1997 Vienna Conference, the Second Austrian Draft included two separate articles governing the destruction of emplaced anti-personnel mines, the first dealing with anti-personnel mines laid within minefields, the second with anti-personnel mines laid in areas outside minefields. The former were to be destroyed within 10 years of entry into force of the Convention for each State Party, the latter contained an obligation to destroy, but without a specific deadline. In theory, the difference between anti-personnel mines located in minefields and those lying outside those areas was that, in the case of minefields, the locations of individual mines would be recorded on maps, and therefore more easily located and removed. By contrast, clearing mines found in other 'mined' areas would be more difficult and time-consuming, as the weapons might be found in a haphazard fashion. In practice, this distinction was found not to be tenable as maps rarely tended to exist in reality and the differences between minefields and other mined areas were often arbitrary.[8]

### Article 5
### Destruction of anti-personnel mines laid within minefields

1. Each State Party undertakes to destroy all anti-personnel mines laid within minefields under its jurisdiction or control, as soon as possible but not later than ten years after the entry into force of this Convention for that State Party.

2. Minefields where anti-personnel mines have been laid shall be marked in accordance with international standards or fenced and shall be monitored until all anti-personnel mines have been removed and destroyed.

### Article 6
### Destruction of anti-personnel mines laid in areas outside minefields

1. Each State Party undertakes to destroy all anti-personnel mines laid in areas under its jurisdiction or control outside minefields.

2. Each State Party shall make every effort to identify areas in which anti-personnel mines are suspected to be present and to provide an immediate and effective warning to the population.

**5.9** Only limited changes were made to the two relevant articles in the Third Austrian Draft of 13 May 1997, notably through the inclusion of an explicit requirement for perimeter marking of minefields and for the clearance 'as soon as possible' of anti-personnel mines laid in areas outside minefields.

---

[8]  There was also a danger of politicizing the Convention, with certain governments being tempted to draw an artificial distinction between their 'good' minefields and the 'bad' mined areas laid by armed opposition groups.

In its comments on the Second Austrian Draft, New Zealand had asked for clarification of the obligation to monitor minefields—specifically, whether it required 24-hour surveillance or just periodic inspections—but the revised draft did not elaborate on the wording.[9] It also suggested that 10 years was too short a time-frame to clear minefields, but the deadline for completion was not amended.[10]

5.10  At the 1997 Brussels Conference, Egypt, which had previously called on a number of occasions for retroactive attribution of responsibility to the parties that had laid mines on its territory during the 1939–45 war, stressed the need to take account of the cost of clearing minefields and the available resources at national and international level.[11] The UK, concerned by the human and financial implications of residual mine contamination in the Falkland Islands, announced that it would be seeking an exception to the requirement to clear anti-personnel mines in situations where there was little or no risk to civilians and the costs and risk involved in clearance were disproportionate to the benefits. The Brussels Declaration, adopted at the Conference, merely called for the destruction of all stockpiled and cleared anti-personnel mines, and thus did not require comprehensive mine clearance.[12]

5.11  While there was some sympathy among Core Group members for the position of the UK, there was also concern that such an exception would lead to a loophole in the Convention that could be exploited by other States Parties. In its comments on the Third Austrian Draft, the ICRC proposed that the provisions be amended to allow States Parties to request an extension period from a Review Conference or Meeting of States Parties in situations where they were unable to complete clearance of mines within minefields within the allotted time-frame.[13] This idea, which is based on a provision in the 1993 Chemical Weapons Convention,[14] was to trigger a significant strengthening of the Convention at the Oslo Diplomatic Conference.

5.12  Indeed, even before the Conference, Core Group members had understood that maintaining a distinction between minefields and other mined areas was going to be difficult. Thus, at an August meeting of the Core Group in Vienna, Canada proposed that the Convention include a general obligation to

---

[9] Note Verbale from New Zealand Ministry of Foreign Affairs addressed to Austrian Embassy (Wellington, 18 Apr. 1997). [10] ibid.

[11] Non-Paper by Egypt, 1997 Brussels Conference, Brussels, undated, p. 2.

[12] See paras. 0.76 and 0.78 above.

[13] 'Comments of the International Committee of the Red Cross on the Third Austrian Draft (13/5/97) of the Convention on the Prohibition of Anti-personnel Mines', reproduced in Maresca and Maslen, *The Banning of Anti-Personnel Landmines*, 551.

[14] See Verification Annex, IV Part IV (C), paras. 24–7, 1993 Chemical Weapons Convention.

clear all anti-personnel mines within a fixed period of time, but giving severely affected States the opportunity to renew the period, in line with the ICRC proposal. The Canadian delegation prepared text to reflect this approach (which is very similar to the final text of Article 5), but did not circulate it. Subsequently, the Philippines put forward informally much of the language dealing with the possibility of renewal as Article 9bis (extension mechanism).

5.13 At the Diplomatic Conference, Ireland served as Friend of the Chair for draft Articles 5 and 6. The proposal to merge the two articles but to provide affected States with the possibility of renewal was generally approved, and quickly became the basis for discussion and agreement.

# Paragraph 1

1. Each State Party undertakes to destroy or ensure the destruction of all anti-personnel mines in mined areas under its jurisdiction or control, as soon as possible but not later than ten years after the entry into force of this Convention for that State Party.

## The Basic Obligations

5.14 A State Party undertakes to destroy or ensure the destruction of all anti-personnel mines located in mined areas under its jurisdiction or control as soon as possible but not later than 10 years after the Convention's entry into force for it. Thus, based on the provision adopted, a mine-affected State depositing its instrument of ratification (or accession) will have 10 years and 6 months to complete the necessary clearance in accordance with Article 5, although it undertakes to complete the requisite clearance 'as soon as possible'.[15] This obligation must be read in conjunction with Article 6(2), (4), and (5),[16] which governs international cooperation and assistance. As of writing, Costa Rica is the only affected State to have declared itself mine-free,[17] and the ICBL has expressed concern that 'at current levels of funding and demining, many mine-affected States Parties will not meet the ten-year deadline for completion of mine clearance'.[18]

---

[15] The term 'as soon as possible' is not defined in the Convention but it may be assumed that it is to be understood both within the context of a State Party's existing resources, and in light of international cooperation and assistance provided in accordance with Article 6.

[16] This provision was included following a proposal by Brazil for Article 5. See below the commentary on Article 6(5).

[17] Statement by Ambassador Jean Lint, Co-Chair, Standing Committee on Mine Clearance, Mine Risk Education and Mine Action Technologies (Geneva, 5 Feb. 2003), available at: www.gichd.ch.

[18] ICBL, *Landmine Monitor Report 2002*, 1.

**5.15** The use of the term 'destroy' is a disarmament term. In the humani-tarian discipline of mine action,[19] the term more usually applied is mine clear-ance, which is part of the broader process of humanitarian demining.[20] This makes it explicit that all cleared anti-personnel mines must be destroyed,[21] although there is no obligation to destroy mines *in situ*. As already noted,[22] the phrase to 'ensure the destruction of' demonstrates that a State Party may call on the services of others—the military forces of another State or commercial dem-ining companies, for instance—to carry out the necessary clearance.

**5.16** The undertaking is to destroy *all*[23] anti-personnel mines[24] located in mined areas under the jurisdiction or control of a State Party.[25] This poses three potential problems—first, the requisite depth of clearance, second, the compre-hensive nature of the clearance, and third, respect for international standards for

[19] According to the International Mine Action Standards (IMAS 4.10; see www.mineactionstandards.org), mine action refers to activities which aim to reduce the social, economic, and environmental impact of mines and UXO. The standard notes that mine action 'is not just about demining; it is also about people and societies, and how they are affected by landmine contamination. The objective of mine action is to reduce the risk from landmines to a level where people can live safe-ly; in which economic, social and health development can occur free from the constraints imposed by landmine contamination, and in which the victims' needs can be addressed. Mine action comprises five complementary groups of activities: (a) mine risk education; (b) humanitarian demining, i.e. mine and UXO survey, mapping, marking and (if necessary) clearance; (c) victim assistance, includ-ing rehabilitation and reintegration; (d) stockpile destruction; and (e) advocacy against the use of anti-personnel mines. It further notes that a number of other enabling activities are required to support these five components of mine action, including: assessment and planning, the mobilisation and prioritisation of resources, information management, human skills development and management training, quality management and the application of effective, appropriate and safe equipment'.

[20] IMAS (04.10) defines demining or humanitarian demining as 'activities which lead to the removal of mine and UXO hazards, including technical survey, mapping, clearance, marking, post-clearance documentation, community mine action liaison and the handover of cleared land'. Accord-ing to IMAS, demining may be carried out by NGOs, commercial companies, national mine action teams or military units as well as others.

[21] The UK proposed both prior to and during the Oslo Diplomatic Conference that the obligation be rephrased as follows: 'Each State Party undertakes to destroy or otherwise eliminate the risk posed by all anti-personnel mines emplaced in its territory or under its control as soon as possible but not later than 10 years'. The proposal was not accepted.                    [22] See above para. 1.80.

[23] A future Review Conference or Meeting of States Parties may yet return to the issue of compre-hensive mine clearance. Currently, international funding for mine action activities, particularly mine clearance operations, remains extremely high, with more than US$1 billion committed to the overall discipline during the 1990s. It is not clear whether such sums will continue to be available in the future. A number of donors have already begun to stress the importance of integrating mine action within broader development initiatives, and competing priorities for shrinking overall resources may result in more use of cost-benefit analysis compared to other rural development projects, not neces-sarily to the benefit of mine action.

[24] Thus, in strict legal terms, a State Party is free to leave anti-vehicle mines and any items of unex-ploded ordnance *in situ*. Whether it would wish to do so is another matter.

[25] Prior to the Oslo Diplomatic Conference, there had been some discussion of the possibility of excepting the obligation to clear existing minefields. This was rejected for a number of reasons, includ-ing the belief that this would fall within the definition of use in the Convention.

mine clearance. With respect to the first of these, it should be borne in mind that clearance operations will only locate and destroy landmines or unexploded ordnance (UXO) up to a certain specified depth. According to the International Mine Action Standards (IMAS):

The specified depth of clearance shall be determined by a technical survey, or from other reliable information which establishes the depth of the mine and UXO hazards and an assessment of the intended land use. In the absence of reliable information on the depth of the local mine and UXO hazard, a default depth for clearance shall be established by the national mine action authority. It should be based on the technical threat from mines and UXO in the country and should also take into consideration the future use to which the land is to be put . . . For buried mines and UXO this depth should normally not be less than 130mm below the original surface level; this figure is based on the effective detection depth of the majority of metal detectors.[26]

Thus, considerable ordnance, including anti-personnel mines, may remain in the ground despite clearance operations. Although they pose no immediate danger to the civilian population, farming or civil construction work may result in deaths or injuries as this ordnance is uncovered.

5.17 With respect to the second issue (that of the comprehensive nature of the clearance), which follows from the first, it is presumably only if a State Party is aware of the specific presence of anti-personnel mines that it must destroy them. Many European nations, for example, are contaminated by UXO, including anti-personnel mines, left over from the 1939–45 war. Their continued presence will not violate the provisions of the Convention, unless an anti-personnel mine is discovered or unearthed and the State Party in question does not clear it as soon as possible. In other words, the obligation in Article 5(2) to 'make every effort to identify all areas under its jurisdiction or control in which anti-personnel mines are known or suspected to be emplaced' must seemingly be tempered by a certain pragmatism, including the availability of resources and even a cost-benefit analysis as to their application. In this regard, a distinction is increasingly made in mine action between making a country mine-impact-free as opposed to mine-free.[27]

5.18 The particular case of Denmark, however, is an interesting one. In its first Article 7 report, submitted on 27 August 1999, Denmark reported as follows:

After the [1939–45 war], there were approximately 1.4 million mines mostly along the coasts of Denmark. Almost all were removed or disarmed in 1945–46. There were also

---

[26] IMAS 09.10 (Clearance Requirements), 1st edn., issued on 1 Oct. 2001, pp. 1–2.

[27] It is likely that discussion of this issue will begin, informally at least, at the first review conference of the Convention in 2004.

deployed mines in the southern part of western Jutland, on a 10-km long peninsula named Skallingen. In 1946, the mine sweeping was ended leaving approximately 1,600 undetected anti-tank mines and 8,300 anti-personnel mines of which many were made of wood. But as Skallingen is not inhabited and mostly consists of a beach, sand dunes and marshland the mines did not constitute any direct risk. . . .

During most of this century Nature has thus been left to itself in forming the shape of Skallingen including the remaining minefields. Consequently big parts of the minefields in the last 55 years have been engulfed into the North Sea. After a heavy storm many mines will have surfaced on the beach or on the slopes, and throughout the years many of these mines have been picked up and removed by officials or others. Furthermore many sheep and some cows have grassed on Skallingen every summer, and could have triggered the personnel mines. But so far no accidents caused by detonating mines have been recorded.

According to the judgement of the Danish Ministry of Defence most of the mines are ineffective today, but there still is a small risk of some being effective. . . . The areas consist of two groups: some long narrow area stretching along the beach from north to south, and a major area at the southern end of Skallingen. Most of the first group is expected to be engulfed into the North Sea within the next two decades. A minor part of the area in the south is also expected to be engulfed within a foreseeable time. . . . When the mapping has been completed, a plan for the handling of the remaining mines will be worked out.[28]

**5.19** Other than the requirement to clear all anti-personnel mines, which suggests the 100 per cent clearance rate typical in humanitarian demining operations, there is no reference to the standards to be applied to mine clearance.[29] The IMAS lay down detailed procedures for demining, including safety, equipment, and, to a lesser degree, appropriate techniques. In international mine action, deminers tend to use the concept of 'toolkit' clearance—an appropriate mix of manual demining, mine detection dogs, and a variety of mechanical mine clearance equipment. Yet, in Cambodia, for instance, so-called village demining is too often the norm, where untrained villagers spontaneously clear mines and UXO for reasons of survival or development.

**5.20** The text of the Convention refers to anti-personnel mines 'located' in mined areas. Thus, it is not necessary that the mines have been emplaced, and *a fortiori* by any particular party to a conflict. The Third Austrian Draft of 14 May 1997 had included the word 'laid' in the provisions regarding mine clearance

---

[28] Article 7 report, submitted on 27 Aug. 1999 for the period 1945–Aug. 1999.

[29] The Canadian Department for National Defense had suggested internally that the article make some reference to the standards for mine clearance, such as a reference to the return of the land to its (safe) original use, but no formal proposal was made.

obligations. The ICRC had asked for the removal of the word, pointing out that mines may arrive in an area for other reasons, such as soil movement or the weather.[30]

5.21 As discussed above, a mined area is defined in Article 2(5) of the Convention as 'an area which is dangerous due to the presence or suspected presence of mines'. It is not entirely clear, however, what is sufficient to constitute a suspected presence of mines—this could range from the simple presence of armed forces in a given area to the identification of mine casings or fuses to, at the extreme end of the spectrum, the physical witnessing of mine-laying.

5.22 The undertaking is to clear anti-personnel mines located in mined areas under the jurisdiction or control of a State Party. The phrase 'jurisdiction or control', which, as in Article 4, refers to alternatives not cumulative requirements, has been discussed in connection with its use in Article 4.[31] It should be noted that in Article 5, the reference is to areas under jurisdiction or control, whereas Article 4 refers to jurisdiction or control over anti-personnel mine stockpiles. Article 5 therefore follows more closely the approach taken in the 1993 Chemical Weapons Convention.

5.23 According to a commentary on the Convention, the phrase jurisdiction or control 'compels States Parties to use jurisdiction with regard to natural and legal persons on its territory, in other places under the jurisdiction outside the territory and on vessels flying its flag or on aircraft registered under the national law, to implement the destruction obligation. The same goes for places under the control of a State Party, that means places over which the State Party exercises factual power or authority, in particular occupied territories. Such places may belong to another State but have an extraterritorial status, or belong to the international parts of the globe. In cases in which the legal status of a place is disputed, for instance in an occupied territory, the State Party actually exercising the control is addressed by this provision'.[32] Thus, the jurisdictional competence of a State is 'primarily territorial', encompassing metropolitan and non-metropolitan areas.[33] Control refers primarily to areas outside

---

[30] 'Comments of the International Committee of the Red Cross on the Third Austrian Draft (13/5/97) of the Convention on the Prohibition of Anti-personnel Mines', reproduced in Maresca and Maslen, *The Banning of Anti-Personnel Landmines*, 550.

[31] Especially in paras. 4.20–4.33.

[32] Krutzsch and Trapp, *A Commentary on the Chemical Weapons Convention*, 16–17.

[33] Thus, for instance, it has been reported in the media that 'hundreds of mines' were emplaced in New Caledonia, a French territory, in 1942–3. If these reports are correct, and the mines are anti-personnel mines, then France will be responsible for clearing them as soon as possible but not later than 1 March 2009. See e.g. 'Territoire miné', *Nouvel Observateur* (20–6 Dec. 2001), 53.

the jurisdictional competence of the State that are none the less within its control, such as occupied territories or zones.

5.24 During the negotiation of the Convention, a number of States reflected on whether the scope of the phrase 'jurisdiction or control' might result in an *ex-post-facto* responsibility for clearance being imposed on their armed forces operating abroad in territories affected by anti-personnel mines or within a multinational operation in which a non-party State was laying anti-personnel mines. It was assumed, however, that in such cases, the State Party would probably not have either jurisdiction or control over the anti-personnel mines or the territory on which they had been emplaced. In the absence of an established government (or party to the conflict in control of the area), it would be the United Nations (UN) that assumed control over the territory or weapons, not the individual troop-contributing nations.

5.25 But the issue is not quite as clear-cut as this. First, there are many different types of UN operations, ranging from military observation to peacekeeping to military enforcement action.[34] The mandates and command structures of these various operations may and do differ widely.[35] Second, there is no reference to 'long-term' control in Article 5, despite a proposal by the USA to include the words in the provision.[36] So although it may safely be assumed that there is no obligation to clear anti-personnel mines in an unsafe environment or a temporary operational context (where the force could not be said to have control),[37] the same is not true where a national contingent of troops is operating over a period of several months or even years in a given area under a broad mandate from the UN Security Council and has *de facto* control of that area in the absence of an effective central government with control of all of its territory. An example of such a context is Kosovo and possibly also Afghanistan.

5.26 States seem, though, to have accepted that an obligation to clear anti-personnel mines in mined areas outside its jurisdiction may occur in certain circumstances. In Canada, for instance, according to the Office of the Judge Advocate General: 'Responsibility for clearing minefields will depend upon the

---

[34] For further discussion of the range of scenarios, see e.g. McCoubrey, H. and White, N. D., *The Blue Helmets: Legal Regulations of United Nations Military Operations* (Aldershot: Dartmouth Publishing, 1996), 1 ff.

[35] Canada, for instance, had discussed internally whether or not to propose a specific exclusion from the provisions of the article for UN peacekeeping forces or other forces acting under a UN mandate which are in 'control' of an area with mines, but this was not done.

[36] APL/CW.11 of 1 Sept. 1997.

[37] Defined generally as 'the act or power of directing or regulating; command, regulating influence'. See e.g. para. 4.20 above.

circumstances. There is no legal obligation to clear mines simply because Canada is conducting operations in an Area of Responsibility (AOR) during peace support or other operations. An obligation may arise at the cessation of hostilities depending upon circumstances such as the degree of control exercised over the territory, the terms of any peace accord or any other bilateral or multilateral agreement'.[38]

## Paragraph 2

> 2. Each State Party shall make every effort to identify all areas under its jurisdiction or control in which anti-personnel mines are known or suspected to be emplaced and shall ensure as soon as possible that all anti-personnel mines in mined areas under its jurisdiction or control are perimeter-marked, monitored and protected by fencing or other means, to ensure the effective exclusion of civilians, until all anti-personnel mines contained therein have been destroyed. The marking shall at least be to the standards set out in the Protocol on Prohibitions or Restrictions on the Use of Mines, Booby-Traps and Other Devices, as amended on 3 May 1996, annexed to the Convention on Prohibitions or Restrictions on the Use of Certain Conventional Weapons Which May Be Deemed to Be Excessively Injurious or to Have Indiscriminate Effects.

5.27　Thus, Article 5(2) requires that a State Party 'make every effort' to identify 'all areas under its jurisdiction or control in which anti-personnel mines are known or suspected to be emplaced'. This obligation is narrower than an obligation to identify all mined areas under its jurisdiction or control containing anti-personnel mines, since it does not require that a State Party seek to identify all areas dangerous due to the presence or suspected presence of mines. Thus, the ICBL has reported that it is suspected that in the south of Peru, Chilean mines laid along its border 'might have been displaced into Peruvian territory by rain and erosion. According to an official at the Ministry of Foreign Affairs, the landmine problem along the border with Chile was not included in the Article 7 Report because Peru had not laid mines there'.[39]

5.28　It is not clear how far the obligation to 'make every effort' extends. The phrase is not defined in the Convention, but it may be assumed that this is to be understood both within the context of a State Party's existing resources, and in light of international cooperation and assistance provided in accordance

---

[38]　Office of the Judge Advocate General, 'The Law of Armed Conflict', 5–10, sect. 4, Annex B, 11(g).

[39]　ICBL, *Landmine Monitor Report 2002*, 403.

with Article 6. Depending on available resources, it could be construed as an obligation upon mine-affected States to carry out, respectively, a general mine action assessment,[40] landmine impact survey,[41] and technical survey[42] of mine-affected or suspected areas.[43]

**5.29** Once the relevant areas have been identified, a State Party must then 'as soon as possible'[44] perimeter mark, monitor,[45] and protect by fencing or other means all anti-personnel mines in mined areas,[46] to ensure the effective exclusion of civilians until clearance operations are completed. This requirement clearly demonstrates that maintenance of minefield protections does not constitute use of mines for the purposes of the present Convention, as long, of course, as the anti-personnel mines contained therein are not replenished.[47] The wording for the provision draws heavily on Article 5(2)(a) of Amended Protocol II,[48] and indeed the marking used shall *at least* be to the standards set out in the Protocol.

**5.30** Surprisingly, there is no obligation to provide an immediate and effective warning to the (civilian) population, despite one being included in draft

[40] A general mine action assessment replaces and amends what was previously called a Level One Survey in mine action lexicon. According to the International Mine Action Standards (IMAS), issued by the UN: 'The purpose of a general mine action assessment is to continually gather, evaluate, analyse and make available sufficient information to assist and update the strategic planning of a national mine action programme. It should provide a source of continually updated data on the nature and extent of the hazards and hazardous areas, the impact of such hazards at community and country level, and other important planning information such as local soil characteristics, vegetation and climate, and safe access routes and local facilities such as water and medical support. The general mine action assessment should also provide an inventory of national capabilities and potential to implement national mine action projects, and to support the work of external organisations and agencies'. IMAS 08.10, Edition 2, 1 Jan. 2003, p. 1, available at: www.mineactionstandards.org.

[41] The Landmine Impact Survey was previously called a Level One Impact Survey. This is a detailed community level survey of suspected areas and a ranking of priority areas based on their socio-economic impact.

[42] Previously called a Level Two Survey. This type of survey verifies the existence of contamination and the outer perimeters of the affected area. See IMAS 08.20, Edition 2, 1 Jan. 2003, available at: www.mineactionstandards.org.

[43] Such surveys can amount to considerable sums of money—a typical landmine impact survey, for instance, costs more than US$1 million and can take one to two years to complete.

[44] Again, it may be assumed that this is to be understood both within the context of a State Party's existing resources, and in light of international cooperation and assistance provided in accordance with Article 6.

[45] In its comments on the Second Austrian Draft, New Zealand had asked for clarification of the obligation to monitor minefields—specifically, whether it required 24-hour surveillance or just periodic inspections—but the revised draft did not elaborate on the wording. Note Verbale from New Zealand Ministry of Foreign Affairs addressed to Austrian Embassy (Wellington, 18 Apr. 1997).

[46] Thus, the obligations to mark, monitor, and protect by fencing or other means are seemingly broader than the preceding requirement to identify affected areas.

[47] See above the commentary on Article 1(1)(a), especially in paras. 1.28–1.29.

[48] Although the obligation in Article 5(2) is stricter than the one contained in the Protocol.

Article 6 before delegates at the Oslo Diplomatic Conference concerning anti-personnel mines in areas outside minefields. It is not known why this provision was not included in the final text. Indeed, in its comments on the Third Austrian Draft, the ICRC had proposed to strengthen the obligation, whereby States Parties would have been obliged to provide an immediate, effective, *and continuous* warning to the civilian population *until such time as the area is known to be clear of mines.*[49]

# Paragraph 3

> 3. If a State Party believes that it will be unable to destroy or ensure the destruction of all anti-personnel mines referred to in paragraph 1 within that time period, it may submit a request to a Meeting of the States Parties or a Review Conference for an extension of the deadline for completing the destruction of such anti-personnel mines, for a period of up to ten years.

5.31 Each State Party undertakes, in accordance with Article 5(1), 'to destroy or ensure the destruction of all anti-personnel mines located in mined areas under its jurisdiction or control as soon as possible but not later than 10 years' after the Convention's entry into force for it. As already discussed, it was generally understood that this objective would not be realistically achieved by certain States—owing to lack of access, insufficiency of resources, and technical feasibility. To address this reality, States Parties are given the possibility under Article 5(3) of requesting an extension of the deadline for a period of up to 10 years. There is no time limit within which a State Party must apply for an extension period, although presumably the application should not be *ex post facto* and should therefore be made no later than the last meeting of States Parties before its deadline elapses.[50]

5.32 To be able to request an extension period, a State Party must simply believe that it will be unable to meet the deadline set down in Article 5(1). This is a purely subjective assessment; there is no need for any rationale to support it, although the content of the written request is governed by Article 5(4) discussed below. Moreover, the inability of the State Party to meet the deadline may be entirely due to its own fault; this will not preclude it from being permitted to submit a request. Any exacerbating factors will, of course, be relevant to the application for an extension period.

---

[49] 'Comments of the International Committee of the Red Cross on the Third Austrian Draft (13/5/97) of the Convention on the Prohibition of Anti-personnel Mines', reproduced in Maresca and Maslen, *The Banning of Anti-Personnel Landmines*, 551.

[50] cf. the provisions in the 1993 Chemical Weapons Convention. See Verification Annex, IV Part IV (C), para. 25, 1993 Chemical Weapons Convention.

# Paragraph 4

4. Each request shall contain:

(a) The duration of the proposed extension;

(b) A detailed explanation of the reasons for the proposed extension, including:

    (i) The preparation and status of work conducted under national demining programs;

    (ii) The financial and technical means available to the State Party for the destruction of all the anti-personnel mines, and

    (iii) Circumstances which impede the ability of the State Party to destroy all the anti-personnel mines in mined areas;

(c) The humanitarian, social, economic, and environmental implications of the extension; and

(d) Any other information relevant to the request for the proposed extension.

5.33 Thus, the request for an extension period under Article 5(3) must contain the following: the duration of the proposed extension; a detailed explanation of the reasons for the proposed extension; the humanitarian, social, economic, and environmental implications of the extension; and any other information relevant to the request for the proposed extension. In accordance with paragraph 3 of the article, the duration of the proposed extension may be for any period up to, but not exceeding, 10 years.

5.34 Under paragraph 4(b), the requesting State Party should presumably demonstrate the existence of a national demining plan and its commitment in human and financial terms to that plan. Typically, mine- and UXO-affected States prepare five-year or 10-year strategic mine action plans that address the type and extent of the contamination, past achievements of the national programme, the actions needed to tackle the remaining contamination, available resources, and the need for outside assistance. Such a plan would appear to fit well with the requirements of the paragraph.[51]

5.35 The UK ostensibly failed in its attempt at the Oslo Diplomatic Conference to secure an explicit exception to the requirement to clear emplaced anti-personnel mines where: '(a) the anti-personnel mines were not laid by the State

---

[51] For the views of the ICBL on reporting under Article 5 more broadly, see for instance 'Opening Intervention on Progress made and Challenges faced in Mine Action by Sara Sekkenes—NPA on behalf of the Mine Action Working Group of the ICBL', Standing Committee on Mine Clearance, Mine Awareness and Related Technologies (Geneva, 5 Feb. 2003), available at: www.gichd.ch/pdf/mbc/SC_feb03/speeches_mc/Sekkenes_MAWG_progress_made.pdf.

Party; (b) the minefield is outside inhabited areas; (c) the risk of death or injury in leaving the minefield undisturbed is outweighed by the risks of clearing it; and (d) the costs of destroying the mines would be wholly disproportionate to the benefit'. The UK accepts that it is obliged under the Convention to demine the Falkland Islands. However, the provisions of Article 5(4)(b)(iii) and (c) may provide an opportunity to delay the implementation of this obligation on the basis that it is extremely physically dangerous as well as being technically difficult to clear mines from land with a high peat content, and that there are other more pressing concerns to be addressed.

5.36 Some progress towards clearance has already been achieved. On 11 October 2001, Argentina and the UK agreed on a Memorandum of Understanding to establish a feasibility study on mine clearance in the islands. A joint working group has been created, but, as of writing, the feasibility study, which will take some 18 months to complete, has yet to be formally initiated.[52]

5.37 The situation is further complicated by Argentina's claim of sovereignty over the Islands, as it too could presumably request an extension on the basis that it does not have the requisite access to carry out demining operations, if clearance is not completed within the specified deadline. Thus, upon ratification of the Convention, Argentina lodged a declaration reaffirming 'its rights of sovereignty over the Malvinas, South Georgia and South Sandwich and the surrounding maritime areas which form an integral part of the territory'. It also declared that since the islands were under 'illegal occupation' by the UK, Argentina was 'effectively prevented from having access to the anti-personnel mines . . . in order to fulfil the obligations undertaken in the . . . Convention'.

## Paragraph 5

> 5. The Meeting of the States Parties or the Review Conference shall, taking into consideration the factors contained in paragraph 4, assess the request and decide by a majority of votes of States Parties present and voting whether to grant the request for an extension period.

5.38 The Review Conference or Meeting of States Parties that assesses the request must take account of the information submitted by the State Party seeking the extension period. Thus, either the first review conference or a subsequent meeting of States Parties should be expected to elaborate more detailed criteria by which an application will be judged. An obvious and relevant factor will be

---

[52] See ICBL, *Landmine Monitor Report 2002*, 820–1.

whether the State Party in question has made a serious effort to meet its obligations under the Convention. The mechanism also gives States Parties the opportunity to call attention to unaddressed needs in accordance with the obligations to provide assistance under Article 6. In general, the States Parties would appear to have broad latitude in reaching a decision whether to grant the request for an extension period.

**5.39** It is unlikely that a well-founded request for an extension would be refused. If it were, however, once the 10-year deadline had elapsed, the State Party would be in violation of its undertakings under the Convention. On the other hand, there is nothing to stop the Meeting of States Parties granting a shorter (or even longer) extension period than that requested by the mine-affected State Party.

**5.40** By virtue of Article 5(3), an extension period may be granted only by a Meeting of the States Parties or a Review Conference. This means that at least one or the other of these meetings must continue to be convened from 2009 and beyond, unless all States Parties are anti-personnel mine-free by that date. A decision on the convening of future Meetings of the States Parties will itself be taken at the first Review Conference in 2004, in accordance with Article 12(2)(b).

# Paragraph 6

> 6. Such an extension may be renewed upon the submission of a new request in accordance with paragraphs 3, 4 and 5 of this Article. In requesting a further extension period a State Party shall submit relevant additional information on what has been undertaken in the previous extension period pursuant to this Article.

**5.41** A State Party that is heavily contaminated may request more than one extension period.[53] Each request for a further extension period may presumably seek a shorter or longer period than the previous one (as long as no single period exceeds 10 years), but must be accompanied by 'relevant additional information on what has been undertaken in the previous extension period'. This will ensure that the other States Parties are able to exercise a degree of ongoing supervision of the State Party's commitment to meeting its obligations.

---

[53] At the Oslo Diplomatic Conference, Belgium had suggested that a second extension should receive a two-thirds majority in favour to be accepted, but this proposal was not supported by the Conference.

# Article 6. International Cooperation and Assistance

Article 6—International cooperation and assistance

1. In fulfilling its obligations under this Convention each State Party has the right to seek and receive assistance, where feasible, from other States Parties to the extent possible.

2. Each State Party undertakes to facilitate and shall have the right to participate in the fullest possible exchange of equipment, material and scientific and technological information concerning the implementation of this Convention. The States Parties shall not impose undue restrictions on the provision of mine clearance equipment and related technological information for humanitarian purposes.

3. Each State Party in a position to do so shall provide assistance for the care and rehabilitation, and social and economic reintegration, of mine victims and for mine awareness programs. Such assistance may be provided, inter alia, through the United Nations system, international, regional or national organizations or institutions, the International Committee of the Red Cross, national Red Cross and Red Crescent societies and their International Federation, non-governmental organizations, or on a bilateral basis.

4. Each State Party in a position to do so shall provide assistance for mine clearance and related activities. Such assistance may be provided, inter alia, through the United Nations system, international or regional organizations or institutions, non-governmental organizations or institutions, or on a bilateral basis, or by contributing to the United Nations Voluntary Trust Fund for Assistance in Mine Clearance, or other regional funds that deal with demining.

5. Each State Party in a position to do so shall provide assistance for the destruction of stockpiled anti-personnel mines.

6. Each State Party undertakes to provide information to the database on mine clearance established within the United Nations system, especially information concerning various means and technologies of mine clearance, and lists of experts, expert agencies or national points of contact on mine clearance.

7. States Parties may request the United Nations, regional organizations, other States Parties or other competent intergovernmental or non-governmental fora to assist its authorities in the elaboration of a national

demining program to determine, inter alia:

(a) The extent and scope of the anti-personnel mine problem;
(b) The financial, technological and human resources that are required for the implementation of the program;
(c) The estimated number of years necessary to destroy all anti-personnel mines in mined areas under the jurisdiction or control of the concerned State Party;
(d) Mine awareness activities to reduce the incidence of mine-related injuries or deaths;
(e) Assistance to mine victims;
(f) The relationship between the Government of the concerned State Party and the relevant governmental, inter-governmental or non-governmental entities that will work in the implementation of the program.

8. Each State Party giving and receiving assistance under the provisions of this Article shall cooperate with a view to ensuring the full and prompt implementation of agreed assistance programs.

# Introduction

## The Purpose of Article 6

**6.1** Under Article 6 of the Anti-Personnel Mine Ban Convention, which draws on the provisions of Article 11 of Amended Protocol II, States Parties accept the obligation to provide international cooperation and assistance to other States Parties to enable them to implement fully their obligations under the Convention. It was understood from the outset of negotiations that a comprehensive package of measures (financial, material, and technical) would be required to ensure that mine clearance, mine awareness, and victim assistance programmes would be strengthened in practice and that severely mine-affected States would feel able to join the Convention without accepting obligations that they would not be able to fulfil.

## The Negotiation of Article 6

**6.2** It is therefore somewhat surprising that none of the earliest drafts of the Convention included specific provisions on international cooperation and assistance, although the draft treaty text prepared by the International Campaign to Ban Landmines (ICBL), circulated in January 1997, included the following: 'Each State Party undertakes to facilitate and shall have the right to participate in the fullest possible exchange of equipment, material and scientific and technological information concerning the implementation of this Convention and means of mine clearance and mine destruction'.[1]

**6.3** At the 1997 Vienna Conference, Afghanistan, Brazil, Canada, Honduras, Mexico, and the International Committee of the Red Cross (ICRC) called for a separate article on assistance for mine clearance to facilitate the implementation

---

[1] Article 6 on Cooperation, Convention on the Prohibition of the Development, Production, Stockpiling, Transfer and Use of Anti-Personnel Mines and on their Destruction, Proposal by the International Campaign to Ban Landmines, ICBL, 20 Dec. 1996.

of the draft provision that would become Article 5.[2] The ICRC remarked that Article 11 of Amended Protocol II would be inappropriate in the context of the present Convention, and called for a new formulation.[3]

6.4 The Second Austrian Draft, however, included a broader and quite detailed article on international cooperation and assistance that went beyond support for mine clearance to include more general cooperation and assistance, and also specified that assistance should be provided for the destruction of stockpiled anti-personnel mines:

1. In fulfilling its obligations under this Convention each State Party has the right to seek and receive assistance from other States Parties to the extent possible.

2. Each State Party undertakes to facilitate and shall have the right to participate in the fullest possible exchange of equipment, material and scientific and technological information concerning the implementation of this Convention.

3. Each State Party in a position to do so shall provide assistance for mine clearance Such assistance may be provided, *inter alia*, through the United Nations System, other international organizations or institutions, regional organizations or on a bilateral basis, or by contributing to the United Nations Voluntary Trust Fund for Assistance in Mine Clearance.

4. Each State Party in a position to do so shall provide assistance for the destruction of stockpiled anti-personnel mines.

5. Each State Party undertakes to provide information to the database on mine clearance established within the United Nations System, especially information concerning various means and technologies of mine clearance, and lists of experts, expert agencies or national points of contact in mine clearance.[4]

The proposed article was unchanged in the Third Austrian Draft of 13 May 1997.

6.5 In its comments on the draft, Switzerland proposed including a provision obliging each State Party in a position to do so to 'provide assistance for the care and rehabilitation of landmine victims and for mine awareness programs'. As mentioned in the Introduction above, the absence of a provision on assistance for landmine victims in the Brussels Declaration had been bitterly contested by a number of African States in particular, and had led to South Africa initially refusing to sign the Declaration.[5] Also, as mentioned above,[6] prior to

---

[2] See paras. 5.4–5.6 above.

[3] For instance, the right to seek and receive technical assistance in Article 11(7) of the Protocol was granted 'with a view to reducing any period of deferral' in meeting the technical specifications for detectability, and self-destruction and self-deactivation of anti-personnel mines.

[4] Article 7 on International Cooperation and Assistance, Second Austrian Draft of 14 Mar. 1997.

[5] See para. 0.78 above.          [6] See para. 1.86 above.

the Oslo Diplomatic Conference, the Philippines, a member of the Core Group, had put forward a proposal to include in Article 1(2) a requirement 'to engage in international cooperation and assistance', giving centre stage to the obligations developed in Article 6. It was dissuaded by other Core Group members from formally proposing the amendment during the Conference.

**6.6** At the Conference itself, Brazil served as the Friend of the Chair on the issue. In comments on the Third Austrian Draft Brazil had previously called for a provision establishing a programme of research and development in mine clearance technology upon entry into force of the Convention, with funding through the UN Voluntary Trust Fund for Assistance in Mine Clearance. On the second day of the Conference, it officially introduced the following proposal:[7]

Article 7 Bis
Research and Development in Mine Clearance Technology

1. A program of research and development in mine clearance technology shall be constituted upon entry into force of this Convention.

2. The program shall be financed by contributions to the United Nations Voluntary Trust Fund for Assistance in Mine Clearance or direct contributions thereto.

3. The Depositary shall be responsible for the program and shall submit annual reports on its implementation to the meetings of States Parties.

4. The States Parties shall have unrestricted access to the research carried out through the Program. Upon request of a State Party, any development in mine clearance technology or knowledge achieved through the program shall be transferred to the requesting State Party on a non-commercial basis.

**6.7** Brazil also introduced a proposal relating to assistance in the elaboration of a National Demining Program:[8]

Article 7 Ter

1. Upon its ratification of, or accession to, this convention, each State Party shall declare to the Depositary whether it has mines laid in areas outside minefields. In case such mines exist, the concerned State Party may request the United Nations, Regional Organisations or other competent intergovernmental fora to assist its authorities in the elaboration of a National Demining Program.

2. The National Demining Program shall determine, inter alia:

    (a) the number of years necessary to destroy all anti-personnel mines laid in areas outside minefields under the jurisdiction or control of the concerned State Party;

[7] APL/CW.29 of 2 Sept. 1997. Several Core Group members were not enthusiastic about the proposal, believing that the money would be better spent on mine clearance.
[8] APL/CW.30 of 2 Sept. 1997.

(b) the financial, technological and human resources that are required for the implementation of the Program;

(c) the appropriate relationship between the Government of the concerned State Party and the relevant governmental, inter-governmental or non-governmental entities that will work in the implementation of the Program.

Following discussion of the proposal in the working group, Brazil introduced a revised proposal,[9] which with further amendment became Article 6(7) in the final treaty text.

**6.8** More heated discussions, though, surrounded the question of victim assistance. At the beginning of the Diplomatic Conference, Norway had put forward the following proposal on assistance to mine victims: 'Each State Party in a position to do so shall provide assistance for the rehabilitation of mine victims. Each State Party undertakes to provide information to a database on victim rehabilitation'.[10] El Salvador also stressed the importance of ensuring effective assistance to the victims of landmines in a proposal introduced on the second day of the Conference.[11]

**6.9** Difficulties arose as NGOs sought the inclusion of a reference to assistance for the social and economic reintegration of mine victims, potentially a far wider provision than simply rehabilitation, which tends to be viewed as only referring to surgery, artificial limb-fitting and physiotherapy, and psychological counselling. As mentioned in relation to the preambular paragraph dealing with the issue of assistance to mine victims, a number of donor governments were said to be concerned about the financial ramifications of such obligations. Germany, in particular, was vocal in opposing the inclusion of the phrase 'social and economic reintegration' although ultimately it was included in both Article 6 and the preamble.[12]

**6.10** At the same time, Germany, which had reportedly been frustrated by practical and financial obstacles in some of its attempts to provide assistance for mine action programmes, introduced the following proposal on the second day of the Conference:

Each State Party receiving assistance under the provisions of this article shall cooperate with a view to ensuring the full and prompt implementation of agreed assistance programmes.

It shall in particular effectively assist seconded experts, provide its own contribution in good time and ensure immediate and cost-free customs clearance of all material supplied on behalf of the assisting party.

---

[9] APL/CW.30/Rev.1 of 3 Sept. 1997.     [10] APL/CW.5 of 1 Sept. 1997.
[11] APL/CW.40 of 2 Sept. 1997.     [12] See paras. 0.109 to 0.111 above.

The first of the two proposed paragraphs was included in the final text as paragraph 8.

# Paragraph 1

> 1. In fulfilling its obligations under this Convention each State Party has the right to seek and receive assistance, where feasible, from other States Parties to the extent possible.

## The Right to Seek and Receive Assistance

**6.11** To support efforts to implement the Convention, each State Party has the right to seek and receive assistance, where feasible, from other States Parties to the extent possible. Thus, the first paragraph of Article 6 sets out the right granted to each State Party to seek and receive assistance from other States Parties in fulfilling its obligations under the Convention. The right to seek assistance arguably exists without the need for any legal underpinning (you can always ask!), the right to receive assistance, on the other hand, is inherently more problematic, as it requires a willing donor.

**6.12** A number of States were concerned about the wording of the text as submitted to the Diplomatic Conference.[13] For this reason, the drafting in paragraph 1 is rather tortuous, using the phrase 'where feasible' as well as 'to the extent possible' to clarify the extent of the right (and thus also the extent of the obligation). It is clear that resources are not infinite, and it is also understood that the level of anti-personnel mine contamination exceeds the resources available to deal with it in a short period of time.[14] The Third Austrian Draft had already included the proviso 'to the extent possible' to avoid an open-ended obligation, but at the Oslo Diplomatic Conference, a number of States pushed for further weakening of the clause and succeeded in inserting the phrase 'where feasible'. Yet, despite the provisos, the scope of the clause is wide, going beyond the provision of funds for mine clearance to address broader financial, legal, managerial, scientific, technical, and technological assistance for mine action.

**6.13** Although the phrase 'where feasible' applies equally to the right to seek assistance, its primary intent is clearly to reduce the legal significance of the

---

[13] 'In fulfilling its obligations under this Convention each State Party has the right to seek and receive assistance from other States Parties to the extent possible'. Article 7(1), Third Austrian Draft.

[14] Experiences in Kosovo and Kuwait, however, have demonstrated clearly that where there is sufficient political will and funding, swift and comprehensive clearance of affected areas is practicable.

right to receive it. The term feasible is not defined under the Convention, although its ordinary meaning is something 'practical' or 'possible',[15] potentially quite a broad concept. The term is used in Amended Protocol II when referring to the precautions to be taken to protect civilians from the effects of mines, booby-traps, and other devices.[16] Feasible precautions are defined in the provision as 'those precautions which are practicable or practically possible taking into account all circumstances ruling at the time, including humanitarian and military considerations'.[17]

6.14 There is a further qualifier to the right to seek and receive assistance from other States Parties—that it is only 'to the extent possible'. It is hard to see in practical terms what this adds (or subtracts) from the previous qualifier 'where feasible', although, of course, not every State Party is in a position to give assistance, and even donor States have limits to the amount of assistance they can provide.

## The Obligation to Provide Assistance

6.15 Logically, however, if each State Party has a right to receive assistance from other States Parties, these States Parties have an obligation to provide it. Many of the remaining paragraphs of the article set out in some detail the scope and ambit of this obligation.

# Paragraph 2

2. Each State Party undertakes to facilitate and shall have the right to participate in the fullest possible exchange of equipment, material and scientific and technological information concerning the implementation of this Convention. The States Parties shall not impose undue restrictions on the provision of mine clearance equipment and related technological information for humanitarian purposes.

---

[15] *The Shorter Oxford English Dictionary.*

[16] 'All feasible precautions shall be taken to protect civilians from the effects of weapons to which this Article applies'. Article 3(10), Amended Protocol II.

[17] It is specified that: 'These circumstances include, but are not limited to: (a) the short- and long-term effect of mines upon the local civilian population for the duration of the minefield; (b) possible measures to protect civilians (for example, fencing, signs, warning and monitoring); (c) the availability and feasibility of using alternatives; and (d) the short- and long-term military requirements for a minefield'. Ibid.

## The Right to Equipment, Material, and Information

**6.16** Paragraph 2, which is taken, with only slight amendment, from Article 11(1) of Amended Protocol II, sets out the right accorded to each State Party to have access to relevant equipment, material, and scientific and technological information to assist its implementation of the Convention.[18] It also sets out the undertaking by States Parties to facilitate the fullest possible exchange of such equipment, material, and information. The remainder of the paragraph, which deals specifically with mine clearance equipment and related technological information, indicates that the main thrust of the paragraph is access to equipment, material, and information that will assist mine detection and destruction.

**6.17** The primary challenge in a mine clearance operation is mine detection, whether of individual mines ('close-in detection'), or of mined areas ('stand-off detection').[19] According to the Geneva International Centre for Humanitarian Demining (GICHD):

Close-in detectors exist in many forms. In general, detection is done either by pushing some form of energy at the mine and measuring the response (prodders, eddy current, radar, infra-red, nuclear etc), or detecting any disturbance caused to the natural conditions by the mine (disturbance of magnetic fields, disturbance of soil, detection of explosive vapour from the mine and its filling) . . . Stand-off [detection] . . . presents an even greater technical challenge, but could provide greater rewards. Some systems, such as air and space photography, infrared detectors, air and space visual light imagery, and remote explosive sensing, have shown potential in this area.[20]

Over the last decade, considerable funds have been devoted to research and development to improve detection equipment and technologies, although the result of this R&D has, so far, been rather disappointing.[21]

## The Prohibition on 'Undue Restrictions'

**6.18** The final sentence of the paragraph repeats the wording of Amended Protocol II, which encourages States Parties to share the fruits of their R&D programmes. The wording 'shall not impose undue restrictions' demonstrates the recognition that there will be 'due' restrictions, on the basis of, at the very least, commercial interest.[22] Undoubtedly, States that receive privileged

---

[18] A similar provision is included in Article X of the 1972 Biological Weapons Convention and Article X of the 1993 Chemical Weapons Convention.

[19] *A Guide to Mine Action.*          [20] ibid.

[21] See e.g. Blagden, P., 'Landmine Detection and Destruction Technologies', in *Mine Action: An Historical Analysis* (Geneva: GICHD, forthcoming).

[22] There may also be some ramifications with respect to patents and copyrights attributed to scientific and technological information emanating from the private sector.

information through bilateral agreements are entitled (and sometimes bound) to maintain confidentiality. There may also be military reasons for a State Party deciding not to share mine clearance equipment and related technological information, as it is acknowledged that certain equipment and technological information is 'dual-use', permitting mine warfare as well as mine clearance activities, although this is less likely to be the case with respect to other parties to the Anti-Personnel Mine Ban Convention than it would with respect to Amended Protocol II.[23]

# Paragraph 3

3. Each State Party in a position to do so shall provide assistance for the care and rehabilitation, and social and economic reintegration, of mine victims and for mine awareness programs. Such assistance may be provided, inter alia, through the United Nations system, international, regional or national organizations or institutions, the International Committee of the Red Cross, national Red Cross and Red Crescent societies and their International Federation, non-governmental organizations, or on a bilateral basis.

## Overview of the Provision

**6.19** This paragraph, which was newly introduced at the Oslo Diplomatic Conference, was only agreed after lengthy debate.[24] It requires that States 'in a position to do so' provide assistance to mine victims and for mine awareness programmes. This phrase is not defined in the Convention, although its inclusion implies that not all States Parties are in such a position. Although assistance is not defined, it presumably includes financial, material, and technical aspects. It may be provided through a wide variety of actors, both governmental and non-governmental.

## The Nature of the Duty to Provide Assistance to Mine Victims

**6.20** According to the GICHD: 'As the responsibility to ensure the well-being of a country's citizens rests with each country's national authorities, the task of providing for the care and rehabilitation needs of a country's landmine

---

[23] This is because Amended Protocol II allows continued use of certain anti-personnel mines under certain circumstances, whereas no use is possible under the Anti-Personnel Mine Ban Convention. However, the same technologies will often be applicable to mines other than anti-personnel mines.

[24] See paras. 6.8 and 6.9 above.

survivors remains a State responsibility'. Yet, as already mentioned,[25] the undertaking in the Convention to provide assistance for the care and rehabilitation, and social and economic reintegration, of mine victims is not an absolute legal obligation. Thus, there is no legal obligation upon a State Party to assist its own victims, and the obligation to provide assistance for victims within the context of international cooperation and assistance is only imposed on States Parties that are 'in a position to do so'. These limitations notwithstanding, the scope of the obligation in paragraph 3 is broad as it applies to all mine victims without exception: no distinction is made between victims of anti-personnel mines and those injured by other landmines.

6.21  The Convention does not, however, define in other respects the scope of the term mine victim, although it is generally assumed that it is restricted to individuals actually injured in a landmine explosion. Beyond the Convention, however, this issue has been the subject of animated debate.[26] The International Mine Action Standards (IMAS), elaborated by the GICHD on behalf of the United Nations Mine Action Service,[27] define a mine victim as 'an individual who has suffered harm as a result of a mine or UXO accident'.[28] This is potentially a very broad definition, as harm could cover not only the physical consequences of a landmine explosion, but also its social, economic, environmental, and psychological implications. This view is partly evidenced by a note to the relevant standard, which states that: 'In the context of victim assistance, the term victim may include dependants of a mine casualty, hence having a broader meaning than survivor'.[29]

6.22  The ICBL similarly defines mine victim broadly to include 'those who, either individually, or collectively, have suffered physical, emotional and psychological injury, economic loss or substantial impairment of their fundamental rights through acts or omissions related to mine utilisation'.[30]

## The Type of Assistance to be Provided

6.23  The care and rehabilitation of mine victims encompasses first aid, surgical treatment of mine injures, and physical and psychological rehabilitation, including physiotherapy and the provision of one or more prostheses. Prostheses

---

[25]  See para. 0.110 above.

[26]  For a brief discussion of the terminological debate see e.g. *The Role of Mine Action in Assistance to Mine and Unexploded Ordnance Victims* (Geneva: GICHD, May 2002).

[27]  The current draft of the IMAS can be accessed at: www.mineactionstandards.org.

[28]  IMAS 04.10, 2nd edn., 1 Jan. 2003, Standard 3.225.          [29]  ibid.

[30]  ICBL, 'Victim Assistance: Contexts, Principles and Issues', Position Paper of the ICBL Working Group on Victim Assistance (2000).

must be regularly replaced, especially in the case of children as their bodies are still growing.[31] Measures to support the social and economic reintegration of mine victims include vocational retraining, education, legislation to protect victims' rights, and measures to reduce discrimination against them.

6.24  According to the IMAS, victim assistance 'refers to all aid, relief, comfort and support provided to victims (including survivors) with the purpose of reducing the immediate and long-term medical and psychological implications of their trauma'.[32] The ICBL defines victim assistance more broadly as including efforts related to the following nine areas of activity:

- emergency medical care;
- continuing medical care;
- physical rehabilitation, prosthesis, and assistive devices;
- psychological and social support;
- employment and economic integration;
- capacity building and sustainability;
- legislation and public awareness;
- access to services; and
- data collection.[33]

Assistance, other than funding, could therefore be usefully provided in the form of legal or technical advice or training, and equipment (e.g. polypropylene, a thermoformable plastic, for the manufacture of prostheses). It should be noted, however, that the provision has also provoked concern that mine victims are receiving 'special treatment' in preference to other civilian victims of war or persons with disability. Thus, the ICRC and WHO published a report in 2000 stating: 'At the field level it is neither practically possible, nor ethically acceptable, to favour one type of victim over another on the basis of the cause of injury. The ICRC and WHO consider that treatment for landmines victims must be integrated into a comprehensive public health care system'.[34]

## The Duty to Provide Assistance for Mine Awareness Programmes

6.25  The combination of victim assistance and mine awareness in the same provision is not a particularly happy one, as the two disciplines differ widely in

---

[31] See e.g. Coupland, R. M., *Assistance for Victims of Anti-Personnel Mines: Needs, Constraints and Strategy* (Geneva: ICRC, 1997).

[32] IMAS 04.10, 2nd, edn., 1 Jan. 2003, Standard 3.226.

[33] ICBL, *Guidelines for the Care and Rehabilitation of Survivors*, Pamphlet of the International Campaign to Ban Landmines Working Group on Victim Assistance (1999).

[34] 'Victim Assistance: A Public Health Response for Landmine Victims', (Geneva: ICRC/WHO, 2000).

terms of service provision and requisite technical skills. The former is a public health concern, the latter more of a communication and community liaison activity.[35]

6.26 There is no explicit obligation upon a State Party to provide mine awareness to anyone at risk from anti-personnel mines on territory under its jurisdiction or control, although it is implicit as States Parties are required by Article 7 to report on 'measures taken to provide an immediate and effective warning to the population in relation to all [mined] areas'.[36] In addition, under Article 6(7)(d) below, States Parties may request assistance from the UN, regional organizations, other States Parties or other competent intergovernmental or non-governmental fora in elaborating mine awareness activities to reduce the incidence of mine-related injuries or deaths within a national demining programme.

6.27 In May 1999, the United Nations adopted international guidelines for mine and unexploded ordnance awareness education, which had been drafted by the United Nations Children's Fund (UNICEF). In the context of the IMAS, UNICEF, the UN's designated focal point for mine awareness,[37] is currently preparing standards for what it now terms 'mine risk education'.[38]

6.28 The type of assistance to be provided for mine awareness programmes could be technical or financial. Mine awareness experts generally reject the importation of materials used in another context as being inappropriate and unadapted to another situation, preferring to harness local resources and capacities to tackling the development of appropriate communication channels and media.[39]

## The Mechanisms for the Provision of Assistance

6.29 A non-exclusive list of mechanisms for the provision of assistance is also included in the paragraph. In addition to bilateral agreements between

---

[35] See e.g. *Communication in Mine Awareness Programmes* (Geneva: GICHD, 2002).

[36] See, below, the commentary on Article 7(1)(i).

[37] 'Mine Action and Effective Coordination: The United Nations Policy', UN Doc. A/53/496, UNMAS (New York, 1998).

[38] According to the UNICEF Project Manager of the standards, the two terms 'mine awareness' and 'mine risk education' are synonyms. Email communication from Ben Lark, Deputy Global Focal Point for Landmines, 4 Feb. 2002. The IMAS defines mine risk education as: 'a process that promotes the adoption of safer behaviours by at-risk groups, and which provides the links between affected communities, other mine action components and other sectors'. It 'is an essential component of mine action. There are two related and mutually reinforcing components: a) community liaison; and b) public education'. It is further noted that 'generally, mine action programmes use both approaches, as they are mutually reinforcing'. IMAS 04.10, 2nd edn., 1 Jan. 2003, Standard 3.126.

[39] See e.g. *Communication in Mine Awareness Programmes*.

States Parties, the list cites the UN, international, regional or national organizations or institutions, the International Committee of the Red Cross (ICRC), national Red Cross and Red Crescent societies and their International Federation, and non-governmental organizations as possible avenues for channelling assistance to mine victims.

**6.30** Under the overall coordination of the UN Mine Action Service (UNMAS), a leading agency for victim assistance within the United Nations system is the World Health Organization,[40] although UNICEF[41] and the United Nations Development Programme (UNDP)[42] also have important roles to play. UNDP, for example, contracted the World Rehabilitation Fund (WRF) to develop Guidelines for the Socio-Economic Reintegration of Landmine Survivors. The resulting guidelines, which were presented in draft form to the Third Meeting of States Parties, found that 'the most acute needs of landmine survivors are not the medical rehabilitation services provided, but assistance in helping the survivors become productive community members and contribute to their families. Socio-economic reintegration, therefore, has been sorely neglected as an issue to be dealt with by national governmental initiatives or by international relief organisation efforts'.[43]

**6.31** The ICRC is probably the world's leading organization in providing assistance to mine victims. In 1979, the ICRC set up a unit for the physical rehabilitation of war victims. Since then, 65 projects have been set up in 25 countries. Two-thirds of the projects are carried out in close cooperation with government authorities. The others are run by the ICRC alone or in partnership with local NGOs or National Red Cross/Red Crescent Societies. Since the unit was formed and up to the end of 2002, more than 160,000 individuals had been fitted with a total of 194,772 prostheses and 87,458 orthoses,[44] while others had received crutches (497,168), wheelchairs (14,834), or physiotherapy.[45]

---

[40] According to a 1998 UN policy document, WHO is 'responsible for the development of appropriate standards and methodologies, as well as the promotion of health service capacity building for sustainable victim assistance, through the Ministries of Health of affected countries. It will provide public technical health support to the various UN partners involved in mine action, and cooperate closely with UNICEF and ICRC'. 'Mine Action and Effective Coordination'.

[41] According to the same policy document: 'UNICEF, in collaboration with WHO, ICRC, and other partners where appropriate, will ensure comprehensive rehabilitation of landmine victims, which includes psychosocial counselling, physical rehabilitation (including the provision of prosthetics and orthotics), and education for those with disabilities'. 'Mine Action and Effective Coordination'.

[42] 'Within the UN system, the United Nations Development Programme will be responsible for addressing the socio-economic consequences of landmine contamination'. Ibid.

[43] World Rehabilitation Fund, Guidelines for the Provision of Socioeconomic Integration of Landmine Survivors (New York: WRF, 2001).

[44] Orthoses are artificial external devices, such as braces or splints, serving to prevent or assist relative movement in the limbs or the spine.

[45] ICRC, *Physical Rehabilitation Programs, Annual Report 2002* (Geneva: ICRC, 2001), 3.

**6.32** Among the NGOs engaged in the delivery of assistance to mine victims are Handicap International France, which has been working in some 40 mine-affected countries and Handicap International Belgium, which in 2003 was delivering services in at least 12 mine-affected countries. The Vietnam Veterans of America Foundation provided physical and social rehabilitation services to civilian victims of conflict in seven mine-affected countries in 2003. Another important organization is the Landmine Survivors Network, which was created by landmine survivors to work directly with those whose lives have been blighted by mines.[46]

# Paragraph 4

4. Each State Party in a position to do so shall provide assistance for mine clearance and related activities. Such assistance may be provided, inter alia, through the United Nations system, international or regional organizations or institutions, non-governmental organizations or institutions, or on a bilateral basis, or by contributing to the United Nations Voluntary Trust Fund for Assistance in Mine Clearance, or other regional funds that deal with demining.

## The Duty to Provide Assistance for Mine Clearance

**6.33** Under paragraph 4, each State Party in a position to do so is required to provide assistance for mine clearance and related activities. This provision recalls Article 11(3) of Amended Protocol II, which provides that: 'Each High Contracting Party in a position to do so shall provide assistance for mine clearance through the United Nations System, other international bodies or on a bilateral basis, or contribute to the United Nations Voluntary Trust Fund for Assistance in Mine Clearance'.

**6.34** Mine clearance is not defined in the Convention, but is defined in the IMAS as: 'the clearance of mines and UXO from a specified area to a predefined standard'.[47] It should be noted that Article 5 refers to the destruction of anti-personnel mines in mined areas rather than their clearance, and that the second preambular paragraph refers to the 'challenge of removing anti-personnel mines placed throughout the world', and to the necessity to assure their destruction.

---

[46] *A Guide to Mine Action*, ch. 8.          [47] IMAS 04.10, 2nd edn., 1 Jan. 2003, Standard 3.127.

6.35 Similarly, what constitute 'related activities' is not defined in the Convention. Again, reference can be made to the IMAS, which notes that mine clearance is considered to be just one part of the (humanitarian) demining process.[48] Humanitarian demining is itself defined as: 'activities which lead to the removal of mine and UXO hazards, including technical survey, mapping, clearance, marking, post-clearance documentation, community mine action liaison and the handover of cleared land'.[49] Logically, the activities cited may all be considered 'related activities' for the purposes of paragraph 4.

## The Type of Assistance to be Provided

6.36 As with assistance for mine victims in paragraph 3 of the article, the type of assistance to be provided for mine clearance and related activities under paragraph 4 is not specified. It presumably includes, in addition to funding, training, technical advice, equipment (even though this is also addressed in paragraph 2 of the article), and other material.[50] Of obvious utility would be mine prodders and detectors,[51] personal protective equipment, such as visors and body armour, mechanical demining equipment, such as flails, tillers or vegetation cutters as well as mine-protected vehicles.[52]

## The Mechanisms for the Provision of Assistance

6.37 A variety of mechanisms for the provision of assistance are included in a non-exclusive list: bilateral assistance between States Parties, the UN system, including the Voluntary Trust Fund for Assistance in Mine Clearance, international or regional organizations or institutions, other regional demining funds, and non-governmental organizations or institutions. The GICHD, for instance, estimates that mine action funding from States Parties in 1997–2002 totals more than $800 million. A further $425 million was donated to mine action by non-party States, most of which was provided by the United States.[53]

---

[48] The terms 'demining' and 'humanitarian demining' are used interchangeably in the IMAS. See IMAS 04.10, 2nd edn., 1 Jan. 2003, Standard 3.42. The term was devised to distinguish humanitarian mine clearance from military breaching. See for instance *A Guide to Mine Action*.

[49] IMAS 04.10, 2nd edn., 1 Jan. 2003, Standard 3.42.

[50] See e.g. *Mine Action Equipment: Study of Global Operational Needs* GICHD (June 2002), available at: www.gichd.ch.

[51] See e.g. *Metal Detectors Catalogue 2003* (Geneva: GICHD, Feb. 2003), available at: www.gichd.ch.

[52] See e.g. *Mechanical Demining Equipment Catalogue 2003* (Geneva: GICHD, Nov. 2002), available at: www.gichd.ch.

[53] Letter from Kerry Brinkert, Manager, Implementation Support Unit, GICHD to the ICRC (Geneva, 6 Aug. 2003).

**6.38** Bilateral assistance is extremely common in mine action, particularly in the case of humanitarian demining, for example through State development bodies, or on a military-to-military basis.[54] This is, of course, not restricted to States Parties to the Convention. Within the UN system, UNDP, UNICEF, the UN Office for Project Services (UNOPS) and the United Nations Mine Action Service (UNMAS) are the key channels (and recipients) for funding for mine action. It has been estimated that in 2000, for example, some US$200 million was donated for mine action activities worldwide, of which about 40 per cent was channelled through the UN system.[55]

**6.39** The Voluntary Trust Fund for Assistance in Mine Action (VTF) was established by the Secretary-General in 1994 to provide resources for mine-action activities where other sources of funding are not immediately available. It is used primarily to finance:

- the conduct of assessment missions to monitor the scope of the landmine threat in affected countries;
- the initiation of emergency humanitarian projects and programmes;
- the bridging of funding gaps in ongoing mine action programmes; and
- the coordination and advocacy work of UNMAS.[56]

Contributions may be made to the VTF by governments, organizations, or individuals. They can be earmarked towards a specific country or project. Responsibility for the Trust Fund lies with the UN Mine Action Service (UNMAS).[57]

**6.40** Since its establishment, the VTF has received more than U.S.$78 million in contributions from 44 donor governments, the European Union, and private donors. These funds have supported mine action activities in most of the severely mine-affected countries, including Afghanistan, Angola, Azerbaijan, Bosnia and Herzegovina, Cambodia, Chad, Croatia, Eritrea, Ethiopia, Guatemala, Kosovo (the Federal Republic of Yugoslavia), Laos, Lebanon, Mozambique, Nicaragua, Somalia, Sri Lanka, Sudan, Thailand, and Yemen.[58]

**6.41** Of the international or regional organizations or institutions involved in supporting demining, one of the most important is the Organization of American States (OAS). The OAS created the Assistance Program for demining in Central America in 1991, in response to requests by Central American

---

[54] For a non-exhaustive overview of military-to-military assistance, see e.g. *The Role of the Military in Mine Action* (Geneva: GICHD, July 2003).

[55] Information on the E-MINE database, available at www.mineaction.org.

[56] ibid. There are also country-specific trust funds, generally managed by UNDP.          [57] ibid.

[58] ibid., but adapted based on table of donations included in the E-MINE database.

countries affected by anti-personnel mines (Costa Rica, Honduras, Guatemala, and Nicaragua).[59]

**6.42** Since May 1995, the general coordination and supervision of the Assistance Program for Demining in Central America (PADCA, by its initials in Spanish) has been provided by the Unit for the Promotion of Democracy (UPD), with the technical support of the Inter American Defense Board (IADB). PADCA has since been subsumed within a new programme area in the UPD, called 'Comprehensive Action against Antipersonnel Mines' (AICMA). This programme serves as a focal point for the OAS General Secretariat and addresses the following:

(a) mine risk awareness education for the civilian population;
(b) support for minefield surveying, mapping, marking, and clearance;
(c) victim assistance, including physical and psychological rehabilitation, and the socio-economic reintegration of cleared zones;
(d) support for a total ban on anti-personnel mines; and
(e) establishment of databases on activities directed against anti-personnel mines.[60]

Costa Rica has now been declared mine-free,[61] and Nicaragua expects to be able to do so by 2005.[62] Operations in Guatemala and Honduras are ongoing, and OAS support for demining is planned for Colombia,[63] Ecuador, and Peru.

**6.43** The most important regional fund for demining is the International Trust Fund for Demining and Mine Victims Assistance (ITF), which focuses on support for mine action in South-East Europe, especially the Balkans.[64] The ITF is a non-profit organization, established in 1998 by the Government of Slovenia, with the aim of helping Bosnia and Herzegovina in its mine clearance and providing assistance to mine victims. Following early success in Bosnia, the ITF expanded to a broader regional role. In the four years to 2002 the ITF raised almost US$100 million from 25 donor countries, cleared more than 29 square kilometres of land, and rehabilitated more than 600 mine victims.[65] As of March 2003, this amount had increased to almost $120 million.[66]

---

[59] Information on OAS website, available at: www.upd.oas.org/lab/demining.  [60] ibid.
[61] See para. 5.14 above.
[62] See e.g. the case study on Nicaragua in *The Role of the Military in Mine Action*.
[63] See e.g. OAS, *El Desminado* (Washington: UPD, Spring 2003), 1.
[64] See the ITF website, at: www.itf-fund.si.
[65] 'The International Trust Fund for Demining and Mine Victims Assistance: An Example of Regional Cooperation in South-East Europe', Address to the Euro-Atlantic Security Workshop by Ambassador Roman Kirn, former Executive Director of the ITF (27 Sept. 2002).
[66] See section on donors on the ITF website, at: www.itf-fund.si.

**6.44** Last, but certainly not least, NGOs have played a crucial role in humanitarian demining and other aspects of mine action, such as victim assistance and mine awareness. A number of international NGOs are dedicated to mine action, such as the HALO Trust,[67] the Mines Advisory Group (MAG),[68] and the Survey Action Center (SAC);[69] others such as Handicap International (HI Belgium, France, Germany, and Luxembourg),[70] Norwegian People's Aid (NPA),[71] and the Vietnam Veterans of America Foundation[72] incorporate a significant mine action component in their other development work.

# Paragraph 5

5. Each State Party in a position to do so shall provide assistance for the destruction of stockpiled anti-personnel mines.

## The Duty to Provide Assistance for Stockpile Destruction

**6.45** As with the clearance of emplaced anti-personnel mines, the destruction of stockpiles carries a significant financial burden (depending on the size of the stockpile). This has sometimes meant that adherence to the Convention is implicitly or explicitly linked to the provision of funding. For instance, the offer of financial assistance for the destruction of Ukraine's huge stockpile of anti-personnel mines[73] appears to have been a key factor in its decision to sign the Convention just prior to its entry into force.[74]

---

[67] See HALO Trust website at: www.halotrust.org. HALO is an acronym for Hazardous Area Life-Support Organization.                              [68] See MAG website at: www.mag.org.uk.

[69] See SAC website at: www.sac-na.org.

[70] See, respectively, the websites as: www.handicapinternational.be; www.handicap-international.org; www.handicap-international.de; and www.handicap-international.lu.

[71] See NPA website at: www.npaid.org/mines.                   [72] See VVAF website at: www.vvaf.org.

[73] Ukrainian President, Leonid Kuchma, claimed that Ukraine had a stock of 7 million anti-personnel mines. See 'Canada to Help Ukraine on Landmine Ban, International Loans', *AFP International* (27 Jan. 1999). The ICBL, citing Canadian government information, claimed that the figure was actually 10.1 million. See ICBL, *Landmine Monitor Report 1999*, 759; see also ICBL, *Landmine Monitor Report 2000*, 786.

[74] As an inducement to join the Convention, Canada offered financial assistance to Ukraine in the destruction of its stockpiles (and help in securing a further loan for Ukraine from the European Bank of Reconstruction and Development to complete two reactors to replace the stricken Chernobyl nuclear power plant). The cost of stockpile destruction was estimated at US$10 million; the proposed loan by the EBRD amounted to some US$200 million. In welcoming the Ukrainian decision, Canadian Prime Minister Jean Chrétien declared that: 'If seven million mines are destroyed [millions of] children, women and men will not suffer any more'. See 'Canada to Help Ukraine on Landmine Ban, International Loans'.

**6.46** As has been discussed with respect to the obligations under Article 4 of the Convention, there are a number of possible ways to destroy anti-personnel mine stockpiles. Each has cost implications, which may differ widely. According to the GICHD:

Physical destruction techniques available range from the relatively simple open burn-ing and open detonation (OBOD) techniques, contained detonation, and crushing, to highly sophisticated industrial processes. According to the IMAS, the costs of demili-tarisation of anti-personnel landmines range from U.S.$2 to U.S.$4 each, depending on the type of mine. Generally, open detonation is likely to be the cheapest means to destroy stockpiles of up to one million anti-personnel landmines, but it requires sig-nificant knowledge of explosives engineering as the shock wave caused by detonation may not destroy the mines but may throw them out and arm them.

Industrial scale demilitarisation has many advantages; mechanical disassembly, incin-eration in environmentally-controlled systems and the ability to operate 24 hours a day, 365 days a year. Their major disadvantage is the high capital set up costs of design, project management, construction and commissioning. Their operating costs are gen-erally lower than OBOD (once amortisation of the development capital is discounted); although high labour costs in developed countries account for a large percentage of the OBOD costs.

Notwithstanding this, OBOD can be a cheaper option dependent on the economy of scale. In the United States (U.S.), for example, average OBOD costs are U.S.$850 per tonne, whereas industrial demilitarisation is U.S.$1,180 per tonne; but it must be recognised that these costs are for all ammunition types, not just anti-personnel mines. The IMAS also notes that salvage of metallic scrap, or explosive waste, can result in an income stream. Some explosive fillings of anti-personnel mines may be useful to the commercial explosive industry, whilst scrap steel is always in demand.

In many cases the development of such purpose built demilitarization facilities to enable State Parties to fulfil their obligation for stockpile destruction will be well beyond avail-able resources and therefore may not be a practical option. Factors such as cost, location and safety may mean that OBOD is the only pragmatic and feasible option.[75]

## The Type of Assistance to be Provided

**6.47** Assistance may typically be provided in the form of funding, equip-ment, and/or technical assistance.[76] For example, the GICHD has a full-time

---

[75] *A Guide to Mine Action.*

[76] In a presentation to the intersessional Standing Committee on Stockpile Destruction on 6 Feb. 2003, Canada referred to three types of technical assistance that it envisages: development of national plans, conduct of destruction, or assessment missions. The presentation is available on the E-MINE database, at: www.mineaction.org/pdf%20file/Canada_assistance.pdf.

staff member dedicated to supporting requests by States for assistance with stockpile destruction. Further, in accordance with Article 3(2) of the Convention,[77] States may accept unlimited transfers of anti-personnel mines for the purpose of destruction within its own facilities or at a private company located on its territory.

## The Mechanisms for the Provision of Assistance

**6.48** No mechanism is suggested for the provision of assistance, although many States Parties have used bilateral means of support, especially through their militaries,[78] or have channelled funds and expertise through the UN system, especially UNDP,[79] or regionally, particularly through the OAS.[80]

# Paragraph 6

> 6. Each State Party undertakes to provide information to the database on mine clearance established within the United Nations system, especially information concerning various means and technologies of mine clearance, and lists of experts, expert agencies or national points of contact on mine clearance.

**6.49** The wording for this paragraph comes from Article 11(2) of Amended Protocol II. The paragraph imposes an obligation on States Parties to provide some, rather than all available information, thereby according a State Party considerable discretion as to which information it will provide. As with paragraph 2 of this article, there may be commercial, contractual, or even political reasons why certain information may be withheld from this database. It is also clear that it was foreseen that access to the database would be open to all

---

[77] See above the commentary on this provision.

[78] For instance, in June 2001 and June 2002, Switzerland organized Stockpile Destruction Management Courses, together with the GICHD 'to put into concrete terms' the obligations established in Articles 4 and 6 of the Convention. Foreword by Dr Erwin Dahinden, Head of Division of Arms Control, Law of Armed Conflict and Verification Cooperation, General Staff of the Swiss Armed Forces, in *1st APM Stockpile Destruction Management Training Course, 11–15 June 2001, Fribourg, Documentation*, General Staff of the Swiss Armed Forces.

[79] Thus, for example, according to the chief of the UN Development Programme (UNDP) Mine Action Team, stockpile destruction should form part of each integrated mine action programme that UNDP supports. Statement by UNDP on the Status of UN Support to Stockpile Destruction to the intersessional Standing Committee on Stockpile Destruction (Geneva, 6 Feb. 2003).

[80] For example, OAS support is ongoing to Ecuador and Peru for the destruction of their anti-personnel mine stockpiles. See www.upd.oas.org/lab/demining/demining.htm.

States, not merely those party to the Anti-Personnel Mine Ban Convention or Amended Protocol II to the Convention on Certain Conventional Weapons.

**6.50** The specific database to which this article refers no longer exists, although UNMAS manages the more general E-MINE[81] database, which has information and documentation on all aspects of mine action. E-MINE, which builds on other mine action databases, information systems, and websites, was launched in September 2001 at the Third Meeting of States Parties. It replaced the original landmines database established by the UN Department of Humanitarian Affairs (DHA) in 1995. In December 2002, in its annual resolution on Assistance in Mine Action,[82] the UN General Assembly requested UNMAS to develop E-MINE further 'as a user-friendly repository of mine-related information and as a means for mine-action programmes to circulate on a regular basis to donors and other partners standard reports on the scope and impact of the mine problem, available mine-action resources and capacities and the progress achieved in the field'.[83]

# Paragraph 7

7. States Parties may request the United Nations, regional organizations, other States Parties or other competent intergovernmental or non-governmental fora to assist its authorities in the elaboration of a national demining program to determine, inter alia:

(a) The extent and scope of the anti-personnel mine problem;

(b) The financial, technological and human resources that are required for the implementation of the program;

(c) The estimated number of years necessary to destroy all anti-personnel mines in mined areas under the jurisdiction or control of the concerned State Party;

(d) Mine awareness activities to reduce the incidence of mine-related injuries or deaths;

(e) Assistance to mine victims;

(f) The relationship between the Government of the concerned State Party and the relevant governmental, inter-governmental or non-governmental entities that will work in the implementation of the program.

---

[81] Electronic Mine Information Network.    [82] UN Doc. A/57/159.
[83] See www.mineaction.org/misc/dynamic_overview.cfm?did=19.

## Introduction

**6.51** As discussed above,[84] paragraph 7 is what remains of two Brazilian proposals[85] regarding a programme of research into mine detection and clearance technologies and assistance with a national demining programme.[86] In fact, in most respects, it does little more than reflect an existing reality, whereby States (whether or not they are party to the Anti-Personnel Mine Ban Convention) are entitled to ask other States, the UN, and relevant regional organizations for assistance to deal with mine contamination.

## Assistance for the Elaboration of a National Demining Programme

**6.52** Although paragraph 7 refers to only to a 'demining programme', the subsequent sub-paragraphs (a) to (f) demonstrate that the programme goes beyond demining to include other components of mine action.[87] These sub-paragraphs detail a series of issues to be included in the national demining plan. They should certainly not be considered comprehensive, as they do not address a number of key issues, such as coordination and management, national legislation for mine action,[88] or stockpile destruction.[89]

**6.53** Thus, it is generally agreed that resources are most effectively and efficiently deployed within an overall mine action programme that is both well coordinated and well targeted.[90] Thus, according to the GICHD: 'An effective national coordinating structure, established by appropriate legislation, is integral to efficient, effective and accountable mine action. As the International Mine Action Standards (IMAS) state: "The primary responsibility for mine action lies with the Government of the mine-affected state. The responsibility

---

[84] See paras. 6.6 and 6.7 above.

[85] Docs. APL/CW.29 of 2 Sept. 1997, APL/CW.30 of 2 Sept. 1997, and APL/CW.30rev1 of 3 Sept. 1997. See Appendix 5 for these proposals.

[86] The second of these two proposals reflected the context of the draft treaty text that served as the basis for negotiations at the Oslo Diplomatic Conference, whereby a distinction was made between mines laid in 'minefields' and mines lying in areas outside minefields. Only the former were subject to a specific deadline for clearance and destruction. The Brazilian proposal was therefore intended to address assistance to deal with the remaining mine contamination.

[87] The term mine action was only formally adopted by the UN in 1998, although it had been widely used prior to that time. Canadians serving in Cambodia in the early 1990s are credited with inventing the phrase. See e.g. *A Guide to Mine Action*.

[88] See e.g. *A Study of National Mine Action Legislation* (Geneva: GICHD, forthcoming).

[89] On 17 Aug. 2000, the UN Inter-agency Co-ordination Group for Mine Action agreed that stockpile destruction be formerly incorporated as the fifth core component of mine action. Accordingly, the International Mine Action Standards (IMAS), developed under UN auspices, also deal with stockpile destruction in its IMAS. See IMAS 11.10, 11.20, and 11.30, 2nd edn., 1 Jan. 2003.

[90] See e.g. *The Role of the Military in Mine Action*.

is normally vested in a national mine action authority, which is charged with the regulation, management and coordination of a national mine action programme".'91

## The Type of Assistance to be Provided

6.54 The type of assistance to be provided is not specified, but given the nature of the task—to elaborate a national demining plan—this would most likely include technical advice and assistance, whether through an assessment mission or a longer-term secondment of qualified staff to a mine-affected State, for example within a national mine action centre.

## The Mechanisms for the Provision of Assistance

6.55 The paragraph refers to United Nations, regional organizations, other States Parties or other competent intergovernmental or non-governmental fora as bodies that might be able to respond favourably to a request from a State Party. This does not, of course, preclude a State Party seeking assistance from another source, for example a commercial company.

## Paragraph 8

> 8. Each State Party giving and receiving assistance under the provisions of this Article shall cooperate with a view to ensuring the full and prompt implementation of agreed assistance programs.

6.56 Paragraph 8, which was amended from a proposal at the Oslo Diplomatic Conference by Germany,92 refers, albeit indirectly, to problems which have sometimes been encountered in importing mine clearance equipment. Customs formalities and duties have not been greatly appreciated by donor States, as these have been unnecessarily time-consuming and expensive.

The paragraph does not resolve these issues, though, as it mentions only a general obligation on donor and recipient States Parties to cooperate so as to ensure the 'full and prompt implementation' of agreed assistance programmes.

---

91 *A Guide to Mine Action*, citing IMAS 01.10, 2nd ean., 1 Jan. 2003, 3.
92 APL/CW.23 of 2 Sept. 1997.

# Article 7. Transparency Measures

Article 7—Transparency measures

1. Each State Party shall report to the Secretary-General of the United Nations as soon as practicable, and in any event not later than 180 days after the entry into force of this Convention for that State Party on:

(a) The national implementation measures referred to in Article 9;

(b) The total of all stockpiled anti-personnel mines owned or possessed by it, or under its jurisdiction or control, to include a breakdown of the type, quantity and, if possible, lot numbers of each type of anti-personnel mine stockpiled;

(c) To the extent possible, the location of all mined areas that contain, or are suspected to contain, anti-personnel mines under its jurisdiction or control, to include as much detail as possible regarding the type and quantity of each type of anti-personnel mine in each mined area and when they were emplaced;

(d) The types, quantities and, if possible, lot numbers of all anti-personnel mines retained or transferred for the development of and training in mine detection, mine clearance or mine destruction techniques, or transferred for the purpose of destruction, as well as the institutions authorized by a State Party to retain or transfer anti-personnel mines, in accordance with Article 3;

(e) The status of programs for the conversion or de-commissioning of anti-personnel mine production facilities;

(f) The status of programs for the destruction of anti-personnel mines in accordance with Articles 4 and 5, including details of the methods which will be used in destruction, the location of all destruction sites and the applicable safety and environmental standards to be observed;

(g) The types and quantities of all anti-personnel mines destroyed after the entry into force of this Convention for that State Party, to include a breakdown of the quantity of each type of anti-personnel mine destroyed, in accordance with Articles 4 and 5, respectively, along with, if possible, the lot numbers of each type of anti-personnel mine in the case of destruction in accordance with Article 4;

(h) The technical characteristics of each type of anti-personnel mine produced, to the extent known, and those currently owned or possessed by a State Party, giving, where reasonably possible, such categories of information as may facilitate identification and clearance of anti-personnel mines; at a minimum, this information shall include the dimensions, fusing, explosive content, metallic content, colour photographs and other information which may facilitate mine clearance; and

(i) The measures taken to provide an immediate and effective warning to the population in relation to all areas identified under paragraph 2 of Article 5.

2. The information provided in accordance with this Article shall be updated by the States Parties annually, covering the last calendar year, and reported to the Secretary-General of the United Nations not later than 30 April of each year.

3. The Secretary-General of the United Nations shall transmit all such reports received to the States Parties.

# Introduction

**7.1** Article 7 addresses obligatory transparency measures included in the Anti-Personnel Mine Ban Convention. Transparency measures form part of a typical disarmament treaty verification and compliance package, but were also included in Amended Protocol II to the 1980 Convention on Certain Conventional Weapons. As part of a cooperative package of measures intended to promote implementation, the Anti-Personnel Mine Ban Convention requires each

State Party to submit an initial report to the Secretary-General of the United Nations (UN) within 180 days after becoming party to the Convention,[1] and then to submit annual reports for each calendar year no later than 30 April the following year. According to the President of the Fourth Meeting of States Parties, the reporting obligation under Article 7 represents 'a valuable source of information to both support cooperation and assess progress'.[2] Implementation of the provision should facilitate the planning of national mine action programmes and decisions about resource allocation; accordingly it should also promote confidence among States Parties, funding agencies, and even the public that the Convention is being effectively implemented.

7.2 Each 'Article 7 report' must document national implementation measures, mined areas, stockpiles of anti-personnel mines and the progress of destruction, details of mines retained or transferred for permitted purposes, details of anti-personnel mines produced (to assist in clearance), and measures taken to warn the civilian population in accordance with Article 5(2).[3] The report is received by the UN Department for Disarmament Affairs[4] on behalf of the Secretary-General, and is then made public through its website.[5] Certain information, however, such as technical details provided to facilitate clearance but which could also be used to manufacture anti-personnel mines, will not be uploaded onto the website.

## Paragraph 1

### Article 7—Transparency measures

1. Each State Party shall report to the Secretary-General of the United Nations as soon as practicable, and in any event not later than 180 days after the entry into force of this Convention for that State Party on:

(a)  The national implementation measures referred to in Article 9;

(b)  The total of all stockpiled anti-personnel mines owned or possessed by

---

[1]  The time-limit was reduced from the one-year deadline specified in the Third Austrian Draft of 13 May 1997 (Article 8).

[2]  Statement by Ambassador Jean Lint to the intersessional Standing Committee on the General Status and Operation of the Convention (Geneva, 12 May 2003), 2, available at: www.gichd.ch.

[3]  The non-governmental organization VERTIC (Verification Research, Training and Information Centre) prepared a guide to the preparation of reports in accordance with Article 7 for the Third Meeting of States Parties in Managua, 18–21 Sept. 2001. *Guide to Reporting under Article 7 of the Ottawa Convention*, VERTIC, London, 2001, available at: www.vertic.org.

[4]  Reports should be sent to the Information Systems Officer at the DDA at malinova@un.org.

[5]  disarmament.un.org/MineBan.nsf. The decision to make the reports publicly available and not merely to the other States Parties was made, after discussion, at the First Meeting of States Parties.

it, or under its jurisdiction or control, to include a breakdown of the type, quantity and, if possible, lot numbers of each type of anti-personnel mine stockpiled;

(c) To the extent possible, the location of all mined areas that contain, or are suspected to contain, anti-personnel mines under its jurisdiction or control, to include as much detail as possible regarding the type and quantity of each type of anti-personnel mine in each mined area and when they were emplaced;

(d) The types, quantities and, if possible, lot numbers of all anti-personnel mines retained or transferred for the development of and training in mine detection, mine clearance or mine destruction techniques, or transferred for the purpose of destruction, as well as the institutions authorized by a State Party to retain or transfer anti-personnel mines, in accordance with Article 3;

(e) The status of programs for the conversion or de-commissioning of anti-personnel mine production facilities;

(f) The status of programs for the destruction of anti-personnel mines in accordance with Articles 4 and 5, including details of the methods which will be used in destruction, the location of all destruction sites and the applicable safety and environmental standards to be observed;

(g) The types and quantities of all anti-personnel mines destroyed after the entry into force of this Convention for that State Party, to include a breakdown of the quantity of each type of anti-personnel mine destroyed, in accordance with Articles 4 and 5, respectively, along with, if possible, the lot numbers of each type of anti-personnel mine in the case of destruction in accordance with Article 4;

(h) The technical characteristics of each type of anti-personnel mine produced, to the extent known, and those currently owned or possessed by a State Party, giving, where reasonably possible, such categories of information as may facilitate identification and clearance of anti-personnel mines; at a minimum, this information shall include the dimensions, fusing, explosive content, metallic content, colour photographs and other information which may facilitate mine clearance; and

(i) The measures taken to provide an immediate and effective warning to the population in relation to all areas identified under paragraph 2 of Article 5.

## The Duty to Provide Information

7.3 Each State is therefore required to submit an initial report to the UN Secretary-General within 180 days of becoming a party to the Convention. An Article 7 'contact group', chaired by Belgium, was established in 2000 to promote compliance with this obligation.[6]

---

[6] See e.g. *A Guide to Mine Action*, ch. 5.

7.4 It was reported that as of May 2003, 114 States Parties had submitted their initial Article 7 report.[7] This represented a rate of compliance with the requirements of the paragraph of almost 90 per cent. Thus, only 14 States Parties were late in fulfilling the requirements of Article 7(1). The quality of reporting has been generally of a high standard, with many reports including considerable detail on the required issues.

### The Voluntary Submission of Information

7.5 In addition, a small number of States not party to the Convention have voluntarily submitted Article 7 reports to the depositary. Thus, in May 2003, Ambassador Jean Lint, the President of the Fourth Meeting of States Parties, informed the intersessional Standing Committee on the General Status and Operation of the Convention that: 'It is worth recalling that on 12 March 2003, Poland, a Signatory State, voluntarily submitted an Article 7 report and that Latvia, which has not acceded to the Convention, did the same on 9 May 2003. Other European States, not yet members of the Convention, have also expressed an interest for this transparency measure'.

## The Information to be Provided

### National Implementation Measures

7.6 Article 9 of the Convention requires that States Parties 'take all appropriate legal, administrative and other measures, including the imposition of penal sanctions, to prevent and suppress any activity prohibited to a State Party under this Convention undertaken by persons or on territory under its jurisdiction or control'. The implementation of this obligation demands much more than the adoption of national legislation criminalizing certain acts, encompassing for example administrative and regulatory measures, such as changes in military doctrine and military manuals, although legislation will generally be a key component in a package of measures.[8] Sub-paragraph (a) requires that States Parties report on the national implementation measures referred to in Article 9.

### Anti-Personnel Mine Stockpiles

7.7 Sub-paragraph (b) is intended to facilitate verification of compliance with Article 4 of the Convention, which requires the destruction of all anti-personnel mines a State owns or possesses or that are under its jurisdiction or control within

---

[7] Statement by Ambassador Jean Lint on Article 7 reporting to the intersessional Standing Committee on the General Status and Operation of the Convention (Geneva, 16 May 2003), 2, available at: www.gichd.ch.

[8] See below the commentary on this provision for a detailed discussion of this obligation.

four years of becoming party to the Convention. Under sub-paragraph (b), States Parties are required to declare the total of all stockpiled anti-personnel mines they own or possess, or that are under its jurisdiction or control. The report should include a breakdown of the type and quantity and, if possible, lot numbers of each type of anti-personnel mine stockpiled.[9]

7.8 In a small number of cases, States Parties deliberately did not include all required information within their report on stockpiles. Thus, for example, with respect to US stockpiles of anti-personnel mines under Norwegian jurisdiction and control, and in accordance with an agreement between the Norwegian Foreign Minister and the US Secretary of State, Norway's Article 7 report on its stockpiles did not include any reference to the number of mines held on behalf of the USA.[10] Norway's report simply states: 'There are pre-stocked U.S. mines on Norwegian territory. Due to previously concluded agreements, information on pre-stocked military material is not available for reporting'.

## Anti-Personnel Mines in Mined Areas

7.9 Sub-paragraph (c) requires States Parties 'to the extent possible'[11] to report the location of all mined areas that contain, or are suspected to contain, anti-personnel mines under its jurisdiction or control.[12] The report is to include 'as much detail as possible regarding the type and quantity of each type of anti-personnel mine in each mined area and when they were emplaced'.

7.10 A number of States still suspected of being contaminated by anti-personnel mines emplaced many decades ago, such as Belgium, which has considerable unexploded ordnance remaining from the 1914–18 and 1939–45 wars, have chosen to declare themselves mine-free.[13] According to

[9] This requirement for specific detail was added at the Oslo Diplomatic Conference, despite concerns by some States that it might impose an unreasonable burden on mine-affected States.

[10] The USA asked NATO nations to allow stockpiling of anti-personnel mines until 2003 and mixed systems including anti-personnel mines indefinitely. Myers, L., 'US Seeks to Keep Landmines', *Philadelphia Inquirer* (1 Mar. 1998), see also 'NATO Treads Carefully on Touchy Landmines Issue', *Reuters* (Brussels, 16 Dec. 1997). It was reported that the United States threatened to remove its military equipment from the country if Norway insisted on the United States removing all its mines. See e.g. 'New U.S. European Commander to Visit Norway', *Agence France Presse* (Oslo, 5 Dec. 1997).

[11] This phrase was added in during the Oslo Diplomatic Conference, following a suggestion by Honduras during the 1997 Brussels Conference, on the basis that there might be situations in which the government was not aware of the existence of particular minefields.

[12] The reference to jurisdiction or control is therefore to the anti-personnel mines rather than the mined areas, in contrast to the provision in Article 5(1), although this is likely to make little practical difference.

[13] See Form C, Article 7 Report by Belgium for calendar year 2002, submitted on 30 Apr. 2003, available at: disarmament.un.org/MineBan.nsf.

France, 'any mined areas on French territory that may remain from the 1914–1918 and 1939–1945 world wars, are not included in this report'.[14]

## *Anti-Personnel Mines Retained under Article 3*

7.11 Under Article 3(1) of the Convention, a State Party is permitted to retain or transfer 'a number of anti-personnel mines for the development of and training in mine detection, mine clearance, or mine destruction techniques', as long as the number does not exceed the minimum number absolutely necessary for those purposes. Article 3(2) allows a State Party to transfer an unlimited number of anti-personnel mines for the purpose of destruction.

7.12 Each State Party must report on the types, quantities and, 'if possible', lot numbers of such anti-personnel mines it retains or transfers, as well as the institutions authorized by a State Party to retain or transfer anti-personnel mines.

## *The Conversion or De-Commissioning of Production Facilities*

7.13 Under Article 1(1)(b), each State Party undertakes never under any circumstances to produce anti-personnel mines.[15] Despite a proposal by the Ivory Coast, however, States Parties are not explicitly required to decommission or destroy any existing production facilities.[16] None the less, such an obligation can be implied from the requirement in Article 7(1)(e) to report on the status of programmes for the conversion or de-commissioning of anti-personnel mine production facilities.

## *The Status of Anti-Personnel Mine Destruction Programmes*

7.14 States Parties are obliged to destroy both stockpiled[17] and emplaced[18] anti-personnel mines within certain deadlines. Typically, anti-personnel mines in mined areas will either be destroyed *in situ*, or together with other mines or munitions at the end of each working day. Stockpiles are more likely to be destroyed in a more planned and systematic process. Sub-paragraph (f) requires States Parties to report generally on the status of destruction programmes in accordance with Articles 4 and 5 of the Convention, and to include in the report details of the destruction methods, the location of all destruction sites, and the applicable safety and environmental standards to be observed.[19]

---

[14] 'D'éventuelles zones minées issues des conflits mondiaux 1914–1918 et 1939–1945, qui pourraient subsister sur le territoire français ne sont pas prises en compte dans ce rapport'. Author's translation of information noted in Form C, Article 7 Report by France for calendar year 2002, submitted on 30 Apr. 2003, available at: disarmament.un.org/MineBan.nsf.

[15] See paras. 1.34–1.35 above.          [16] See para. 1.85 above.

[17] See above the commentary on Article 4.          [18] See above the commentary on Article 5.

[19] This phrase was added following comments by France at the 1997 Bonn Conference as well as the options paper on compliance submitted by Germany in connection with that conference.

**7.15** The Convention does not lay down any specific destruction methods or safety and environmental standards to be observed,[20] although, as the Geneva International Centre for Humanitarian Demining (GICHD) has noted: 'Concerns have been expressed as to the environmental consequences of destroying certain mines by open detonation, both by the State holding the stockpiles and also potential donors, which may fall foul of national or international environmental legislation and guidelines'.[21] Thus, for instance, the GICHD notes[22] that the NATO Maintenance and Supply Agency (NAMSA), which has supported stockpile destruction in a number of countries, including Albania, Moldova, and the Ukraine, will not award contracts for stockpile destruction by open detonation.

## Progress in Anti-Personnel Mine Destruction

**7.16** Sub-paragraph (g) continues the requirements contained in (f) above, this time requiring States Parties to report on the progress in destruction programmes. The report must include the types and quantities of all anti-personnel mines destroyed after a State has become a party to the Convention. In the case of the destruction of stockpiles in accordance with Article 4, States Parties should, if possible, detail the lot numbers of each type of anti-personnel mine destroyed.

## Characteristics of Anti-Personnel Mines Produced

**7.17** Under sub-paragraph (h), States Parties must report on the technical characteristics of each type of anti-personnel mine produced by it in the past 'to the extent known', as well as those it currently owns or possesses, giving 'where reasonably possible' all categories of information that 'may facilitate identification and clearance of anti-personnel mines'. This must include, 'at a minimum', the 'dimensions, fusing, explosive content, metallic content, colour photographs and other information which may facilitate mine clearance'. For States Parties with major producers of anti-personnel mines on its territory, considerable efforts may be required to fulfil this obligation.

## Warning Measures

**7.18** Although States Parties are not specifically required to undertake mine awareness programmes for the benefit of the civilian population affected by

---

[20] This omission contrasts with Article II of the 1972 Biological Weapons Convention dealing with destruction of biological weapons or toxins, which states *inter alia* that: 'In implementing the provisions of this article, all necessary safety precautions shall be observed to protect populations and the environment'.    [21] *A Guide to Mine Action*, Ch. 9.
[22] ibid.

anti-personnel mines[23] (or, indeed, the military), sub-paragraph (i) implies that they should provide 'an immediate and effective warning' on the basis of confirmed or suspected mined areas containing anti-personnel mines.

## Voluntary Reporting

**7.19** In order to provide States Parties with the opportunity to report voluntarily on matters pertaining to compliance and implementation not covered by the formal reporting requirements contained in Article 7, it was recommended at the Second Meeting of States Parties that the Article 7 reporting format be amended to include an additional form J entitled 'Other relevant matters'.[24] It was further recommended that States Parties consider using this form to report on activities undertaken with respect to Article 6, in particular to report on assistance provided for the care and rehabilitation, and social and economic reintegration, of mine victims.[25]

## Other Issues

**7.20** Although States Parties are not required to provide such information, the ICBL has encouraged Article 7 reporting on the measures taken to ensure that Claymore-type devices are not used in tripwire-mode,[26] which is prohibited by the Convention. Sweden, for example, has voluntarily done so.[27] Landmine Monitor has reported that 20 States Parties 'are known to be retaining operational stocks of Claymore-type mines'.[28]

**7.21** The ICBL has also called for States Parties to report on intended purposes and actual uses of mines retained under Article 3 (the ICBL notes that about a dozen States have done so), and foreign stockpiles of anti-personnel mines. In May 2003, it commended Tajikistan for having done so, with respect to Russian anti-personnel mines stockpiled on its territory.[29]

---

[23]  See para. 6.26 above.

[24]  President's Paper on Amending the Article 7 Reporting Format, Annex III to Final Report of the Second Meeting of the States Parties to the Anti-Personnel Mine Ban Convention, Doc. APLC/MSP.2/2000/1 (18 Sept. 2000), 2, available at: www.gichd.ch.

[25]  ibid. Prior to the Oslo Diplomatic Conference, the NGO, Landmine Survivors Network, had proposed that States be required to report on the status of programmes for medical care, physical rehabilitation, and socio-economic reintegration of mine victims. The proposal did not draw widespread support due to the administrative onus it would have required.

[26]  See e.g. Intervention on Article 7 by Stephen Goose, Head of ICRC Delegation, to the Standing Committee on General Status and Operation of the Convention (Geneva, 16 May 2003), available at: www.gichd.ch.

[27]  See Article 7 report by Sweden for the period 1 Apr. 2001–1 Apr. 2002, submitted on 25 Apr. 2002, available at: disarmament.un.org/MineBan.nsf.

[28]  Human Rights Watch, 'Claymore-Type Mines', Landmine Monitor Fact Sheet (Geneva, 7 Feb. 2003), 1.                                                                  [29]  ibid.

## The Mechanism for Submitting Information

7.22 In May 1999, at the First Meeting of States Parties in Maputo, Austria proposed a standard format for Article 7 reports.[30] This follows the order of the sub-paragraphs as set out in Article 7(1) of the Convention. As discussed above,[31] this format was further refined at the Second Meeting of States Parties in Geneva in September 2000. A copy of the current format is included in Appendix 7 to this commentary.[32]

7.23 Article 7 reports may be submitted in any UN language, and, for reasons of cost, are not subsequently translated by the UN Secretariat. The UN Department for Disarmament Affairs has stressed the importance of providing it with an electronic copy of the report to expedite its inclusion on their website.[33]

## Paragraph 2

2. The information provided in accordance with this Article shall be updated by the States Parties annually, covering the last calendar year, and reported to the Secretary-General of the United Nations not later than 30 April of each year.

7.24 Thus, each State Party is required to update its Article 7 reports to cover the last calendar year. They are given until 30 April of the following year to submit the updated annual report to the UN Secretary-General. According to Human Rights Watch, at the beginning of May 2002, 12 States Parties had failed to submit an annual update for calendar years 2000 and 2001.[34]

## Paragraph 3

3. The Secretary-General of the United Nations shall transmit all such reports received to the States Parties.

[30] See 'Reporting Formats for Article 7', Annex II to Final Report of the First Meeting of the States Parties to the Anti-Personnel Mine Ban Convention, Doc. APLC/MSP.1/1999/1 of 20 May 1999, available at: www.gichd.ch/docs/minebantreaty/index_1msp.htm.

[31] See para. 7.19 above.

[32] The form in the various UN languages can be downloaded from the website of the Department for Disarmament Affairs, at: disarmament.un.org/MineBan.nsf.

[33] Oral remarks to the intersessional Standing Committee on the General Status and Operation of the Convention (Geneva, 16 May 2003). See e.g. ICBL, 'Intersessional Daily Update 5' (29 May 2003), available at: www.icbl.org.

[34] Andorra, Antigua and Barbuda, Belize, Bolivia, Fiji, Guatemala, Jamaica, Lesotho, the Former Yugoslav Republic of Macedonia, Saint Kitts and Nevis, Swaziland, and Tunisia. Information provided by Mark Hiznay, Human Rights Watch, in email communication of 3 May 2002.

**7.25** The Secretary-General of the UN is requested to transmit all reports received to the States Parties. This is done by posting them on a website of the Department for Disarmament Affairs, where they are also available to the public. To save time and money (and trees!), hard copies are not distributed to all States Parties.

# Article 8.  Facilitation and Clarification of Compliance

Article 8—Facilitation and clarification of compliance

1. The States Parties agree to consult and cooperate with each other regarding the implementation of the provisions of this Convention, and to work together in a spirit of cooperation to facilitate compliance by States Parties with their obligations under this Convention.

2. If one or more States Parties wish to clarify and seek to resolve questions relating to compliance with the provisions of this Convention by another State Party, it may submit, through the Secretary-General of the United Nations, a Request for Clarification of that matter to that State Party. Such a request shall be accompanied by all appropriate information. Each State Party shall refrain from unfounded Requests for Clarification, care being taken to avoid abuse. A State Party that receives a Request for Clarification shall provide, through the Secretary-General of the United Nations, within 28 days to the requesting State Party all information which would assist in clarifying this matter.

3. If the requesting State Party does not receive a response through the Secretary-General of the United Nations within that time period, or deems the response to the Request for Clarification to be unsatisfactory, it may submit the matter through the Secretary-General of the United Nations to the next Meeting of the States Parties. The Secretary-General of the United Nations shall transmit the submission, accompanied by all appropriate information pertaining to the Request for Clarification, to all States Parties. All such information shall be presented to the requested State Party which shall have the right to respond.

4. Pending the convening of any meeting of the States Parties, any of the States Parties concerned may request the Secretary-General of the United Nations to exercise his or her good offices to facilitate the clarification requested.

5. The requesting State Party may propose through the Secretary-General of the United Nations the convening of a Special Meeting of the States Parties to consider the matter. The Secretary-General of the United Nations shall thereupon communicate this proposal and all information submitted by the States Parties concerned, to all States Parties with a request that they indicate whether they favour a Special Meeting of the States Parties, for the purpose of considering the matter. In the event that within 14 days from the date of such communication, at least one-third of the States Parties favours

such a Special Meeting, the Secretary-General of the United Nations shall convene this Special Meeting of the States Parties within a further 14 days. A quorum for this Meeting shall consist of a majority of States Parties.

6. The Meeting of the States Parties or the Special Meeting of the States Parties, as the case may be, shall first determine whether to consider the matter further, taking into account all information submitted by the States Parties concerned. The Meeting of the States Parties or the Special Meeting of the States Parties shall make every effort to reach a decision by consensus. If despite all efforts to that end no agreement has been reached, it shall take this decision by a majority of States Parties present and voting.

7. All States Parties shall cooperate fully with the Meeting of the States Parties or the Special Meeting of the States Parties in the fulfilment of its review of the matter, including any fact-finding missions that are authorized in accordance with paragraph 8.

8. If further clarification is required, the Meeting of the States Parties or the Special Meeting of the States Parties shall authorize a fact-finding mission and decide on its mandate by a majority of States Parties present and voting. At any time the requested State Party may invite a fact-finding mission to its territory. Such a mission shall take place without a decision by a Meeting of the States Parties or a Special Meeting of the States Parties to authorize such a mission. The mission, consisting of up to 9 experts, designated and approved in accordance with paragraphs 9 and 10, may collect additional information on the spot or in other places directly related to the alleged compliance issue under the jurisdiction or control of the requested State Party.

9. The Secretary-General of the United Nations shall prepare and update a list of the names, nationalities and other relevant data of qualified experts provided by States Parties and communicate it to all States Parties. Any expert included on this list shall be regarded as designated for all fact-finding missions unless a State Party declares its non-acceptance in writing. In the event of non-acceptance, the expert shall not participate in fact-finding missions on the territory or any other place under the jurisdiction or control of the objecting State Party, if the non-acceptance was declared prior to the appointment of the expert to such missions.

10. Upon receiving a request from the Meeting of the States Parties or a Special Meeting of the States Parties, the Secretary-General of the United Nations shall, after consultations with the requested State Party, appoint the members of the mission, including its leader. Nationals of States Parties requesting the fact-finding mission or directly affected by it shall not be appointed to the mission. The members of the fact-finding mission shall enjoy privileges and immunities under Article VI of the Convention on the Privileges and Immunities of the United Nations, adopted on 13 February 1946.

11. Upon at least 72 hours notice, the members of the fact-finding mission shall arrive in the territory of the requested State Party at the earliest opportunity. The requested State Party shall take the necessary administrative measures to receive, transport and accommodate the mission, and shall be responsible for ensuring the security of the mission to the maximum extent possible while they are on territory under its control.

12. Without prejudice to the sovereignty of the requested State Party, the fact-finding mission may bring into the territory of the requested State Party the necessary equipment which shall be used exclusively for gathering information on the alleged compliance issue. Prior to its arrival, the mission will advise the requested State Party of the equipment that it intends to utilize in the course of its fact-finding mission.

13. The requested State Party shall make all efforts to ensure that the fact-finding mission is given the opportunity to speak with all relevant persons who may be able to provide information related to the alleged compliance issue.

14. The requested State Party shall grant access for the fact-finding mission to all areas and installations under its control where facts relevant to the compliance issue could be expected to be collected. This shall be subject to any arrangements that the requested State Party considers necessary for:

(a) The protection of sensitive equipment, information and areas;

(b) The protection of any constitutional obligations the requested State Party may have with regard to proprietary rights, searches and seizures, or other constitutional rights; or

(c) The physical protection and safety of the members of the fact-finding mission.

In the event that the requested State Party makes such arrangements, it shall make every reasonable effort to demonstrate through alternative means its compliance with this Convention.

15. The fact-finding mission may remain in the territory of the State Party concerned for no more than 14 days, and at any particular site no more than 7 days, unless otherwise agreed.

16. All information provided in confidence and not related to the subject matter of the fact-finding mission shall be treated on a confidential basis.

17. The fact-finding mission shall report, through the Secretary-General of the United Nations, to the Meeting of the States Parties or the Special Meeting of the States Parties the results of its findings.

18. The Meeting of the States Parties or the Special Meeting of the States Parties shall consider all relevant information, including the report

submitted by the fact-finding mission, and may request the requested State Party to take measures to address the compliance issue within a specified period of time. The requested State Party shall report on all measures taken in response to this request.

19. The Meeting of the States Parties or the Special Meeting of the States Parties may suggest to the States Parties concerned ways and means to further clarify or resolve the matter under consideration, including the initiation of appropriate procedures in conformity with international law. In circumstances where the issue at hand is determined to be due to circumstances beyond the control of the requested State Party, the Meeting of the States Parties or the Special Meeting of the States Parties may recommend appropriate measures, including the use of cooperative measures referred to in Article 6.

20. The Meeting of the States Parties or the Special Meeting of the States Parties shall make every effort to reach its decisions referred to in paragraphs 18 and 19 by consensus, otherwise by a two-thirds majority of States Parties present and voting.

# Introduction

**8.1** Article 8, which provides a mechanism for the 'facilitation and clarification of compliance', was one of the hardest provisions to agree on as the negotiating positions of certain States on the twin issues of verification and compliance were often far apart. The divide, which at times appeared like a chasm,[1] crystallized at the Oslo Diplomatic Conference, with positions polarized between Germany and Mexico in particular, but was a subject of contention throughout the negotiations. The outcome represents a compromise between the intrusive verification measures typical of disarmament treaties[2] and the relatively light model traditionally favoured by international humanitarian law.[3]

**8.2** Indeed, the end result of the negotiations allowed both 'camps' to claim victory. There is provision for fact-finding without consent (a key objective of

---

[1] Those who opposed intrusive verification measures were motivated not only by ideology and philosophy but also by politics and pragmatism. Thus, although there was a view that extensive verification was neither necessary nor appropriate to the treaty, there was also a concern that the issue of verification might be used and abused by certain States that wished to see a total prohibition on anti-personnel mines watered down. There was also a fear on the part of some, which subsequently appears to have been overblown, that verification would deter adherence to the Convention.

[2] A number of States considered verification essential to the credibility of the Convention. According to the German Federal Minister of Foreign Affairs, for instance, 'experience has shown that an agreement without verification can be easily broken. Doubt and mistrust are the consequences. Verification, on the other hand, creates transparency and trust. For this reason simple, effective control measures should be incorporated into the banning agreement. This applies to the production, storage, transfer and destruction or clearing of mines'. Speech of Dr Klaus Kinkel to the opening of the International Meeting of Experts on Verification Issues regarding an International Agreement to Ban Anti-Personnel Mines (Königswinter, 24 Apr. 1997), 4.

[3] Switzerland, for instance, argued that the Convention would be 'primarily an instrument of international humanitarian law. Any provisions on compliance should be adapted to the nature of the treaty . . . In the framework of the Ottawa Process, it has been agreed up to now that the new Convention must be lean and simple. *Therefore*, one should avoid the introduction of a sophisticated intrusive mechanism, which would unduly complicate the Convention'. Switzerland, 'International Convention for Total Ban of Antipersonnel Mines, Provisions on Compliance', *Working Paper*, distributed at the Expert Meeting on Possible Verification Measures for a Convention to Ban Anti-Personnel Landmines (Bonn, 24–5 Apr. 1997).

Germany and its supporters), but no easy path to it, and certainly no challenge inspections.

## The Negotiation of the Provision

8.3 The issue of verification and compliance was addressed from the outset of the negotiations. Thus, the first Austrian draft text had two articles dealing with compliance. Article 6 was entitled 'Compliance with the Convention', and Article 7 was entitled 'Verification of Compliance'.[4] As set out below, the latter included provision for challenge inspections 'in the case of serious doubts about compliance'.

### Article 6
#### Compliance with the Convention

1. Each High Contracting Party shall take all appropriate legal and other measures, including the imposition of penal sanctions to prevent and suppress breaches of this Convention by persons or on territory under its jurisdiction or control.

2. The provisions of the Geneva Conventions of 12 August 1949 relating to measures for the repression of breaches and grave breaches shall apply to breaches and grave breaches of this Convention. Any act or omission occurring during armed conflict in violation of this Convention, if committed wilfully or wantonly and causing death or serious injury, shall be treated as a grave breach.

3. The High Contracting Parties undertake to consult each other and to cooperate with each other to resolve any problems that may arise with regard to the implementation and application of the provisions of this Article.

### Article 7
#### Verification of Compliance

*Notifications*

1. Each High Contracting Party shall notify to the Depositary within 60 days after the individual entering into force of this Convention:

(a) all anti-personnel mines under its control, be it either in stockpile or employed.

This notification shall contain complete information about number, type, use, maps of areas of deployment (Minefields or mined areas), type of fuse, lifetime and other relevant information;

---

[4] Thus, the original draft of the Convention first set out national implementation measures (Article 6) and then measures for international verification (Article 7). At least one leading authority on the Convention regrets that in the treaty as adopted, this order is reversed, giving apparent primacy to concerns about compliance over the obligation at national level to implement the Convention.

(b) its general plan for clearing and destroying deployed anti-personnel mines.

These notifications shall be updated by the HCP on an annual basis until all anti-personnel mines have been destroyed.

*Challenge inspections*

2. In the case of serious doubts about compliance each High Contracting Party has the right to request an on-site challenge inspection of any facility or location in the territory or in any other place under the jurisdiction or control of any other High Contracting Party for the sole purpose of clarifying and resolving any questions concerning possible non-compliance with the provisions of this Convention.

Such a request, accompanied by evidence, shall be addressed to a Board of Eminent Experts, appointed by the Secretary-General of the United Nations, for immediate processing.

If the Board of Eminent Experts considers the request not to be frivolous, abusive or clearly beyond the scope of this Convention and the evidence sufficient, it may decide not later than 24 hours after having received the inspection request to order an inspection in the framework of a clear mandate.

Such an inspection will be made by an inspection team nominated by the Board of Eminent Experts and under its responsibility.

The inspected State, which has the right to demonstrate its compliance, shall assist the inspection team throughout the challenge inspection and facilitate its task. The report of the Board of Eminent Experts on the result of the inspection shall be addressed via the Secretary-General of the United Nations to all High Contracting Parties and shall, in the case of abuse, contain recommendations on appropriate measures to redress the situation.

The inspection will be financed by the requesting High Contracting Party. If, however, the non-compliance with the Convention is established in the report of the Board of Eminent Experts, then the inspected High Contracting Party shall refund the cost of the inspection.

**8.4** The ICBL, in its proposed treaty text of 20 December 1996, included provisions for reporting and transparency, national implementation, consultation and fact-finding, including an Annex on Fact-finding regarding use or transfer of anti-personnel mines,[5] which were clearly one of the sources of inspiration for much of what would ultimately be adopted in Articles 7, 8, and 9 of the Anti-Personnel Mine Ban Convention.[6]

---

[5] Draft Articles 7, 8, and 9, Convention on the Prohibition of the Development, Production, Stockpiling, Transfer and Use of Anti-Personnel Mines and on their Destruction, Proposal by the International Campaign to Ban Landmines, ICBL (20 Dec. 1996). See Appendix 4 for a copy of the text.

[6] The ICBL draft Article 10, however, which dealt with the consequences of violations, went beyond what would be acceptable to States Parties.

**8.5** Interventions by States at the 1997 Vienna Conference, however, made it obvious that the issue of verification and compliance would be 'potentially the most difficult one and would require further and deeper consideration'.[7] At the Conference, the ICRC suggested that the best method would be to set up an independent mechanism to investigate credible reports of the use of anti-personnel mines following the entry into force of the new treaty, although it cautioned against allowing the issue to stand in the way of a clear norm prohibiting anti-personnel mines. It reminded States that although earlier norms of humanitarian law prohibiting the use of specific weapons had been enacted without provisions on verification, this had not prevented them from being very largely respected.[8]

**8.6** Not all governments were convinced, though, and Germany, a long-time enthusiast of verification, offered to host a meeting devoted to the issue.[9] In the Second Austrian Draft, a footnote was added to the effect that the draft provisions on verification, which were unchanged from those in the first draft, would be reviewed following a conference dedicated to the issue, to be held in Bonn in April 1997.

**8.7** The International Expert Meeting on Possible Verification Measures to Ban Anti-Personnel Landmines, the second formal follow-up gathering to the 1996 Ottawa Conference, was held in Bonn on 24–5 April 1997. In advance of the meeting, Germany circulated an 'Options Paper for a possible verification scheme for a convention to ban anti-personnel landmines', which implied a desire to see significant and intrusive verification measures common in disarmament treaties.[10] During the conference, Canada put forward proposals for a 'Cooperative Implementation Commission' to be composed of a small, representative group of experts to facilitate the implementation of the future Convention and to review compliance by States Parties with their treaty obligations.[11] Although there was interest in the collaborative aspect of the proposal, its substance received relatively scant support from within the Core Group.

**8.8** As noted above, the Second Draft of the Convention did not include a provision on grave breaches, a potentially significant tool in the implementation of international humanitarian law. At the Bonn Conference, the ICRC had

---

[7] Hajnoczi, T., Desch, T., and Chatsis, D., 'The Ban Treaty', in Cameron *et al.*, *To Walk without Fear*, 301.     [8] Statement of the ICRC to the Vienna Expert Meeting (12 Feb. 1997).

[9] This is said in some quarters to have been the quid pro quo for its leaving the 'hard core' of States opposed to a fast-track negotiation of a total ban treaty and joining the Ottawa Process.

[10] Yet, even Germany understood that there were limits to the extent of verification that would be acceptable and achievable, especially given the tight deadlines of the process.

[11] Canada, 'International Agreement to ban Anti-Personnel (AP) Mines: Compliance Issues', unpublished document, undated, but 1997.

circulated an informal draft article on national implementation measures. Central to this draft was the following proposed provision:

Each State Party shall search for all persons on its territory or under its jurisdiction or control, being nationals of a State party to this Convention, alleged to have used, or to have ordered the use of, anti-personnel mines, in violation of this Convention, regardless of the place where such acts were committed, and shall either bring such persons before its own courts or hand such persons over for trial to another State Party.

**8.9** A total of 121 States were represented at the Bonn Conference, and views were divided, as they had been in Vienna two months previously, between States who believed that detailed verification was essential to ensure that any agreement was effective,[12] and others that argued that the proposed agreement was essentially humanitarian in character, stressing the overriding importance of a clear norm prohibiting anti-personnel mines.[13] Diplomats intimately involved in the negotiation of the Convention noted afterwards that:

While some progress was achieved, no convergence of minds was in sight. Having dodged this controversial issue in the second version, the final Austrian draft had to find a viable middle ground. After numerous consultations, Austria presented a compromise solution that did not satisfy any side fully, but was conceptually acceptable for everyone.[14]

**8.10** The summary of the meeting, however, prepared by Germany, was more upbeat:

During the debate some support began to emerge for a middle course combining comprehensive cooperation and transparency measures with the possibility of effective fact-finding. Important areas of a future convention—production, export, use, destruction of stockpiles and the treatment of minefields—may require differentiated verification measures. Routine inspections were given little chance of realization in statements at the conference.[15]

---

[12] Australia, France, Italy, the UK, and the USA, although the USA warned against imposing unrealistic standards which might block conclusion of an agreement.

[13] Austria, Belgium, Canada, Ireland, Mexico, Norway, the Netherlands, South Africa, and Switzerland. This was also the position of the ICRC. For its part, the ICBL had changed the position it had held during the negotiation of Amended Protocol II. It now maintained that extensive verification was not crucial to the treaty and should not be used as a pretext to weaken the scope of a total ban.

[14] Hajnoczi *et al.*, 'The Ban Treaty', in Cameron *et al.*, *To Walk without Fear*, 301. Ambassador Molander of Sweden, on the other hand, complained subsequently that the Anti-Personnel Mine Ban Convention 'contains provisions on verification which make an unusual combination of total intrusiveness in principle and considerable weakness in practice'. Molander, J., 'Foreword' to Maresca and Maslen, *The Banning of Anti-Personnel Landmines*, p. xxv.

[15] 'Summary', International Meeting of Experts on Verification Issues regarding an International Agreement to Ban Anti-Personnel Mines (Königswinter, 24 Apr. 1997).

**8.11** None the less, the significant difficulties—and divergences of opinion—that remained, became evident in the elaboration of the relevant text for the Third Austrian Draft. As it had with its Second Draft, Austria circulated its proposed text first to the core group for comment. In the case of the article on facilitation and clarification of compliance, the provision read as follows:

Article 9
Facilitation and clarification of compliance

1. The States Parties agree to establish at the First Meeting of the States Parties a Commission of Experts to facilitate the implementation of the provisions of this Convention by States Parties and to review compliance by the States Parties with their obligations under this Convention.

2. The Commission is to be comprised of 15 experts of high moral standing and acknowledged impartiality, elected by the Meeting of the States Parties for a tenure of five years based on equitable geographic distribution. The members of the Commission shall serve in their personal capacity. Outgoing members may be re-elected for one immediate consecutive term. The Meeting of the States Parties shall adopt the Rules of Procedure of the Commission. The Commission shall elect its own President, Vice-President and Rapporteur in accordance with the Rules of Procedure.

3. The Commission shall, unless it decides otherwise, meet twice a year. The Depositary shall arrange for and service the meetings of the Commission. The costs of the Commission shall be borne by the States Parties in accordance with the United Nations scale of assessment adjusted appropriately.

4. All States Parties shall cooperate fully with the Commission in the fulfilment of its tasks.

5. The Commission shall:

(a) consider ways and means of facilitating the compliance by States Parties with their obligations under this Convention, taking into account, inter alia, Article 7;

(b) receive and review any submission to the Depositary made by a State Party or States Parties regarding non-compliance with this Convention.

6. If one or more States Parties wish to clarify and seek to resolve questions relating to compliance with the provisions of this Convention by another State Party, it may submit through the Depositary, a Request for Clarification of that matter to that State Party. Such a request shall be accompanied by all relevant information. A State Party that receives a Request for Clarification shall provide through the Depositary, within 30 days at the latest, to the requesting State Party all information necessary which will assist in clarifying this matter.

7. If the requesting State Party does not receive a response through the Depositary within the time-span provided for in paragraph 6, or deems the response to the Request for Clarification to be unsatisfactory, it may submit, through the Depositary, the matter to the Commission. This submission shall include all relevant information. The Commission shall consider the matter within one month after having received the submission.

8. The Commission may request additional information from any State party on matters under consideration. A State Party that receives such a request shall provide to the Commission, within 30 days at the latest, the information requested.

9. If the Commission concludes that further information is required to clarify the matter, the Commission may undertake a fact-finding mission to collect additional information on the spot or in other places directly related to this matter under the jurisdiction or control of the State Party concerned.

10. The Commission shall report through the Depositary the results of its findings, in accordance with the provisions of this Article, including any recommendations it considers appropriate in order to facilitate compliance with this Convention, to the State Party or States Parties concerned and to the Meeting of the States Parties.

**8.12** The reaction from the Core Group was less than enthusiastic. Norway, in particular, was critical of the Austrian proposals, which it felt had 'now departed considerably from the concept originally agreed upon, according to which the Convention was to put emphasis on humanitarian objectives and take its provisions concerning compliance primarily from international humanitarian law. The proposed wording of Article 9 also seems to conflict with what we perceived to be a growing convergence during the Bonn meeting on this issue, namely that transparency and confidence building measures, rather than intrusive and extensive verification regime in the traditional sense, should be the key elements of the Convention'.[16]

**8.13** Norway proposed the deletion of any reference to a commission of experts and fact-finding, and to concentrate on establishing the right of States Parties to request clarification on possible non-compliance.[17] It also rejected the idea of a cooperative implementation commission, along the lines of the Canadian proposal, on the basis that it was not convinced that it 'would be particularly helpful in promoting cooperation and assistance' but rather 'an extra bureaucratic burden'.[18] It supported Switzerland's view that 'to entrust the regular Meetings of the States Parties . . . with tasks pertaining to transparency, facilitation and compliance would be a more cost-effective and practicable solution. This would also be tactically more useful'.[19]

**8.14** After taking other soundings from Core Group members, Austria redrafted the article significantly, removing any reference to a commission of experts, but retaining the option of a fact-finding mission. It then circulated the Second Austrian Draft to States with draft Article 9 as set out below. The fundamental basis of the final agreement on what would become Article 8 was

---

[16]  Fax from Royal Ministry of Foreign Affairs, Oslo, to Thomas Hajnoczi (10 May 1997), 1–2.
[17]  ibid. 3.         [18]  ibid.         [19]  ibid.

now in place. The details of the article, however, would only be finally resolved in the first week of the Oslo Diplomatic Conference.

Article 9
Facilitation and clarification of compliance

1. The States Parties agree to consult and cooperate with each other regarding the implementation of the provisions of this Convention, and to facilitate compliance by States Parties with their obligations under this Convention.

2. If one or more States Parties wish to clarify and seek to resolve questions relating to compliance with the provisions of this Convention by another State Party, it may submit, through the Depositary, a Request for Clarification of that matter to that State Party. Such a request shall be accompanied by all relevant information. A State Party that receives a Request for Clarification shall provide through the Depositary, within 30 days to the requesting State Party all information which would assist in clarifying this matter.

3. If the requesting State Party does not receive a response through the Depositary within the time period provided for in paragraph 2, or deems the response to the Request for Clarification to be unsatisfactory, it may submit, through the Depositary, the matter to a Meeting of the State Parties. This submission shall include all relevant information. The Meeting of State Parties shall consider the matter at its next meeting.

4. The requesting State Party may propose to the Depositary to convene a special Meeting of the States Parties to consider the matter. The Depositary shall thereupon communicate this proposal to the States Parties with a request that they indicate whether they favour a Special Meeting of the States Parties, for the purpose of considering the matter. In the event that within 30 days from the date of such communication at least one third of the States Parties favour such a special Meeting, the Depositary shall convene this Special Meeting of the States Parties.

5. All States Parties shall cooperate fully with the Meeting of States Parties in the fulfilment of its review of the matter.

6. The Meeting of States Parties may request additional information from a State Party on matters under its consideration. If it concludes that it is necessary, the Meeting of States Parties may authorize a fact-finding mission to collect additional information on the spot or in other places directly related to the alleged compliance issue under the jurisdiction or control of the concerned State Party.

7. The fact-finding mission shall report, through the Depositary, to the States Parties and the Meeting of the States Parties the results of its findings, including any recommendations it considers appropriate in order to facilitate compliance with this Convention.

**8.15** The Austrian text did not satisfy either side of the debate. France and Germany wanted a more 'effective' system, that is, one that was more intrusive and time-sensitive. Others within the core group, such as Mexico, Norway, and South Africa, did not want any type of compulsory fact-finding as they feared it would delay, if not impede, negotiations on the Convention, and in any event, was not appropriate for the context.

**8.16** Accordingly, in the time between the issuing of the Third Austrian Draft and the Oslo Diplomatic Conference, informal negotiations were ongoing, in particular between Germany and Mexico. Germany, which had already accepted privately that there was insufficient support for more general inspections, proposed more detail on procedural and voting matters, including a one-third minority vote for an enquiry[20] and included an annex outlining the procedures to be used for on-site inspections.[21] Mexico put forward a variant of the Third Austrian Draft in which the threshold for authorizing a fact-finding mission would be higher (two-thirds of the States Parties present and voting) and visits would only take place with the consent of the interested States Parties.[22] To complicate matters further, the USA, which had decided to join the Ottawa Process in August 1997, made strengthening the verification regime in the Convention one of its five 'red lines'—preconditions for its future signature of the Convention. Indeed, it is probably the only one of these five areas of concern where it could feel that its efforts had resulted in any success.

**8.17** It is generally agreed by the key actors that the turning point of the negotiations on Article 8 occurred during the first few days of the Oslo Diplomatic Conference, where, under the auspices and encouragement of the Canadian Friend of the Chair, the respective heads of delegation of Germany and Mexico agreed to merge their two texts into one. Compulsory fact-finding, a key German demand, was part of this agreement, but the path to fact-finding would be encumbered by a series of 'red lights' and 'green lights'.[23]

## Overview of the Compliance Procedure

### *The Spirit of Cooperation*

**8.18** As Article 8(1) makes clear, the provision on facilitation and clarification of compliance is founded on a desire by States Parties to 'work together in a

---

[20] See the proposal by Germany circulated at the Oslo Diplomatic Conference—APL/CW.25 of 2 Sept. 1997.

[21] The Annex on Clarification initially included two variants, one for the Meeting of the States Parties, the other for a 'Clarification Commission'. The first variant was subsequently circulated at the Oslo Diplomatic Conference as APL/CW.24 of 2 Sept. 1997.

[22] The document was subsequently issued at the Oslo Diplomatic Conference as APL/CW.6 of 1 Sept. 1997.

[23] The language, which came from the negotiations of the Comprehensive Test Ban Treaty, was confusing to some of the delegations.

spirit of cooperation to facilitate compliance by States Parties with their obligations' under the Convention. This could include a number of approaches, including informal discussions in a meeting of States Parties or intersessional meeting, and governmental demarches. If, however, at some time in the future this spirit of cooperation fails to resolve a particular issue of implementation of the Convention, a detailed compliance procedure is laid out in the remaining paragraphs of Article 8. A good overview of the compliance procedure has been given by three lawyers, two Austrian and one Canadian, who were intimately involved in the drafting of the Convention. They summarize the process in the following five stages.[24]

## *The 'Five Stages' of Compliance*

**8.19** The *first stage* is a request from one or more States Parties ('the requesting State') for information regarding allegations of non-compliance.[25] The 'requested State Party' has 28 days to respond to these allegations.

**8.20** The *second stage* follows in the event of a failure by the 'requested State Party' to respond satisfactorily (or at all) to the allegations. The requesting State or States may then refer the matter to the next Meeting of States Parties[26] or call for a Special Meeting of States Parties.[27] A Special Meeting would be convened if one-third of the States Parties agree (within 14 days).[28]

**8.21** The *third stage* is the meeting itself, at which a decision can be taken to authorize a fact-finding mission[29] by simple majority of those present and voting (though every effort must be taken to reach a decision by consensus).[30] A requested State Party may also invite such a mission at any stage without the need for a specific decision to be taken.[31]

**8.22** The fact-finding mission itself is the *fourth stage* in the process. The mission shall consist of up to nine experts drawn from a list submitted by States Parties and held by the UN Secretary-General.[32] The Secretary-General is responsible for nominating the members of the mission, after consultation with the requested State Party.[33] That State has the right to withhold access to certain areas for reasons of security, but if it does so, must make every reasonable effort to demonstrate through alternative means its compliance with the Convention.[34] In the absence of consent, the mission may remain in the territory of the requested State Party for no more than 14 days, including a maximum of seven days at any one site.[35]

---

[24] Hajnoczi *et al.*, 'The Ban Treaty' in Cameron *et al.*, *To Walk without Fear*, 301–4.
[25] Article 8(2).   [26] Article 8(3).   [27] Article 8(5).   [28] ibid.
[29] Article 8(8).   [30] Article 8(6).   [31] Article 8(8).   [32] Article 8(9).
[33] Article 8(10).   [34] Article 8(14).   [35] Article 8(15).

**8.23** The *fifth stage* in the process (and the final one) is the review of information collected by the fact-finding mission, which is to report to the Meeting of States Parties through the Secretary-General.[36] If the mission finds that the requested State Party has not complied with the Convention, the Meeting 'may suggest to the States Parties concerned ways and means to further clarify or resolve the matter under consideration, including the initiation of appropriate procedures in conformity with international law'.[37] The Meeting must make every effort to reach decisions by consensus, but if this is not possible, they will be taken by a two-thirds majority of States Parties present and voting.[38]

*Summary*

**8.24** In sum, Article 8 'allows for a formal exchange of information between States Parties, allowing them to clarify situations in which they have reason to believe another State Party may not be complying with its Convention obligations. In the event that this exchange of information does not sufficiently clarify the situation, the Convention allows for the possibility of a fact-finding mission of experts to the territory of the State in question to gather more information'.[39]

## The Implementation of the Provision

**8.25** Article 8 has never formally been invoked, although its first paragraph has, informally at least, been followed in a number of instances. In January 2000, at the intersessional Standing Committee meeting on the General Status and Operation of the Convention, the ICBL stressed the need to 'urgently' put in place the structures and methodology necessary to carry out Article 8 on compliance, and called upon States to use the possibility of calling for clarification regarding possible violations 'whenever appropriate, and not to only use it in the most dire situations'.[40] The co-chairs of the working group agreed to coordinate a group of interested states to produce a document aimed at 'operationalising' Article 8.[41]

---

[36]  Article 8(17).　　　[37]  Article 8(19).　　　[38]  Article 8(20).

[39]  Hajnoczi *et al.*, 'The Ban Treaty', in Cameron *et al.*, *To Walk without Fear*, 302.

[40]  Email correspondence from Liz Bernstein, ICBL Coordinator (12 May 2000). The second annual Landmine Monitor report, published in August 2000, called upon States Parties to make detailed requests for clarification from Rwanda, Uganda, and Zimbabwe as to their alleged use of anti-personnel mines in the Democratic Republic of Congo. 'Even if those States Parties have not used anti-personnel mines themselves, they may have engaged in co-operative military action with armed forces that have laid anti-personnel mines, which could also constitute a treaty violation'. ICBL, *Landmine Monitor Report 2000*, 5, 198, 200. It is unclear, for example, what action the States Parties will take in case of a wilful refusal by a requesting State Party to demonstrate good faith in the application and implementation of Article 5. Corruption or at least poor management of mine action has already been noted in a number of States Parties, with a resultant impact on funding and operations.

[41]  Email correspondence from Liz Bernstein, ICBL Coordinator (12 May 2000).

**8.26** Following an agreement at the intersessional Standing Committee meetings in May 2000, Canada took the lead[42] in attempting to draft a document acceptable to all, but has struggled to make significant progress.[43] At a workshop in New York on 3 November 2000, Ambassador Dan Livermore remarked 'what is probably obvious to all of us—that resorting to the full procedures contained in Article 8 would be relatively rare . . . Nevertheless, States Parties need to discuss implementation of Article 8 provisions to clarify a number of matters, including financial, procedural, logistical and administrative issues related to Special Meetings of the States Parties and fact-finding missions'.[44]

**8.27** By 31 May 2002, Canada felt able to claim that:

In terms of the dialogue to date, considerable progress has been made. There is growing agreement on the need to continue to make concerted efforts to cooperate and offer assistance to ensure full implementation. And a sense appears to exist that States Parties should be prepared to respond in ways that are flexible, cooperative, adaptive and in accordance with the provisions of the Convention to allegations related to possible violations of the most serious actions prohibited by the Convention—those that may have serious humanitarian impacts and/or undermine the Convention. On the advisability of, and willingness to establish mechanisms not already mentioned in the Convention, however, a broad range of divergent views persists.[45]

**8.28** Yet, the issue of compliance continues to be highly charged. In 2002, the non-governmental organization, VERTIC (Verification Research, Training and Information Centre) published its *Guide to Fact-Finding Missions under the Ottawa Convention*, billed as 'another contribution to the continuing dialogue on clarifying how the . . . Convention's compliance procedures may be used'.[46] The guide 'is intended to assist States Parties in their advance

---

[42] For a time, France advocated the establishment of a committee of States that would act as a filter for possible concerns about compliance. Given the discussions surrounding a Commission of experts in the negotiation of the Convention, it is highly improbable that this will be acceptable to many States. Information provided by Thomas Wagner, Permanent Mission of France to the United Nations in Geneva, 24 Apr. 2002. According to the President of France's National Commission for the Elimination of Anti-Personnel Mines, the Convention is a disarmament treaty but contains only a 'rudimentary verification mechanism'. Statement of Brigitte Stern during the debate on Article 8 at the Third Meeting of States Parties in Managua, Sept. 2001, reproduced in Commission nationale pour l'élimination des mines antipersonnel, *Rapport 2000*, CNEMA (Paris, 2001), 129.

[43] See e.g. the presentation by Canada, 'Article 8 and the Facilitation and Clarification of Compliance', to the Standing Committee on the General Status and Operation of the Convention, Geneva, dated 2 May 2001, and intervention by Canada on 11 May 2001, available at: www.gichd.ch.

[44] Informal notes on intervention by the Canadian Ambassador for Mine Action, Dan Livermore (New York, 3 Nov. 2000).

[45] Report to the Standing Committee on the General Status and Operation of the Convention (Geneva, 31 May 2002), 4.

[46] VERTIC, *Guide to Fact-Finding Missions under the Ottawa Convention* (London: Dec. 2002), VERTIC/Diana, Princess of Wales Memorial Fund, 3.

planning and preparations for receiving a fact-finding mission under Article 8'.[47] In fact, the guide provoked a visceral reaction from Brazil, which delivered a candid statement to the intersessional Standing Committee meeting on the General Status and Operation of the Convention in February 2003:

### Article 8: Guide for Fact-Finding Missions

Brazil is doubtful whether there is a real sense of need for a Guide of Fact-Finding Missions as suggested by Vertic.

Contrary to what happens in other treaties involving arms control, in which Vertic may have found inspiration, a fact-finding mission under the Mine Ban Treaty would not be a routine, but a highly exceptional eventuality.

It is not certain that, as Vertic states, engaging in advance planning and preparation for the eventuality of a fact-finding mission would demonstrate a State Party's commitment to the implementation of all aspects of the Ottawa Convention. An adverse effect could be the introduction of an element of suspicion, not consistent with the spirit of cooperation that has always characterized the Ottawa Process.

Vertic suggests provisions on the mandate of a fact-finding mission, on the length of the days it would stay, on the rights and responsibilities of the receiving State, on the extent of access, etc. The mandate of an eventual fact-finding mission is to be negotiated and determined jointly by the States Parties.

Vertic makes precisions on some provisions of the Convention, giving its own interpretation and sometimes reinterpreting them in a manner not consistent with the letter of the Convention.

Brazil takes note of Vertic's Guide. For us, nevertheless, all efforts regarding compliance should lie in victim assistance and mine clearance, areas in which the mine action community has been giving an extremely valuable contribution and where there is a lot of work to done before the 2009 deadline.

**8.29** In the subsequent intersessional meetings in May 2003, the ICBL delivered the following intervention:

We would like to begin by noting our extreme disappointment that, as just reported by Canada, no State Party has put forward a topic or initiative to move the compliance discussion forward. The ICBL's views are well-known: States Parties should put a high priority on operationalizing Article 8 and on finding a new mechanism or a new way of ensuring a more coordinated, systematic and effective response to compliance concerns. This should be done by the time of the 2004 Review Conference.

Earlier the ICBL expressed its concern about Turkmenistan and its failure to fully meet its stockpile destruction obligation. We also want to inform delegates that Landmine

---

[47]  VERTIC, *Guide to Fact-Finding Missions under the Ottawa Convention.*

Monitor is currently investigating two allegations of use of antipersonnel mines by States Parties. We receive such allegations every year, and while some have been quite serious, happily none have been definitively confirmed.

# Paragraph 1

1. The States Parties agree to consult and cooperate with each other regarding the implementation of the provisions of this Convention, and to work together in a spirit of cooperation to facilitate compliance by States Parties with their obligations under this Convention.

## The Nature of the Duty to Consult and Cooperate

**8.30** This first paragraph of Article 8 sets out the general intent of the States Parties to address issues of implementation of the Convention through consultation and cooperation.[48] In particular, States Parties agree to 'work together in a spirit of cooperation' in order to facilitate compliance.[49] The paragraph does not specifically refer to such a spirit applying also to the clarification of compliance, a mechanism for which is set out in the remaining paragraphs of the article. The procedure does not, formally at least, apply to signatories to the Convention.[50]

**8.31** There is no ostensible role for the Secretary-General of the United Nations (UN) in addressing implementation issues amicably at this stage, although, as seen below, the Secretary-General has a major role to play if consultation and cooperation fails to resolve the concerns, including the use of his or her 'good offices'.[51]

# Paragraph 2

2. If one or more States Parties wish to clarify and seek to resolve questions relating to compliance with the provisions of this Convention by another State Party, it may submit, through the Secretary-General of the United Nations, a Request for Clarification of that matter to that State Party. Such

---

[48] Broadly similar provisions are included in Article V of the 1972 Biological Weapons Convention and Article IX of the 1993 Chemical Weapons Convention.

[49] As of writing, the determination of the States Parties will be put to the test by the decision of Turkmenistan to retain nearly 70,000 anti-personnel mines, a quantity that appears excessive with regard to Article 3 of the Convention. See further the commentary on this provision.

[50] Angola admitted using anti-personnel mines while a signatory to the Convention. See para. 1.8 above and the commentary on Article 15 below.

[51] See below Article 8(4) and the accompanying commentary.

a request shall be accompanied by all appropriate information. Each State Party shall refrain from unfounded Requests for Clarification, care being taken to avoid abuse. A State Party that receives a Request for Clarification shall provide, through the Secretary-General of the United Nations, within 28 days to the requesting State Party all information which would assist in clarifying this matter.

## The Nature of a Request for Clarification

**8.32** According to paragraph 2, one or more States Parties wishing to clarify and seek to resolve questions relating to compliance with the provisions of the Convention by another State Party may submit a 'Request for Clarification'. It is implicit rather than explicit in paragraph (1) above that concerns should first be raised with the State Party at issue before issuing such a request.

**8.33** The Request for Clarification must be accompanied by 'all appropriate information', that is, supporting documentation that calls into question the level of compliance of the requested State Party. Although the term 'appropriate' is not defined in the Convention, it presumably allows a requesting State Party certain discretion to withhold relevant information, for instance for reasons of national security or safety of personnel.

## The Mechanism for Submission of a Request for Clarification

**8.34** The Request for Clarification must be submitted to the State Party whose compliance is in question, through the Secretary-General of the United Nations (UN). From this point on, the UN plays a central role throughout any process of facilitation and clarification of compliance.

## The Duty to Refrain from Unfounded Requests

**8.35** States Parties are obliged to refrain from unfounded Requests for Clarification and must take care 'to avoid abuse'.[52] It seems unlikely, however, that any State Party or States Parties would want to initiate a Request for Clarification and the procedure it entails without highly credible evidence of a significant violation of the Convention. In addition to use or transfer of

---

[52] See Article IX(9) of the 1993 Chemical Weapons Convention, from which this provision is adapted. To avoid unfounded or abusive inspection requests, the Organization for the Prohibition of Chemical Weapons has specified the information that must be provided. See Kellman and Tanzman, *Manual for National Implementation of the Chemical Weapons Convention*, 133.

anti-personnel mines (other than for the purpose of destruction, of course),[53] new production of the weapons would surely constitute such a violation.

## The Duty on the Requested State Party to Respond

**8.36** Once it has received a Request for Clarification, the requested State Party is required, within 28 days, to provide the requesting State Party with 'all information' which would assist in clarifying the matter. Once again, the information must be submitted through the UN Secretary-General.

## Paragraph 3

3. If the requesting State Party does not receive a response through the Secretary-General of the United Nations within that time period, or deems the response to the Request for Clarification to be unsatisfactory, it may submit the matter through the Secretary-General of the United Nations to the next Meeting of the States Parties. The Secretary-General of the United Nations shall transmit the submission, accompanied by all appropriate information pertaining to the Request for Clarification, to all States Parties. All such information shall be presented to the requested State Party which shall have the right to respond.

## Submission of the Matter to the Meeting of States Parties

**8.37** According to paragraph 3, if the requesting State Party does not receive a response to its Request for Clarification through the Secretary-General within 28 days, or if it deems any response unsatisfactory, it may submit the matter through the Secretary-General to the next Meeting of the States Parties. Of course, it is under no obligation to do so. If it decides to proceed, however, the Secretary-General is now required to transmit to all the States Parties the original Request for Clarification, 'accompanied by all appropriate information pertaining' to it.

## The Right of the Requested State Party to Respond

**8.38** The requested State Party has the 'right to respond' to the information circulated to the States Parties. As the mechanism for any such response is not specified in the paragraph, the requested State Party may presumably

---

[53] See Article 3(2) above and the accompanying commentary.

choose whether or not to continue to transmit information through the UN Secretary-General, although it would be logical to do so.

# Paragraph 4

4. Pending the convening of any meeting of the States Parties, any of the States Parties concerned may request the Secretary-General of the United Nations to exercise his or her good offices to facilitate the clarification requested.

## The 'Good Offices' of the UN Secretary-General

**8.39** In the interim between the convening of a meeting of the States Parties and the meeting taking place, any of the States Parties concerned may request the UN Secretary-General to exercise his or her good offices to facilitate the clarification requested. The reference to the States Parties concerned seemingly limits those who have the right to involve the UN Secretary-General to the requesting State Party or States Parties and the requested State Party.[54]

# Paragraph 5

5. The requesting State Party may propose through the Secretary-General of the United Nations the convening of a Special Meeting of the States Parties to consider the matter. The Secretary-General of the United Nations shall thereupon communicate this proposal and all information submitted by the States Parties concerned, to all States Parties with a request that they indicate whether they favour a Special Meeting of the States Parties, for the purpose of considering the matter. In the event that within 14 days from the date of such communication, at least one-third of the States Parties favours such a Special Meeting, the Secretary-General of the United Nations shall convene this Special Meeting of the States Parties within a further 14 days. A quorum for this Meeting shall consist of a majority of States Parties.

## The Right of the Requested State Party to Request a Special Meeting of the States Parties

**8.40** Notwithstanding any involvement of the good offices of the UN Secretary-General, the requesting State Party may propose the convening of a 'Special Meeting of the States Parties'. According to paragraph 6, there does

---

[54] Though see VERTIC, *Guide to Fact-Finding Missions under the Ottawa Convention*, 14.

not need to be any particular justification for such a proposal, although it would presumably be invoked in the case of a suspected serious violation of the Convention when time is of the essence, or if a meeting of States Parties is not scheduled to take place for many months or even a year or more.[55]

## The Procedure for Convening a Special Meeting of the States Parties

**8.41** The requesting State Party seeking the convening of a Special Meeting of the States Parties must make a proposal through the UN Secretary-General, who in turn will communicate the proposal and all information submitted by the States Parties concerned, to all States Parties. The communication will include a request that States Parties indicate whether they support the convening of a Special Meeting of the States Parties to consider the matter. If, within 14 days of the communication, at least one-third of the States Parties support the proposal, the UN Secretary-General will then convene a Special Meeting of the States Parties within a further 14 days.

## The Quorum for the Meeting

**8.42** A majority of the States Parties must be present at a Special Meeting of the States Parties for a quorum to be constituted. Thus, on the basis of the level of adherence to the Convention as at June 2003, this would already require the attendance of more than 65 States Parties.

## Paragraph 6

6. The Meeting of the States Parties or the Special Meeting of the States Parties, as the case may be, shall first determine whether to consider the matter further, taking into account all information submitted by the States Parties concerned. The Meeting of the States Parties or the Special Meeting of the States Parties shall make every effort to reach a decision by consensus. If despite all efforts to that end no agreement has been reached, it shall take this decision by a majority of States Parties present and voting.

## The Role of the Meeting or Special Meeting of the States Parties

**8.43** The first task of the Meeting of the States Parties or Special Meeting of the States Parties, as the case may be, is to determine whether to consider the

---

[55] According to Article 11 of the Convention, States Parties must meet 'regularly' and meetings of the States Parties are to be held annually only until the first review conference, which will take place in late 2004. According to Article 12(2)(b), the review conference must then decide on the 'need for and the interval between further Meetings of the States Parties'. See below the commentary on these provisions.

matter further, taking into account all information submitted by the States Parties concerned. Although it is not stipulated, presumably the requested State Party will be given an opportunity to deliver a statement to the States Parties before they reach a decision.

### The Decision-Making Process

**8.44**  States Parties must make every effort to reach a decision by consensus on whether to consider the matter further. If they fail to reach consensus, the decision will be taken by a majority of States Parties present and voting. The requested State Party is seemingly not prevented from taking an active part in the discussions, even to the extent of blocking a consensus on any decision to consider the matter further, although under paragraph 7 below, 'all States Parties shall cooperate fully with the Meeting of the States Parties or the Special Meeting of the States Parties in the fulfilment of its review of the matter'.

## Paragraph 7

> 7. All States Parties shall cooperate fully with the Meeting of the States Parties or the Special Meeting of the States Parties in the fulfilment of its review of the matter, including any fact-finding missions that are authorized in accordance with paragraph 8.

### The Duty on States Parties to Cooperate

**8.45**  Thus, all States Parties are obliged to 'cooperate fully' with the Meeting of the States Parties or Special Meeting of the States Parties 'in the fulfilment of its review of the matter, including any fact-finding missions that are authorized in accordance with paragraph 8'. As discussed in commentary paragraph 9.23 below, the UK is one of a number of States Parties that has 'rehearsed' the conduct of a fact-finding mission on its territory.

## Paragraph 8

> 8. If further clarification is required, the Meeting of the States Parties or the Special Meeting of the States Parties shall authorize a fact-finding mission and decide on its mandate by a majority of States Parties present and voting. At any time the requested State Party may invite a fact-finding

mission to its territory. Such a mission shall take place without a decision by a Meeting of the States Parties or a Special Meeting of the States Parties to authorize such a mission. The mission, consisting of up to 9 experts, designated and approved in accordance with paragraphs 9 and 10, may collect additional information on the spot or in other places directly related to the alleged compliance issue under the jurisdiction or control of the requested State Party.

## The Decision to Authorize a Fact-Finding Mission

**8.46** According to paragraph 8, if further clarification is required, the Meeting of the States Parties or the Special Meeting of the States Parties shall authorize a fact-finding mission and decide on its mandate by a majority of States Parties present and voting. As already noted, this provision was the crux of the disagreement between Germany and Mexico throughout the negotiations and especially in the build-up to, and during, the Oslo Diplomatic Conference.[56] Germany sought a provision requiring only a one-third minority of States Parties present and voting to authorize a fact-finding mission. Mexico, on the other hand, proposed that the threshold for authorizing a fact-finding mission be set at two-thirds of States Parties present and voting, and further that visits would only take place with the consent of the concerned States Parties.[57]

**8.47** As VERTIC points out, the Convention does not specify the precise circumstances under which fact-finding missions might be authorized. The organization suggests that it is only likely to be in situations where: the alleged activity would be a significant breach; there is little information available to confirm or refute the alleged violation; and the State has not cooperated in clarifying the matter.[58]

## The Right of the Requested State Party to Invite a Fact-Finding Mission

**8.48** Paragraph 8 specifically authorizes the requested State Party 'at any time' to invite a fact-finding mission to its territory. Such a mission will take place without a decision by a Meeting of the States Parties or a Special Meeting of the States Parties to authorize such a mission.

[56] See para. 8.17 above.

[57] Mexico had initially suggested using the International Fact-Finding Commission established by Article 90 of Additional Protocol I to the 1949 Geneva Conventions to conduct any authorized fact-finding mission.

[58] VERTIC, *Guide to Fact-Finding Missions under the Ottawa Convention*, 19.

## The Conduct of the Mission

**8.49** Irrespective of whether the fact-finding mission is authorized or invited to its territory by the requested State Party, the conduct of the mission remains the same. The mission will consist of no more than nine experts, who are 'designated and approved in accordance with paragraphs 9 and 10'. According to paragraph 8, the experts are authorized to 'collect additional information on the spot or in other places directly related to the alleged compliance issue under the jurisdiction or control of the requested State Party'.[59]

# Paragraph 9

9. The Secretary-General of the United Nations shall prepare and update a list of the names, nationalities and other relevant data of qualified experts provided by States Parties and communicate it to all States Parties. Any expert included on this list shall be regarded as designated for all fact-finding missions unless a State Party declares its non-acceptance in writing. In the event of non-acceptance, the expert shall not participate in fact-finding missions on the territory or any other place under the jurisdiction or control of the objecting State Party, if the non-acceptance was declared prior to the appointment of the expert to such missions.

## The List of Experts

**8.50** According to paragraph 9, the UN Secretary-General is responsible for preparing and updating a list of qualified experts[60] to participate in any fact-finding mission. The names of experts are to be provided by States Parties, and it does not appear that the UN will have any formal role in suggesting qualified experts.

**8.51** The list and its updates must be communicated to all States Parties.[61] Any expert included on the list can be considered for all fact-finding missions

---

[59] This language was taken by Austria from the text of the Compliance Annex drafted by the US delegation to the First Review Conference of the Convention on Certain Conventional Weapons. UN Doc. CCW/CONF.I/CRP.9/Rev.1 of 2 May 1996. The proposed annex was not accepted by the States Parties.

[60] The term is not defined in the Convention. VERTIC suggests that a wide range of skills and experience is likely to be required, and it suggests a number of these in its guide to fact-finding missions. See VERTIC, *Guide to Fact-Finding Missions under the Ottawa Convention*, 17.

[61] The UN Department for Disarmament Affairs has provided a template form which States Parties may use to submit details of their national experts for the roster. The Department requests this information from States Parties each year, following a Meeting of States Parties. On the basis of these submissions, it updates the roster and circulates it to the States Parties at the next Meeting of States Parties. VERTIC, *Guide to Fact-Finding Missions under the Ottawa Convention*, 17–18.

unless a State Party declares in writing that it will not accept him or her. In the event of non-acceptance, the expert shall not participate in any fact-finding mission on the territory or any other place under the jurisdiction or control of the objecting State Party. The declaration of non-acceptance must, however, be declared prior to the appointment of the expert to such a mission.

# Paragraph 10

10. Upon receiving a request from the Meeting of the States Parties or a Special Meeting of the States Parties, the Secretary-General of the United Nations shall, after consultations with the requested State Party, appoint the members of the mission, including its leader. Nationals of States Parties requesting the fact-finding mission or directly affected by it shall not be appointed to the mission. The members of the fact-finding mission shall enjoy privileges and immunities under Article VI of the Convention on the Privileges and Immunities of the United Nations, adopted on 13 February 1946.

## Appointment of the Members of a Fact-Finding Mission

**8.52** Upon receiving a request from the Meeting of the States Parties or a Special Meeting of the States Parties, the UN Secretary-General will, after consulting with the requested State Party, appoint the members of the mission, including its leader. Nationals of States Parties requesting the fact-finding mission or directly affected by it will not be appointed to the mission.

## The Privileges and Immunities of a Fact-Finding Mission

**8.53** The members of the fact-finding mission will benefit from the privileges and immunities laid down in Article VI of the Convention on the Privileges and Immunities of the United Nations, adopted on 13 February 1946. This article provides as follows:

Article VI
Experts on missions for the United Nations

*Section 22*

Experts (other than officials coming within the scope of Article V) performing missions for the United Nations shall be accorded such privileges and immunities as are necessary for the independent exercise of their functions during the period of their missions, including the time spent on journeys in connexion with their missions. In particular, they shall be accorded:

(a) immunity from personal arrest or detention and from seizure of their personal baggage;
(b) in respect of words spoken or written and acts done by them in the course of the performance of their mission, immunity from legal process of every kind. This immunity from legal process shall continue to be accorded notwithstanding that the persons concerned are no longer employed on missions for the United Nations;
(c) inviolability for all papers and documents;
(d) for the purpose of their communications with the United Nations, the right to use codes and to receive papers or correspondence by courier or in sealed bags;
(e) the same facilities in respect of currency or exchange restrictions as are accorded to representatives of foreign governments on temporary official missions;
(f) the same immunities and facilities in respect of their personal baggage as are accorded to diplomatic envoys.

*Section 23*

Privileges and immunities are granted to experts in the interests of the United Nations and not for the personal benefit of the individuals themselves. The Secretary-General shall have the right and the duty to waive the immunity of any expert in any case where, in his opinion, the immunity would impede the course of justice and it can be waived without prejudice to the interests of the United Nations.

# Paragraph 11

11. Upon at least 72 hours notice, the members of the fact-finding mission shall arrive in the territory of the requested State Party at the earliest opportunity. The requested State Party shall take the necessary administrative measures to receive, transport and accommodate the mission, and shall be responsible for ensuring the security of the mission to the maximum extent possible while they are on territory under its control.

## The Arrival of a Fact-Finding Mission

8.54  The requested State Party must be given at least 72 hours' notice prior to the arrival of any fact-finding mission, but thereafter the mission must arrive on its territory 'at the earliest opportunity'. During the negotiation of this paragraph, a number of States regretted the delay in the arrival of a fact-finding mission, but recognized that, in the case of the alleged use of anti-personnel mines at least, comprehensive clearance within such a short time was unlikely to be a feasible option open to the requested State Party.

## The Role of the Host State Party

8.55 The requested State Party must take the 'necessary administrative measures to receive, transport and accommodate the mission, and shall be responsible for ensuring the security of the mission to the maximum extent possible while they are on territory under its control'. It is acknowledged that no State Party can absolutely guarantee the safety of any mission, especially if there is ongoing armed conflict on its territory—and therefore potentially the presence of other armed actors not under its control.

# Paragraph 12

12. Without prejudice to the sovereignty of the requested State Party, the fact-finding mission may bring into the territory of the requested State Party the necessary equipment which shall be used exclusively for gathering information on the alleged compliance issue. Prior to its arrival, the mission will advise the requested State Party of the equipment that it intends to utilize in the course of its fact-finding mission.

## The Equipment for the Mission

8.56 Without prejudice to the sovereignty of the requested State Party, the fact-finding mission is entitled to bring into the territory of the requested State Party equipment it needs for gathering information on the alleged compliance issue. The equipment must, however, be used exclusively for these purposes.

## The Duty to Inform the Host State Party

8.57 Prior to its arrival, the fact-finding mission is required to advise the requested State Party of the equipment that it intends to use in the course of its mission.

# Paragraph 13

13. The requested State Party shall make all efforts to ensure that the fact-finding mission is given the opportunity to speak with all relevant persons who may be able to provide information related to the alleged compliance issue.

## The Duty of the Host State Party to Facilitate Interlocutors

**8.58** The requested State Party is required to make 'all efforts to ensure that the fact-finding mission is given the opportunity to speak with all relevant persons who may be able to provide information related to the alleged compliance issue'. As was clearly evidenced during the UN weapons inspections in Iraq in early 2003, the issue of interlocutors is not as simple as it might at first appear.

# Paragraph 14

14. The requested State Party shall grant access for the fact-finding mission to all areas and installations under its control where facts relevant to the compliance issue could be expected to be collected. This shall be subject to any arrangements that the requested State Party considers necessary for:

(a) The protection of sensitive equipment, information and areas;
(b) The protection of any constitutional obligations the requested State Party may have with regard to proprietary rights, searches and seizures, or other constitutional rights; or
(c) The physical protection and safety of the members of the fact-finding mission.

In the event that the requested State Party makes such arrangements, it shall make every reasonable effort to demonstrate through alternative means its compliance with this Convention.

## The Duty to Grant Access

**8.59** The requested State Party must grant access for the fact-finding mission to all areas and installations under its control where facts relevant to the compliance issue could be expected to be collected. The areas are presumably defined by the fact-finding mission in consultation with all relevant parties.

**8.60** The requested State Party does, however, have the right to restrict access to equipment, information, and areas it deems sensitive, and to protect its constitutional obligations with regard to proprietary rights, searches and seizures, or other constitutional rights. Further, the requested State Party may determine that the physical protection and safety of the members of the fact-finding mission may be unduly put at risk by granting access into certain areas.

**8.61** VERTIC suggests that a State Party use recognized 'managed access techniques',[62] such as: switching off computers in areas where the mission will have access; negotiating a number of areas to which the mission will have access within a sensitive location; negotiating a number of storage containers to which the mission will have access within a sensitive location ('random selective access'); and shrouding equipment or components that are not relevant to the Convention.[63]

## The Duty to Demonstrate Compliance through Alternative Means

**8.62** In the event that the requested State Party decides not to grant access on the basis of one or more of the three specific exceptions laid down in paragraph 14, it must make 'every reasonable effort' to demonstrate its compliance with the Convention through alternative means.

# Paragraph 15

15. The fact-finding mission may remain in the territory of the State Party concerned for no more than 14 days, and at any particular site no more than 7 days, unless otherwise agreed.

## The Right of the Mission to Remain in Country

**8.63** Unless otherwise agreed, the fact-finding mission is entitled to remain in the territory of the requested State Party for no more than 14 days.

## The Right of the Mission to Remain at a Particular Site

**8.64** Unless otherwise agreed, the fact-finding mission is entitled to remain at any particular site for no more than 7 days.

# Paragraph 16

16. All information provided in confidence and not related to the subject matter of the fact-finding mission shall be treated on a confidential basis.

---

[62] In the case of the 1993 Chemical Weapons Convention, ' "managed access" is an important process to limit the scope of challenge inspections in order to protect sensitive equipment, data, or areas not related to chemical weapons. The inspection team and the challenged State Party will negotiate the extent of access, the performance of activities, and the provision of information, but if the inspection team finds evidence of non-compliance, it will not be bound to the managed access agreement'. Kellman and Tanzman, *Manual for National Implementation of the Chemical Weapons Convention*, 139.

[63] VERTIC, *Guide to Fact-Finding Missions under the Ottawa Convention*, 21.

## The Duty of Confidentiality

**8.65** All information provided in confidence to the fact-finding mission and which is not related to the subject-matter of the mission must be treated on a confidential basis. This is narrower than the informal proposal by Colombia, made prior to the Oslo Diplomatic Conference, whereby all information received in the course of an investigation would be treated as confidential. States Parties were keen to avoid unduly restricting the ability of the fact-finding teams to gather information and prepare their reports.

# Paragraph 17

17. The fact-finding mission shall report, through the Secretary-General of the United Nations, to the Meeting of the States Parties or the Special Meeting of the States Parties the results of its findings.

## The Duty to Report the Findings

**8.66** The fact-finding mission must submit a report detailing the results of its findings to the Meeting of the States Parties or the Special Meeting of the States Parties. The report is to be sent through the UN Secretary-General. No deadline is given for the report of the submission. The proceedings of the Meeting of the States Parties or the Special Meeting of the States Parties are presumably suspended to allow the fact-finding mission to take place and the report to be submitted, as time is likely to be of the essence. The relevant meeting may therefore reconvene to consider the situation, as set out in paragraph 18.

# Paragraph 18

18. The Meeting of the States Parties or the Special Meeting of the States Parties shall consider all relevant information, including the report submitted by the fact-finding mission, and may request the requested State Party to take measures to address the compliance issue within a specified period of time. The requested State Party shall report on all measures taken in response to this request.

## Consideration by the Meeting or Special Meeting

**8.67** The Meeting of the States Parties or the Special Meeting of the States Parties is obliged to consider all relevant information, including, but not limited to, the report submitted by the fact-finding mission.

## The Right to Request Measures to Address Compliance

**8.68** The meeting is authorized to request the State Party concerned to take measures to address the compliance issue within a specified period of time. In accordance with paragraph 20 below, the meeting must make every effort to reach its decision by consensus, otherwise by a two-thirds majority of States Parties present and voting.

## The Duty on the Requested State Party to Report on Measures Taken

**8.69** The requested State Party is required, presumably only once any specified period of time has elapsed, to report on all the measures it has taken in response to the request.

# Paragraph 19

19. The Meeting of the States Parties or the Special Meeting of the States Parties may suggest to the States Parties concerned ways and means to further clarify or resolve the matter under consideration, including the initiation of appropriate procedures in conformity with international law. In circumstances where the issue at hand is determined to be due to circumstances beyond the control of the requested State Party, the Meeting of the States Parties or the Special Meeting of the States Parties may recommend appropriate measures, including the use of cooperative measures referred to in Article 6.

## The Right to Suggest Further Measures

**8.70** Notwithstanding any decision under paragraph 18, the Meeting of the States Parties or the Special Meeting of the States Parties may also suggest to the States Parties concerned 'ways and means to further clarify or resolve the matter under consideration, including the initiation of appropriate procedures in conformity with international law'.[64] This suggests that a proposal will be put to the requesting as well as the requested State Party or States Parties to resolve the issue. This could, for example, be a request for an advisory opinion

---

[64] At the Oslo Diplomatic Conference, Japan put forward a proposal for a new article, entitled 'Measures, including sanctions to redress a situation and to ensure compliance'. This included provision for the Meeting of the States Parties, in cases of particular gravity, to 'bring the issue, including relevant information and conclusions, to the attention of the United Nations General Assembly and the United Nations Security Council'. See APL/CW.20 of 2 Sept. 1997.

from the International Court of Justice, where the compliance issue concerned differing legal interpretations of a particular provision of the Convention.[65]

8.71 In accordance with paragraph 20 below, the meeting must make every effort to reach its decision by consensus, otherwise by a two-thirds majority of States Parties present and voting.

## Circumstances beyond the Control of the State Party

8.72 In circumstances where the compliance issue is deemed to be due to circumstances beyond the control of the requested State Party, the Meeting of the States Parties or the Special Meeting of the States Parties may recommend 'appropriate measures, including the use of cooperative measures referred to in Article 6'. Thus, for example, if a State Party has been unable to fulfil the deadline laid down in Article 4 for the destruction of anti-personnel mine stockpiles for technical reasons or because it does not have the necessary financial resources, international cooperation and assistance could help to resolve this.

8.73 A more difficult situation to address would be one where a State Party had used anti-personnel mines in violation of Article 1 of the Convention and now seeks international funding from other States Parties to clear those mines in accordance with Article 6.

# Paragraph 20

20. The Meeting of the States Parties or the Special Meeting of the States Parties shall make every effort to reach its decisions referred to in paragraphs 18 and 19 by consensus, otherwise by a two-thirds majority of States Parties present and voting.

## The Decision-Making Process

8.74 As already noted, under paragraph 20 the Meeting of the States Parties or the Special Meeting of the States Parties must make every effort to reach the decisions referred to in paragraphs 18 and 19 above by consensus, otherwise by a two-thirds majority of States Parties present and voting.

---

[65] According to the NGO, VERTIC: 'Ultimately, as in other serious cases of non-compliance with an international treaty, the UN Security Council may be called on to consider the matter'. VERTIC, *Guide to Fact-Finding Missions under the Ottawa Convention*, 16. This appears rather unlikely, at least for the foreseeable future, not least given the presence of three non-party States among the five permanent members of the Security Council.

# Article 9. National Implementation Measures

Article 9—National implementation measures

Each State Party shall take all appropriate legal, administrative and other measures, including the imposition of penal sanctions, to prevent and suppress any activity prohibited to a State Party under this Convention undertaken by persons or on territory under its jurisdiction or control.

## Introduction

**9.1** According to one of the basic tenets of international treaty law: 'Every treaty in force is binding upon the parties to it and must be performed by them in good faith'.[1] Further, a party 'may not invoke the provisions of its internal law as justification for its failure to perform a treaty'.[2] Article 9 of the Anti-Personnel Mine Ban Convention, which addresses national implementation measures, sets out the requirement to 'take all appropriate legal, administrative and other measures, including the imposition of penal sanctions, to prevent and suppress any activity prohibited to a State Party' under the Convention 'undertaken by persons or on territory under its jurisdiction or control'. It is potentially broad in ambit but considerable discretion is left to States Parties.

**9.2** As explained below, efforts to incorporate even a modified form of compulsory universal jurisdiction in the Convention were ultimately unsuccessful. Compulsory universal jurisdiction, sometimes referred to by the Latin *aut*

---

[1] This fundamental principle, known also under its Latin nomenclature, *pacta sunt servanda*, is reproduced in Article 26 of the 1969 Vienna Convention on the Law of Treaties.

[2] Article 27, 1969 Vienna Convention on the Law of Treaties.

*dedere aut iudicare*, obliges States to prosecute or extradite persons who have committed acts contrary to the provisions of a Convention that includes it, no matter where the acts have been committed. Under international humanitarian law States are already required to exercise universal jurisdiction in respect of 'grave breaches' of the 1949 Geneva Conventions and their Additional Protocol I of 1977, which refer to acts such as wilful killing, torture, or inhuman treatment committed against protected persons in situations of armed conflict or making the civilian population or individual civilians the object of attack. Similarly, in the context of human rights law, General Pinochet of Chile was arrested and held in the UK for several months on the basis of acts of torture for which he had been responsible in Chile in the 1980s and 1990s, as the 1994 UN Convention against Torture contains a provision detailing compulsory universal jurisdiction.[3]

## The Negotiation of the Article

**9.3**  Dr Werner Ehrlich's draft treaty text deliberately omitted the details of any compliance mechanism. The First Austrian Draft Text, however, which built on his work, included an article entitled Compliance with the Convention, as set out below:

Article 6

Compliance with the Convention

1.  Each High Contracting Party shall take all appropriate legal and other measures, including the imposition of penal sanctions to prevent and suppress breaches of this Convention by persons or on territory under its jurisdiction or control.

2.  The provisions of the Geneva Conventions of 12 August 1949 relating to measures for the repression of breaches and grave breaches shall apply to breaches and grave breaches of this Convention. Any act or omission occurring during armed conflict in violation of this Convention, if committed wilfully or wantonly and causing death or serious injury, shall be treated as a grave breach.

3.  The High Contracting Parties undertake to consult each other and to cooperate with each other to resolve any problems that may arise with regard to the implementation and application of the provisions of this Article.

**9.4**  Paragraph 1 of the draft text is very close to what was ultimately adopted in Article 9. The intent of Paragraph 2, which resembled a proposal by the USA for Amended Protocol II in the preparation for the First Review Conference of

---

[3] Article 7, Convention against Torture, and Other Cruel, Inhuman or Degrading Treatment or Punishment, adopted by UN General Assembly Resolution 39/64 of 10 Dec. 1984.

the Convention on Certain Conventional Weapons,[4] was not accepted in any form by the States Parties. Paragraph 3 was included, with amendment, as Article 10(1) of the Convention.

9.5 The Belgian draft treaty text included a more elaborate provision, based on Article VII of the 1993 Chemical Weapons Convention. It appears to have had little bearing on the negotiation of Article 9.

Article 7
National implementation measures

1. Each State Party shall, in accordance with its constitutional processes, take any necessary measures to implement its obligations under the present Convention. In particular, it shall take any necessary measures:

(a) To prohibit natural and legal persons anywhere on its territory or in any other place under its jurisdiction as recognized by international law from undertaking any activity prohibited to a State Party under the present Convention.

(b) To prohibit natural and legal persons from undertaking any such activity anywhere under its control.

(c) To prohibit, in conformity with international law, natural persons possessing its nationality from undertaking any such activity anywhere.

2. Each State Party shall cooperate with other States Parties and afford the appropriate form of legal assistance to facilitate the implementation of the obligations under paragraph 1.

3. Each State Party shall inform the Organization of the measures taken pursuant to this Article.

9.6 The ICBL draft treaty text also includes a provision on national implementation measures, which is surprisingly weak, making no reference to compulsory universal jurisdiction.[5] It did, however, lay down a deadline—one year after ratification—for taking 'the necessary legislative, administrative and other measures to implement its obligations' under the Convention.[6]

---

[4] The proposal was subsequently watered down and incorporated as Article 14(2) of Amended Protocol II: 'The measures envisaged in paragraph 1 of this Article include appropriate measures to ensure the imposition of penal sanctions against persons who, in relation to an armed conflict and contrary to the provisions of this Protocol, wilfully kill or cause serious injury to civilians and to bring such persons to justice'.

[5] 'Each State Party shall, within one year after ratification of this Convention, take the necessary legislative, administrative and other measures to implement its obligations under this Convention. This obligation includes the adoption of legal measures to prevent persons and entities within its jurisdiction or control from engaging in conduct prohibited by this Convention'.

[6] Article 8, Convention on the Prohibition of the Development, Production, Stockpiling, Transfer and Use of Anti-Personnel Mines and on their Destruction, Proposal by the International Campaign to Ban Landmines, ICBL, 20 Dec. 1996.

**9.7** Following discussions within the Core Group, the Second Austrian Draft Text had removed any reference to grave breaches, and the language used was almost identical to the article as ultimately adopted. The intent of the second paragraph of the draft article is reflected in Article 7(1)(a) of the Convention.

Article 10
National implementation measures

1. Each State Party shall take all appropriate legal, administrative and other measures, including the imposition of penal sanctions to prevent and suppress any activity prohibited to a State Party under this Convention undertaken by persons or on territory under its jurisdiction or control.

2. All measures taken under paragraph 1 shall be reported to the Depositary annually, covering the last calendar year, not later than six months before the next Meeting of the States Parties.

**9.8** Thus, the Third Austrian Draft Text moved the content of the second paragraph to the article on transparency measures, and merely added a comma after 'sanctions' for grammatical reasons. Despite considerable discussion at the Oslo Diplomatic Conference, the article was adopted unchanged from the one contained in the draft put before it.

**9.9** The main issue at the Diplomatic Conference was whether or not to include compulsory universal jurisdiction for violations of the Convention. As mentioned above in paragraph 8.8, at the 1997 Bonn Conference,[7] the ICRC had already circulated an informal draft article containing such a proposal:

Each State Party shall search for all persons on its territory or under its jurisdiction or control, being nationals of a State party to this Convention, alleged to have used, or to have ordered the use of, anti-personnel mines, in violation of this Convention, regardless of the place where such acts were committed, and shall either bring such persons before its own courts or hand such persons over for trial to another State Party.

**9.10** In the run-up to the Oslo Diplomatic Conference, Switzerland, with support from Mexico and Sweden, pushed hard for violations of the Convention to be classified as 'grave breaches', language used in the 1949 Geneva Conventions and Additional Protocol I that invokes compulsory universal jurisdiction. But a number of Core Group members were reluctant to countenance this, because they considered the requirement to take legislative measures sufficient for the purposes of national implementation,[8] because they viewed the instrument as one of disarmament rather than humanitarian law, or because they were concerned

---

[7] See paras. 0.64 to 0.66 above for a brief summary of the Conference.

[8] Although many States will not consider extraterritorial jurisdiction in the absence of an international agreement to do so.

about the legal and political implications. One State, for instance, questioned the application of the provision to military personnel serving abroad on an exchange with the military of a State not party to the Convention.

**9.11** At the Diplomatic Conference, Switzerland put forward a proposal, which it later revised, that avoided the use of the term 'grave breaches' but maintained its intent:

Each State Party shall search for any national of a State Party alleged to have used, or to have ordered to use anti-personnel mines and shall have such a person tried by its courts. It also may, in accordance with its legislation, hand over such a person for trial to another State Party concerned or to such international tribunal as may have jurisdiction.[9]

**9.12** When Switzerland, supported orally by Belgium, Colombia, Ghana, Mexico, and Venezuela, introduced its proposal to the plenary, many States expressed their reservations. They argued that this would require instructions from capitals, was not appropriate to the current context, and, based on their disarmament background, was potentially breaking new legal ground. The proposal was not accepted.

**9.13** In June 1998, however, the year following the Oslo Diplomatic Conference, States were in Rome negotiating the Statute for a permanent international criminal court. The Preparatory Committee in December 1997 had added anti-personnel mines to a list of weapons whose use could be conferred to the jurisdiction of the Court.[10]

**9.14** At the Rome Diplomatic Conference itself, Nigeria was one of a number of States that supported including landmines within the jurisdiction of the court, declaring that the use of anti-personnel mines and 'other weapons of mass destruction' should be considered as war crimes.[11] As there was widespread agreement, however, that a prohibition on the use of anti-personnel mines was not part of the corpus of customary international law, many States supportive of the Anti-Personnel Mine Ban Convention, including Canada itself, did not pursue the issue actively.

## 'Appropriate' Legal, Administrative, and Other Measures

**9.15** Each State Party is required to take all *appropriate* legal, administrative, and other measures. The term appropriate is not defined, but appears to

---

[9] APL/CW.42 of 2 Sept. 1997. See also APL/CW.42/Rev.1 of 9 Sept. 1997.

[10] See UN Doc. A/AC.249/1997/L.9/Rev.1 (1997), 8–11.

[11] 'Use of weapons of mass destruction should be included in Criminal Court's definition of war crimes, say several conference speakers', UN press release L/ROM.14, available at www.un.org/icc.

leave considerable discretion to the State Party in question.[12] Thus, for example, Norway is said to have agreed on a specific exemption from penal sanctions for foreigners, primarily military personnel, whose own country has not ratified the treaty, arguing that 'a possible prosecution of allies[13] in such a situation cannot be seen as appropriate'.[14] Other States Parties have sought to ensure a 'shield against unreasonable prosecution' to soldiers serving alongside forces from the United States.[15]

# Legal Measures

**9.16** For most States Parties, implementing legislation is necessary to give effect at national level to the obligations undertaken by States at international level.[16] According to the International Committee of the Red Cross, the provisions of Article 9 will entail for most States[17] the adoption of criminal legislation.[18] Excepted would be States that had already implemented a prohibition on

---

[12] The term 'appropriate' was employed in Article 14 of 1996 Amended Protocol II, the provision on which this article is based. Article VII(1) of the 1993 Chemical Weapons Convention, on the other hand, uses the phrase 'necessary measures to implement [State Party] obligations' under the Convention, which is clearly much stronger.                                      [13] i.e. the USA.

[14] ICBL, *Landmine Monitor Report 1999*, 635.

[15] Secretary of State for Foreign Affairs, Robin Cook, cited in Morrison, J., 'Britain Accused of Watering Down Landmines Ban', *Reuters* (London, 10 July 1998). Thus, Clause 5 of the United Kingdom Landmines Act provides a defence against prosecution if the accused is able to prove that: '(a) the conduct was in the course of, or for the purposes of, a military operation or the planning of a military operation; (b) the conduct was not the laying of an anti-personnel mine; (c) at the time of the conduct he believed, on reasonable grounds, that the operation was or would be an operation to which this section applies; and (d) he did not suspect, and had no grounds for suspecting, that the conduct related to the laying of anti-personnel mines in contravention of the Ottawa Convention'.

[16] In a number of countries, such as the USA and many European States, certain 'self-executing' treaties (or certain provisions contained within such treaties) that are adhered to by the executive, bind the courts without the need for any further specific act of incorporation into domestic law. The inclusion of an article on national implementation suggests that the Convention is not to be considered as self-executing; also relevant is the reference to penal sanctions.

[17] Mexico, for instance, has adopted no implementing legislation because once the Convention was promulgated and published in the Official Federal Gazette, it became part of domestic law. Similarly, Qatar has stated that by virtue of its ratification of the Convention the provisions had become 'part and parcel of the national laws of the State of Qatar'. Letter of Saad Mohamed Al-Kobaisi, Ambassador of Qatar, to Landmine Monitor (9 Sept. 1999).

[18] ICRC, Implementing the Ottawa Treaty: National Legislation (Geneva: ICRC, Apr. 1999). The ICRC also pointed out the likelihood of the need for 'other regulatory measures such as changes in military doctrine and procedures, the notification of organisations and corporations involved in anti-personnel mine production and sale and instructions to the relevant ministries to rescind export licences which may involve anti-personnel mines'.

anti-personnel mines in national legislation that was at least as wide in its ambit as the Anti-Personnel Mine Ban Convention.[19]

**9.17** Significant latitude is left to States Parties as to the type of legal measures they will impose, on whom, and to which degree.[20] Article 9 specifically refers to 'legal . . . measures, including the imposition of penal sanctions', but does not stipulate what those must be, other than that they be appropriate. At a minimum, penal legislation should apply to the undertakings contained in Article 1 of the Convention. They could also apply to acts, such as obstructing a fact-finding mission authorized in accordance with Article 8. State practice is varied with regard to the penalties national legislation imposes for violations.[21]

**9.18** As already mentioned, Article 9 does not require extraterritorial jurisdiction for prohibited acts, though there is no impediment to doing so.[22] Thus, according to the legislation adopted by Germany, extraterritorial offences 'count as offences irrespective of the national law of the scene of the crime . . . if the perpetrator is German'.[23]

**9.19** According to the ICRC, as of May 2003, 35 States Parties had adopted national legislation to implement the Convention: Australia, Austria, Belgium, Brazil, Burkina Faso, Cambodia, Canada, Colombia, Costa Rica, the Czech Republic, France, Germany, Guatemala, Honduras, Hungary, Iceland, Italy, Japan, Liechtenstein, Luxembourg, Malaysia, Mali, Malta, Monaco, Mauritius, New Zealand, Nicaragua, Norway, Romania, Spain, Sweden, Switzerland,

---

[19] Thus, for example, Austrian national legislation prohibiting anti-personnel mines, which predated the adoption and entry into force of the Convention, served also as its implementing legislation for the Convention without the need for further legislative measures. Spain's 'Law Banning Anti-personnel Landmines as well as those Arms with similar Effects', Law 33/1998, does not include any penal sanctions. In an annex to the Law, it was stated that sanctions would be developed in subsequent implementing legislation.

[20] The ICRC has prepared an 'Information Kit on the Development of National Legislation to Implement the Convention on the Prohibition of Anti-Personnel Mines'. The kit is available in hard copy from the ICRC or online at: www.icrc.org.

[21] See e.g. the Austrian Federal Law on the Ban of Anti-personnel Mines (BGBI I No. 13/97), which imposes a penalty on whoever, and even by negligence, contravenes the prohibition of Article 2 of the Federal Law (Article 7 Report, 1 Mar.–30 Apr. 1999, Form A). Paragraph 5 of the Norwegian Act relating to the implementation of the Ottawa Convention, Act No. 54/1998, dated 17 July 1998, reads as follows: 'Any person who contravenes this Act or regulations issued pursuant thereto is liable to a fine or to imprisonment for a term not exceeding two years. A negligent act is punishable by a fine or imprisonment for a term not exceeding six months. An accomplice shall be liable to the same penalty'. The Italian Law No. 374 of 29 Oct. 1997 on the Ban of Anti-Personnel Mines allows a reduction of the penalty by half if the offence is not particularly serious (sect. 7, § 3). Under the amended Swedish Penal Code, the offence of 'Unlawful Dealing with Mines' (Penal Code, ch. 22 sect. 6 b), can be punished by up to four years' imprisonment or, if the crime is serious, ten years' or life imprisonment (Article 7 Report, 1 May–30 Sept. 1999, Form A).

[22] Hajnoczi *et al.*, 'The Ban Treaty', in Cameron *et al.*, *To Walk without Fear*, 306.

[23] *Bundesgesetzblatt Teil I*, no. 43 (9 July 1998), 1778.

Trinidad and Tobago, the United Kingdom, and Zimbabwe.[24] A further 20 States Parties were in the process of adopting legislation: Albania, Argentina, Bangladesh, Benin, Bosnia and Herzegovina, Botswana, El Salvador, Kenya, Mauritania, Mexico, Niger, Peru, the Philippines, the Seychelles, South Africa, Swaziland, Thailand, Togo, Uganda, and Yemen.[25] A total of 13 States Parties had declared that their existing laws were sufficient to give effect to the Convention: Bulgaria, Croatia, Denmark, the Holy See, Ireland, Jordan, the Netherlands, Panama, Samoa, Senegal, St Vincent and the Grenadines, Thailand, and Tunisia.[26]

## Administrative Measures

**9.20** Administrative measures are actions determined or instructions issued by the executive but which do not necessarily have the force of law. The UK has identified a number of these in a non-exhaustive list: organizing stockpile destruction and/or placing of relevant contracts; issuing a clear command to all troops on the new responsibilities; rewriting military doctrine where appropriate; changing training procedures and rewriting military manuals; and refocusing the relevant parts of training programmes for foreign forces.[27] In addition, various administrative measures are required in support of legislation, such as: establishing a mechanism to grant permission to hold landmines for purposes permitted by the Convention; and putting in place procedures and allocating responsibilities to facilitate fact-finding missions.[28]

**9.21** There has been State practice in a number of these areas,[29] especially regarding military doctrine, manual, and training. Thus, for example, a number of States have adapted military doctrine and manuals and conducted training to familiarize the armed forces with obligations under the Convention. Australia, for instance, has prepared a Training Information Bulletin (TIB), No. 86, entitled 'The Ottawa Convention: A Commander's Guide', which was promulgated in October 1999 within the Australian Defence Force. The document aims to provide commanders and staff with an interpretation of

---

[24] Presentation by the ICRC to the Standing Committee on the General Status and Operation of the Convention (Geneva, 16 May 2003), available at: www.gichd.ch.                     [25] ibid.

[26] ibid.

[27] Information provided by Peter Balmer, UK Ministry of Defence, in facsimile to the author (18 June 2002).

[28] ibid. According to Peter Balmer, the UK has already taken all of the above steps.

[29] See VERTIC, *Guide to Reporting under Article 7 of the Ottawa Convention* (London: VERTIC, 2001), available at: www.vertic.org.

revised policy on landmines, booby-traps, and improvised explosive devices and their application to military operations.[30] In Brazil, on 11 August 1999, the Ministry of Defence of Brazil formally instructed the Navy, Army, and Air Force Commanders to disseminate the text of the Convention in military school instruction courses, at the Graduation, Advanced, and Staff levels.[31] In 2001, Canada's Office of the Judge Advocate General issued a new document, *The Law of Armed Conflict at the Operational and Tactical Level—Annotated*, which includes doctrine and policy towards the Anti-Personnel Mine Ban Convention.[32]

## Other Measures

**9.22** Beyond the administrative measures referred to above, the NGO, VERTIC, has noted that it 'would be helpful' if experts nominated by States to serve on fact-finding missions received regular or periodic training.[33] Civil law States typically publish details of the Convention in the official journal (Gazette),[34] or even in the newspapers, as was done on a number of occasions by Liechtenstein, in order to inform the general public of the obligations stemming from the Convention.

**9.23** More practically, States can usefully 'rehearse' hosting a fact-finding mission. Thus, for example, in January 2002, the UK Ministry of Defence simulated an investigation, based on Article 8 compliance processes, into hypothetical breaches of the Convention in the UK.[35] The three-day exercise, Operation Partlett, was intended to present an opportunity for different parties to learn

---

[30] The Department of Defence also produced an information document, Defgram No. 196/99, entitled 'Ottawa Landmines Convention—Defence Implications and Obligations'. A Defgram is a publication disseminated within the Defence Organization. Defgram 196/99 is an information document, conveying to the Defence Organization its obligations under the Ottawa Convention. Form A, Article 7 Report for the period 1 June–27 Dec. 1999, submitted on 23 Dec. 1999.

[31] Form A, Article 7 Report for the period Oct. 1999–Mar. 2000, submitted on 30 Apr. 2001.

[32] Office of the Judge Advocate General, The Law of Armed Conflict, Department of National Defence (Canada, 21 Mar. 2001).

[33] VERTIC, *Guide to Fact-Finding Missions under the Ottawa Convention*, 25.

[34] In Brazil, on 5 Aug. 1999, the text of the Convention was published in the *Union's Official Diary* (the Federal Government's official journal), along with Presidential Decree No. 3128, whereby the President of the Republic promulgated the Convention. 'Promulgation' is a necessary procedure under Brazilian Constitutional Law, whereby an international treaty previously ratified by Brazil is formally incorporated into the corpus of domestic law. The publication of the treaty's text in the Federal Government's official journal also constitutes a national dissemination measure. Form A, Article 7 Report for the period Oct. 1999–Mar. 2000, submitted on 30 Apr. 2001.

[35] ICBL, *Landmine Monitor Report 2002*, 508.

about the processes of both conducting and hosting an investigation. The main parties involved were a fact-finding mission, National Authority representatives, the Joint Arms Control Implementation Group, staff at the Defence Munitions depot in Plymouth, and a number of observers, including NGOs. The hypothetical breach being investigated was a claim that the UK had allowed transshipment by the USA of anti-personnel mines through UK bases during mobilization for the conflict in Afghanistan. This was the third such exercise to be undertaken at different military premises in the UK.[36] It was subsequently repeated in Febuary 2003 and there are likely to be similar exercises in future.[37]

## Persons or on Territory under its Jurisdiction or Control

9.24 Article 9 does not specify whether the term 'persons' covers legal persons (i.e. companies or corporations) as well as natural persons (human beings). The issue of sanctioning a corporation criminally falls under the concept of domestic jurisdiction of States[38] and thus varies from one State to another.[39] The object and purpose of the Convention would suggest a broad reading of the term; its ordinary meaning would lean towards a narrower understanding, excluding companies from the obligatory scope of the provision. In addition, during the Oslo Diplomatic Conference, the USA put forward a proposal to cover legal persons under the article, but this was not accepted.[40] State practice is varied but tends to focus on the individual.[41]

9.25 A State Party has to take the above-mentioned measures against prohibited acts undertaken 'by persons or on territory under its jurisdiction or control'. At a minimum, a State Party has 'jurisdiction' over conduct that takes

---

[36] ICBL, *Landmine Monitor Report 2002*, 508.

[37] Information provided by Peter Balmer, UK Ministry of Defence, in email of 16 July 2003.

[38] For an overview of recent developments in this field of law, see e.g. Kamminga, M. T. and Zia-Zarifi, S. (eds.), *Liability of Multilateral Corporations under International Law* (The Hague: Kluwer Law International, 2000).

[39] See Kellman and Tanzman, *Manual for National Implementation of the Chemical Weapons Convention*, 54 ff.          [40] APL/CW.14 of 1 Sept. 1997.

[41] The Canadian Anti-Personnel Mines Convention Implementation Act, for example, contains penalties for 'individuals' only, who are found guilty of contravening provisions of the Act (Article 7 Report for the period 1 Aug. 1999–14 Mar. 2000). In contrast, the Czech Act No. 305/1999 on the prohibition of the use, stockpiling, production, and transfer of anti-personnel mines and their destruction and on the amendment to Act No. 140/1961 (Criminal Code), which entered into force on 3 Dec. 1999, bans both natural and legal persons from developing in the territory of the Czech Republic activities violating the provisions of the Convention (Article 7 Report for the period 1 Jan.–31 Dec. 2001).

place or has harmful effects within its territorial boundaries, including relevant coastal waters and seabed areas (the so-called 'territorial theory' of jurisdiction). The term 'control' suggests extension of this authority to conduct that takes place at embassies, military installations, and other locations within another nation's jurisdiction, including occupied territory, but which are nevertheless under a State Party's legal control.[42]

---

[42] Kellman and Tanzman, *Manual for National Implementation of the Chemical Weapons Convention*, 7.

# FINAL CLAUSES

## Article 10.  Settlement of Disputes

Article 10—Settlement of disputes

1.  The States Parties shall consult and cooperate with each other to settle any dispute that may arise with regard to the application or the interpretation of this Convention. Each State Party may bring any such dispute before the Meeting of the States Parties.

2.  The Meeting of the States Parties may contribute to the settlement of the dispute by whatever means it deems appropriate, including offering its good offices, calling upon the States Parties to a dispute to start the settlement procedure of their choice and recommending a time-limit for any agreed procedure.

3.  This Article is without prejudice to the provisions of the Convention on facilitation and clarification of compliance.

## Introduction

**10.1** As has been remarked, 'Treaties give rise to numerous disputes about their interpretation or application. Although the two terms are usually mentioned in the same breath, strictly speaking when the meaning is clear the text is applied; when it is not clear, it has to be interpreted'.[1] International law typically seeks to resolve such disputes[2] not through enforcement

---

[1] Aust, *Modern Treaty Law and Practice*, 285, citing McNair, *Law of Treaties*, 365.

[2] A 'dispute' has been defined by the Permanent Court of International Justice as 'a disagreement on a point of law or fact, a conflict of legal views or interests between persons'. *Mavrommatis case*, Permanent Court of International Justice, 1924, Ser. A, No. 2, pp. 11–12. A more recent statement by the

mechanisms, at least initially, but through diverse, pacific means of dispute settlement.[3]

**10.2** It has been claimed that: 'A well-drafted dispute settlement article provides an element of stability in any treaty regime. It does this by specifying the range of procedures which any disputants will be expected to follow, and by giving formal recognition to the wider international interest which entitles those treaty institutions to take the initiative in offering some form of intermediary intervention or encouraging direct negotiation'.[4] Thus, it is common practice to include a provision dealing with the settlement of disputes in treaties;[5] this is recommended by the 1982 Manila Declaration on the Peaceful Settlement of Disputes, which was annexed to United Nations (UN) General Assembly resolution 37/190.[6]

**10.3** In the case of the Anti-Personnel Mine Ban Convention, there have been differences of opinion as to both the interpretation and application of a number of its provisions, although Article 10 has never been formally invoked.[7] It could also be applied with respect to administrative and procedural disputes arising from the interpretation and application of the Convention.

**10.4** The Convention does not set out any formal mechanism for adjudication of any disputes. The UN Charter requires parties to 'any dispute, the

International Court of Justice suggested that a dispute 'is a disagreement on a point of law, a conflict of legal views or interests between parties'. Case Concerning East Timor (Portugal v. Australia), *ICJ Reports*, 1995, pp. 90, 99, cited by Clark, R. S., 'Article 119—Settlement of Disputes', in Triffterer, O. (ed.), *Commentary on the Rome Statute of the International Criminal Court: Observers' Notes, Article by Article* (Baden-Baden: Nomos Verlagsgesellschaft, 1999), 1242–3.

[3] See Article 2(3) of the UN Charter: 'All Members shall settle their international disputes by peaceful means in such a manner that international peace and security, and justice, are not endangered'.

[4] Sims, N. A., 'Article XII: Settlement of Disputes', Bradford Evaluation Paper, Department of Peace Studies, University of Bradford (Bradford, Nov. 1999), 5, para. 9, available at: www.brad.ac.uk/acad/sbtwc/briefing/bw-briefing.htm.

[5] Schachter, O., *International Law in Theory and Practice* (Leiden: Brill Publishers, 1991), 184; see Myjer, E. P. J., 'The Settlement of Disputes under the Chemical Weapons Convention and the Case of the Confidentiality Commission', in Bardonnet, D. (ed.), *The Convention on the Prohibition and Elimination of Chemical Weapons: A Breakthrough in Multilateral Disarmament, Workshop, The Hague 24–26 November 1994* (Dordrecht: Martinus Nijhoff, 1995), 541ff.

[6] Paragraph 9 of the Declaration recommends that 'States . . . should also include in . . multilateral conventions to be concluded, as appropriate, effective provisions for the peaceful settlement of disputes arising from the interpretation and application thereof'. Cited in Krutzsch and Trapp, *A Commentary on the Chemical Weapons Convention*, 232 and n. 2.

[7] A draft provision on the settlement of disputes was first included as Article 11 of the Second Austrian Draft Text. It stated simply that: 'The States Parties undertake to consult each other and to cooperate with each other to resolve any problems that may arise with regard to the application and implementation of this Convention. Each State Party may bring any such problem to the attention of the Meeting of the States Parties'.

continuance of which is likely to endanger the maintenance of international peace and security' to seek a pacific settlement by 'negotiation, enquiry, mediation, conciliation, arbitration, judicial settlement, resort to regional agencies or arrangements, or other peaceful means of their own choice'.[8]

# Paragraph 1

1. The States Parties shall consult and cooperate with each other to settle any dispute that may arise with regard to the application or the interpretation of this Convention. Each State Party may bring any such dispute before the Meeting of the States Parties.

**10.5** Article 10(1) of the Convention provides broadly for two avenues to settle disputes relating to application and interpretation of its provisions: consultation and cooperation between States Parties, and referral of the dispute to a Meeting of the States Parties.[9] In the case of concerns about the application of the Convention by a State Party, these avenues should presumably be exhausted before resort is made to the more formal mechanisms set up by Article 8, unless it concerns an alleged serious violation of one or more of the Convention's provisions.[10]

**10.6** Thus, States Parties are first required 'to consult and cooperate with each other' to settle any dispute as to the application or interpretation of the Convention.[11] Broadly similar requirements are included in the 1993 Chemical Weapons Convention,[12] the 1996 Comprehensive Nuclear-Test-Ban Treaty,[13] and the 1972 Biological Weapons Convention.[14] In contrast to these

---

[8]  Article 33, United Nations Charter.

[9]  Compare with the provisions included in the 1977 Geneva Protocol relating to the Protection of Victims of International Armed Conflicts (Protocol I). Article 7 provides that: 'The depositary of this Protocol shall convene a meeting of the High Contracting Parties, at the request of one or more of the said Parties and upon the approval of the majority of the said Parties, to consider general problems concerning the application of the Conventions and of the Protocol'.

[10]  Indeed, Article 8(1) provides that: 'The States Parties agree to consult and cooperate with each other regarding the implementation of the provisions of this Convention, and to work together in a spirit of cooperation to facilitate compliance by States Parties with their obligations under this Convention'.

[11]  This is similar to the provision in Amended Protocol II to the 1980 Convention on Certain Conventional Weapons, which requires that: 'The High Contracting Parties undertake to consult and cooperate with each other on all issues related to the operation of this Protocol'. Article 13(1), Amended Protocol II.

[12]  Article XIV(2) provides that: 'When a dispute arises between two or more States Parties, or between one or more States Parties and the Organization, relating to the interpretation or application of this Convention, the parties concerned shall consult together with a view to the expeditious settlement of the dispute by negotiation or by other peaceful means of the parties' choice'.

[13]  Article VI(2).          [14]  Article V.

agreements, however, there is no recommendation to consider referral, by mutual consent, to the International Court of Justice.

**10.7** Any State Party[15] is also entitled (though not obliged) to bring any dispute as to the application or interpretation of the Convention before a Meeting of the States Parties. Article 11, which governs the Meetings of the States Parties, provides that the States Parties 'shall meet regularly in order to consider any matter with regard to the application or implementation of this Convention' and then sets out a non-exhaustive list of such matters.[16] Although it would have been appropriate to include the term 'interpretation' in the *chapeau* of Article 11, its omission does not preclude a State bringing such a dispute before the Meeting in accordance with Article 10.

## Paragraph 2

2. The Meeting of the States Parties may contribute to the settlement of the dispute by whatever means it deems appropriate, including offering its good offices, calling upon the States Parties to a dispute to start the settlement procedure of their choice and recommending a time-limit for any agreed procedure.

**10.8** The role of the Meeting of the States Parties is clearly set out in this provision. It 'may contribute to the settlement of the dispute by whatever means it deems appropriate, including offering its good offices, calling upon the States Parties to a dispute to start the settlement procedure of their choice and recommending a time-limit for any agreed procedure'. This provision is taken almost verbatim from the 1993 Chemical Weapons Convention.[17] The language of the paragraph suggests that the Meeting does not have the authority to impose a settlement on the parties to the dispute, although the parties could of course agree, in advance or *ex post*, to accept a decision of the Meeting as binding upon them.[18]

## Paragraph 3

3. This Article is without prejudice to the provisions of the Convention on facilitation and clarification of compliance.

---

[15] i.e., not only the State Parties involved directly in the dispute.
[16] Article 11(1); see the commentary on this provision.    [17] Article XIV(3).
[18] See also Krutzsch and Trapp, *A Commentary on the Chemical Weapons Convention*, 236.

**10.9** Although the precise nature of the relationship between Article 8 and Article 10 is not entirely clear, it remains open to a State Party to pursue concerns about the compliance of one or more other States Parties through the procedures laid down in Article 8. Article 8(1) provides that the States Parties 'agree to consult and cooperate with each other regarding the implementation of the provisions of this Convention, and to work together in a spirit of cooperation to facilitate compliance by States Parties with their obligations under this Convention'. In accordance with the general spirit of the Convention, the emphasis is put strongly on a consultative and cooperative, rather than a confrontational, approach to resolving disputes.

# Article 11. Meetings of the States Parties

Article 11—Meetings of the States Parties

1. The States Parties shall meet regularly in order to consider any matter with regard to the application or implementation of this Convention, including:

(a) The operation and status of this Convention;
(b) Matters arising from the reports submitted under the provisions of this Convention;
(c) International cooperation and assistance in accordance with Article 6;
(d) The development of technologies to clear anti-personnel mines;
(e) Submissions of States Parties under Article 8; and
(f) Decisions relating to submissions of States Parties as provided for in Article 5.

2. The First Meeting of the States Parties shall be convened by the Secretary-General of the United Nations within one year after the entry into force of this Convention. The subsequent meetings shall be convened by the Secretary-General of the United Nations annually until the first Review Conference.

3. Under the conditions set out in Article 8, the Secretary-General of the United Nations shall convene a Special Meeting of the States Parties.

4. States not parties to this Convention, as well as the United Nations, other relevant international organizations or institutions, regional organizations, the International Committee of the Red Cross and relevant non-governmental organizations may be invited to attend these meetings as observers in accordance with the agreed Rules of Procedure.

# Introduction

## Overview

11.1  The meetings of the States Parties were intended to give a permanence to the Convention in the absence of a secretariat, thereby going beyond the limited role of the Annual Conferences of States Parties to Amended Protocol II to the Convention on Certain Conventional Weapons. They were also foreseen as a mechanism to track implementation and compliance and to provide an opportunity for mine-affected States to present their respective situations. As will be seen, the meetings have become a major decision-making event, turning the Anti-Personnel Mine Ban Convention and its implementation mechanisms into a more dynamic process. States Parties have, for instance, set up intersessional Standing Committee meetings,[1] contact groups on Article 7 reporting, universalization, and mobilization of resources, and an 'Implementation Support Unit', to support implementation and encourage universalization of the Convention.

## The Negotiation of the Article

11.2  The suggestion to provide for a regular meeting of States Parties was first made at the 1997 Vienna Conference, and a provision to that effect was subsequently included in the Second Austrian Draft Text.[2] A similar forum, the Annual Conference of States Parties, had already been included in Article 13 of 1996 Amended Protocol II to the Convention on Certain Conventional Weapons (CCW),[3] after Western Group proposals for a detailed fact-finding

---

[1]  Currently, there are four Standing Committees—General Status and Operation of the Convention; Mine Clearance, Mine Awareness, and Mine Action Technologies; Stockpile Destruction; and Victim Assistance—each meeting twice yearly in Geneva.

[2]  Article 12, Second Austrian Draft Text of 14 Mar. 1997.

[3]  The work of the Annual Conference of States Parties includes: the review of the 'operation and status' of the Protocol; consideration of 'matters arising' from annual reports to be submitted by States Parties; preparation for review conferences; and consideration of the development of technologies to protect civilians against indiscriminate effects of mines. Article 13(3)(a)–(d).

and inter-State 'Verification Commission' had failed to gain acceptance at the First CCW Review Conference in 1995–6.

**11.3** An advance draft of the Second Austrian Draft Text circulated in early March to the Core Group had proposed that meetings of States Parties be held annually for an indefinite period of time, but South Africa was opposed on the basis that it might place an excessive burden on developing States, and that, as time went by and stockpiles were destroyed and emplaced anti-personnel mines cleared, there would be less need for such regular meetings. As a result, it was decided to hold annual meetings only until the First Review Conference of the Convention, which takes place in 2004, when a decision will be taken on the need for and interval between future meetings.[4]

**11.4** In accordance with Article 14(1) of the Anti-Personnel Mine Ban Convention, the costs of the Meetings of the States Parties and any Special Meeting of the States Parties[5] are met by the States Parties participating therein. The burden of costs is calculated in accordance with the United Nations scale of assessment, adjusted to take account of the fact that not all members of the United Nations are party to the Convention.

**11.5** The annual Meetings of the States Parties have been supported by 'intersessional' meetings of 'Standing Committees of Experts' (now renamed simply Standing Committees), in accordance with a decision taken by the First Meeting of the States Parties.[6] It was understood that it would be important to maintain the momentum that had been generated through the Ottawa Process in achieving universality of the Convention and promoting its effective implementation.[7] The Geneva International Centre for Humanitarian Demining, opened by the Swiss government in 1998, offered to support the intersessional meetings.[8]

---

[4] See, below, the commentary on Article 12.

[5] See para. 11.19 below and, above, the commentary on Article 8

[6] 'Final Report', UN Doc. APLC/MSP.1/1999/1, of 20 May 1999.

[7] The President's Paper on the Intersessional Work Programme suggested that the meetings could enable: 'In-depth consideration of relevant questions for improving Mine Action within the above categories and outlining specific activities . . . Facilitating and supporting the effective functioning of the Convention as an instrument of Mine Action by maintaining practical work at a high level and with particular emphasis on international cooperation among governments, international organizations and non-governmental organizations (NGOs). The role of the intersessional Work Programme undertaken by the SCEs should be an essential element in maintaining the momentum and cohesion behind the global humanitarian Mine Action effort. The work of the SCEs should support, inter alia, the coordination role played by the United Nations Mine Action Service (UNMAS) as the focal point for United Nations Mine Action, and encourage the active participation of the United Nations and regional organizations active in Mine Action'. See 'President's Paper on Intersessional Work', APLC/MSP.1/1999/Informal 2, Annex IV to the Final Report of the Meeting.     [8] See ibid.

**11.6** There are currently four Standing Committees[9]—the Standing Committee on the General Status and Operation of the Convention; the Standing Committee on Victim Assistance and Socio-Economic Reintegration; the Standing Committee on Mine Clearance, Mine Awareness, and Mine Action Technologies; and the Standing Committee on Stockpile Destruction—each meeting twice a year in 2002 and 2003.[10] It is likely that the Review Conference will decide on the future frequency of the Standing Committee meetings, and that this decision will be, indirectly at least, linked to the frequency of Meetings of the States Parties.[11]

**11.7** The intersessional meetings are supported by an 'Implementation Support Unit', which was set up following a decision of the Third Meeting of States Parties.[12] The Unit is hosted by the Geneva International Centre for Humanitarian Demining and has a small permanent staff. The duties of the Implementation Support Unit (ISU) are to support Coordinating Committee (CC) meetings[13] and the current President and incoming President of the Meeting of States Parties; carry out communication and liaison relating to the Convention; provide assistance in administrating the sponsorship programme, budgeting and planning functions, and collecting, collating, storing, and retrieving documentation on the Convention and its implementation.[14]

**11.8** The Convention as a whole, however, did not provide for a formal secretariat. It was argued that resources should be devoted to mine clearance and

---

[9] Initially there were five: Mine Clearance; Victim Assistance, Socio-Economic Reintegration, and Mine Awareness; Stockpile Destruction; Technologies for Mine Action; and General Status and Operation of the Convention.

[10] Standing Committee meetings have been well attended. For example, in 2001–2, more than 80 States Parties, 30 non-party States, as well as the ICRC, ICBL and 'numerous' other international and non-governmental organizations participated in one or more of the Standing Committee meetings on the General Status and Operation of the Convention. See APLC/MSP.4/2002/SC.4/1 of 19 July 2002, p. 1, available at: www.gichd.ch.          [11] See below the commentary on Article 12(2)(b).

[12] According to the Final Report of the meeting: 'States Parties endorsed the President's Paper on the Establishment of an Implementation Support Unit, as contained in Annex II to this report. States Parties warmly welcomed the establishment, within the GICHD, of an Implementation Support Unit to further enhance the operation and the implementation of the Convention. States Parties expressed their appreciation to the GICHD for its cooperation in the establishment of this unit, encouraged States in a position to do so to make voluntary contributions in support of the unit and mandated the President of the Third Meeting, in consultation with the Coordinating Committee, to finalise an agreement with the GICHD on the functioning of the unit'. APLC/MSP.3/2001/1 of 10 Jan. 2002, p. 7, para. 31.

[13] The Coordinating Committee is a mechanism established by the Second Meeting of States Parties. It brings together the co-chairs and the co-rapporteurs from the intersessional Standing Committees with the President of the Meeting of States Parties. The ICBL and the ICRC are extended an invitation as observers, as is the Manager of the Implementation Support Unit.

[14] For a detailed list of the tasks to be performed see Annex II to APLC/MSP.3/2001/1 of 10 Jan. 2002, p. 16, sect. B.

victim assistance rather than to set up new structures,[15] although there is also a sense that in addition to this, certain States Parties did not wish to see decision-making power ceded to an outside body.[16]

# Paragraph 1

1. The States Parties shall meet regularly in order to consider any matter with regard to the application or implementation of this Convention, including:

(a)  The operation and status of this Convention;
(b)  Matters arising from the reports submitted under the provisions of this Convention;
(c)  International cooperation and assistance in accordance with Article 6;
(d)  The development of technologies to clear anti-personnel mines;
(e)  Submissions of States Parties under Article 8; and
(f)  Decisions relating to submissions of States Parties as provided for in Article 5.

**11.9**  The Convention does not lay down detailed decision-making rules for the Meetings of the States Parties, leaving it to the Rules of Procedure of each Meeting. At the Fourth Meeting of States Parties, in Geneva, in September 2002, the Rules of Procedure provided that:

Chapter V.  Decision-Making

*Promotion of general agreement*
*Rule 11*

The Meeting of the States Parties shall make every effort to reach general agreement on matters of substance.

*Voting rights*
*Rule 12*

Each State Party participating at the Meeting of the States Parties shall have one vote.

---

[15]  Funding is clearly an issue. Even after the events of 11 September 2001, the head of the OPCW was warning that it lacked the necessary financial support. See e.g. Simons, M., 'Money Short for Battle on Chemicals Use in War', *The New York Times* (5 Oct. 2001), p. A9.

[16]  A number of States Parties have privately noted their concern that the authority of States Parties might have been compromised by a separate institution capable of taking substantive decisions relating to the Convention.

*Quorum*
*Rule 13*

The presence of representatives of 30 of the participating States Parties shall be required for any decision to be taken.

*Majority required*[17]
*Rule 14*

1. Decisions of the Meeting of the States Parties on all matters of substance shall be taken by a two-thirds majority of the representatives of States Parties present and voting.

2. Decisions of the Meeting of the States Parties on matters of procedure shall be taken by a majority of the representatives of States Parties present and voting.

3. If the question arises whether a matter is one of procedure or of substance, the President of the Meeting of the States Parties shall rule on the question. An appeal against this ruling shall be put to the vote immediately and the President's ruling shall stand unless overruled by a majority of the representatives of States Parties present and voting.[18]

## The Duty to Meet Regularly

**11.10** States Parties *shall* meet regularly, defined as once a year until the convening of the first Review Conference of the Convention. This implies that the Review Conference may not decide not to convene any more meetings of States Parties, although 'regularly' is not capable of precise definition. It does not, though, necessarily mean 'often'. It has been suggested by the President of the Fourth Meeting of States Parties that there be two meetings a year, made up of intersessional meetings and/or a meeting of States Parties. This will be decided at the first Review Conference.[19]

## The Application or Implementation of the Convention

**11.11** States Parties can consider *any* matter with regard to the application or implementation of the Convention. It is made explicit that the list of specific matters to be considered is not exclusive. None the less, paragraph 1 enumerates a list of specific issues some or all of which may be considered by the Meeting. These are: the operation and status of the Convention; matters arising from the Article 7 Reports;[20] international cooperation and assistance in accordance with Article 6; the development of technologies to clear

---

[17] This rule is subject to the rules for decision-making laid down in Articles 5 and 8.

[18] Rules of Procedure, APLC/MSP.4/2002/L.3, available at: www.gichd.ch.

[19] As of writing, discussions were ongoing, with a difference of opinion between a number of States from the North and the South.     [20] See further, above, the commentary on Article 7.

anti-personnel mines; submissions of States Parties under Article 8;[21] and decisions relating to requests for an extension of the deadline for clearance of anti-personnel mines under Article 5.[22]

## Paragraph 2

2. The First Meeting of the States Parties shall be convened by the Secretary-General of the United Nations within one year after the entry into force of this Convention. The subsequent meetings shall be convened by the Secretary-General of the United Nations annually until the first Review Conference.

### The First Meeting of the States Parties

**11.12** In accordance with United Nations (UN) General Assembly resolution 53/77 of 12 January 1999, the Secretary-General of the UN convened the First Meeting of the States Parties in Maputo, Mozambique, from 3–7 May 1999. Article 13(2) of the Convention required that the meeting take place within a year of its entry into force; in fact, it was held just over two months after the Convention had become binding under international law for the first 44 States that adhered to it.[23]

**11.13** A total of 43 States Parties were represented at the meeting in Maputo,[24] together with 18 that had ratified but for which the Convention had not yet entered into force,[25] and 47 States not party to the Convention.[26] As noted above, the Meeting decided *inter alia* to set up the Intersessional Work Programme.

---

[21] To date, no State Party has made a submission under Article 8.

[22] To date, no request has been submitted.

[23] See, below, the commentary on Article 17(1).

[24] Austria, Belgium, Benin, Bolivia, Bosnia and Herzegovina, Bulgaria, Burkina Faso, Canada, Croatia, Denmark, France, Germany, Guinea, the Holy See, Honduras, Hungary, Ireland, Jamaica, Japan, Jordan, Malawi, Mali, Mauritius, Mexico, Mozambique, Namibia, Nicaragua, Norway, Panama, Paraguay, Peru, San Marino, Senegal, Slovenia, South Africa, Sweden, Switzerland, Thailand, the former Yugoslav Republic of Macedonia, Turkmenistan, the United Kingdom, Yemen, and Zimbabwe. There were at that time 55 States Parties to the Convention.

[25] Antigua and Barbuda, Australia, Brazil, Chad, Ecuador, El Salvador, Guatemala, Italy, Lesotho, Malaysia, the Netherlands, New Zealand, Niger, Portugal, Slovakia, Spain, Swaziland, and Uganda.

[26] Albania, Algeria, Angola, Argentina, Bangladesh, Burundi, Cambodia, Cameroon, Cape Verde, Chile, China, Colombia, Côte d'Ivoire, Cuba, Cyprus, Czech Republic, Dominican Republic, Ethiopia, Finland, Gabon, Georgia, Ghana, Greece, Iceland, Indonesia, Israel, Kazakhstan, Kenya, Libyan Arab Jamahiriya, Lithuania, Luxembourg, Mauritania, Morocco, Nepal, Philippines, Poland, Romania, Rwanda, Saint Vincent and the Grenadines, Singapore, Sri Lanka, Sudan, Togo, Turkey, Ukraine, Tanzania, and Zambia.

## The Second Meeting of the States Parties

11.14 The Second Meeting of States Parties was held in Geneva on 11–15 September 2000.[27] A total of 62 States Parties participated in the Meeting.[28] In addition, seven States that ratified the Convention, but for which the Convention had not yet entered into force, participated in the Meeting as observers.[29] The Meeting decided *inter alia* to set up the Coordinating Committee.

## The Third Meeting of the States Parties

11.15 The Third Meeting of States Parties was hosted by Nicaragua in Managua on 18–21 September 2001.[30] A total of 67 States Parties participated in the Meeting.[31] In addition, six States that had ratified the Convention, but for which the Convention had not yet entered into force,[32] participated in the Meeting as observers.[33] Eleven signatories participated in the Meeting as observers,[34] as did 11 States not parties to the Convention.[35] The Meeting decided *inter alia* to set up the Implementation Support Unit, to be hosted at the Geneva International Centre for Humanitarian Demining.

---

[27] See the Final Report of the Meeting, APLC/ MSP.2/2000/1 of 18 Sept. 2002, available at: www.gichd.ch.

[28] Albania, Argentina, Australia, Austria, Belgium, Benin, Bolivia, Bosnia and Herzegovina, Brazil, Bulgaria, Burkina Faso, Cambodia, Canada, Costa Rica, Croatia, Czech Republic, Denmark, Ecuador, El Salvador, France, Germany, Guatemala, Guinea, Holy See, Honduras, Hungary, Ireland, Italy, Jamaica, Japan, Jordan, Liberia, Liechtenstein, Luxembourg, Madagascar, Malaysia, Mali, Mexico, Monaco, Mozambique, the Netherlands, New Zealand, Nicaragua, Norway, Panama, Peru, Philippines, Portugal, Qatar, Senegal, Slovakia, Slovenia, South Africa, Spain, Sweden, Switzerland, Thailand, Tunisia, the UK, Venezuela, Yemen, and Zimbabwe.

[29] Bangladesh, Colombia, Côte d'Ivoire, Dominican Republic, Gabon, Ghana, and Mauritania.

[30] See the Final Report of the Meeting, APLC/MSP.3/2001/1 of 10 Jan. 2002, available at: www.gichd.ch.

[31] Albania, Argentina, Australia, Austria, Belgium, Belize, Benin, Bolivia, Bosnia and Herzegovina, Brazil, Bulgaria, Cambodia, Canada, Chad, Colombia, Costa Rica, Croatia, Czech Republic, Denmark, Dominican Republic, Ecuador, El Salvador, France, Germany, Ghana, Guatemala, Holy See, Honduras, Hungary, Ireland, Italy, Japan, Jordan, Kenya, Lesotho, Malaysia, Mali, Mauritania, Mexico, Mozambique, the Netherlands, New Zealand, Nicaragua, Norway, Panama, Peru, Philippines, Portugal, Qatar, Republic of Moldova, Romania, Rwanda, Senegal, Slovakia, South Africa, Spain, Sweden, Switzerland, Thailand, Togo, Uganda, the UK, Uruguay, Venezuela, Yemen, Zambia, and Zimbabwe.

[32] Chile, the Republic of Congo, Guinea-Bissau, Malta, Saint Vincent and the Grenadines, and Sierra Leone.

[33] In accordance with Article 11(4) of the Convention, and Rule 1, para. 1 of the Rules of Procedure of the Meeting.

[34] Algeria, Angola, Burundi, Cameroon, Cyprus, Ethiopia, Greece, Indonesia, Lithuania, Poland, and Sudan.

[35] Belarus, Cuba, Finland, Kuwait, Lao People's Democratic Republic, Morocco, Oman, Russian Federation, Syrian Arab Republic, Turkey, and Yugoslavia.

## The Fourth Meeting of the States Parties

**11.16** The Fourth Meeting of States Parties took place in Geneva on 16–20 September 2002. Eighty-nine States parties participated in the Meeting.[36] Five States that had ratified or acceded to the Convention, but for which the Convention had not yet entered into force, participated in the Meeting as observers.[37] Eleven signatories that have not ratified the Convention participated in the Meeting as observers,[38] as did 27 States not parties to the Convention.[39]

## The Fifth Meeting of the States Parties

**11.17** Thailand hosted the Fifth Meeting of States Parties in Bangkok on 15–19 September 2003. This was the final such Meeting prior to the first Review Conference of the Convention in 2004.[40]

## Future Meetings of the States Parties

**11.18** As noted below, the First Review Conference has the explicit task of deciding on the need for, and intervals between, future Meetings of the States Parties.

# Paragraph 3

3. Under the conditions set out in Article 8, the Secretary-General of the United Nations shall convene a Special Meeting of the States Parties.

---

[36] Albania, Algeria, Argentina, Australia, Austria, Bangladesh, Barbados, Belgium, Benin, Bolivia, Bosnia and Herzegovina, Brazil, Bulgaria, Burkina Faso, Cambodia, Canada, Chad, Chile, Colombia, Congo, Costa Rica, Côte d'Ivoire, Croatia, Czech Republic, Denmark, Dominican Republic, Ecuador, El Salvador, Equatorial Guinea, France, Germany, Ghana, Guatemala, Guinea, Guinea-Bissau, Holy See, Honduras, Hungary, Iceland, Ireland, Italy, Jamaica, Japan, Jordan, Kenya, Luxembourg, Former Yugoslav Republic of Macedonia, Madagascar, Malawi, Malaysia, Mali, Malta, Mauritania, Mauritius, Mexico, the Republic of Moldova, Monaco, Mozambique, the Netherlands, New Zealand, Nicaragua, Nigeria, Norway, Panama, Paraguay, Peru, Philippines, Portugal, Qatar, Romania, Rwanda, Senegal, Slovakia, Slovenia, South Africa, Spain, Sweden, Switzerland, Tajikistan, Thailand, Tunisia, Uganda, the UK, the United Republic of Tanzania, Uruguay, Venezuela, Yemen, Zambia, and Zimbabwe.

[37] Afghanistan, Angola, Cameroon, Comoros, and the Democratic Republic of Congo.

[38] Brunei Darussalam, Burundi, Cyprus, Ethiopia, Gambia, Greece, Haiti, Lithuania, Poland, Sudan, and Ukraine.

[39] Armenia, Azerbaijan, Belarus, Central African Republic, Cuba, Estonia, Finland, Georgia, Iraq, Israel, Kazakhstan, Kuwait, Kyrgyzstan, Latvia, Lebanon, the Libyan Arab Jamahiriya, Mongolia, Morocco, Nepal, Oman, Papua New Guinea, Saudi Arabia, Singapore, Sri Lanka, Syrian Arab Republic, Turkey, and Yugoslavia. [40] See, below, the commentary on Article 12.

## The Convening of a Special Meeting of the States Parties

**11.19** In accordance with Article 8(5), a requesting State Party may propose through the UN Secretary-General the convening of a Special Meeting of the States Parties to consider questions relating to the compliance of another State Party. If at least one-third of the States Parties indicate their support for such a meeting within 14 days of a communication from the Secretary-General regarding the proposal, he shall convene the meeting within a further 14 days. To date, no such proposal has been made.

# Paragraph 4

> 4. States not parties to this Convention, as well as the United Nations, other relevant international organizations or institutions, regional organizations, the International Committee of the Red Cross and relevant non-governmental organizations may be invited to attend these meetings as observers in accordance with the agreed Rules of Procedure.

## Participation in the Meeting of the States Parties

**11.20** States that are not parties to the Convention, including signatory States, the United Nations, 'other relevant international organisations or institutions, regional organisations, the International Committee of the Red Cross and relevant non-governmental organisations' *may* be invited to attend Meetings of the States Parties and any Special Meeting of the States Parties as observers. Although several members of the Core Group were in favour of an automatic invitation to non-governmental organizations to attend these meetings, there was concern on the part of others that this would not be acceptable to all States.[41] Consequently, it was decided to leave the decision to the States Parties when elaborating the rules of procedure for the meetings.[42]

---

[41] Given this concern, it is surprising that participation was not separated out into distinct provisions, as signatory States and non-governmental organizations are treated on exactly the same footing, even though a signatory State may be asked to respond to claims that it has committed acts 'which would defeat the object and purpose' of the Convention.

[42] A similar approach had previously been adopted with respect to participation in the Annual Conferences of States Parties to Amended Protocol II to the 1980 Convention on Certain Conventional Weapons. Article 13(2) of the Protocol provides simply that: 'Participation in the annual conferences shall be determined by their agreed Rules of Procedure'.

**11.21** According to the draft Rules of Procedure for the Fifth Meeting of States Parties:[43]

Chapter I. Participation in the Meeting of the States Parties

*Participation in the Meeting of the States Parties*

*Rule 1*

1. States Parties present at the Meeting of the States Parties will be participants. Other States may participate in the Meeting of the States Parties as observers.

2. Relevant international organizations or institutions and regional organizations may attend the Meeting of the States Parties as observers.

3. The United Nations Secretary-General, the UNHCR, UNDP, UNICEF, WHO, WFP, the International Committee of the Red Cross and the International Federation of the Red Cross and Red Crescent Societies, the Sovereign Order of Malta, the International Campaign to Ban Landmines, and the Geneva International Centre for Humanitarian Demining may attend the Meeting of the States Parties as observers.

4. Others that have received an invitation from the Coordinating Committee of Co-Chairs may attend the Meeting of the States Parties as observers, subject to approval of the Meeting of States Parties.

---

[43] www.gichd.ch/pdf/mbc/SC_feb03/Draft_Rules_of_Procedure_5MSP.pdf.

# Article 12. Review Conferences

Article 12—Review Conferences

1. A Review Conference shall be convened by the Secretary-General of the United Nations five years after the entry into force of this Convention. Further Review Conferences shall be convened by the Secretary-General of the United Nations if so requested by one or more States Parties, provided that the interval between Review Conferences shall in no case be less than five years. All States Parties to this Convention shall be invited to each Review Conference.

2. The purpose of the Review Conference shall be:

(a) To review the operation and status of this Convention;

(b) To consider the need for and the interval between further Meetings of the States Parties referred to in paragraph 2 of Article 11;

(c) To take decisions on submissions of States Parties as provided for in Article 5; and

(d) To adopt, if necessary, in its final report conclusions related to the implementation of this Convention.

3. States not parties to this Convention, as well as the United Nations, other relevant international organizations or institutions, regional organizations, the International Committee of the Red Cross and relevant non-governmental organizations may be invited to attend each Review Conference as observers in accordance with the agreed Rules of Procedure.

# Introduction

## Overview

**12.1** Many treaties provide for their review after a set period of time, particularly when it is clear that future developments may affect the subject-matter of the treaty or require amendment or expansion of its terms. For example, the 1980 Convention on Certain Conventional Weapons (CCW), to which three Protocols were originally annexed,[1] provided for the possibility of amending the Convention and its Protocols at a specially convened conference.[2] If, as occurred, no conference were convened after a period of 10 years following the entry into force of the Convention, any State Party was entitled to request the depositary to convene a conference 'to review the scope and operation' of the Convention and Protocols.[3] The Anti-Personnel Mine Ban Convention is slightly different, in so far as the Review Conference is not an amendment conference—the possibility of amendments is specifically foreseen in a separate procedure laid down in Article 14 of the Convention.

## The Negotiation of the Article

**12.2** A draft article on the convening of review conferences was first included in the Second Austrian Draft Text of 14 March 1997. It did not change substantively in the Third Austrian Draft Text:

1. A Review Conference shall be convened by the Depositary five years after the entry into force of this Convention, and thereafter regularly at five year intervals. All States Parties to this Convention shall be invited to each Review Conference.

2. The purpose of the Review Conference shall be to:

(a) review the operation and status of this Convention;

(b) consider any proposals for amendments to this Convention;

---

[1] Protocol on Non-Detectable Fragments (Protocol I); Protocol on Prohibitions or Restrictions on the Use of Mines, Booby-Traps and Other Devices (1980 Protocol II); Protocol on Prohibitions or Restrictions on the Use of Incendiary Weapons (Protocol III).

[2] Article 8(1) and (2), 1980 Convention on Certain Conventional Weapons.

[3] Article 8(3), 1980 Convention on Certain Conventional Weapons. On 3 May 1996, at the conclusion of the first Review Conference of the Convention in Geneva, States Parties agreed to convene a second Review Conference in five years' time. This took place in Geneva in December 2001, at which they agreed to hold a third Review Conference not later than 2006, i.e. after a further period of five years. The Final Declaration of the Second Review Conference provides that: 'The Conference agrees that future Review Conferences should continue to be held on a regular basis . . . The Conference decides, consistent with Article 8(3)(c) to convene a further Conference five years following the entry into force of the amendments adopted at the Second Review Conference, but in any case not later than 2006, with preparatory meetings starting as early as 2005, if necessary.' UN Doc. CCW/CONF.II/2, p. 8.

(c) consider the need for and the interval between further Meetings of the States Parties referred to in Article 12.

3. States not parties to this Convention, as well as the United Nations, other relevant international organizations or institutions, regional organizations, the International Committee of the Red Cross and relevant non-governmental organizations may be invited to attend each Review Conference as observers in accordance with the agreed Rules of Procedure.

4. The costs of the Review Conference shall be borne by the States Parties and States not parties to this Convention participating in the Review Conference, in accordance with the United Nations scale of assessment adjusted appropriately.[4]

**12.3** At the Oslo Diplomatic Conference, there were a number of amendments to the provision. First, the UK objected in the plenary to the automaticity of the review conferences[5] and proposed language that was subsequently incorporated to allow one or more State Parties to request a review conference, as long as the interval between conferences was not less than five years. The UK was supported by Australia, Canada, Spain, and Sweden. Only the International Committee of the Red Cross (ICRC) objected, pointing out that automaticity was important to promote both universality and implementation of the Convention.

**12.4** In the same plenary,[6] Slovenia proposed a new sub-paragraph for paragraph 2 whereby the review conference was authorized: 'To adopt, if necessary, in its final report conclusions related to the implementation of this Convention'. This proposal was accepted by the Diplomatic Conference. In addition, two other sections of the draft article were deleted: the provision for consideration of amendments, as a separate article was drafted to deal with this issue;[7] and the provision on costs, as all issues related to costs were placed in a new article.[8] It is not made clear whether a review conference could transform itself into an amendment conference, should it so decide.

# Paragraph 1

1. A Review Conference shall be convened by the Secretary-General of the United Nations five years after the entry into force of this Convention. Further Review Conferences shall be convened by the Secretary-General of the United Nations if so requested by one or more States Parties, provided that the interval between Review Conferences shall in no case be

---

[4] Article 13, Third Austrian Draft Text of 13 May 1997.
[5] It had previously raised the issue at the 1997 Brussels Conference.     [6] On 2 Sept. 1997.
[7] See, below, the commentary on Article 13.     [8] See, below, the commentary on Article 14.

less than five years. All States Parties to this Convention shall be invited to
each Review Conference.

**12.5** Thus, the Anti-Personnel Mine Ban Convention provides for one
automatic Review Conference,[9] which, as set out below, will take place from
29 November to 3 December 2004, and future review conferences upon request
of one or more State Parties, as long as the interval between conferences is not
less than five years. The functions of the Review Conference are set out in
paragraph 2 of this article.

**12.6** There is no formal process to prepare the First Review Conference of
the Convention. An informal process was launched by the Fourth Meeting of
States Parties whereby the President of the Meeting 'was mandated to undertake informal open-ended consultations on matters related to a preparatory
process for the First Review Conference—matters which could then be considered by States Parties at the Fifth Meeting of the States Parties. First open-
ended consultations were held in Geneva on 31 January 2003 and attended by
more than eighty participants from States Parties, representatives of non-
governmental organizations, international organizations and observers.[10]

**12.7** The results of the consultations included a recommendation that the
Review Conference be held over a period of five days in September 2004 or later,
depending on the UN calendar of events and meetings. With regard to the timing and duration of the preparatory process, Ambassador Lint declared that:

The States Parties have stated that, during preparatory meetings, they wish to
discuss:

(i) Administrative matters such as a draft agenda, a programme of work, rules
of procedure and cost estimates;
(ii) The nature and form of the review of the operation and status of the Convention, taking into account what has been achieved during the previous
meetings of States Parties and the intersessional programme of work;
(iii) The preliminary considerations of the need for and the interval between
Meetings of the States Parties that would take place after the First Review

---

[9] In the case of the 1972 Biological Weapons Convention, Article XII similarly provided for a
review conference to be convened five years after its entry into force. Subsequently, the States Parties
decided to meet 'at least' every five years. Goldblat, J., 'The Biological Weapons Convention: An
Overview', *International Review of the Red Cross*, no. 318 (30 June 1997), 262.

[10] Informal Open-ended Consultations held in Geneva on 31 January 2003 on matters related to a
Preparatory Process for the Mine-Ban Convention's First Review Conference, Non-Paper by the President of the Fourth Meeting of States Parties, presented on 7 February 2003 by Ambassador Jean Lint of
Belgium to the Standing Committee on the General Status and Operation of the Convention, available
at: www.gichd.ch/pdf/mbc/SC_feb03/speeches_gs/JeanLint%20informal%20consultations.pdf.

Conference, as mandated by Article 12, para 2, point 2. Preliminary views were exchanged about the appropriate interval between Meetings of States Parties, including the future intersessional work programme, taking into account the importance of achieving the humanitarian aims of the Convention and the universalization process.

(iv) Adjustments to the implementation mechanisms that have been established by the States Parties since the entry-into-force of the Convention, taking into account the decisions which will be made in relation to the interval between Meetings of States Parties.

(v) Preliminary considerations concerning any conclusions related to the implementation of the Convention, including the Final documents of the Review Conference.[11]

**12.8**  In a presentation following that by Ambassador Lint, Brazil noted that it was 'certain that the States Parties will continue to conduct the Ottawa Process through transparent and inclusive decision processes, consistent with the nature of the mandates established by the Convention'.[12]

**12.9**  By May 2003, a number of issues appeared to have been resolved. Thus, the Review Conference would be held at the United Nations facilities in Nairobi, Kenya, from 29 November to 3 December 2004.[13] The nationality of the President of the Review Conference would be other than Kenyan, but the Secretary-General of the Conference would be a representative of the host country.[14] It was planned to hold two preparatory meetings: on 13 February 2004 and 21–2 June 2004.[15] No Meeting of the States Parties will be held during 2004.

## Paragraph 2

2. The purpose of the Review Conference shall be:

(a) To review the operation and status of this Convention;

(b) To consider the need for and the interval between further Meetings of the States Parties referred to in paragraph 2 of Article 11;

---

[11] Informal Open-ended Consultations held in Geneva on 31 January 2003 on matters related to a Preparatory Process for the Mine-Ban Convention's First Review Conference, Non-Paper by the President of the Fourth Meeting of States Parties, presented on 7 February 2003 by Ambassador Jean Lint of Belgium to the Standing Committee on the General Status and Operation of the Convention, available at: www.gichd.ch/pdf/mbc/SC_feb03/speeches_gs/JeanLint%20informal%20consultations.pdf.

[12] Statement by Brazil to the Standing Committee on the General Status and Operation of the Convention, Geneva, 7 Feb. 2003.

[13] 'Update on the President's Consultations held in Geneva on 12 May 2003 on Preparing for the Convention's First Review Conference', Geneva, 15 May 2003, p. 1.                    [14] ibid.

[15] ibid.

(c) To take decisions on submissions of States Parties as provided for in Article 5; and

(d) To adopt, if necessary, in its final report conclusions related to the implementation of this Convention.

## Overview

**12.10** Paragraph 2 sets out an exhaustive list of purposes for the review conferences. Two of the four issues listed are broad, the two remaining are specific. The review of the operation and status of the Convention is potentially an extremely broad topic, covering both the interpretation and application of its provisions. Similarly, the possibility to 'adopt, if necessary, in its final report conclusions related to the implementation of this Convention' may cover a wide range of issues.

## Review of the Operation and Status of the Convention

**12.11** The intersessional Standing Committee on the General Operation and Status of the Convention has addressed a broad range of issues. Thus, the report of the Standing Committee to the Third Meeting of States Parties, held in Managua in September 2001, addresses the intersessional work programme, the 'Sponsorship Programme',[16] the role of the 'Coordinating Committee',[17] the preparation of the Third Meeting of States Parties, the establishment of an Implementation Support Unit,[18] as well as issues of universalization and interpretation of a number of provisions in the Convention.[19]

## Future Meetings of the States Parties

**12.12** As discussed, above, in the commentary on Article 11, the Convention provides for annual meetings of States Parties until the Review Conference. Given the financial burden imposed on developing States, it was agreed that the decision on the frequency of future meetings would be taken at the Review Conference. Given the requirement in Article 11(1) for States Parties 'to meet regularly', it does not appear possible for the Review Conference to decide that there will be no further meetings. It is assumed that decisions will be taken in accordance with the agreed Rules of Procedure. To date, all decisions in the Meetings of the States Parties have been taken by consensus,

---

[16] A programme established prior to the Second Meeting of States Parties to facilitate a broader participation of mine-affected countries in intersessional Standing Committee meetings

[17] See, above, the commentary on Article 11 for details of the Coordinating Committee.

[18] See, above, the commentary on Article 11 for details of the Implementation Support Unit.

[19] See 'Report of the Standing Committee on the General Status and Operation of the Convention to the Third Meeting of States Parties', Annex III, Doc. APLC/MSP.3/2001/1, pp. 38–41.

although there is provision for a decision to be taken on procedural matters by simple majority, and on substantive issues, by a two-thirds majority.[20]

## Extension of the Deadline for Clearance of Emplaced Anti-Personnel Mines

**12.13** The Review Conference is also authorized to decide on a request by a State Party for an extension to the deadline of 10 years from entry into force of the Convention for that State Party for the clearance of all anti-personnel mines in mined areas under its jurisdiction or control, in accordance with Article 5(3)–(6).[21] The decision is to be taken by a majority of votes of States Parties present and voting.[22]

## Conclusions Relating to the Implementation of the Convention

**12.14** Finally, the Review Conference is to adopt 'if necessary' in its final report 'conclusions related to the implementation' of the Convention. In addition to addressing the implementation of the 'core humanitarian aims' of the Convention (e.g. mine clearance, stockpile destruction, and victim assistance), this could presumably cover concerns about the compliance of any State Party. It is not clear whether implementation covers also the interpretation of the provisions of the Convention.

# Paragraph 3

> 3. States not parties to this Convention, as well as the United Nations, other relevant international organizations or institutions, regional organizations, the International Committee of the Red Cross and relevant non-governmental organizations may be invited to attend each Review Conference as observers in accordance with the agreed Rules of Procedure.

**12.15** Similar to the provision on participation in the Meetings of the States Parties and Amendment Conferences, States that are not parties to the Convention, including signatory States, the UN, 'other relevant international organisations or institutions, regional organisations, the International Committee of the Red Cross and relevant non-governmental organisations' may be invited to attend the Review Conference as observers in accordance with the agreed Rules of Procedure.

---

[20] See the Rules of Procedure and Articles 5 and 8.
[21] See, above, the commentary on Article 5.
[22] See, above, the commentary on Article 5(5).

# Article 13. Amendments

Article 13—Amendments

1. At any time after the entry into force of this Convention any State Party may propose amendments to this Convention. Any proposal for an amendment shall be communicated to the Depositary, who shall circulate it to all States Parties and shall seek their views on whether an Amendment Conference should be convened to consider the proposal. If a majority of the States Parties notify the Depositary no later than 30 days after its circulation that they support further consideration of the proposal, the Depositary shall convene an Amendment Conference to which all States Parties shall be invited.

2. States not parties to this Convention, as well as the United Nations, other relevant international organizations or institutions, regional organizations, the International Committee of the Red Cross and relevant non-governmental organizations may be invited to attend each Amendment Conference as observers in accordance with the agreed Rules of Procedure.

3. The Amendment Conference shall be held immediately following a Meeting of the States Parties or a Review Conference unless a majority of the States Parties request that it be held earlier.

4. Any amendment to this Convention shall be adopted by a majority of two-thirds of the States Parties present and voting at the Amendment Conference. The Depositary shall communicate any amendment so adopted to the States Parties.

5. An amendment to this Convention shall enter into force for all States Parties to this Convention which have accepted it, upon the deposit with the Depositary of instruments of acceptance by a majority of States Parties. Thereafter it shall enter into force for any remaining State Party on the date of deposit of its instrument of acceptance.

## Introduction

**13.1** The Second and Third Austrian Draft Texts had allocated responsibility to a Review Conference to consider any proposal for amendment.[1] The relevant provision gave no indication, however, as to how amendments were to be adopted, nor how they would become binding on States Parties. The provision on amendment included as a separate article in the Anti-Personnel Mine Ban Convention was negotiated at the Oslo Diplomatic Conference following a proposal introduced by Austria.[2] The text as adopted did not differ materially from that proposal. Amendment of the Convention is only possible in accordance with the provisions of Article 13.

**13.2** It is not entirely clear why the provisions for dealing with amendments are separated from the Review Conference, although it does appear to serve to discourage the proposing of amendments.[3] Two other reasons have been advanced: the first financial, the second, that in the case of an urgent need to amend the Convention, Article 12 might prevent this occurring, given that a review conference is to be convened on request and only if the interval between review conferences is at least five years. If it proves impossible to agree on common understandings regarding key articles, it may be that a number of States Parties will consider using the amendment procedure in Article 13 to address the issue.

## Paragraph 1

1. At any time after the entry into force of this Convention any State Party may propose amendments to this Convention. Any proposal for an amendment shall be communicated to the Depositary, who shall circulate it to all States Parties and shall seek their views on whether an Amendment Conference should be convened to consider the proposal. If a majority of the States Parties notify the Depositary no later than 30 days after its circulation that they support further consideration of the proposal, the Depositary shall convene an Amendment Conference to which all States Parties shall be invited.

**13.3** Since the Convention has already entered into force, any State Party may propose an amendment through the Secretary-General of the United

---

[1] See e.g. Article 13(2)(b) of the Third Austrian Draft Text of 13 May 1997.

[2] APL/CW.35 of 1 Sept. 1997.

[3] Although, of course, the term 'review' does not necessarily mean 'revision'.

Nations (UN), as Depositary of the Convention.[4] Upon receipt of a proposed amendment, the Depositary will circulate it to all States Parties. If a majority indicate to the Depositary that they wish to consider further the proposal within 30 days of its circulation, the Depositary will convene an 'Amendment Conference' to which all States Parties will be invited. In accordance with Article 14 of the Convention, the costs related to the Amendment Conferences shall be borne by the States Parties and States not parties to this Convention participating therein, in accordance with the UN scale of assessment adjusted appropriately.

13.4 The amendment can seemingly be of any nature, substantive, technical, financial, or procedural. It is not clear, however, if, procedurally, further proposals for amendments can be made by the proposing State Party or any other State Party during the Amendment Conference itself.

## Paragraph 2

> 2. States not parties to this Convention, as well as the United Nations, other relevant international organizations or institutions, regional organizations, the International Committee of the Red Cross and relevant non-governmental organizations may be invited to attend each Amendment Conference as observers in accordance with the agreed Rules of Procedure.

13.5 Similar to the provision on participation in the Meetings of the States Parties and Review Conferences, States that are not parties to the Convention, including signatory States, the UN, 'other relevant international organizations or institutions, regional organizations, the International Committee of the Red Cross and relevant non-governmental organizations' may be invited to attend any Amendments Conference as observers in accordance with the agreed Rules of Procedure.

## Paragraph 3

> 3. The Amendment Conference shall be held immediately following a Meeting of the States Parties or a Review Conference unless a majority of the States Parties request that it be held earlier.

13.6 The Amendment Conference shall be held immediately following a Meeting of the States Parties or a Review Conference unless a majority of the

---

[4] To date, however, none has done so.

States Parties request that it be held earlier. In contrast to the 1998 Rome Statute on the International Criminal Court,[5] there are no time-limits specified between the decision to convene an Amendment Conference and the Conference itself.

# Paragraph 4

4. Any amendment to this Convention shall be adopted by a majority of two-thirds of the States Parties present and voting at the Amendment Conference. The Depositary shall communicate any amendment so adopted to the States Parties.

**13.7** At a specially convened Amendment Conference any proposed amendment will be adopted by a majority of two-thirds of the States Parties present and voting.[6] The UN Secretary-General as depositary will communicate any amendment adopted to all the States Parties.

# Paragraph 5

5. An amendment to this Convention shall enter into force for all States Parties to this Convention which have accepted it, upon the deposit with the Depositary of instruments of acceptance by a majority of States Parties. Thereafter it shall enter into force for any remaining State Party on the date of deposit of its instrument of acceptance.

**13.8** Subsequently, States Parties notify the depositary of their consent to be bound by the amendment through the deposit of an instrument of acceptance. Once a majority of the States Parties have accepted the amendment, it will enter into force for all those who have deposited an instrument of acceptance. Subsequently, the amendment will enter into force for each remaining State Party immediately upon deposit of its instrument of acceptance. There is, however, no obligation on any State Party to accept any amendment.[7]

---

[5] Article 121(2).

[6] This threshold is the same as that required by Article 121 of the 1998 Rome Statute of the International Criminal Court.

[7] It has been noted, though, that: 'It may . . . be destabilising to a treaty for some States Parties to adhere to the treaty as amended and others to the unamended treaty, because this introduces two sets of obligations within the same treaty'. Pearson, G. S. and Sims, N., 'Article XIV: Amendments', Bradford Evaluation Paper, Department of Peace Studies, University of Bradford (Bradford, Jan. 2000), 5, para. 7.

**13.9** It is assumed that the UN Secretary-General will, in accordance with established practice, inform all States Parties of instruments of acceptance and of the entry into force of any amendments.[8]

---

[8] See Clark, R. S., 'Article 121—Amendments', in Triffterer, *Commentary on the Rome Statute of the International Criminal Court*, p. 1271.

# Article 14. Costs

Article 14—Costs

1. The costs of the Meetings of the States Parties, the Special Meetings of the States Parties, the Review Conferences and the Amendment Conferences shall be borne by the States Parties and States not parties to this Convention participating therein, in accordance with the United Nations scale of assessment adjusted appropriately.

2. The costs incurred by the Secretary-General of the United Nations under Article 7 and 8 and the costs of any fact-finding mission shall be borne by the States Parties in accordance with the United Nations scale of assessment adjusted appropriately.

## Introduction

**14.1** The Convention on the Prohibition of Anti-Personnel Mines is somewhat unusual among disarmament and humanitarian law treaties in including a separate article on costs. The proposal for a separate article on costs was first made by Austria at the Oslo Diplomatic Conference. Previous draft texts had not included a separate provision.[1]

**14.2** What is interesting is the difference between the two paragraphs of the article. Article 14(1) is, in substantive effect, no different from a provision governing the costs of the annual Conference of High Contracting Parties in Amended Protocol II to the 1980 Convention on Certain Conventional Weapons.[2] Article 14(2), however, which deals with costs incurred by the UN

---

[1] See APL/CW.39 of 2 Sept. 1997.

[2] 'The costs of the Conference of High Contracting Parties shall be borne by the High Contracting Parties and States not parties participating in the work of the Conference, in accordance with the United Nations scale of assessment adjusted appropriately.' Article 13(5), Amended Protocol II. NB: There is a small textual error in the provision as included in Roberts and Guelff, *Documents on the Laws of War*, 548.

with respect to Article 7 transparency reports and the compliance mechanism under Article 8, including any fact-finding missions, allocates all the costs to the States Parties.

**14.3** The Convention makes no provision for States Parties to finance the Intersessional Standing Committee meetings, nor the Implementation Support Unit (ISU) established by a decision of the Third Meeting of States Parties held in Managua, Nicaragua, in September 2001.[3] As discussed above,[4] during the negotiation of the Convention States decided not to set up a secretariat to support its implementation.[5]

## Paragraph 1

> 1. The costs of the Meetings of the States Parties, the Special Meetings of the States Parties, the Review Conferences and the Amendment Conferences shall be borne by the States Parties and States not parties to this Convention participating therein, in accordance with the United Nations scale of assessment adjusted appropriately.

**14.4** The costs of the various gatherings envisaged by the Convention[6] are to be met by States Parties participating in them, and, on the basis of their participation, non-party States.[7] The burden of costs is calculated in accordance with the UN scale of assessment adjusted to take account of the fact that not all UN members are party to the Anti-Personnel Mine Ban Convention.

## Paragraph 2

> 2. The costs incurred by the Secretary-General of the United Nations under Article 7 and 8 and the costs of any fact-finding mission shall be borne by the States Parties in accordance with the United Nations scale of assessment adjusted appropriately.

---

[3] Accordingly, the costs of the intersessional meetings and the ISU are met through voluntary contributions to the GICHD, which hosts both the meetings and the Unit.

[4] See, above, the commentary on Article 11.

[5] Compare the 1993 Chemical Weapons Convention, in which the issue of costs is addressed in the article that establishes the Organization for the Prohibition of Chemical Weapons, and the provisions also set out the voting sanctions in the event of unjustifiable non-payment of costs. Article VIII (7) and (8), 1993 Chemical Weapons Convention. See Krutzsch and Trapp, *A Commentary on the Chemical Weapons Convention*, 124, 130–2.

[6] Under Articles 8(5), 11, 12, and 13. For example, the Fourth Meeting of States Parties, held in Geneva in September 2002, cost US$255,800. See www.gichd.ch/pdf/mbc/4msp/4MSP_Cost_Estimates.pdf.

[7] Thus, at the Second Meeting of States Parties, held in Geneva in September 2000, the USA was reduced to watching from the public gallery, as it was not willing to pay its requisite share of the costs.

**14.5** The costs incurred by the UN Secretariat in receiving and transmitting reports submitted by States Parties under Article 7 of the Convention are to be borne by the States Parties in accordance with the UN scale of assessment adjusted to take account of the fact that not all UN members are party to the Convention. A similar burden is imposed on States Parties with respect to costs incurred by the UN in facilitating compliance under Article 8, including any fact-finding mission that may be conducted.

# Article 15. Signature

Article 15—Signature

This Convention, done at Oslo, Norway, on 18 September 1997, shall be open for signature at Ottawa, Canada, by all States from 3 December 1997 until 4 December 1997, and at the United Nations Headquarters in New York from 5 December 1997 until its entry into force.

## Introduction

**15.1** Most multilateral treaties have a specific article on signature.[1] Typically, however, signature alone does not constitute consent to be bound by a treaty but, as in the present Convention, is typically subject to ratification.[2] This approach is followed in the Anti-Personnel Mine Ban Convention.[3]

**15.2** An article allowing for signature of the Convention, for a period of 12 months, was included in the first draft text by Werner Ehrlich. No such article, however, was included in the First Austrian Draft Text, although this seems to have been merely an oversight.[4] The Second Austrian Draft Text provided that: 'This Convention shall be open to all States for signature before its entry into force'.[5] The draft provision was unchanged in the Third Austrian Draft Text of 14 May 1997.

---

[1] Aust, *Modern Treaty Law and Practice*, 348.

[2] Thus, it is generally inappropriate to refer to Signatory States as meaning States that have consented to be bound by a given treaty.      [3] See below the commentary on Article 16(1).

[4] As draft Article 8 states that the Convention 'is subject to ratification, acceptance or approval of the Signatories'.

[5] Article 14, Second Austrian Draft Text. The Belgian Draft Text similarly restricted signature to before entry into force of the Convention. The ICBL Draft Convention, however, allowed all States to sign the Convention without restriction.

**15.3** Following the announcement by Canada during the 1997 Brussels Conference that the treaty signing conference would be held in Ottawa on 3–4 December 1997,[6] the UN suggested, and the Core Group agreed, prior to the Oslo Diplomatic Conference, that the article should be redrafted as follows: 'This Convention shall be open for signature at Ottawa, Canada, by all States from 2 December 1997 until 4 December 1997, and at the United Nations Headquarters in New York from 5 December 1997 until its entry into force'. On 2 September 1997, in a plenary session of the Conference, Austria proposed these changes, which were accepted.

**15.4** One further addition was proposed at the Conference, Tanzania suggesting that credit be given in the Convention to Norway for their 'wonderful hospitality' in organizing the Conference and the words 'done at Oslo, on 18 September 1997' [7] were included in Article 15. [8]

## The 'Testimonium'

**15.5** The Convention is somewhat unusual among multilateral treaties in that it does not have a *testimonium*. A '*testimonium*' is the Latin name for the last, formal part of a treaty beneath which the plenipotentiaries sign.[9] Instead, the Convention merely includes the words 'done at Oslo, Norway, on 18 September 1997'. At the Oslo Diplomatic Conference, the UN pointed out that such a clause normally came at the end of the Convention.

## The Treaty Signing Conference in Ottawa

**15.6** A total of 121 States signed the Convention at the Treaty Signing Ceremony in Ottawa on 3–4 December 1997.[10] An additional 12 States signed the

---

[6] See para. 0.77 above.

[7] The International Committee of the Red Cross noted that 'done' was not the usual word employed, but the proposal was accepted none the less.

[8] Thus, the Convention could be known informally as the Oslo Treaty as well as the Ottawa Treaty.

[9] Aust, *Modern Treaty Law and Practice*, 352. Thus e.g. the final article of the 1993 Chemical Weapons Convention, Article XXIV, which deals with the authentic texts of the Convention, is followed by the *testimonium*: 'IN WITNESS THEREOF the undersigned, being duly authorized to that effect, have signed this Convention. Done at Paris on the thirteenth day of January, one thousand nine hundred and ninety-three'. See e.g. Bassiouni, M. C., *A Manual on International Humanitarian Law and Arms Control Agreements*, International and Comparative Criminal Law Series (Ardsley, NY: Transnational Publishers, 2000), 432.

[10] Algeria, Andorra, Angola, Antigua and Barbuda, Argentina, Australia, Austria, Bahamas, Barbados, Belgium, Benin, Bolivia, Bosnia and Herzegovina, Botswana, Brazil, Brunei Darussalam,

Convention at the UN in New York,[11] before it entered into force on 1 March 1999 in accordance with its Article 17. The last of these was Ukraine, which signed five days prior to entry into force. Since 1 March 1999, non-signatory States wishing to become parties to the Anti-Personnel Mine Ban Convention have to accede directly, in accordance with Article 16(2).

## Signature until Entry into Force

15.7  International humanitarian law, and many other multilateral treaties, have tended to set a time-limit within which a State can sign.[12] A number of human rights treaties impose no time-limit on signature.[13] The Anti-Personnel Mine Ban Convention has followed a trend evident in disarmament or arms control treaties by allowing signature only until the date of entry into force.[14] Given that a number of States with significant military power and possessing

Bulgaria, Burkina Faso, Burundi, Cambodia, Cameroon, Canada, Cape Verde, Chile, Colombia, Cook Islands, Costa Rica, Côte d'Ivoire, Croatia, Cyprus, Czech Republic, Denmark, Djibouti, Dominica, Dominican Republic, Ecuador, El Salvador, Ethiopia, Fiji, France, Gabon, Gambia, Germany, Ghana, Greece, Grenada, Guatemala, Guinea, Guinea-Bissau, Guyana, Haiti, Holy See, Honduras, Hungary, Iceland, Indonesia, Ireland, Italy, Jamaica Japan, Lesotho, Liechtenstein, Luxembourg, Madagascar, Malawi, Malaysia, Mali, Malta, Marshall Islands, Mauritania, Mauritius, Mexico, Monaco, Mozambique, Namibia, the Netherlands, New Zealand, Nicaragua, Niger, Niue, Norway, Panama, Paraguay, Peru, Philippines, Poland, Portugal, Qatar, Republic of Moldova, Romania, Rwanda, Saint Kitts and Nevis, Saint Lucia, Saint Vincent and the Grenadines, Samoa, San Marino, Senegal, Seychelles, Slovakia, Slovenia, Solomon Islands, South Africa, Spain, Sudan, Suriname, Swaziland, Sweden, Switzerland. Thailand, Togo, Trinidad and Tobago, Tunisia, Turkmenistan, Uganda, the United Kingdom, United Republic of Tanzania, Uruguay, Vanuatu, Venezuela, Yemen, and Zimbabwe.

[11] Albania, Bangladesh, Belize, Chad, Jordan, Kenya, Lithuania, the Maldives, Sao Tomé and Príncipé, Sierra Leone, Ukraine, and Zambia.

[12] See e.g. Article 151, Geneva Convention Relative to the Protection of Civilian Persons in Time of War of August 12, 1949 (Geneva Convention IV); Article 92, 1977 Geneva Protocol I Additional to the Geneva Conventions of 12 August 1949, and Relating to the Protection of Victims of International Armed Conflicts. Note also the 1998 Rome Statute of the International Criminal Court, Article 125(1): 'This Statute shall be open for signature by all States in Rome, at the headquarters of the Food and Agriculture Organization of the United Nations, on 17 July 1998. Thereafter, it shall remain open for signature in Rome at the Ministry of Foreign Affairs in Italy until 17 October 1998. After that date, the Statute shall remain open for signature in New York, at the United Nations Headquarters, until 31 December 2000'.

[13] See e.g. Article 48, International Covenant on Civil and Political Rights.

[14] Thus e.g. the 1993 Chemical Weapons Convention, Article XVIII provides that: 'This Convention shall be open for signature for all States before its entry into force'. Broadly similar provisions are included in the 1996 Comprehensive Nuclear-Test-Ban Treaty (Article 11), the 1963 Partial Test Ban Treaty (Article III, para. 1), and the 1972 Biological Weapons Convention (Article XIV, para. 1).

huge stockpiles of anti-personnel mines remain outside the Convention,[15] which will likely require considerable time to destroy, it is perhaps regrettable that it is no longer possible to sign the Convention.[16]

## The Consequences of Signature

**15.8** Even though a State's signature is subject to ratification, acceptance, or approval in order to constitute consent to be bound by the provisions, there are significant obligations that result from signing a treaty. According to the 1969 Vienna Convention:

Article 18

*Obligation not to defeat the object and purpose of a treaty prior to its entry into force*

A State is obliged to refrain from acts which would defeat the object and purpose of a treaty when:

(a)  it has signed the treaty or has exchanged instruments constituting the treaty subject to ratification, acceptance or approval, until it shall have made its intention clear not to become a party to the treaty; or

(b)  it has expressed its consent to be bound by the treaty, pending the entry into force of the treaty and provided that such entry into force is not unduly delayed.

**15.9** Thus, a signatory State to the Anti-Personnel Mine Ban Convention is obliged to refrain from acts which would defeat its object and purpose unless and until it makes its intention clear not to become a party to the treaty.[17] At the end of May 2003, these constraints applied to the 13 remaining signatory States: Brunei, Burundi, Cook Islands, Ethiopia, Greece, Guyana, Haiti, Indonesia, the Marshall Islands, Poland, Sudan, Ukraine, and Vanuatu.

**15.10** In seeking to ascertain the object and purpose of the Convention, a good starting-point is its title. The full, formal title is the Convention on the Prohibition of the Use, Stockpiling, Production and Transfer of Anti-Personnel Mines and on their Destruction. The apparent primacy accorded in the title to the prohibition on the 'use' of anti-personnel mines is supported by the opening preambular paragraph, which records that the States Parties are 'determined to put an end to the suffering and casualties caused by anti-personnel

---

[15]  According to the International Campaign to Ban Landmines (ICBL), for example, China has some 110 million anti-personnel mines, and Russia has some 60–70 million. ICBL, *Landmine Monitor Report 2002*, 8.      [16]  Although it is argued that it is better for universalization.

[17]  To date, none has done so. Under international law, it is generally believed to be not possible to withdraw a signature once appended to an international treaty, as the USA purported to do with respect to the 1998 Rome Statute of the International Criminal Court.

mines' (i.e. their use), and by Article 1 of the Convention (General Obligations), which separates out the obligation 'never under any circumstances' to use anti-personnel mines[18] from the remaining general obligations.[19] The prohibition on use is immediate and is not subject to any exception.

15.11 Thus, any hostile emplacement[20] by a signatory State of anti-personnel mines, as defined by the Convention, should be considered an act 'which would defeat the object and purpose of a treaty' and thereby represent a violation of that State's obligations under international law. This position is further evidenced by the 'Maputo Declaration' made by States Parties to the Convention at the conclusion of the First Meeting of States Parties. Paragraph 11 of the Declaration includes the following appeal: 'To those few signatories who continue to use these weapons, this is a violation of the object and purpose of the Convention that you solemnly signed. We call upon you to respect and implement your commitments'.[21]

15.12 It is also arguable that the development, production,[22] or acquisition of anti-personnel mines by a signatory State or, other than for one of the purposes specifically excepted in Article 3, the transfer of anti-personnel mines to another State or non-State entity, would likewise engage the international responsibility of the State concerned. Continued stockpiling of anti-personnel mines, however, would not constitute such an act, since it is lawful for a State Party to retain stockpiles for up to four years following the Convention's entry into force for it (although they are also obliged to destroy stockpiles 'as soon as possible').[23]

15.13 As discussed in relation to Article 7 above, there is no obligation upon signatories to submit a transparency report, although a number have voluntarily done so.[24]

---

[18] Article 1(1)(a).    [19] Article 1(1)(b) and (c) and Article 1(1)2.

[20] As opposed to emplacement of anti-personnel mines for training purposes in accordance with Article 3 of the Convention.

[21] Final Report of the First Meeting of States Parties, Maputo, 3–7 May 1999, Part II, Maputo Declaration, Maputo, Mozambique, 7 May 1999, para. 11.

[22] Or even the opening of new anti-personnel mine production facilities, without production actually being initiated. During the Oslo Diplomatic Conference, one State suggested privately that this was the *only* act that would defeat the object and purpose of the Convention!

[23] See, above, the commentary on Article 4.    [24] See paras. 3.29 and 7.5 above

# Article 16.  Ratification, Acceptance, Approval, or Accession

Article 16—Ratification, acceptance, approval or accession

1. This Convention is subject to ratification, acceptance or approval of the Signatories.

2. It shall be open for accession by any State which has not signed the Convention.

3. The instruments of ratification, acceptance, approval or accession shall be deposited with the Depositary.

## Introduction

**16.1**  According to the 1969 Vienna Convention: 'The consent of a State to be bound by a treaty may be expressed by signature, exchange of instruments constituting a treaty, ratification, acceptance, approval or accession, or by any other means if so agreed'.[1] In accordance with Article 16 of the Anti-Personnel Mine Ban Convention, States wishing to become party to it must ratify, accept, or approve their signature,[2] or, if they are not a signatory, must accede directly.

**16.2**  According to the 1969 Vienna Convention, ' "ratification", "acceptance", "approval" and "accession" mean in each case the international act so named whereby a State establishes on the international plane its consent to be bound by a treaty'.[3] The mechanism of ratification was originally devised to guard against the dangers of a State's plenipotentiary exceeding his powers or the instructions from his capital with regard to a particular treaty.[4] Formerly a function of the sovereign, it is now subject to the constitutional control of the Executive.[5]

---

[1] Article 11, 1969 Vienna Convention.

[2] In accordance with Article 15, signature must have occurred prior to 1 Mar. 1999, the date of entry into force of the Convention.       [3] Article 1(b), 1969 Vienna Convention.

[4] Shaw, M. N., *International Law*, 4th edn. (Cambridge: Cambridge University Press, 1997), 639–40.       [5] ibid., 640.

**16.3** In comparison, the terms 'acceptance' and 'approval' are 'more a matter of terminology than of substance. Acceptance and approval perform the same function on the international plane as ratification and accession; in particular they give a State time to consider a treaty at length before deciding whether to be bound. The main reason for the popularity of these terms is that they enable a State to evade provisions in its own constitution requiring the consent of the legislature for ratification'.[6]

**16.4** Accession has the same effect as signature and ratification combined.[7] In the view of one authority, accession is 'primarily the means for a State to become a party if, for whatever reason, it is unable to sign the treaty'.[8]

## Paragraph 1

1. This Convention is subject to ratification, acceptance or approval of the Signatories.

**16.5** Article 16(1) makes it clear that signature of the Anti-Personnel Mine Ban Convention does not amount to consent to be bound by its provisions. A signatory State must ratify, approve, or accept the Convention in order to become a State Party.[9] At the end of May 2003, only two States had accepted the Convention,[10] and one had approved it.[11]

## Paragraph 2

2. It shall be open for accession by any State which has not signed the Convention.

**16.6** Any State that has not signed the Convention may accede to it at any time.[12] Thus, the Convention allowed a State wishing to become a party

---

[6] Malanczuk, P., *Akehurst's Modern Introduction to International Law*, 7th rev. edn. (London: Routledge, 1997), 134.          [7] ibid., p. 133.

[8] Aust, *Modern Treaty Law and Practice*, 88. For a brief discussion of the case of the Former Yugoslav Republic of Macedonia, see below the commentary on para. 3 of this article.

[9] At 1 January 2004, 9 signatory States had yet to ratify: Brunei, Cook Islands, Ethiopia, Haiti, Indonesia, the Marshall Islands, Poland, Ukraine, and Vanuatu.

[10] Japan and the Netherlands.          [11] Slovakia.

[12] At 1 January 2004, 44 States had neither signed nor acceded nor become a party to the Convention: Armenia, Azerbaijan, Bahrain, Bhutan, China, Cuba, the Democratic People's Republic of Korea, Egypt, Estonia, Finland, Georgia, India, Iran, Iraq, Israel, Kazakhstan, the Republic of Korea, Kuwait, Kyrgyzstan, the Lao People's Democratic Republic, Latvia, Lebanon, the Libyan

to the Convention to accede rather than to sign and then ratify, approve, or accept it.[13]

**16.7** At the Oslo Diplomatic Conference, the UK, with support from Mexico, had called for accession to be possible only *after* entry into force. Austria pointed out, however, that the 1969 Vienna Convention allows accession before entry into force, and stated its belief that the provision as drafted would speed adherence.[14] Moreover, according to the UN Secretariat, this is consistent with the final clauses of most other treaties deposited with the Secretary-General of the UN.[15]

# Paragraph 3

> 3. The instruments of ratification, acceptance, approval or accession shall be deposited with the Depositary.

**16.8**  Each State wishing to become party to the Anti-Personnel Mine Ban Convention must deposit an instrument of ratification, acceptance, approval, or accession, as appropriate, with the depositary.[16] This is normal practice for multilateral treaties. The instrument should identify the treaty by its title and the date when and place where it was concluded; give the name and title of the person signing the instrument; and state when and where the instrument was issued.[17] By virtue of Article 21 of the Convention, the Secretary-General of the UN has been designated the depositary of the Convention.[18]

---

Arab Jamahariya, Micronesia, Mongolia, Morocco, Myanmar, Nepal, Oman, Pakistan, Palau, Papua New Guinea, the Russian Federation, Saudi Arabia, Singapore, Somalia, Sri Lanka, Syria, Tonga, Tuvalu, United Arab Emirates, the USA, Uzbekistan, and Vietnam.

[13]  At 1 January 2004 the following States had acceded to the Convention: Afghanistan, Belarus, the Central African Republic, Comoros, the Republic of Congo, the Democratic Republic of Congo, East Timor, Equatorial Guinea, Eritrea, Kiribati, Liberia, the Former Yugoslav Republic of Macedonia, Nauru, Nigeria, Serbia and Montenegro, Tajikistan, and Turkey.

[14]  Only two States, Equatorial Guinea and the Former Yugoslav Republic of Macedonia, took advantage of this possibility. It was, however, of considerable significance for the latter of the two, since the government has refused to sign a treaty under that name but was able to accede as the UN has accepted instruments of ratification under its preferred name, the Republic of Macedonia.

[15]  'Comments by the United Nations Secretariat on the Draft Convention on the Prohibition of the Use, Stockpiling, Production and Transfer of Anti-Personnel Mines and on their Destruction', attached to Note of the Secretary-General to the Permanent Representative of Austria to the United Nations (New York, 15 Aug. 1997), point 1(e). But compare the 1993 Chemical Weapons Convention, Article XX (Accession) of which provides that: 'Any State which does not sign this Convention before its entry into force may accede to it at any time thereafter'.

[16]  The International Committee of the Red Cross has prepared a ratification kit for the Convention in the six UN languages. See www.icrc.org.          [17]  Aust, *Modern Treaty Law and Practice*, 86.

[18]  See, below, the commentary on Article 21.

# Article 17.   Entry into Force

Article 17—Entry into force

1. This Convention shall enter into force on the first day of the sixth month after the month in which the 40th instrument of ratification, acceptance, approval or accession has been deposited.

2. For any State which deposits its instrument of ratification, acceptance, approval or accession after the date of the deposit of the 40th instrument of ratification, acceptance, approval or accession, this Convention shall enter into force on the first day of the sixth month after the date on which that State has deposited its instrument of ratification, acceptance, approval or accession.

## Introduction

**17.1**  The 1969 Vienna Convention provides that a treaty 'enters into force in such manner and upon such date as it may provide or as the negotiating States may agree'.[1] From the date of entry into force 'treaties start producing their effect and become binding on the parties thereto'.[2] In the case of the Anti-Personnel Mine Ban Convention, States Parties decided to select 40 ratifications or accessions as the threshold for entry into force, the same number as Austria has included in its first draft text.

**17.2**  Even before entry into force of a treaty, however, certain provisions among those included in the final clauses have legal effect.[3] Thus, Article 24(4)

---

[1] Article 24(1).

[2] United Nations, 'Summary of Practice of the Secretary-General as Depositary of Multilateral Treaties', Prepared by the Treaty Section of the Office of Legal Affairs, UN Doc. ST/LEG/3, undated, p. 66, cited by Roucounas, E., 'Uncertainties regarding the Entry into Force of some Multilateral Treaties', in Wellens, K. (ed.), *International Law: Theory and Practice, Essays in Honour of Eric Suy* (The Hague: Martinus Nijhoff, 1998), 179.

[3] For a brief discussion of this 'peculiarity' of the law of treaties see Roucounas, 'Uncertainties regarding the Entry into Force of some Multilateral Treaties', 182.

of the 1969 Vienna Convention provides as follows:

The provisions of a treaty regulating the authentication of its text, the establishment of the consent of States to be bound by the treaty, the manner or date of its entry into force, reservations, the functions of the depositary and other matters arising necessarily before the entry into force of the treaty apply from the time of the adoption of its text.[4]

Accordingly, in the case of the Anti-Personnel Mine Ban Convention, the articles addressing: signature; ratification, acceptance, approval, or accession; entry into force; provisional application; reservations; the depositary; and authentic texts,[5] all applied from the date of the adoption of the Convention, that is, 18 September 1997.

**17.3**  The choice of 40 States as the trigger threshold for entry into force corresponds to the number proposed by the Third Austrian Draft of 13 May 1997, which served as the basis of negotiations at the Oslo Diplomatic Conference. In its comments on the Third Austrian Draft, the International Committee of the Red Cross had stated its view that the threshold of 40 ratifications for entry into force was 'too high, particularly given that the threshold for the . . . [Convention on Certain Conventional Weapons] was only 20. Humanitarian law instruments such as the Geneva Conventions and Additional Protocols of 1977 entered into force upon the deposit of two ratifications.'[6]

**17.4**  Discussions at the Conference were complicated by a formal US request for the inclusion of an optional nine-year deferral period for entry into force as a new paragraph 3 of Article 16:

In the event that a State Party determines that it cannot immediately comply with the provisions of paragraphs 1(a), 1(b) of Article 1, as they relate to retention, stockpiling, transfer not involving transfer of title to or control over, and use of anti-personnel mines, it may declare at the time of the deposit of its instrument of ratification, acceptance, approval or accession to the Convention that it will defer compliance with those provisions for a period not to excess [sic] nine years from the entry into force of this Convention.[7]

After introducing the proposal, the USA received support from Australia, Chile, Ecuador, Japan, and Poland. However, Belgium, Colombia, Guinea, the Holy See, Norway, and South Africa opposed its inclusion. With the US proposal defeated, discussions focused on the number of ratifications needed for entry into force. Some 20 States proposed reducing the requisite number of ratifications required to 20,[8] while a broadly similar number of States sought to

---

    4  Article 24(4).        5  Articles 15, 16, 17, 18, 19, 21, and 22, respectively.
    6  'Comments of the International Committee of the Red Cross on the Third Austrian Draft (13/5/97) of the Convention on the Prohibition of Anti-personnel Mines', reproduced in Maresca and Maslen, *The Banning of Anti-Personnel Landmines*, 553.        7  APL/CW.15 of 1 Sept. 1997.
    8  Typically those States that favoured an approach more akin to humanitarian law than to disarmament.

raise it to 60 or more.[9] The number agreed upon and ultimately adopted represents a general compromise.[10]

# Paragraph 1

1. This Convention shall enter into force on the first day of the sixth month after the month in which the 40th instrument of ratification, acceptance, approval or accession has been deposited.

## The Date of Entry into Force of the Convention

**17.5** Thus, in accordance with Article 17(1), the Anti-Personnel Mine Ban Convention required 40 States to accede to, or sign and ratify, accept or approve, the Convention in order for it to enter into force. This occurred on 1 March 1999, less than 15 months after the Convention was first opened for signature,[11]—the first day of the sixth month after the month in which Burkina Faso became the fortieth State to consent to be bound by its provisions.[12]

**17.6** In accordance with Article 17, on 1 March 1999, the Anti-Personnel Mine Ban Convention became binding international law for a total of 45 States: Andorra, Austria, Bahamas, Belgium, Belize, Benin, Bolivia, Bosnia and Herzegovina, Bulgaria, Burkina Faso, Canada, Croatia, Denmark, Djibouti, Equatorial Guinea, Fiji, the Former Yugoslav Republic of Macedonia, France, Germany, Grenada, Holy See, Honduras, Hungary, Ireland, Jamaica, Japan, Malawi, Mali, Mauritius, Mexico, Mozambique, Namibia, Niue, Norway, Peru, Samoa, San Marino, Senegal, South Africa, Switzerland, Trinidad and Tobago, Turkmenistan, the UK, Yemen, and Zimbabwe.

# Paragraph 2

2. For any State which deposits its instrument of ratification, acceptance, approval or accession after the date of the deposit of the 40th instrument

[9] The USA had proposed that the Convention should only enter into force after 75 States had consented to be bound by its provisions, including the five Permanent Members of the UN Security Council. Sweden had proposed that 65 States be required to trigger entry into force, the same number as the 1993 Chemical Weapons Convention.

[10] Caflisch, L., and Godet, F., 'De la réglementation à l'interdiction des mines antipersonnel', *Revue suisse de droit international et de droit européen* (1998), 32.

[11] According to Emmanuel Roucounas, entry into force of multilateral treaties deposited with the Secretary-General of the United Nations normally occurs between three and five years after signature. Roucounas, 'Uncertainties regarding the Entry into Force of some Multilateral Treaties', 185.

[12] Burkina Faso deposited its instrument of ratification on 16 Sept. 1998.

of ratification, acceptance, approval or accession, this Convention shall enter into force on the first day of the sixth month after the date on which that State has deposited its instrument of ratification, acceptance, approval or accession.

## Entry into Force for other States Parties

17.7 Thus, each State that has notified the depositary of its consent to be bound by the Convention after its entry into force has become a State Party on the first day of the sixth month after the date on which it deposited its instrument of ratification, acceptance, approval, or accession. Pending entry into force, a State may declare that it will provisionally apply Article 1(1) of the Convention, in accordance with the provisions of Article 18 (see overleaf).

# Article 18.  Provisional Application

Article 18—Provisional application

Any State may at the time of its ratification, acceptance, approval or accession, declare that it will apply provisionally paragraph 1 of Article 1 of this
Convention pending its entry into force.

## Introduction

**18.1**  According to the 1969 Vienna Convention: 'A treaty or a part of a treaty
is applied provisionally pending its entry into force if: (a) the treaty itself so provides; or (b) the negotiating States have in some other manner so agreed'.[1] Thus,
provisional application may extend to a treaty as a whole or only to part of it.[2]

**18.2**  An article on the provisional application of the Anti-Personnel Mine
Ban Convention was first proposed by Belgium during the Oslo Diplomatic
Conference in response to the relatively high number of ratifications necessary
for entry into force; it had not been included in any of the draft treaty texts prepared by Austria. The original Belgian proposal was much stricter than the article
as ultimately adopted, applying automatically to all States and to the treaty as a
whole: 'The States Parties to this Convention decide of [*sic*] its provisional application from the time of their ratification, acceptance, approval or accession
pending its entry into force'.[3] This was unacceptable to the majority of delegations, although there was broad support for the general principle.

**18.3**  A revised proposal restricted the application to Article 1, but maintained its automatic imposition on all adhering States.[4] This, too, was not
accepted by the Conference as a number of States continued to express

---

[1] Article 25, 1969 Vienna Convention. See generally Aust, *Modern Treaty Law and Practice*,
139–41.
[2] See Lefeber, R., 'The Provisional Application of Treaties', in Klabbers J. (ed.), *Essays on the Law
of Treaties* (The Hague: Martinus Nijhoff, 1998), 84.      [3] See APL/CW.47 of 2 Sept. 1997.
[4] See APL/CW.47/rev.1 of 3 Sept. 1997.

concern. Japan and Spain called for the application to be optional. The UK objected on the basis that it was a 'Pandora's Box'. France claimed that provisional application was not satisfactory from a legal standpoint. Canada also objected, affirming that it might delay ratification or entry into force of the Convention.

**18.4** Austria, El Salvador, and Mexico, however, offered their support to the proposal, but in a spirit of compromise called for the provisional application to be optional. As a result, Belgium introduced a second revised proposal.[5] It was subsequently adopted with only minor amendment (to allow a State acceding to the Convention, as well as one ratifying, accepting, or approving it, to provisionally apply Article 1(1)).

## Provisional Application of the Convention

**18.5** Thus, under Article 18 of the Anti-Personnel Mine Ban Convention, a State is explicitly given the opportunity,[6] when it deposits its instrument of ratification, acceptance, approval or accession, to declare that it will apply provisionally the following general obligations:

1. Each State Party undertakes never under any circumstances:

(a) To use anti-personnel mines;
(b) To develop, produce, otherwise acquire, stockpile, retain or transfer to anyone, directly or indirectly, anti-personnel mines;
(c) To assist, encourage or induce, in any way, anyone to engage in any activity prohibited to a State Party under this Convention.[7]

Accordingly, the provisional application does not apply to the undertaking in Article 1(2) to 'destroy or ensure the destruction of all anti-personnel mines'.

**18.6** The same opportunity was not given explicitly to States upon signature of the Convention, though presumably, in accordance with the right of States to make unilateral declarations at any time, there was nothing to preclude a State from doing so.

---

[5] APL/CW.47/rev.2 of 9 Sept. 1997.

[6] Similar 'opt-in' provisions were included in the 1986 International Atomic Energy Authority Convention on Early Notification of a Nuclear Incident (Article 13) and the 1994 International Tropical Timber Agreement (Article 40). See Lefeber, 'The Provisional Application of Treaties', in Klabbers, *Essays on the Law of Treaties*, 85.

[7] See, above, the commentary on Article 1 for a discussion of the implications of these provisions.

## States having Accepted Provisional Application

**18.7** In accordance with Article 18, the following States declared that they would provisionally apply Article 1(1) pending the entry into force of the Convention: Austria, Mauritius, New Zealand, South Africa, Sweden, and Switzerland. Perhaps surprisingly, Belgium, which proposed the inclusion of the article, did not make such a declaration upon deposit of its instrument of ratification.[8]

---

[8] This may be attributed to the fact that Belgium had had national legislation prohibiting anti-personnel mines in place since 1995 (the first country in the world to adopt such legislation), but the explanation is not wholly satisfactory.

# Article 19.  Reservations

Article 19—Reservations

The Articles of this Convention shall not be subject to reservations.

## Introduction

**19.1** It is common practice for States to make reservations to treaties.[1] This is particularly so with respect to international humanitarian law treaties,[2] less so in the case of disarmament or international criminal law. Thus, the 1998 Rome Statute of the International Criminal Court provides that: 'No reservations may be made to this Statute'.[3] Similarly, the 1993 Chemical Weapons Convention prohibits reservations to the Convention, although it allows reservations to be made to its Annexes on the condition that they are not 'incompatible with its object and purpose'.[4]

**19.2** A provision prohibiting reservations to the Anti-Personnel Mine Ban Convention was first included in the First Austrian Draft Text of October 1996.[5]

---

[1] According to Article 19 of the 1969 Vienna Convention, a State may, 'when signing, ratifying, accepting, approving or acceding to a treaty, formulate a reservation unless . . . (a) the reservation is prohibited by the treaty'. In the view of one international lawyer: 'The legal instrument of reservations to international multilateral treaties is deemed to strike a balance between the rigidity and integrity of a multilateral treaty and the objective to bring as many States as possible under the umbrella of this treaty'. Hafner, G., 'Article 120: Reservations', in Triffterer, *Commentary on the Rome Statute of the International Criminal Court*, 1255.

[2] Thus, neither the Geneva Conventions of August 12, 1949 nor the two 1977 Protocols Additional to the Geneva Conventions prohibit reservations to its provisions, and States have typically made a number of reservations to them upon adherence.              [3] Article 120.

[4] Article XXII, 1993 Chemical Weapons Convention. A similar provision is included in Article XV of the 1996 Comprehensive Nuclear-Test-Ban Treaty. The 1972 Biological Weapons Convention does not, however, prohibit reservations.

[5] In Article 10. Similar provisions were proposed in the Belgian Draft Text of October 1996 and the ICBL proposal for an Anti-Personnel Mine Ban Convention of December 1996.

The draft article was maintained in the Second and Third Austrian Draft Texts unchanged. At the Oslo Diplomatic Conference, the USA sought the deletion of the prohibition on reservations,[6] but was unsuccessful. Belgium, Burkina Faso, Cameroon, Croatia, Denmark, El Salvador, Germany, Italy, Kenya, Mexico, Norway, Sudan, South Africa, and the UK, all opposed the US proposal.[7]

**19.3** Accordingly, it is prohibited to make any reservations to the Convention, and hence also to any amendments that may be adopted by the States Parties in the future[8] in accordance with Article 13 (unless, of course, the amendment in question be the deletion of Article 19). As noted above in the commentary on the respective provisions, upon adherence to the Convention, a number of States have sought to make what they have termed interpretive declarations to one or more of its provisions.[9]

## Determining a Reservation

**19.4** The 1969 Vienna Convention on the Law of Treaties defines a reservation as a 'unilateral statement, however phrased or named, made by a State, when signing, ratifying, accepting, approving or acceding to a treaty, whereby it purports to exclude or to modify the legal effect of certain provisions of the treaty in their application to that State'.[10] In the event of a dispute as to whether any of the interpretative declarations made by States to the Anti-Personnel Mine Ban Convention constitute reservations, the procedures laid down in Article 10 for the settlement of disputes shall apply.

**19.5** Article 10 of the Convention does not, though, preclude a State Party from seeking an Advisory Opinion from the International Court of Justice,[11]

---

[6] APL/CW.16 of 1 Sept. 1997. It did recognize, however, that under customary law, reservations incompatible with the object and purpose of the Convention would be unlawful.

[7] France had previously sought the deletion of the prohibition on reservations. See para. 0.67 above.

[8] See also Hafner, 'Article 120: Reservations', in Triffterer, *Commentary on the Rome Statute of the International Criminal Court*, 1257.

[9] See e.g. commentary paras. 1.55, 1.64, 1.67, 1.69–1.70.

[10] Article 2(1)(d), 1969 Vienna Convention.

[11] In addition, by virtue of Article 65(1) of the Statute of the International Court of Justice: 'The Court may give an advisory opinion on any legal question at the request of whatever body may be authorised by or in accordance with the Charter of the United Nations to make such a request'. At present, the following are authorized to request advisory opinions under the UN Charter (see www.icj-cij.org): the General Assembly and the Security Council, three other UN organs (the Economic and Social Council, Trusteeship Council, and Interim Committee of the General Assembly), and 16 UN specialized agencies, where so authorized by the General Assembly. Thus, for instance, the World Health Organization asked for an advisory opinion on the legality of the threat or use of nuclear weapons.

even if the Meeting of the States Parties is seized of the affair. As noted in the commentary on that article, it is regrettable that there is no provision for an arbitration or adjudication mechanism laid down in the Convention.[12]

**19.6** It also appears possible for a State Party to consider an unlawful reservation by another State Party as a 'question relating to compliance' with the Convention, and therefore to invoke the provisions of Article 8. In accordance with Article 8(1), this would require efforts to resolve the issue through consultation and cooperation.

## The Consequences of Unlawful Reservations

**19.7** The legal consequences under international law of inadmissible reservations are unclear, although there are two main, opposing schools of thought.[13] According to the first, inadmissible reservations affect the consent to be bound and consequently destroy its legal effect making the State in question not a party to the treaty. According to the second, an inadmissible reservation is to be considered as not having been made and therefore does not in any way affect the consent to be bound. The issue remains unresolved in international treaty law.[14]

**19.8** The issue has, however, also arisen in international human rights law. Thus, the European Court of Human Rights decided in the *Belilos* case that so-called 'interpretive declarations' made by Switzerland upon adherence to the European Convention for the Protection of Human Rights and Fundamental Freedoms in reality had to be treated as reservations.[15] The Court decided that the reservations should be simply disregarded, leaving Switzerland bound by

---

[12]  See e.g. Aust, *Modern Treaty Law and Practice*, 290–4.

[13]  See Hafner, 'Article 120: Reservations', in Triffterer, *Commentary on the Rome Statute of the International Criminal Court*, 1262.

[14]  Thus, the Special Rapporteur of the International Law Commission on Reservations to Treaties elaborated the following series of questions to which he was unable to provide conclusive answers: 'Must the reservation be regarded as void, but the expression of consent to be bound by the treaty as valid? On the contrary, does the impermissibility of the reservation affect the reliability of the expression of consent itself? Does the impermissibility of the reservation produce effects independently of any objections which may be raised to it? At most, have the other contracting States (or international organisations) an obligation in such circumstances to raise an objection to an impermissible reservation? Or may they, rather, accept such a reservation, either expressly or tacitly?' Ibid., citing Pellet, A., 'First Report on Reservations to Treaties', UN Doc. A/CN.4/470, 52.

[15]  See *Publications of the European Court of Human Rights*, Series A, vol. 132, Judgment of 29 Apr. 1988, p. 22.

the Convention in full.[16] Under the Convention, Switzerland had the right to withdraw from it, but chose not to.[17]

## The Legality of Interpretive Declarations

**19.9** Although reservations are prohibited by Article 19 of the Anti-Personnel Mine Ban Convention, a State is seemingly free to make one or more interpretative declarations to the Convention.[18] It appears that such declarations can be made at any time—during negotiatons, when signing or ratifying, or later during ensuing practice.[19]

**19.10** There is, however, no universally accepted definition of an interpretative declaration under international law. The Special Rapporteur of the International Law Commission on Reservations to Treaties, Alain Pellet, has defined them as unilateral declarations 'however phrased or named, made by a State or by an international organization whereby that State or that organization purports to clarify the meaning or scope attributed by the declarant to the treaty or to certain of its provisions'.[20]

**19.11** The Special Rapporteur has also suggested that 'when reservations were prohibited under a treaty, it would seem that there were grounds for presuming, again not irrefragably, that the author of an interpretive declaration with the same object had acted in good faith and had made what was indeed an interpretive declaration'.[21] It is clear, however, that the description applied by

[16] Although it is argued that this conclusion should be seen 'in the light of the particular circumstances'. Aust, *Modern Treaty Law and Practice*, 118–19; see also Marks, S., 'Reservations Unhinged: The Belilos Case before the European Court of Human Rights', *International and Comparative Law Quarterly* (1990), 300–27.

[17] In similar circumstances, under Article 20 of the Anti-Personnel Mine Ban Convention, a State could likewise opt to withdraw, although there would presumably be a political cost to pay.

[18] See Hafner, 'Article 120: Reservations', in Triffterer, *Commentary on the Rome Statute of the International Criminal Court*, 1258. Hafner notes that although a number of international treaties, 'in particular those on human rights', contain a clause on the prohibition of reservations, States Parties nevertheless have not abstained from entering declarations without their being contested by the other States Parties or the relevant treaty body. He refers to Article 21 of the 1987 European Convention for the Prevention of Torture and Inhuman or Degrading Treatment or Punishment to which declarations were made by Germany, Italy, the Netherlands, and the UK, and Article 6(3) of the Additional Protocol to the 1975 European Convention on Extradition to which declarations were made by Hungary and the Netherlands, among others. Ibid. 1258 n. 45. The 1969 Vienna Convention is silent on the issue of interpretive declarations.

[19] See also *Yearbook of the International Law Commission* (1998), vol. ii, part 2, UN doc. A/CN.4/SER.A/1998/Add.1 (Part 2), p. 96.

[20] Pellet, 'Third Report on Reservations to Treaties', Addendum, UN Doc. A/CN.4/491/Add.4, p. 33.

[21] *Yearbook of the International Law Commission* (1998), 95.

the State making a statement is not determinant as to its status. According to the International Law Commission, 'States . . . not infrequently make declarations as to their understanding of some matter or as to their interpretation of a particular provision. Such a declaration may be a mere clarification of the State's position or it may amount to a reservation, according as it does or does not vary or exclude the application of the terms of the treaty as adopted.'[22] Thus, 'the test is not the nomenclature but the effect the statement purports to have. The test is whether the statement seeks to "exclude or to modify the legal effect of certain provisions of the treaty"'.[23]

**19.12** It is also important to distinguish between a reservation and an interpretive declaration 'with regard to the burden of proof as to the binding effect'. The State invoking a reservation only has to show inaction by other States (i.e. *tacit acceptance*). For an interpretive declaration, on the other hand, it is a matter of showing acquiescence in the declaration by the confronted States.[24]

---

[22] *Yearbook of the International Law Commission* (1966), vol. ii. 189–90, para. 11.

[23] Bowett, D. W., 'Reservations to Non-restricted Multilateral Treaties', *British Yearbook of International Law* (1976–1977), vol. xlviii. 68. See also *Yearbook of the International Law Commission* (1998), 95–6.

[24] Lysén, G., *The International Regulation of Armaments: The Law of Disarmament* (Sweden: Iustus Förlag, 1970), 168.

# Article 20. Duration and Withdrawal

Article 20—Duration and withdrawal

1. This Convention shall be of unlimited duration.

2. Each State Party shall, in exercising its national sovereignty, have the right to withdraw from this Convention. It shall give notice of such withdrawal to all other States Parties, to the Depositary and to the United Nations Security Council. Such instrument of withdrawal shall include a full explanation of the reasons motivating this withdrawal.

3. Such withdrawal shall only take effect six months after the receipt of the instrument of withdrawal by the Depositary. If, however, on the expiry of that six-month period, the withdrawing State Party is engaged in an armed conflict, the withdrawal shall not take effect before the end of the armed conflict.

4. The withdrawal of a State Party from this Convention shall not in any way affect the duty of States to continue fulfilling the obligations assumed under any relevant rules of international law.

## Introduction

**20.1** Article 20 deals with the duration of the Anti-Personnel Mine Ban Convention and withdrawal from it. It is not uncommon to allow a State Party to denounce a treaty[1] or to withdraw from it, although the act itself of withdrawal is extremely rare.[2] 'Denunciation denotes a unilateral act by which a

---

[1] Thus e.g. Article 9(1) of the 1980 Convention on Certain Conventional Weapons allows a State Party to denounce the Convention or any of its annexed Protocols by so notifying the Depositary'.

[2] Thus e.g. amid international concern, on 13 Dec. 2001, the USA announced that it would withdraw from the 1972 Anti-Ballistic Missile treaty with Russia. On 10 Jan. 2003, the Democratic

party seeks to terminate its participation in a treaty. Lawful denunciation of a bilateral treaty terminates it. Although denunciation is also used in relation to a multilateral treaty, the better term is withdrawal. Withdrawal of a party from a multilateral treaty will not normally result in its termination.'[3] Withdrawal from a treaty is specifically authorized by the 1969 Vienna Convention under certain circumstances.[4]

**20.2**  States participating in the 1997 Vienna Conference had recommended the inclusion of a provision on withdrawal in the future Anti-Personnel Mine Ban Convention. Accordingly, the Second Austrian Draft of 14 March 1997 proposed to allow a State Party to withdraw from the Convention on a year's notice to all other States Parties, the depositary, and the United Nations (UN) Security Council if it decided that 'extraordinary events, related to the subject matter of this Convention, have jeopardized the supreme interests of its country'.[5]

**20.3**  However, concern about the risk of a State Party withdrawing in order to employ anti-personnel mines in an armed conflict[6] led to changes in the Third Austrian Draft Text of 13 May 1997. Article 18(3) of the draft provided as follows:

In case a State Party should withdraw from this Convention, the withdrawal shall only take effect one year after receipt of the instrument of withdrawal by the Depositary. If, however, on the expiry of that year the withdrawing State Party is engaged in an armed conflict the withdrawal shall not take effect before the end of the armed conflict.[7]

---

Republic of Korea announced that it was withdrawing from the Nuclear Non-Proliferation Treaty. Furthermore, the Democratic Republic of Korea claimed that since it had given just under the requisite three months' notice in a previous dispute with the USA in 1993, this time period meant that on this occasion its withdrawal was effective almost immediately.

   [3]  Aust, *Modern Treaty Law and Practice*, 224.

   [4]  Thus, according to Article 54, 1969 Vienna Convention: 'The termination of a treaty or the withdrawal of a party may take place: (a) in conformity with the provisions of the treaty; or (b) at any time by consent of all the parties after consultation with the other contracting States'.

   [5]  Article 18 of the Second Austrian Draft provided as follows: '1. This Convention shall be of unlimited duration. 2. Each State Party shall, in exercising its national sovereignty, have the right to withdraw from this Convention if it decides that extraordinary events, related to the subject matter of this Convention, have jeopardized the supreme interests of its country. It shall give notice of such withdrawal one year in advance to all other States Parties, to the Depositary and to the United Nations Security Council. Such notice shall include a statement of the extraordinary events it regards as having jeopardized its supreme interests. 3. The withdrawal of a State Party from this Convention shall not in any way affect the duty of States to continue fulfilling the obligations assumed under any relevant rules of international law.'

   [6]  It has been rumoured that at least two States Parties have considered withdrawing from the Convention, at least one of which was actively engaged in an armed conflict at the time, although to date, none has done so.

   [7]  The provision draws on Article 99(1), Protocol Additional to the Geneva Conventions of 12 August 1949, and Relating to the Protection of Victims of International Armed Conflicts (Protocol I), and Article 9(1) of the 1980 Convention on Certain Conventional Weapons.

**20.4** At the Oslo Diplomatic Conference, a number of States sought to reduce the period of notice required and to delete the provision barring effective withdrawal during an armed conflict.[8] The USA, for instance, introduced a formal proposal in this sense, requiring only 90 days' notice prior to a withdrawal taking effect.[9] Chile proposed that: 'Each State Party shall, in exercising its national sovereignty, have the right to withdraw from this Protocol. It shall give notice of such withdrawal six months in advance to all other States Parties and to the Depositary. The withdrawal shall only take effect six months after receipt of the instrument of withdrawal by the Depositary.'[10]

**20.5** Similarly, Ecuador tabled a proposal to delete paragraph 3 of the article and to replace paragraph 2 with the following text:

Each State Party, in the exercise of its national sovereignty, shall have the right to renounce this Protocol, if it determines that extraordinary events, relating to the very subject of this Protocol, have imperilled the paramount interests of its country. It shall notify its renunciation to the Depositary, including a statement of the extraordinary events which have put its paramount interests at risk.[11]

In the Article as adopted, however,[12] although the period of notice was reduced to six months, the provision barring effective withdrawal during an armed conflict was maintained, largely due to the determination of African and Central American States.[13] In many ways, this was a crucial provision, testing States' resolve to adopt a Convention with, in the words of the ICBL, 'No exceptions, no reservations, no loopholes!'.

## Paragraph 1

1. This Convention shall be of unlimited duration.

---

[8] In the plenary discussion on 10 Sept. 1997, for instance, both Australia and the UK declared their support for removing the obstacle to withdrawal during an armed conflict. In addition, as already discussed, Spain had introduced a proposal seeking to allow continued use of anti-personnel mines 'as a temporary arrangement' in accordance with the international laws of armed conflict. See para. 1.14 above.

[9] See APL/CW.15 of 1 Sept. 1997. See also Caflisch and Godet, 'De la réglementation à l'interdiction des mines antipersonnel', 33. Towards the end of the Oslo Diplomatic Conference, the USA also circulated informally a proposal whereby the limitation on withdrawal before the end of an armed conflict would not apply 'if the withdrawing State Party or its ally is a victim of armed aggression in violation of the UN Charter'.　　　　　　　　　　　　　　　[10] APL/CW.21 of 2 Sept. 1997.

[11] APL/CW.44 of 2 Sept. 1997.

[12] The adoption of the article followed discussions in a meeting of a 'Friend of the Conference', which was chaired by the French Ambassador, Joëlle Bourgeois.

[13] This is in harmony with the undertaking in Article 1(1)(a) of the Convention, 'never under any circumstances to use anti-personnel mines'.

**20.6** The Convention is of 'unlimited' duration. This provision is identical to one included in the 1993 Chemical Weapons Convention.[14] As set out in paragraphs 2 to 4 of the article, however, a State Party has the right to withdraw from the Convention.

## Paragraph 2

> 2. Each State Party shall, in exercising its national sovereignty, have the right to withdraw from this Convention. It shall give notice of such withdrawal to all other States Parties, to the Depositary and to the United Nations Security Council. Such instrument of withdrawal shall include a full explanation of the reasons motivating this withdrawal.

**20.7** Thus, each State Party, 'in exercising its national sovereignty' has the right to withdraw from the Convention. It is obliged to give notice of withdrawal to all other States Parties, the depositary, and the UN Security Council. The 'instrument of withdrawal' must include a full explanation of the reasons motivating the withdrawal, but, in contrast to the 1993 Chemical Weapons Convention, there are no criteria for judging whether these reasons are well-founded and presumably any reasons would suffice.[15]

## Paragraph 3

> 3. Such withdrawal shall only take effect six months after the receipt of the instrument of withdrawal by the Depositary. If, however, on the expiry of that six-month period, the withdrawing State Party is engaged in an armed conflict, the withdrawal shall not take effect before the end of the armed conflict.

**20.8** A withdrawal by a State Party will only take effect at the end of the six-month notice period if it is not engaged in an armed conflict at the end of that period.[16] This provision is intended in particular to prevent a State engaged in an armed conflict announcing its withdrawal from the treaty with a view to using anti-personnel mines as soon as the notice period elapses.[17]

---

[14]  Article XVI, 1993 Chemical Weapons Convention.

[15]  Cf. Article XVI (2) of the 1993 Chemical Weapons Convention, which requires that there be 'extraordinary events . . . related to the subject matter' of the Convention that a State Party considers have 'jeopardized the supreme interests of its country'. Thus, the provision contains both an objective and a subjective element.                     [16]  The armed conflict may be international or internal.

[17]  See also the proposal by Austria at the Oslo Diplomatic Conference. APL/CW.36 of 2 Sept. 1997.

**20.9** The provision, which was keenly contested at the Oslo Diplomatic Conference, does not clarify what constitutes an armed conflict for the purposes of the Convention. Although the term is well known to international humanitarian law,[18] there remains dispute as to its scope and ambit and States have been particularly reluctant to categorize any internal disputes involving the use of armed force as armed conflicts, preferring to deem them acts of terrorism.[19] Thus, in 1977 Additional Protocol II, it is provided that: 'This Protocol shall not apply to situations of internal disturbances and tensions, such as riots, isolated and sporadic acts of violence and other acts of a similar nature, as not being armed conflicts'.[20]

# Paragraph 4

4. The withdrawal of a State Party from this Convention shall not in any way affect the duty of States to continue fulfilling the obligations assumed under any relevant rules of international law.

## The Consequences of Withdrawal

**20.10** Once a State Party has effectively withdrawn from the Anti-Personnel Mine Ban Convention, it is still bound by 'the obligations assumed under any relevant rules of international law'. Thus, a State that has already consented to be bound by 1980 Protocol II and/or 1996 Amended Protocol II to the 1980 Convention on Certain Conventional Weapons remains constrained by the provisions of the respective Protocol(s), as well as by the provisions of customary international law applicable to all weapons, including landmines.[21]

---

[18] The Geneva Convention Relative to the Protection of Civilian Persons in Time of War of 12 Aug. 1949, for instance, refers in its Article 2 to the application of the Convention to 'all cases of declared war or of any other armed conflict'. Similar provisions are included in the three other Geneva Conventions of 12 Aug. 1949.

[19] Thus, at the Oslo Diplomatic Conference, the representative of the UN Secretariat pointed out that the Depositary could not make a determination as to whether a State Party wishing to withdraw was engaged in an armed conflict or not.

[20] Article 1(2), Protocol Additional to the Geneva Conventions of 12 Aug. 1949, and Relating to the Protection of Victims of Non-International Armed Conflicts (Protocol II).

[21] As noted above in the commentary on the final preambular paragraph, the International Campaign to Ban Landmines believes that landmines are inherently indiscriminate and their use is therefore already prohibited by customary international law. This is not generally accepted by States. As and when the various obligations under the Anti-Personnel Mine Ban Convention become part of customary international law, withdrawal from the Convention will not allow a State to avoid these obligations.

**20.11** Indeed, many States Parties to the Anti-Personnel Mine Ban Convention are also parties to 1980 Protocol II[22] or 1996 Amended Protocol II.[23] In general, 1980 Protocol II adds little to the customary law obligations applicable to the use of all conventional weapons, but 1996 Amended Protocol II has significant restrictions on the use and transfer of anti-personnel mines.

**20.12** With regard to customary international law, the final preambular paragraph of the Convention on the Prohibition of Anti-Personnel Mines recalls 'the principle of international humanitarian law that the right of the parties to an armed conflict to choose methods or means of warfare is not unlimited . . . the principle that prohibits the employment in armed conflicts of weapons, projectiles and materials and methods of warfare of a nature to cause superfluous injury or unnecessary suffering and . . . the principle that a distinction must be made between civilians and combatants.'[24]

**20.13** In addition, the Martens Clause will continue to be relevant.[25] Thus, the International Court of Justice in its *Nuclear Weapons Advisory Opinion* declared that it 'would likewise refer, in relation to these [cardinal] principles [of international humanitarian law], to the Martens Clause, which was first included in the Hague Convention II with Respect to the Laws and Customs of War on Land of 1899 and which has proved to be an effective means of

[22] Protocol on Prohibitions or Restrictions on the Use of Mines, Booby-Traps and Other Devices (1980 Protocol II). At 1 January 2004, 82 States had consented to be bound by the Protocol: Argentina, Australia, Austria, Bangladesh, Belarus, Belgium, Bolivia, Bosnia and Herzegovina, Brazil, Bulgaria, Burkina Faso, Cambodia, Canada, Cape Verde, China, Colombia, Costa Rica, Croatia, Cuba, Cyprus, the Czech Republic, Denmark, Djibouti, Ecuador, El Salvador, Finland, France, Germany, Georgia, Greece, Guatemala, Holy See, Honduras, Hungary, India, Ireland, Israel, Italy, Japan, Lao People's Democratic Republic, Latvia, Lesotho, Liechtenstein, Luxembourg, Maldives, Mali, Malta, Mauritius, Mexico, Moldova, Mongolia, Morocco, Nauru, the Netherlands, New Zealand, Niger, Norway, Pakistan, Panama, the Philippines, Poland, Portugal, Romania, the Russian Federation, Seychelles, Slovakia, Slovenia, South Africa, Spain, Sweden, Switzerland, the Former Yugoslav Republic of Macedonia, Tajikistan, Togo, Tunisia, Uganda, Ukraine, the UK, Uruguay, the USA, Uzbekistan, and the Federal Republic of Yugoslavia.

[23] Amended Protocol on Prohibitions or Restrictions on the Use of Mines, Booby-Traps and Other Devices (1996 Amended Protocol II). At 1 January 2004, 74 States had consented to be bound by the Protocol: Albania, Argentina, Australia, Austria, Bangladesh, Belgium, Bolivia, Bosnia and Herzegovina, Brazil, Bulgaria, Burkina Faso, Cambodia, Canada, Cape Verde, Chile, China, Colombia, Costa Rica, Croatia, Cyprus, the Czech Republic, Denmark, Ecuador, El Salvador, Estonia, Finland, France, Germany, Greece, Guatemala, Holy See, Honduras, Hungary, India, Ireland, Israel, Italy, Republic of Korea, Japan, Jordan, Latvia, Liechtenstein, Lithuania, Luxembourg, Maldives, Mali, Moldova, Monaco, Morocco, Nauru, the Netherlands, New Zealand, Nicaragua, Norway, Pakistan, Panama, Peru, the Philippines, Poland, Portugal, Romania, Senegal, Seychelles, Slovakia, Slovenia, South Africa, Spain, Sweden, Switzerland, Tajikistan, Ukraine, the UK, Uruguay, and the USA.

[24] See, above, the commentary on this preambular provision, in paras. 0.131–0.139.

[25] See paras. 0.123–0.124 above.

addressing the rapid evolution of military technology'.[26] As noted above,[27] the preamble to the 1980 Convention on Certain Conventional Weapons includes a version of the Martens Clause whereby:

*Confirming* their determination that in cases not covered by this Convention and its annexed Protocols, the civilian population and the combatants shall at all times remain under the protection and authority of the principles of international law derived from established custom, from the principles of humanity and from the dictates of public conscience.

[26] *Nuclear Weapons Advisory Opinion*, para. 78, *ICJ Reports*, 1996.
[27] See paras. 0.123–0.124 above.

# Article 21. Depositary

Article 21—Depositary

The Secretary-General of the United Nations is hereby designated as the Depositary of this Convention.

## Introduction

**21.1** Article 21 nominates the Secretary-General of the United Nations (UN) as the depositary of the Anti-Personnel Mine Ban Convention. This is in harmony with the 1969 Vienna Convention, which expressly allows the Chief Administrative Officer of an international organization to be designated as the depositary of a treaty, and for the designation to be made in the treaty itself.[1]

## The Choice of the Depositary

**21.2** There was a political decision to choose the Secretary-General of the UN as depositary in order to give further legitimacy to the Ottawa Process. Prior to the Oslo Diplomatic Conference, the Secretary-General had indicated his willingness to accept a request to perform traditional depositary functions.[2] In principle, the policy of the Secretary-General has been to restrict the assumption of depositary functions to open multilateral treaties of worldwide interest, usually adopted by the General Assembly or concluded by plenipotentiary conferences convened by the United Nations, or regional treaties drawn up within the framework of the

---

[1] Thus Article 76(1) provides that: 'The designation of the depositary of a treaty may be made by the negotiating States, either in the treaty itself or in some other manner. The depositary may be one or more States, an international organization or the chief administrative officer of the organization.'

[2] 'Note of the Secretary-General to the Permanent Representative of Austria to the United Nations' (New York, 15 Aug. 1997). In practice, the depositary duties of the Secretary-General are performed by the Treaty Section of the Office of Legal Affairs in the UN Secretariat. Aust, *Modern Treaty Law and Practice*, 264.

UN regional commissions.[3] However, the Secretary-General has the discretion to accept depositary functions for any multilateral treaty he deems appropriate.[4]

## The Functions of the Depositary

**21.3** The principal functions of a depositary are listed in detail in Article 77(1) of the 1969 Vienna Convention.[5] They include: keeping the original text and certified copies of the treaty; receiving any signatures and receiving and keeping custody of any instruments of ratification, acceptance, approval, accession, or succession, and ensuring that they are in due and proper form; receiving and keeping custody of all other communications relating to the treaty; and registering the treaty following entry into force.[6]

**21.4** As one authority remarks: 'Now that depositary functions are so well established and largely codified in the [1969 Vienna] Convention, it is enough simply to designate a depositary on the understanding that the duties will be performed in accordance with the law of treaties and established practice'.[7] Thus, following suggested text put forward by the UN Secretariat prior to the Oslo Diplomatic Conference,[8] the Anti-Personnel Mine Ban Convention does not list

[3] UN Secretariat, 'Summary of Practice of the Secretary-General as Depositary of Multilateral Treaties', UN Doc. ST/LEG/8, UN (New York, 1994).

[4] In the Secretary-General's Note in which he indicated his willingness to accept, he referred to 'the greatest importance' he attached 'to the achievement of a total ban of anti-personnel mines', and remarked that the UN had been 'closely involved in raising international consciousness of the need for a total ban.' 'Note of the Secretary-General to the Permanent Representative of Austria to the United Nations' (New York, 15 Aug. 1997).

[5] Article 77(1) provides as follows: 'The functions of a depositary, unless otherwise provided in the treaty or agreed by the contracting States, comprise in particular: (a) keeping custody of the original text of the treaty and of any full powers delivered to the depositary; (b) preparing certified copies of the original text and preparing any further text of the treaty in such additional languages as may be required by the treaty and transmitting them to the parties and to the States entitled to become parties to the treaty; (c) receiving any signatures to the treaty and receiving and keeping custody of any instruments, notifications and communications relating to it; (d) examining whether the signature or any instrument, notification or communication relating to the treaty is in due and proper form and, if need be, bringing the matter to the attention of the State in question. (e) informing the parties and the States entitled to become parties to the treaty of acts, notifications and communications relating to the treaty; (f) informing the States entitled to become parties to the treaty when the number of signatures or of instruments of ratification, acceptance, approval or accession required for the entry into force of the treaty has been received or deposited; (g) registering the treaty with the Secretariat of the United Nations; (h) performing the functions specified in other provisions of the present Convention.'

[6] Aust, *Modern Treaty Law and Practice*, 267–8.    [7] ibid. 269.

[8] 'Comments by the United Nations Secretariat on the Draft Convention on the Prohibition of the Use, Stockpiling, Production and Transfer of Anti-Personnel Mines and on their Destruction', attached to Note of the Secretary-General to the Permanent Representative of Austria to the United Nations (New York, 15 Aug. 1997).

the depositary tasks to be performed by the Secretary-General.[9] A number of such tasks had, however, been included in the Third Austrian Draft forwarded to the Oslo Diplomatic Conference.[10]

**21.5** The Anti-Personnel Mine Ban Convention also assigns a number of what are termed 'administrative functions' to the Secretary-General. These include assisting in the organization of fact-finding missions under Article 8, and convening Meetings of States Parties (Article 11(2) ) and Review Conferences (Article 12(1) ).

[9] Article 10 of the 1980 Convention on Certain Conventional Weapons lists a number tasks 'in addition to his usual functions' to be performed by the Secretary-General of the United Nations in his capacity as depositary of that Convention. See for instance Roberts and Guelff, *Documents on the Laws of War*, 526.

[10] Article 19 of the Third Austrian Draft provided as follows: 'The Secretary-General of the United Nations is hereby designed as the Depositary of this Convention and shall, inter alia: (a) Promptly inform all signatory and acceding States of the date of each signature, the date of deposit of each instrument of ratification, acceptance, approval or accession and the date of the entry into force of this Convention; (b) Transmit duly certified copies of this Convention to the Governments of all signatory and acceding States; (c) Register this Convention pursuant to Article 102 of the Charter of the United Nations; (d) Transmit to the States Parties as well as to the Commission of Experts, where appropriate, not later than two months before the next Meeting of the States Parties the reports received under Articles 8 and 10; and (e) Convene the Meetings of the State Parties referred to in Article 12 and the Review Conferences referred to in Article 13.'

# Article 22. Authentic Texts

Article 22—Authentic Texts

The original of this Convention, of which the Arabic, Chinese, English, French, Russian and Spanish texts are equally authentic, shall be deposited with the Secretary-General of the United Nations.

## Introduction

**22.1**  A provision on authentic texts is standard in an international treaty. Yet, as one authority remarks, 'language as a means of communication is fraught with ambiguities, mistakes and deception. These problems may be alleviated or exacerbated by drafting texts in multiple languages. On the one hand, a comparison of different texts may help to resolve an ambiguity inherent in a term or phrase used in one language, making clearer the intention of the drafters . . . On the other hand, the lack of precise linguistic equivalents and differences in legal systems throughout the globe make it virtually certain that multiple language versions will include terminological differences that lead to conflicting interpretations of the text.'[1]

**22.2**  Despite the inherent risks, international treaties are often authenticated in more than one language.[2] In such cases, Article 33 of the 1969 Vienna Convention provides that the text is equally authoritative in each language, unless otherwise agreed, and the terms of the treaty are presumed to have the same meaning in each authentic text.[3] Where all the texts are equally authentic but a

---

[1] Shelton, D., 'Reconcilable Differences? The Interpretation of Multilingual Treaties', *Hastings International and Comparative Law Review*, 20 (1997), 611–12 (footnotes omitted).

[2] See e.g. Aust, *Modern Treaty Law and Practice*, 202, 352.

[3] Article 33, 1969 Vienna Convention, provides that: '1. Where a treaty has been authenticated in two or more languages, the text is equally authoritative in each language, unless the treaty provides or the parties agree that, in a case of divergence, a particular text shall prevail. 2. A version of the treaty in a language other than one of those in which the text was authenticated shall be considered an authentic text only if the treaty so provides or the parties so agree. 3. The terms of the treaty are presumed to

comparison of them reveals a difference of meaning which is not resolved by interpretation in accordance with Articles 31 and 32 of the 1969 Vienna Convention, 'the meaning which best reconciles the texts, having regard to the object and purpose of the treaty, shall be adopted'.[4]

**22.3**  In accordance with its Article 22, the Anti-Personnel Mine Ban Convention is authenticated in the six working languages of the United Nations (UN)—Arabic,[5] Chinese, English, French, Russian, and Spanish.[6] The formulation employed is similar, though not identical, to that contained in the 1993 Chemical Weapons Convention.[7] There is no provision or agreement for any language version to prevail in the case of any inconsistency,[8] although in practice it is likely that particular attention will be paid to the English version of the Convention since most of the oral and written treaty negotiation was conducted in English.[9]

# The Process of Authentication

**22.4**  Authentication is the process by which a treaty text is certified to be the definitive and authentic text.[10] In the case of the Anti-Personnel Mine Ban Convention, this demanded not only a copy-edit of the text adopted by

have the same meaning in each authentic text. 4. Except where a particular text prevails in accordance with paragraph 1, when a comparison of the authentic texts discloses a difference of meaning which the application of articles 31 and 32 does not remove, the meaning which best reconciles the texts, having regard to the object and purpose of the treaty, shall be adopted.'

[4]  See further Shaw, *International Law*, 660.

[5]  It has been claimed that there is an error in the Arabic text of the Convention, which has omitted to refer to 'the Secretary-General of the UN' with respect to the requirement to submit transparency reports in accordance with Article 7.

[6]  A broadly similar provision was already included in the first draft text of the Convention by Werner Ehrlich in April 1996.

[7]  Article XXIV provides that: 'This Convention, of which the Arabic, Chinese, English, French, Russian and Spanish texts are equally authentic, shall be deposited with the Secretary-General of the United Nations'.

[8]  For example, a 1955 Protocol amending the 1929 Warsaw Convention has three authentic texts—English, French, and Spanish—but provides that 'in the case of any inconsistency, the text in the French language, in which language the Convention was drawn up, shall prevail'. Aust, *Modern Treaty Law and Practice*, 204.

[9]  Prior to the Oslo Diplomatic Conference, draft treaty texts were negotiated only in English. At the Conference itself, negotiations and written proposals were available only in English, French, and Spanish. In comparison, the proceedings of the UN General Assembly and its committees are conducted in the six official UN languages (although informal meetings and drafting is often done only in English). Aust, *Modern Treaty Law and Practice*, 203. For example, the 1980 Convention on Certain Conventional Weapons (CCW) and all annexed Protocols were likewise negotiated in the six official languages.                          [10]  See Aust, *Modern Treaty Law and Practice*, 71–3.

the Oslo Diplomatic Conference in English, French, and Spanish, but also translation of the text into the three remaining authentic languages: Arabic, Chinese, and Russian. Thus, the formal Report of the Oslo Diplomatic Conference records that:

The Conference agreed to request the Secretary General to the United Nations [*sic*] to translate the agreed text into Arabic, Chinese and Russian. The Conference agreed that the translated texts should be circulated to all potential signatory States. The final versions of the Convention, in the six authentic languages, will be forwarded to Ottawa, Canada, by the last week of November for signature there from 3 December 1997 until 4 December 1997.[11]

## The Obligation of the Depositary

**22.5** In contrast to certain other international law treaties,[12] the Anti-Personnel Mine Ban Convention imposes no express obligation on the Secretary-General of the UN, in his capacity as depositary, to send certified copies of the treaty to all States. A certified copy is usually needed for the purpose of official publication and any requisite parliamentary procedure.[13] An explicit obligation to do so had been included in the Third Austrian Draft Text submitted to the Oslo Diplomatic Conference,[14] but was removed on the suggestion of the UN Secretariat, seemingly on the basis that it fell within traditional depositary functions and therefore did not need to be included.[15]

---

[11] APL/CRP.5 of 18 Sept. 1997.

[12] e.g. the 1998 Rome Statute of the International Criminal Court; 1977 Additional Protocol I; and the 1980 Convention on Certain Conventional Weapons. Thus, Article 128 of the Rome Statute of the International Criminal Court provides that: 'The original of this Statute, of which the Arabic, Chinese, English, French, Russian and Spanish texts are equally authentic, shall be deposited with the Secretary-General of the United Nations, who shall send certified copies thereof to all States'.

[13] Aust, *Modern Treaty Law and Practice*, 268.    [14] Article 19.

[15] 'Comments by the United Nations Secretariat on the Draft Convention on the Prohibition of the Use, Stockpiling, Production and Transfer of Anti-Personnel Mines and on their Destruction', attached to Note of the Secretary-General to the Permanent Representative of Austria to the United Nations (New York, 15 Aug. 1997).

# Bibliography

## Books

Aust, A., *Modern Treaty Law and Practice* (Cambridge: Cambridge University Press, 2000).

Bassiouni, M. C., *A Manual on International Humanitarian Law and Arms Control Agreements*, International and Comparative Criminal Law Series (Ardsley, NY: Transnational Publishers, 2000).

Best, G., *Humanity in Warfare* (New York: Columbia University Press, 1980).

Cameron, M. A., Lawson, R. J., and Tomlin, B. W. (eds.), *To Walk without Fear: The Global Movement to Ban Landmines* (Toronto: Oxford University Press, 1998).

CETS (Commission on Engineering and Technical Systems), *Alternative Technologies to Replace Antipersonnel Landmines* (Washington: National Academies Press, 2001).

Cornish, P., *Anti-Personnel Mines: Controlling the Plague of 'Butterflies'* (London: Royal Institute for International Affairs, 1994).

Croll, M., *The History of Landmines* (Barnsley: Leo Cooper, 1998).

de la Guardia, E., *Derecho de los tratados internacionales* (Buenos Aires: Abaco de Rodolfo Depalma, 1997).

Dupuy, T. N. (ed.), *The International Military and Defence Encyclopaedia*, iv (London: Brassey's, 1993).

Fleck, D. (ed.), *The Handbook of Humanitarian Law in Armed Conflicts* (New York: Oxford University Press, 1995).

Harris, D. J., *Cases and Materials on International Law*, 5th edn. (London: Sweet & Maxwell, 1998).

Healy, M., *Kursk 1943: The Tide Turns in the East* (London: Osprey Military, 1997).

Heyman, Major C., *Trends in Landmine Warfare* (Coulden, UK: Jane's Information Group, 1995).

Human Rights Watch and Physicians for Human Rights, *Landmines: A Deadly Legacy* (New York: Human Rights Watch, Oct. 1993).

International Campaign to Ban Landmines, *Landmine Monitor Report 2002: Toward a Mine-Free World* (Washington: Human Rights Watch, Aug. 2002).

—— *Landmine Monitor Report 2001: Toward a Mine-Free World* (Washington: Human Rights Watch, Sept. 2001).

—— *Landmine Monitor Report 2000: Toward a Mine-Free World* (Washington: Human Rights Watch, Aug. 2000).

—— *Landmine Monitor Report 1999: Toward a Mine-Free World* (Washington: Human Rights Watch, Apr. 1999).

Kamminga, M. T., and Zia-Zarifi, S. (eds.), *Liability of Multilateral Corporations under International Law* (The Hague: Kluwer Law International, 2000).

Klabbers, J. (ed.), *Essays on the Law of Treaties* (The Hague: Martinus Nijhoff, 1998).

Krutzsch, W., and Trapp, R., *A Commentary on the Chemical Weapons Convention* (Dordrecht: Martinus Nijhoff, 1994).

Lenarcic, D. A., *Knight-Errant? Canada and the Crusade to Ban Anti-Personnel Land Mines*, Contemporary Affairs No. 2 (Toronto: Irwin Publishing, 1998).

Lysén, G., *The International Regulation of Armaments: The Law of Disarmament* (Sweden: Iustus Förlag, 1970).

McCoubrey, H., and White, N. D., *The Blue Helmets: Legal Regulations of United Nations Military Operations* (Aldershot: Dartmouth Publishing, 1996).

McGrath, R., *Landmine and Unexploded Ordnance: A Resource Book* (London: Pluto Press, 2000).

McManners, Captain H., *Falklands Commando* (London: William Kimber, 1984).

McNair, A., *Law of Treaties*, 2nd edn. (Oxford: Clarendon Press, 1961).

Malanczuk, P., *Akehurst's Modern Introduction to International Law*, 7th rev. edn. (London: Routledge, 1997).

Maresca, L., and Maslen, S. (eds.), *The Banning of Anti-Personnel Landmines: The Work of the International Committee of the Red Cross 1955–1999* (Cambridge: Cambridge University Press, 2000).

Oman, C., *The Art of War in the Middle Ages, Volume One: 378–1278AD* (London: Greenhill, 1991).

O'Connell, D. P., *International Law*, 2nd edn., vol. ii (London: Steven & Sons, 1970).

Perry, M. F., *Infernal Machines: The Story of Confederate Submarine and Mine Warfare* (Baton Rouge, La.: Louisiana State University Press, 1985).

Pictet, J. S. (ed.), *Commentary, III Geneva Convention Relative to the Treatment of Prisoners of War* (Geneva: International Committee of the Red Cross, 1960).

—— (ed.), *Commentary to the I Geneva Convention* (Geneva: ICRC, 1952).

Reuter, P., *Introduction au droit des traités*, 3rd edn. (Geneva: Publications de l'Institut Universitaire des Hautes Etudes Internationales—Genève, 1995).

Roberts, A., and Guelff, R., *Documents on the Laws of War*, 3rd edn. (Oxford: Clarendon Press, 2001).

Roberts, S., and Williams, J., *After the Guns Fall Silent: The Enduring Legacy of Landmines* (Washington: Vietnam Veterans of America Foundation, 1995).

Sandoz, Y., Swinarski, C., and Zimmerman, B. (eds.), *Commentary on the Additional Protocols of 8 June 1977 to the Geneva Conventions of 12 August 1949* (Geneva: ICRC/Martinus Nijhoff, 1987).

Schachter, O., *International Law in Theory and Practice* (Leiden: Brill Publishers, 1991).

School of Military Engineering, *The Work of the Royal Engineers in the European War 1914–19* (Chatham: SME, 1924).

Shaw, M. N., *International Law*, 4th edn. (Cambridge: Cambridge University Press, 1997).

Sinclair, I., *The Vienna Convention on the Law of Treaties*, 2nd edn. (Manchester: Manchester University Press, 1984).

Sloan, Lieutenant-Colonel C. E. E., *Mine Warfare on Land* (London: Brassey's, 1986), 36.

Swinarski, C. (ed.), *Studies and Essays on International Humanitarian Law and Red Cross Principles* (Geneva/The Hague: ICRC/Martinus Nijhoff, 1984).

Triffterer, O. (ed.), *Commentary on the Rome Statute of the International Criminal Court: Observers' Notes, Article by Article* (Baden-Baden: Nomos Verlagsgesellschaft, 1999).

US Department of State, *Hidden Killers: The Global Problem with Uncleared Landmines: A Report on International Demining* (Washington: Bureau of Political-Military Affairs, Department of State Publication 10098, July 1993).

Wulff, T., *Barriers against Weapons: Development of Weapons and Restrictions on their Use* (Stockholm: Swedish Red Cross, 1984).

## Dictionaries and Reference Works

Brown, L. (ed.), *The New Shorter Oxford English Dictionary*, i (Oxford: Clarendon Press, 1993).

Pearsall, J. (ed.), *The New Oxford Dictionary of English* (Oxford: Clarendon Press, 1998).

*The Shorter Oxford English Dictionary*, 5th edn. on CD-ROM (Oxford: Oxford University Press).

US Department of Defense, Joint Chiefs of Staff, *Dictionary of Military Terms* (London: Greenhill Books, 1999).

Verri, P., *Dictionary of the International Law of Armed Conflict* (Geneva: ICRC, 1992).

## Articles, Monographs, and Reports

*A Guide to Mine Action* (Geneva: Geneva International Centre for Humanitarian Demining (GICHD), July 2003).

*Anti-Personnel Landmines: Friend or Foe?* (Geneva: International Committee of the Red Cross, Mar. 1996).

Association of Military-Political and Military-Historic Research, 'The Position of Russia as Regards the Problem of Use of Anti-Personnel Mines Considering the Conferences in Brussels and Oslo' (Moscow, 1997).

*A Study of National Mine Action Legislation* (Geneva: GICHD, forthcoming).

*Banning Anti-Personnel Mines: The Ottawa Treaty Explained* (Geneva: ICRC, 1998).

Beale, J. H. 'The Jurisdiction of a Sovereign State', *Harvard Law Review*, 36 (1923).

Blagden, P., 'Landmine Detection and Destruction Technologies', in *Mine Action: An Historical Analysis* (Geneva: GICHD, forthcoming).

Bowett, D. W., 'Reservations to Non-restricted Multilateral Treaties', *British Yearbook of International Law, 1976–1977*, xlviii (Oxford: Oxford University Press, 1978).

Caflisch, L., and Godet, F., 'De la réglementation à l'interdiction des mines antipersonnel', *Revue suisse de droit international et de droit européen* (1998).

Canadian Department of Foreign Affairs and International Trade, 'A Global Ban on Landmines', Fact Sheet, undated but 1997.

Canadian Department of National Defence, 'The Canadian Forces and Anti-Personnel Landmines', Department of National Defence (Ottawa, 13 Feb. 2002).

Capece, C. M., 'The Ottawa Treaty and its Impact on U.S. Military Policy and Planning', *Brookings Journal of International Law*, 25/1 (1999).

Cassese, A., 'The Status of Rebels under the 1977 Geneva Protocol on Non-international Armed Conflicts', *International and Comparative Law Quarterly*, 30 (Apr. 1981).

Ceva, L., 'The Influence of Mines and Minefields in the North African Campaign of 1940–1943', Paper presented to the Symposium on Material Remnants of the Second World War on Libyan Soil (Geneva, 28 Apr.–1 May 1981).

Chief of the Defence Staff, 'Anti-Personnel Mines: Restrictions on Canadian Forces Personnel' (11 Aug. 1998).

Commission nationale pour l'élimination des mines antipersonnel, *Rapport 2000*, CNEMA (Paris, 2001).

*Communication in Mine Awareness Programmes* (Geneva: GICHD, 2002).

Coupland, R. M., *Assistance for Victims of Anti-Personnel Mines: Needs, Constraints and Strategy* (Geneva: ICRC, 1997).

—— 'Technical Aspects of War Wound Excision', *British Journal of Surgery*, 76 (July 1989).

—— and Korver, A., 'Injuries from Antipersonnel Mines: The Experience of the International Committee of the Red Cross', *British Medical Journal*, 303 (14 Dec. 1991).

Daoust, I., 'ICRC Expert Meeting on Legal Reviews of Weapons and the SIrUS Project', *International Review of the Red Cross*, no. 842 (Geneva: ICRC, 30 June 2001).

Davies, P., 'Mines and Unexploded Ordnance in Cambodia and Laos: Understanding the Costs', in Kumar, K. (ed.), *Rebuilding Societies after Civil War: Critical Roles for International Assistance* (Boulder, Colo.: Lynne Rienner, 1997).

Department of Defense, 'Landmines in the Department of Defense', South African National Defence Forces, Logistical Division (20 May 1997).

Department of Foreign Affairs and Trade, Conventional and Nuclear Disarmament Section, International Security Division, 'National Interest Analysis: Convention on the Prohibition of the Use, Stockpiling, Production and Transfer of Anti-Personnel Mines and on their Destruction', tabled on 26 May 1998, available at: www.austlii.edu.au/au/other/dfat/nia/1998/1998019n.html.

Dupuy Institute, 'Military Consequences of Landmine Restrictions' (Washington, Apr. 1996).

Faulkner, F., 'Anti-Personnel Landmines: A Necessary Evil?' *International Relations*, 13/4 (Apr. 1997).

Fenrick, W. J., 'The Conventional Weapons Convention A Modest but Useful Treaty', *International Review of the Red Cross*, no. 279 (Nov.–Dec. 1990).

—— 'New Developments in the Law concerning the Use of Conventional Weapons in Armed Conflict', *Canadian Yearbook of International Law*, 19/19 (1981).

Fenrick, W. J., 'The Law of Armed Conflict: The CUSHIE Weapons Treaty', *Canadian Defence Quarterly*, 11 (1981).

Fitch, Colonel E., Presentation to the ICRC Seminar on the Humanitarian Impact and Military Utility of Anti-Personnel Mines (Budapest, 26–8 Mar. 1998).

Gard Jr., R. G., 'Alternatives to Anti-Personnel Mines', Vietnam Veterans Monograph Series, 1/1 (Washington, spring 1999).

General Accounting Office, 'Military Operations: Information on U.S. Use of Land Mines in the Persian Gulf War', Report No. GAO-02-1003 (Washington, 30 Sept. 2002), available at: www.access.gpo.gov/su_docs/aces/aces160.shtml.

Goldblat, J., 'The Biological Weapons Convention: An Overview', *International Review of the Red Cross*, no. 318 (30 June 1997).

Goose, S., 'The Diplomatic History regarding Anti-Vehicle Mines with Anti-Handling Devices', Attachment 3 to Human Rights Watch Memorandum for Delegates: Anti-Vehicle Mines with Sensitive Fuzes or Anti-Handling Devices (1 Feb. 2002).

—— 'Anti-Personnel Mines and the Conference on Disarmament', ICBL (Washington, Feb. 1999).

—— 'The Ottawa Process and the 1997 Mine Ban Treaty', *Yearbook of International Humanitarian Law* (The Hague: Asser Press, 1998).

Gravett, R., 'Report on the Technical Expert Meeting on Anti-Vehicle Mines with Sensitive Fuzes or with Sensitive Anti-Handling Devices, Hosted by the ICRC in Geneva, 13–14 March 2001' (Apr. 2001).

Greenwood, C., 'Humanitarian Law and Laws of War', Centennial of the First International Peace Conference, Preliminary Report (June 1998).

Guide to Reporting under Article 7 of the Ottawa Convention, VERTIC (London, 2001), available at: www.vertic.org.

Herby, P., 'Third Session of the Review Conference of States Parties to the 1980 United Nations Convention on Certain Conventional Weapons (CCW): Geneva, 22 April–3 May 1996', *International Review of the Red Cross*, no. 312 (May–June 1996).

Hewish, M., and Pengelley, R., 'In Search of a Successor to the Anti-Personnel Landmine, Non-lethal Weapons, Precision Weapons and Close Surveillance', *Jane's International Defense Review* (Mar. 1998).

Human Rights Watch, 'Claymore-Type Mines', Landmine Monitor Fact Sheet (Geneva, 7 Feb. 2003).

—— 'Mines Retained for Training and Development', Landmine Monitor Fact Sheet (Geneva, 7 Feb. 2003), available at: www.icbl.org.

—— 'Antivehicle Mines with Sensitive Fuzes or Antihandling Devices', Memorandum for Delegates to the Fifth Meeting of the Intersessional Standing Committee on the General Status and Operation of the 1997 Mine Ban Treaty, Human Rights Watch (Washington, 1 Feb. 2002).

Institute for Defense Analyses, 'The Military Utility of Landmines: Implications for Arms Control', Doc. D–1559 (Washington, June 1994).

International Campaign to Ban Landmines, 'Victim Assistance: Contexts, Principles and Issues', Position Paper of the ICBL Working Group on Victim Assistance (2000).

—— *Guidelines for the Care and Rehabilitation of Survivors.* Pamphlet of the International Campaign to Ban Landmines Working Group on Victim Assistance (1999).

International Committee of the Red Cross, *Physical Rehabilitation Programs, Annual Report 2002* (Geneva: ICRC, 2001).

—— 'Information Kit on the Development of National Legislation to Implement the Convention on the Prohibition of Anti-Personnel Mines' (Geneva: ICRC, 2001).

—— ICRC Fact Sheet on the Convention on the Prohibition of Anti-Personnel Mines and on their Destruction (Geneva: ICRC, 2000).

—— 'Implementing the Ottawa Treaty: National Legislation', Information Paper (Geneva: ICRC, Apr. 1999).

—— 'Progress towards a Ban on Anti-Personnel Landmines: Measures by Countries and Organizations', ICRC (Geneva, 17 Jan. 1997).

—— 'Report of the ICRC for the Review Conference of the 1980 UN Convention on Certain Conventional Weapons', *International Review of the Red Cross* (Geneva: ICRC, Mar.–Apr. 1994).

—— *Report on the Conference of Government Experts on the Use of Certain Conventional Weapons, Second Session (Lugano, 28 January–26 February 1976)* (Geneva: ICRC, 1976).

—— *Report on the Conference of Government Experts on the Use of Certain Conventional Weapons (Lucerne, 24 September–18 October 1974)* (Geneva: ICRC, 1975).

—— *Draft Rules for the Protection of the Civilian Population from the Dangers of Indiscriminate Warfare* (Geneva: ICRC, June 1955).

Kellman, B., and Tanzman, E. A., *Manual for National Implementation of the Chemical Weapons Convention*, 2nd edn. (Chicago: International Criminal Justice and Weapons Control Center, Feb. 1998).

King, C., 'Legislation and the Landmine', *Jane's Intelligence Review*, Special Report No. 16 (UK, Nov. 1997).

Krawciv, N., 'Banning of Antipersonnel Mines', Memorandum (2 Jan. 1997).

*Land Mines in Cambodia: The Coward's War*, Asia Watch & Physicians for Human Rights (USA, 1991).

Levie, H. S., 'Prohibitions and Restrictions on the Use of Conventional Weapons', *St John's Law Review*, 68 (summer 1994).

Marks, S., 'Reservations Unhinged: The Belilos Case before the European Court of Human Rights', *International and Comparative Law Quarterly* (1990).

Matthews, R. J., and McCormack, T. L. H., 'The Influence of Humanitarian Principles in the Negotiation of Arms Control Treaties', *International Review of the Red Cross*, 81/834 (1999).

*Mechanical Demining Equipment Catalogue 2003* (Geneva: GICHD, Nov. 2002), available at: www.gichd.ch.

Meron, T., 'The Continuing Role of Custom in the Formation of International Humanitarian Law', Editorial Comment, *The American Journal of International Law*, 90/238 (Apr. 1996).

*Metal Detectors Catalogue 2003* (Geneva: GICHD, Feb. 2003), available at: www.gichd.ch.

*Mine Action Equipment: Study of Global Operational Needs*, GICHD (June 2002), available at: www.gichd.ch.

'Mine Action and Effective Coordination: The United Nations Policy', UN Doc. A/53/496, UNMAS (New York, 1998).

Myjer, E. P. J., 'The Settlement of Disputes under the Chemical Weapons Convention and the Case of the Confidentiality Commission', in Bardonnet, D. (ed.), *The Convention on the Prohibition and Elimination of Chemical Weapons: A Breakthrough in Multilateral Disarmament, Workshop, The Hague, 24–26 November 1994* (Dordrecht: Martinus Nijhoff, 1995).

Nash, M., 'Contemporary Practice of the United States Relating to International Law', *American Journal of International Law*, 91 (Apr. 1997).

'Non-Paper by the President of the Fourth Meeting of States Parties', presented on 7 Feb. 2003 by Ambassador Jean Lint of Belgium to the Standing Committee on the General Status and Operation of the Convention, available at: www.gichd.ch.

Office of the Judge Advocate General, 'The Law of Armed Conflict at the Operational and Tactical Level', Department of National Defence (Canada, 21 Mar. 2001).

Organization of American States, *El Desminado* (Washington: UPD, spring 2003).

Oxman, B. H., 'Jurisdiction of States', in *Encyclopaedia of Public International Law*, iii (Amsterdam: Elsevier, 1997).

Pearson, G. S., and Sims, N., 'Article XIV: Amendments', Bradford Evaluation Paper, Department of Peace Studies, University of Bradford (Bradford, Jan. 2000).

Pellet, A., 'First Report on Reservations to Treaties', UN Doc. A/CN.4/470, 52.

Pellet, A., 'Third Report on Reservations to Treaties', Addendum, UN Doc. A/CN.4/491/Add.4.

'President's Paper on Intersessional Work', APLC/MSP.1/1999/Informal 2, Annex IV to the Final Report of the Meeting.

Pustogarov, V., 'Fyodor Fyodorovich Martens (1845–1909): A Humanist of Modern Times', *International Review of the Red Cross*, no. 312 (Geneva, May–June 1996).

Report to the Secretary of Defense on the Status of DOD's Implementation of the US Policy on Anti-personnel Landmines, Office of the Under Secretary of Defense for Policy (May 1997).

Roach, Capt. J. A., 'Certain Conventional Weapons Convention: Arms Control or Humanitarian Law', *Military Law Review*, 105 (summer 1984).

Robblee Jr., Captain P. A., 'The Legitimacy of Modern Conventional Weaponry', *The Military Law and Law of War Review*, 16/4 (1977).

Rogers, Lieutenant-Colonel A. P. V., 'A Commentary on the Protocol on Prohibitions or Restrictions on the Use of Mines, Booby-Traps and Other Devices', *Military Law and Law of War Review*, 26 (1987).

Rossouw, Colonel A. J., 'Rethinking Military Doctrine: Making War without Anti-Personnel Landmines', unpublished paper, undated.

Roucounas, E., 'Uncertainties regarding the Entry into Force of some Multilateral Treaties', in Wellens, K. (ed.), *International Law: Theory and Practice, Essays in Honour of Eric Suy* (The Hague: Martinus Nijhoff, 1998).

Roy, R. L., 'Tactical Impact of Removing Antipersonnel Landmines', Research Note RN 0005, Department of National Defence (Kingston, Canada, Nov. 2000).

Sage, Lieutenant-Colonel J., 'Anti-Personnel Mines, their Military Utility and Humanitarian Considerations', *Journal of the Royal Military College of Science* (UK, July 1995).

Shaw, M., 'The United Nations Convention on Prohibitions or Restrictions on the Use of Certain Conventional Weapons, 1981', *Review of International Studies*, 9/2 (1983).

Shelton, D., 'Reconcilable Differences? The Interpretation of Multilingual Treaties', *Hastings International and Comparative Law Review* 20 (1997).

Short, N., 'International Efforts to Ban Landmines: The Vienna Conference', Briefing Notes, Centre for European Security and Disarmament (Brussels, 4 Mar. 1997).

Sims, N. A., 'Article XII: Settlement of Disputes', Bradford Evaluation Paper, Department of Peace Studies, University of Bradford (Bradford, Nov. 1999), available at: www.brad.ac.uk/acad/sbtwc/briefing/bw-briefing.htm.

Smith, Dr C. (ed.), *The Military Utility of Landmines . . .?* North-South Defence and Security Programme, Centre for Defence Studies, King's College, University of London (June 1996).

Standing Committee on Stockpile Destruction, 'Update on Implementation of Article 4' (30 May 2002), available at: www.gichd.ch.

*Still Killing: Landmines in Southern Africa*, Human Rights Watch (USA, 1997).

Submission of the African National Congress to the Truth and Reconciliation Commission in Reply to the Section 30 (2) of Act 34 of 1996 on the TRC 'Findings on the African National Congress' (Oct. 1998).

'Summary', International Meeting of Experts on Verification Issues regarding an International Agreement to Ban Anti-Personnel Mines (Königswinter, 24 Apr. 1997).

Suy, E., 'Reflexions sur la distinction entre la Souveraineté et la compétence territorial', in *Internationale Festschrift für Alfred Verdross zum 80. Geburtstag* (Munich/Salzburg: Wilhelm Fink Verlag, 1971).

'Swedish Position on the Significance of Article 1(c) of the Ottawa Convention as regards Participation in International Peace Operations', Memorandum, Ministry of Foreign Affairs (1 Sept. 2001).

Switzerland, 'International Convention for Total Ban of Antipersonnel Mines, Provisions on Compliance', Working Paper, distributed at the Expert Meeting on Possible Verification Measures for a Convention to Ban Anti-Personnel Landmines (Bonn, 24–5 Apr. 1997).

Szasz, P., 'The Conference on Excessively Injurious or Indiscriminate Weapons', *American Journal of International Law*, 74 (Jan. 1980).

*The Role of Mine Action in Victim Assistance* (Geneva: GICHD, 2001).

*The Role of the Military in Mine Action* (Geneva: GICHD, June 2003).

*The Worldwide Epidemic of Landmine Injuries: The ICRC's Health Oriented Approach* (Geneva: ICRC, 1995).

Ticehurst, R., 'The Martens Clause and the Laws of Armed Conflict', *International Review of the Red Cross*, no. 317 (Mar.–Apr. 1997).

United Kingdom Permanent Representation to the Conference on Disarmament, 'APL Mine Stockpiles and their Destruction: A Progress Report: Landmine Monitor Fact Sheet' (11 May 2001).

United Nations, 'Summary of Practice of the Secretary-General as Depositary of Multilateral Treaties', Prepared by the Treaty Section of the Office of Legal Affairs, UN Doc. ST/LEG/8, undated.

—— *Humanitarian Demining, Terminology Bulletin No. 349*, ST/CS/SER.F/349 (New York: UN, 1997).

—— *Landmines*, 1.4 (Sept. 1996).

—— Department for Humanitarian Affairs, 'Fact Sheet on Manufacturing and Trade' (New York, 1996).

—— 'Summary of Negotiations Leading to the Conclusion of the Convention on Prohibitions or Restrictions on the Use of Certain Conventional Weapons which may be Deemed to be Excessively Injurious or to have Indiscriminate Effects and of Subsequent Developments related to the Convention', UN Doc. CCW/CONF.I/GE/5 (6 May 1994).

US Army, Office of the Chief of Staff, 'Certain Victory: United States Army in the Gulf War', Desert Storm Study Project (US Army, 1993).

US Defense Intelligence Agency and US Army Foreign Science and Technology Center, 'Landmine Warfare: Trends and Projections (U)', DST-1160S-019-92 (Washington, Dec. 1992).

'Update on the President's Consultations held in Geneva on 12 May 2003 on Preparing for the Convention's First Review Conference' (Geneva, 15 May 2003).

VERTIC, *Guide to Fact-Finding Missions under the Ottawa Convention* (London: VERTIC/Diana, Princess of Wales Memorial Fund, Dec. 2002).

—— *Guide to Reporting under Article 7 of the Ottawa Convention* (London: VERTIC, 2001), available at: www.vertic.org.

Victim Assistance: A Public Health Response for Landmine Victims' (Geneva: ICRC/WHO, 2000).

Wilkinson, A., 'Evaluating Destruction Techniques for PFM APM' (Geneva: GICHD, Dec. 2000), available at: www.gichd.ch.

World Rehabilitation Fund, 'Guidelines for the Provision of Socioeconomic Integration of Landmine Survivors' (New York: WRF, 2001).

## Conference Statements

Intervention on Article 7 by Stephen Goose, Head of ICRC Delegation, to the Standing Committee on General Status and Operation of the Convention (Geneva, 16 May 2003), available at: www.gichd.ch.

Landmine Survivors Network, 'Landmine Survivors Call on Governments to Address the Plight of Mine Victims Worldwide', Statement to the Brussels Conference (Brussels, 26 June 1997).

'Opening Intervention on Progress made and Challenges faced in Mine Action by Sara Sekkenes: NPA on behalf of the Mine Action Working Group of the ICBL', Standing Committee on Mine Clearance, Mine Awareness and Related Technologies (Geneva, 5 Feb. 2003), available at: www.gichd.ch/pdf/mbc/SC_feb03/speeches_mc /Sekkenes_MAWG_progress_made.pdf.

Presentation by Canada, 'Article 8 and the Facilitation and Clarification of Compliance', to the Standing Committee on the General Status and Operation of the Convention (Geneva, dated 2 May 2001).

Speech of Belgian Foreign Minister Eric Derycke, Chairman of the International Meeting on Demining (Geneva, 6 July 1995).

Speech of Dr Klaus Kinkel to the opening of the International Meeting of Experts on Verification Issues regarding an International Agreement to Ban Anti-Personnel Mines (Königswinter, 24 Apr. 1997).

Statement by Ambassador Jean Lint, Co-Chair, Standing Committee on Mine Clearance, Mine Risk Education and Mine Action Technologies (Geneva, 5 Feb. 2003), available at: www.gichd.ch.

Statement by Ambassador Jean Lint on Article 7 reporting to the intersessional Standing Committee on the General Status and Operation of the Convention (Geneva, 16 May 2003), available at: www.gichd.ch.

Statement by Brazil on Issues concerning Article 1 (General Obligations) of the Anti-Personnel Mine Ban Convention to the Standing Committee on General Status and Operation of the Convention (Geneva, 1 Feb. 2002).

Statement by Brazil on Issues concerning Article 1 (General Obligations) of the Mine Ban Convention to the intersessional Standing Committee on General Status and Operation of the Convention (1 Feb. 2002).

Statement by the Permanent Representative of Germany to the Conference on Disarmament, Ambassador Volker Heinsberg, to the Fourth Meeting of States Parties to the Convention on the Prohibition of the Use, Stockpiling, Production and Transfer of Anti-Personnel Mines and on their Destruction (Geneva, 17 Sept. 2002).

Statement by UNDP on the Status of UN Support to Stockpile Destruction to the Standing Committee on Stockpile Destruction (Geneva, 6 Feb. 2003).

Statement by the United Kingdom on Article 2 of the Convention on the Prohibition of the Use, Stockpiling, Production and Transfer of Anti-Personnel Mines and on their Destruction, Standing Committee on the General Status and Operation of the Convention (Geneva, 30 May 2002).

Statement by Zimbabwe on Issues concerning Article 1 (General Obligations) of the Anti-Personnel Mine Ban Convention to the Standing Committee on the General Status and Operation of the Convention (Geneva, 31 May 2002), available at: www.gichd.ch/pdf/mbc/SC_may02/speeches_gs/Statement_Zimbabwe.pdf.

Statement of the Canadian Ambassador to the Conference on Disarmament (Geneva, 6 Feb. 1997).

Statement of Deputy Minister of Foreign Affairs of the Republic of Zambia to the Second Meeting of States Parties (Geneva, 12 Sept. 2000).

Statement of Eric Roethlisberger, Vice-President of the ICRC, to the closing session of the First Review Conference of the 1980 Convention on Certain Conventional Weapons (3 May 1996).

Statement of Germany to the Standing Committee on the General Operation and Status of the Convention (Geneva, 27 May 2002).

Statement of the International Campaign to Ban Landmines to the Standing Committee on the General Status and Operation of the Convention (Geneva, 16 May 2003), available at: www.gichd.ch/pdf/mbc/SC_may03/speeches_gs/ICBL_Art2.pdf.

Statement of the International Committee of the Red Cross on Article 2 of the Convention to the Third Meeting of States Parties (Managua, 20 Sept. 2001).

Statement of the International Committee of the Red Cross to the Standing Committee on the General Status and Operation of the Convention (Geneva, 16 May 2003), available at: www.gichd.ch/pdf/mbc/SC_may03/speeches_gs/ICRC_Art2.pdf.

Statement of the International Committee of the Red Cross to the Standing Committee on the General Status and Operation of the Convention (Geneva, 16 May 2003), available at: www.gichd.ch/pdf/mbc/SC_may03/speeches_gs/ICRC_Best_Practices.pdf.

Statement of the Secretary-General of the UN to the Diplomatic Conference on an International Total Ban on Anti-Personnel Land Mines (Oslo, 3 Sep. 1997).

'The International Trust Fund for Demining and Mine Victims Assistance: An Example of Regional Cooperation in South-East Europe', Address to the Euro-Atlantic Security Workshop by Ambassador Roman Kirn, former Executive Director of the ITF (27 Sept. 2002).

## Press Articles, Releases, and Reports

'600-Year-Old Mines Unearthed in Inner Mongolia', *Xinhua Press Agency* (Hohhot, Mongolia, 11 Apr. 2001).

'Apartheid Indictment finds Fault on all Sides', CNN (Pretoria, 29 Oct. 1998), available at: www.cnn.com/WORLD/africa/9810/29/truth.commission.03/.

'Axworthy Announces Dates for Landmine Treaty Conference', News Release, Canadian Embassy (Brussels, 27 June 1997).

Ayllón, L., 'España insiste a EE. UU. para que destruya sus minas antipersonal', *ABC* (2 Nov. 1998).

Bonner, R., 'How a Group of Outsiders Moved Nations to Ban Landmines', *New York Times* (20 Sept. 1997).

—— 'New US Terms on Mine Ban are Called Unacceptable', *New York Times* (16 Sept. 1997).

'Border Landmines kill 35 South Koreans: Minister', *Agence France Presse* (2 Oct. 1997).

'Britain Calls for Ban on Landmine Exports', *Financial Times* (31 Jan. 1997).

'Canada to Help Ukraine on Landmine Ban, International Loans', *AFP International* (27 Jan. 1999).

'Chemical Weapons Destruction Complete on Johnston Atoll', Press Release No. 715-00, Office of the Assistant Secretary of Defense (Public Affairs) (Washington, 30 Nov. 2000).

'Desactivan explosive en balón', *El Tiempo* (9 Jan. 2003).

'Disarmament Conference hears Further Calls for Bans on Landmines and Fissile Materials, Establishment of Negotiating Committee on Nuclear Disarmament', UN Press release DCF/283 (Geneva, 23 Jan. 1997).

'Disarmament Conference hears Statements on Anti-Personnel Landmines Nuclear Disarmament and Fissile Material Cut-Off', UN Press release DCF/311 (Geneva, 15 Aug. 1997).

'Forces will have to Destroy all Landmines', *The Times* (22 May 1997).

Gertz, B., 'Clinton Resisted Pressure to Join Ban on Landmines', *Washington Times* (20 Sept. 1997).

'La Suède se félicite sur l'accord sur les mines antipersonnel', *Agence France Presse* (Stockholm, 3 May 1996).

Mannion, J., 'US Wants Talks on Landmine Ban held in Geneva', *Agence France Presse* (Washington, 17 Jan. 1997).

Morrison, J., 'Britain Accused of Watering down Landmines Ban', *Reuters* (London, 10 July 1998).

Myers, L., 'US Seeks to Keep Landmines', *Philadelphia Inquirer* (1 Mar. 1998).

'NATO Treads Carefully on Touchy Landmines Issue', *Reuters* (Brussels, 16 Dec. 1997).

NATO/SFOR Press Briefing (12 Dec. 2002), available at: www.nato.int/sfor/trans/2002/t021212a.htm.

'New U.S. European Commander to Visit Norway', *Agence France Presse* (Oslo, 5 Dec. 1997).

Nivat, A., 'Tadjikistan: la sale frontière', *Le Nouvel observateur* (*TéléCinéObs*) (26 Dec. 2002).

'North Korea against Landmine Ban Exclusion', *Reuters* (Moscow, 14 Sept. 1997).

Pinon, B., 'Les Etats Unis accusés de vouloir "saboter" la Conférence de Bruxelles', *Agence France Presse* (Brussels, 26 June 1997).

Priest, D., 'Mine Decision Boosts Clinton–Military Relations', *Washington Post* (21 Sept. 1997).

' "Safe" Landmine', *The Times* (24 Apr. 2003).

Simons, M., 'Money Short for Battle on Chemicals Use in War', *The New York Times* (5 Oct. 2001).

'Territoire miné', *Nouvel Observateur* (20–6 Dec. 2001).

'Un "coordonnateur" pour les négociations sur les mines anti-personnel', *Agence France Presse* (Geneva, 26 June 1997).

'United States Announces Next Step on Anti-Personnel Landmines', Statement by the Press Secretary, Office of the Press Secretary, The White House (Washington, 17 Jan. 1997).

'United States to Join Ottawa Process', Statement by the Press Secretary (Martha's Vineyard: Mass., 18 Sept. 1997).

'US Wins more Time for Landmines Pact', *Financial Times* (17 Sept. 1997).

Williams, F., 'UN Fails to Agree Outright Ban on Landmines', *Financial Times* (4 May 1996).

## List of Legal Cases

*Bankovic et* al. v. *Belgium et* al., European Court of Human Rights, Application No. 52207/99, para. 59, available at: www.hudoc.echr.coe.int.

Nuclear Weapons Advisory Opinion, *ICJ Reports*, 1996.

'Pershing II and Cruise Missile . . . Decision 1', BVerfGE 66, 39, 2 BvR 1160/83 *et al.*, available at: www.ucl.ac.uk.

*Prosecutor* v. *Tadíc, Case No. IT-94-1-AR72*, Appeal on Jurisdiction, 2 Oct. 1995.

Publications of the European Court of Human Rights, Series A, Vol. 132, Judgment of 29 Apr. 1988.

*Territorial Dispute* (*Libyan Arab Jamahariya/Chad*) case, *ICJ Reports*, 1994.

## Other Documents

Letter from Knut Vollbaeck, Norwegian Minister of Foreign Affairs, to US Secretary of State, Madeleine Albright (20 May 1998).

'Note of the Secretary-General to the Permanent Representative of Austria to the United Nations' (New York, 15 Aug. 1997).

Note Verbale from New Zealand Ministry of Foreign Affairs to the Austrian Embassy (Wellington, 18 Apr. 1997).

1st APM stockpile Destruction Management Training Course, 11–15 June 2001, Fribourg, Documentation, General Staff of the Swiss Armed Forces.

# APPENDIXES

# APPENDIX 1

# Key Provisions of Treaty Interpretation

## VIENNA CONVENTION ON THE LAW OF TREATIES

Signed at Vienna, 23 May 1969

Entry into force: 27 January 1980

The States Parties to the present Convention

. . .

Noting that the principles of free consent and of good faith and the pacta sunt servanda rule are universally recognized,

Affirming that disputes concerning treaties, like other international disputes, should be settled by peaceful means and in conformity with the principles of justice and international law,

. . .

Affirming that the rules of customary international law will continue to govern questions not regulated by the provisions of the present Convention,

Have agreed as follows:

## PART I: INTRODUCTION

### Article 1. Scope of the present Convention

The present Convention applies to treaties between States.

### Article 2. Use of terms

1. For the purposes of the present Convention:

(a) 'treaty' means an international agreement concluded between States in written form and governed by international law, whether embodied in a single instrument or in two or more related instruments and whatever its particular designation;

(b) 'ratification', 'acceptance', 'approval' and 'accession' mean in each case the international act so named whereby a State establishes on the international plane its consent to be bound by a treaty;

(c) 'full powers' means a document emanating from the competent authority of a State designating a person or persons to represent the State for negotiating, adopting or authenticating the text of a treaty, for expressing the consent of the State to be bound by a treaty, or for accomplishing any other act with respect to a treaty;

(d) 'reservation' means a unilateral statement, however phrased or named, made by a State, when signing, ratifying, accepting, approving or acceding to a treaty, whereby it purports to exclude or to modify the legal effect of certain provisions of the treaty in their application to that State;

(e) 'negotiating State' means a State which took part in the drawing up and adoption of the text of the treaty;

(f) 'contracting State' means a State which has consented to be bound by the treaty, whether or not the treaty has entered into force;

(g) 'party' means a State which has consented to be bound by the treaty and for which the treaty is in force;

. . .

## PART II: CONCLUSION AND ENTRY INTO FORCE OF TREATIES

### Section 1.  Conclusion of Treaties

### Article 6.  Capacity of States to conclude treaties

Every State possesses capacity to conclude treaties.

### Article 9.  Adoption of the text

1.  The adoption of the text of a treaty takes place by the consent of all the States participating in its drawing up except as provided in paragraph 2.

2.  The adoption of the text of a treaty at an international conference takes place by the vote of two-thirds of the States present and voting, unless by the same majority they shall decide to apply a different rule.

### Article 10.  Authentication of the text

The text of a treaty is established as authentic and definitive:

(a) by such procedure as may be provided for in the text or agreed upon by the States participating in its drawing up; or

(b) failing such procedure, by the signature, signature ad referendum or initialling by the representatives of those States of the text of the treaty or of the Final Act of a conference incorporating the text.

### Article 11.  Means of expressing consent to be bound by a treaty

The consent of a State to be bound by a treaty may be expressed by signature, exchange of instruments constituting a treaty, ratification, acceptance, approval or accession, or by any other means if so agreed.

## Article 14. Consent to be bound by a treaty expressed by ratification, acceptance or approval

1. The consent of a State to be bound by a treaty is expressed by ratification when:

(a) the treaty provides for such consent to be expressed by means of ratification;

(b) it is otherwise established that the negotiating States were agreed that ratification should be required;

(c) the representative of the State has signed the treaty subject to ratification; or

(d) the intention of the State to sign the treaty subject to ratification appears from the full powers of its representative or was expressed during the negotiation.

2. The consent of a State to be bound by a treaty is expressed by acceptance or approval under conditions similar to those which apply to ratification

## Article 15. Consent to be bound by a treaty expressed by accession

The consent of a State to be bound by a treaty is expressed by accession when:

(a) the treaty provides that such consent may be expressed by that State by means of accession;

(b) it is otherwise established that the negotiating States were agreed that such consent may be expressed by that State by means of accession; or

(c) all the parties have subsequently agreed that such consent may be expressed by that State by means of accession.

## Article 18. Obligation not to defeat the object and purpose of a treaty prior to its entry into force

A State is obliged to refrain from acts which would defeat the object and purpose of a treaty when:

(a) it has signed the treaty or has exchanged instruments constituting the treaty subject to ratification, acceptance or approval, until it shall have made its intention clear not to become a party to the treaty; or

(b) it has expressed its consent to be bound by the treaty, pending the entry into force of the treaty and provided that such entry into force is not unduly delayed.

### Section 2.  Reservations

## Article 19.  Formulation of reservations

A State may, when signing, ratifying, accepting, approving or acceding to a treaty, formulate a reservation unless:

(a) the reservation is prohibited by the treaty;

(b) the treaty provides that only specified reservations, which do not include the reservation in question, may be made; or

(c) in cases not falling under sub-paragraphs (a) and (b), the reservation is incompatible with the object and purpose of the treaty.

## Section 3. Entry into Force and Provisional Application of Treaties

### Article 24. Entry into force

1. A treaty enters into force in such manner and upon such date as it may provide or as the negotiating States may agree.

2. Failing any such provision or agreement, a treaty enters into force as soon as consent to be bound by the treaty has been established for all the negotiating States.

3. When the consent of a State to be bound by a treaty is established on a date after the treaty has come into force, the treaty enters into force for that State on that date, unless the treaty otherwise provides.

4. The provisions of a treaty regulating the authentication of its text, the establishment of the consent of States to be bound by the treaty, the manner or date of its entry into force, reservations, the functions of the depositary and other matters arising necessarily before the entry into force of the treaty apply from the time of the adoption of its text.

### Article 25. Provisional application

1. A treaty or a part of a treaty is applied provisionally pending its entry into force if:

(a) the treaty itself so provides; or

(b) the negotiating States have in some other manner so agreed.

2. Unless the treaty otherwise provides or the negotiating States have otherwise agreed, the provisional application of a treaty or a part of a treaty with respect to a State shall be terminated if that State notifies the other States between which the treaty is being applied provisionally of its intention not to become a party to the treaty.

## PART III: OBSERVANCE, APPLICATION AND INTERPRETATION OF TREATIES

### Section 1. Observance of Treaties

### Article 26. Pacta sunt servanda

Every treaty in force is binding upon the parties to it and must be performed by them in good faith.

### Article 27. Internal law and observance of treaties

A party may not invoke the provisions of its internal law as justification for its failure to perform a treaty. This rule is without prejudice to article 46.

### Section 2. Application of Treaties

### Article 28. Non-retroactivity of treaties

Unless a different intention appears from the treaty or is otherwise established, its provisions do not bind a party in relation to any act or fact which took place or any situation which ceased to exist before the date of the entry into force of the treaty with respect to that party.

### Article 29. Territorial scope of treaties

Unless a different intention appears from the treaty or is otherwise established, a treaty is binding upon each party in respect of its entire territory.

### Article 30. Application of successive treaties relating to the same subject-matter

1. Subject to Article 103 of the Charter of the United Nations, the rights and obligations of States parties to successive treaties relating to the same subject-matter shall be determined in accordance with the following paragraphs.

2. When a treaty specifies that it is subject to, or that it is not to be considered as incompatible with, an earlier or later treaty, the provisions of that other treaty prevail.

3. When all the parties to the earlier treaty are parties also to the later treaty but the earlier treaty is not terminated or suspended in operation under article 59, the earlier treaty applies only to the extent that its provisions are compatible with those of the latter treaty.

4. When the parties to the later treaty do not include all the parties to the earlier one:

(a) as between States parties to both treaties the same rule applies as in paragraph 3;

(b) as between a State party to both treaties and a State party to only one of the treaties, the treaty to which both States are parties governs their mutual rights and obligations.

5. Paragraph 4 is without prejudice to article 41, or to any question of the termination or suspension of the operation of a treaty under article 60 or to any question of responsibility which may arise for a State from the conclusion or application of a treaty, the provisions of which are incompatible with its obligations towards another State under another treaty.

### Section 3. Interpretation of Treaties

### Article 31. General rule of interpretation

1. A treaty shall be interpreted in good faith in accordance with the ordinary meaning to be given to the terms of the treaty in their context and in the light of its object and purpose.

2. The context for the purpose of the interpretation of a treaty shall comprise, in addition to the text, including its preamble and annexes:

(a) any agreement relating to the treaty which was made between all the parties in connexion with the conclusion of the treaty;

(b) any instrument which was made by one or more parties in connexion with the conclusion of the treaty and accepted by the other parties as an instrument related to the treaty.

3. There shall be taken into account, together with the context:

(a) any subsequent agreement between the parties regarding the interpretation of the treaty or the application of its provisions;

(b)  any subsequent practice in the application of the treaty which establishes the agreement of the parties regarding its interpretation;

(c)  any relevant rules of international law applicable in the relations between the parties.

4.  A special meaning shall be given to a term if it is established that the parties so intended.

### Article 32.  Supplementary means of interpretation

Recourse may be had to supplementary means of interpretation, including the preparatory work of the treaty and the circumstances of its conclusion, in order to confirm the meaning resulting from the application of article 31, or to determine the meaning when the interpretation according to article 31:

(a)  leaves the meaning ambiguous or obscure; or

(b)  leads to a result which is manifestly absurd or unreasonable.

### Article 33.  Interpretation of treaties authenticated in two or more languages

1.  When a treaty has been authenticated in two or more languages, the text is equally authoritative in each language, unless the treaty provides or the parties agree that, in case of divergence, a particular text shall prevail.

2.  A version of the treaty in a language other than one of those in which the text was authenticated shall be considered an authentic text only if the treaty so provides or the parties so agree.

3.  The terms of the treaty are presumed to have the same meaning in each authentic text.

4.  Except where a particular text prevails in accordance with paragraph 1, when a comparison of the authentic texts discloses a difference of meaning which the application of articles 31 and 32 does not remove, the meaning which best reconciles the texts, having regard to the object and purpose of the treaty, shall be adopted.

### Section 4. Treaties and Third States

### Article 34.  General rule regarding third States

A treaty does not create either obligations or rights for a third State without its consent.

### Article 38.  Rules in a treaty becoming binding on third States through international custom

Nothing in articles 34 to 37 precludes a rule set forth in a treaty from becoming binding upon a third State as a customary rule of international law, recognized as such.

## Part IV: Amendment and Modification of Treaties

### Article 39.  General rule regarding the amendment of treaties

A treaty may be amended by agreement between the parties. The rules laid down in Part II apply to such an agreement except in so far as the treaty may otherwise provide.

## Depositaries, Notifications, Corrections and Registration

### Article 77.  Functions of depositaries

1.  The functions of a depositary, unless otherwise provided in the treaty or agreed by the contracting States, comprise in particular:

(a)  keeping custody of the original text of the treaty and of any full powers delivered to the depositary;

(b)  preparing certified copies of the original text and preparing any further text of the treaty in such additional languages as may be required by the treaty and transmitting them to the parties and to the States entitled to become parties to the treaty;

(c)  receiving any signatures to the treaty and receiving and keeping custody of any instruments, notifications and communications relating to it;

(d)  examining whether the signature or any instrument, notification or communication relating to the treaty is in due and proper form and, if need be, bringing the matter to the attention of the State in question;

(e)  informing the parties and the States entitled to become parties to the treaty of acts, notifications and communications relating to the treaty;

(f)  informing the States entitled to become parties to the treaty when the number of signatures or of instruments of ratification, acceptance, approval or accession required for the entry into force of the treaty has been received or deposited;

(g)  registering the treaty with the Secretariat of the United Nations;

(h)  performing the functions specified in other provisions of the present Convention.

2.  In the event of any difference appearing between a State and the depositary as to the performance of the latter's functions, the depositary shall bring the question to the attention of the signatory States and the contracting States or, where appropriate, of the competent organ of the international organization concerned.

### Article 79.  Correction of errors in texts or in certified copies of treaties

1.  Where, after the authentication of the text of a treaty, the signatory States and the contracting States are agreed that it contains an error, the error shall, unless they decide upon some other means of correction, be corrected:

(a)  by having the appropriate correction made in the text and causing the correction to be initialled by duly authorized representatives;

(b)  by executing or exchanging an instrument or instruments setting out the correction which it has been agreed to make; or

(c)  by executing a corrected text of the whole treaty by the same procedure as in the case of the original text.

2.  Where the treaty is one for which there is a depositary, the latter shall notify the signatory States and the contracting States of the error and of the proposal to correct it and

shall specify an appropriate time-limit within which objection to the proposed correction may be raised. If, on the expiry of the time-limit:

(a) no objection has been raised, the depositary shall make and initial the correction in the text and shall execute a procès-verbal of the rectification of the text and communicate a copy of it to the parties and to the States entitled to become parties to the treaty;

(b) an objection has been raised, the depositary shall communicate the objection to the signatory States and to the contracting States.

3. The rules in paragraphs 1 and 2 apply also where the text has been authenticated in two or more languages and it appears that there is a lack of concordance which the signatory States and the contracting States agree should be corrected.

4. The corrected text replaces the defective text ab initio, unless the signatory States and the contracting States otherwise decide.

5. The correction of the text of a treaty that has been registered shall be notified to the Secretariat of the United Nations.

6. Where an error is discovered in a certified copy of a treaty, the depositary shall execute a procès-verbal specifying the rectification and communicate a copy of it to the signatory States and to the contracting States.

### Article 80. Registration and publication of treaties

1. Treaties shall, after their entry into force, be transmitted to the Secretariat of the United Nations for registration or filing and recording, as the case may be, and for publication.

2. The designation of a depositary shall constitute authorization for it to perform the acts specified in the preceding paragraph.

# APPENDIX 2
# United Nations General Assembly Resolutions

## 48/75. GENERAL AND COMPLETE DISARMAMENT
## K
## MORATORIUM ON THE EXPORT OF ANTI-PERSONNEL LAND-MINES

*The General Assembly,*

*Noting* that there are as many as 85 million uncleared land-mines throughout the world, particularly in rural areas,

*Expressing deep concern* that such mines kill or maim hundreds of people each week, mostly unarmed civilians, obstruct economic development and have other severe consequences, which include inhibiting the repatriation of refugees and the return of internally displaced persons,

*Recalling with satisfaction* its resolution 48/7 of 19 October 1993, by which it, inter alia, requested the Secretary-General to submit a comprehensive report on the problems caused by mines and other unexploded devices,

*Convinced* that a moratorium by States exporting anti-personnel land-mines that pose grave dangers to civilian populations would reduce substantially the human and economic costs resulting from the use of such devices and would complement the aforementioned initiative,

*Noting with satisfaction* that several States have already declared moratoriums on the export, transfer or purchase of anti-personnel land-mines and related devices

1. Calls upon States to agree to a moratorium on the export of anti-personnel land-mines that pose grave dangers to civilian populations;

2. Urges States to implement such a moratorium;

3. Requests the Secretary-General to prepare a report concerning progress on this initiative, including possible recommendations regarding further appropriate measures to limit the export of anti-personnel land-mines, and to submit it to the General Assembly at its forty-ninth session under the item entitled 'General and complete disarmament'.

81st plenary meeting
16 December 1993

## 49/75. GENERAL AND COMPLETE DISARMAMENT
### D
### MORATORIUM ON THE EXPORT OF
### ANTI-PERSONNEL LAND-MINES

*The General Assembly,*

*Recalling with satisfaction* its resolution 48/75 K of 16 December 1993, by which it, *inter alia,* called upon States to agree to a moratorium on the export of anti-personnel land-mines that pose grave dangers to civilian populations, and urged States to implement such a moratorium,

*Noting* that there are approximately 85 million or more anti-personnel land-mines in the ground throughout the world and that many thousands of such mines continue to be laid in an indiscriminate manner,

*Expressing deep concern* that anti-personnel land-mines kill or maim hundreds of people every week, mostly unarmed civilians, obstruct economic development and reconstruction and have other severe consequences, which include inhibiting the repatriation of refugees and the return of internally displaced persons,

*Welcoming* the programmes of assistance which exist for demining and humanitarian support for the victims of anti-personnel land-mines,

*Gravely concerned* with the suffering and casualties caused to non-combatants as a result of the proliferation, as well as the indiscriminate and irresponsible use, of anti-personnel land-mines,

*Recognizing* that States can move most effectively towards the ultimate goal of the eventual elimination of anti-personnel land-mines as viable and humane alternatives are developed,

*Recalling with satisfaction* the report of the Secretary-General\* concerning progress on the initiative in the aforementioned resolution,

*Convinced* that moratoriums by States exporting anti-personnel land-mines that pose grave dangers to civilian populations are important measures in helping to reduce substantially the human and economic costs resulting from the use of such devices,

*Noting with satisfaction* that many States already have declared moratoriums on the export, transfer or sale of anti-personnel land-mines and related devices, with many of these moratoriums being declared as a result of the aforementioned resolution,

*Believing* that ongoing efforts to strengthen the Convention on Prohibitions or Restrictions on the Use of Certain Conventional Weapons Which May Be Deemed to Be Excessively Injurious or to Have Indiscriminate Effects,\*\* particularly its Protocol II,\*\*\* are an important part of the overall effort to address problems caused by anti-personnel land-mines,

*Recalling with satisfaction* its resolution 48/7 of 19 October 1993 calling for assistance in mine clearance,

1. Welcomes the moratoriums already declared by certain States on the export of anti-personnel land-mines;

2. Urges States that have not yet done so to declare such moratoriums at the earliest possible date;

3. Requests the Secretary-General to prepare a report on steps taken by Member States to implement such moratoriums and to submit it to the General Assembly at its fiftieth session under the item entitled 'General and complete disarmament';

4. Emphasizes the importance of the Convention on Prohibitions or Restrictions on the Use of Certain Conventional Weapons Which May Be Deemed to Be Excessively Injurious or to Have Indiscriminate Effects and its Protocols as the authoritative international instrument governing the responsible use of anti-personnel land-mines and related devices;

5. Urges States that have not done so to adhere to the Convention and its Protocols;

6. Encourages further international efforts to seek solutions to the problems caused by anti-personnel land-mines, with a view to their eventual elimination.

   \* A/49/275 of 27 July 1994 and Add.1 of 31 October 1994.
  \*\* See *The United Nations Disarmament Yearbook*, vol. 5: 1980 (United Nations publication, Sales No. E.81.IX.4), appendix VII.
\*\*\* *Ibid*, Protocol on Prohibitions or Restrictions on the Use of Mines, Booby Traps and Other Devices.

90th plenary meeting
15 December 1994

## 50/70. GENERAL AND COMPLETE DISARMAMENT
### O
### MORATORIUM ON THE EXPORT OF ANTI-PERSONNEL LAND-MINES

*The General Assembly,*

*Recalling with satisfaction* its resolutions 48/75 K of 16 December 1993 and 49/75 D of 15 December 1994, in which it, *inter alia*, called upon States to agree to a moratorium on the export of anti-personnel land-mines that pose grave dangers to civilian populations, and urged States to implement moratoria on the export of anti-personnel land-mines,

*Also recalling with satisfaction* its resolution 49/75 D, in which it, *inter alia*, established as a goal of the international community the eventual elimination of anti-personnel land-mines,

*Noting* that, according to the 1994 report of the Secretary-General entitled 'Assistance in mine clearance',\* it is estimated that there are more than one hundred and ten million land-mines in the ground in more than sixty countries throughout the world,

*Noting also* that, according to the same report, the global land-mine crisis continues to worsen as an estimated two to five million new land-mines are laid each year, while only an estimated one hundred thousand were cleared in 1994,

*Expressing deep concern* that anti-personnel land-mines kill or maim hundreds of people every week, mostly innocent and defenceless civilians, obstruct economic development and reconstruction, and have other severe consequences for years after emplacement, which include inhibiting the repatriation of refugees and the return of internally displaced persons,

*Gravely concerned* over the suffering and casualties caused to non-combatants as a result of the proliferation, as well as the indiscriminate and irresponsible use, of anti-personnel land-mines,

*Recalling with satisfaction* its resolutions 48/7 of 19 October 1993 and 49/215 A of 23 December 1994 calling for assistance in mine clearance,

*Welcoming* the programmes of assistance that exist for demining and humanitarian support for the victims of anti-personnel land-mines,

*Welcoming also* the International Meeting on Mine Clearance, held at Geneva from 5 to 7 July 1995, and noting the statement of the Secretary-General at the meeting that the international community must take specific and tangible steps to address the intolerable situation caused by the proliferation of anti-personnel land-mines throughout the world,

*Recalling with satisfaction* the report of the Secretary-General concerning progress on the initiative in resolution 49/75 D,\*\*

*Convinced* that moratoria by States on the export of anti-personnel landmines that pose grave dangers to civilian populations are important measures in helping to reduce substantially the human and economic costs resulting from the proliferation, as well as the indiscriminate and irresponsible use, of such devices,

*Noting with satisfaction* that more than twenty-five States already have declared moratoria on the export, transfer or sale of anti-personnel landmines, with many of these moratoria being declared as a result of the aforementioned resolutions,

*Believing* that ongoing efforts to strengthen the Convention on Prohibitions or Restrictions on the Use of Certain Conventional Weapons Which May Be Deemed to Be Excessively Injurious or to Have Indiscriminate Effects,\*\*\* in particular Protocol II thereto,\*\*\*\* are an essential part of the overall effort to address problems caused by the proliferation, as well as the indiscriminate and irresponsible use, of anti-personnel land-mines,

*Noting* the efforts that were made at the Review Conference of the States Parties to the Convention, held at Vienna from 25 September to 13 October 1995, to strengthen prohibitions and restrictions in Protocol II governing land-mine use and transfer, and urging parties to build consensus towards agreement on such prohibitions and restrictions when the Review Conference reconvenes in January and April 1996,

*Believing* that, in addition to Protocol II, other measures to control the production, stockpiling and transfer of anti-personnel land-mines are also necessary to address problems caused by anti-personnel land-mines, especially the indiscriminate or illegal use of anti-personnel land-mines that continue to inflict harm on civilian populations long after emplacement,

*Recognizing* that States can move most effectively towards the goal of the eventual elimination of anti-personnel land-mines as viable alternatives are developed that significantly reduce the risk to the civilian population, and emphasizing the need for States to work on developing such alternatives on an urgent basis,

1. Welcomes the moratoria already declared by certain States on the export of anti-personnel land-mines;

2. Urges States that have not yet done so to declare such moratoria at the earliest possible date;

3. Requests the Secretary-General to prepare a report on steps taken by Member States to implement such moratoria, and to submit it to the General Assembly at its fifty-first session under the item entitled 'General and complete disarmament';

4. Emphasizes the importance of the Convention on Prohibitions or Restrictions on the Use of Certain Conventional Weapons Which May Be Deemed to Be Excessively Injurious or to Have Indiscriminate Effects and Protocol II thereto as the authoritative international instrument governing the responsible use of anti-personnel land-mines and related devices, and urges parties to build consensus towards an agreement when the Review Conference reconvenes;

5. Encourages the widest possible accession to the Convention and to Protocol II thereto, and further urges all States to comply immediately and fully with the applicable rules of Protocol II;

6. Also encourages further immediate international efforts to seek solutions to the problems caused by anti-personnel land-mines, with a view to the eventual elimination of anti-personnel land-mines.

* A/49/357 and Add.1 and 2.
** A/50/701.
*** See *The United Nations Disarmament Yearbook*, vol. 5: 1980 (United Nations publication, Sales No. E.81.IX.4), appendix VII.
**** Protocol on Prohibitions or Restrictions on the Use of Mines, Booby Traps and Other Devices (see *The United Nations Disarmament Yearbook*, vol. 5: 1980 (United Nations publication, Sales No. E.81.IX.4), appendix VII).

90th plenary meeting
12 December 1995

## 51/45. GENERAL AND COMPLETE DISARMAMENT
## S
## AN INTERNATIONAL AGREEMENT TO BAN
## ANTI-PERSONNEL LANDMINES

*The General Assembly,*

*Recalling with satisfaction* its resolutions 48/75 K of 16 December 1993, 49/75 D of 15 December 1994 and 50/70 O of 12 December 1995, in which it, *inter alia*, urged States to implement moratoriums on the export of anti-personnel landmines,

*Also recalling with satisfaction* its resolutions 49/75 D and 50/70 O, in which it, *inter alia*, established as a goal of the international community the eventual elimination of anti-personnel landmines,

*Noting* that, according to the 1995 report of the Secretary-General entitled 'Assistance in mine clearance',\* it is estimated that there are one hundred and ten million landmines in the ground in more than sixty countries throughout the world,

*Noting also* that, according to the same report, the global landmine crisis continues to worsen as an estimated two million new landmines are laid each year, while only an estimated one hundred and fifty thousand were cleared in 1995,

*Expressing deep concern* that anti-personnel landmines kill or maim hundreds of people every week, mostly innocent and defenceless civilians and especially children, obstruct economic development and reconstruction, inhibit the repatriation of refugees and the return of internally displaced persons, and have other severe consequences for years after emplacement,

*Gravely concerned* about the suffering and casualties caused to non-combatants as a result of the proliferation, as well as the indiscriminate and irresponsible use, of anti-personnel landmines,

*Recalling with satisfaction* its resolutions 48/7 of 19 October 1993, 49/215 A of 23 December 1994 and 50/82 of 14 December 1995 calling for assistance in mine clearance,

*Welcoming* the recent decisions taken at the Review Conference of the States Parties to the Convention on Prohibitions or Restrictions on the Use of Certain Conventional Weapons Which May Be Deemed to Be Excessively Injurious or to Have Indiscriminate Effects, particularly with respect to the amended Protocol II\*\* to the Convention, and believing that the amended Protocol is an essential part of the global effort to address problems caused by the proliferation, as well as the indiscriminate and irresponsible use, of anti-personnel landmines,

*Welcoming also* the adoption of the declaration entitled 'Towards a Global Ban on Anti-Personnel Mines' by participants at the Ottawa International Strategy Conference on 5 October 1996,\*\*\* including its call for the earliest possible conclusion of a legally binding international agreement to ban anti-personnel landmines, and further welcoming the follow-on conference at Brussels in June 1997,

*Welcoming* further the recent decisions taken by States to adopt various bans, moratoriums or other restrictions on the use, stockpiling, production and transfer of anti-personnel landmines, and other measures taken unilaterally as well as multilaterally,

*Recognizing the need* to conclude an international agreement to ban all anti-personnel landmines as soon as possible,

1. Urges States to pursue vigorously an effective, legally binding international agreement to ban the use, stockpiling, production and transfer of anti-personnel landmines with a view to completing the negotiation as soon as possible;

2. Urges States that have not yet done so to accede to the Convention on Prohibitions or Restrictions on the Use of Certain Conventional Weapons Which May Be Deemed to Be Excessively Injurious or to Have Indiscriminate Effects**** and Protocol II as amended on 3 May 1996,** and urges all States immediately to comply to the fullest extent possible with the applicable rules of Protocol II as amended

3. Welcomes the various bans, moratoriums or other restrictions already declared by States on anti-personnel landmines;

4. Calls upon States that have not yet done so to declare and implement such bans, moratoriums or other restrictions—particularly on operational use and transfer—at the earliest possible date;

5. Requests the Secretary-General to prepare a report on steps taken to complete an international agreement banning the use, stockpiling, production and transfer of anti-personnel landmines, and on other steps taken by Member States to implement such bans, moratoriums or other restrictions and to submit it to the General Assembly at its fifty-second session under the item entitled 'General and complete disarmament';

6. Requests Member States to provide the requested information for the report of the Secretary-General on steps taken to complete an international agreement banning the use, stockpiling, production and transfer of anti-personnel landmines, and on other steps taken to implement bans, moratoriums or other restrictions on anti-personnel landmines and to submit such information to the Secretary-General by 15 April 1997.

* A/50/408.
** Protocol on Prohibitions or Restrictions on the Use of Mines, Booby Traps and Other Devices (see *The United Nations Disarmament Yearbook*, vol. 5: 1980 (United Nations publication, Sales No. E.81.IX.4), appendix VII).
*** A/C.1/51/10, annex.
**** See *The United Nations Disarmament Yearbook*, vol. 5: 1980 (United Nations publication, Sales No. E.81.IX.4), appendix VII.

79th plenary meeting
10 December 1996

## 52/38. GENERAL AND COMPLETE DISARMAMENT
### A
### CONVENTION ON THE PROHIBITION OF THE USE, STOCKPILING, PRODUCTION AND TRANSFER OF ANTI-PERSONNEL MINES AND ON THEIR DESTRUCTION

*The General Assembly,*

*Determined* to put an end to the suffering and casualties caused by anti-personnel mines that kill or maim hundreds of people every week, mostly innocent and defenceless civilians and especially children, obstruct economic development and reconstruction, inhibit the repatriation of refugees and internally displaced persons, and have other severe consequences for years after emplacement,

*Believing it necessary* to do the utmost to contribute in an efficient and coordinated manner to facing the challenge of removing anti-personnel mines placed throughout the world, and to assure their destruction,

*Wishing* to do the utmost in assuring assistance for the care and rehabilitation, including the social and economic reintegration, of mine victims,

*Recalling* its resolution 51/45 S of 10 December 1996 urging all States to pursue vigorously an effective, legally binding international agreement to ban the use, stockpiling, production and transfer of anti-personnel landmines with a view to completing the negotiation as soon as possible,

*Stressing* the role of public conscience in furthering the principles of humanity as evidenced by the call for a total ban on anti-personnel mines, and recognizing the efforts to that end undertaken by the International Red Cross and Red Crescent Movement, the International Campaign to Ban Landmines and numerous other non-governmental organizations around the world,

*Recalling* the Ottawa Declaration of 5 October 1996* and the Brussels Declaration of 27 June 1997** urging the international community to negotiate an international and legally binding agreement prohibiting the use, stockpiling, production and transfer of anti-personnel mines,

*Emphasizing* the desirability of attracting the adherence of all States to the Convention on the Prohibition of the Use, Stockpiling, Production and Transfer of Anti-personnel Mines and on Their Destruction, and determined to work strenuously towards the promotion of its universalization in all relevant forums including, *inter alia*, the United Nations, the Conference on Disarmament, regional organizations and groupings, and review conferences of the Convention on Prohibitions or Restrictions on the Use of Certain Conventional Weapons Which May Be Deemed to Be Excessively Injurious or to Have Indiscriminate Effects,***

*Basing itself* on the principle of international humanitarian law that the right of the parties to an armed conflict to choose methods or means of warfare is not unlimited, on the principle that prohibits the employment in armed conflicts of weapons, project-iles and materials and methods of warfare of a nature to cause superfluous injury or unnecessary suffering and on the principle that a distinction must be made between civilians and combatants,

*Welcoming* the conclusion of negotiations on 18 September 1997 at Oslo on the Convention on the Prohibition of the Use, Stockpiling, Production and Transfer of Anti-personnel Mines and on Their Destruction,

1. Invites all States to sign the Convention on the Prohibition of the Use, Stockpiling, Production and Transfer of Anti-personnel Mines and on Their Destruction, which was open for signature at Ottawa on 3 and 4 December 1997 and at Headquarters in New York on 5 December 1997, and which shall remain open for signature thereafter at Headquarters until its entry into force;

2. Urges all States to ratify the Convention without delay subsequent to their signatures;

3. Calls upon all States to contribute towards the full realization and effective implementation of the Convention to advance the care and rehabilitation, and the social and economic reintegration of mine victims, and mine-awareness programmes, and the removal of anti-personnel mines placed throughout the world and the assurance of their destruction;

4. Requests the Secretary-General to render the necessary assistance and to provide such services as may be necessary to fulfil the tasks entrusted to him by the Convention;

5. Decides to include in the provisional agenda of its fifty-third session an item entitled 'Convention on the Prohibition of the Use, Stockpiling, Production and Transfer of Anti-personnel Mines and on Their Destruction'.

> \* A/C.1/51/10, annex I.
> \*\* See CD/1467.
> \*\*\* See *The United Nations Disarmament Yearbook*, vol. 5: 1980 (United Nations publication, Sales No. E.81.IX.4), appendix VII.

67th plenary meeting
9 December 1997

## 53/77. GENERAL AND COMPLETE DISARMAMENT

### N

### CONVENTION ON THE PROHIBITION OF THE USE, STOCKPILING, PRODUCTION AND TRANSFER OF ANTI-PERSONNEL MINES AND ON THEIR DESTRUCTION

*The General Assembly,*

*Recalling* its resolution 52/38 A of 9 December 1997,

*Reaffirming its determination* to put an end to the suffering and casualties caused by anti-personnel mines, which kill or maim hundreds of people every week, mostly innocent and defenceless civilians and especially children, obstruct economic development and reconstruction, inhibit the repatriation of refugees and internally displaced persons, and have other severe consequences for years after emplacement,

*Believing it necessary* to do the utmost to contribute in an efficient and coordinated manner to facing the challenge of removing anti-personnel mines placed throughout the world, and to assure their destruction,

*Wishing* to do the utmost in assuring assistance for the care and rehabilitation, including the social and economic reintegration, of mine victims,

*Recalling* the conclusion of negotiations on 18 September 1997 at Oslo on the Convention on the Prohibition of the Use, Stockpiling, Production and Transfer of Anti-personnel Mines and on Their Destruction* and the opening for signature of the Convention at Ottawa, on 3 and 4 December 1997, and thereafter at Headquarters in New York until its entry into force,

*Welcoming* the addition of new States signatories to the Convention since its opening for signature, the rapid ratification by many signatories and the early achievement of the fortieth ratification of the Convention on 16 September 1998, which, according to the provisions of article 17 of the Convention, will result in the entry into force of the Convention on 1 March 1999,

*Emphasizing* the desirability of attracting the adherence of all States to the Convention, and determined to work strenuously towards the promotion of its universalization,

1. Invites all States that have not yet done so to sign or, after entry into force, to accede to the Convention on the Prohibition of the Use, Stockpiling, Production and Transfer of Anti-personnel Mines and on Their Destruction;*

2. Urges all States that have not yet done so to ratify the Convention without delay subsequent to their signature;

3. Renews its call upon all States to contribute towards the full realization and effective implementation of the Convention to advance the care and rehabilitation, and the social and economic reintegration of mine victims, and mine awareness programmes, and the removal of anti-personnel mines placed throughout the world and the assurance of their destruction;

4. Welcomes the generous offer by the Government of Mozambique to act as host for the First Meeting of the States Parties;

5. Requests the Secretary-General, in accordance with article 11, paragraph 2, of the Convention, to undertake the preparations necessary to convene the First Meeting of the States Parties, to take place in Maputo during the week of 3 May 1999;

6. Invites all States parties to the First Meeting of the States Parties and, in accordance with article 11, paragraph 4, of the Convention, States not parties to the Convention,

as well as the United Nations, other relevant international organizations or institutions, regional organizations, the International Committee of the Red Cross and relevant non-governmental organizations to attend the Meeting as observers in accordance with the agreed rules of procedure.

\* See CD/1478.

79th plenary meeting
4 December 1998

## 54/54. GENERAL AND COMPLETE DISARMAMENT

### B

## IMPLEMENTATION OF THE CONVENTION ON THE PROHIBITION OF THE USE, STOCKPILING, PRODUCTION AND TRANSFER OF ANTI-PERSONNEL MINES AND ON THEIR DESTRUCTION

*The General Assembly,*

*Recalling* its resolution 53/77 N of 4 December 1998,

*Reaffirming its determination* to put an end to the suffering and casualties caused by anti-personnel mines, which kill or maim hundreds of people every week, mostly innocent and defenceless civilians and especially children, obstruct economic development and reconstruction, inhibit the repatriation of refugees and internally displaced persons, and have other severe consequences for years after emplacement,

*Believing it necessary* to do the utmost to contribute in an efficient and coordinated manner to facing the challenge of removing anti-personnel mines placed throughout the world, and to assure their destruction,

*Wishing* to do the utmost in ensuring assistance for the care and rehabilitation, including the social and economic reintegration, of mine victims,

*Welcoming* the entry into force on 1 March 1999 of the Convention on the Prohibition of the Use, Stockpiling, Production and Transfer of Anti-personnel Mines and on Their Destruction,\*

*Recalling* the First Meeting of the States Parties to the Convention, held at Maputo from 3 to 7 May 1999, and the reaffirmation made in the Maputo Declaration\*\* of a commitment to the total eradication of anti-personnel mines,

*Noting with satisfaction* the addition of new States signatories to the Convention, the rapid ratification by many signatories, and the accession to the Convention by other States, bringing the total number of States that have signed to one hundred and thirty-three, and that eighty-nine States have ratified or acceded to the Convention in the two years since it was opened for signature,

*Emphasizing* the desirability of attracting the adherence of all States to the Convention, and determined to work strenuously towards the promotion of its universalization,

*Noting with regret* that anti-personnel mines continue to be used in conflicts around the world, causing human suffering and impeding post-conflict development,

1. Invites all States that have not signed the Convention on the Prohibition of the Use, Stockpiling, Production and Transfer of Anti-personnel Mines and on Their Destruction* to accede to it without delay;

2. Urges all States that have signed but not ratified the Convention to ratify it without delay;

3. Stresses the importance of the full and effective implementation of, and compliance with, the Convention;

4. Urges all States parties to provide the Secretary-General with complete and timely information, as required in article 7 of the Convention in order to promote transparency and compliance with the Convention;

5. Invites all States that have not ratified the Convention or acceded to it to provide, on a voluntary basis, information to make global mine action efforts more effective;

6. Renews its call upon all States and other relevant parties to work together to promote, support and advance the care, rehabilitation and social and economic reintegration of mine victims, mine awareness programmes, and the removal of anti-personnel mines placed throughout the world and the assurance of their destruction;

7. Invites and encourages all interested States, the United Nations, other relevant international organizations or institutions, regional organizations, the International Committee of the Red Cross and relevant non-governmental organizations to participate in the programme of inter-sessional work established at the First Meeting of States Parties to the Convention;

8. Requests the Secretary-General, in accordance with article 11, paragraph 2, of the Convention, to undertake the preparations necessary to convene the Second Meeting of the States Parties to the Convention at Geneva, from 11 to 15 September 2000, and, on behalf of States parties and according to article 11, paragraph 4, of the Convention, to invite States not parties to the Convention, as well as the United Nations, other relevant international organizations or institutions, regional organizations, the International Committee of the Red Cross and relevant non-governmental organizations to attend the Meeting as observers;

9. Decides to include in the provisional agenda of its fifty-fifth session the item entitled 'Implementation of the Convention on the Prohibition of the Use, Stockpiling, Production and Transfer of Anti-personnel Mines and on Their Destruction'.

 * See CD/1478.
** APLC/MSP.1/1999/1, part II.

69th plenary meeting
1 December 1999

# 55/33. GENERAL AND COMPLETE DISARMAMENT
## V
## IMPLEMENTATION OF THE CONVENTION ON THE PROHIBITION OF THE USE, STOCKPILING, PRODUCTION AND TRANSFER OF ANTI-PERSONNEL MINES AND ON THEIR DESTRUCTION

*The General Assembly,*

*Recalling* its resolution 54/54 B of 1 December 1999,

*Reaffirming* its determination to put an end to the suffering and casualties caused by anti-personnel mines, which kill or maim hundreds of people every week, mostly innocent and defenceless civilians and especially children, obstruct economic development and reconstruction, inhibit the repatriation of refugees and internally displaced persons, and have other severe consequences for years after emplacement,

*Believing* it necessary to do the utmost to contribute in an efficient and coordinated manner to facing the challenge of removing anti-personnel mines placed throughout the world, and to assure their destruction,

*Wishing* to do the utmost in ensuring assistance for the care and rehabilitation, including the social and economic reintegration, of mine victims,

*Welcoming* the entry into force on 1 March 1999 of the Convention on the Prohibition of the Use, Stockpiling, Production and Transfer of Anti-personnel Mines and on Their Destruction,* and noting with satisfaction the work undertaken to implement the Convention and the substantial progress made towards addressing the global landmine problem,

*Recalling* the First Meeting of the States Parties to the Convention, held at Maputo from 3 to 7 May 1999, and the reaffirmation made in the Maputo Declaration** of a commitment to the total eradication of anti-personnel mines,

*Recalling* also the Second Meeting of States Parties to the Convention, held at Geneva from 11 to 15 September 2000, and the Declaration of the Second Meeting of States Parties reaffirming the commitment to implement completely and fully all provisions of the Convention,***

*Noting with satisfaction* that additional States have ratified or acceded to the Convention, bringing the total number of States that have formally accepted the obligations of the Convention to one hundred and eight,

*Emphasizing* the desirability of attracting the adherence of all States to the Convention, and determined to work strenuously towards the promotion of its universalization,

*Noting with regret* that anti-personnel mines continue to be used in conflicts around the world, causing human suffering and impeding post-conflict development,

1. Invites all States that have not signed the Convention on the Prohibition of the Use, Stockpiling, Production and Transfer of Anti-personnel Mines and on Their Destruction* to accede to it without delay;

2. Urges all States that have signed but not ratified the Convention to ratify it without delay;

3. Stresses the importance of the full and effective implementation of, and compliance with, the Convention;

4. Urges all States parties to provide the Secretary-General with complete and timely information, as required in article 7 of the Convention, in order to promote transparency and compliance with the Convention;

5. Invites all States that have not ratified the Convention or acceded to it to provide, on a voluntary basis, information to make global mine action efforts more effective;

6. Renews its call upon all States and other relevant parties to work together to promote, support and advance the care, rehabilitation and social and economic reintegration of mine victims, mine awareness programmes, and the removal of antipersonnel mines placed throughout the world and the assurance of their destruction;

7. Invites and encourages all interested States, the United Nations, other relevant international organizations or institutions, regional organizations, the International Committee of the Red Cross and relevant non-governmental organizations to participate in the programme of inter-sessional work established at the First Meeting of States Parties to the Convention and further developed at the Second Meeting of States Parties to the Convention;

8. Welcomes the generous offer of the Government of Nicaragua to host the Third Meeting of States Parties to the Convention;

9. Requests the Secretary-General, in accordance with article 11, paragraph 2, of the Convention, to undertake the preparations necessary to convene the Third Meeting of States Parties to the Convention at Managua, from 18 to 21 September 2001, and, on behalf of States parties and in accordance with article 11, paragraph 4, of the Convention, to invite States not parties to the Convention, as well as the United Nations, other relevant international organizations or institutions, regional organizations, the International Committee of the Red Cross and relevant non-governmental organizations to attend the Meeting as observers;

10. Decides to include in the provisional agenda of its fifty-sixth session the item entitled 'Implementation of the Convention on the Prohibition of the Use, Stockpiling, Production and Transfer of Anti-personnel Mines and on Their Destruction'.

* See CD/1478.
** APLC/MSP.1/1999/1, part II.
*** APLC/MSP/2/2000/1, part II.

69th plenary meeting
20 November 2000

## 56/24. GENERAL AND COMPLETE DISARMAMENT

## M

## IMPLEMENTATION OF THE CONVENTION ON THE PROHIBITION OF THE USE, STOCKPILING, PRODUCTION AND TRANSFER OF ANTI-PERSONNEL MINES AND ON THEIR DESTRUCTION

*The General Assembly,*

*Recalling* its resolutions 54/54 B of 1 December 1999 and 55/33 V of 20 November 2000,

*Reaffirming* its determination to put an end to the suffering and casualties caused by anti-personnel mines, which kill or maim hundreds of people every week, mostly innocent and defenceless civilians and especially children, obstruct economic development and reconstruction, inhibit the repatriation of refugees and internally displaced persons, and have other severe consequences for years after emplacement,

*Believing it necessary* to do the utmost to contribute in an efficient and coordinated manner to facing the challenge of removing anti-personnel mines placed throughout the world, and to ensure their destruction,

*Wishing* to do the utmost in ensuring assistance for the care and rehabilitation, including the social and economic reintegration, of mine victims,

*Welcoming* the entry into force on 1 March 1999 of the Convention on the Prohibition of the Use, Stockpiling, Production and Transfer of Anti-personnel Mines and on Their Destruction,* and noting with satisfaction the work undertaken to implement the Convention and the substantial progress made towards addressing the global landmine problem,

*Recalling* the First Meeting of States Parties to the Convention, held at Maputo from 3 to 7 May 1999, and the reaffirmation made in the Maputo Declaration of a commitment to the total eradication of anti-personnel mines,**

*Recalling also* the Second Meeting of States Parties to the Convention, held at Geneva from 11 to 15 September 2000, and the Declaration of the Second Meeting of States Parties reaffirming the commitment to implement completely and fully all provisions of the Convention,***

*Recalling further* the Third Meeting of States Parties to the Convention, held at Managua from 18 to 21 September 2001, and the Declaration of the Third Meeting of States Parties reaffirming the unwavering commitment both to the total eradication of anti-personnel mines and to addressing the insidious and inhumane effects of those weapons,****

*Noting with satisfaction* that additional States have ratified or acceded to the Convention, bringing the total number of States that have formally accepted the obligations of the Convention to one hundred and twenty-two,

*Emphasizing* the desirability of attracting the adherence of all States to the Convention, and determined to work strenuously towards the promotion of its universalization,

*Noting with regret* that anti-personnel mines continue to be used in conflicts around the world, causing human suffering and impeding post-conflict development,

1. Invites all States that have not signed the Convention on the Prohibition of the Use, Stockpiling, Production and Transfer of Anti-personnel Mines and on Their Destruction* to accede to it without delay;

2. Urges all States that have signed but not ratified the Convention to ratify it without delay;

3. Stresses the importance of the full and effective implementation of, and compliance with, the Convention;

4. Urges all States parties to provide the Secretary-General with complete and timely information, as required under article 7 of the Convention, in order to promote transparency and compliance with the Convention;

5. Invites all States that have not ratified the Convention or acceded to it to provide, on a voluntary basis, information to make global mine action efforts more effective;

6. Renews its call upon all States and other relevant parties to work together to promote, support and advance the care, rehabilitation and social and economic reintegration of mine victims, mine awareness programmes, and the removal of anti-personnel mines placed throughout the world and the assurance of their destruction;

7. Invites and encourages all interested States, the United Nations, other relevant international organizations or institutions, regional organizations, the International Committee of the Red Cross and relevant non-governmental organizations to participate in the programme of inter-sessional work established at the First Meeting of States Parties to the Convention and further developed at the Second and Third Meetings of States Parties to the Convention;

8. Requests the Secretary-General, in accordance with article 11, paragraph 2, of the Convention, to undertake the preparations necessary to convene the Fourth Meeting of States Parties to the Convention at Geneva from 16 to 20 September 2002, and, on behalf of States parties and in accordance with article 11, paragraph 4, of the Convention, to invite States not parties to the Convention, as well as the United Nations, other relevant international organizations or institutions, regional organizations, the International Committee of the Red Cross and relevant non-governmental organizations to attend the Meeting as observers;

9. Decides to include in the provisional agenda of its fifty-seventh session the item entitled 'Implementation of the Convention on the Prohibition of the Use, Stockpiling, Production and Transfer of Anti-personnel Mines and on Their Destruction'.

\* See CD/1478.
\*\* APLC/MSP.1/1999/1, part II.
\*\*\* APLC/MSP/2/2000/1, part II.
\*\*\*\* See APLC/MSP.3/2001/1, part II.

68th plenary meeting
29 November 2001

# 57/74. GENERAL AND COMPLETE DISARMAMENT
## A
## IMPLEMENTATION OF THE CONVENTION ON THE PROHIBITION OF THE USE, STOCKPILING, PRODUCTION AND TRANSFER OF ANTI-PERSONNEL MINES AND ON THEIR DESTRUCTION

*The General Assembly,*

*Recalling* its resolutions 54/54 B of 1 December 1999, 55/33 V of 20 November 2000 and 56/24 M of 29 November 2001,

*Reaffirming* its determination to put an end to the suffering and casualties caused by anti-personnel mines, which kill or maim hundreds of people every week, mostly innocent and defenceless civilians and especially children, obstruct economic development and reconstruction, inhibit the repatriation of refugees and internally displaced persons, and have other severe consequences for years after emplacement,

*Believing it necessary* to do the utmost to contribute in an efficient and coordinated manner to facing the challenge of removing anti-personnel mines placed throughout the world, and to assure their destruction,

*Wishing* to do the utmost in ensuring assistance for the care and rehabilitation, including the social and economic reintegration, of mine victims,

*Welcoming* the entry into force, on 1 March 1999, of the Convention on the Prohibition of the Use, Stockpiling, Production and Transfer of Anti-personnel Mines and on Their Destruction,* and noting with satisfaction the work undertaken to implement the Convention and the substantial progress made towards addressing the global landmine problem,

*Recalling* the First Meeting of the States Parties to the Convention, held at Maputo from 3 to 7 May 1999, and the reaffirmation made in the Maputo Declaration of a commitment to the total eradication of anti-personnel mines,**

*Recalling also* the Second Meeting of States Parties to the Convention, held at Geneva from 11 to 15 September 2000, and the Declaration of the Second Meeting of States Parties reaffirming the commitment to implement completely and fully all provisions of the Convention,***

*Recalling further* the Third Meeting of States Parties to the Convention, held at Managua from 18 to 21 September 2001, and the Declaration of the Third Meeting of States Parties reaffirming the unwavering commitment both to the total eradication of anti-personnel mines and to addressing the insidious and inhumane effects of those weapons,****

*Recalling* the Fourth Meeting of States Parties to the Convention, held at Geneva from 16 to 20 September 2002, and the Declaration of the Fourth Meeting of States Parties reaffirming the commitment of the States parties to intensify further their efforts in those areas most directly related to the core humanitarian objectives of the Convention,*****

*Noting with satisfaction* that additional States have ratified or acceded to the Convention, bringing the total number of States that have formally accepted the obligations of the Convention to one hundred and twenty-nine,

*Emphasizing* the desirability of attracting the adherence of all States to the Convention, and determined to work strenuously towards the promotion of its universalization,

*Noting with regret* that anti-personnel mines continue to be used in conflicts around the world, causing human suffering and impeding post-conflict development,

1. Invites all States that have not signed the Convention on the Prohibition of the Use, Stockpiling, Production and Transfer of Anti-Personnel Mines and on Their Destruction* to accede to it without delay;

2. Urges all States that have signed but not ratified the Convention to ratify it without delay;

3. Stresses the importance of the full and effective implementation of, and compliance with, the Convention;

4. Urges all States parties to provide the Secretary-General with complete and timely information as required under article 7 of the Convention, in order to promote transparency and compliance with the Convention;

5. Invites all States that have not ratified the Convention or acceded to it to provide, on a voluntary basis, information to make global mine action efforts more effective;

6. Renews its call upon all States and other relevant parties to work together to promote, support and advance the care, rehabilitation and social and economic reintegration of mine victims, mine risk education programmes, and the removal of anti-personnel mines placed throughout the world and the assurance of their destruction;

7. Invites and encourages all interested States, the United Nations, other relevant international organizations or institutions, regional organizations, the International Committee of the Red Cross and relevant non-governmental organizations to participate in the programme of intersessional work established at the First Meeting of States Parties to the Convention and further developed at the Second, Third and Fourth Meetings of States Parties to the Convention;

8. Requests the Secretary-General, in accordance with article 11, paragraph 2, of the Convention, to undertake the preparations necessary to convene the Fifth Meeting of States Parties to the Convention at Bangkok from 15 to 19 September 2003, and, on behalf of States parties and in accordance with article 11, paragraph 4, of the Convention, to invite States not parties to the Convention, as well as the United Nations, other relevant international organizations or institutions, regional organizations, the International Committee of the Red Cross and relevant non-governmental organizations to attend the Meeting as observers;

9. Decides to include in the provisional agenda of its fifty-eighth session the item entitled 'Implementation of the Convention on the Prohibition of the Use, Stockpiling, Production and Transfer of Anti-personnel Mines and or Their Destruction'.

\* See CD/1478.
\*\* APLC/MSP.1/1999/1, part II.
\*\*\* APLC/MSP/2/2000/1, part II.
\*\*\*\* See APLC/MSP.3/2001/1, part II.
\*\*\*\*\* See APLC/MSP.4/2002/1, part II.

57th plenary meeting
22 November 2002

# APPENDIX 3

# Conference Declarations

## OTTAWA INTERNATIONAL STRATEGY CONFERENCE, 3–5 OCTOBER 1996

### DECLARATION OF THE OTTAWA CONFERENCE, CANADA, 3–5 OCTOBER 1996

Following consultations with relevant international agencies, international organizations and non-governmental organizations, the states represented at the Ottawa conference, the 'Ottawa Group', have agreed to enhance cooperation and coordination of efforts on the basis of the following concerns and goals with respect to anti-personnel mines:

1. a recognition that the extreme humanitarian and socio-economic costs associated with the use of anti-personnel mines requires urgent action on the part of the international community to ban and eliminate this type of weapon.

2. a conviction that until such a ban is achieved, states must work to encourage universal adherence to the prohibitions or restrictions on anti-personnel mines as contained in the amended Protocol II of the Convention on Certain Conventional Weapons.

3. an affirmation of the need to convince mine affected states to halt all new deployments of anti-personnel mines to ensure the effectiveness and efficiency of mine-clearance operations.

4. a recognition that the international community must provide significantly greater resources to mine-awareness programs, mine-clearance operations and victim assistance.

5. a commitment to work together to ensure:

- the earliest possible conclusion of a legally-binding international agreement to ban anti-personnel mines;
- progressive reductions in new deployments of anti-personnel mines with the urgent objective of halting all new deployments of anti-personnel mines;
- support for an UNGA 51 resolution calling upon member states, inter alia, to implement national moratoria, bans or other restrictions, particularly on the operational use and transfer of anti-personnel mines at the earliest possible date;
- regional and sub-regional activities in support of a global ban on anti-personnel mines; and,
- a follow-on conference hosted by Belgium in June 1997 to review the progress of the international community in achieving a global ban on anti-personnel mines.

# Towards a Global Ban on Anti-Personnel Mines

## Chairman's Agenda for Action on Anti-Personnel (AP) Mines

Participants in the Ottawa Conference have re-affirmed their commitment to seek the earliest possible conclusion of a legally-binding agreement to ban the production, stockpiling, transfer and use of anti-personnel (AP) mines. This agreement will be achieved most rapidly through increased co-operation within the international community.

The purpose of the Ottawa Conference was to catalyze practical efforts to move toward a ban and create partnerships between states, international organizations and agencies and non-governmental organizations essential to building the necessary political will to achieve a global ban on AP mines.

The following Agenda for Action captures the dynamism of the discussions in Ottawa, the recognition that movement toward a global ban has already begun and details concrete activities to be undertaken by the international community—on an immediate and urgent basis—to build upon the Ottawa Declaration and to move this process ahead in preparation for the follow-up meeting which will be hosted by Belgium in 1997.

This Agenda for Action reflects the interrelationship of the global ban, mine clearance and victim assistance agendas. It highlights the need to reach out beyond the already committed to engage the broader international community in the global ban effort. It also recognizes that action must be taken at the global, regional, sub-regional and national levels to achieve a rapid global ban on AP mines.

## A. Global Action

Building the necessary political will for a new legally-binding international agreement banning AP mines will require more nations to adopt national bans or moratoria, on the production, stockpiling, use and transfer of AP mines. Nations which are not AP mine producers should also consider adopting bans on the imports of AP mines. These actions will also have the effect of reducing the total number of new deployments of AP mines—deployments which would create new victims and increase the costs of mine clearance operations.

Global actions suggested by participants in this conference include:

1. The passage of an UNGA 51 Resolution promoting an international agreement to ban AP mines.

Recognizing that a key vehicle for building international support for a global ban will be the development of overwhelming support for the resolution being proposed by the United States at the current session of the General Assembly, the following activities were identified as key opportunities to develop political support for the resolution:

- 'Potential co-sponsors' meeting—10 October 1996, New York (4 PM, UN Conference Room 9)
- Inter-Parliamentary Union Meeting at the UN—22 October

- Parliamentarians for Global Action—Annual General Meeting, October 1996, New York
- Landmine Panel, NGO, Committee on Disarmament, 24 October 1996, New York
- Work in regional or sub-regional groupings, as well as bilaterally, to build support for the resolution

2. Building public awareness and political will for a global AP mine ban.

Building increased public awareness of the social, economic and human costs of AP mines is essential to develop and sustain the necessary political will for a global AP mine ban. Opportunities for building political will and public awareness include:

- Launch of the Machel Study in response to Resolution A/RES/48/157 of the 48th session of UNGA on the Impact of Armed Conflict (and Land Mines) on Children, New York at the UN and by Archbishop Tutu in South Africa—11 November 1996
- Adoption of the Machel Report by the UNGA and implementation of its recommendations
- Reports on progress in the development of national AP mines policies in national reporting on the implementation of the Convention on the Rights of the Child to the Geneva-based Committee on the Rights of the Child
- Engaging military experts in the study of the military utility/humanitarian costs of AP mine use
- Adding the AP mine issue to the agenda of appropriate United Nations fora

3. Encourage rapid entry into force and universal adherence to the prohibitions and restrictions on AP mines as contained in the amended Protocol II of the Convention on Certain Conventional Weapons.

4. Increased exchanges of information and data on AP mines and national AP mine policies to build the confidence and transparency necessary for rapid progress towards a global AP mine ban, including:

- The development and publication of a global data-base on national AP mine policies (to be circulated by Canada in the fall of 1996)
- Studies by experts on the international production and legal and illicit trade of AP mines

5. To lay the necessary groundwork for a legally-binding international agreement to ban AP mines, Austria will produce a first draft and Canada will produce a possible framework for the verification of such an agreement.

6. Suggested follow-up conferences to the Ottawa Conference include:

- Belgium, June 1997
- Norway, Germany, Switzerland

## B. Regional Action

Actions at the sub-regional and regional levels will be instrumental in catalyzing the development of political will for a global ban on AP mines. To build upon the recent decision by the Central American Council of Ministers for Foreign Affairs to ban the production, use and trade in AP mines—thus creating the world's first regional AP mine-free zone—participants in the Conference suggested the following actions:

- Increased funding for mine clearance and victim assistance for those regions and sub-regions which have taken concrete steps to create 'AP mine-free zones'.

Within Africa:

- Efforts to enhance the de-mining capacities of African countries with priority given to heavily mine-affected countries. This will include a Conference of African Experts in Demining and Assistance to Victims of Landmines (1997)
- Meetings to engage military/national security experts on AP mines issues at the sub-regional level—including an ICRC seminar in Southern Africa (1997)
- 4th ICBL Conference on Landmines: Toward a Mine-Free [Southern] Africa, Feb. 25–28, 1997 Maputo, Mozambique
- Work towards the implementation of the three-part program of the Union Inter-africain des droits de l'homme

Within Asia:

- Meetings to engage military/national security experts on AP mines issues at the sub-regional level—including a planned ICRC/Philippines seminar (proposed for the first half of 1997)
- ICBL Conference, 1998
- Work toward consideration of AP mine issues within the ARF framework, including an ARF intersessional meeting on Demining for UN Peacekeepers, to be held in New Zealand in March/April 1997

Within the Americas:

- Defence Ministerial of the Americas, Bariloche, Argentina, October 6–9, 1996— seek support for follow-up to the OAS resolution on 'The Western Hemisphere as an Antipersonnel Land Mine-Free Zone'
- Special meeting at the end of October or early November 1996 of the Organization of American States' Committee on Hemispheric Security to promote imple-mentation of OAS General Assembly Resolution 'The Western Hemisphere as an Antipersonnel Land Mine-Free Zone' including:
  - ○ information exchanges on national AP mine policies
  - ○ provision of information to establish a hemispheric AP mine registry
- Regional ICBL Conference—Fall 1997
- Possible discussion in the Rio Group on AP mines under the topic of conventional arms control
- Meetings to engage military authorities on AP mines issues at the regional and sub-regional level
- Include anti-personnel landmines trade in discussions on illicit traffic in arms
- Encourage development of CBM regimes to replace AP mines in border areas.

Within Europe:

Implementation by the European Union (EU) of the joint action on AP mines adopted by the EU on 1 October 1996, in which the EU clearly asserts its determination to pursue the total elimination of AP mines. To this end:

- the EU will pursue efforts to ensure full implementation of the results of the Review Conference of the 1980 Convention on the one hand, and support for international efforts to ban AP mines on the other hand;
- the EU is committed to the goal of the total elimination of AP mines and shall work actively towards the achievement at the earliest possible date of an effective international agreement to ban these weapons world-wide;
- the EU shall seek to raise without delay the issue of a total ban in the most appropriate international forum;
- the Member States of the EU shall implement a common moratorium on the export of all AP mines to all destinations and shall refrain from issuing new licences for the transfer of technology to enable the manufacture of AP mines in third countries;
- EU Member States shall endeavour to implement national restrictions or bans additional to those contained in Protocol II of the CCW Convention;
- the EU will reinforce its contribution to international mine clearance.

A budget of 7 million ECU is to be provided for initiatives to be launched in the period up to the end of 1997, in the form of contributions to the UN Voluntary Trust Fund for assistance in mine clearance and/or specific EU actions providing assistance for mine clearance in response to the request of a regional organization or a third country's authorities. In addition, the Commission of the European Communities intends to continue the Community's support for activity in the field of mine clearance in the context of humanitarian aid, reconstruction and development co-operation.

- The EU will invite the Associate countries of Central and Eastern Europe, the Associate countries Cyprus and Malta and the EFTA countries, members of the European Economic Area to align themselves with initiatives taken in pursuit of the aims of its joint action
- Support will be sought within the OSCE for participating States to work towards a ban on all AP mines as soon as possible

In addition, other European countries:

- have taken concrete steps in terms of destroying their stocks of AP mines or have made decisions to do so within a specific timeframe;
- are introducing national legal regulations prohibiting exports and imports of AP mines and their components;
- are strengthening their capacity to carry out demining activities;
- are making contributions to strengthen the ability of the UN to initiate and coordinate demining activities in other regions, and;

- in the field of developing demining technology, Norway has started a pilot mine clearance programme in the former Yugoslavia utilizing a new mechanical mine clearance machine.

### C. Land Mine Clearance, Mine Awareness and Victim Assistance

Delegates highlighted the need to take special action to deal with the humanitarian crisis caused by AP mines, while recognizing that without a ban, mine clearance and victim assistance programs will always be insufficient to deal with the crisis.

In this regard, in addition to the announcement of many states of increased financial commitments to clearance, awareness and assistance efforts, the following specific initiatives and ideas were discussed to foster international technical co-operation and to make further progress to improve and share mine clearance technology, equipment and expertise; to improve mine awareness efforts and to enhance victim assistance programmes. These initiatives include:

- Meeting of Technical Experts on De-mining Technology, in preparation for the Tokyo meeting—Germany, early 1997
- Development of Canadian capacities in humanitarian demining and assistance to victims—Winnipeg, Canada—early 1997
- Demining and victim assistance—Tokyo, March 1997
- Cooperation on victim assistance (Canada-Mexico and Cuban, South African offer of their expertise)
- Increased international co-operation in AP mine stockpile destruction
- Efforts to develop standard procedures for mine-awareness education
- Include consideration of humanitarian mine clearance within peace accords
- Strengthening the efforts by Central America to achieve a land-mine free zone by the year 2000
- Establishment of a centre at James Madison University to act as a database to assist in co-ordinating international demining efforts
- Submission by the Presidency of the European Union of an UNGA 51 Resolution on assistance with mine clearance

In addition to the above, a number of countries indicated that other events are being planned and that appropriate details will soon be forthcoming.

## FINAL DECLARATION OF THE 4TH INTERNATIONAL NGO CONFERENCE ON LANDMINES: TOWARD A MINE FREE SOUTHERN AFRICA

### Maputo, Mozambique, 25–28 February 1997

Remembering the tens of thousands of men, women, and children killed and maimed by landmines each year, and

Commending the courage and commitment of the humanitarian deminers who daily risk their lives to remove this deadly weapon from the ground, the following statement was issued on behalf of the more than 450 participants from 60 countries attending the 4th international NGO conference on landmines in Maputo, Mozambique:

Recognizing the urgent need for a comprehensive global ban on antipersonnel landmines and greatly expanded programs for mine clearance and victim assistance;

Noting that a comprehensive ban rests on the pillars of an international ban treaty, humanitarian mine clearance and victim assistance;

Recognizing the particular importance of this year as the international community moves toward the signing of a total ban treaty in Ottawa, Canada in December 1997;

Convinced that the Ottawa process is the most clear expression of the will of the international community as stated in the 10 December 1996 United Nations General Assembly resolution calling for the conclusion of an international ban treaty 'as soon as possible' and that other negotiating fora, such as the Conference on Disarmament, will not fulfill that will in a timely fashion;

Welcoming the initiative taken by the government of Austria in formulating a draft ban treaty and in convening the first international meeting in February of this year to discuss the elements of a comprehensive treaty to ban antipersonnel landmines;

Welcoming the important roles of the governments of Belgium and Norway in the Ottawa process in their hosting treaty negotiating sessions in June and September of this year;

Appreciating the preparatory work for this conference by the regional steering committee and the Mozambique Campaign Against Landmines;

Noting the launching of new landmine ban campaigns in Angola, Kenya, Somalia, Zambia and Zimbabwe in the run-up to the conference;

Noting the successful pre-conference seminar held by the campaigns from the south and welcoming recommendations from the south to make consistent efforts to include southern campaigns in ICBL planning meetings;

Welcoming the pre-conference announcement by the government of South Africa of its ban on the use, production, development, trade and stockpiling of antipersonnel landmines;

Appreciating the opening of the conference by president Joaquim Chissano of Mozambique as a clear expression of commitment by the government to a global ban on antipersonnel landmines;

Welcoming the announcement at the conference by the government of Mozambique of its ban on the use, production, and trade of antipersonnel landmines;

Welcoming the participation in the conference by many regional and other governmental representatives;

Appreciating the important support for the conference by its patrons and donors;

Noting the widespread endorsement of the conference by political, religious and social leaders worldwide; and

Noting the widespread regional and international attention to the landmines crisis generated by the conference;

The 4th international NGO conference on landmines, calls on all governments:

To publicly commit to the objective of signing an international treaty banning all antipersonnel landmines in December 1997;

To actively participate during 1997 in the process of negotiating a simple, clear and unambiguous treaty that bans all antipersonnel landmines and not just those weapons 'primarily' designed or adapted to be exploded by the presence, proximity or contact of a person;

To open all meetings of the Ottawa process to participation by an ICBL delegation, and additionally, to invite NGO representatives to form part of government delegations to these meetings;

To take unilateral and regional steps to ban AP mines to continue to build momentum toward the signing of the Ottawa treaty;

Of the South African development community (SADC) to take all measures to make the region a mine free zone;

In Africa to implement the OAU resolutions urging a continent wide ban on antipersonnel landmines, using appropriate fora such as the OAU landmine meeting in South Africa in May and the OAU summit in Zimbabwe in June;

Of mine-affected countries to follow the lead of Mozambique and take unilateral steps to ban antipersonnel landmines;

To increase greatly resources for mine clearance for all mine-contaminated countries, and particularly in those nations and regions that have banned the weapon in order to encourage other countries to do the same;

To increase greatly resources for victim assistance for all mine-contaminated countries;

Who have produced and supplied mines to accept their responsibility and to assist with clearance and victim assistance programs;

and

For the governments of mine-contaminated countries to develop and implement national mine clearance policies that are transparent and include the needs of all sectors of society.

Calls upon members of the ICBL:

To present this declaration to their governments, at regional and continent-wide meetings such as upcoming SADC and OAU summits;

To press governments to participate in the Ottawa process and sign the ban treaty in December 1997;

To attend the treaty preparatory conferences in Brussels in June, Oslo in September and Ottawa in December;

To increase networking and communication among campaigns in the south and within regions;

To take the initiative to help generate and support new campaigns and pro-ban initiatives throughout their regions;

To broaden the base of participation by civil society in national campaigns by including organizations such as student groups, trade unions, women's organizations, professional groups, disability advocacy groups and others not yet actively involved in the campaign;

To make particular effort to empower landmine survivors to participate actively in national campaigns and speak out for a ban at international fora;

To give particular emphasis to the empowerment of landmine survivors;

To increase networking and communication between campaigns in the north and the south, and take measures to ensure that campaigns in the south can fully participate in the Ottawa process;

To encourage national campaigns and NGOS to document the socio-economic impact of APMS on their societies to provide critical information to raise public awareness to strengthen ICBL advocacy efforts for humanitarian mine clearance and victim assistance;

To begin strategizing and planning for campaign work beyond the signing of the comprehensive ban treaty in Ottawa in December 1997 in order to universalize the treaty, to ensure the complete eradication of landmines throughout the world and that assistance to mine victims be comprehensive to ensure their reintegration into society.

## TOKYO CONFERENCE ON ANTI-PERSONNEL LANDMINES, MARCH 1997

### CHAIRMAN'S SUMMARY

**Tokyo, Japan, March 7, 1997**

1. Responding to the initiative of Prime Minister Ryutaro Hashimoto at the 1996 Lyon Summit, the 'Tokyo Conference on Anti-Personnel Landmines' was held on Thursday, March 6 and Friday, March 7, 1997. This Conference was attended by 27 countries, the European Union and 10 international organizations. Participants undertook a comprehensive discussion to strengthen international efforts on the problems of anti-personnel landmines.

### I. General Remarks

2. Recognizing the problem of anti-personnel landmines as a humanitarian concern, a threat to peace and stability, and an obstacle to reconstruction and development, the

conference emphasized the strong need to further address the problems of anti-personnel landmines through international cooperation. In addition, the participants noted the need to make efforts to work toward the total ban on anti-personnel landmines.

## II. Establishing a Goal

3. The participants expressed their will to work toward substantially reducing the number of mine victims, with the ultimate goal of zero victims. In the meantime, the international community should seek to bring adequate medical care to a much greater proportion of injury victims.

## III. Guidelines for Landmine Clearance by the UN and Other Organizations

4. The participants of this Conference acknowledged the following basic principles of the United Nations mine action program: (1) to get involved early, (2) to make mine action a feature of the peace process, (3) to take an integrated approach to mine action from the start, (4) to emphasize the principle of comparative advantage when several partners cooperate towards the same humanitarian goal, (5) to move toward the ownership of the mine action program by the concerned State, as proposed by the UN Department of Humanitarian Affairs.

5. Noting the importance of partnership among the international community, the participants emphasized the need for better coordination among the UN agencies, other international organizations, mine-infested countries, donor countries, and NGOs in the process of implementing mine programs. It was pointed out that mine-infested countries should play a key role based on the idea of ownership.

6. Reiterating the role of the UNDHA as a focal point in assisting mine clearance activities, the participants shared the view that the ways and means of strengthening the UNDRA should be further discussed.

7. The participants endorsed the broad priorities set out by the ICRC and the UNDHA, while noting that specific priorities would need to be set for each country's program. Taking into consideration the impact of the anti-personnel landmine problem on the process of reconstruction and development, development agencies, including the UNDP and the World Bank, were invited to discuss the priority of mine programs.

## IV. Guidelines for Development of New Technology for Mine Detection and Removal

8. The participants concurred to strengthen international efforts to develop usable and cost-effective technologies for humanitarian reasons and for promoting reconstruction and development in mine-infested countries.

9. The participants took note of the following five guidelines for technology development to clear mines, as proposed by both the UNDHA and UNDPKO: (1) to define specifications, (2) to develop field sensor technology, (3) to develop protective clothing, (4) to promote the transfer of technologies, and (5) to integrate the tool-box approach.

10. Addressing the difficulties of developing new demining technologies, the participants recognized the imperative for a 'two-track' approach. In a short-term track, it is crucial to determine the most appropriate, effective method of combining existing technologies (a tool-box approach, plus the utilization of dogs), suited to the given conditions. In a mid-term track, developing new technologies is still required to expedite mine-clearance activities and increase their effectiveness.

11. The participants confirmed that at an early stage in developing new senior and demining technologies, feasibility testing should be conducted in the actual minefields, due to the varying conditions and circumstances of given sites.

12. The participants recognized the necessity to share information on technologies for mine detection and removal. For this purpose, the participants indicated the desirability of registering with the UNDHA as much information as possible on the results of testing and the development of technologies.

13. The participants recognized the importance of information transfer and the exchange of experience among mine-infested nations. Cambodia and South Africa showed their willingness to cooperate in this field.

### V. Guidelines for Assistance to Victims

14. The participants noted that the international community's primary objective in assisting the victims of anti-personnel landmines is to develop national capacities to manage and execute comprehensive programs.

The programs consist of first aid, surgery, manufacturing of artificial limbs, rehabilitation, vocational and reintegration training for victims.

15. The International Committee of the Red Cross proposed the establishment of a mines information system to collect and analyze information at the local level for the purpose of assisting victims and preventing further human suffering by anti-personnel landmines.

Noting the importance of promoting information exchanges on anti-personnel landmines, the participants endorsed the ICRC proposal of a mine information system. They requested that the ICRC elaborate the proposal for presentation to the international community.

16. The participants noted the desirability of fostering and sustaining a high public awareness level of the urgent need to address the problems of anti-personnel landmines.

## ANTI-PERSONNEL MINES: WHAT FUTURE FOR SOUTHERN AFRICA? REGIONAL SEMINAR FOR THE STATES OF THE SOUTHERN AFRICA DEVELOPMENT COMMUNITY

### Sponsored by the International Committee of the Red Cross in cooperation with the Organisation of African Unity and the Republic of Zimbabwe

### Harare, 21–23 April 1997

**Final Declaration of Participants**

(representing: Angola, Botswana, Lesotho, Malawi, Mauritius, Mozambique, Namibia, South Africa, Swaziland, Tanzania, Zambia, Zimbabwe) Participants call upon States of the Southern Africa Development Community to take the following steps, on the national, regional and global levels, towards ending the scourge of anti-personnel mines.

1. to launch an initiative, in the context of the Southern African Development Community, for the establishment of a regional zone free of anti-personnel mines;

2. in this context to establish within the SADC Organ on Politics, Defence and Security a Sub-Committee on Landmines supported by a working group of experts to promote and coordinate as a matter of urgency:

(a) planning of humanitarian mine clearance;

(b) joint training of mine clearance personnel;

(c) technological cooperation to facilitate more rapid and cost effective clearance operations in the region;

(d) adoption of a SADC code of ethics and standards for humanitarian mine clearance (quality assurance);

(e) mine awareness campaign programs;

(f) support of national programs for victim assistance;

(g) creation of a SADC data bank on landmine matters; and

(h) funding for humanitarian mine clearance, victim assistance, rehabilitation programs and mine awareness;

3. to immediately end all new deployments of anti-personnel mines and to establish national prohibitions, such as those already adopted in the region, on their production, stockpiling, transfer and use;

4. for those States which are not yet Parties, to adhere to the 1980 United Nations Convention on Certain Conventional Weapons, including its Protocol II on landmines (as amended on 3 May 1996); for current States party to this Convention to

adhere to its amended Protocol II at the earliest possible date to ensure its early entry into force;

5.  to participate actively in the Conference of the Organisation of African Unity on 'A Landmine Free Africa: The OAU and the Legacy of Anti-personnel Mines' to be held in Johannesburg from 19–21 May 1997 and to take into account there the results of this seminar;

6.  to promote the strongest possible resolution on anti-personnel mines at the OAU Summit Meeting in Harare from 2–4 June 1997; and

7.  to declare, at an early date, that they will participate actively in the Brussels conference (24–26 June 1997) of the Ottawa Group of States supporting a global ban and officially to endorse there the conclusion of a new treaty comprehensively prohibiting the production, stockpiling, transfer and use of anti-personnel mines to be signed by the end of 1997.

Participants appeal to the international community, including governments, international agencies and non-governmental organisations to assist the Southern Africa region in becoming permanently free of the scourge of anti-personnel mines, in particular through the provision of technical, financial and other assistance in the clearance and destruction of mines, assistance to victims and mine awareness programs.

Participants express their thanks to the International Community of the Red Cross for convening the seminar, and for its ongoing efforts on behalf of war victims in many of the countries of the region, to the Organisation of African Unity for its active leadership on the mines issue in Africa and to the Republic of Zimbabwe for its generous hospitality in hosting them in Harare.

Harare, 23 April 1997

# FIRST CONTINENTAL CONFERENCE OF AFRICAN EXPERTS ON LANDMINES

## Plan of Action

The first Continental Conference of African Experts on Landmines was held in Kempton Park, Republic of South Africa, from 19 to 21 May 1997. The Conference, which was attended by forty member states of the OAU, UN, specialised agencies, a wide spectrum of representatives of the donor community and non-government organisations, adopted the following Plan of Action:

### I. On Policy on Landmines

The Conference discussed African policies on anti-personnel landmines, the momentum towards a global ban on anti-personnel landmines, legal aspects of humanitarian law pertaining to landmines, landmine-free zones with reference to the Organisation of American States (OAS) and Africa as a landmine-free zone.

Within the framework of the implementation of the relevant Organisation of African Unity (OAU) resolution, participants agreed:

- to stress the need that the problem be addressed in a co-ordinated and multifaceted manner banning comprehensively anti-personnel landmines and intensifying efforts with regard to mine clearance and mine victim assistance;
- to adopt as a goal the elimination of all anti-personnel landmines and the establishment of Africa as an Anti-Personnel Landmine Free Zone;
- all states should end all deployments of anti-personnel landmines in Africa and to establish national prohibitions such as those already adopted on the African continent, on their use, production, stockpiling, transfer and their destruction;
- urged all states to participate actively in the Brussels Conference, 24–27 June 1997, the Oslo Conference in September 1997, which are both integral to the process leading to the negotiation and signature of a legally binding international agreement to ban anti-personnel landmines in Ottawa in December 1997;
- for those states which are not yet parties, to adhere to the 1980 United Nations Convention on Certain Conventional Weapons (CCW), including the Protocol II on landmines (as amended on 3 May 1996); for current states party to this Convention to adhere to its amended Protocol II at the earliest possible date to assure its earliest possible entry into force; and
- to promote the strongest possible resolution on the banning of anti-personnel landmines to be considered by Heads of State and Government at the OAU Summit Meeting in Harare, Zimbabwe, 2–4 June 1997.

## II. On Mine Clearance

The Conference discussed at length mine clearance issues which included the building of national capacities for mine clearance, setting local priorities, standards and technologies and inter-African co-operation.

Noting the crucial link between the drive for the total ban on landmines and mine clearance the Conference agreed on the following:

- In building capacity for mine clearance there is a need to create national, subregional and regional co-ordinating and strategic planning bodies. Subregional organisations such as SADC, IGAD and others and also the OAU, could play such a role. Further, national capacities for mine clearance should be simple, manageable and sustainable.
- The challenge in demining is the development of institutions rather than mine clearance itself; full attention should, therefore, be devoted to this task.
- Data bases should be established at the national, subregional and regional levels which would create the necessary management information systems on the extent of mine problems, on techniques of demining, on the results of demining, the assessment of surveys and the movement of illegal mine transfers.

- At present demining is a slow process—methods and technology must be created to increase the rate of demining; with regards to this, the need for the employment of integrated technology is of importance.
- The task of mine clearance in Africa is so cast that the public sector and commercial enterprises should operate in parallel reinforcing each other's efforts. Further, the armed forces of Africa states should be allowed to play a proper role in demining.
- There is a need to involve national authorities, at various levels, in the building of national capacities.
- In building capacities, finance will be a critical constraint. Hence, there is a need to exert efforts to mobilise financial resources. But requests for financial assistance should be backed by appropriate project feasibility studies.
- The aim of mine awareness should be to reduce mine risk through the adoption of sustainable safe behaviour, and to ensure the close involvement of the affected community, to ensure that priorities in mine awareness programmes are set by the members of the community themselves; lessons learned and experiences gained must be institutionalised, and interactive communication must be adopted.
- Efficient and effective demining efforts should be made to develop standards and guidelines for deminers and independent quality assurance and quality control established.
- For successful demining, inter-African co-operation is seen as a vital and crucial element; such co-operation should cover areas, such as political/diplomatic action, logistics, technical, financial, clearing operations, research and development, as well as the transfer of technology.

### III. On Landmine Survivors Assistance

The Conference discussed a wide range of issues relating to landmine survivors assistance. The following aspects, inter alia, were covered:

- rehabilitation and social integration;
- training;
- resources: human, facilities, funds; and
- development of (a) data bases(s).

Against the background of efforts to achieve a total ban on anti-personnel mines, and to clear Africa of existing landmines, the participants agreed as follows:

- Governments in Africa, and the OAU, should address the plight of victims and survivors and take renewed cognisance of their problems with a view to meet the health and social needs of all landmine survivors in Africa.
- To be optimally effective in bringing more and higher quality assistance to landmine survivors in the long term, a structured flow and analysis of information about the entire mine problem in any given country are needed.
- Priorities for the allocation of scarce resources among mine clearance projects, community mine awareness programmes, and the provision for the health and social needs of landmine survivors, can only be set by co-operative and co-ordinated

efforts on the part of:

- ○ local authorities and national governments;
- ○ the OAU and its specialised agencies, such as ARI;
- ○ the UN system and its agencies;
- ○ the NGO community; and
- ○ the ICRC and National Red Crescent or Red Cross Societies.

—to urge governments to adopt a policy aiming at the establishment of national mine information systems

—to urge governments to include the active participation of landmine survivors in the formulation, decision-making process and the execution of national policy and legislation in respect of articles that affect them. Concomitantly, survivors should influence their governments' positions in the formulation of international humanitarian treaties; and

—to encourage communities and the health services of mine-infested countries to maintain and increase their readiness to deal with mine injuries long after armed conflict has ended. At the same time, they must build their social and institutional capacities to deal with an ever-increasing number of disabled.

- • The relevant regional and national institutions should be urged to co-ordinate their efforts and to exchange information on their available medical facilties and capacities, and to provide modes of accessing them through a central African clearing-house in order to improve and increase assistance to landmine survivors.
- • Support to all training centres and institutes should be increased for the combined or joint use of all medical, social, psychological and other relevant measures and regular regional and continental training sessions should be organised for civilian and/or military health workers on the treatment and rehabilitation of the mine-injured.
- • In order to meet the psychological and social need of mine survivors, the Conference urges governments to quantify the numbers of survivors and encourages local NGOs or National Red Cross/Red Crescent societies to initiate appropriate programmes, with rehabilitation for all victims and survivors in countries at war or affected by landmines in the post-conflict period.
- • Governments should establish national support funds for landmine survivors and international donors should contribute to these funds.

## IV. On International Co-operation and Finance

On international co-operation and finance, the Conference:

- • reiterated the appeal of the OAU to the international community, international financial agencies, and the private sector working in the military field, to provide African countries affected by mines with all the necessary assistance for the demining of their countries. As an essential component of the efforts towards the elimination of mines, this assistance should comprise financial and technical components, as well as the training of deminers;

- underscored the moral responsibility of the powers which laid the mines during the Second World War and independence wars, and wished that these powers should devote a reasonable percentage of their military budgets to mine clearance in the African countries concerned;
- underlined the need for international co-operation, including close South-South co-operation, in order to support efforts towards demining and assistance to victims with a view to accelerating the realisation of the objectives of total elimination of mines; and
- requested the General Secretariat of the OAU, bearing in mind the relevant experience of other international organisations, to establish a mechanism to enhance the mobilisation of the international community in order to assist the African countries affected by anti-personnel landmines.

## ASHGABAT CENTRAL ASIAN REGIONAL CONFERENCE ON A GLOBAL BAN ON ANTI-PERSONNEL MINES

### June 10–12, 1997

#### Final Communiqué

Participants in the Ashgabat Conference met 10–12 June, 1997, to explore and discuss regional and global issues related to anti-personnel mines.

In the course of the Conference, numerous aspects of the problem were discussed, and various proposals and opinions were heard. Participants have agreed on the urgency of further drawing the attention of the world community to the AP mine problem and have called upon the world community to do its utmost for mine clearance, rendering humanitarian aid to mine victims and creating conditions of normal life for the civilian population.

All participants highly appreciated the initiative of Turkmenistan to hold the Conference.

Ashgabat, June 12, 1997

## BRUSSELS INTERNATIONAL CONFERENCE FOR A COMPREHENSIVE BAN ON ANTI-PERSONNEL LANDMINES

### 24–27 June 1997

#### Declaration of the Brussels Conference on Anti-Personnel Landmines

The following States met in Brussels from June 24 to 27, 1997 to pursue an enduring solution to the urgent humanitarian crisis caused by anti-personnel landmines. They are convinced that this solution must include the early conclusion of a comprehensive ban on anti-personnel landmines.

They recall that United Nations Assembly resolution 51/45 S. supported by 156 States, urged the vigorous pursuit of 'an effective, legally binding international agreement to ban the use, stockpiling, production and transfer of anti-personnel landmines.'

In that spirit they affirm that the essential elements of such an agreement should include:

- A comprehensive ban on the use, stockpiling, production and transfer of anti-personnel landmines,
- The destruction of stockpiled and removed anti-personnel landmines,
- International cooperation and assistance in the field of mine clearance in affected countries.

The following States:

encouraged by the work of the Brussels Conference;

encouraged further by numerous national and regional initiatives and measures taken to eliminate anti-personnel landmines;

encouraged by the attention given to this subject by the United Nations and by other fora;

encouraged, finally, by the active support of the International Committee of the Red Cross, the International Campaign to Ban Landmines and numerous other Non-Governmental Organisations;

welcome the convening of a Diplomatic Conference by the Government of Norway in Oslo on 1 September 1997 to negotiate such an agreement;

also welcome the important work done by the Government of Austria on the text of a draft agreement which contains the essential elements identified above and decide to forward it to the Oslo Diplomatic Conference in order to be considered together with other relevant proposals which may be put forward there;

affirm their objective of concluding the negotiation and signing of such an agreement banning anti-personnel landmines before the end of 1997 in Ottawa;

invite all other States to join them in their efforts towards such an agreement.

List of countries associated with the Political Declaration of the Brussels International Conference for a Comprehensive Ban on Anti-Personnel Landmines, June 27, 9.30 a.m.

Angola, Antigua and Barbuda (Caricom), Austria, Bahamas (Caricom), Barbados, Belgium, Belize (Caricom), Benin, Bolivia, Bosnia-Herzegovina, Botswana, Brazil, Burkina Faso, Cambodia, Cameroon, Canada, Cape Verde, Chad, Colombia. Republic of Congo, Costa Rica, Croatia, Czech Republic, Denmark, Dominica (Caricom), El Salvador, Ecuador, Ethiopia, Fiji, France, Gabon, Germany, Ghana. Grenada (Caricom), Great Britain, Guatemala, Guinea, Guyana (Caricom), Haiti, The Holy See, Honduras, Hungary, Ireland, Italy, Ivory Coast, Jamaica (Caricom), Jordan, Lesotho, Liechtenstein, Luxembourg, The Former Yugoslav Republic of Macedonia. Malaysia, Malawi, Mali, Malta, Mauritania, Mexico, Moldova, Monaco, Mozambique, Namibia, The Netherlands, Nicaragua, Norway, New Zealand, Panama, Papua New Guinea,

Paraguay, Peru, The Philippines, Portugal, Qatar, Rwanda, Saint Kitts and Nevis (Caricom), Saint Lucia (Caricom), San Marino, Saint Vincent and the Grenadines (Caricom), Senegal, Seychelles, Slovakia, Slovenia, South Africa, Spain, Sudan, Surinam (Caricom), Swaziland, Sweden, Switzerland, Tanzania, Togo, Trinidad and Tobago (Caricom), Turkmenistan, Uruguay, Venezuela, Yemen, Zambia, Zimbabwe

## LIST OF PARTICIPANTS

(OBS = Observer)

| | |
|---|---|
| Albania (OBS) | Democratic Republic of the Congo |
| Algeria (OBS) | Costa Rica |
| Angola | Côte d'Ivoire |
| Argentina (OBS) | Croatia |
| Armenia (OBS) | Cuba (OBS) |
| Australia | Czech Republic |
| Austria | Denmark |
| Azerbaijan (OBS) | Dominica |
| Bangladesh (OBS) | Dominican Republic |
| Barbados | Ecuador |
| Belarus | Egypt |
| Belgium | El Salvador |
| Belize | Eritrea |
| Benin | Estonia |
| Bolivia | Ethiopia |
| Bosnia-Herzegovina | Fiji |
| Botswana | Finland (OBS) |
| Brazil | France |
| Bulgaria (OBS) | Gabon |
| Burkina Faso | The Gambia |
| Burundi | Georgia |
| Cambodia | Germany |
| Cameroon | Great Britian |
| Canada | Greece |
| Cape Verde | Guatemala |
| Central African Republic | Guinea |
| Chad | Guinea-Bissau |
| Chile (OBS) | Guyana |
| Cyprus (OBS) | Haiti |
| Colombia | Holy See (OBS) |
| Republic of the Congo | Honduras |

Hungary
Iceland
India (OBS)
Indonesia (OBS)
Iran (OBS)
Ireland
Israel (OBS)
Italy
Jamaica
Japan (OBS)
Jordan
Kazakhstan (OBS)
Republic of Korea (OBS)
Kuwait
Kyrgyzstan
Latvia
Lebanon
Lesotho
Liberia
Libya (OBS)
Liechtenstein
Lithuania
Luxembourg
Former Yugoslav Republic of Macedonia
Malaysia
Malawi
Mali
Malta
Mauritania
Mauritius
Mexico
Moldova
Monaco
Mongolia
Morocco (OBS)
Mozambique
Namibia
Nepal
Netherlands
Netherlands (Presidency of European Union)

Netherlands (European Commission)
New Zealand
Nicaragua
Niger
Nigeria
Norway
Oman
Pakistan
Panama
Papua New Guinea
Paraguay
Peru
Philippines
Poland (OBS)
Portugal
Qatar
Romania (OBS)
Russian Federation (OBS)
Rwanda
Saint Vincent and the Grenadines
San Marino
Saudi Arabia (OBS)
Senegal
Seychelles
Slovakia
Slovenia
South Africa
Spain
Sri Lanka (OBS)
Sudan
Surinam
Sweden
Swaziland
Switzerland
Tanzania
Thailand (OBS)
Togo
Trinidad and Tobago
Tunisia (OBS)
Turkey (OBS)
Turkmenistan

Uganda
Ukraine (OBS)
United States of America (OBS)
Uzbekistan (OBS)
Venezuela
Vietnam (OBS)
Yemen
Yugoslav Federal Republic
Zimbabwe

**Observer Organisations**

United Nations
United Nations High Commissioner for
 Refugees

United Nations Children's Fund
Organisation of American States
Organisation for African Unity
International Committee of the Red
 Cross
International Federation of Red Cross
 and Red Crescent Societies
The Grand Magistry of the Sovereign
 Military Order of Malta
International Campaign to Ban Land-
 mines
Palestinian Authority
European Parliament

## ANTI-PERSONNEL MINES: WHAT FUTURE FOR ASIA?

**Regional Seminar for Asian Military and Strategic Studies Experts sponsored by the International Committee of the Red Cross in cooperation with the Government of the Republic of the Philippines and the Philippine National Red Cross Society**

**Manila, 20–23 July 1997**

### FINAL DECLARATION OF PARTICIPANTS

The undersigned Asian military and strategic studies analysts from 14 countries gathered in Manila to examine the experience of anti-personnel mine use in the region. The analysts discussed the military effectiveness of anti-personnel mines based on their actual combat performance in Asian and other conflicts. The military value of AP mines was considered in the context of the long-term human, social and economic costs incurred in many of the conflicts in which this weapon has been used. Particular attention was given to the difficulties and extremely high costs of post-conflict mine clearance.

The seminar sought to develop recommendations which will promote and broaden dialogue within Asian military and political circles on the question of anti-personnel mines. It is hoped that the work of the Manila seminar can contribute to the development of a common approach within the region to the humanitarian problems which anti-personnel mines have caused in Asia and globally. The following statement was adopted by participants acting in their personal capacities.

The undersigned participants in the regional seminar 'Anti-personnel Landmines: What Future for Asia?' agree that:

1. The global scourge of anti-personnel landmines, which kill and injure some 2,000 persons per month, most of whom are civilians, is unacceptable and must be stopped. These mines not only kill and maim combatants in an inhumane way, but also indiscriminately affect civilians and inflict on them enormous physical and psychological damage long after the conflict is over. This must be a grave and continuous concern of the international community;

2. In most conflicts, the appalling humanitarian consequences of the use of anti-personnel mines have far outweighed their military utility;

3. The use of anti-personnel landmines in internal armed conflicts, either by State or non-State actors, should not be condoned;

4. The cases considered during the seminar, and the personal experience of participants, lead to some initial conclusions concerning traditionally emplaced mines:

- Establishing, monitoring and maintaining extensive border minefields is time-consuming, expensive and dangerous. In order to be effective they need to be under continuous observation and direct fire, which is not always possible. Because of these practical difficulties some armed forces have entirely refrained from using such minefields. Moreover, these minefields have not always proved successful in preventing infiltration.
- Under battlefield conditions the use, marking, mapping and removal of mines in accordance with classical military doctrine and international humanitarian law is extremely difficult, even for professional armed forces. History indicates that effective marking, mapping and removal of mines have rarely occurred.[1] The cost to forces using anti-personnel mines, in terms of casualties to one's own forces and civilians, the limitation of tactical flexibility and the loss of sympathy of the indigenous population is higher than has been generally acknowledged.
- Use in accordance with traditional military doctrine appears to have occurred infrequently and only when the following specific conditions were met:

  —both parties to the conflict were disciplined professional armies with a high sense of responsibility and engaged in a short-lived international conflict,—the tactical situations were fairly static,—mines were not a major component of the conflict,—forces possessed adequate time and resources to mark, monitor and maintain minefields in accordance with law and doctrine,—mined areas were of sufficient economic or military value to ensure that mine clearance occurred,— parties had sufficient resources to ensure clearance and it was carried out without delay, and—the political will existed to limit strictly the use of mines and to clear them as indicated above;

5. Remotely delivered anti-personnel mines are not exclusively defensive weapons. They can easily be used in an offensive manner behind frontlines to prevent reinforcement and escape, and to saturate target areas.

Remotely delivered anti-personnel mines can cause vastly increased civilian casualties, even if such mines are designed to be self-destructing and self-deactivating, for the following reasons:

• they will be dangerous during their intended active life-time, • the fencing and marking of such mines will be virtually impossible, • in extended conflicts minefields may be re-laid many times, • self-destructing and deactivating devices may be unreliable, • inactive mines, as unexploded ordnance, can still be dangerous, and • the mere presence of mined areas will produce fear, keeping civilians out of areas important for their livelihood:

6. Some barrier systems and other methods offer more humane alternatives to anti-personnel mines under certain circumstances. Additional alternatives should be pursued rather than further development of any new anti-personnel mine technologies. Developments which further increase, rather than reduce, the lethality of anti-personnel mines are to be deplored and are unnecessary;

7. Those who have used and those who have supplied anti-personnel mines bear a joint responsibility to ensure the clearance of these weapons and the provision of adequate care to their victims;

8. Improved mine clearance technologies for military, humanitarian and civilian agencies that are affordable and easy to use should be vigorously developed with a goal of making the use of anti-personnel mines progressively less useful;

9. Since resources are not currently available even to clear mines currently in the ground, any attempt to deploy additional anti-personnel mines is likely to impose an unacceptable level of cost on countries that are least able to bear it;

10. Countries in Asia, including Afghanistan, Cambodia, Laos and Vietnam are among those most affected by anti-personnel mines and similar remnants of war; and

11. Notwithstanding successive UN resolutions since 1994 calling for increased assistance by all States to mine-affected countries, the actual assistance rendered has fallen far short of the requirements.

The undersigned participants therefore call upon States of the Asian region to consider the following urgent measures:

• The adoption of national prohibitions on the production, stockpiling, transfer and use of anti-personnel mines;
• For those States which are not yet Parties, adherence to the 1980 United Nations Convention on Certain Conventional Weapons, including its Protocol II on landmines (as amended on 3 May 1996), and for current States party to this Convention that have not yet done so adherence to its amended Protocol II at the earliest possible date to ensure its early entry into force;
• A substantial increase in assistance to mine-affected countries in the region, including Afghanistan, Cambodia, Laos and Vietnam. Such assistance might include

provision of trained manpower, specialized equipment and funds to cope with the problems of landmines laid in those countries. The delivery of such assistance should be considered a purely humanitarian measure, should be free of political considerations, and should not be at the expense of other forms of humanitarian assistance;

- The initiation, through all appropriate institutions, including the Asian Development Bank, of programs of regional cooperation in the fields of mine clearance, mine-risk education and victim assistance;
- The rapid adoption of a regional agreement to prohibit remotely delivered anti-personnel landmines in Asia so as to prevent an escalation of mine warfare in the region and even higher levels of civilian casualties; and
- Participation in upcoming negotiations aimed at the conclusion of a new treaty comprehensively prohibiting anti-personnel landmines by the end of 1997.
- To build on and work towards the implementation of United Nations General Assembly Resolution 51/45S calling for the conclusion of a legally-binding agreement totally prohibiting anti-personnel landmines.

The undersigned participants appeal to the international community:

- To pursue as a matter of urgency the prohibition and elimination of anti-personnel mines;
- For those States which are not yet Parties, to adhere to the 1980 United Nations Convention on Certain Conventional Weapons, including its Protocol II on landmines (as amended on 3 May 1996), and for current States party to this Convention that have not yet done so to adhere to its amended Protocol II at the earliest possible date to ensure its early entry into force;
- To recognize that the use of anti-personnel landmines in internal armed conflicts, either by State or non-State actors, should not be condoned;
- To explore how non-State actors involved in internal armed conflicts can be encouraged to end the use of anti-personnel mines;
- To assist mine-affected countries in Asia in ending the scourge of anti-personnel mines on their soil, in particular through the provision of technical, financial and other assistance in the clearance and destruction of mines, assistance to victims and mine awareness programs; and
- To adopt a compassionate approach to the reunification of mine victims with family members living in mine-free countries.

Participants express their thanks to the International Committee of the Red Cross for convening the seminar, and for its ongoing efforts on behalf of war victims in many of the countries of the region and to the Government of the Republic of the Philippines and Philippine National Red Cross for the generous hospitality they have provided in Manila.

Manila, 23 July 1997

*Notes*:

   * Some participants shared the humanitarian concerns expressed in this document but consider that the proposed prohibitions and restrictions on anti-personnel landmines should be pursued on a step-by-step basis according to the prevailing conditions faced by their countries.

   ¹ According to a number of participants these requirements were successfully carried out in the India-Pakistan wars.

# OSLO DIPLOMATIC CONFERENCE ON AN INTERNATIONAL TOTAL BAN ON ANTI-PERSONNEL LANDMINES

## Oslo, 1–19 September 1997

### REPORT

### 1. Opening of the Conference

The Plenary met on September 1 1997 at 11.00 hrs. The Conference was addressed by Mr. Jan Egeland, State Secretary of Norway and H.E. Mr. Bjørn Tore Godal, Minister of Foreign Affairs of Norway.

### 2. Election of the President

H.E. Ambassador J.S. Selebi, Permanent Representative of South Africa in Geneva, was elected President by acclamation.

### 3. Adoption of the Agenda

The agenda was adopted by consensus.

### 4. Adoption of the Rules of Procedure

The Rules of Procedure were adopted by consensus.

### 5. Election of the Vice-Presidents

The following delegates were elected Vice-Presidents by acclamation:

H.E. Mr. Andre Mernier, Belgium
Mr. Mahama Savadogo, Burkina Faso
Dr. Maria Francisca Arias, Colombia
Ms. Lam Mai Peng, Malaysia
H.E. Mr. Antonio de Icaza, Mexico
H.E. Mr. Johan Løvald, Norway
Hon. José U. Fernandez, Philippines
Mr. G. Punungwe, Zimbabwe

## 6. Organization of the Work

The President outlined how he planned to divide the work between the Plenary, the Committee of the Whole and the Friends of the Chair.

## 7. International Convention on a Total Ban on Anti-Personnel Land Mines

The President adjourned the Plenary meeting in order for the Conference to work in the Committee of the Whole and Friends of the Chair groups.

The Plenary was convened again on Wednesday September 3 at 16.30 hrs. to hear an address by the Secretary General of the United Nations, Mr. Kofi Annan.

The Plenary met again on Tuesday September 16 at 12.00 hrs. Based on rule 25 of the Rules of Procedure, the Plenary accepted a proposal of the United States to suspend the Plenary for 24 hours for further consultations.

The Plenary met again on Wednesday September 17 at 12.00 hrs. and agreed to adopt the text.

The Plenary met again on Thursday September 18 at 10.00 hrs and formally adopted the attached text of the Convention. Delegations made statements which are attached to this report.

The Conference agreed to request the Secretary General to the United Nations to translate the agreed text into Arabic, Chinese and Russian. The Conference agreed that the translated texts should be circulated to all potential Signatory States. The final versions of the Convention, in the six authentic languages, will be forwarded to Ottawa, Canada, by the last week of November for signature there from 3 December 1997 until 4 December 1997.

## 8. Closure of the Conference

The Plenary met Thursday September 18 at 12.00 hrs. The President of the Conference handed over the text of the Convention to H.E. Mr. Bjørn Tore Godal, Minister of Foreign Affairs of Norway. The Minister of Foreign Affairs addressed the Conference. The President closed the Conference.

## LIST OF PARTICIPANTS

### Participants

Algeria
Angola
Antigua and Barbuda
Argentina
Australia
Austria
Barbados

Belgium
Bolivia
Bosnia and Herzegovina
Botswana
Brazil
Burkina Faso
Cambodia

Cameroon
Canada
Cape Verde
Chile
Colombia
Costa Rica
Côte d'Ivoire
Croatia
Czech Republic
Denmark
Dominican Republic
Ecuador
El Salvador
Ethiopia
France
Gabon
Germany
Ghana
Guatemala
Guinea
Holy See
Honduras
Hungary
Iceland
Ireland
Italy
Japan
Jordan
Kenya
Kuwait
Lesotho
Liechtenstein
Luxembourg/EU
Macedonia (Fyrom)
Malaysia
Mali
Malta
Mauritania
Mauritius
Mexico
Monaco
Mozambique
Netherlands

New Zealand
Nicaragua
Norway
Papua New Guinea
Paraguay
Peru
Philippines
Poland
Portugal
Qatar
San Marino
Senegal
Seychelles
Slovakia
Slovenia
South Africa
Spain
Sudan
Swaziland
Sweden
Switzerland
Tanzania
Turkmenistan
Uganda
United Arab Emirates
United Kingdom
United States
Uruguay
Venezuela
Yemen
Zambia
Zimbabwe

**Observer States**

Albania
Bangladesh
Belarus
Brunei Darussalam
Bulgaria
Egypt
Estonia
Finland
Georgia

Greece
India
Indonesia
Islamic Republic of Iran
Latvia
Libyan Arab Jamahiriya
Lithuania
Morocco
Nepal
Oman
Pakistan
Panama
Republic of Korea
Romania
Russian Federation
Saudi Arabia
Serbia and Montenegro
Singapore

Sri Lanka
Thailand
Tunisia
Turkey
Ukraine

**Observer Organisations**

United Nations
UNHCR
UNICEF
WFP
OAS
OAU
ICRC
IFRC
The Grand Magistry of the Sovereign
    Military Order of Malta
ICBL

# SANA'A REGIONAL SEMINAR ON LANDMINES

### Organized by Swedish Save the Children Fund (Rädda Barnen)
### Sana'a, Republic of Yemen
### 3–4 November 1997

## DECLARATION OF SANA'A

Declaration adopted by the participants to the Regional Seminar on Landmines

In view of the increasing humanitarian efforts and the mounting solidarity of the international community to end the humanitarian suffering caused by anti-personnel landmines which leave behind tens of thousands of civilians killed or handicapped every year all over the world;

Since there are more than 54 million landmines laid in several countries of the region—which is around 45% of the total landmines scattered all over the world—something that continues to pose a grave threat to the lives of people in the region;

We the participants in the Regional Seminar on Anti-Personnel Mines held in Sana'a, the Republic of Yemen, between 3 and 4 November 1997;

Express our gratitude to the Government and the People of the Republic of Yemen for hosting this seminar.

Voice our support for the Yemeni Government's efforts to eliminate the laid landmines and do hope that the support and solidarity of the donor countries, international governmental organizations and NGOs to Yemen would constitute a good example for international regional humanitarian cooperation.

Appeal to the international community, particularly the landmines producing and exporting countries, to shoulder their humanitarian responsibilities in assisting the affected countries in general, and Yemen in particular, to get rid of this weapon.

Underline the significance of continuing the international humanitarian efforts, which started with the global appeal issued in Ottawa 1996, to bring about a total ban on land-mines, which is in line with the new trend of the international community to achieve world peace and security; the two essential objectives of the world nations and states.

Highly appreciate and welcome all individual and collective efforts in this very direction by various world states, the UN, governmental and non-governmental organizations for convening international and regional conferences meetings—that started in Ottawa in October 1996, Vienna in February 1997, Mozambique in February 1997, Bonn in April 1997, Brussels in June 1997, and Oslo in September 1997—in order to attain the noble humanitarian goal to have a world free of landmines and their tragedies. In this respect, we salute the initiative of the Canadian, South African and Norwegian governments in destroying the remaining personnel landmines in their stock.

Invite governments to consider signing the anti-personnel mine ban treaty in Ottawa, Canada, on 3–4 December 1997, or thereafter at the UN headquarters in New York, or at minimum, to adhere to the Protocol II, as amended and annexed to the 1980 UN Convention on Certain Conventional Weapons.

Wish that those countries, unable to sign the upcoming Ottawa Treaty for certain reasons, will continue to benefit from the available technical demining assistance.

Hope that this seminar, which is the last activity prior to the Ottawa Conference, would create the appropriate environment for cooperation in humanitarian issues and the exchange of expertise and data on the elimination of Anti-personnel landmines.

Call upon the international community to increase its influential contribution towards the complete elimination of suffering and tragedies that innocent civilians face as a result of this blind weapon all over the world.

# CONVENTION SIGNING CONFERENCE AND MINE ACTION FORUM

### 2–4 December 1997
### Ottawa, Canada

## A PROGRAM FOR MINE ACTION: FINAL CONFERENCE DOCUMENT

At the Ottawa Conference, States Parties to the Convention on the Prohibition of the Use, Stockpiling, Production and Transfer of Anti-Personnel Mines and on their

Destruction were joined by others in considering the elements of a global action plan to ensure progress on the issue of anti-personnel mines during the period leading up to entry into force of the Convention. In plenary sessions for the Ministerial Conference and Mine Action Forum, the following initiatives were circulated or announced.

### General Mine Action Initiatives

In signing the Convention, States Parties expressed their determination to put an end to the suffering and casualties caused by anti-personnel mines.

**Canada** Establishment of a $100 million fund. This fund will support early ratification and entry into force of the Convention and universal acceptance and compliance with its provisions, and support mine-affected countries in the areas of capacity building for indigenous mine action programs, mine awareness education, and assistance to victims.

**Central America** Central America 2000 initiative to declare the region mine-free by the year 2000.

**EU** Revised Joint Action on AP mines to provide a further EU contribution to demining and victim assistance as well as a moratorium on the transfer and production of anti-personnel mines.

**OSCE** The Forum for Security Co-operation will circulate annually among participating States a questionnaire on anti-personnel landmines, with responses due by March 15, 1998 and subsequently by December 15 each year.

**UNDPKO** As focal point for mine action within the UN, and through the activities of the newly-created Mine Action Service, to set up new programs and support existing ones, manage information, promote new techniques and technologies, and play an advocacy role. These new functions are in addition to the demining responsibilities that have traditionally been part of peacekeeping missions.

**ICRC** Organize regional seminars and national roundtables of military and political leaders on the military utility/humanitarian costs of AP mines (Central/Eastern Europe and Asia).

### Entry Into Force

Participants in the Ottawa Conference stressed the need for governments to take the necessary national steps to ratify the Convention as soon as possible in order to bring this instrument into force and make effective its provisions. Canada, Ireland and Mauritius presented to the UN Secretary General their instruments of ratification, becoming the first three states to ratify the Convention. Importance was attached to ensuring that states have the technical capacity to comply.

**Austria** Ratify in 1998 Initiative, using bilateral and multilateral contacts to encourage signatories to ratify the Convention in 1998.

**African Topics** African Topics Magazine will produce a special issue on the Ottawa Conference (March 1998), and a journalists' handbook on the Ottawa Conference, the Convention and ratification process.

**ICBL** Public campaign Entry into Force During 1998. Lobby the UN to proclaim the year 2000 as International Year of the Eradication of Landmines.

**ICRC** Global promotion and distribution of ratification kits, including a summary of the Convention for parliamentarians and the public and guidelines for state adherence and implementation.

- Publication of a layman's guide to the Ottawa treaty.

**IPU** Circulation of a survey to member states of the Inter-Parliamentary Union on what parliamentarians can do to ensure the implementation of the landmines ban.

**UNICEF** Lobby non-signatories to sign the Convention; promote early ratification by signatories.

### Stockpile Destruction

The Convention calls for the destruction of all stockpiled anti-personnel mines owned by signatories as soon as possible, but not later than four years after entry into force.

**Denmark** Destruction of existing stocks to be completed by the year 2000.

**France** Destruction of stockpiled anti-personnel mines to be completed before the year 2000.

**Hungary** Under the 'package of unilateral measures', all remaining stockpiles will be destroyed by December 31, 2000.

**Ukraine** Ready to begin partial destruction of its APM stockpiles, with the first stocks to be destroyed by the end of 1997.

**ICBL** Work with governments to establish a base line of mine-related information against which to measure the accuracy of data provided on entry into force.

### Mine Clearance

Participants in the Ottawa Conference recognized the importance of removing anti-personnel mines already in the ground. Signatories to the Convention agreed to destroy all anti-personnel mines in mined areas under their control not later than 10 years after entry into force and, where possible, to assist others in mine clearance and related activities.

**Australia** Continuation of multi-year demining programs.

- The Australian Defence Science and Technology Organization will spend AUS $4 million over the next five years on research into improved mine detection and neutralization.

**Austria** Creation of a new Mine Information Centre of the Austrian Armed Forces for the dissemination of know-how on demining.

—Increase assistance to demining, mine awareness and victim-rehabilitation programs, and increase the number of Armed Forces instructors for international demining operations.

**Belgium** Increased contribution to the UN Voluntary Fund and to the ICRC; continuation of research into high technology demining solutions, including a continued contribution to the pilot project 'Airborne Minefield Detection in Angola'. Additional contributions will amount to more than BF 63 million, bringing the annual global contribution to more than BF 100 million.

**China** Second massive demining campaign in the border regions of Yunnan province. (November 97–December 99)

**EU** US$40 million in 1998 for demining (European Commission); plus up to ECU 4.5 million in other contributions to international and regional organizations; plus ECU 15 million for development of appropriate technologies for humanitarian demining (European Commission).

- Convening an End User Forum on demining in January 1998, probably at the Joint Research Centre (JRC) in Ispra, Italy.
- Convening an International Symposium and Exhibition on demining technology at the JRC in Ispra on September 29, 1998.

**Finland** Initiating a two-year mine clearance program, in cooperation with the Cambodian Mine Action Centre. A Finnish mine-clearing group will be deployed; total cost, FM 9.2 million.

**France** To open the doors of the Ministry of Defence's Engineering Academy in Angers (Ecole Supérieure du Génie) to foreign trainees and members of NGCs.

- To promote the establishment of a world data bank on the world's mined areas.

**Germany** To host an International Experts Conference on Demining, focused on mechanical mine clearance and detection technologies (early June 1998).

- To increase its current level of bilateral funding for demining activity, including mine-related education and awareness building (to approximately DM 20 million per annum).

**Italy** To provide US $5.9 million for demining in 1998. An additional US $1.25 million is expected for multilateral demining assistance.

**Japan** Within the framework of the Tokyo Guidelines, to extend ¥10 billion in assistance over the next five years in the fields of demining, vocational assistance and victim assistance.

- To make possible the provision of equipment or technologies necessary for humanitarian mine clearance.

**Netherlands** Commitment to step up efforts at demining, including the launch of a training program for 80 mine clearance instructors for humanitarian mine clearance operations.

- Research and development program looking at new, improved techniques for humanitarian mine clearance; first tangible results expected by the year 2000.

**Norway** US$100 million contribution over five years, for mine clearance and awareness and mine victim assistance.

**Romania** Donation of demining equipment, a mine-related radiological laboratory and a mobile medical unit, to Angola.

**Slovenia**  To assist Bosnia and Herzegovina in demining; and, in the context of mine action in Bosnia and Herzegovina, to establish an International Trust Fund for Demining, Mine Clearance and Assistance to Mine Victims.

**Solomon Islands**  To undertake a study, with assistance from the UNDP, to determine the feasibility of removing unexploded ordnance left behind on the seabed from World War II.

**Sweden**  Increase funding for demining to approximately Cdn $28 million.
 • Increase funding for R&D (multi-sensor mines detector) by approximately Cdn $3 million. Start-up R&D project on the use of mine dogs, in co-operation with the Cambodian Mine Action Centre.
 • Complete the establishment of a national mine clearance centre.
 • Work on a database to complement that of the UN.

**Switzerland**  To establish the Geneva International Centre for Humanitarian Demining directed toward practical solutions to the operational problems posed by humanitarian demining, including creation of a database and management training courses. (Official creation of the centre March 1998; pilot seminar of directors of humanitarian demining programs in April/May 1998; annual conferences of demining program directors.)
 • To host a two-day International Expert Conference on Demining Policy Planning and Implementation. This conference is designed to give impetus to cooperation among signatories to the Ottawa Convention by providing a forum for contacts, the clarification of obligations, and the exchange of field experience and relevant information (early September 1998).

**Thailand**  To help demine Thailand's entire common border with Cambodia within the next three years.

**UK**  To double its resources for demining to £10 million per year over the next three years. Resources will be committed to new technology that improves safety standards and speeds up clearance.

**USA**  Demining 2010 Initiative. A global demining campaign to remove landmines by 2010. This will involve a panel of distinguished Americans to advise and mobilize support, and will include the hosting of an international conference in Washington May 21–22, 1998 to develop strategies for eliminating the landmine threat to civilians by the year 2010.
 • USA Department of Defense-hosted conference to gain appreciation for operational and environmental conditions confronting Mine Action Centres and demining NGOs, and obtain a 'wish list' of technology they would like to see US and other R&D establishments pursue (January 20–22, 1998 at Ft. Belvoir, Virginia).
 • Demining Conference at James Madison University, Washington DC (December 15–16). Focus will be on NGOs involved in demining and their informational requirements.
 • The USA will increase its financial contributions to global demining to approximately US $82 million in 1998. The goal is to increase to $1 billion per year

worldwide resources devoted to landmine related issues, including mine awareness education, mine and unexploded ordnance clearance, and mine victim assistance.

- The USA will work to expand the number of countries supported by its humanitarian demining program to 21 in 1998, with more considered in 1999.

**CAW** Contribution of Cdn $1.25 million by the Canadian Auto Workers for demining in Mozambique.

**OAS** Launching a mine clearing program in Guatemala.

- Expanding the number of trained deminers who could be made available to the international community after the year 2000.

**OAU** Implementation of the Plan of Action adopted at The First Continental Conference of African Experts on Landmines at Kempton Park.

**Physicians for Human Rights** Offer to convene a meeting to establish standardized methods to collect information and report on mine incidents, with NGO, International Agency and state involvement.

**UNA-USA** 'Adopt-a-Minefield' program, by which minefields identified by the UN will be paired with adoptive communities in the USA and abroad that will raise funds for their demining.

**UNDP** Proposed establishment of a Mine Action Centre, in a mine-infested developing country, to focus on training of trainers in survey, minefield information systems, mine awareness, assistive devices and networking. The Centre would promote the sustainability of global efforts through the development of national capacities. It would increase coordination among programs worldwide by providing a forum for sharing lessons learned.

**UNICEF** Promote mine awareness through international distribution and promotion of the animated video *The Silent Shout: Helping Children Learn About Landmines* (with Canada's assistance).

**Mine Victim Assistance**

The Convention clearly recognizes the need to provide assistance for the care, rehabilitation and social and economic reintegration of mine victims.

**EU** Contribution of up to ECU 8 million to the ICRC for assistance to mine victims.

**Holy See** Contribution of US$100,000 to the ICRC for victim assistance.

**Norway** Norwegian Mine Victim Support Strategy. In support of the ICRC's comprehensive mine victim assistance program, Norway will contribute US$20 million over a five-year period.

**ICBL** National campaigns to promote the establishment of an international day for mine victims.

**ICRC** Continued support to health facilities treating patients injured by mines.

- Continuation of a series of war surgery seminars to train surgeons in the surgical treatment of mine injuries.

- Undertake a study of the psychological and socio-economic needs of disabled mine victims.
- Organize an international technical and cooperation meeting of key agencies providing field assistance to mine victims.
- Further develop programs of mine awareness in affected countries; convene an international conference on mine awareness (Sarajevo, February 1998).

**LSN** Establish in 1998 support services for landmine survivors by developing locally-run networks in 12 mined countries, providing an international training conference for Landmine Survivors Network (LSN) associates, and launching an easy-to-use database on victim assistance over the Internet. LSN will also work closely with donor governments, private industry and international NGOs to raise US$3 billion for a range of effective survivor assistance over 10 years.

### Coordinating/Assessing Progress

There is widespread agreement on the need for effective coordination of international efforts by states, international organizations and NGOs, and for transparency in tracking progress made.

**Austria** European seminar on the implementation of treaty obligations with regard to APM in the armed forces. (Summer 1998 in Vienna.)

**Canada** Host a senior working-level meeting in March 1998 to discuss how the international community might best manage the humanitarian demining and victim assistance agendas during the coming months and years, and to seek agreement on a coordinated global approach to utilizing the resources and energy committed, with maximum results and cost effectiveness.

**EU** To promote greater international coordination through a Steering Committee, and working groups for appropriate technology, information management, and afflicted country actions.

**Hungary** To consider co-sponsoring a regional conference to promote dialogue and encourage joint action.

**Ireland** To host an international meeting in autumn 1998 in Dublin to assess the current state of the anti-personnel mine problem as well as international progress on mine action (in cooperation with Canada and the ICBL).

**CIET** A Mine Action Tracking System will be established by Community Information, Empowerment and Transparency in every mine-affected country, once funding is secured. Mine action tracking obtains data in a way that precipitates effective local action; it provides reliable operational accounting of mine action impact, benchmarks the reduction in mine events and changes in food security, and identifies points where the gains in mine action have levelled out.

**ICBL** Meeting in Bosnia and Herzegovina (early 1998).
- Second NGO Tokyo Conference (January 31–February 1, 1998).
- Meeting in South Korea (Late January–early February).

- Demining in Southern Africa Seminar, co-hosted by GEM, SACBL, MAG (South Africa, February 1998).
- West African NGO strategy workshop (February 1998).
- Regional government/NGO seminar in Budapest (March 1998).
- Meeting in Moscow, ICBL/IPPNW (May 1998).
- Meeting in Burkina Faso parallel to OAU Summit (June 1998).
- Seminar on Non-state Actors and the Ban (June 1998).
- 5th International ICBL Conference (tentative; Fall 1998).

Calendar of Mine Action Events [omitted]

# Draft Treaty Texts

## CONVENTION ON THE PROHIBITION OF ANTI-PERSONNEL MINES (1ST. DRAFT BY W. EHRLICH, APRIL 1996)

The High Contracting parties

Recalling that . . .

Have agreed as follows:

### Article 1. Scope of application

This Convention shall apply to anti-personnel mines as defined in paragraph 3 of article 2 of Protocol II of the CCW-Convention as amended on 3 May 1996.

This Convention shall apply in all circumstances including armed conflict and times of peace.

### Article 2. Relations with other international agreements

Nothing in this Convention shall be invoked as affecting the purposes and principles contained in the United Nations Charter or as detracting from other obligations imposed upon the High Contracting Parties by international humanitarian law.

### Article 3. Prohibitions

It is prohibited to employ, produce, transfer or stockpile anti-personnel mines.

### Article 4. Exceptions

The acquisition and stockpiling of small amounts of anti-personnel mines is not prohibited if they are exclusively used for the development and the teaching of mine detection or mine-clearance techniques and if the amount and the types are registered with the Depositary of this Convention.

### Article 5. Destruction of stocks

(a) Existing stockpiles of anti-personnel mines going beyond the amount covered by the exceptions or article 4 shall be destroyed by the HCP within one year of the coming into force of this Convention for the HCP.

(b) Anti-personnel mines already laid in the ground shall be destroyed by the High Contracting Parties within five years of the coming into force of this convention for the HCP.

(c) If an HCP cannot comply with these obligations in time, it may defer compliance for one year in the case of paragraph (a) and for two years in the case of paragraph (b) and for two years in the case of paragraph (c) but only if the amount and the types of mines respectively and the location of the minefields already laid are notified with the Depositary of this Convention.

## Article 6. Compliance with the Convention

## Article 7. Signature

This Convention shall be open for signature by all States at United Nations Headquarters in New York for a period of twelve months from . . .

## Article 8. Ratification, acceptance, approval or accession

This Convention is subject to ratification, acceptance or approval of the Signatories. Any State which has not signed this Convention may accede to it.

The instruments of ratification, acceptance, approval or accession shall be deposited with the Depositary.

## Article 9. Entry into force

This convention shall enter into force six months after the date of deposit of the 40th instrument of ratification, acceptance, approval or accession.

For any State which deposits its instrument of ratification, acceptance, approval or accession after the date of the deposit of the 40th instrument of ratification, acceptance, approval or accession, this Convention shall enter into force six months after the date on which that State has deposited its instrument of ratification, acceptance, approval or accession.

## Article 10. Depositary

The Secretary General of the United Nations shall be the Depositary of this Convention.

In addition to his usual functions the Depository shall inform all States of:

(a) signatures affixed to this Convention under article 7
(b) deposits of instruments of ratification, acceptance or approval or of accession to this Convention deposited under article 8,
(c) the dates of entry into force of this Convention
(d) notifications received under article 5c.

## Article 11. Authentic texts

The original of this Convention of which the Arabic, Chinese, English, French, Russian and Spanish texts are equally authentic, shall be deposited with the Depositary who shall transmit certified true copies thereof to all States.

# (ICBL DRAFT) CONVENTION ON THE PROHIBITION OF THE DEVELOPMENT, PRODUCTION, STOCKPILING, TRANSFER AND USE OF ANTI-PERSONNEL MINES AND ON THEIR DESTRUCTION

### (Proposal by the International Campaign to Ban Landmines, ICBL) 20 December 1996

The States Parties to the present Convention,

*Deeply concerned* by the worsening landmine crisis, and its devastating effects upon developing communities and the environment,

*Convinced* that the only solution to this humanitarian disaster is a total prohibition of the development, production, stockpiling, transfer and use of anti-personnel mines, as well as increased and improved assistance for demining and victim assistance,

*Recognizing* the need to prevent the use of weapons which violate international law principles, which prohibit *inter alia* weapons which cause indiscriminate effects and are incapable of distinguishing civilian and military targets, or are of a nature to cause superfluous injury or unnecessary suffering, and recognizing that anti-personnel mines are of such a nature,

. . .

Have agreed as follows:

### Article 1. Scope of application

This Convention shall apply in all circumstances including armed conflict and times of peace. In the case of an armed conflict involving one of the States Parties to this Convention, each party to the conflict shall be bound to apply the Convention. In peacetime this Convention shall apply to each State Party to the Convention and all persons and entities operating on the territory or under the control or jurisdiction of a State Party to the Convention.

### Article 2. Prohibition of anti-personnel mines

Each State Party to this Convention undertakes never under any circumstance:

(a) To develop, produce, stockpile or transfer, directly or indirectly, anti-personnel mines or components intended for use in anti-personnel mines;
(b) To use anti-personnel mines;
(c) To permit, assist, encourage or induce in any way, anyone to engage in any activity prohibited to a State Party under this Convention.

### Article 3. Definitions

1. 'Anti-personnel mine' means a munition designed or adapted to be exploded by the presence, proximity or contact of a person and that can incapacitate, injure or kill one

or more persons, including:

(a) any mine fitted with a device intended to protect the mine and which is part of, linked to, attached to or placed under the mine and which activates when an attempt is made to tamper with the mine ('all mines with anti-handling devices');
(b) any device or material which is designed, constructed or adapted to kill or injure, and which functions unexpectedly when a person disturbs or approaches an apparently harmless object or performs an apparently safe act ('booby-trap').

## Article 4. Destruction of stockpiles

Each State Party undertakes to destroy all anti-personnel mines in its possession, or in locations under its jurisdiction or control, within two years after the entry into force of this Convention.

## Article 5. Removal of emplaced anti-personnel mines

1. Each State Party which has anti-personnel mines on its territory or in places under its jurisdiction or control undertakes to clear these mines and destroy them. The mine-fields shall be recorded, marked, fenced and continuously monitored until they have been cleared. Until the mine-fields have been cleared, the State Party shall provide the Depositary with the information in accordance with Article 7 of this Convention.

2. With respect to anti-personnel mines laid by a party in areas controlled by another state, such party shall provide to the State in control of the area technical and material assistance necessary to remove and destroy the anti-personnel mines.

## Article 6. Cooperation

Each State Party undertakes to facilitate and shall have the right to participate in the fullest possible exchange of equipment, material and scientific and technological information concerning the implementation of this Convention and means of mine clearance and mine destruction.

## Article 7. Reporting and transparency measures

1. Each State Party shall, six months after the entry into force of this Convention, and thereafter on an annual basis, provide the Depositary with the following information:

(a) the number and types of anti-personnel mines stockpiled by the State Party;
(b) the number and types of anti-personnel mines destroyed by the State Party;
(c) the geographical location of minefields on the territory of the State Party, or on locations under the jurisdiction or control of the State Party;
(d) the estimated number and types of anti-personnel mines in these minefields;
(e) measures taken to record, mark, fence and monitor these minefields;
(f) a time-table for the destruction of anti-personnel mines in stockpiles and for the clearance of mine-fields;
(g) progress achieved in clearing minefields;

(h) pursuant to Article 8 of this Convention, a description of the legislative and other measures adopted to implement this Convention.

2. The Depositary shall, on an annual basis, make publicly available the information provided under paragraph 1 of this Article.

3. States Parties shall allow on-site observation by Representatives of other States Parties when stockpiled anti-personnel mines are destroyed.

### Article 8. National implementation measures

Each State Party shall, within one year after ratification of this Convention, take the necessary legislative, administrative and other measures to implement its obligations under this Convention. This obligation includes the adoption of legal measures to prevent persons or entities within its jurisdiction or control from engaging in conduct prohibited by this Convention.

### Article 9. Consultation and fact-finding

1. States Parties undertake to consult and to cooperate with each other in order to resolve any problems that may arise in the implementation of this Convention.

2. Each State Party has the right to request the Depositary to obtain clarification from another State Party in resolving any situation which may be considered ambiguous or which gives rise to a concern about the implementation of this Convention.

3. The Depositary shall forward the request for clarification to the State Party concerned not later than 5 days after its receipt. The requested State Party shall provide the clarification to the Depositary no later than 14 days after the receipt of the request. The Depositary shall take note of the clarification and forward it to the requesting State Party no later than 5 days after its receipt.

4. If the requesting State Party deems the clarification to be inadequate, it shall have the right to request the Depositary to convene a Team of Experts, provided that at least two other State Parties support the request. The sole purpose of convening the Team of Experts shall be to collect and examine data concerning the possible use or transfer of anti-personnel mines.

5. The Depositary shall convene the Team of Experts within ten days after receiving the request supported by at least two other States Parties. For this purpose, the Depositary shall keep up to date a list of qualified experts who shall carry out their functions in accordance with the Annex on Fact-finding. The Annex shall be considered an integral part of this Convention.

### Article 10. Compliance

1. If the report of the Team of Experts, referred to in the Annex on Fact-finding, concludes that a State Party has used or transferred anti-personnel mines, or that the State Party knowingly has permitted the use or transfer of anti-personnel mines to or from territory under its jurisdiction or control, the responsible State Party shall be required

to take all appropriate measures to remedy the situation and, in particular, to ensure the removal and destruction of the mines and minefields. The responsible State Party shall also impose penal sanctions against the person or persons responsible for the violation.

2. The provisions of the Geneva Conventions of 1949 regarding the measures each State Party must take to suppress and punish grave breaches of the Geneva Conventions shall also apply to this Convention. Any wilful use or transfer of anti-personnel mines shall be considered as a grave breach.

3. If a dispute arises between two or more States Parties relating to the interpretation or application of this Convention, the parties concerned shall consult together with a view to the expeditious settlement of the dispute by negotiation or by other peaceful means of the parties' choice, including, by mutual consent, referral to the International Court of Justice in conformity with the statute of the Court. The States Parties shall keep the Depositary informed of actions being taken.

4. If the dispute cannot be settled, a State Party may request the Depositary to convene a Commission of States Parties, provided that the request is supported by two other States Parties. Each State Party may appoint one representative to the Commission, which shall meet no later than one week after the Depositary has received the request from the requesting State Party. The Commission shall prepare a report which shall be made public, and shall consider what action to take, such as bringing the question to the attention of the Security Council of the United Nations. The Commission shall take its decisions by consensus if possible, but otherwise by a majority of members present and voting.

### Article 11. Relations with other international agreements

Nothing in this Convention shall be interpreted as detracting from other obligations imposed upon the States Parties by international law.

### Article 12. Signature

This Convention is open for signature by all States.

### Article 13. Ratification

This Convention is subject to ratification or accession by the Signatories. Any State which has not signed this Convention may accede to it. The instrument of ratification or accession shall be deposited with the Depositary.

### Article 14. Entry into force

1. This Convention shall enter into force three months after the date of deposit of the twentieth instrument of ratification or accession.

2. For any State ratifying or acceding to this Convention after its entry into force, the Convention shall enter into force three months after the date of deposit of its own instrument of ratification or accession.

3. Pending the entry into force of this Convention, the States signatories undertake immediately not to transfer, produce or use any anti-personnel mines.

### Article 15. Consultative meetings, review and amendments

1. A Consultative Meeting of States Parties shall be convened by the Depositary annually for the first three years after the entry into force of this Convention. The purpose of the Consultative Meeting shall be to examine progress made in implementing the Convention, and to explore ways of expanding the number of States Parties. All States Parties to the Convention shall be invited to the Consultative Meetings. States not parties, inter-governmental organizations and non-governmental organizations shall be invited as observers.

2. A Review Conference shall be convened by the Depositary five years after the adoption of this Convention. The purpose of the Review Conference shall be to review the scope and operation of this Convention and consider any proposal for amendments of the Convention. All States Parties shall be invited to the Review Conference. The Conference shall take its decisions by consensus if possible, but otherwise by a majority of members present and voting. States not parties, inter-governmental organizations and non-governmental organizations shall be invited as observers.

3. In addition to the regular Review Conferences, any State Party may at any time after the entry into force of this Convention propose amendments to this Convention. Any proposal for an amendment shall be communicated to the Depositary, who shall notify it to all States Parties and shall seek their views on whether a conference shall be convened to consider the proposal. If a majority, that shall not be less than eighteen of the States Parties, so agrees, he shall promptly convene a conference to which all States Parties shall be invited. States not parties, inter-governmental organizations and non-governmental organizations shall be invited as observers.

### Article 16. Duration and withdrawal

1. This Convention shall be of unlimited duration.

2. Each State Party shall have the right to withdraw from this Convention if it decides that extraordinary events have jeopardized the supreme interests of its country. It shall give notice of such withdrawal 90 days in advance to all other States Parties, the Depositary and the United Nations Security Council. Such notice shall include a statement of the extraordinary events it regards have jeopardized its supreme interests. Withdrawal shall take effect one year after the date of receipt of the notification to the Depositary. If however, on the expiry of that year, the withdrawing State Party is engaged in an armed conflict, the withdrawal shall not take effect. A withdrawal shall not have the effect of releasing the State Party from its obligations under this Convention prior to the date at which the withdrawal becomes effective.

### Article 17. Reservations

This Convention shall not be subject to reservations.

### Article 18. Depositary

The [. . .] is designated as Depositary of this Convention.

### Article 19. Authentic texts

This Convention, of which the Arabic, Chinese, English, French, Russian and Spanish texts are equally authentic, shall be deposited with the Depositary, who shall transmit certified copies thereof to all States Parties to the Convention.

## ANNEX

### Fact-finding regarding Use or Transfer of Anti-personnel Mines

1. In accordance with Article 9 of this Convention, each State Party shall be entitled to ask the Depositary to convene a Team of Experts, within a period of ten days, to conduct an inquiry in order to clarify and resolve any questions relating to the possible use or transfer of anti-personnel mines by a State Party. The request for an inquiry must be supported by at least two other States Parties. The request for an inquiry shall be accompanied by all relevant information and all possible evidence confirming its accuracy.

2. The costs of the Team of Experts' activities shall be covered by the States Parties in accordance with the United Nations scale of assessments, adjusted to allow for differences between the number of States members of the United Nations and the number of States Parties to this Convention.

3. The depositary shall inform all States Parties of the decision to convene a Team of Experts as soon as possible. For the purposes of the inquiry, the Team of Experts shall seek useful assistance and relevant information from States Parties and international organizations concerned and from any other appropriate source.

4. The Team of Experts may decide that the inquiry has to be supplemented by evidence collected on the spot and in a location under the jurisdiction or control of the State Party concerned. In such cases, the Team of Experts shall notify the State Party concerned of the decision to send a team of experts to conduct an inquiry on the spot. The Team of Experts shall notify the State Party concerned at least 24 hours before the team is expected to arrive, and shall inform all States Parties of the decision taken as soon as possible.

5. For the purpose of paragraph 1 of this Annex, the Depositary shall keep up to date a list of qualified experts supplied by the States Parties, on whom the Depositary may call with a minimum of notice to conduct an inquiry.

6. The State Party concerned shall make the necessary arrangements to receive, transport and accommodate the Team of Experts on its territory.

7. For the purposes of the inquiry conducted on the spot, the Team of Experts may hear a statement of information by the authorities of the State Party concerned and may question any person likely to be connected with the alleged violation. The Team of Experts shall have the right of access to all areas and installations where evidence of violations of this Convention could be collected.

8.  The Team of Experts shall complete its mission within a reasonable period. It shall submit a report to the Depositary not later than one week after leaving the territory of the State Party concerned. The Depositary shall communicate this report to the States Parties within a period of one week.

## BELGIAN DRAFT OF A CONVENTION ON THE TOTAL PROHIBITION OF ANTI-PERSONNEL MINES

The States Parties to the present Convention

Preamble

Have agreed as follows:

### Art. 1: Scope of Application

The object of this Convention is to prohibit anti-personnel mines as defined in article 2 hereafter.

The present Convention is of application in all circumstances in peacetime as well as in armed conflicts.

### Art. 2: Definition

For the purpose of this Convention

- 'Anti-personnel mine' means a mine primarily designed to be exploded by the presence, proximity or contact of a person and that will incapacitate, injure or kill one or more persons.
- 'Mine' means a munition designed to be placed under, on or near the ground or other surface area and to be exploded by the presence, proximity or contact of a person or a vehicle.

### Art. 3: Prohibition of anti-personnel mines

It is prohibited to use, manufacture, stockpile or transfer anti-personnel mines.

### Art. 4: Exception

The present Convention knows only one exception to its article 3. This exception allows States Parties to acquire and stockpile a limited amount of anti-personnel land-mines for the sole purpose of training and research.

### Art. 5: Destruction of stockpiles

States Parties undertake to destroy this stockpile of anti-personnel mines within three years after the date of deposit of their instrument of ratification or accession to this Convention.

## Art. 6: Existing anti-personnel minefields

States Parties will communicate to the Depository of the Convention the geographical location as well as the amount of APL mines in the existing anti-personnel minefields under their control.

This communication is made annually from the date of deposit of their instrument of ratification or accession to the present Convention.

This communication will also include the intention of the State Party concerned, about the removal of these minefields.

This article concerns only the minefields which already exist before the deposit of the instrument of ratification or accession to the present Convention by the State Party concerned; it cannot be interpreted as detracting from the general prohibition imposed by art. 3.

## Art. 7: National implementation measures

1. Each State Party shall, in accordance with its constitutional processes, take any necessary measures to implement its obligations under the present Convention. In particular, it shall take any necessary measures:

(a) To prohibit natural and legal persons anywhere on its territory or in any other place under its jurisdiction as recognized by international law from undertaking any activity prohibited to a State Party under the present Convention.

(b) To prohibit natural and legal persons from undertaking any such activity anywhere under its control.

(c) To prohibit, in conformity with international law, natural persons possessing its nationality from undertaking any such activity anywhere.

2. Each State Party shall cooperate with other States Parties and afford the appropriate form of legal assistance to facilitate the implementation of the obligations under paragraph 1.

3. Each State Party shall inform the Organization of the measures taken pursuant to this Article.

## Art. 8: Confidence building measures

Upon deposit of its instrument of ratification or accession to the present Convention, each State Party will communicate to the depositary the number and technical data of anti-personnel mines in its detention. This communication is made annually and when appropriate must be completed

- by the number and technical data of the anti-personnel mines destroyed during the year in review
- by the number and technical data of the anti-personnel mines acquired during the year in review for the purpose of training and research.

When appropriate, this communication includes the information described in art. 6.

### Art. 9: Entry into Force

The present Convention shall enter into force ninety days after the date of deposit of the twentieth instrument of ratification or accession.

For any State whose instrument of ratification or accession is deposited after the entry into force of the present Convention, the Convention will enter into force ninety days after the deposit of its own instrument of ratification or accession.

### Art. 10: Signature

The present Convention shall be open to States for signature before its entry into force.

### Art. 11: Ratification

The present Convention shall be subject to ratification by States Signatories according to their respective constitutional processes.

### Art. 12: Accession

Any State which does not sign this Treaty before its entry into force may accede to it at any time thereafter.

### Art. 13: Reservation

The articles of the present Convention shall not be subject to reservation.

### Art. 14: Duration and withdrawal

1. The present Convention shall be of unlimited duration.

2. Each State Party shall, in exercising its national sovereignty, have the right to withdraw from the present Convention if it decides that extraordinary events related to the subject matter of this Treaty have jeopardized its supreme interests.

3. Withdrawal shall be effected by giving notice six months in advance to all other States Parties, and to the Depositary. Notice of withdrawal shall include a statement of the extraordinary event or events which a State Party regards as jeopardizing its supreme interests.

### Art. 15: Depositary

1. The Secretary-General of the United Nations shall be the Depositary of this Convention and shall receive signatures, instruments of ratification and instruments of accession.

2. The Depositary shall promptly inform all States Signatories and acceding States of the date of each signature, the date of deposit of each instrument of ratification or accession, the date of the entry into force of the Convention as of the reception of all information foreseen in art. 7.

3. The Depositary shall send duly certified copies of this Convention to the Governments of the States Signatories and acceding States.

4. The Convention shall be registered by the Depositary pursuant to Article 102 of the Charter of the United Nations.

### Art. 16: Authentic texts

This Convention, of which the Arabic, Chinese, English, French, Russian and Spanish texts are equally authentic, shall be deposited with the Secretary-General of the United Nations.

## CONVENTION ON THE PROHIBITION OF ANTI-PERSONNEL MINES (FIRST AUSTRIAN DRAFT TEXT)

### Article 1. Scope of application

This Convention shall apply to anti-personnel mines as defined in Article 2.

This Convention shall apply in all circumstances including armed conflict and times of peace.

### Article 2. Definitions

1. 'Anti-personnel mine' means a mine primarily designed to be exploded by the presence, proximity, or contact of a person and that will incapacitate, injure or kill one or more persons.

2. 'Mine' means a munition designed to be placed under, on or near the ground or other surface area and to be exploded by the presence, proximity or contact of a person or a vehicle.

### Article 3. Prohibitions

It is prohibited to use anti-personnel mines as they are deemed to be excessively injurious and to have indiscriminate effects.

Each High Contracting Party to this Convention undertakes never:

(a) To develop, produce, otherwise acquire, stockpile, retain or transfer, directly or indirectly, anti-personnel mines to anyone.
(b) To permit, assist, encourage or induce in any way, anyone to engage in any activity prohibited to a High Contracting Party under this Convention.

### Article 4. Exceptions

The acquisition or retention of small amounts of anti-personnel mines is not prohibited if they are exclusively used for the development and the teaching of mine detection, mine clearance, or mine destruction techniques and if the responsible institutions, the amount and the types are registered with the Depositary of this Convention.

### Article 5. Destruction of stocks

1. Each High Contracting Party undertakes to destroy stockpiles of anti-personnel mines it owns or possesses, or that are located in any place under its jurisdiction or

control, within one year and anti-personnel mines already employed within five years of the individual entry into force of this Convention for the High Contracting Party.

2. If a High Contracting Party cannot comply with this obligation in time, it may declare this when depositing its instrument of ratification, acceptance, approval or accession and defer such destruction, in addition to the periods mentioned in paragraph one, for one year in the case of stockpiles and for two years in the case of employed anti-personnel mines, if all relevant data are notified with the Depositary.

### Article 6. Compliance with the Convention

1. Each High Contracting Party shall take all appropriate legal and other measures, including the imposition of penal sections to prevent and suppress breaches of this Convention by persons or on territory under its jurisdiction or control.

2. The provisions of the Geneva Conventions of 12 August 1949 relating to measures for the repression of breaches and grave breaches shall apply to breaches and grave breaches of this Convention. Any act or omission occurring during armed conflict in violation of this Convention, if committed wilfully or wantonly and causing death or serious injury, shall be treated as a grave breach.

3. The High Contracting Parties undertake to consult each other and to cooperate with each other to resolve any problems that may arise with regard to the implementation and application of the provisions of this Article.

### Article 7. Verification of compliance

*Notifications*

1. Each High Contracting Party shall notify to the Depositary within 60 days after the individual entering into force of this Convention:

(a) all anti-personnel mines under its control, be it either in stockpile or employed.

This notification shall contain complete information about number, type, use, maps of areas of deployment (minefields or mined areas), type of fuse, lifetime and other relevant information;

(b) its general plan for clearing and destroying deployed anti-personnel mines.

These notifications shall be updated by the HCP on an annual basis until all anti-personnel mines have been destroyed.

*Challenge inspections*

2. In the case of serious doubts about compliance each High Contracting Party has the right to request an on-site challenge inspection of any facility or location in the territory or in any other place under the jurisdiction or control of any other High Contracting Party for the sole purpose of clarifying and resolving any questions concerning possible non-compliance with the provisions of this Convention.

Such a request, accompanied by evidence, shall be addressed to a Board of Eminent Experts, appointed by the Secretary-General of the United Nations, for immediate processing.

If the Board of Eminent Experts considers the request not to be frivolous, abusive or clearly beyond the scope of this Convention and the evidence sufficient, it may decide not later than 24 hours after having received the inspection request to order an inspection in the framework of a clear mandate.

Such an inspection will be made by an inspection team nominated by the Board of Eminent Experts and under its responsibility.

The inspected State, which has the right to demonstrate its compliance, shall assist the inspection team throughout the challenge inspection and facilitate its task. The report of the Board of Eminent Experts on the result of the inspection shall be addressed via the Secretary-General of the United Nations to all High Contracting Parties and shall, in the case of abuse, contain recommendations on appropriate measures to redress the situation.

The inspection will be financed by the requesting High Contracting Party. If, however, the non-compliance with the Convention is established in the report of the Board of Eminent Experts, then the inspected High Contracting Party shall refund the cost of the inspection.

### Article 8. Ratification, acceptance, approval or accession

This Convention is subject to ratification, acceptance or approval of the Signatories. Any State which has not signed the Convention may accede to it.

The instruments of ratification, acceptance, approval or accession shall be deposited with the Depositary.

### Article 9. Entry into force

This Convention shall enter into force on the first day of the sixth month after the month in which the 40th instrument of ratification, acceptance, approval or accession has been deposited.

For any State which deposits its instrument of ratification, acceptance, approval or accession after the date of the deposit of the 40th instrument of ratification, acceptance, approval or accession, this Convention shall enter into force six months after the date on which that State has deposited its instrument of ratification, acceptance, approval or accession.

### Article 10. Reservations

The Articles of this Convention shall not be subject to reservations.

### Article 11. Duration and withdrawal

1. This Convention shall be of unlimited duration.

2. Each High Contracting Party shall, in exercising its national sovereignty, have the right to withdraw from this Convention if it decides that extraordinary events, related to the subject-matter of this Convention, have jeopardized the supreme interests of its

country. It shall give notice of such withdrawal 90 days in advance to all other HCP, to the Depositary and to the Security Council of the United Nations. Such notice shall include a statement of the extraordinary events it regards as having jeopardized its supreme interests.

3. The withdrawal of a High Contracting Party from this Convention shall not in any way affect the duty of States to continue fulfilling the obligations assumed under any relevant rules of international law.

### Article 12.  Depositary

The Secretary-General of the United Nations is hereby designed as the Depositary of this Convention and shall, inter alia:

(a) Promptly inform all signatory and acceding States of the date of each signature, the date of deposit of each instrument of ratification, acceptance, approval or accession and the date of the entry into force of this Convention.
(b) Promptly inform all High Contracting Parties of all notifications received under Articles 4, 5 and 7.
(c) Assume the tasks assigned to him by Article 7.

### Article 13.  Authentic texts

The original of this Convention, of which the Arabic, Chinese, English, French, Russian and Spanish texts are equally authentic, shall be deposited with the Secretary-General of the United Nations.

## CONVENTION ON THE PROHIBITION OF THE USE, STOCKPILING, PRODUCTION AND TRANSFER OF ANTI-PERSONNEL MINES AND ON THEIR DESTRUCTION (SECOND AUSTRIAN DRAFT TEXT)

The States Parties

Recalling that . . .

Have agreed as follows:

### Article 1.  General Obligations

1. Each State party undertakes never under any circumstances:

(a) To use anti-personnel mines;
(b) To develop, produce, otherwise acquire, stockpile, retain or transfer to anyone, directly or indirectly, anti-personnel mines;
(c) To assist, encourage or induce, in any way, anyone to engage in any activity prohibited to a State Party under this Convention.

2. Each State Party undertakes to destroy all anti-personnel mines in accordance with the provisions of this Convention.

## Article 2. Definitions

1. 'Anti-personnel mine' means a mine designed to be exploded by the presence, proximity or contact of a person and that will incapacitate, injure or kill one or more persons. Mines designed to be detonated by the presence, proximity or contact of a vehicle as opposed to a person, that are equipped with anti-handling devices, are not considered anti-personnel mines as a result of being so equipped.

2. 'Mine' means a munition designed to be placed under, on or near the ground or other surface area and to be exploded by the presence, proximity or contact of a person or a vehicle.

3. 'Anti-handling device' means a device intended to protect a mine and which is part of, linked to, attached to or placed under the mine and which activates when an attempt is made to tamper with the mine.

4. 'Transfer' involves, in addition to the physical movement of anti-personnel mines into or from national territory, the transfer of title to and control over the mines, but does not involve the transfer of territory containing emplaced anti-personnel mines.

5. 'Minefield' is a defined area in which mines have been emplaced.

## Article 3. Exceptions

1. Notwithstanding the general obligations under Article 1, a State Party may retain or transfer a number of anti-personnel mines necessary for the development and teaching of mine detection, mine clearance, or mine destruction techniques. The number of such mines shall not exceed that absolutely necessary for the above mentioned purposes.

2. The transfer of anti-personnel mines for the purpose of destruction is permitted.

## Article 4. Destruction of stockpiled anti-personnel mines

Each State Party undertakes to destroy all stockpiled anti-personnel mines it owns or possesses, or that are under its jurisdiction or control, as soon as possible but not later than three years after the entry into force of this Convention for that State Party.

## Article 5. Destruction of anti-personnel mines laid within minefields

1. Each State Party undertakes to destroy all anti-personnel mines laid within minefields under its jurisdiction or control, as soon as possible but not later than ten years after the entry into force of this Convention for that State Party.

2. Minefields where anti-personnel mines have been laid shall, until all anti-personnel mines contained therein have been destroyed, be perimeter-marked, monitored and protected by fencing or other means, to ensure the effective exclusion of civilians. The marking must be of a distinct and durable character and must at least be visible to a person who is about to enter the minefield.

### Article 6.  Destruction of anti-personnel mines laid in areas outside minefields

1.  Each State Party undertakes to destroy, as soon as possible, all anti-personnel mines laid in areas under its jurisdiction or control outside minefields.

Each State Party shall make every effort to identify areas under its jurisdiction or control in which anti-personnel mines are known or suspected to be present and to provide an immediate and effective warning to the population.

### Article 7.  International cooperation and assistance

1.  In fulfilling its obligations under this Convention each State Party has the right to seek and receive assistance from other States Parties to the extent possible.

2.  Each State Party undertakes to facilitate and shall have the right to participate in the fullest possible exchange of equipment, material and scientific and technological information concerning the implementation of this Convention.

3.  Each State Party in a position to do so shall provide assistance for mine clearance. Such assistance may be provided, inter alia, through the United Nations System, other international organizations or institutions, regional organizations, or on a bilateral basis, or by contributing to the United Nations Voluntary Trust Fund for Assistance in Mine Clearance.

4.  Each State Party in a position to do so shall provide assistance for the destruction of stockpiled anti-personnel mines.

5.  Each State Party undertakes to provide information to the database on mine clearance established within the United Nations System, especially information concerning various means and technologies of mine clearance, and lists of experts, expert agencies or national points of contact on mine clearance.

### Article 8.  Transparency measures

1.  Each State Party shall report to the Depositary not later than one year after the entry into force of this Convention for that State Party on:

(a)  the national implementation measures referred to in Article 10;

(b)  the types and quantities of all stockpiled anti-personnel mines owned or possessed by it, or under its jurisdiction or control;

(c)  the location of all minefields under its jurisdiction or control containing anti-personnel mines;

(d)  to the extent possible, the location of all areas outside minefields in which anti-personnel mines are known or suspected to be present;

(e)  the types and quantities of all anti-personnel mines retained or transferred for the development and teaching of mine detection, mine clearance or mine destruction techniques, or transferred for the purpose of destruction, as well as the names and the institutions authorized by a State Party to retain or transfer anti-personnel mines, in accordance with Article 3;

(f)  the status of programmes for the conversion or de-commissioning of anti-personnel mine production facilities; and

(g) the status of programmes for the destruction of anti-personnel mines in accordance with Articles 4, 5 and 6, including applicable safety and environmental standards to be observed.

(h) The information provided in accordance with this Article shall be updated by the States Parties annually, covering the last calendar year, and reported to the Depositary not later than 1 March.

### Article 9. Facilitation and clarification of compliance

1. The States Parties agree to consult and cooperate with each other regarding the implementation of the provisions of this Convention, and to facilitate compliance by States Parties with their obligations under this Convention.

2. If one or more States Parties wish to clarify and seek to resolve questions relating to compliance with the provisions of this Convention by another State Party, it may submit, through the Depositary, a Request for Clarification of that matter to that State Party. Such a request shall be accompanied by all relevant information. A State Party that receives a Request for Clarification shall provide through the Depositary, within 30 days to the requesting State Party all information necessary which would assist in clarifying this matter.

3. If the requesting State Party does not receive a response through the Depositary within the time period provided for in para 2, or deems the response to the Request for Clarification to be unsatisfactory, it may submit, through the Depositary, the matter to a Meeting of the States Parties. This submission shall include all relevant information. The Meeting of States Parties shall consider the matter at its next meeting.

4. The requesting State Party may propose to the Depositary to convene a Special Meeting of the States Parties to consider the matter. The Depositary shall thereupon communicate this proposal to the States Parties with a request that they indicate whether they favour a Special Meeting of the States Parties, for the purpose of considering the matter. In the event that within 30 days from the date of such communication, at least one third of the States Parties favour such a Special Meeting, the Depositary shall convene this Special Meeting of the States Parties.

5. All States Parties shall cooperate fully with the Meeting of States Parties in the fulfilment of its review of the matter.

6. The Meeting of States Parties may request additional information from a State Party on matters under its consideration. If it concludes that it is necessary, the Meeting of States Parties may authorize a fact-finding mission to collect additional information on the spot or in other places directly related to the alleged compliance issue under the jurisdiction or control of the concerned State Party.

7. The fact-finding mission shall report, through the Depositary, to the States Parties and the Meeting of the States Parties the results of its findings, including any recommendations it considers appropriate in order to facilitate compliance with this Convention.

### Article 10.  National implementation measures

Each State Party shall take all appropriate legal, administrative and other measures, including the imposition of penal sanctions to prevent and suppress any activity prohibited to a State Party under this Convention undertaken by persons or on territory under its jurisdiction or control.

### Article 11.  Settlement of Disputes

The States Parties undertake to consult each other and to cooperate with each other to resolve any problems that may arise with regard to the application and implementation of this Convention. Each State Party may report any such problem to the Meeting of the States Parties.

### Article 12.  Meetings of the States Parties

1.  The States Parties shall meet regularly in order to discuss any matter with regard to the application or implementation of this Convention, including:

 (a)  the operation and status of this Convention;
 (b)  matters arising from the reports submitted under the provisions of this Convention;
 (c)  international cooperation and assistance in accordance with Article 7;
 (d)  the development of technologies to clear anti-personnel mines;
 (e)  submissions of States Parties under Article 9.

2.  The First Meeting of the States Parties shall be convened by the Depositary within one year after the entry into force of this Convention. The subsequent meetings shall be convened by the Depositary annually until the first Review Conference.

3.  Under the conditions set out in Article 9, the Depositary shall convene a Special Meeting of the States Parties.

4.  States not parties to this Convention, as well as the United Nations, other relevant international organizations or institutions, regional organizations, the International Committee of the Red Cross and relevant non-governmental organizations may be invited to attend these meetings as observers in accordance with the agreed Rules of Procedure.

5.  The costs of the Meeting of the States Parties shall be borne by the States Parties and States not parties to this Convention participating in the meeting, in accordance with the United Nations scale of assessment adjusted appropriately.

### Article 13.  Review Conferences

1.  A Review Conference shall be convened by the Depositary five years after the entry into force of this Convention, and thereafter at five year intervals. All States Parties to this Convention shall be invited to the Review Conference.

2.  The purpose of the Review Conference shall be to:

 (a)  review the operation and status of this Convention;
 (b)  consider any proposal for amendments to this Convention;

(c) consider the need for and the interval between further Meetings of the States Parties referred to in para 2 of Article 12.

3. States not parties to this Convention, as well as the United Nations, other relevant international organizations or institutions, regional organizations, the International Committee of the Red Cross and relevant non-governmental organizations may be invited to attend the Review Conference as observers in accordance with the agreed Rules of Procedure.

4. The costs of the Review Conference shall be borne by the States Parties and States not parties to this Convention participating in the Review Conference, in accordance with the United Nations scale of assessment adjusted appropriately.

### Article 14. Signature

This Convention shall be open to all States for signature before its entry into force.

### Article 15. Ratification, acceptance, approval or accession

This Convention is subject to ratification, acceptance or approval of the Signatories. Any State which has not signed the Convention before its entry into force may accede to it at any time.

### Article 16. Entry into force

1. This Convention shall enter into force on the first day of the sixth month after the month in which the 40th instrument of ratification, acceptance or approval has been deposited.

2. For any State which deposits its instrument of ratification, acceptance, approval or accession after the date of the deposit of the 40th instrument of ratification, acceptance, approval or accession, this Convention shall enter into force six months after the date on which that State has deposited its instrument of ratification, acceptance, approval or accession.

### Article 17. Reservations

The Articles of this Convention shall not be subject to reservations.

### Article 18. Duration and withdrawal

1. This Convention shall be of unlimited duration.

2. Each State Party shall, in exercising its national sovereignty, have the right to withdraw from this Convention if it decides that extraordinary events, related to the subject-matter of this Convention, have jeopardized the supreme interests of its country. It shall give notice of such withdrawal one year in advance to all other States Parties, to the Depositary and to the United Nations Security Council. Such notice shall include a statement of the extraordinary events it regards as having jeopardized its supreme interests.

3. In case a State Party should withdraw from this Convention, the withdrawal shall only take effect one year after the receipt of the instrument of withdrawal by the Depositary.

If, however, on the expiry of that year the withdrawing State Party is engaged in an armed conflict the withdrawal shall not take effect before the end of the armed conflict.

4. The withdrawal of a State Party from this Convention shall not in any way affect the duty of States to continue fulfilling the obligations assumed under any relevant rules of international law.

### Article 19. Depositary

The Secretary-General of the United Nations is hereby designated as the Depositary of this Convention and shall, inter alia,

(a) Promptly inform all signatory and acceding States of the date of each signature, the date of deposit of each instrument of ratification, acceptance, approval or accession and the date of the entry into force of this Convention;

(b) Transmit duly certified copies of this Convention to the Governments of all signatory and acceding States;

(c) Register this Convention pursuant to Article 102 of the Charter of the United Nations;

(d) Transmit to the States Parties not later than two months before the next Meeting of the States Parties the reports received under Article 8;

(e) Transmit to the States Parties the submissions received under Article 9; and

(f) Convene the Meetings of the States Parties referred to in Article 12 and the Review Conferences referred to in Article 13.

### Article 20. Authentic texts

The original of this Convention, of which the Arabic, Chinese, English, French, Russian and Spanish texts are equally authentic, shall be deposited with the Secretary-General of the United Nations.

## CONVENTION ON THE PROHIBITION OF THE USE, STOCKPILING, PRODUCTION AND TRANSFER OF ANTI-PERSONNEL MINES AND ON THEIR DESTRUCTION (THIRD AUSTRIAN DRAFT TEXT)

### Austrian draft 13 May 1997

The States Parties

Recalling that . . .

Have agreed as follows:

### Article 1. General obligations

1. Each State Party undertakes never under any circumstances:

(a) To use anti-personnel mines;

(b) To develop, produce, otherwise acquire, stockpile, retain or transfer to anyone, directly or indirectly, anti-personnel mines;

(c) To assist, encourage or induce, in any way, anyone to engage in any activity prohibited to a State Party under this Convention.

2. Each State Party undertakes to destroy all anti-personnel mines in accordance with the provisions of this Convention.

## Article 2. Definitions

1. 'Anti-personnel mine' means a mine designed to be exploded by the presence, proximity, or contact of a person and that will incapacitate, injure or kill one or more persons. Mines designed to be detonated by the presence, proximity or contact of a vehicle as opposed to a person, that are equipped with anti-handling devices, are not considered anti-personnel mines as a result of being so equipped.

2. 'Mine' means a munition designed to be placed under, on or near the ground or other surface area and to be exploded by the presence, proximity or contact of a person or a vehicle.

3. 'Anti-handling device' means a device intended to protect a mine and which is part of, linked to, attached to or placed under the mine and which activates when an attempt is made to tamper with the mine.

4. 'Transfer' involves, in addition to the physical movement of anti-personnel mines into or from national territory, the transfer of title to and control over the mines, but does not involve the transfer of territory containing emplaced anti-personnel mines.

5. 'Minefield' is a defined area in which mines have been emplaced.

## Article 3. Exceptions

1. Notwithstanding the general obligations under Article 1, a State Party may retain or transfer a number of anti-personnel mines necessary for the development and teaching of mine detection, mine clearance, or mine destruction techniques. The number of such mines shall not exceed that absolutely necessary for the above mentioned purposes.

2. The transfer of anti-personnel mines for the purpose of destruction is permitted.

## Article 4. Destruction of stockpiled anti-personnel mines

Each State Party undertakes to destroy all stockpiled anti-personnel mines it owns or possesses, or that are under its jurisdiction or control, as soon as possible but not later than three years after the entry into force of this Convention for that State Party.

## Article 5. Destruction of anti-personnel mines laid within minefields

1. Each State Party undertakes to destroy all anti-personnel mines laid within minefields under its jurisdiction or control, as soon as possible but not later than ten years after the entry into force of this Convention for that State Party.

2. Minefields where anti-personnel mines have been laid shall, until all anti-personnel mines contained therein have been destroyed, be perimeter-marked, monitored and protected by fencing or other means, to ensure the effective exclusion of civilians. The marking must be of a distinct and durable character and must at least be visible to a person who is about to enter the minefield.

### Article 6. Destruction of anti-personnel mines laid in areas outside minefields

1. Each State Party undertakes to destroy, as soon as possible, all anti-personnel mines laid in areas under its jurisdiction or control outside minefields.

2. Each State Party shall make every effort to identify areas under its jurisdiction or control in which anti-personnel mines are known or suspected to be present and to provide an immediate and effective warning to the population.

### Article 7. International cooperation and assistance

1. In fulfilling its obligations under this Convention each State Party has the right to seek and receive assistance from other States Parties to the extent possible.

2. Each State Party undertakes to facilitate and shall have the right to participate in the fullest possible exchange of equipment, material and scientific and technological information concerning the implementation of this Convention.

3. Each State Party in a position to do so shall provide assistance for mine clearance. Such assistance may be provided, inter alia, through the United Nations System, other international organizations or institutions, regional organizations, or on a bilateral basis, or by contributing to the United Nations Voluntary Trust Fund for Assistance in Mine Clearance.

4. Each State Party in a position to do so shall provide assistance for the destruction of stockpiled anti-personnel mines.

5. Each State Party undertakes to provide information to the database on mine clearance established within the United Nations System, especially information concerning various means and technologies of mine clearance, and lists of experts, expert agencies or national points of contact on mine clearance.

### Article 8. Transparency measures

1. Each State Party shall report to the Depositary not later than one year after the entry into force of this Convention for that State Party on:

(a) The national implementation measures referred to in Article 10;
(b) The types and quantities of all stockpiled anti-personnel mines owned or possessed by it, or under its jurisdiction or control;
(c) The location of all minefields under its jurisdiction or control containing anti-personnel mines;
(d) To the extent possible, the location of all areas outside minefields in which anti-personnel mines are known or suspected to be present;

(e) The types and quantities of all anti-personnel mines retained or transferred for the development and teaching of mine detection, mine clearance or mine destruction techniques, or transferred for the purpose of destruction, as well as the names of the institutions authorized by a State Party to retain or transfer anti-personnel mines, in accordance with Article 3;

(f) The status of programmes for the conversion or de-commissioning of anti-personnel mine production facilities; and

(g) The status of programmes for the destruction of anti-personnel mines in accordance with Articles 4, 5 and 6, including applicable safety and environmental standards to be observed.

2. The information provided in accordance with this Article shall be updated by the States Parties annually, covering the last calendar year, and reported to the Depositary not later than 1 March.

**Article 9.  Facilitation and clarification of compliance**

1. The States Parties agree to consult and cooperate with each other regarding the implementation of the provisions of this Convention, and to facilitate compliance by States Parties with their obligations under this Convention.

2. If one or more States Parties wish to clarify and seek to resolve questions relating to compliance with the provisions of this Convention by another State Party, it may submit, through the Depositary, a Request for Clarification of that matter to that State Party. Such a request shall be accompanied by all relevant information. A State Party that receives a Request for Clarification shall provide, through the Depositary, within 30 days to the requesting State Party all information which would assist in clarifying this matter.

3. If the requesting State Party does not receive a response through the Depositary within the time period provided for in paragraph 2, or deems the response to the Request for Clarification to be unsatisfactory, it may submit, through the Depositary, the matter to the Meeting of the States Parties. This submission shall include all relevant information. The Meeting of the States Parties shall consider the matter at its next meeting.

4. The requesting State Party may propose to the Depositary to convene a Special Meeting of the States Parties to consider the matter. The Depositary shall thereupon communicate this proposal to the States Parties with a request that they indicate whether they favour a Special Meeting of the States Parties, for the purpose of considering the matter. In the event that within 30 days from the date of such communication, at least one third of the States Parties favours such a Special Meeting, the Depositary shall convene this Special Meeting of the States Parties.

5. All States Parties shall cooperate fully with the Meeting of the States Parties fulfillment of its review of the matter.

6. The Meeting of the States Parties may request additional information from a State Party on matters under its consideration. If it concludes that it is necessary, the Meeting of the States Parties may authorize a fact-finding mission to collect additional information on the spot or in other places directly related to the alleged compliance issue under the jurisdiction or control of the concerned State Party.

7. The fact-finding mission shall report, through the Depositary, to the States Parties and the Meeting of the States Parties the results of its findings, including any recommendations it considers appropriate in order to facilitate compliance with this Convention.

### Article 10.  National implementation measures

Each State Party shall take all appropriate legal, administrative and other measures, including the imposition of penal sanctions, to prevent and suppress any activity prohibited to a State Party under this Convention undertaken by persons or on territory under its jurisdiction or control.

### Article 11.  Settlement of disputes

The States Parties undertake to consult each other and to cooperate with each other to resolve any problem that may arise with regard to the application and interpretation of this Convention. Each State Party may report any such problem to the Meeting of the States Parties.

### Article 12.  Meetings of the States Parties

1. The States Parties shall meet regularly in order to consider any matter with regard to the application or implementation of this Convention, including:

(a)  The operation and status of this Convention;
(b)  Matters arising from the reports submitted under the provisions of this Convention;
(c)  International cooperation and assistance in accordance with Article 7;
(d)  The development of technologies to clear anti-personnel mines; and
(e)  Submissions of States Parties under Article 9.

2. The First Meeting of the States Parties shall be convened by the Depositary within one year after the entry into force of this Convention. The subsequent meetings shall be convened by the Depositary annually until the first Review Conference.

3. Under the conditions set out in Article 9, the Depositary shall convene a Special Meeting of the States Parties.

4. States not parties to this Convention, as well as the United Nations, other relevant international organizations or institutions, regional organizations, the International Committee of the Red Cross and relevant non-governmental organizations may be invited to attend these meetings as observers in accordance with the agreed Rules of Procedure.

5. The costs of the Meetings of the States Parties shall be borne by the States Parties and States not parties to this Convention participating in the meeting, in accordance with the United Nations scale of assessment adjusted appropriately.

### Article 13. Review Conferences

1. A Review Conference shall be convened by the Depositary five years after the entry into force of this Convention, and thereafter at five years interval. All States Parties to this Convention shall be invited to the Review Conference.

2. The purpose of the Review Conference shall be:

(a) To review the operation and status of this Convention;
(b) To consider any proposal for amendments to this Convention; and
(c) To consider the need for and the interval between further Meetings of the States Parties referred to in paragraph 2 of Article 12.

3. States not parties to this Convention, as well as the United Nations, other relevant international organizations or institutions, regional organizations, the International Committee of the Red Cross and relevant non-governmental organizations may be invited to attend the Review Conference as observers in accordance with the agreed Rules of Procedure.

4. The costs of the Review Conference shall be borne by the States Parties and States not parties to this Convention participating in the Review Conference, in accordance with the United Nations scale of assessment adjusted appropriately.

### Article 14. Signature

This Convention shall be open to all States for signature before its entry into force.

### Article 15. Ratification, acceptance, approval or accession

This Convention is subject to ratification, acceptance or approval of the Signatories. Any State which has not signed this Convention before its entry into force may accede to it at any time.

### Article 16. Entry into force

1. This Convention shall enter into force on the first day of the sixth month after the month in which the 40th instrument of ratification, acceptance, approval or accession has been deposited.

2. For any State which deposits its instrument of ratification, acceptance, approval or accession after the date of the deposit of the 40th instrument of ratification, acceptance, approval or accession, this Convention shall enter into force six months after the date on which that State has deposited its instrument of ratification, acceptance, approval or accession.

### Article 17. Reservations

The Articles of this Convention shall not be subject to reservations.

**Article 18.  Duration and withdrawal**

1.  This Convention shall be of unlimited duration.

2.  Each State Party shall, in exercising its national sovereignty, have the right to withdraw from this Convention if it decides that extraordinary events, related to the subject-matter of this Convention, have jeopardized the supreme interests of its country. It shall give notice of such withdrawal one year in advance to all other States Parties, to the Depositary and to the United Nations Security Council. Such notice shall include a statement of the extraordinary events it regards as having jeopardized its supreme interests.

3.  In case a State Party should withdraw from this Convention, the withdrawal shall only take effect one year after receipt of the instrument of withdrawal by the Depositary. If, however, on the expiry of that year the withdrawing State Party is engaged in an armed conflict the withdrawal shall not take effect before the end of the armed conflict.

4.  The withdrawal of a State Party from this Convention shall not in any way affect the duty of States to continue fulfilling the obligations assumed under any relevant rules of international law.

**Article 19.  Depositary**

The Secretary-General of the United Nations is hereby designated as the Depositary of this Convention and shall, inter alia:

(a)  Promptly inform all signatory and acceding States of the date of each signature, the date of deposit of each instrument of ratification, acceptance, approval or accession and the date of the entry into force of this Convention;
(b)  Transmit duly certified copies of this Convention to the Governments of all signatory and acceding States;
(c)  Register this Convention pursuant to Article 102 of the Charter of the United Nations;
(d)  Transmit to the States Parties not later than two months before the next Meeting of the States Parties the reports received under Article 8;
(e)  Transmit to the States Parties the submissions received under Article 9; and
(f)  Convene the Meetings of the States Parties referred to in Article 12 and the Review Conferences referred to in Article 13.

**Article 20.  Authentic texts**

The original of this Convention, of which the Arabic, Chinese, English, French, Russian and Spanish texts are equally authentic, shall be deposited with the Secretary-General of the United Nations.

# APPENDIX 5
## Oslo Diplomatic Conference Documentation

PROPOSALS TABLED AT THE DIPLOMATIC
CONFERENCE ON AN INTERNATIONAL TOTAL BAN
ON ANTI-PERSONNEL LAND MINES

APL/CW.01
1 September 1997

ARTICLES 8, 9, 12, 13 AND 19
PROPOSAL SUBMITTED BY AUSTRIA

The proposed Convention assigns a number of functions to the Secretary-General of the United Nations as 'Depositary' of this Convention. While the functions assigned under Articles 18 (2) and (3), 19 (a)–(c) and 20 correspond to the traditional depositary functions as specified in Article 77 (1) of the 1969 Vienna Convention on the Law of Treaties, the functions assigned under Articles 8 (1) and (2), 9 (2)–(4) and (7), 12 (2) and (3), 13 (1) and 19 (d)–(f) are usually not considered to be depositary functions. It is therefore suggested that these Articles refer to the 'Secretary-General of the United Nations' as the executing authority, and not to the 'Depositary'. Furthermore, the non-depositary functions assigned to the Secretary-General in Article 19 (d)–(f) should be transferred to other Articles or be entirely omitted as repetitious (proposed changes are printed in bold letters, comments in italics, deletions in square brackets):

### Article 8. Transparency measures

1. Each State Party shall report to the Secretary-General of the United Nations not later than one year after the entry into force of this Convention for that State Party on:

. . .

2. The information provided in accordance with this Article shall be updated by the States Parties annually, covering the last calendar year, and reported to the **Secretary-General of the United Nations** not later than 1 March. **The latter shall transmit the reports to the States Parties not later than two months before the next Meeting of the States Parties** *(language taken from former Art. 19 para. (d))*.

### Article 9. Facilitation and clarification of compliance

. . .

2. If one or more States Parties wish to clarify and seek to resolve questions relating to compliance with the provisions of this Convention by another State Party, it may

submit, through the **Secretary-General of the United Nations**, a Request for Clarification of that matter to that State Party. Such a request shall be accompanied by all relevant information. A State Party that receives a Request for Clarification shall provide, through the **Secretary-General of the United Nations**, within 30 days to the requesting State Party all information which would assist in clarifying this matter.

3. If the requesting State Party does not receive a response through the **Secretary-General of the United Nations** within the time period provided for in paragraph 2, or deems the response to the Request for Clarification to be unsatisfactory, it may submit, through the **Secretary-General of the United Nations who shall transmit the submission received to the States Parties** *(language taken from former Art. 19 para. (e))*, the matter to the Meeting of the States Parties. This submission shall include all relevant information. The Meeting of the States Parties shall consider the matter at its next meeting.

4. The requesting State Party may propose to the **Secretary-General of the United Nations** to convene a Special Meeting of the States Parties to consider the matter. The **Secretary-General of the United Nations** shall thereupon communicate this proposal to the States Parties with a request that they indicate whether they favour a Special Meeting of the States Parties, for the purpose of considering the matter. In the event that within 30 days from the date of such communication, at least one third of the States Parties favours such a Special Meeting, the **Secretary-General of the United Nations** shall convene this Special Meeting of the States Parties.

7. The fact-finding mission shall report, through the **Secretary-General of the United Nations**, to the States Parties and the Meeting of the States Parties the results of its findings, including any recommendations it considers appropriate in order to facilitate compliance with this Convention.

### Article 12. Meetings of the States Parties

. . .

2. The First Meeting of the States Parties shall be convened by the **Secretary-General of the United Nations** within one year after the entry into force of this Convention. The subsequent meetings shall be convened by the **Secretary-General of the United Nations** annually until the first Review Conference.

3. Under the conditions set out in Article 9, the **Secretary-General of the United Nations** shall convene a Special Meeting of the States Parties.

### Article 13. Review Conferences

1. A Review Conference shall be convened by the **Secretary-General of the United Nations** five years after the entry into force of this Convention, and thereafter at five years interval. All States Parties to this Convention shall be invited to the Review Conference.

. . .

**Article 19 Depositary**

The Secretary-General of the United Nations is hereby designated as the Depositary of this Convention [. . .].

**APL/CW.02**
**1 September 1997**

## ARTICLE 2 (DEFINITIONS): PROPOSED AMENDMENTS (AUSTRALIA)

'Anti-personnel mine' means a mine designed to be triggered automatically and solely by the presence, proximity or contact of a person and whose effect cannot be exclusively limited to combatants, including mines designed to be detonated by the presence, proximity or contact of a vehicle whose triggering device may be configured so as to be triggered by the presence, proximity or contact of a person and whose effects cannot be exclusively limited to combatants. Mines designed to be detonated by the presence, proximity or contact of a vehicle as opposed to a person that are equipped with anti-handling devices, are not considered anti-personnel as a result of being so equipped.

'Mine' means a munition designed to be placed under, on, near or suspended above the ground or other surface area and to be triggered automatically and solely by the presence, proximity or contact of a person or vehicle.

'Designed' means both the manufacturer's technical specifications and any intentional modification, adaptation or improvisation of any other munition or explosives so as to operate as a mine.

**APL/CW.03**
**1 September 1997**

## THE NORWEGIAN DELEGATION PROPOSAL FOR THE PREAMBLE, 1 SEPTEMBER 1997

**Preamble:**

'The States Parties,

*Expressing deep concern* about the suffering and casualties caused to non-combatants as a result of the proliferation and use of anti-personnel landmines,

*Gravely concerned* that these mines kill or maim hundreds of people every week, mostly innocent and defenceless civilians and especially children, obstruct economic development and reconstruction, inhibit the repatriation of refugees and internally displaced persons, and have other severe consequences for years after emplacement,

*Welcoming* that the United Nations General Assembly in its resolution 51/45 S *urged States to pursue vigorously an effective, legally-binding international agreement to ban the use, stockpiling, production and transfer of anti-personnel landmines.*

Have agreed as follows:

Article 1

etc. . . . .'

## APL/CW.04
### 1 September 1997

### THE NORWEGIAN DELEGATION PROPOSAL FOR AMENDMENT TO ARTICLE 2, 1 SEPTEMBER 1997

**Article 2:**

Exchange the second sentence of Article 2.1 with 'Mines designed to be detonated by the presence, proximity or contact of a vehicle as opposed to a person, including those which are equipped with anti-handling devices, are not considered anti-personnel mines'.

## APL/CW.05
### 1 September 1997

### THE NORWEGIAN DELEGATION PROPOSAL FOR AMENDMENT TO ARTICLE 7, 1 SEPTEMBER 1997

**Article 7:**

Insert the following after Article 7.3: (3. bis): 'Each State Party in a position to do so shall provide assistance for the rehabilitation of mine victims. Each State Party undertakes to provide information to a database on victim rehabilitation.'

## APL/CW.06
### 1 September 1997

### MEXICO
### PROPOSAL FOR AMENDMENT (CHANGES APPEAR IN ITALICS AND BOLD CHARACTERS)

**Article 9 Facilitation and Clarification of Compliance**

(. . .)

3. If the requesting State Party does not receive a response through the Depositary within the time period provided for in paragraph 2, or deems the response to the request for clarification to be unsatisfactory, it may submit, through the Depositary, the matter to the Meeting of States Parties. The submission shall ***be accompanied by all evidence of the alleged facts constituting the basis for the request for clarification. All evidence shall be fully disclosed to the State Party concerned which shall have the right to challenge such evidence***. The Meeting of the States Parties shall consider the matter at its next meeting.

*3 bis. Pending the convening of any Meeting of the States Parties, the Depositary shall offer his good offices to the States Parties concerned to facilitate the clarification requested.*

*4 bis. Any meeting of the States Parties which is due to consider a request for clarification shall decide in the first place whether such a request is founded. In so doing, it will evaluate all information and evidence submitted by the States Parties concerned. The Meeting of the States Parties shall make every effort to reach its decisions by general agreement. If despite all efforts to that end no agreement has been reached, voting shall take place and decisions shall be taken by a two thirds majority of the States Parties present and voting.*

6. *If the Meeting of the States Parties has determined that the request for clarification is founded, in trying to clarify the matter under consideration it may ask any of the States Parties concerned to submit additional information. If it concludes that information submitted by any of the States Parties concerned does not sufficiently clarify the matter under consideration,* the Meeting of the States Parties may authorize a fact-finding mission to collect additional information on the spot or in other places direct-ly *related to the matter under consideration, with the previous consent of the State Party concerned.*

*6 bis. When authorizing a fact-finding mission in accordance with the preceding paragraph, the Meeting of the States Parties shall also decide on the composition and mandate entrusted to the mission. The costs of the mission shall be borne by the States Parties, in accordance with the United Nations scale of assessment adjusted appropriately, unless the Meeting of the State Parties decides otherwise.*

*6 ter. Whenever it deems it appropriate, the Meeting of the States Parties may suggest to the States Parties concerned ways and means to further clarify the matter under consideration, including the initiation of appropriate international procedures in conformity with international law.*

APL/CW.07
1 September 1997

SPANISH DELEGATION
PROPOSAL FOR A TEMPORARY ARRANGEMENT

'Notwithstanding the general obligations under Article 1 and the exceptions under Articles 3 and 17, a State Party, under exceptional circumstances for its National Security, may resort to the use of antipersonnel mines in accordance with the International Laws of armed conflict and in full compliance with the amended Protocol II on landmines annexed to the 1980 Convention.

The use of antipersonnel mines would never be authorised in conflicts amongst States Parties to this Convention.

This is a temporary arrangement which will cease to apply when the Meeting of States Parties so decides'.

**APL/CW.08**
**1 September 1997**

US Proposal

### Article 3.  Exceptions

3.  *The general obligations under Article 1 shall not apply to activities in support of a United Nations command or its successor, by a State Party participating in that command, where a military armistic agreement had been concluded by a United Nations command.*

With respect to this Article 3 amendment, the U.S. proposes the following change to Article 13, Article 13 bis, and Article 16, to accommodate an amendment process.

### Article 13

*2 bis. The Review Conference convened by the Depositary five years after entry into force of this Convention and, as necessary, each subsequent Review Conference shall review the operation of paragraph 3 of Article 3 in light of the importance of proceeding toward the complete elimination of anti-personnel mines and of whether permanent peace arrangements are in place in the region where a military armistic agreement had been concluded by a United Nations command. If a Review Conference decides that paragraph 3 of Article 3 should be modified or deleted, it shall commence work without delay, with a view to recommending to States Parties for adoption an appropriate amendment to this Convention. Any such proposed amendment shall be considered in accordance with the provisions of {Article 13 bis and} Article 16.*

### Article 13 bis

1.  *Any State Party may propose amendments to this Convention, including its Annex on Clarification. The Depositary shall circulate any proposals for amendments to all States Parties 90 days in advance of the next Review Conference. Any such proposed amendments shall be considered at the next Review Conference convened pursuant to Article 13.*

2.  *Amendments shall be adopted by a Review Conference by a two-thirds majority of all States Parties. Amendments so adopted shall be promptly circulated by the Depositary to all States Parties and shall enter into force for those States Parties that approve them in accordance with Article 16.*

3.  *In order to ensure the viability and effectiveness of this Convention, the Annex on Clarification shall be subject to changes in accordance with paragraph 4, if the proposed changes are related only to matters of an administrative or technical nature. All other provisions of the Convention and Annex shall not be subject to changes in accordance with paragraph 4.*

*4. Proposed changes referred to in paragraph 3 shall be made in accordance with the following procedures:*

(a) *Any State Party may propose changes to the Annex on Clarification. The Depository shall circulate any proposals for changes to all States Parties 45 days in advance of the next Meeting of the States Parties. The text of such proposed changes shall be considered at the next meeting of the States Parties convened pursuant to Article 12;*

(b) *If the Meeting of the States Parties recommends that the proposal be adopted, the Depository shall notify the Meeting of the States Parties recommendation, with appropriate explanations including a discussion of why the proposal fulfills the requirements of paragraph 3, to all States Parties for consideration. States Parties shall acknowledge receipt within 10 days;*

(c) *If no State Party objects to the proposal within 90 days after receipt of the recommendation, the Depository shall notify all States Parties that no objection has been received and the proposal shall be effective 30 days after the date of notification.*

(d) *If any State Party objects to the proposal within 90 days after receipt of the recommendation, the proposal may be considered at the next Review Conference convened pursuant to article 13, under the procedures in paragraph 2.*

### Article 16. Entry into Force

1. This Convention **and any amendments to this Convention** shall enter into force on the first day of the sixth month after the month in which the 40th instrument of ratification, acceptance or approval has been deposited.

2. For any State which deposits its instrument of ratification, acceptance or approval or accession after the date of the deposit of the 40th instrument of ratification, acceptance, approval or accession, this Convention **and any amendments to this Convention** shall enter into force six months after the date on which the State has deposited its instrument of ratification, acceptance, approval or accession.

### APL/CW.09
### 1 September 1997

## US Proposal

### Article 2. Definitions

The U.S. Delegation proposes that the first-paragraph be divided into two subparagraphs. The second sentence in the current draft would be incorporated into subparagraph b as outlined below:

*1(b) Mines designed to be detonated by the presence, proximity or contact of a vehicle, as opposed to a person, that are equipped with anti-handling devices, are not considered anti-personnel landmines as a result of being so equipped. Likewise, mines that are integral submunitions in a munition that is designed for other than anti-personnel purposes (e.g. anti-tank, anti-vehicle, or runway denial) are not considered to be anti-personnel mines, provided that all such mines have self-destruction and self deactivation features in compliance with paragraph 3(a) of the Technical Annex to the Protocol on Prohibitions or Restrictions on the Use of Mines, Booby-Traps and Other Devices as Amended on 3 May 1996, whether or not such mines are remotely-delivered.*

. . .

5. 'Minefield' is a defined area in which mines have been emplaced. *'Phony minefield' means an area free of mines that simulates a minefield. The term 'minefield' includes phony minefields.*

6. *'Use' means the act of emplacement.*

APL/CW.09/Rev.1
8 September 1997

## Revised US Proposal

### Article 2. Definitions

1. 'Anti-personnel mine' means a mine designed to be exploded by the presence proximity, or contact of a person and that will incapacitate, injure or kill one or more persons. Mines designed to be detonated by the presence, proximity or contact of a vehicle as opposed to a person, *as well as any* anti-handling devices *associated with those mines*, are not considered anti-personnel mines.

2. 'Mine' means a munition designed to be placed under, on or near the ground or other surface area and to be exploded by the presence, proximity or contact of a person or a vehicle.

3. 'Anti-handling device' means a device or submunition intended to protect a mine *other than an anti-personnel mine* and which is part of, linked to, attached to, placed under, or *deployed as a constituent element of a munition containing* the mine and which activates when an attempt is made to tamper with the mine, *provided that any submunition deployed as a constituent element of a munition containing the mine has self-destruction and self-deactivation features in compliance with paragraph 3(a) of the Technical Annex to the Protocol on Prohibitions or Restrictions on the Use of Mines, Booby-Traps and Other Devices as Amended on 3 May 1996, whether or not such mines are remotely-delivered.*

APL/CW.10
1 September 1997

## US Proposal

### Article 4. Destruction of stockpiled anti-personnel mines

Each State Party undertakes to destroy all stockpiled anti-personnel mines it owns or possesses, or that are under its jurisdiction or control, as soon as possible but not later than three years after the entry into force of this Convention for that State Party. *These provisions apply to anti-personnel mines that are owned or possessed by natural or legal persons on the territory of the State Party. These provisions do not apply to anti-personnel mines that are owned or possessed by a State not Party to this Convention, provided that such mines are not also owned or possessed by the State Party.*

**APL/CW.11**
**1 September 1997**

## US PROPOSAL

### Article 5. Destruction of anti-personnel mines laid within minefields

1. Each State Party undertakes to destroy all anti-personnel mines laid within minefields under its jurisdiction or *long term* control, as soon as possible but not later than ten years after the entry into force of this Convention for that State Party.

**APL/CW.12**
**1 September 1997**

## US PROPOSAL

### Article 6. Destruction of anti-personnel mines laid in areas outside minefields

1. Each State Party undertakes to destroy, as soon as possible, all anti-personnel mines laid in areas under its jurisdiction or *long term* control outside minefields.

**APL/CW.13**
**1 September 1997**

## US PROPOSAL

### Article 8. Transparency measures

1. *Each State Party shall report to the Depositary not later than one year after the entry into force of this Convention for that State Party on*:

(a) *the national implementation measures referred to in Article 10;*

(b) *the total of all stockpiled anti-personnel mines owned or possessed by it, or under its jurisdiction or control to include a breakdown of the quantity and lot number of each type of anti-personnel mine stockpiled;*

(c) *the location of all minefields under its jurisdiction or control containing anti-personnel mines, to include the type and quantity of each type of anti-personnel mine in each minefield and when they were emplaced, in so far as possible;*

(d) *to the extent possible, the location of all areas outside minefields in which anti-personnel mines are known or suspected to be present, to include the type and quantity of each type of anti-personnel mine in each area and when they were emplaced, in so far as possible;*

(e) *separate from the reporting required by subparagraph (b), the types and quantities of all anti-personnel mines retained in accordance with paragraph 1 of Article 3 for the development and teaching of mine detection, mine clearance or mine destruction techniques, to include a breakdown identifying locations authorized to store such anti-personnel mines, along with the quantity and lot number of each type of anti-personnel mine stored at each location;*

(f)  *the types and quantities of all anti-personnel mines transferred to another State Party in accordance with paragraph 1 of Article 3 for the purpose of the development and teaching of mine detection, mine clearance or mine destruction techniques, to include, in each case, the date of the transfer, destination, point of origin, and the quantity and lot number of each type of anti-personnel mine transferred;*

(g)  *the types and quantities of all anti-personnel mines transferred to another State Party in accordance with paragraph 2 of Article 3 for the purpose of destruction, to include, in each case, the date of the transfer, destination, point of origin, and the quantity and lot number of each type of anti-personnel mine transferred;*

(h)  *the quantities of anti-personnel mines involved in activities conducted in accordance with paragraph 3 of Article 3;*

(i)  *the status of programmes for the conversion or de-commissioning of anti-personnel mine production facilities:*

(j)  *the status of programmes for the destruction of anti-personnel mines in accordance with Articles 4, 5, and 6, including applicable safety and environmental standards to be observed;*

(k)  *the types and quantities of all anti-personnel mines destroyed, to include a breakdown of the quantity of each type of anti-personnel mine destroyed, in accordance with Articles 4, 5, and 6, respectively, along with the lot number of each type of anti-personnel mine in the case of destruction in accordance with Article 4;*

(l)  *the technical characteristics of each type of anti-personnel mine owned or possessed by a State Party, to include information found in the 'Mine Facts' available from the United Nations, in order to facilitate recognition of anti-personnel mines and their probable manufacturers, and to help facilitate implementation of Article 7; and*

(m)  *the location, to include geographic coordinates, of anti-personnel mine production facilities, as well as notifications of cessation of production of anti-personnel mines at these facilities.*

2.  *The information provided in accordance with this Article shall be updated by the States Parties annually, covering the last calendar year, and reported to the Depositary not later than 1 March.*

3.  *Transparency measures discussed in subparagraphs (b)–(d) of paragraph 1 of this Article shall not apply to mines involved in activities conducted in accordance with paragraph 3 of Article 3.*

**APL/CW.13/Rev.1**
**3 September 1997**

### REVISED US PROPOSAL

**Article 8.  Transparency measures**

1.  Each State Party shall report to the Depositary not later than one year after the entry into force of this Convention for that State Party on:

(a)  the national implementation measures referred to in Article 10;

(b)  *the total* of all stockpiled anti-personnel mines owned or possessed by it, or under its jurisdiction or control, *to include a breakdown of the quantity and lot numbers of each type of anti-personnel mine stockpiled;*

(c)  the location of all minefields under its jurisdiction or control containing anti-personnel mines, *to include the type and quantity of each type of anti-personnel mine in each minefield and when they were emplaced, in so far as possible;*

(d)  *to the extent possible, the location of all areas outside minefields in which anti-personnel mines are known or suspected to be present, to include the type and quantity of each type of anti-personnel mine in each area and when they were emplaced, in so far as possible;*

(e)  *separate from the reporting required by subparagraph (b), the types and quantities of all anti-personnel mines retained in accordance with paragraph 1 of Article 3 for the development and teaching of mine detection, mine clearance or mine destruction techniques, to include a breakdown identifying locations authorized to store such antipersonnel mines, along with the quantity and lot numbers of each type of anti-personnel mine stored at each location;*

(f)  *the types and quantities of all anti-personnel mines transferred to another State Party in accordance with paragraph 1 of Article 3 for the purpose of the development and teaching of mine detection, mine clearance or mine destruction techniques, to include, in each case, the date of the transfer, destination, point of origin, and the quantity and lot numbers of each type of anti-personnel mine transferred;*

(g)  *the types and quantities of all anti-personnel mines transferred to another State Party in accordance with paragraph 2 of Article 3 for the purpose of destruction, to include, in each case, the date of the transfer, destination, point of origin, and the quantity and lot numbers of each type of anti-personnel mine transferred;*

(h)  *the quantities of anti-personnel mines involved in activities conducted in accordance with paragraph 3 of Article 3;*

(i)  the status of programmes for the conversion or de-commissioning of anti-personnel mine production facilities:

(j)  the status of programmes for the destruction of anti-personnel mines in accordance with Articles 4, 5, and 6, including applicable safety and environmental standards to be observed;

(k)  *the types and quantities of all anti-personnel mines destroyed, to include a breakdown of the quantity of each type of anti-personnel mine destroyed, in accordance with Articles 4, 5, and 6, respectively, along with the lot number of each type of anti-personnel mine in the case of destruction in accordance with Article 4;*

(l)  *the technical characteristics of each type of anti-personnel mine owned or possessed by a State Party, to include information found in the 'Mine Facts' available from the United Nations, in order to facilitate recognition of anti-personnel mines and their probable manufacturers, and to help facilitate implementation of Article 7; and*

(m)  *the location, to include geographic coordinates and the names, of anti-personnel mine production facilities that produced anti-personnel mines at any time since*

> *January 1, 1990, as well as notifications of cessation of production of anti-personnel mines at these facilities.*

2. The information provided in accordance with this Article shall be updated by the States Parties annually, covering the last calendar year, and reported to the Depositary not later than 1 March.

3. *Transparency measures discussed in subparagraphs (b), (c) or (d) of paragraph 1 of this Article shall not apply to anti-personnel mines involved in activities conducted in accordance with paragraph 3 of Article 3.*

APL/CW.14
1 September 1997

## US Proposal

### Article 10. National implementation measures

Each State Party shall take all appropriate legal, administrative and other measures, including the imposition of penal sanctions to prevent and suppress any activity prohibited to a State Party under this Convention undertaken *on its territory by natural and legal persons and anywhere else by natural persons possessing its nationality, in conformity with international law.*

APL/CW.15
1 September 1997

## US Proposal

### Article 16. Entry into force

3. In the event that a State Party determines that it cannot immediately comply with the provisions of paragraphs 1(a), 1(b) or Article 1, as they relate to retention, stockpiling, transfer not involving transfer of title to or control over, and use of anti-personnel mines, it may declare at the time of the deposit of its instrument of ratification, acceptance, approval or accession to the Convention that it will defer compliance with those provisions for a period not to excess [sic] nine years from the entry into force of this convention.

APL/CW.16
1 September 1997

## US Proposal

### Article 17. Reservations

The U.S. delegation proposes the deletion of this article.

APL/CW.17
1 September 1997

## US Proposal

**Article 18. Duration and withdrawal**

2. . . . notice of such withdrawal *90 days* in advance to all . . .

3. In case a State Party should withdraw from this Convention, the withdrawal shall only take effect *90 days* after receipt of the instrument of withdrawal by the Depositary. ~~If, however, on the expiry of that year the withdrawing State Party is engaged in an armed conflict the withdrawal shall not take effect before the end of the armed conflict.~~

APL/CW.18
2 September 1997

## Japan Proposal for Amendment

**Article 4**

**Add the following underlined phrase to the present Article 4.**

*Without prejudice to the rules and practices of international law*, each State Party undertakes to destroy all stockpiled anti-personnel mines it owns or possesses, or that are under its jurisdiction or control, . . .

APL/CW.19
2 September 1997

## Japan Proposal for Amendment

**Article 8**

1. **Add the following underlined phrases to the present Article 8.1 (b), (c) and (d).**

(b) *to the extent possible under the rules and practices of international law*, the types and quantities of all stockpiled anti-personnel mines . . .

(c) *to the extent possible under the rules and practices of international law*, the location of all minefields . . .

(d) *to the extent possible under the rules and practices of international law*, the location of all areas outside minefields . . .

2. **Delete Article 8. 1 (g) and provide a following new Article 6 bis.**

**Article 6 bis**

Each State Party, during the destruction of anti-personnel mines, shall assign the highest priority to ensuring the safety of the people and to protecting the environment. Each State Party shall destroy anti-personnel mines in accordance with its national standards for safety and emissions.

**APL/CW.20**
**2 September 1997**

JAPAN PROPOSAL FOR AMENDMENT

Provide the following new *Article 9 bis.*

**Article 9 bis Measures, including sanctions to redress a situation and to ensure compliance**

1. The meeting of the State Parties shall take the necessary measures, as set forth in paragraphs 2, 3 and 4, to ensure compliance with this Convention and to redress and remedy any situation which contravenes the provisions of this Convention.

2. In case of non-compliance by a State Party, the Meeting of the States Parties may restrict or suspend that State Party's rights and privileges under this Convention until it undertakes necessary actions to conform with its obligations under this Convention.

3. In cases where serious damage to the object and purpose of this Convention may result from activities prohibited under this Convention, the Meeting of the States Parties may recommend collective measures to States Parties in conformity with international law.

4. The Meeting of the States Parties shall in cases of particular gravity bring the issue, including relevant information and conclusions, to the attention of the United Nations General Assembly and the United Nations Security Council.

5. The Meeting of the States Parties shall take decisions on taking the necessary measures of paragraphs 2, 3 and 4 as far as possible by consensus. If consensus is not attainable when an issue comes up for decision, the Chairman of the Meeting of the States Parties shall defer any vote for 24 hours and during this period of deferment shall make every effort to facilitate achievement of consensus, and shall report to the Meeting before the end of this period. If consensus is not possible at the end of 24 hours, the Meeting of States Parties shall take the decision by two-thirds majority of members present and voting.

**APL/CW.21**
**2 September 1997**

PROPOSED CHILE AMENDMENT

Chile proposes the following amendment:

Article 18

Duration and withdrawal

Replace paragraphs 2 and 3:

'Each State Party shall, in exercising its national sovereignty, have the right to withdraw from this Protocol. It shall give notice of such withdrawal six months in advance to all other States Parties and to the Depositary. The withdrawal shall only take effect six months after receipt of the instrument of withdrawal by the Depositary.'

**APL/CW.22**
**2 September 1997**

### Proposal of France

The States Parties

- Strongly determined to put an end to the humanitarian disaster caused by the proliferation and indiscriminate use against civilian populations of anti-personnel mines,
- Recalling the determination shown by the international community, particularly through United Nations General Assembly resolutions 49/75 D, 50/70 0 and 51/45 S, to achieve a definitive ban on anti-personnel mines,
- Welcoming the recent measures taken over the past years, both unilaterally and multilaterally, aiming at prohibiting, restricting or suspending the use, stockpiling, production and transfer of anti-personnel mines,
- Welcoming also the adoption, on May 3rd 1996, of the revised Protocol 2 to the Convention on prohibitions or restrictions on the use of certain conventional weapons which may be deemed to be excessively injurious or to have indiscriminate effects, and calling for the early ratification of this protocol by all countries who have not yet done so,
- Recognising the complementary efforts undertaken in the Conference on disarmament towards achieving a world-wide solution for the total and definitive elimination of anti-personnel mines,
- Recalling the Ottawa declaration of October 5th 1996 urging the international community to negotiate an international and legally binding agreement prohibiting the use, stockpiling, production and transfer of anti-personnel mines,
- Convinced of the necessity to conclude such an agreement to prohibit as soon as possible all anti-personnel mines,

Have agreed as follows:

**APL/CW.23**
**2 September 1997**

### Proposal of Germany

**Article 7, para 6**

Each State Party receiving assistance under the provisions of this article shall cooperate with a view to ensuring the full and prompt implementation of agreed assistance programmes.

It shall in particular effectively assist seconded experts, provide its own contribution in good time and ensure immediate and cost-free customs clearance of all material supplied on behalf of the assisting party.

**APL/CW.24**
**2 September 1997**

PROPOSAL OF GERMANY

**Annex on Clarification**

1. The fact finding mission stipulated in article 9 of the Treaty shall be undertaken by a team of experts.

2. To this end the Depositary shall prepare and update a list of qualified experts provided by Parties and communicate it to all Parties. Any expert not objected by a Party within 30 days after communication of this list shall be regarded as designated.

3. Upon receiving a request from the Meeting of States Parties the Depositary shall appoint a team of no more than five designated experts, one of them as team leader. Nationals of Parties requesting the enquiry or concerned by it shall not be appointed. The team shall have diplomatic immunity.

4. The Depositary shall dispatch the team of experts at the earliest opportunity and shall notify the host State Party at least 48 hours before the team is expected to arrive. The host State Party shall make the necessary arrangements including administrative decisions to receive, transport and accommodate the team of experts. It shall be responsible for ensuring the security of the team of experts at all times while they are on territory under its control.

5. The team of experts may bring the equipment necessary to be used exclusively for gathering information on the alleged compliance issue. The list of the equipment will be adopted by the Meeting of the States Parties.

6. After arrival, the team may hear statements by official representatives of the Party and question persons connected with the alleged compliance issue.

7. The host State Party shall grant access for the team of experts to all areas and installations under its control where facts relevant to the compliance issue could be expected to be collected. The team of experts may collect samples of relevant mines as well as copies of documents relevant to them. It may enter minefields at its discretion.

These rights shall be subject to any arrangements that the Party concerned considers necessary for:

- the protection of sensitive equipment, information and areas;
- the protection of any constitutional obligations the Party concerned may have with regard to proprietary rights, searches and seizures, or other constitutional rights,
- the physical protection and safety of the team of experts;

In the event that any of these arrangements apply, the Party concerned shall make every effort to satisfy the legitimate needs of the team of experts through other means.

8. The team of experts may remain in the territory of the Party concerned for no more than two weeks, and at any particular site no more than one week unless otherwise agreed.

9. All costs of the team of experts shall be covered by the States Parties in accordance with the United Nations scale of assessments adjusted appropriately.

**APL/CW.25**
**2 September 1997**

## Proposal of Germany

### Article 9. Facilitation and clarification of compliance

1. The States Parties agree to consult and cooperate with each other regarding the implementation of the provisions of this Convention, and to facilitate compliance by States Parties with their obligations under this Convention.

2. If one or more State Parties wish to clarify and seek to resolve questions relating to compliance with the provisions of this Convention by another State Party, it may submit, through the Depositary, a request for Clarification of that matter to that State Party. Such a request shall be accompanied by all *appropriate* information. *Each State Party shall refrain from unfounded Requests for Clarification, care being taken to avoid abuse.* A State Party that receives a request for Clarification shall provide through the Depositary, within *21* days to the requesting State Party all information which would assist in clarifying this matter.

3. If the requesting State Party does not receive a response through the Depositary within the time period provided for in paragraph 2, or deems the response to the request for Clarification to be unsatisfactory, it may submit, through the Depositary, the matter to a Meeting of the State Parties. This submission shall include all *appropriate* information. The meeting of State Parties shall consider the matter at its next meeting and *hold an enquiry if at least one third of the States Parties agrees.*

4. The requesting State Party may propose to the Depositary to convene a Special Meeting of the States Parties to *hold an inquiry.* The Depositary shall thereupon communicate this proposal to the States Parties with a request that they indicate whether they favour a Special Meeting of States Parties, for the purpose of considering the matter. In the event that within *14* days from the date of such communication, at least one third of the States Parties favours such a Special Meeting, the Depositary shall convene this Special Meeting of the State Parties *in New York within two weeks to hold an inquiry.*

5. All States Parties shall cooperate fully with the Meeting of States Parties in the fulfillment of its review of the matter.

6. *The Meeting of States Parties shall make every effort to reach its decisions by consensus, otherwise by a majority of Parties present and voting unless stipulated otherwise herein. Upon request of a State Party it shall authorize in the framework of its inquiry a fact-finding mission to collect additional information on the spot or in other places directly related to the alleged compliance issue under the jurisdiction or control of the concerned State Party unless a two-third majority of Parties present and voting decides otherwise.*

*7. The fact-finding mission shall proceed in accordance with Annex 1 to this Treaty (Annex on Clarification). It shall report, through the Depositary, to the States Parties and the Meeting of the States Parties the results of its findings.*

*8. The Meetings of States Parties shall consider all relevant information and facts available, including the report submitted by the team of experts. It may request the concerned State Party to take measures to redress the situation within a specified time. The State Party shall report to the Meeting of State Parties within the specified time on the measures it has taken to redress the situation. If the concerned State Party fails to fulfill this request within the specified time, a Meeting of States Parties may recommend to States Parties measures which are in conformity with international law. The meeting of States Parties may bring the issue, including relevant information, to the attention of the United Nations.*

**APL/CW.26**
**2 September 1997**

## Proposal of Cambodia

**Article 2. Definitions**

5. 'Minefield' is a ***clearly mapped*** area in which mines have been emplaced.

**APL/CW.27**
**2 September 1997**

## Proposal of Slovenia

**Article 11. Settlement of disputes**

1. The States Parties shall settle any dispute (between them) that may arise concerning the interpretation or application of this Convention by peaceful means in accordance with the (relevant) provisions of this Convention and in conformity with the provisions of the Charter of the United Nations (Article 2, paragraph 3 of the Charter of the United Nations and, to this end shall seek a solution by means indicated in Article 33 paragraph 1 of the Charter of the United Nations).

2. When a dispute arises between two or more States Parties concerning the interpretation or application of this Convention, the parties to the dispute shall consult together with a view to the expeditious settlement of the dispute by negotiations, or by other peaceful means of the parties' choice, including recourse to the Meeting of the State Parties and, by mutual consent, referral to the International Court of Justice in conformity with the Statute of the Court.

3. The States Parties involved in a dispute shall report any such dispute to the Meeting of the States Parties and keep it informed of actions being taken.

4. The Meeting of the States Parties shall contribute to the settlement of a dispute by offering its good offices, calling upon States Parties to a dispute to start the

settlement procedure of their choice and recommending a time limit for any agreed procedure.

**APL/CW.28**
**2 September 1997**

## Proposal of Slovenia

**Preamble (Amendment)**

**The States Parties,**

- Understanding anti-personnel mines as a primarily defence weapon, their total prohibition is to be observed as an important confidence building measure.

**APL/CW.29**
**2 September 1997**

## Proposal of Brazil

**Article 7 bis Research and development in mine clearance technology**

1. A program of research and development in mine clearance technology shall be constituted upon entry into force of this Convention.

2. The program shall be financed by contributions to the United Nations Voluntary Trust Fund for Assistance in Mine Clearance or direct contributions thereto.

3. The Depositary shall be responsible for the program and shall submit annual reports on its implementation to the meetings of States Parties.

4. The States Parties shall have unrestricted access to the research carried out through the Program. Upon request of a State Party, any development in mine clearance technology or knowledge achieved through the program shall be transferred to the requesting State Party on a non-commercial basis.

**APL/CW.30**
**2 September 1997**

## Proposal of Brazil

**Article 7 ter**

1. Upon its ratification of, or accession to, this convention, each State Party shall declare to the Depositary whether it has mines laid in areas outside minefields. In case such mines exist, the concerned State Party may request the United Nations, Regional Organisations or other competent intergovernmental fora to assist its authorities in the elaboration of a National Demining Program.

2. The National Demining Program shall determine, inter alia:

(a) the number of years necessary to destroy all anti-personnel mines laid in areas outside minefields under the jurisdiction or control of the concerned State Party;

(b) the financial, technological and human resources that are required for the implementation of the Program;

(c) the appropriate relationship between the Government of the concerned State Party and the relevant governmental, inter-governmental or nongovernmental entities that will work in the implementation of the Program.

**APL/CW.30/Rev.1**
**3 September 1997**

PROPOSAL OF BRAZIL

**Article 7 ter**

1. A State Party in whose territory there are mines laid outside minefields may request the United Nations, Regional Organisations or other competent intergovernmental or non-governmental fora to assist its authorities in the elaboration of a National Demining Program to determine, inter alia:

(a) the extent and scope of the problem;

(b) the financial, technological and human resources that are required for the implementation of the Program;

(c) the estimated number of years necessary to destroy all anti-personnel mines laid in areas outside minefields under the jurisdiction or control of the concerned State Party;

(d) mine awareness activities to reduce the incidence of mine related injuries or deaths;

(e) assistance to victims of landmines;

(f) the appropriate relationship between the Government of the concerned State Party and the relevant governmental, inter-governmental or non-governmental entities that will work in the implementation of the Program.

**APL/CW.31**
**2 September 1997**

PROPOSAL OF UNITED KINGDOM

The United Kingdom proposes the replacement of Article 8 of the draft Treaty with the following:

1. Each State Party shall report to the Depositary as soon as practicable and, in any event, not later than ninety days after the entry into force of this Convention for that the State Party on:

(a) The National implementation measures referred to in Article 10;

(b) Full technical details, including specifications of the dimensions, fusing and explosive content of all anti-personnel mines manufactured by or on behalf of the State Party, or in use, or intended to be used, by the State Party, together with photographs and details of the procedures used to render safe such anti-personnel mines;

(c) the location, including details of the types and quantities at each location, of all stock-piled anti-personnel mines owned or possessed by it, or under its control;

(d) the location of all minefields under its control containing anti-personnel land-mines, including as much detail as possible of the types and quantities of anti-personnel mines in each minefield;

(e) to the extent possible, the location of all areas outside minefields in which anti-personnel mines are known or suspected to be present, including as much detail as possible of the types and quantities of anti-personnel mines known or suspected to be present at each location;

(f) the measures taken to provide an immediate and effective warning to the population in relation to any areas identified under Article 6.2;

(g) [paragraph (e) of the third Austrian draft]

(h) [paragraph (f) of the third Austrian draft]

(j) the status of programmes for the destruction of anti-personnel mines in accordance with Articles 4, 5, and 6, including details of the methods which will be used in destruction, the location of all destruction sites and the applicable safety and environmental standards to be observed.

2. The information provided in accordance with this Article shall be updated annually by each State Party in respect of the previous calendar year. Such updated reports shall be submitted to the Secretary General of the United Nations by 1 March of each year. The Secretary General of the United Nations shall transmit all such reports received by him to the States Parties.

**APL/CW.32**
**2 September 1997**

### PROPOSAL OF UNITED KINGDOM

The United Kingdom proposes the following amendment to Article 2, paragraph 3 of the draft Treaty:

'. . . tamper with *or otherwise disturb* the mine'.

**APL/CW.33**
**2 September 1997**

### PROPOSAL OF UNITED KINGDOM

The United Kingdom proposes the following revision to paragraph 1 of Article 13 of the draft Treaty:

1. A Review Conference shall be convened by the Secretary General of the United Nations five years after the entry into force of this Convention. *Further Review Conferences shall be convened by the Secretary General of the United Nations if so requested by one or more State Parties, provided that the interval between Review Conferences*

*shall in no case be less than 5 years*. All States Parties to this Convention shall be invited to *each* Review Conference.

**APL/CW.34**
**2 September 1997**

### Proposal of United Kingdom

The United Kingdom proposes the following addition to Article 15:

This Convention is subject to ratification, acceptance or approval of the signatories. Any State which has not signed this Convention before its entry into force may accede to it at any time thereafter.

**APL/CW.35**
**2 September 1997**

### Proposal of Austria

**Article 13 bis Amendments**

1. At any time after the entry into force of this Convention any State Party may propose amendments to this Convention. Any proposal for an amendment shall be communicated to the Depositary, who shall circulate it to all States Parties and shall seek their views on whether an Amendment Conference should be convened to consider the proposal. If a majority of the States Parties notify the Depositary no later than 30 days after its circulation that they support further consideration of the proposal, the Depositary shall convene an Amendment Conference to which all States Parties shall be invited.

2. States not parties to this Convention, as well as the United Nations, other relevant international organizations or institutions, regional organizations, the International Committee of the Red Cross and relevant non-governmental organizations may be invited to attend the Amendment Conference as observers in accordance with the agreed Rules of Procedure.

3. The Amendment Conference shall be held immediately following a Meeting of the States Parties or a Review Conference unless a majority of the States Parties request that it be held earlier.

4. Any amendment to this Convention shall be adopted by a majority of two thirds of the States Parties present and voting at the Amendment Conference or at the Review Conference dealing with the amendment. The Depositary shall communicate any amendment so adopted to the States Parties.

5. An amendment to this Convention shall enter into force for all States Parties to this Convention which have accepted it, upon the deposit with the Depositary of instruments of acceptance by a majority of States Parties. Thereafter it shall enter

into force for any remaining State Party on the date of deposit of its instrument of acceptance.

## APL/CW.36
## 2 September 1997

### PROPOSAL OF AUSTRIA

**Article 18**

. . .

2. Each State Party shall, in exercising its national sovereignty, have the right to withdraw from this Convention if it decides that extraordinary events, related to the subject-matter of this Convention, have jeopardized the supreme interests of its country. It shall give notice of such withdrawal one year in advance to all other States Parties, to the Depositary and to the United Nations Security Council. Such **instrument of withdrawal** shall include a statement of the extraordinary events it regards as having jeopardized its supreme interests.

3. In case a State Party **proceeds as described in paragraph 2,** the withdrawal from this Convention shall __ take effect one year after **the** receipt of the instrument of withdrawal by the Depositary. If, however, on the expiry of that year the withdrawing State Party is engaged in an armed conflict, **its obligations under this Convention** shall not **cease** before the end of the armed conflict.

## APL/CW.37
## 2 September 1997

### PROPOSAL OF AUSTRIA

**Article 15**

1. This Convention is subject to ratification, acceptance or approval of the Signatories. **It shall be open for accession by any State not signatory.**

2. **The instruments of ratification, acceptance, approval or accession shall be deposited with the Depositary.**

## APL/CW.38
## 2 September 1997

### PROPOSAL OF AUSTRIA

**Article 14**

This Convention shall be open for signature **at Ottawa, Canada, by** all States **from 3 December 1997 until 4 December 1997, and at the United Nations Headquarters in New York from 5 December 1997 until** its entry into force.

APL/CW.39
2 September 1997

## PROPOSAL OF AUSTRIA

### Article 13 ter Costs

1. The costs of the Meetings of the States Parties, the Special Meetings of the States Parties, the Review Conferences and the Amendment Conferences shall be borne by the States Parties and States not parties to this Convention participating therein, in accordance with the United Nations scale of assessment adjusted appropriately.

2. The costs incurred by the Secretary-General of the United Nations under Articles 8 and 9 shall be borne by the States Parties in accordance with the United Nations scale of assessment adjusted appropriately.

APL/CW.40
2 September 1997

## PROPOSAL OF EL SALVADOR

As we indicated at the time of the Brussels meeting, this Protocol should address the humanitarian aspect, specifically in respect of aid to victims of anti-personnel mines. We must think of those who are already living out this tragedy, as well as of those who will unfortunately fall into the tragic trap of mines still in existence. In this sense, we recall what was expressed by Ambassador Mernier, who in his report affirmed that aid to victims should be an integral part of the Protocol under discussion.

And so, the Delegation of El Salvador proposes that Article 7 might be drafted as follows:

### Article 7
### International Cooperation and Assistance with the Destruction of Mines and Rehabilitation of Victims of Accidents with Anti-Personnel Mines

In Numeral 4, the following alternative wording is proposed:

'Each State Party in a position to do so shall lend assistance in the destruction of stockpiled anti-personnel mines, whenever one of the States Parties officially solicits such assistance.'

6. 'The States Parties in a position to contribute to an integral solution of the grave consequences inflicted on former combatants and civilian persons who fall victim to mine accidents, will provide financial cooperation and assistance to other States Parties who need them, with the aim of contributing to the efforts being extended by the latter through the local programs they are implementing, or are about to implement, for the physical and psychological rehabilitation of the victims of anti-personnel mine accidents.'

APL/CW.41
2 September 1997

## Proposal of Sweden

**New article 14**

Under article 13(b) of the Austrian draft, Review Conferences may consider proposals for amendments. The procedure for amendments needs to be specified in the Convention. The following is therefore proposed:

### Article 14. Amendments

1. State Parties may propose amendments to this Convention. The depositary shall communicate any proposed amendments to the State Parties. Unless, within six months of the communication of a proposal for such amendments, one third of the State Parties object, the Depositary shall convene a meeting of experts open to all State Parties to study the proposal or proposals and to forward their recommendations to the Review Conference. The meeting of technical experts shall strive to agree on their recommendations by consensus. Should a consensus prove impossible to achieve, the meeting of technical experts may adopt their recommendations by a majority of two thirds of those participating in the meeting.

2. States which have not ratified the Convention, the United Nations, the UNHCR, UNICEF and the ICRC shall be invited to attend the meeting of technical experts as observers with the right to make their views known orally or in writing.

3. The Review Conference may adopt the proposed amendments by a majority of two thirds of the State Parties.

4. The depositary shall communicate any amendment so adopted to the State Parties. An amendment shall be considered to have been accepted at the end of one year after having been so communicated, unless, within that period, a declaration of non-acceptance of the amendment has been communicated to the Depositary by not less than one third of the State Parties.

APL/CW.42
2 September 1997

## Proposal of Switzerland

**Article 10**

New paragraph

Each State Party shall search for any national of a State party alleged to have used or to have ordered to use anti-personnel mines and shall have a person tried by its courts. It also may, in accordance with its legislation, hand over such a person for trial to another State Party concerned or such international tribunal as may have jurisdiction.

**APL/CW.42/Rev.1**
**9 September 1997**

## Proposal of Switzerland

**Article 10**

New paragraph 2

Each State Party shall search for persons suspected to have used, or to have ordered the use of, anti-personnel mines and shall have persons tried by its courts, whatever their nationality. It may also, in accordance with its legislation, extradite them to another State Party concerned or hand them over to such international criminal tribunal as may have jurisdiction.

**APL/CW.43**
**2 September 1997**

## Proposal of Ecuador

**Article 8**

(h) the quantities of mines produced, exported and/or re-exported to other States, indicating the final destination of such exports.

**APL/CW.44**
**2 September 1997**

## Proposal of Ecuador

**Article 18**

2. Each State Party, in the exercise of its national sovereignty, shall have the right to renounce this Protocol if it determines that extraordinary events, relating to the very subject of this Protocol, have imperilled the paramount interests of its country. It shall notify its renunciation to the Depositary, including a statement of the extraordinary events which have put its paramount interests at risk.

3. ELIMINATE.

**APL/CW.45**
**3 September 1997**

## Revised US Proposal

**Article 5. Destruction of anti-personnel mines laid within minefields**

1. Each State Party undertakes to destroy all anti-personnel mines laid within minefields under its jurisdiction or *long-term* control, as soon as possible but not later than ten years after the entry into force of this Convention for that State Party.

2. Minefields where anti-personnel mines have been laid shall, until all anti-personnel mines contained therein have been destroyed, be perimeter-marked, monitored and protected by fencing or other means, to ensure effective exclusion of civilians. The marking must be of a distinct and durable character and must at least be visible to a person who is about to enter the minefield. *Such marking shall comply with paragraph 4 of the Technical Annex to the Protocol on Prohibitions or Restrictions on the Use of Mines, Booby-Traps and Other Devices as Amended on 3 May 1996.*

**APL/CW.46**
**3 September 1997**

## PROPOSAL OF COLOMBIA

**Article 10 bis. Relation to other international agreements**

Nothing in this Convention shall be invoked as in any way limiting or detracting from the obligations assumed by any State Party under all applicable norms of International Humanitarian Law. In particular, this Convention shall apply to situations and to parties mentioned in article 3 common to the Geneva Conventions of 12 August 1949 and their additional Protocols of 1977.

**APL/CW.47**
**2 September 1997**

## PROPOSAL OF BELGIUM

**Article 16 bis**

The States Parties to this Convention decide on its provisional application from the time of their ratification, acceptance, approval or accession pending its entry into force.

*Rationale: this possibility is open by the article 25 of the Vienna Convention on the Law of Treaties (1969).*

**APL/CW.47/Rev.1**
**3 September 1997**

## REVISED PROPOSAL OF BELGIUM

**Article 16 bis**

Pending the entry into force of this Convention, article 1 will be applied provisionally by the States at the time of the deposit of their instrument of ratification, acceptance, approval or accession.

*Rationale: this possibility is open by the article 25 of the Vienna Convention on the Law of Treaties (1969).*

APL/CW.47/Rev.2
9 September 1997

## REVISED PROPOSAL OF BELGIUM

**Article 16 bis**

Any State may at the time of its ratification, acceptance, approval or accession, declare that it will apply provisionally paragraph 1 of Article 1 of this Convention pending its entry into force.


APL/CW.48
3 September 1997

## PROPOSAL OF JAPAN

**Article 2**

*For the purposes of this Convention,*

1. 'Anti-personnel mine' means . . .


APL/CW.49
3 September 1997

## PROPOSAL OF SLOVENIA

**Article 13. Review Conferences (Amendment)**

2. The Purpose of the Review Conference shall be:

(d) To adopt, if necessary, in its Final Report, conclusions related to the implementation of this Convention.


APL/CW.50
3 September 1997

## PROPOSAL OF JAPAN

**Article 2**

5. 'Minefield' is *an area in which mines have been emplaced and the perimeter of which is shown by the State Party which has jurisdiction or control over the area through fencing or other means marking its perimeter and recording of its location or other means. In cases where another State Party can show an area with its perimeter in which mines have been emplaced and the Meeting of State Parties approves of it, such area will also be deemed as a minefield.*

APL/CW.51
10 September 1997

## Proposal of Austria

### Article 11. Settlement of disputes

1. The States Parties **shall** consult and cooperate with each other to **settle** any **dispute** that may arise with regard to the application **or the** interpretation of this Convention. Each State Party may **bring** any such **dispute before** the Meeting of the States Parties.

2. The Meeting of the States Parties **may contribute to the settlement of the dispute by whatever means it deems appropriate, including offering its good offices, calling upon the States Parties to a dispute to start the settlement procedure of their choice and recommending a time-limit for any agreed procedure.**

3. **This Article is without prejudice to the provisions of this Convention on facilitation and clarification of compliance.**

APL/CW.51/Corr.1
10 September 1997

## Proposal of Austria and Slovenia

### Article 11. Settlement of disputes

1. The States Parties **shall** consult and cooperate with each other to **settle** any **dispute** that may arise with regard to the application **or the** interpretation of this Convention. Each State Party may **bring** any such **dispute before** the Meeting of the States Parties.

2. The Meeting of the States Parties **may contribute to the settlement of the dispute by whatever means it deems appropriate, including offering its good offices, calling upon the States Parties to a dispute to start the settlement procedure of their choice and recommending a time-limit for any agreed procedure.**

3. **This Article is without prejudice to the provisions of this Convention on facilitation and clarification of compliance.**

# APPENDIX 6

# Meetings of the States Parties Documentation

## FIRST MEETING OF STATES PARTIES
## (MAPUTO, 3–7 MAY 1999)

### FINAL REPORT

APLC/MSP.1/1999/1 of 20 May 1999

The Final Report of the First Meeting of the States Parties to the Convention on the Prohibition of the Use, Stockpiling, Production and Transfer of Anti Personnel Mines and on Their Destruction consists of two parts and five annexes as follows:

I.  Organization and Work of the First Meeting
II.  Maputo Declaration

Annexes:
    Annex I: List of Documents
    Annex II: Reporting Formats for Article 7
    Annex III: President's Paper on Circulation of Article 7 Reports
    Annex IV: President's Paper on Intersessional Work
    Annex V: Statement by His Excellency Mr. Joaquim Alberto Chissano, President of the Republic of Mozambique, at the opening ceremony of the First Meeting

### Part I.  Organization and Work of the First Meeting

#### A.  Introduction

1. The Convention on the Prohibition of the Use, Stockpiling, Production and Transfer of Anti Personnel Mines and on Their Destruction provides in Article 11, paragraphs 1 and 2:

'1.  The States Parties shall meet regularly in order to consider any matter with regard to the application or implementation of this Convention, including:

(a)  The operation and status of this Convention;
(b)  Matters arising from the reports submitted under the provisions of this Convention;
(c)  International cooperation and assistance in accordance with Article 6;
(d)  The development of technologies to clear anti personnel mines;
(e)  Submissions of States Parties under Article 8; and
(f)  Decisions relating to submissions of States Parties as provided for in Article 5.

'2. The First Meeting of the States Parties shall be convened by the Secretary General of the United Nations within one year after the entry into force of this Convention. The subsequent meetings shall be convened by the Secretary General of the United Nations annually until the First Review Conference.'

2. At its fifty third session, the General Assembly of the United Nations in resolution 53/77 N welcomed the generous offer by the Government of the Republic of Mozambique to act as host for the First Meeting of the States Parties, and requested the Secretary General, in accordance with Article 11, paragraph 2, of the Convention, to undertake the preparations necessary to convene the First Meeting of the States Parties, to take place in Maputo during the week of 3 May 1999.

3. To prepare for the First Meeting, States Parties convened two rounds of open ended informal consultations at the Palais des Nations, Geneva, to which they also invited States not parties to the Convention, as well as the United Nations, other relevant international organizations or institutions, regional organizations, the International Committee of the Red Cross and relevant non governmental organizations.

4. The first round of informal consultations was held on 1 March 1999, the day the Convention entered into force. During the consultations, participants considered a number of issues relating to the organization of the First Meeting including papers containing a draft provisional agenda, a draft programme of work, draft rules of procedure, and provisional estimated costs for convening the First Meeting. No objections were raised in connection with any of the papers considered and it was agreed that they would be finalized in all six languages of the Convention to be put before the First Meeting.

5. The second set of informal consultations took place on 13 April 1999. At that meeting, participants reviewed elements for a proposed draft political declaration to be issued on the occasion of the First Meeting; possible modalities for intersessional work under the Convention; practical ways of circulating the reports to be submitted under Article 7 of the Convention; and the issue of the venue and format of future meetings of the States Parties.

## B. Organization of the First Meeting

6. The First Meeting was opened on 3 May 1999 by His Excellency Mr. Joaquim Alberto Chissano, President of the Republic of Mozambique. The opening statement of the President of the Republic of Mozambique is contained in annex V to this report. The First Meeting elected by acclamation the Minister of Foreign Affairs and Cooperation of the Republic of Mozambique, Dr. Leonardo Santos Simão, as its President in accordance with rule 7 of the Draft Rules of Procedure.

7. At the opening session, statements were made by Mrs. Louise Fréchette, Deputy Secretary General of the United Nations; Dr. Salim Ahmed Salim, Secretary General of the Organization of African Unity; His Royal Highness Prince Zeid Ra'ad Zeid Al Hussein delivering a message to the First Meeting from Her Majesty Queen Noor of the Hashemite Kingdom of Jordan; Ms. Jody Williams, Ambassador for the International Campaign to Ban Landmines; and Ms. Fárida Gulamo of the Mozambican

Campaign Against Landmines. In addition, the President of the Meeting read a message addressed to the First Meeting by the President of the United States of America, Mr. William Jefferson Clinton.

8. At its first plenary meeting, on 3 May 1999, the First Meeting adopted its agenda as contained in document APLC/MSP.1/1999/L.1. On the same occasion, the First Meeting adopted its Rules of Procedure as contained in document APLC/MSP.1/ 1999/L.3, the estimated costs for convening the First Meeting as contained in document APLC/MSP.1/1999/L.5, and its programme of work as contained in document APLC/MSP.1/1999/L.2.

9. Also at its first plenary meeting, the Meeting elected by acclamation the representatives of Honduras, Jordan, Norway and Turkmenistan as Vice Presidents of the First Meeting in accordance with rule 7 of the Rules of Procedure.

10. The Meeting unanimously confirmed the nomination of Mr. Carlos dos Santos, Ambassador and Permanent Representative of the Republic of Mozambique to the United Nations in New York, as the Secretary General of the Meeting. The nomination had been the result of informal consultations among States Parties.

### C. Participation and Credentials in the First Meeting

11. Forty three States Parties participated in the Meeting: Austria, Belgium, Benin, Bolivia, Bosnia and Herzegovina, Bulgaria, Burkina Faso, Canada, Croatia, Denmark, France, Germany, Guinea, Holy See, Honduras, Hungary, Ireland, Jamaica, Japan, Jordan, Malawi, Mali, Mauritius, Mexico, Mozambique, Namibia, Nicaragua, Norway, Panama, Paraguay, Peru, San Marino, Senegal, Slovenia, South Africa, Sweden, Switzerland, Thailand, The former Yugoslav Republic of Macedonia, Turkmenistan, United Kingdom of Great Britain and Northern Ireland, Yemen and Zimbabwe.

12. Eighteen States which had ratified the Convention, but for which the Convention had not yet entered into force, participated in the Meeting as observers, in accordance with Article 11, paragraph 4, of the Convention and rule 1, paragraph 1, second sentence, of the Rules of Procedure of the Meeting: Antigua and Barbuda, Australia, Brazil, Chad, Ecuador, El Salvador, Guatemala, Italy, Lesotho, Malaysia, the Netherlands, New Zealand, Niger, Portugal, Slovakia, Spain, Swaziland and Uganda.

13. A further forty seven States not parties to the Convention participated in the Meeting as observers, in accordance with Article 11, paragraph 4, of the Convention and rule 1, paragraph 1, second sentence, of the Rules of Procedure of the Meeting: Albania, Algeria, Angola, Argentina, Bangladesh, Burundi, Cambodia, Cameroon, Cape Verde, Chile, China, Colombia, Côte d'Ivoire, Cuba, Cyprus, Czech Republic, Dominican Republic, Ethiopia, Finland, Gabon, Georgia, Ghana, Greece, Iceland, Indonesia, Israel, Kazakhstan, Kenya, Libyan Arab Jamahiriya, Lithuania, Luxembourg, Mauritania, Morocco, Nepal, Philippines, Poland, Romania, Rwanda, Saint Vincent and the Grenadines, Singapore, Sri Lanka, Sudan, Togo, Turkey, Ukraine, United Republic of Tanzania and Zambia.

14. Credentials issued by the Head of State or Government or by the Minister for Foreign Affairs or by a person authorized by one of the above, as required by rule 4 of the Rules of Procedure of the Meeting, or credentials in the form of photocopies or facsimiles of such a document, or credentials in the form of information concerning the appointment of representatives to the Meeting received in the form of letters or notes verbales or facsimiles thereof from embassies, permanent missions to the United Nations or other intergovernmental organizations or other government offices or authorities, were received from all 108 States mentioned in paragraphs 11 through 13 above.

15. The Meeting accepted the credentials of the representatives of all of the States mentioned in paragraphs 11 through 13 above.

16. In accordance with Article 11, paragraph 4, of the Convention and rule 1, paragraphs 2 and 3, of the Rules of Procedure, the following international organizations and institutions, regional organizations, entities and non governmental organizations attended the Meeting as observers: Palestine, United Nations, United Nations Children's Fund, United Nations Development Programme, United Nations Office for Project Services, World Food Programme, United Nations High Commissioner for Refugees, United Nations Institute for Disarmament Research, World Health Organization, European Commission, Organization of African Unity, Organization of American States, International Organization of The Francophonie, International Committee of the Red Cross, International Federation of Red Cross and Red Crescent Societies, Sovereign Military Order of Malta and International Campaign to Ban Landmines.

17. A list of all delegations to the First Meeting is contained in document APLC/MSP.1/1999/INF.1.

## D. Work of the First Meeting

18. The First Meeting held seven plenary meetings from 3 to 7 May, when it concluded its work.

19. The first four plenary meetings were devoted to the general exchange of views under agenda item 10. Eighty three delegations to the First Meeting made statements in the general exchange of views.

20. At the fifth plenary meeting, on 5 May 1999, the Meeting considered the submission of requests under Article 5 of the Convention. The President informed the Meeting that he had not been notified that any State wished to make such a request at the First Meeting. The Meeting took note of this.

21. At the same meeting, the Meeting considered the submission of requests under Article 8 of the Convention. The President informed the Meeting that he had not been notified that any State wished to make such a request at the First Meeting. The Meeting took note of this.

22. In addition to the plenary meetings, the Meeting held informal consultations on issues related to the operation of the Convention. These included the consideration of

international cooperation and assistance in accordance with Article 6 on the topics of mine clearance, victim assistance, socio economic reintegration and mine awareness, destruction of stockpiled anti personnel mines, and development of technologies for mine action.

### E. Decisions and recommendations

23. At its fifth plenary meeting, on 5 May 1999, the Meeting considered matters arising from and in the context of reports to be submitted under Article 7, including consideration and adoption of the reporting formats. The reporting formats were adopted as amended and are contained in annex II to this report.

24. At its sixth plenary meeting, on 6 May 1999, the Meeting agreed that the content of the President's Paper on Circulation of Article 7 Reports as amended (APLC/MSP.1/1999/Informal 3/Rev.1) should guide the technical ways and means of circulation of the reports. That Paper is contained in annex III to this report.

25. Following consultations on the President's Paper on Intersessional Work (APLC/MSP.1/1999/Informal 2), the Meeting recognized the importance of having intersessional Standing Committees of Experts on issues related to the operation of the Convention. Subsequently, at its seventh plenary meeting, on 7 May 1999, the Meeting decided that the intersessional work would be guided by the President's Paper which is contained in annex IV to this report. Further consultations identified the following States Parties as Co-chairs and Rapporteurs for the intersessional work programme:

*Mine clearance*

Mozambique and the United Kingdom of Great Britain and Northern Ireland, Co-Chairs;

Peru and the Netherlands, Rapporteurs.

*Victim assistance, socio-economic reintegration and mine awareness*

Mexico and Switzerland, Co-Chairs;

Nicaragua and Japan, Rapporteurs.

*Stockpile destruction*

Hungary and Mali, Co-Chairs;

Malaysia and the Slovak Republic, Rapporteurs.

*Technologies for mine action*

Cambodia and France, Co-Chairs;

Yemen and Germany, Rapporteurs.

*General status and operation of the Convention*

South Africa and Canada, Co-Chairs;

Zimbabwe and Belgium, Rapporteurs.

26. The Meeting further noted that the first sessions of the Standing Committees of Experts would take place in Geneva on the following dates:

Mine clearance 13–15 September 1999

Victim assistance socio economic reintegration and mine awareness 15–17 September 1999

Stockpile destruction 9–10 December 1999

Technologies for mine action 13–14 December 1999

General status and operation of the Convention 10–11 January 2000

27. At its seventh plenary meeting, the Meeting agreed that the Second Meeting of the States Parties would be held on 11–15 September 2000 in Geneva.

28. At the same plenary meeting, the Meeting adopted the Maputo Declaration, which is contained in part II of this report.

## F. Documentation

29. A list of documents of the First Meeting is contained in annex I to this report.

## G. Adoption of the Final Report and conclusion of the First Meeting

30. At its seventh and final plenary meeting on 7 May 1999, the Meeting adopted its Final Report as contained in document APLC/MSP.1/1999/L.7 and as orally amended by the President.

## Part II. Maputo Declaration

### Maputo, Mozambique

### 7 May, 1999

1. We, the States Parties to the Convention on the Prohibition of the Use, Stockpiling, Production and Transfer of Anti-Personnel Mines and on Their Destruction, together with signatory States, are gathered in Maputo, Mozambique, joined by international organizations and institutions and non governmental organizations, to reaffirm our unwavering commitment to the total eradication of an insidious instrument of war and terror: anti-personnel mines.

2. Even now, at the end of the century, anti-personnel mines continue to maim and kill countless innocent people each day; force families to flee their lands and children to abandon their schools and playgrounds; and prevent long suffering refugees and displaced persons from returning to rebuild their homes and their lives. The real or suspected presence of anti-personnel mines continues to deny access to much needed resources and services and cripples normal social and economic development.

3. We raise our serious concern at the continued use of anti-personnel mines in areas of instability around the world. Such acts are contrary to the aims of the Convention; they exacerbate tensions, undermine confidence and impede diplomatic efforts to find peaceful solutions to conflicts.

4. Therefore, even as we celebrate this First Meeting of the States Parties two months after the rapid entry into force of the Convention, we recognize that the enduring value of this unique international instrument rests in fully realizing the obligations and the promise contained within the Convention

- to ensure no new use;
- to eradicate stocks;
- to cease development, production and transfers;
- to clear mined areas and thus free the land from its deadly bondage;
- to assist the victims to reclaim their lives and to prevent new victims.

5. We believe these to be common tasks for humanity and therefore call on governments and people everywhere to join us in this effort.

6. To those who continue to use, develop, produce, otherwise acquire, stockpile, retain and transfer these weapons: cease now, and join us in this task.

7. To those who can offer technical and financial assistance to meet the enormous challenges of humanitarian mine action: intensify your efforts and help build the capacity of mine affected countries themselves to increasingly take on these tasks.

8. To those who can offer assistance: help with the physical and psycho social treatment and social and economic reintegration of mine victims, support mine awareness education programmes, and help those States in need to meet treaty obligations to demine and to destroy stockpiles, thus facilitating the widest possible adherence to the Convention.

9. To those that have not yet joined this community of States Parties: accede quickly to the Convention. To those who have signed: ratify. If ratification will take more time: provisionally apply the terms of the Convention while you put in place the necessary domestic legislation.

10. To the international community: promulgate, implement and universalise the Convention, the new international standard and norm of behaviour it is establishing.

11. In this spirit, we voice our outrage at the unabated use of anti-personnel mines in conflicts around the world. To those few signatories who continue to use these weapons, this is a violation of the object and purpose of the Convention that you solemnly signed. We call upon you to respect and implement your commitments.

12. Know that, as a community dedicated to seeing an end to the use of anti-personnel mines, our assistance and cooperation will flow primarily to those who have foresworn the use of these weapons forever through adherence to and implementation of the Convention.

13. Driven by the sad reality that the people of the world will continue to suffer the consequences of the use of anti-personnel mines for many years to come, we believe it crucial that we use this First Meeting of the States Parties to ensure that we make continued, measurable progress in our future efforts to eradicate anti-personnel mines and to alleviate the humanitarian crisis caused by them.

14. We recognize that anti-personnel mines represent a major public health threat. The plight of mine victims has revealed the inadequacy of assistance for victims in the countries most affected. Such assistance must be integrated into broader public health and socio economic strategies to ensure not simply short term care for victims, but special attention to the serious long term needs for social and economic reintegration. Mine victims must be permitted to realize, with dignity, their place within their families and their societies. These issues must be accorded the highest political importance and practical commitment by States Parties and all those in the international community who care about this issue.

15. To this end, we commit ourselves to mobilise resources and energies to universalise the Convention, alleviate and eventually eradicate the human suffering caused by anti-personnel mines, including by striving to meet the goal of 'zero victims'.

16. For these purposes, we, the States Parties, will implement an intersessional work programme to take us steadily forward to the next Meeting of the States Parties, which will take place in Geneva from 11 to 15 September 2000. This will enable us to focus and advance our mine action efforts and to measure progress made in achieving our objectives. This work will be based on our tradition of inclusivity, partnership, dialogue, openness and practical cooperation. In this regard, we invite all interested governments, international organizations and institutions and non governmental organizations to join us in this task.

17. Our work programme will draw together experts, building on the discussions held here in Maputo, to address the key thematic issues of:

the general status and operation of the Convention;
mine clearance;
victim assistance and mine awareness;
stockpile destruction; and,
technologies for mine action.

This intersessional work will, inter alia, assist us in developing, with the United Nations, a global picture of priorities consistent with the obligations and time frames contained within the Convention, including with regard to international cooperation and assistance. It will also take into account important work done at the international, regional and sub regional levels.

18. The work of our experts will begin just four months from now, in Geneva. We appreciate and accept the offer of the Geneva International Centre for Humanitarian Demining to support our efforts. Our work will complement and reinforce the important mine action activities being undertaken by mine affected States working in partnership with other States, international and regional organizations, non-governmental organizations and the private sector also recognizing the United Nations system as an important actor in global mine action efforts.

19. Meeting here in one of the most mine affected continents on earth and in a country which has experienced the ravages wreaked by these weapons on the Mozambican people and the social fabric of the nation, we focus our minds and strengthen our conviction on

the need to make the killing fields of anti personnel mines that have terrorized, maimed and killed people, destroyed lives and hope for too long, a relic of the past.

We are determined to succeed in our common task.

We are determined to work in partnership to this end.

We are determined to apply the principle of international humanitarian law, enunciated in the final preambular paragraph of the Convention itself that '. . . the right of the parties to an armed conflict to choose methods or means of warfare is not unlimited . . .'

This is our firm pledge to future generations.

[Annexes omitted]

## SECOND MEETING OF STATES PARTIES (GENEVA, 11–15 SEPTEMBER 2000)

### FINAL REPORT

APLC/MSP.2/2000/1

The Final Report of the Second Meeting of the States Parties to the Convention on the Prohibition of the Use, Stockpiling, Production and Transfer of Anti-Personnel Mines and on Their Destruction consists of two parts and five annexes as follows:

Part I   Organization and Work of the Second Meeting
Part II  Declaration of the Second Meeting of the States Parties

Annexes:
   Annex I List of Documents
   Annex II President's Paper on Revisions to the Intersessional Work Programme
   Annex III President's Paper on Amending the Article 7 Reporting Format
   Annex IV Final Reports of the Standing Committees of Experts
   Annex V President's Action Programme

### Part I. Organization and Work of the Second Meeting

#### A. Introduction

1. The Convention on the Prohibition of the Use, Stockpiling, Production and Transfer of Anti-Personnel Mines and on Their Destruction provides in Article 11, paragraphs 1 and 2, that:

'The States Parties shall meet regularly in order to consider any matter with regard to the application or implementation of this Convention, including:

(a)  The operation and status of this Convention;
(b)  Matters arising from the reports submitted under the provisions of this Convention;

(c) International cooperation and assistance in accordance with Article 6;

(d) The development of technologies to clear anti-personnel mines;

(e) Submissions of States Parties under Article 8; and

(f) Decisions relating to submissions of States Parties as provided for in Article 5'; and,

Meetings subsequent to the First Meeting of the States Parties 'shall be convened by the Secretary-General of the United Nations annually until the first Review Conference'.

2. At its fifty-fourth session, the General Assembly of the United Nations in resolution 54/54 B requested the Secretary-General, 'in accordance with Article 11, paragraph 2, of the Convention, to undertake the preparations necessary to convene the Second Meeting of the States Parties to the Convention at Geneva, from 11 to 15 September 2000, and, on behalf of States Parties and according to Article 11, paragraph 4, of the Convention, to invite States not parties to the Convention, as well as the United Nations, other relevant international organizations or institutions, regional organizations, the International Committee of the Red Cross and relevant non-governmental organizations to attend the Meeting as observers'.

3. To prepare for the Second Meeting, the Standing Committee of Experts (SCE) on the General Status and Operation of the Convention, established by the First Meeting of the States Parties, held two meetings, to which all interested States Parties, States not parties to the Convention, as well as the United Nations, other relevant international organizations or institutions, regional organizations, the International Committee of the Red Cross and relevant non-governmental organizations were encouraged to attend.

4. The first meeting of the SCE was held 10–11 January 2000. During the meeting, participants considered a number of issues relating to the organization of the Second Meeting, including a draft provisional agenda, a draft programme of work, draft rules of procedure and provisional estimated costs for convening the Second Meeting. No objections were raised in connection with the proposals made with respect to the draft rules of procedure, provisional estimated costs and the venue for the Second Meeting, and it was agreed that they, along with all other conference documents with the exception of reports submitted under Article 7 of the Convention, would be finalized in all six languages of the Convention to be put before the Second Meeting. It was also agreed that the record of work of the five Standing Committees of Experts would be communicated to the Second Meeting in the form of a five-page report prepared by each Committee.

5. The second meeting of the SCE was held 29–30 May 2000. During the meeting, no objections were made with respect to the draft provisional agenda and draft programme of work, and it was agreed that they would be put before the Second Meeting. In addition, no objections were made with respect to five-page SCE reports serving as the basis for discussion during the informal consultations to be held at the Second

Meeting under agenda item 15 (with the exception of the report of the SCE on the General Status and Operation of the Convention, which would serve as the basis for discussion under agenda item 11).

6. Between the First and Second Meetings of the States Parties, the Standing Committees of Experts received considerable support from the Geneva International Centre for Humanitarian Demining (GICHD). States Parties expressed their appreciation for this assistance and the GICHD's contribution to the successful operation of the intersessional work programme. In addition, States Parties recognized that the work of the Standing Committees of Experts benefited greatly from the active participation of relevant non-governmental, regional and international organizations. States Parties expressed their gratitude to these organizations for their substantive involvement in the intersessional work programme.

7. The opening of the Second Meeting was preceded by a ceremony at which statements were delivered by the following: Vladimir Petrovsky, Director-General of the United Nations Office at Geneva; Adolf Ogi, President of Switzerland; Martine Brunschwig Graf, State Councillor of the Republic and Canton of Geneva; Alain Vaissade, Mayor of the City of Geneva; Her Royal Highness, Princess Astrid of Belgium; Elisabeth Reusse-Decrey, President of the Swiss Campaign against Landmines; Sir Paul McCartney and Heather Mills. In addition, a presentation was made by 18 landmine survivors from 14 countries.

## B. Organization of the Second Meeting

8. The Second Meeting was opened on 11 September 2000 by the President of the First Meeting of the States Parties, the Minister of Foreign Affairs and Cooperation of the Republic of Mozambique, Dr. Leonardo Santos Simão. The Second Meeting elected by acclamation Ambassador Steffen Kongstad of Norway as its President in accordance with rule 7 of the draft rules of procedure.

9. At the opening session, a message addressed to the Second Meeting by the Secretary-General of the United Nations was read by the Director-General of the United Nations Office at Geneva, and statements were made by Jakob Kellenberger, President of the International Committee of the Red Cross, and Jody Williams, Ambassador for the International Campaign to Ban Landmines.

10. At its first plenary meeting on 11 September 2000, the Second Meeting adopted its agenda as contained in document APLC/MSP.2/2000/L.1. On the same occasion, the Second Meeting adopted its rules of procedure as contained in document APLC/MSP.2/2000/L.3, the estimated costs for convening the Second Meeting as contained in document APLC/MSP.2/2000/L.4, and its programme of work as contained in document APLC/MSP.2/2000/L.2.

11. Also at its first plenary meeting, representatives from Cambodia, Canada, France, Hungary, Mali, Mexico, Mozambique, South Africa, Switzerland and the United Kingdom were elected by acclamation as Vice-Presidents of the Second Meeting.

12. The Meeting unanimously confirmed the nomination of Ambassador Christian Faessler of Switzerland as the Secretary-General of the Meeting.

## C. Participation and credentials in the Second Meeting

13. Sixty-two States Parties participated in the Meeting: Albania, Argentina, Australia, Austria, Belgium, Benin, Bolivia, Bosnia and Herzegovina, Brazil, Bulgaria, Burkina Faso, Cambodia, Canada, Costa Rica, Croatia, Czech Republic, Denmark, Ecuador, El Salvador, France, Germany, Guatemala, Guinea, Holy See, Honduras, Hungary, Ireland, Italy, Jamaica, Japan, Jordan, Liberia, Liechtenstein, Luxembourg, Madagascar, Malaysia, Mali, Mexico, Monaco, Mozambique, the Netherlands, New Zealand, Nicaragua, Norway, Panama, Peru, Philippines, Portugal, Qatar, Senegal, Slovakia, Slovenia, South Africa, Spain, Sweden, Switzerland, Thailand, Tunisia, the United Kingdom of Great Britain and Northern Ireland, Venezuela, Yemen and Zimbabwe.

14. Seven States that ratified the Convention, but for which the Convention had not yet entered into force, participated in the Meeting as observers, in accordance with Article 11, paragraph 4, of the Convention and rule 1, paragraph 1, second sentence, of the rules of procedure of the Meeting: Bangladesh, Colombia, Côte d'Ivoire, Dominican Republic, Gabon, Ghana and Mauritania.

15. A further forty-one States not parties to the Convention participated in the Meeting as observers, in accordance with Article 11, paragraph 4, of the Convention and rule 1, paragraph 1, second sentence, of the rules of procedure of the Meeting: Afghanistan, Algeria, Angola, Azerbaijan, Belarus, Brunei Darussalam, Burundi, Bhutan, Cameroon, Cape Verde, Chile, China, Cuba, Cyprus, Estonia, Finland, Georgia, Greece, Indonesia, Iraq, Israel, Kenya, Libyan Arab Jamahiriya, Lithuania, Malta, Morocco, Nepal, Oman, Poland, Romania, Saudi Arabia, Singapore, Somalia, Sri Lanka, Sudan, Turkey, Ukraine, United Arab Emirates, Uruguay, Viet Nam and Zambia.

16. Credentials issued by the Head of State or Government or by the Minister for Foreign Affairs or by a person authorized by one of the above, as required by rule 4 of the rules of procedure of the Meeting, or credentials in the form of photocopies or facsimiles of such a document, or credentials in the form of information concerning the appointment of representatives to the Meeting received in the form of letters or notes verbales or facsimiles thereof from embassies, permanent missions to the United Nations or other intergovernmental organizations or other government offices or authorities, were received from all 110 States mentioned in paragraphs 13 to 15 above.

17. The Meeting accepted the credentials of the representatives of all of the States mentioned in paragraphs 13 to 15 above.

18. In accordance with Article 11, paragraph 4, of the Convention and rule 1, paragraphs 2 and 3 of the rules of procedure, the following international organizations and institutions, regional organizations, entities and non-governmental organizations

attended the Meeting as observers: European Union; International Atomic Energy Agency (IAEA); International Campaign to Ban Landmines (ICBL); International Committee of the Red Cross (ICRC); Organization of American States (OAS); Sovereign Military Order of Malta; United Nations Organization: United Nations Secretariat (Department of Peace-Keeping Operations/United Nations Mine Action Service (UNMAS) and Office for the Coordination of Humanitarian Affairs), United Nations Children's Fund (UNICEF), United Nations Development Programme (UNDP), United Nations High Commissioner for Refugees (UNHCR), United Nations Office for Project Services (UNOPS), United Nations Institute for Disarmament Research (UNIDIR), World Health Organization (WHO); World Bank. In accordance with rule 1.4, the following organizations attended the Meeting as observers on the invitation of the Meeting: Geneva Foundation, Geneva International Centre for Humanitarian Demining (GICHD), Green Earth Organization, International Development Research Centre (IDRC), League of Arab States, Organisation Internationale de la Francophonie, Organization of the Islamic Conference, PRIO (International Peace Research Institute, Oslo) and SOLIDEST.

19. A list of all delegations to the Second Meeting is contained in document APLC/MSP.2/2000/INF.3.

## D. Work of the Second Meeting

20. The Second Meeting held eight plenary meetings from 11 to 15 September 2000.

21. The first three and a half plenary meetings were devoted to the general exchange of views under agenda item 10. Delegations of 34 States Parties, 15 observer States and 7 observer organizations made statements in the general exchange of views, including rights of reply.

22. At the fourth plenary meeting, on 13 September 2000, the Meeting reviewed the general status and operation of the Convention, expressing satisfaction that 107 States have formally accepted the obligations of the Convention, that 22 States Parties have completed destruction of stockpiled anti-personnel mines and a further 23 States Parties are in the process of stockpile destruction, that the new international norm established by the Convention is taking hold as demonstrated by the behaviour of many States not parties to the Convention, and that approximately US$250 million has been allocated by donors over the past year to address the global landmine problem. The Meeting also expressed satisfaction that efforts to implement the Convention are making a difference, with considerable areas of mined land having been cleared over the past year, with casualty rates having been reduced in several of the world's most mine-affected States, and with more and better efforts being undertaken to assist landmine victims.

23. As part of the above-mentioned review, the Meeting reviewed the work of the Standing Committee of Experts on the General Status and Operation of the Convention, as recorded in its report contained in annex IV, and focused its attention on actions recommended by the Committee.

24. At the fifth plenary meeting, on 13 September 2000, the Meeting considered the submission of requests under Article 5 of the Convention. The President notified the Meeting that he had not been informed that any State wished to make such a request at the Second Meeting. The Meeting took note of this.

25. At the same plenary, the Meeting considered the submission of requests under Article 8 of the Convention. The President notified the Meeting that he had not been informed that any State wished to make such a request at the Second Meeting. The Meeting took note of this.

26. In addition, within the framework of the fifth to the seventh plenary meetings, the Meeting held informal consultations on international cooperation and assistance in accordance with Article 6 on the following topics: mine clearance; victim assistance, socio-economic reintegration and mine awareness; the destruction of stockpiled anti-personnel mines; and the development of technologies for mine action. These consultations involved a review of the work of the relevant Standing Committees of Experts, as recorded in their reports contained in annex IV, with a focus on the actions recommended by the Committees.

### E. Decisions and recommendations

27. At its fifth plenary meeting, on 13 September 2000, the Meeting considered matters arising from and in the context of reports to be submitted under Article 7, including consideration of an amendment to the reporting format. The amendment to the format was adopted and is contained in annex III to this report. In addition, the Meeting reviewed the technical ways and means of circulating reports as adopted at the First Meeting, without making any changes to these, with the exception of encouraging States Parties to submit reports electronically and, when submitting an annual update, to highlight changes in relation to earlier reports.

28. Further to the recommendations made by the Standing Committee of Experts on the General Status and Operation of the Convention, the Meeting recognized the continuing importance of the intersessional work programme and, at its fifth plenary meeting, on 13 September 2000, agreed that the second intersessional work programme would be adjusted according to the President's paper, which is contained in annex II. Further consultations identified the following States Parties as the Committee Co-Chairs and Rapporteurs until the end of the Third Meeting of the States Parties:

*Mine Clearance and Related Technologies*

Netherlands and Peru (Co-Chairs);

Germany and Yemen (Rapporteurs);

*Victim Assistance, Socio-Economic Reintegration and Mine Awareness*

Japan and Nicaragua (Co-Chairs);

Canada and Honduras (Rapporteurs);

*Stockpile Destruction*

Malaysia and Slovakia (Co-Chairs);

Australia and Croatia (Rapporteurs);

*General Status and Operation of the Convention*

Belgium and Zimbabwe (Co-Chairs);

Norway and Thailand (Rapporteurs).

29. States Parties recognized that the work of the Standing Committees would require a high degree of coordination between the Co-Chairs to ensure that their work would facilitate the successful implementation of the Convention. In this context the States Parties established a Coordinating Committee of Co-Chairs, which will meet on an ad hoc basis under the chairmanship of the current President of the Meeting of the States Parties. This Committee will serve to coordinate matters relating to and flowing from the work of the Standing Committees with the work of the Meetings of the States Parties. As appropriate, the Committee can call upon any relevant party to assist in its work, including past Presidents, past Co-Chairs, and representatives of other States Parties and organizations.

30. The Meeting also noted the work undertaken by interested States Parties to establish a sponsorship programme to ensure more widespread representation at meetings of the Convention.

31. States Parties endorsed, and expressed satisfaction with, the work of the Standing Committees of Experts, warmly welcoming the reports of the Standing Committees of Experts, as contained in annex IV. The Meeting was in general agreement with the recommendations made by the Standing Committees of Experts and urged States Parties and all other relevant parties, where appropriate, to act with urgency on these recommendations.

32. At its eighth plenary meeting, on 15 September 2000, the Meeting agreed that the Third Meeting of the States Parties would be held on 18 to 21 September 2001 in Managua, Nicaragua.

33. At the same plenary, the Meeting adopted the Declaration of the Second Meeting of the States Parties, which is contained in Part II of this report. In addition, the Meeting warmly welcomed the President's Action Programme, contained in annex V, as a practical means of facilitating implementation of the Convention in accordance with the recommendations made by the Standing Committees of Experts.

## F. Documentation

34. A list of documents of the Second Meeting is contained in annex I to this report.

## G. Adoption of the Final Report and conclusion of the Second Meeting

35. At its eighth and final plenary meeting, on 15 September 2000, the Meeting adopted its draft Final Report, contained in document APLC/MSP.2/2000/L.8.

## Part II. Declaration of the Second Meeting of the States Parties

1. We, the States Parties to the Convention on the Prohibition of the Use, Stockpiling, Production and Transfer of Anti-Personnel Mines and on Their Destruction, along with other States, international organizations and institutions and non-governmental organizations, are gathered in Geneva, Switzerland to reaffirm our unwavering commitment both to the total eradication of anti-personnel mines and to addressing the insidious and inhumane effects of these weapons.

2. We celebrate the ongoing growth in support for the Convention and our satisfaction with the general status and operation of it: over 100 States have formally accepted the obligations of the Convention; over 20 States Parties have completed destruction of stockpiled anti-personnel mines and a further 23 States Parties are in the process of destroying stockpiles; the new international norm established by the Convention is taking hold as demonstrated by the behaviour of many States not parties to the Convention; and approximately US$250 million has been allocated by donors over the past year to address the global landmine problem.

3. We recognize that much work remains. However, we are pleased that our efforts are making a difference: considerable areas of mined land have been cleared over the past year; casualty rates have been reduced in several of the world's most mine-affected States; and more and better efforts are being undertaken to assist landmine victims.

4. While we celebrate the success of the Convention, we remain deeply concerned that anti-personnel mines continue to kill, maim and threaten the lives of countless innocent people each day; that the terror of mines prevents individuals from reclaiming their lives; and that the lasting impact of these weapons denies communities the opportunity to rebuild long after conflicts have ended.

5. We deplore the continued use of anti-personnel mines. Such acts are contrary to the aims of the Convention and exacerbate the humanitarian problems already caused by the use of these weapons. We call upon all those who continue to use anti-personnel mines, as well as those who develop, produce, otherwise acquire, stockpile, retain and transfer these weapons, to cease now and to join us in the task of eradicating these weapons.

6. We implore those States that have declared their commitment to the object and purpose of the Convention and that continue to use anti-personnel mines to recognize that this is a clear violation of their solemn commitment. We call upon all States concerned to respect their commitments.

7. We celebrate this Second Meeting of the States Parties. But we recognize that achieving the promise of this unique and important humanitarian instrument rests in continuing to be tireless in our efforts to end the use of anti-personnel mines, to eradicate stockpiles, to cease development, production and transfers of these weapons, to clear mined areas in order to free land from its deadly bondage, to assist victims to reclaim their lives and to prevent new victims.

8. We also recognize that these are common tasks for humanity and therefore call upon all governments and people everywhere to join us in this effort. We call upon those in a

position to do so to provide technical and financial assistance to meet the enormous challenges of mine action, and, whenever relevant, to integrate these efforts into development planning and programming. We call upon those States that have not formally accepted the obligations of the Convention to ratify or accede to it promptly. We call upon all States that are in the process of formally accepting the obligations of the Convention to apply provisionally the terms of the Convention. And we call upon one another as States Parties to effectively implement the Convention and to comply fully with its provisions.

9.  We reiterate that, as a community dedicated to seeing an end to the use of anti-personnel mines, our assistance and cooperation will flow primarily to those who have foresworn the use of these weapons forever through adherence to and implementation of the Convention.

10.  While we realize that our task is huge, we warmly welcome the substantial progress that has been made during the intersessional work programme and the accomplishments of this programme's Standing Committees of Experts.

11.  We recall that the intersessional work programme was established at the First Meeting of the States Parties to focus and advance the international community's mine action efforts and to measure progress made in achieving its objectives. We express our satisfaction that the intersessional work programme has lived up to this promise, has assisted in developing a global picture of priorities consistent with the obligations and time-frames contained within the Convention, and has been undertaken in a manner consistent with the Convention's tradition of inclusivity, partnership, dialogue, openness and practical cooperation.

12.  We acknowledge that the progress made during the intersessional work programme was significantly enhanced by the substantive participation of the International Campaign to Ban Landmines and other relevant non-governmental organizations, and by regional and international organizations, including the International Committee of the Red Cross. We express our gratitude to these organizations for their important contributions and we thank the Geneva International Centre for Humanitarian Demining for its support of the first intersessional work programme and its commitment to continuing to support future intersessional work.

13.  Building upon the accomplishments of the intersessional work programme, including increased participation in the work of the Convention by mine-affected States, we call upon all interested parties to continue to participate in the work of the Standing Committees between now and the next Meeting of the States Parties, which will take place on 18 to 21 September 2001 in Managua, Nicaragua.

14.  In reflecting upon our progress and accomplishments, and in considering the work that lies ahead, we reconfirm our conviction to make anti-personnel mines objects of the past, our obligation to assist those who have fallen victim to this terror, and our shared responsibility to the memories of those whose lives have been lost as a result of the use of these weapons, including those killed as a result of their dedication to helping others by clearing mined areas or providing humanitarian assistance.

[Annexes omitted]

# THIRD MEETING OF STATES PARTIES
## (MANAGUA, 11–15 SEPTEMBER 2001)

### FINAL REPORT

APLC/MSP.3/2001/1

The Final Report of the Third Meeting of the States Parties to the Convention on the Prohibition of the Use, Stockpiling, Production and Transfer of Anti-Personnel Mines and on Their Destruction consists of two parts and four annexes as follows:

Part I  Organization and Work of the Third Meeting
Part II  Declaration of the Third Meeting of the States Parties

Annexes:
  Annex I List of Documents
  Annex II President's Paper on the Establishment of the Implementation Support Unit
  Annex III Final Reports of the Standing Committees
  Annex IV President's Action Programme


### Part I. Organization and Work of the Third Meeting

#### A. Introduction

1. The Convention on the Prohibition of the Use, Stockpiling, Production and Transfer of Anti-Personnel Mines and on Their Destruction provides in Article 11, paragraphs 1 and 2, that: 'The States Parties shall meet regularly in order to consider any matter with regard to the application or implementation of this Convention, including:

(a)  The operation and status of this Convention;
(b)  Matters arising from the reports submitted under the provisions of this Convention;
(c)  International cooperation and assistance in accordance with Article 6;
(d)  The development of technologies to clear anti-personnel mines;
(e)  Submissions of States Parties under Article 8; and
(f)  Decisions relating to submissions of States Parties as provided for in Article 5'; and,

Meetings subsequent to the First Meeting of the States Parties 'shall be convened by the Secretary-General of the United Nations annually until the first Review Conference'.

2. At its fifty-fifth session, the General Assembly of the United Nations in resolution 55/33 V requested the Secretary-General, 'in accordance with Article 11, paragraph 2, of the Convention, to undertake the preparations necessary to convene the Third Meeting of the States Parties to the Convention at Managua, from 18 to 21 September 2001, and, on behalf of States Parties and according to Article 11, paragraph 4, of the Convention, to invite States not parties to the Convention as well as the United Nations, other relevant international organizations or institutions, regional organizations,

the International Committee of the Red Cross and relevant non-governmental organizations to attend the Meeting as observers'.

3. To prepare for the Third Meeting, the Standing Committee on the General Status and Operation of the Convention, established by the First Meeting of the States Parties, held two meetings, to which all interested States Parties, States not parties to the Convention, as well as the United Nations, other relevant international organizations or institutions, regional organizations, the International Committee of the Red Cross, the International Campaign to Ban Landmines and relevant non-governmental organizations were encouraged to attend.

4. The first meeting of the Standing Committee was held on 8 December 2000. During the meeting, participants considered a number of issues relating to the organization of the Third Meeting, including a draft provisional agenda, a draft programme of work, draft rules of procedure and provisional estimated costs for convening the Third Meeting. No objections were raised in connection with the proposals made with respect to the draft rules of procedure, draft provisional agenda, draft programme of work and the venue for the Third Meeting, and it was agreed that they, along with all other conference documents with the exception of reports submitted under Article 7 of the Convention, would be finalized in all six languages of the Convention to be put before the Third Meeting. It was also agreed that the record of work of the four Standing Committees would be communicated to the Third Meeting in the form of a five-page report prepared by each Committee.

5. The second meeting of the Standing Committee was held on 11 May 2001. During the meeting, no objections were made with respect to the provisional estimated costs, and it was agreed that they would be put before the Third Meeting.

6. Between the Second and the Third Meetings of the States Parties, the Standing Committees received considerable support from the Geneva International Centre for Humanitarian Demining (GICHD). States Parties expressed their appreciation for this assistance and the GICHD's contribution to the successful operation of the intersessional work programme. In addition, States Parties recognized that the work of the Standing Committees benefited greatly from the active participation of relevant non-governmental, regional and international organizations. States Parties expressed their gratitude to these organizations for their substantive involvement in the intersessional work programme.

7. The opening of the Third Meeting was preceded by a ceremony at which statements were delivered by the following: Francisco Xavier Aguirre Sacasa, Minister of Foreign Affairs of the Republic of Nicaragua; Colonel William McDonough with a message of the Secretary-General from the OAS; Jesus Martinez, a landmine survivor from El Salvador, with a message from Her Majesty Queen Noor of Jordan; Enrique Larenas, father of a landmine survivor in Chile, Juan Carlos Varela, deminer of the Nicaraguan Army and landmine survivor; Pablo Ubilla, President of the National Post Office of Nicaragua; Gema María Peña Navarrete, winner of the organized painting contest; and

Arnoldo Aleman, President of the Republic of Nicaragua. In addition, Jonas Patin, an indigenous Nicaraguan and landmine survivor introduced the documentary entitled 'Mine victims in Nicaragua' in his native Misquito language. The ceremony served to remind States Parties of the central importance of supporting the care and rehabilita-tion, and social and economic reintegration, of landmine survivors.

## B. Organization of the Third Meeting

8. The Third Meeting was opened on 18 September 2001 by the President of the Second Meeting of the States Parties, Ambassador Steffen Kongstad of Norway. The Third Meeting elected by acclamation Francisco Xavier Aguirre Sacasa, Minister of Foreign Affairs of the Republic of Nicaragua, as its President in accordance with rule 7 of the draft rules of procedure.

9. At the opening session, a message addressed to the Third Meeting by the Secretary-General of the United Nations was read by Under Secretary-General for Disarmament Affairs, Jayantha Dhanapala, and a statement was made by Jody Williams, Ambassador for the International Campaign to Ban Landmines.

10. At its first plenary meeting on 18 September 2001, the Third Meeting adopted its agenda as contained in document APLC/MSP.3/2001/L.1. On the same occasion, the Third Meeting adopted its rules of procedure as contained in document APLC/MSP.3/2001/L.3, the estimated costs for convening the Third Meeting as con-tained in document APLC/MSP.3/2001/L.4, and its programme of work as contained in document APLC/MSP.3/2001/L.2.

11. Also at its first plenary meeting, representatives from Belgium, Japan, Malaysia, the Netherlands, Norway, Peru, Slovakia and Zimbabwe were elected by acclamation as Vice-Presidents of the Third Meeting.

12. The Meeting unanimously confirmed the nomination of Mrs. Bertha Marina Argüello, Vice Minister of Foreign Affairs of the Republic of Nicaragua, as the Secretary-General of the Meeting. The Meeting also took note that the Republic of Nicaragua had appointed Mr. Kerry Brinkert as Deputy Secretary-General.

## C. Participation in the Third Meeting

13. Sixty-seven States Parties participated in the Meeting: Albania, Argentina, Australia, Austria, Belgium, Belize, Benin, Bolivia, Bosnia and Herzegovina, Brazil, Bulgaria, Cambodia, Canada, Chad, Colombia, Costa Rica, Croatia, Czech Republic, Denmark, Dominican Republic, Ecuador, El Salvador, France, Germany, Ghana, Guatemala, Holy See, Honduras, Hungary, Ireland, Italy, Japan, Jordan, Kenya, Lesotho, Malaysia, Mali, Mauritania, Mexico, Mozambique, the Netherlands, New Zealand, Nicaragua, Norway, Panama, Peru, Philippines, Portugal, Qatar, Republic of Moldova, Romania, Rwanda, Senegal, Slovakia, South Africa, Spain, Sweden, Switzerland, Thailand, Togo, Uganda, the United Kingdom of Great Britain and Northern Ireland, Uruguay, Venezuela, Yemen, Zambia and Zimbabwe.

14. Six States that ratified the Convention, but for which the Convention had not yet entered into force, participated in the Meeting as observers, in accordance with Article 11, paragraph 4, of the Convention and rule 1, paragraph 1 of the rules of procedure of the Meeting: Chile, Congo, Guinea-Bissau, Malta, Saint Vincent and the Grenadines and Sierra Leone.

15. Eleven signatories that have not ratified the Convention participated in the Meeting as observers, in accordance with Article 11, paragraph 4, of the Convention and rule 1, paragraph 1 of the rules of procedure of the Meeting: Algeria, Angola, Burundi, Cameroon, Cyprus, Ethiopia, Greece, Indonesia, Lithuania, Poland and Sudan.

16. A further eleven States not parties to the Convention participated in the Meeting as observers, in accordance with Article 11, paragraph 4, of the Convention and rule 1, paragraph 1 of the rules of procedure of the Meeting: Belarus, Cuba, Finland, Kuwait, Lao People's Democratic Republic, Morocco, Oman, Russian Federation, Syrian Arab Republic, Turkey and Yugoslavia.

17. Delegation information submitted in accordance with rule 4 of the rules of procedure of the Meeting was received from 95 States mentioned in paragraphs 13 to 16 above.

18. The Meeting accepted the delegation information of the representatives of all of the States mentioned in paragraphs 13 to 16 above.

19. In accordance with Article 11, paragraph 4, of the Convention and rule 1, paragraphs 2 and 3 of the rules of procedure, the following international organizations and institutions, regional organizations, entities and non-governmental organizations attended the Meeting as observers: European Commission; Geneva International Centre for Humanitarian Demining; International Campaign to Ban Landmines; International Committee of the Red Cross; International Federation of Red Cross and Red Crescent Societies; Organization of American States; Pan American Health Organization; United Nations Organization: United Nations Secretariat (Department of Peace-Keeping Operations/United Nations Mines Action Service (UNMAS)), United Nations Children's Fund (UNICEF), United Nations Development Programme (UNDP), United Nations Disarmament Research (UNIDIR), World Food Programme (WPF), World Bank and World Health Organization (WHO). In accordance with rule 1.4, the following organizations attended the Meeting as observers on the invitation of the Meeting: Asociación de Asistencia Técnica en Educación y Discapacidad (ASCATED/UNICEF); Association of Free Children from Landmines in Japan; Emergency, Life Support for Civilian War Victims; Instituto de Ecologia Política; Instituto Uruguayo para el Desarrollo; International Peace Research Institute, Oslo (PRIO); Junta Interamericana de Defensa; Swedish Fellowship for Reconciliation; Civil Society Nicaragua: Acción Médica Cristiana, CENAPRORTO, Centro de Estudios Estratégicos de Nicaragua (CEEN), Centro de Estudios Internacionales (CEI), Centro de Información y Servicios de Asesoria en Salud (CISAS), Centro Inter-Eclesial de Estudio Tecnológico y Sociales (CIEETS), Centro Nicaraguense de Derechos Humanos (CENIDH), Coalición para el desminado humanitario, Comité Internacional de Solidaridad con los Pueblos (CIS), Coordinador Civil para la

Emergencia y la Reconstrucción, Federación de Coordinadora de Organismos por la Rehabilitación e Integración (FECONORI), Fundación M. Morales, Fundación Participación y Desarrollo (PARDES), Marshall Legacy and Walking Unidos.

20. A list of all delegations to the Third Meeting is contained in document APLC/MSP.3/2001/INF/7.

### D. Work of the Third Meeting

21. The Third Meeting held seven plenary meetings from 18 to 21 September 2001.

22. The second, third and fourth plenary meetings were devoted to the general exchange of views under agenda item 10. Delegations of 39 States Parties, 12 observer States and 9 observer organizations made statements in the general exchange of views, including rights of reply.

23. At the fifth plenary meeting, on 20 September 2001, the Meeting reviewed the general status and operation of the Convention, expressing satisfaction that 120 States have formally accepted the obligations of the Convention, that 30 States Parties have completed destruction of stockpiled anti-personnel mines and a further 17 States Parties are in the process of stockpile destruction. The Meeting also expressed that the new international norm established by the Convention is taking hold as demonstrated by the behaviour of many States not parties to the Convention. The Meeting also expressed satisfaction that efforts to implement the Convention are making a difference, with considerable areas of mined land having been cleared over the past year, with casualty rates having been reduced in several of the world's most mine-affected States, and with more and better efforts being undertaken to assist landmine victims.

24. At the fifth plenary meeting, on 20 September 2001, the Meeting considered the submission of requests under Article 5 of the Convention. The President notified the Meeting that he had not been informed that any State wished to make such a request at the Third Meeting. The Meeting took note of this.

25. At the same plenary, the Meeting considered the submission of requests under Article 8 of the Convention. The President notified the Meeting that he had not been informed that any State wished to make such a request at the Third Meeting. The Meeting took note of this.

26. In addition, within the framework of the sixth and seventh plenary meetings, the Meeting held informal consultations on international cooperation and assistance in accordance with Article 6 on the following topics: mine clearance and related technologies; victim assistance, socioeconomic reintegration and mine awareness; and the destruction of stockpiled anti-personnel mines. These consultations involved a review of the work of the relevant Standing Committees, as recorded in their reports contained in Annex III, with a focus on the actions recommended by the Committees.

### E. Decisions and recommendations

27. At its fifth plenary meeting, on 20 September 2001, the Meeting considered matters arising from and in the context of reports to be submitted under Article 7, including matters pertaining to the reporting process. States Parties expressed their continued

satisfaction with the technical ways and means of circulating reports as adopted at the First Meeting and as amended at the Second Meeting. States Parties encouraged the submission of reports electronically and, when submitting an annual update, the highlighting of changes in relation to earlier reports. In addition, States Parties recognized and expressed their appreciation for the efforts of Belgium and the non-governmental organization VERTIC to develop and distribute an Article 7 reporting guide. States Parties also encouraged the use of optional Form J, especially for matters such as victim assistance programmes and mine action funding.

28. Further to the recommendations made by the Standing Committee on the General Status and Operation of the Convention, the Meeting recognized the continuing importance of the intersessional work programme. States Parties accepted the minor change to the structure of the intersessional work programme with the Standing Committee on Mine Clearance and Related Technologies becoming the Standing Committee on Mine Clearance, Mine Awareness and Mine Action Technologies and the Standing Committee on Victim Assistance, Socio-Economic Reintegration and Mine Awareness becoming the Standing Committee on Victim Assistance and Socio-Economic Reintegration. In addition, pursuant to further consultations the following States Parties were identified as the Committee Co-Chairs and Co-Rapporteurs until the end of the 4th Meeting of the States Parties:

*Mine Clearance, Mine Awareness and Mine Action Technologies*

Germany and Yemen (Co-Chairs);

Belgium and Kenya (Co-Rapporteurs);

*Victim Assistance and Socio-Economic Reintegration*

Canada and Honduras (Co-Chairs);

Colombia and France (Co-Rapporteurs);

*Stockpile Destruction*

Australia and Croatia (Co-Chairs);

Romania and Switzerland (Co-Rapporteurs);

*General Status and Operation of the Convention*

Norway and Thailand (Co-Chairs);

Austria and Peru (Co-Rapporteurs).

29. States Parties recognized the value and importance of the Coordinating Committee in the effective functioning and implementation of the Convention and requested that the Coordinating Committee consider further improvements in the format, timing and work of the Standing Committees in order to ensure the identification of concrete and practical outcomes. States Parties agreed that the President, as chairperson of the Coordinating Committee, would report on its functioning to the intersessional meetings and also to the annual meetings of States Parties.

30. The Meeting also noted the work undertaken by interested States Parties through the establishment of a sponsorship programme had helped to ensure more widespread representation at meetings of the Convention.

31. States Parties endorsed, and expressed satisfaction with, the work of the Standing Committees, warmly welcoming the reports of the Standing Committees, as contained in Annex III. The Meeting was in general agreement with the recommendations made by the Standing Committees and urged States Parties and all other relevant parties, where appropriate, to act with urgency on these recommendations.

32. At its final plenary meeting, on 21 September 2001, the Meeting agreed that the 4th Meeting of the States Parties would be held from 16 to 20 September 2002 in Geneva, Switzerland, and nominated Ambassador Jean Lint of Belgium as President of the Fourth Meeting of States Parties.

33. States Parties endorsed the President's Paper on the Establishment of an Implementation Support Unit, as contained in Annex II to this report. States Parties warmly welcomed the establishment, within the GICHD, of an Implementation Support Unit to further enhance the operation and the implementation of the Convention. States Parties expressed their appreciation to the GICHD for its cooperation in the establishment of this unit, encouraged States in a position to do so to make voluntary contributions in support of the unit and mandated the President of the Third Meeting, in consultation with the Coordinating Committee, to finalize an agreement with the GICHD on the functioning of the unit.

34. At the same plenary, the Meeting adopted the Declaration of the Third Meeting of the States Parties, which is contained in Part II of this report. In addition, the Meeting warmly welcomed the President's Action Programme, contained in Annex IV, as a practical means of facilitating implementation of the Convention in accordance with the recommendations made by the Standing Committees.

35. The Meeting took note of the Statement by Francisco X. Aguirre-Sacasa, President of the Third Meeting of States Parties to the Ottawa Convention regarding terrorist attacks on the United States of America.

### F. Documentation

36. A list of documents of the Third Meeting is contained in Annex I to this report.

### G. Adoption of the Final Report and conclusion of the Third Meeting

37. At its seventh and final plenary meeting, on 21 September 2001, the Meeting adopted its draft Final Report, contained in document APLC/MSP.3/2001/L.7.

### Part II. Declaration of the Third Meeting of the States Parties

1. We, the States Parties to the Convention on the Prohibition of the Use, Stockpiling, Production and Transfer of Anti-Personnel Mines and on Their Destruction, along

with other States, international organizations and institutions and non-governmental organizations, gathered in Managua, Nicaragua, reaffirm our unwavering commitment both to the total eradication of anti-personnel mines and to addressing the insidious and inhumane effects of these weapons.

2. Meeting in Nicaragua, one of the most mine-affected countries in the Americas, we are witness to the devastating effects of this weapon on individuals and their communities. We are also witness to the importance of our work in addressing the problems faced by the Nicaraguan people, and countless others in countries around the world. We are reminded of the long journey ahead towards a mine-free world, as well as the significant steps already secured to reach our goal.

3. We celebrate the growing support for the Convention, ratified or acceded to by 120 States. With an additional 21 countries having signed, but not yet ratified the Convention, the number of States Parties and signatories now totals 141, including more than 40 mine-affected States. We call upon those that have not done so, to ratify or accede to the Convention. We also call upon all States in the process of formally accepting the obligations of the Convention, to provisionally apply the terms of the Convention.

4. We recognize that the new international norm established by the Convention is being demonstrated by the successful record of implementation of the Convention, including the conduct of many States not party to the Convention respecting the provisions therein. This includes the complete destruction of stockpiled anti-personnel mines in 30 countries, with 17 States Parties in the process of destroying stockpiles. Furthermore, approximately 220 million US$ has been allocated by donors over the past year to address the global landmine problem, in addition to the resources being allocated by mine-affected countries themselves.

5. We are pleased that over the past year, a considerable amount of land was cleared of anti-personnel mines, that casualty rates in several of the world's most mine-affected States have decreased, that landmine victim assistance has improved, and that our cooperative efforts continue to contribute to this progress.

6. While celebrating the success of the Convention, we remain deeply concerned that anti-personnel mines continue to kill, maim and threaten the lives of countless innocent people each day, that the terror of mines prevents individuals from reclaiming their lives and that the lasting impact of these weapons denies communities the opportunity to rebuild long after conflicts have ended.

7. We deplore any use of anti-personnel mines. Such acts are contrary to the object and purpose of the Convention and exacerbate the humanitarian problems already caused by the use of these weapons. We urge all those who continue to use, develop, produce, otherwise acquire, stockpile, retain and/or transfer anti-personnel landmines, to cease immediately and to join us in the task of eradicating these weapons.

8. We expect those States, which have declared their commitment to the object and purpose of the Convention and which continue to use anti-personnel mines, to

recognize that this is a clear violation of their solemn commitment. We call upon all States concerned to respect their commitments.

9. Recognizing the need to secure full compliance with all obligations of the Convention, we reaffirm our commitment to effectively implement the Convention and to comply fully with its provisions. We do so in the spirit of cooperation and collaboration that has characterized this process. In this context, we recall that the four-year maximum time period for the destruction of stockpiled anti-personnel mines is rapidly approaching for many States Parties. We also recall that as soon as possible, but not later than ten years after the entry into force of this Convention, each State party undertakes to destroy or ensure the destruction of all anti-personnel mines in mined areas under its jurisdiction or control. We encourage national, regional and international initiatives aimed at fulfilling these obligations.

10. We call upon all governments and people everywhere to join in the common task to meet the enormous challenges of mine action, including victim assistance, to provide the technical and financial assistance required, and, where appropriate, to integrate these efforts into development planning and programming. As States Parties bound to the eradication of anti-personnel mines, we reiterate that assistance and cooperation for practical mine action will flow primarily to those that have forsworn the use of these weapons forever through adherence to, implementation of, and compliance with the Convention.

11. We recognize that to achieve the promise of this unique and important humanitarian instrument, we must continue working tirelessly in all parts of the world to end the use of anti-personnel mines, to destroy stockpiles, to cease development, production and transfers of these weapons, to clear mined areas to free land from its deadly bondage, to assist victims to reclaim their lives with dignity and to prevent new victims.

12. We also recognize that progress to free the world from anti-personnel mines would be promoted by the commitment by non-State actors to cease and renounce their use in line with the international norm established by this Convention.

13. We warmly welcome the substantial progress made during the intersessional work programme. This programme continues to focus and advance the international community's mine action efforts, it greatly assists in our collective aim to implement the Convention and it provides a forum for mine-affected and other States to share experiences, acquire knowledge and enhance efforts to implement the Convention at the national level. We express our satisfaction that the intersessional work programme has been carried out in the Convention's tradition of partnership, dialogue, openness and practical cooperation. We welcome the increased participation of mine-affected States in the intersessional work and the valuable contribution of the Sponsorship Programme.

14. Recognizing the importance of the challenge to reach the goal set by the Americas to convert the 'Western Hemisphere into an anti-personnel landmine free zone' as soon as possible, which is a determining factor in the efforts to make the Convention both universal and fully operative, achieving this goal will be an example to the world of the Convention's effectiveness and an inspiration for other affected regions.

15. To further enhance the intersessional process, we must build upon its accomplishments, strengthen its outcomes and focus on providing States and other relevant international actors with the tools required to carry out the promise of the Convention. We continue to encourage the active participation of mine-affected and other interested States, as well as other relevant actors in the Intersessional Work Programme.

16. We acknowledge the positive work of the Coordinating Committee tasked with the coordination of the intersessional work programme, and its role in the strengthening of the intersessional process.

17. We call upon the States Parties to continue participating in the work of the Standing Committees established by the meetings of the States Parties to the Convention.

18. We express our gratitude to the International Campaign to Ban Landmines and other relevant non-governmental organizations, to regional and international organizations, including the International Committee of the Red Cross, for their important and substantive contribution to the intersessional process and to the overall implementation and consolidation of the Convention. We also thank all those agencies involved in mine clearance, mine awareness, victim assistance, stockpile destruction and other efforts to this end.

19. We thank the Geneva International Centre for Humanitarian Demining for its essential support and its commitment to enhance its support to the intersessional process through the establishment of an implementation unit.

20. In reflecting upon our progress and accomplishments, and in considering the work that lies ahead, we reconfirm our conviction to make anti-personnel mines objects of the past, our obligation to assist those who have fallen victim to this terror, and our shared responsibility to the memories of those whose lives have been lost as a result of the use of these weapons, including those killed as a result of their dedication to helping others by clearing mined areas or providing humanitarian assistance.

[Annexes omitted]

## FOURTH MEETING OF STATES PARTIES (GENEVA, 16–20 SEPTEMBER 2002)

### FINAL REPORT

APLC/MSP.4/2002/1

The Final Report of the Fourth Meeting of the States Parties to the Convention on the Prohibition of the Use, Stockpiling, Production and Transfer of Anti-Personnel Mines and on Their Destruction consists of two parts and nine annexes as follows:

Part I    Organization and Work of the Fourth Meeting
Part II   Declaration of the Fourth Meeting of the States Parties

Annexes:

Annex I List of Documents
Annex II President's Paper on the Intersessional Work Programme
Annex III President's Paper on Article 7 Reporting
Annex IV President's Paper on Developing a Process to Prepare for the Convention's First Review Conference
Annex V Final Reports of the Standing Committees
Annex VI President's Action Programme
Annex VII Report on the Functioning of the Implementation Support Unit
Annex VIII Managua Appeal
Annex IX Declaration of the Human Security Network on Promoting the Universalization of the Convention

## Part I. Organization and Work of the Fourth Meeting

### A. Introduction

1. The Convention on the Prohibition of the Use, Stockpiling, Production and Transfer of Anti-Personnel Mines and on Their Destruction provides in article 11, paragraphs 1 and 2, that: 'The States parties shall meet regularly in order to consider any matter with regard to the application or implementation of this Convention, including:

(a)  The operation and status of this Convention;

(b)  Matters arising from the reports submitted under the provisions of this Convention;

(c)  International cooperation and assistance in accordance with article 6;

(d)  The development of technologies to clear anti-personnel mines;

(e)  Submissions of States parties under article 8; and

(f)  Decisions relating to submissions of States parties as provided for in article 5'; and,

Meetings subsequent to the First Meeting of the States Parties 'shall be convened by the Secretary-General of the United Nations annually until the first Review Conference'.

2.  At its fifty-sixth session, the General Assembly of the United Nations in resolution 56/24 M requested the Secretary-General, 'in accordance with article 11, paragraph 2, of the Convention, to undertake the preparations necessary to convene the Fourth Meeting of the States Parties to the Convention in Geneva, from 16 to 20 September 2002, and, on behalf of States Parties and according to article 11, paragraph 4, of the Convention, to invite States not parties to the Convention, as well as the United Nations, other relevant international organizations or institutions, regional organizations, the International Committee of the Red Cross and relevant non-governmental organizations to attend the Meeting as observers'.

3.  To prepare for the Fourth Meeting, the Standing Committee on the General Status and Operation of the Convention, established by the First Meeting of the States Parties, held two meetings, to which all interested States Parties, States not parties to the

Convention, as well as the United Nations, other relevant international organizations or institutions, regional organizations, the International Committee of the Red Cross, the International Campaign to Ban Landmines and relevant non-governmental organizations were encouraged to attend.

4. The first meeting of the Standing Committee was held on 1 February 2002. During the meeting, participants considered a number of issues relating to the organization of the Fourth Meeting, including a draft provisional agenda, a draft programme of work, draft rules of procedure and provisional estimated costs for convening the Fourth Meeting. No objections were raised in connection with the proposals made with respect to the draft rules of procedure, draft provisional agenda, draft programme of work and the venue for the Fourth Meeting, and it was agreed that they, along with all other conference documents with the exception of reports submitted under article 7 of the Convention, would be finalized in all six languages of the Convention to be put before the Fourth Meeting. It was also agreed that the record of work of the four Standing Committees would be communicated to the Fourth Meeting in the form of final reports prepared by the Co-Chairs of each Standing Committee.

5. The second meeting of the Standing Committee was held on 27 and 31 May 2002. During the meeting, no objections were made with respect to the provisional estimated costs, and it was agreed that they would be put before the Fourth Meeting.

6. The opening of the Fourth Meeting was preceded by a ceremony at which statements were delivered by the President of the Swiss Confederation, Mr. Kaspar Villiger, and Her Royal Highness, Princess Astrid of Belgium. This ceremony also illustrated, through an interpretative dance piece performed by Nomades, the daily terror of landmines faced by thousands throughout the world, and featured testimonies provided by landmine survivors Ms. Felicidade Maria de Jesus from Angola and Mr. Marick Ngueradjim from Chad.

**B. Organization of the Fourth Meeting**

7. The Fourth Meeting was opened on 16 September 2002 by the Vice-President of the Republic of Nicaragua, Mr. José Rizo Castellón, on behalf of the President of the Third Meeting of the States Parties, who also presented the Conference with the 'Managua Appeal' which was adopted in Managua on 28 August 2002 at the Conference on Progress in Demining in the Americas (contained in Annex VIII). The Fourth Meeting elected by acclamation Ambassador Jean Lint of Belgium as its President in accordance with rule 7 of the draft rules of procedure.

8. At the opening session, a message addressed to the Fourth Meeting by the Secretary-General of the United Nations was read by Under-Secretary-General and High Commissioner for Human Rights, Mr. Sergio Vieira de Mello, and a statement was made by Jody Williams, 1997 Nobel Peace Prize Laureate and Ambassador for the International Campaign to Ban Landmines. In addition, a message of the President of the International Committee of the Red Cross was read by Mr. Jean de Courten.

9. At its first plenary meeting on 16 September 2002, the Fourth Meeting adopted its agenda as contained in document APLC/MSP.4/2002/L.1. On the same occasion, the Fourth Meeting adopted its rules of procedure as contained in document APLC/MSP.4/2002/L.3, the estimated costs for convening the Fourth Meeting as contained in document APLC/MSP.4/2002/L.4, and its programme of work as contained in document APLC/MSP.4/2002/L.2.

10. Also at its first plenary meeting, representatives from Australia, Canada, Croatia, Germany, Honduras, Norway, Thailand and Yemen were elected by acclamation as Vice-Presidents of the Fourth Meeting.

11. The Meeting unanimously confirmed the nomination of Ambassador Christian Faessler of Switzerland as the Secretary-General of the Meeting. The Meeting also took note of the appointment by the United Nations Secretary-General of Mr. Enrique Roman-Morey, Director of the Geneva Branch of the United Nations Department for Disarmament Affairs, as Executive Secretary of the Meeting, and the appointment by the President of Mr. Kerry Brinkert, Manager of the Implementation Support Unit, as the President's Executive Coordinator.

### C. Participation in the Fourth Meeting

12. Eighty-nine States parties participated in the Meeting: Albania, Algeria, Argentina, Australia, Austria, Bangladesh, Barbados, Belgium, Benin, Bolivia, Bosnia and Herzegovina, Brazil, Bulgaria, Burkina Faso, Cambodia, Canada, Chad, Chile, Colombia, Congo, Costa Rica, Côte d'Ivoire, Croatia, Czech Republic, Denmark, Dominican Republic, Ecuador, El Salvador, Equatorial Guinea, France, Germany, Ghana, Guatemala, Guinea, Guinea-Bissau, Holy See, Honduras, Hungary, Iceland, Ireland, Italy, Jamaica, Japan, Jordan, Kenya, Luxembourg, Macedonia (former Yugoslav Republic of), Madagascar, Malawi, Malaysia, Mali, Malta, Mauritania, Mauritius, Mexico, Moldova (Republic of), Monaco, Mozambique, the Netherlands, New Zealand, Nicaragua, Nigeria, Norway, Panama, Paraguay, Peru, Philippines, Portugal, Qatar, Romania, Rwanda, Senegal, Slovakia, Slovenia, South Africa, Spain, Sweden, Switzerland, Tajikistan, Thailand, Tunisia, Uganda, the United Kingdom of Great Britain and Northern Ireland, United Republic of Tanzania, Uruguay, Venezuela, Yemen, Zambia and Zimbabwe.

13. Five States that had ratified or acceded to the Convention, but for which the Convention had not yet entered into force, participated in the Meeting as observers, in accordance with article 11, paragraph 4, of the Convention and rule 1, paragraph 1 of the rules of procedure of the Meeting: Afghanistan, Angola, Cameroon, Comoros and Democratic Republic of Congo.

14. Eleven signatories that have not ratified the Convention participated in the Meeting as observers, in accordance with article 11, paragraph 4, of the Convention and rule 1, paragraph 1 of the rules of procedure of the Meeting: Brunei Darussalam, Burundi, Cyprus, Ethiopia, Gambia, Greece, Haiti, Lithuania, Poland, Sudan and Ukraine.

15. A further 27 States not parties to the Convention participated in the Meeting as observers, in accordance with article 11, paragraph 4, of the Convention and rule 1, paragraph 1 of the rules of procedure of the Meeting: Armenia, Azerbaijan, Belarus, Central African Republic, Cuba, Estonia, Finland, Georgia, Iraq, Israel, Kazakhstan, Kuwait, Kyrgyzstan, Latvia, Lebanon, Libyan Arab Jamahiriya, Mongolia, Morocco, Nepal, Oman, Papua New Guinea, Saudi Arabia, Singapore, Sri Lanka, Syrian Arab Republic, Turkey, and Yugoslavia.

16. Delegation information submitted in accordance with rule 4 of the rules of procedure of the Meeting was received from 132 States mentioned in paragraphs 12 to 15 above.

17. The Meeting took note of the delegation information of the representatives of all of the States mentioned in paragraphs 12 to 15 above.

18. In accordance with article 11, paragraph 4, of the Convention and rule 1, paragraphs 2 and 3 of the rules of procedure, the following international organizations and institutions, regional organizations, entities and non-governmental organizations attended the Meeting as observers: European Commission, European Parliament, Geneva International Centre for Humanitarian Demining, International Campaign to Ban Landmines, International Committee of the Red Cross, International Federation of Red Cross and Red Crescent Societies, Order of Malta, Organization of American States, International Labour Office, United Nations Development Programme (UNDP), UNICEF, United Nations Department for Disarmament Affairs, United Nations Institute for Disarmament Research (UNIDIR), United Nations Mine Action Service (UNMAS), United Nations Office for Project Services (UNOPS), and the World Health Organization (WHO). In accordance with rule 1, paragraph 4, the following organizations attended the Meeting as observers at the invitation of the Meeting: Canadian International Demining Corps (Canada), Emergency Life Support for Civilian War Victims (Italy), HAMAP Demineurs—Halte aux Mines Antipersonnel (Switzerland), International Committee for the Respect and Application of the African Charter on Human and People's Rights (Switzerland), International Trust Fund for Demining and Mine Victims Assistance (Slovenia), Mine Action Information Centre, James Madison University (United States), NAMSA—the NATO Maintenance and Supply Agency (Luxembourg), PRIO—International Peace Research Institute, Oslo (Norway), Solidest (Switzerland), South African Institute of International Affairs (South Africa), VERTIC—the Verification Research, Training and Information Centre (United Kingdom).

19. A list of all delegations to the Fourth Meeting is contained in documents APLC/MSP.4/2002/INF.2 and APLC/MSP.4/2002/INF.2/Add.1.

## D. Work of the Fourth Meeting

20. The Fourth Meeting held eight plenary meetings from 16 to 20 September 2002.

21. The first, second, third and fifth plenary meetings were devoted to the general exchange of views under agenda item 10. Delegations of 50 States parties, 14 observer

States and 5 observer organizations made statements in the general exchange of views, including rights of reply.

22. At the fourth plenary meeting, on 18 September 2002, the Meeting reviewed the general status and operation of the Convention, expressing satisfaction that 126 States have ratified or acceded to the Convention. The Meeting also expressed satisfaction that the new international norm established by the Convention is taking held as demonstrated by the behaviour of many States not parties to the Convention. In addition, the Meeting expressed satisfaction that efforts to implement the Convention are making a difference, that 88 States parties no longer possess stockpiled anti-personnel mines, that considerable areas of mined land have been cleared over the past year that casualty rates have been reduced in several of the world's most mine-affected States, and that more and better efforts are being undertaken to assist landmine victims. The Meeting also heard of efforts in the area of universalization, including the action taken by the Human Security Network, the Declaration of which can be found in Annex IX.

23. Also in the context of reviewing the general status and operation of the Convention, States parties took note of the challenges that remain in achieving the Convention's core humanitarian aims, expressing their will to work tirelessly to ensure that mined areas are cleared and stockpiles destroyed within the time limits contained in the Convention, to further assist landmine victims for as long as assistance is required, and to vigorously promote formal acceptance of the Convention, particularly by those States that continue to produce and/or use anti-personnel mines.

24. Also in the context of reviewing the general status and operation of the Convention, and in the context of a subsequent discussion on assistance and cooperation, it was recalled that States parties in a position to do so committed themselves on a long-term basis to sustain the process of achieving the Convention's humanitarian aims, and that States parties should continue to give high priority to mine action within their development and humanitarian policies, particularly with a view to the Convention's 10-year time frame for mine clearance.

25. Also in the context of reviewing the general status and operation of the Convention, the delegations of Austria, Canada, Germany and Norway expressed interest in hosting the Review Conference of the Convention in 2004.

26. At the fourth plenary meeting, on 18 September 2002, the Meeting considered the submission of requests under article 5 of the Convention. The President notified the Meeting that he had not been informed that any State wished to make such a request at the Fourth Meeting. The Meeting took note of this.

27. At the same plenary, the Meeting considered the submission of requests under article 8 of the Convention. The President notified the Meeting that he had not been informed that any State wished to make such a request at the Fourth Meeting. The Meeting took note of this.

28. In addition, within the framework of the sixth and seventh plenary meetings, the Meeting held informal consultations on international cooperation and assistance in

accordance with article 6 on the following topics: resource mobilization, mine clearance and related technologies; victim assistance, socio-economic reintegration and mine awareness; and the destruction of stockpiled anti-personnel mines. These consultations involved a review of the work of the relevant Standing Committees, as recorded in their reports contained in Annex V, with a focus on the actions recommended by the Committees.

### E. Decisions and recommendations

29. At its fourth plenary meeting, on 18 September 2002, the Meeting considered matters arising from and in the context of reports to be submitted under article 7, including matters pertaining to the reporting process. States parties expressed their continued satisfaction with the technical ways and means of circulating reports as adopted at the First Meeting and as amended at the Second Meeting. On the basis of suggestions contained in the President's Paper on article 7 reporting as contained in Annex III, the Meeting encouraged States parties to maximize the potential of the reporting format as an important tool to measure progress and communicate needs and, in this context, expressed their appreciation for and agreed to act upon, as appropriate, the suggestions made in the President's Paper. This would include submitting reports electronically and, as relevant, using the suggested cover page.

30. Further to the recommendations made by the Standing Committee on the General Status and Operation of the Convention, the Meeting recognized the continuing importance of the Intersessional Work Programme and expressed that on the basis of the President's Paper on the Intersessional Work Programme as contained in Annex II, the Programme in the lead-up to the Convention's First Review Conference should focus with even greater clarity on those areas most directly related to the core humanitarian objectives of the Convention. In addition, States Parties expressed that the Intersessional Work Programme should proceed in a manner consistent with the principles that have well served the Programme to date, particularly the informal, inclusive and cooperative nature of the process.

31. Further to a proposal made by the President, States parties agreed to change the name of the Standing Committee on Mine Clearance, Mine Awareness and Mine Action Technologies to the Standing Committee on Mine Clearance, Mine Risk Education and Mine Action Technologies. Pursuant to extensive consultations, States parties also identified the following States parties as the Committee Co-Chairs and Co-Rapporteurs until the end of the Fifth Meeting of the States Parties:

- Mine Clearance, Mine Risk Education and Mine Action Technologies: Belgium and Kenya (Co-Chairs); Cambodia and Japan (Co-Rapporteurs);
- Victim Assistance and Socio-Economic Reintegration: Colombia and France (Co-Chairs); Australia and Croatia (Co-Rapporteurs);
- Stockpile Destruction: Romania and Switzerland (Co-Chairs); Guatemala and Italy (Co-Rapporteurs);
- General Status and Operation of the Convention: Austria and Peru (Co-Chairs); Mexico and the Netherlands (Co-Rapporteurs).

32. Further to a proposal made by the President, States parties agreed to set the dates of the 2003 meetings of the Standing Committees from 3 to 7 February and from 12 to 16 May.

33. States parties again recognized the value and importance of the Coordinating Committee in the effective functioning and implementation of the Convention and for operating in an open and transparent manner, requested that the Coordinating Committee, in a manner consistent with its mandate, continue to be practical-minded and apply the principle of flexibility with respect to the format of Standing Committee meetings, and their sequencing and respective time allocation, continue with its practice to make available summary reports of its meetings on the web site of the GICHD, and, requested the President, as Chair of the Coordinating Committee, to continue to report on the Coordinating Committee's functioning.

34. The Meeting noted the Director of the GICHD's report on the activities of the Implementation Support Unit (ISU), contained in Annex VII. States parties expressed their appreciation to the GICHD for the prompt manner in which it established the ISU and for its ongoing support for the Intersessional Work Programme, and to the ISU for quickly demonstrating its effectiveness and value to States Parties.

35. The Meeting again noted the work undertaken by interested States Parties through the establishment of a sponsorship programme, which had helped to ensure more widespread representation at meetings of the Convention and of the intersessional meetings. States Parties expressed their appreciation of the sponsorship programme and of the efficient management thereof by the GICHD.

36. On the basis of the President's Paper on Developing a Process to Prepare for the Convention's First Review Conference as contained in Annex IV, the Meeting agreed to mandate the President to facilitate consultations leading to consideration of a variety of matters at the Fifth Meeting on preparations for the Convention's First Review Conference.

37. States parties endorsed, and expressed satisfaction with, the work of the Standing Committees, welcoming the reports of the Standing Committees, as contained in Annex V. The Meeting was in general agreement with the recommendations made by the Standing Committees and urged States parties and all other relevant parties, where appropriate, to act with urgency on these recommendations.

38. At its final plenary meeting, on 20 September 2002, the Meeting agreed that the Fifth Meeting of the States Parties would be held, in accordance with the provisions of article 11 of the Convention, from 15 to 19 September 2003 in Bangkok, Thailand.

39. At the same plenary, the Meeting adopted the Declaration of the Fourth Meeting of the States Parties, which is contained in Part II of this report. In addition, the Meeting warmly welcomed the President's Action Programme, contained in Annex VI, as a practical means of facilitating implementation of the Convention in accordance with the recommendations made by the Standing Committees.

## F. Documentation

40. A list of documents of the Fourth Meeting is contained in Annex I to this report.

## G. Adoption of the Final Report and conclusion of the Fourth Meeting

41. At its eighth and final plenary meeting, on 20 September 2002, the Meeting adopted its draft Final Report, contained in document APLC/MSP.4/2002/CRP.5.

### Part II. Declaration of the Fourth Meeting of the States Parties

1. We, the States parties to the Convention on the Prohibition of the Use, Stockpiling, Production and Transfer of Anti-Personnel Mines and on Their Destruction, along with other States, international organizations and institutions and non-governmental organizations, gathered in Geneva, reaffirm our unwavering commitment to the total eradication of anti-personnel mines and to addressing the insidious and inhumane effects of these weapons. We commit ourselves to intensify our efforts in those areas most directly related to the core humanitarian objectives of the Convention.

2. We celebrate the growing support for the Convention, ratified by 116 States and acceded to by another 12. With an additional 17 countries having signed, but not yet ratified the Convention, the number of States parties and signatories now totals 145, including more than 40 mine-affected States. We call upon those that have not done so, to ratify or accede to the Convention. We also call upon all States in the process of formally accepting the obligations of the Convention, to provisionally apply the terms of the Convention.

3. We recognize that the new international norm established by the Convention is being demonstrated by the successful record of implementation of the Convention, including the conduct of many States not party to the Convention respecting the provisions therein. A total of 88 States parties no longer possess stockpiled anti-personnel mines, including 34 which have completed stockpile destruction since the entry into force of the Convention. A further 22 State parties are in the process of destroying their stockpiles. Furthermore, over US$1 billion has been allocated since the Convention was negotiated to address the global landmine problem, in addition to the resources being allocated by mine-affected countries themselves.

4. We feel encouraged by the fact that over the past year, a considerable amount of land was cleared of anti-personnel mines, that casualty rates in several of the world's most mine-affected States have again decreased, that landmine victim assistance has improved, and that our cooperative efforts continue to contribute to this progress.

5. While recognizing the success of the Convention, we remain deeply concerned that anti-personnel mines continue to kill, maim and threaten the lives of countless innocent people each day, that the terror of mines prevents individuals from reclaiming their lives and that the lasting impact of these weapons denies communities the opportunity to rebuild long after conflicts have ended.

6. We deplore any use of anti-personnel mines. Such acts are contrary to the object and purpose of the Convention and exacerbate the humanitarian problems already caused by the use of these weapons. We urge all those who continue to use, produce, otherwise acquire, stockpile, retain and/or transfer anti-personnel landmines, to cease immediately and to join us in the task of eradicating these weapons. We particularly call upon the States outside the Convention, which have recently used anti-personnel mines and/or continue to produce to stop these activities.

7. We expect those States, which have declared their commitment to the object and purpose of the Convention and which continue to use anti-personnel mines, to recognize that this is a clear violation of their solemn commitment. We call upon all States concerned to respect their commitments.

8. Recognizing the need to secure full compliance with all obligations of the Convention, we reaffirm our commitment to effectively implement the Convention and to comply fully with its provisions. We do so in the spirit of cooperation and collaboration that has characterized this process. In the event of serious concerns of non-compliance with any of the obligations of the Convention, we acknowledge our responsibility to seek clarification of these concerns, in this cooperative spirit.

9. We recall that the four-year maximum time period for the destruction of stockpiled anti-personnel mines is less than one year away for those States which became parties in 1999. We also recall that as soon as possible, but not later than 10 years after the entry into force of this Convention, each State party must undertake to destroy or ensure the destruction of all anti-personnel mines in mined areas under its jurisdiction or control. We encourage continuing national, regional and international initiatives aimed at fulfilling these obligations. At the same time, we congratulate those States parties that have already destroyed their stockpiles of anti-personnel mines and those that have made substantial progress in clearing mined areas.

10. We call upon all Governments and people everywhere to join in the common task to meet the enormous challenges of mine action, including victim assistance, to provide the technical and financial assistance required, and, where appropriate, to integrate these efforts into national development strategies. As States parties committed to the eradication of anti-personnel mines, we reiterate that assistance and cooperation for mine action will flow primarily to those that have forsworn the use of these weapons forever through adherence to, implementation of, and compliance with the Convention.

11. We recognize that to achieve the promise of this unique and important humanitarian instrument, we must continue working tirelessly in all parts of the world to end the use of anti-personnel mines, to destroy stockpiles, to cease development, production and transfers of these weapons, to clear mined areas to free land from its deadly bondage, to assist victims to reclaim their lives with dignity and to prevent new victims.

12. We reaffirm that progress to free the world from anti-personnel mines would be promoted by the commitment by non-State actors to cease and renounce their use in line with the international norm established by this Convention. We urge all non-State actors

to cease and renounce the use, stockpiling, production and transfer of anti-personnel mines according to the principles and norms of International Humanitarian Law.

13. We warmly welcome the substantial progress made during the intersessional work programme. This programme continues to focus and advance the international community's mine action efforts, it greatly assists in our collective aim to implement the Convention and it provides a forum for mine-affected and other States to share experiences, acquire knowledge and enhance efforts to implement the Convention. We express our satisfaction that the intersessional work programme has been carried out in the Convention's tradition of partnership, dialogue, openness and practical cooperation. We welcome the increasing participation of mine-affected States in the intersessional work programme and the valuable contribution of the Sponsorship Programme.

14. To further enhance the intersessional process, we commit ourselves to intensify our efforts in those areas most directly related to the core humanitarian objectives of the Convention. We recommit ourselves to proceed with our work in a manner consistent with the principles that have well served the intersessional programme to date, particularly informality and cooperation. We furthermore call upon all States parties and other interested actors to continue to participate actively in the work of the Standing Committees.

15. We acknowledge the positive work of the Coordinating Committee tasked with the coordination of the intersessional work programme, and its role in the strengthening of the intersessional process. We thank the Geneva International Centre for Humanitarian Demining (GICHD) for its essential support and its commitment to the intersessional process. And we express our appreciation to the GICHD for the prompt manner in which it established the Implementation Support Unit (ISU) in accordance with the decision taken by the States parties at the Third Meeting of the States Parties and to the ISU for quickly demonstrating its effectiveness and value to States parties.

16. We acknowledge the contributory role of the United Nations agencies involved in Mine Action.

17. We express our gratitude to the International Campaign to Ban Landmines (ICBL) and other relevant non-governmental organizations, the International Committee of the Red Cross (ICRC) and to regional and national organizations and agencies for their important and substantive contribution to the intersessional process and to the overall implementation and consolidation of the Convention.

18. In reflecting upon our progress and accomplishments, and in considering the work that lies ahead, we reconfirm our conviction to make anti-personnel mines objects of the past, our obligation to assist those who have fallen victim to this terror, and our shared responsibility to the memories of those whose lives have been lost as a result of the use of these weapons, including those killed as a result of their dedication to helping others by clearing mined areas or providing humanitarian assistance.

[Annexes omitted]

# APPENDIX 7

# Model for an Article 7 Report

## CONVENTION ON THE PROHIBITION OF THE USE, STOCKPILING, PRODUCTION AND TRANSFER OF ANTI-PERSONNEL MINES AND ON THEIR DESTRUCTION

**Reporting Formats for Article 7**[1]

State Party     _____

Date of Submission   _____

Point of Contact     _____

                      (Organization, telephones, fax, email)

                      (Only for the purposes of clarification)

## Form A. National implementation measures

Article 7.1 'Each State Party shall report to the Secretary-General . . . on:

(a) The national implementation measures referred to in Article 9.'

*Remark:* In accordance with Article 9, 'Each State Party shall take all appropriate legal, administrative and other measures, including the imposition of penal sanctions, to prevent and suppress any activity prohibited to a State Party under this Convention undertaken by persons or on territory under its jurisdiction or control.'

State [Party] _____ reporting for time period from _____ to _____

| Measures | Supplementary information (e.g. effective date of implementation and text of legislation attached) |
|---|---|
|  |  |

## Form B. Stockpiled anti-personnel mines

Article 7. 1 'Each State Party shall report to the Secretary-General . . . on:

(b) The total of all stockpiled anti-personnel mines owned or possessed by it, or under its

---

[1] These reporting formats informally provided by Austria on disk are based on document APLC/MSP.1/1999/L.4 of 31 March 1999, as amended and decided upon by the First Meeting of the States Parties to the Convention on the Prohibition of the Use, Stockpiling, Production and Transfer of Anti-Personnel Mines and on their Destruction, held in Maputo from 3 to 7 May 1999. Tables of formats may be expanded as desired.

jurisdiction or control, to include a breakdown of the type, quantity and, if possible, lot numbers of each type of anti-personnel mine stockpiled.'

State [Party] _____ reporting for time period from _____ to_____

| Type | Quantity | Lot no. (if possible) | Supplementary information |
|------|----------|----------------------|---------------------------|
|      |          |                      |                           |
|      |          |                      |                           |
| TOTAL |        |                      |                           |

### Form C.  Location of mined areas

Article 7.1 'Each State Party shall report to the Secretary-General . . . on:

(c) To the extent possible, the location of all mined areas that contain, or are suspected to contain, anti-personnel mines under its jurisdiction or control, to include as much detail as possible regarding the type and quantity of each type of anti-personnel mine in each mined area and when they were emplaced.'

State [Party] _____ reporting for time period from _____ to _____

1. Areas that contain mines*

| Location | Type | Quantity | Date of emplacement | Supplementary information |
|----------|------|----------|---------------------|---------------------------|
|          |      |          |                     |                           |
|          |      |          |                     |                           |

2. Areas suspected to contain mines*

| Location | Type | Quantity | Date of emplacement | Supplementary information |
|----------|------|----------|---------------------|---------------------------|
|          |      |          |                     |                           |
|          |      |          |                     |                           |

* If necessary, a separate table for each mined area may be provided.

### Form D.  APMs retained or transferred

Article 7.1 'Each State Party shall report to the Secretary-General . . . on:

(d) The types, quantities and, if possible, lot numbers of all anti-personnel mines retained or transferred for the development of and training in mine detection, mine clearance or mine destruction techniques, or transferred for the purpose of destruction, as well as the institutions authorized by a State Party to retain or transfer anti-personnel mines, in accordance with Article 3.'

State [Party] _____ reporting for time period from _____ to _____

1. Retained for development of and training in (Article 3, para. 1)

| Institution authorized by State Party | Type | Quantity | Lot no. (if possible) | Supplementary information |
|---|---|---|---|---|
| | | | | |
| | | | | |
| TOTAL | | | | |

2. Transferred for development of and training in (Article 3, para. 1)

| Institution authorized by State Party | Type | Quantity | Lot no. (if possible) | Supplementary information: e.g. transferred from, transferred to |
|---|---|---|---|---|
| | | | | |
| | | | | |
| TOTAL | | | | |

3. Transferred for the purpose of destruction (Article 3, para. 2)

| Institution authorized by State Party | Type | Quantity | Lot no. (if possible) | Supplementary information: e.g. transferred from, transferred to |
|---|---|---|---|---|
| | | | | |
| | | | | |
| TOTAL | | | | |

## Form E. Status of programs for conversion or de-commissioning of APM production facilities

Article 7.1 'Each State Party shall report to the Secretary-General . . . on:

(e) The status of programs for the conversion or de-commissioning of anti-personnel mine production facilities.'

State [Party] _____ reporting for time period from _____ to _____

| Indicate if to 'convert' or 'de-commission' | Status (indicate if 'in process' or 'completed') | Supplementary information |
|---|---|---|
|  |  |  |
|  |  |  |

### Form F. Status of programs for destruction of APMs

Article 7.1 'Each State Party shall report to the Secretary-General . . . on:

(f) The status of programs for the destruction of anti-personnel mines in accordance with Articles 4 and 5, including details of the methods which will be used in destruction, the location of all destruction sites and the applicable safety and environmental standards to be observed.'

State [Party] _____ reporting for time period from _____ to _____

1. Status of programs for destruction of stockpiled APMs (Article 4)

| Description of the status of programs including: |  |
|---|---|
| Location of destruction sites | Details of: |
|  | Methods |
|  | Applicable safety standards |
|  | Applicable environmental standards |

2. Status of programs for destruction of APMs in mined areas (Article 5)

| Description of the status of programs including: |  |
|---|---|
| Location of destruction sites | Details of: |
|  | Methods |
|  | Applicable safety standards |
|  | Applicable environmental standards |

### Form G. APMs destroyed after entry into force

Article 7.1 'Each State Party shall report to the Secretary-General . . . on:

(g) The types and quantities of all anti-personnel mines destroyed after the entry into force of this Convention for that State Party, to include a breakdown of the quantity of each type of anti-personnel mine destroyed, in accordance with Articles 4 and 5, respectively, along with, if possible, the lot numbers of each type of anti-personnel mine in the case of destruction in accordance with Article 4.'

State [Party] _____ reporting for time period from _____ to _____

## 1. Destruction of stockpiled APMs (Article 4)

| Type | Quantity | Lot no. (if possible) | Supplementary information |
|---|---|---|---|
|  |  |  |  |
|  |  |  |  |
| TOTAL |  |  |  |

## 2. Destruction of APMs in mined areas (Article 5)

| Type | Quantity | Supplementary information |
|---|---|---|
|  |  |  |
|  |  |  |
| TOTAL |  |  |

## Form H. Technical characteristics of each type produced/owned or possessed

Article 7.1 'Each State Party shall report to the Secretary-General . . . on:

(h) The technical characteristics of each type of anti-personnel mine produced, to the extent known, and those currently owned or possessed by a State Party, giving, where reasonably possible, such categories of information as may facilitate identification and clearance of anti-personnel mines; at a minimum, this information shall include the dimensions, fusing, explosive content, metallic content, colour photographs and other information which may facilitate mine clearance.'

State [Party] _____ reporting for time period from _____ to _____

## 1. Technical characteristics of each APM-type produced

| Type | Dimensions | Fusing | Explosive content | | Metallic content | Colour photo attached | Supplementary information to facilitate mine clearance |
|---|---|---|---|---|---|---|---|
|  |  |  | type | grams |  |  |  |
|  |  |  |  |  |  |  |  |
|  |  |  |  |  |  |  |  |

2. Technical characteristics of each APM-type currently owned or possessed

| Type | Dimensions | Fusing | Explosive content | | Metallic content | Colour photo attached | Supplementary information to facilitate mine clearance |
|---|---|---|---|---|---|---|---|
| | | | type | grams | | | |
| | | | | | | | |
| | | | | | | | |

### Form I. Measures to provide warning to the population

Article 7.1 'Each State Party shall report to the Secretary-General . . . on:

(i) The measures taken to provide an immediate and effective warning to the population in relation to all areas identified under paragraph 2 of Article 5.'

*Remark*: In accordance with Article 5, para. 2: 'Each State Party shall make every effort to identify all areas under its jurisdiction or control in which anti-personnel mines are known or suspected to be emplaced and shall ensure as soon as possible that all anti-personnel mines in mined areas under its jurisdiction or control are perimeter-marked, monitored and protected by fencing or other means, to ensure the effective exclusion of civilians, until all anti-personnel mines contained therein have been destroyed. The marking shall at least be to the standards set out in the Protocol on Prohibitions or Restrictions on the Use of Mines, Booby-Traps and Other Devices, as amended on 3 May 1996, annexed to the Convention on Prohibitions or Restrictions on the Use of Certain Conventional Weapons Which May Be Deemed to Be Excessively Injurious or to Have Indiscriminate Effects'.

State [Party] _____ reporting for time period from _____ to _____

[Narrative:]

### Form J. Other relevant matters

*Remark*: States Parties may use this form to report voluntarily on other relevant matters, including matters pertaining to compliance and implementation not covered by the formal reporting requirements contained in Article 7. States Parties are encouraged to use this form to report on activities undertaken with respect to Article 6, and in particular to report on assistance provided for the care and rehabilitation, and social and economic reintegration, of mine victims.

State [Party] _____ reporting for time period from _____ to _____

[Narrative/reference to other reports]

# APPENDIX 8
# List of States Parties and Signatories to the Convention[1]

| States Parties | Date of entry into force |
|---|---|
| Afghanistan | 1 March 2003 |
| Albania | 1 August 2000 |
| Algeria | 1 April 2002 |
| Andorra | 1 March 1999 |
| Angola | 1 January 2003 |
| Antigua and Barbuda | 1 November 1999 |
| Argentina | 1 March 2000 |
| Australia | 1 July 1999 |
| Austria | 1 March 1999 |
| Bahamas | 1 March 1999 |
| Bangladesh | 1 March 2001 |
| Barbados | 1 July 1999 |
| Belarus | 1 March 2004 |
| Belgium | 1 March 1999 |
| Belize | 1 March 1999 |
| Benin | 1 March 1999 |
| Bolivia | 1 March 1999 |
| Bosnia and Herzegovina | 1 March 1999 |
| Botswana | 1 September 2000 |
| Brazil | 1 October 1999 |
| Bulgaria | 1 March 1999 |
| Burkina Faso | 1 March 1999 |
| Burundi | 1 April 2004 |
| Cambodia | 1 January 2000 |
| Cameroon | 1 March 2003 |
| Canada | 1 March 1999 |
| Cape Verde | 1 November 2001 |
| Central African Republic | 1 May 2003 |
| Chad | 1 November 1999 |
| Chile | 1 March 2002 |
| Colombia | 1 March 2001 |

[1] The list of States Parties is correct as at 1 April 2004 and the list of Signatories is correct as at 1 February 2004.

| | |
|---|---|
| Comoros | 1 March 2003 |
| Republic of the Congo | 1 November 2001 |
| Costa Rica | 1 September 1999 |
| Côte d'Ivoire | 1 December 2000 |
| Croatia | 1 March 1999 |
| Cyprus | 1 July 2003 |
| Czech Republic | 1 April 2000 |
| Democratic Republic of the Congo | 1 November 2002 |
| Denmark | 1 March 1999 |
| Djibouti | 1 March 1999 |
| Dominica | 1 September 1999 |
| Dominican Republic | 1 December 2000 |
| Ecuador | 1 October 1999 |
| El Salvador | 1 July 1999 |
| Equatorial Guinea | 1 March 1999 |
| Eritrea | 1 February 2002 |
| Fiji | 1 March 1999 |
| Former Yugoslav Republic of Macedonia | 1 March 1999 |
| France | 1 March 1999 |
| Gabon | 1 March 2001 |
| The Gambia | 1 March 2003 |
| Germany | 1 March 1999 |
| Ghana | 1 December 2000 |
| Greece | 1 March 2004 |
| Grenada | 1 March 1999 |
| Guatemala | 1 September 1999 |
| Guinea | 1 April 1999 |
| Guinea-Bissau | 1 November 2001 |
| Guyana | 1 February 2004 |
| Holy See | 1 March 1999 |
| Honduras | 1 March 1999 |
| Hungary | 1 March 1999 |
| Iceland | 1 November 1999 |
| Ireland | 1 March 1999 |
| Italy | 1 October 1999 |
| Jamaica | 1 March 1999 |
| Japan | 1 March 1999 |
| Jordan | 1 May 1999 |
| Kenya | 1 July 2001 |
| Kiribati | 1 March 2001 |
| Lesotho | 1 June 1999 |
| Liberia | 1 June 2000 |

| | |
|---|---|
| Liechtenstein | 1 April 2000 |
| Lithuania | 1 November 2003 |
| Luxembourg | 1 December 1999 |
| Madagascar | 1 March 2000 |
| Maldives | 1 March 2001 |
| Malaysia | 1 October 1999 |
| Malawi | 1 March 1999 |
| Mali | 1 March 1999 |
| Malta | 1 November 2001 |
| Mauritania | 1 January 2001 |
| Mauritius | 1 March 1999 |
| Mexico | 1 March 1999 |
| Republic of Moldova | 1 March 2001 |
| Monaco | 1 May 1999 |
| Mozambique | 1 March 1999 |
| Nauru | 1 February 2001 |
| Namibia | 1 March 1999 |
| Netherlands | 1 October 1999 |
| New Zealand | 1 July 1999 |
| Nicaragua | 1 May 1999 |
| Niger | 1 September 1999 |
| Nigeria | 1 March 2002 |
| Niue | 1 March 1999 |
| Norway | 1 March 1999 |
| Panama | 1 April 1999 |
| Paraguay | 1 May 1999 |
| Peru | 1 March 1999 |
| Philippines | 1 August 2000 |
| Portugal | 1 August 1999 |
| Qatar | 1 April 1999 |
| Romania | 1 May 2001 |
| Rwanda | 1 December 2000 |
| Saint Kitts and Nevis | 1 June 1999 |
| Saint Lucia | 1 October 1999 |
| Saint Vincent and the Grenadines | 1 February 2002 |
| Samoa | 1 March 1999 |
| San Marino | 1 March 1999 |
| São Tomé e Principe | 1 September 2003 |
| Senegal | 1 March 1999 |
| Serbia and Montenegro | 1 March 2004 |
| Seychelles | 1 December 2000 |
| Sierra Leone | 1 October 2001 |

| | |
|---|---|
| Slovakia | 1 August 1999 |
| Slovenia | 1 April 1999 |
| Solomon Islands | 1 July 1999 |
| South Africa | 1 March 1999 |
| Spain | 1 July 1999 |
| Sudan | 1 April 2004 |
| Surinam | 1 November 2002 |
| Swaziland | 1 June 1999 |
| Sweden | 1 May 1999 |
| Switzerland | 1 March 1999 |
| Tajikistan | 1 April 2000 |
| Tanzania | 1 May 2001 |
| Thailand | 1 May 1999 |
| Timor Leste | 1 November 2003 |
| Togo | 1 September 2000 |
| Trinidad and Tobago | 1 March 1999 |
| Tunisia | 1 January 2000 |
| Turkey | 1 March 2004 |
| Turkmenistan | 1 March 1999 |
| Uganda | 1 August 1999 |
| United Kingdom | 1 March 1999 |
| Uruguay | 1 December 2001 |
| Venezuela | 1 October 1999 |
| Yemen | 1 March 1999 |
| Zambia | 1 August 2001 |
| Zimbabwe | 1 March 1999 |

## SIGNATORIES TO THE CONVENTION

| State | Date of Signature |
|---|---|
| Brunei Darussalam | 4 December 1997 |
| Cook Islands | 3 December 1997 |
| Ethiopia | 3 December 1997 |
| Haiti | 3 December 1997 |
| Indonesia | 4 December 1997 |
| Marshall Islands | 4 December 1997 |
| Poland | 4 December 1997 |
| Ukraine | 4 December 1997 |
| Vanuatu | 4 December 1997 |

# APPENDIX 9

# Declarations to the Convention

(Unless otherwise indicated, the declarations were made upon ratification, acceptance, approval or accession.)[1]

## ARGENTINA

*Interpretative declaration*:

The Argentine Republic declares that in its territory, in the Malvinas, there are anti-personnel mines. This situation was brought to the attention of the Secretary-General of the United Nations when providing information within the framework of General Assembly resolutions 48/7; 49/215; 50/82; and 51/149 concerning 'Assistance in mine clearance'.

Since this part of the Argentine territory is under illegal occupation by the United Kingdom of Great Britain and Northern Ireland, the Argentine Republic is effectively prevented from having access to the anti-personnel mines placed in the Malvinas in order to fulfil the obligations undertaken in the present Convention.

The United Nations General Assembly has recognized the existence of a dispute concerning sovereignty over the Malvinas, South Georgia and South Sandwich and has urged the Argentine Republic and the United Kingdom of Great Britain and Northern Ireland to maintain negotiations in order to find as soon as possible a peaceful and lasting solution to the dispute, with the good offices of the Secretary-General of the United Nations, who is to report to the General Assembly on the progress made (resolutions 2065 (XX), 3160 (XXVIII), 31/49, 37/9, 38/12, 39/6, 40/21, 41/40, 42/19 and 43/25). The Special Committee on decolonization has taken the same position, and has adopted a resolution every year stating that the way to put an end to this colonial situation is the lasting settlement, on a peaceful and negotiated basis, of the sovereignty dispute, and requesting both Governments to resume negotiations to that end. The most recent of these resolutions was adopted on 1 July 1999.

The Argentine Republic reaffirms its rights of sovereignty over the Malvinas, South Georgia and South Sandwich and the surrounding maritime areas which form an integral part of its national territory.

## AUSTRALIA

*Declarations*:

'It is the understanding of Australia that, in the context of operations, exercises or other military activity authorised by the United Nations or otherwise conducted in accordance with international law, the participation by the Australian Defence Force, or individual Australian citizens or residents, in such operations, exercises or other military activity conducted in combination with the armed forces of States not party to the Convention which engage in activity prohibited under the Convention would not, by itself, be considered to be in violation of the Convention.

It is the understanding of Australia that, in relation to Article 1(a), the term "use" means the actual physical emplacement of anti-personnel mines and does not include receiving an indirect or incidental benefit from anti-personnel mines laid by another State or person. In Article 1(c) Australia will interpret the word "assist" to mean the actual and direct physical participation in any activity prohibited by the Convention but does not include permissible indirect support such as the provision of security for the personnel of a State not party to the Convention engaging in such activities, "encourage" to mean the actual request for the commission of any activity prohibited by the Convention, and "induce" to mean the active engagement in the offering of threats or incentives to obtain the commission of any activity prohibited by the Convention.

It is the understanding of Australia that in relation to Article 2(1), the definition of "anti-personnel mines" does not include command detonated munitions.

In relation to Articles 4, 5(1) and (2), and 7(1)(b) and (c), it is the understanding of Australia that the phrase "jurisdiction or control" is intended to mean within the sovereign territory of a State Party or over which it exercises legal responsibility by virtue of a United Nations mandate or arrangement with another State and the ownership or physical possession of anti-personnel mines, but does not include the temporary occupation of, or presence on, foreign territory where anti-personnel mines have been laid by other States or persons.'

## CANADA

*Understanding*:

'It is the understanding of the Government of Canada that, in the context of operations, exercises or other military activity sanctioned by the United Nations or otherwise conducted in accordance with international law, the mere participation by the Canadian Forces, or individual Canadians, in operations, exercises or other military activity conducted in combination with the armed forces of States not party to the Convention which engage in activity prohibited under the Convention would not, by itself, be considered to be assistance, encouragement or inducement in accordance with the meaning of those terms in article 1, paragraph 1 (c).'

## CHILE

*Declaration*:

The Republic of Chile declares that it will apply provisionally paragraph 1 of article 1 of the Convention.

## Czech Republic

*Declaration*:

'It is the understanding of the Government of the Czech Republic that the mere participation in the planning or execution of operations, exercises or other military activities by the Armed Forces of the Czech Republic, or individual Czech Republic nationals, conducted in combination with the armed forces of States not party to the [Convention], which engage in activities prohibited under the Convention, is not, by itself, assistance, encouragement or inducement for the purposes of Article 1, paragraph 1 (c) of the Convention.'

## Greece

*Upon signature*:

*Declaration*:

'Greece fully subscribes to the principles enshrined within the [Convention] and declares that ratification of this Convention will take place as soon as conditions relating to the implementation of its relevant provisions are fulfilled.'

## Lithuania

*Upon signature*:

*Declaration*:

'The Republic of Lithuania subscribes to the principles and purposes of the [Convention] and declares that ratification of the Convention will take place as soon as [the] relevant conditions relating to the implementation of the provisions of the Convention are fulfilled.'

## United Kingdom of Great Britain and Northern Ireland[2]

*Declaration*:

'It is the understanding of the Government of the United Kingdom that the mere participation in the planning or execution of operations, exercises or other military activity by the United Kingdom's Armed Forces, or individual United Kingdom nationals, conducted in combination with the armed forces of States not party to the [said Convention], which engage in activity prohibited under that Convention, is not, by itself, assistance, encouragement or inducement for the purposes of Article 1, paragraph (c) of the Convention.'

*Notes*

¹ The Netherlands ratified the Convention on behalf of the Kingdom in Europe.

² On 4 December 2001: Extension to the following territories for whose international relations the United Kingdom is responsible: Anguilla, Bermuda, British Antarctic Territory, British Indian Ocean Territory, British Virgin Islands, Cayman Islands, Falkland Islands, Montserrat, Pitcairn, Henderson, Ducie and Oeno Islands, St. Helena and Dependencies, South Georgia and the South Sandwich Islands, Sovereign Base Areas of Akrotiri and Dhekelia and Turks and Caicos Islands.

On 3 April 2002: Extension to the Bailiwick of Guernsey, Bailiwick of Jersey and the Isle of Man.

# Declaration of Provisional Application of Article 1 (1) in Accordance with Article 18 of the Convention

Austria
Mauritius
South Africa
Sweden
Switzerland

# APPENDIX 10

# Anti-Personnel Mine Ban Convention

## CONVENTION ON THE PROHIBITION OF THE USE, STOCKPILING, PRODUCTION AND TRANSFER OF ANTI-PERSONNEL MINES AND ON THEIR DESTRUCTION

### Preamble

The States Parties,

*Determined* to put an end to the suffering and casualties caused by anti-personnel mines, that kill or maim hundreds of people every week, mostly innocent and defenceless civilians and especially children, obstruct economic development and reconstruction, inhibit the repatriation of refugees and internally displaced persons, and have other severe consequences for years after emplacement,

*Believing* it necessary to do their utmost to contribute in an efficient and coordinated manner to face the challenge of removing anti-personnel mines placed throughout the world, and to assure their destruction,

*Wishing* to do their utmost in providing assistance for the care and rehabilitation, including the social and economic reintegration of mine victims,

*Recognizing* that a total ban of anti-personnel mines would also be an important confidence-building measure,

*Welcoming* the adoption of the Protocol on Prohibitions or Restrictions on the Use of Mines, Booby-Traps and Other Devices, as amended on 3 May 1996, annexed to the Convention on Prohibitions or Restrictions on the Use of Certain Conventional Weapons Which May Be Deemed to Be Excessively Injurious or to Have Indiscriminate Effects, and calling for the early ratification of this Protocol by all States which have not yet done so,

*Welcoming* also United Nations General Assembly Resolution 51/45 S of 10 December 1996 urging all States to pursue vigorously an effective, legally-binding international agreement to ban the use, stockpiling, production and transfer of anti-personnel landmines,

*Welcoming* furthermore the measures taken over the past years both unilaterally and multilaterally, aiming at prohibiting, restricting or suspending the use, stockpiling, production and transfer of anti-personnel mines,

*Stressing* the role of public conscience in furthering the principles of humanity as evidenced by the call for a total ban of anti-personnel mines and recognizing the efforts to that end undertaken by the International Red Cross and Red Crescent Movement, the International Campaign to Ban Landmines and numerous other non-governmental organizations around the world,

*Recalling* the Ottawa Declaration of 5 October 1996 and the Brussels Declaration of 27 June 1997 urging the international community to negotiate an international and legally binding agreement prohibiting the use, stockpiling, production and transfer of anti-personnel mines,

*Emphasizing* the desirability of attracting the adherence of all States to this Convention, and determined to work strenuously towards the promotion of its universalization in all relevant fora including, inter alia, the United Nations, the Conference on Disarmament, regional organizations, and groupings, and review conferences of the Convention on Prohibitions or Restrictions on the Use of Certain Conventional Weapons Which May Be Deemed to Be Excessively Injurious or to Have Indiscriminate Effects,

*Basing* themselves on the principle of international humanitarian law that the right of the parties to an armed conflict to choose methods or means of warfare is not unlimited, on the principle that prohibits the employment in armed conflicts of weapons, projectiles and materials and methods of warfare of a nature to cause superfluous injury or unnecessary suffering and on the principle that a distinction must be made between civilians and combatants,

Have agreed as follows:

### Article 1. General obligations

1. Each State Party undertakes never under any circumstances:

(a) To use anti-personnel mines;
(b) To develop, produce, otherwise acquire, stockpile, retain or transfer to anyone, directly or indirectly, anti-personnel mines;
(c) To assist, encourage or induce, in any way, anyone to engage in any activity prohibited to a State Party under this Convention.

2. Each State Party undertakes to destroy or ensure the destruction of all anti-personnel mines in accordance with the provisions of this Convention.

### Article 2. Definitions

1. 'Anti-Personnel mine' means a mine designed to be exploded by the presence, proximity or contact of a person and that will incapacitate, injure or kill one or more persons. Mines designed to be detonated by the presence, proximity or contact of a vehicle as opposed to a person, that are equipped with anti-handling devices, are not considered anti-personnel mines as a result of being so equipped.

2. 'Mine' means a munition designed to be placed under, on or near the ground or other surface area and to be exploded by the presence, proximity or contact of a person or a vehicle.

3. 'Anti-handling device' means a device intended to protect a mine and which is part of, linked to, attached to or placed under the mine and which activates when an attempt is made to tamper with or otherwise intentionally disturb the mine.

4. 'Transfer' involves, in addition to the physical movement of anti-personnel mines into or from national territory, the transfer of title to and control over the mines, but does not involve the transfer of territory containing emplaced anti-personnel mines.

5. 'Mined area' means an area which is dangerous due to the presence or suspected presence of mines.

### Article 3. Exceptions

1. Notwithstanding the general obligations under Article 1, the retention or transfer of a number of anti-personnel mines for the development of and training in mine detection, mine clearance, or mine destruction techniques is permitted. The amount of such mines shall not exceed the minimum number absolutely necessary for the above-mentioned purposes.

2. The transfer of anti-personnel mines for the purpose of destruction is permitted.

### Article 4. Destruction of stockpiled anti-personnel mines

Except as provided for in Article 3, each State Party undertakes to destroy or ensure the destruction of all stockpiled anti-personnel mines it owns or possesses, or that are under its jurisdiction or control, as soon as possible but not later than four years after the entry into force of this Convention for that State Party.

### Article 5. Destruction of anti-personnel mines in mined areas

1. Each State Party undertakes to destroy or ensure the destruction of all anti-personnel mines in mined areas under its jurisdiction or control, as soon as possible but not later than ten years after the entry into force of this Convention for that State Party.

2. Each State Party shall make every effort to identify all areas under its jurisdiction or control in which anti-personnel mines are known or suspected to be emplaced and shall ensure as soon as possible that all anti-personnel mines in mined areas under its jurisdiction or control are perimeter-marked, monitored and protected by fencing or other means, to ensure the effective exclusion of civilians, until all anti-personnel mines contained therein have been destroyed. The marking shall at least be to the standards set out in the Protocol on Prohibitions or Restrictions on the Use of Mines, Booby-Traps and Other Devices, as amended on 3 May 1996, annexed to the Convention on Prohibitions or Restrictions on the Use of Certain Conventional Weapons Which May Be Deemed to Be Excessively Injurious or to Have Indiscriminate Effects.

3. If a State Party believes that it will be unable to destroy or ensure the destruction of all anti-personnel mines referred to in paragraph 1 within that time period, it may submit a request to a Meeting of the States Parties or a Review Conference for an extension of the deadline for completing the destruction of such anti-personnel mines, for a period of up to ten years.

4. Each request shall contain:

(a) The duration of the proposed extension;

(b) A detailed explanation of the reasons for the proposed extension, including:
   (i) The preparation and status of work conducted under national demining programs;
   (ii) The financial and technical means available to the State Party for the destruction of all the anti-personnel mines; and
   (iii) Circumstances which impede the ability of the State Party to destroy all the anti-personnel mines in mined areas;

(c) The humanitarian, social, economic, and environmental implications of the extension; and

(d) Any other information relevant to the request for the proposed extension.

5. The Meeting of the States Parties or the Review Conference shall, taking into consideration the factors contained in paragraph 4, assess the request and decide by a majority of votes of States Parties present and voting whether to grant the request for an extension period.

6. Such an extension may be renewed upon the submission of a new request in accordance with paragraphs 3, 4 and 5 of this Article. In requesting a further extension period a State Party shall submit relevant additional information on what has been undertaken in the previous extension period pursuant to this Article.

### Article 6. International cooperation and assistance

1. In fulfilling its obligations under this Convention each State Party has the right to seek and receive assistance, where feasible, from other States Parties to the extent possible.

2. Each State Party undertakes to facilitate and shall have the right to participate in the fullest possible exchange of equipment, material and scientific and technological information concerning the implementation of this Convention. The States Parties shall not impose undue restrictions on the provision of mine clearance equipment and related technological information for humanitarian purposes.

3. Each State Party in a position to do so shall provide assistance for the care and rehabilitation, and social and economic reintegration, of mine victims and for mine awareness programs. Such assistance may be provided, inter alia, through the United Nations system, international, regional or national organizations or institutions, the International Committee of the Red Cross, national Red Cross and Red Crescent societies and their International Federation, non-governmental organizations, or on a bilateral basis.

4. Each State Party in a position to do so shall provide assistance for mine clearance and related activities. Such assistance may be provided, inter alia, through the United Nations system, international or regional organizations or institutions, non-governmental organizations or institutions, or on a bilateral basis, or by contributing to the United Nations Voluntary Trust Fund for Assistance in Mine Clearance, or other regional funds that deal with demining.

5. Each State Party in a position to do so shall provide assistance for the destruction of stockpiled anti-personnel mines.

6. Each State Party undertakes to provide information to the database on mine clearance established within the United Nations system, especially information concerning various means and technologies of mine clearance, and lists of experts, expert agencies or national points of contact on mine clearance.

7. States Parties may request the United Nations, regional organizations, other States Parties or other competent intergovernmental or non-governmental fora to assist its authorities in the elaboration of a national demining program to determine, inter alia:

(a) The extent and scope of the anti-personnel mine problem;

(b) The financial, technological and human resources that are required for the implementation of the program;

(c) The estimated number of years necessary to destroy all anti-personnel mines in mined areas under the jurisdiction or control of the concerned State Party;

(d) Mine awareness activities to reduce the incidence of mine-related injuries or deaths;

(e) Assistance to mine victims;

(f) The relationship between the Government of the concerned State Party and the relevant governmental, inter-governmental or non-governmental entities that will work in the implementation of the program.

8. Each State Party giving and receiving assistance under the provisions of this Article shall cooperate with a view to ensuring the full and prompt implementation of agreed assistance programs.

### Article 7. Transparency measures

1. Each State Party shall report to the Secretary-General of the United Nations as soon as practicable, and in any event not later than 180 days after the entry into force of this Convention for that State Party on:

(a) The national implementation measures referred to in Article 9;

(b) The total of all stockpiled anti-personnel mines owned or possessed by it, or under its jurisdiction or control, to include a breakdown of the type, quantity and, if possible, lot numbers of each type of anti-personnel mine stockpiled;

(c) To the extent possible, the location of all mined areas that contain, or are suspected to contain, anti-personnel mines under its jurisdiction or control, to include as much detail as possible regarding the type and quantity of each type of anti-personnel mine in each mined area and when they were emplaced;

(d) The types, quantities and, if possible, lot numbers of all anti-personnel mines retained or transferred for the development of and training in mine detection, mine clearance or mine destruction techniques, or transferred for the purpose of destruction, as well as the institutions authorized by a State Party to retain or transfer anti-personnel mines, in accordance with Article 3;

(e) The status of programs for the conversion or de-commissioning of anti-personnel mine production facilities;

(f) The status of programs for the destruction of anti-personnel mines in accordance with Articles 4 and 5, including details of the methods which will be used in destruction, the location of all destruction sites and the applicable safety and environmental standards to be observed;

(g) The types and quantities of all anti-personnel mines destroyed after the entry into force of this Convention for that State Party, to include a breakdown of the quantity of each type of anti-personnel mine destroyed, in accordance with Articles 4 and 5, respectively, along with, if possible, the lot numbers of each type of anti-personnel mine in the case of destruction in accordance with Article 4;

(h) The technical characteristics of each type of anti-personnel mine produced, to the extent known, and those currently owned or possessed by a State Party, giving, where reasonably possible, such categories of information as may facilitate identification and clearance of anti-personnel mines; at a minimum, this information shall include the dimensions, fusing, explosive content, metallic content, colour photographs and other information which may facilitate mine clearance; and

(i) The measures taken to provide an immediate and effective warning to the population in relation to all areas identified under paragraph 2 of Article 5.

2. The information provided in accordance with this Article shall be updated by the States Parties annually, covering the last calendar year, and reported to the Secretary-General of the United Nations not later than 30 April of each year.

3. The Secretary-General of the United Nations shall transmit all such reports received to the States Parties.

### Article 8. Facilitation and clarification of compliance

1. The States Parties agree to consult and cooperate with each other regarding the implementation of the provisions of this Convention, and to work together in a spirit of cooperation to facilitate compliance by States Parties with their obligations under this Convention.

2. If one or more States Parties wish to clarify and seek to resolve questions relating to compliance with the provisions of this Convention by another State Party, it may submit, through the Secretary-General of the United Nations, a Request for Clarification of that matter to that State Party. Such a request shall be accompanied by all appropriate information. Each State Party shall refrain from unfounded Requests for Clarification, care being taken to avoid abuse. A State Party that receives a Request for Clarification shall provide, through the Secretary-General of the United Nations,

within 28 days to the requesting State Party all information which would assist in clarifying this matter.

3. If the requesting State Party does not receive a response through the Secretary-General of the United Nations within that time period, or deems the response to the Request for Clarification to be unsatisfactory, it may submit the matter through the Secretary-General of the United Nations to the next Meeting of the States Parties. The Secretary-General of the United Nations shall transmit the submission, accompanied by all appropriate information pertaining to the Request for Clarification, to all States Parties. All such information shall be presented to the requested State Party which shall have the right to respond.

4. Pending the convening of any meeting of the States Parties, any of the States Parties concerned may request the Secretary-General of the United Nations to exercise his or her good offices to facilitate the clarification requested.

5. The requesting State Party may propose through the Secretary-General of the United Nations the convening of a Special Meeting of the States Parties to consider the matter. The Secretary-General of the United Nations shall thereupon communicate this proposal and all information submitted by the States Parties concerned, to all States Parties with a request that they indicate whether they favour a Special Meeting of the States Parties, for the purpose of considering the matter. In the event that within 14 days from the date of such communication, at least one-third of the States Parties favours such a Special Meeting, the Secretary-General of the United Nations shall convene this Special Meeting of the States Parties within a further 14 days. A quorum for this Meeting shall consist of a majority of States Parties.

6. The Meeting of the States Parties or the Special Meeting of the States Parties, as the case may be, shall first determine whether to consider the matter further, taking into account all information submitted by the States Parties concerned. The Meeting of the States Parties or the Special Meeting of the States Parties shall make every effort to reach a decision by consensus. If despite all efforts to that end no agreement has been reached, it shall take this decision by a majority of States Parties present and voting.

7. All States Parties shall cooperate fully with the Meeting of the States Parties or the Special Meeting of the States Parties in the fulfilment of its review of the matter, including any fact-finding missions that are authorized in accordance with paragraph 8.

8. If further clarification is required, the Meeting of the States Parties or the Special Meeting of the States Parties shall authorize a fact-finding mission and decide on its mandate by a majority of States Parties present and voting. At any time the requested State Party may invite a fact-finding mission to its territory. Such a mission shall take place without a decision by a Meeting of the States Parties or a Special Meeting of the States Parties to authorize such a mission. The mission, consisting of up to 9 experts, designated and approved in accordance with paragraphs 9 and 10, may collect additional information on the spot or in other places directly related to the alleged compliance issue under the jurisdiction or control of the requested State Party.

9. The Secretary-General of the United Nations shall prepare and update a list of the names, nationalities and other relevant data of qualified experts provided by States Parties and communicate it to all States Parties. Any expert included on this list shall be regarded as designated for all fact-finding missions unless a State Party declares its non-acceptance in writing. In the event of non-acceptance, the expert shall not participate in fact-finding missions on the territory or any other place under the jurisdiction or control of the objecting State Party, if the non-acceptance was declared prior to the appointment of the expert to such missions.

10. Upon receiving a request from the Meeting of the States Parties or a Special Meeting of the States Parties, the Secretary-General of the United Nations shall, after consultations with the requested State Party, appoint the members of the mission, including its leader. Nationals of States Parties requesting the fact-finding mission or directly affected by it shall not be appointed to the mission. The members of the fact-finding mission shall enjoy privileges and immunities under Article VI of the Convention on the Privileges and Immunities of the United Nations, adopted on 13 February 1946.

11. Upon at least 72 hours notice, the members of the fact-finding mission shall arrive in the territory of the requested State Party at the earliest opportunity. The requested State Party shall take the necessary administrative measures to receive, transport and accommodate the mission, and shall be responsible for ensuring the security of the mission to the maximum extent possible while they are on territory under its control.

12. Without prejudice to the sovereignty of the requested State Party, the fact-finding mission may bring into the territory of the requested State Party the necessary equipment which shall be used exclusively for gathering information on the alleged compliance issue. Prior to its arrival, the mission will advise the requested State Party of the equipment that it intends to utilize in the course of its fact-finding mission.

13. The requested State Party shall make all efforts to ensure that the fact-finding mission is given the opportunity to speak with all relevant persons who may be able to provide information related to the alleged compliance issue.

14. The requested State Party shall grant access for the fact-finding mission to all areas and installations under its control where facts relevant to the compliance issue could be expected to be collected. This shall be subject to any arrangements that the requested State Party considers necessary for:

(a) The protection of sensitive equipment, information and areas;
(b) The protection of any constitutional obligations the requested State Party may have with regard to proprietary rights, searches and seizures, or other constitutional rights; or
(c) The physical protection and safety of the members of the fact-finding mission.

In the event that the requested State Party makes such arrangements, it shall make every reasonable effort to demonstrate through alternative means its compliance with this Convention.

15. The fact-finding mission may remain in the territory of the State Party concerned for no more than 14 days, and at any particular site no more than 7 days, unless otherwise agreed.

16. All information provided in confidence and not related to the subject matter of the fact-finding mission shall be treated on a confidential basis.

17. The fact-finding mission shall report, through the Secretary-General of the United Nations, to the Meeting of the States Parties or the Special Meeting of the States Parties the results of its findings.

18. The Meeting of the States Parties or the Special Meeting of the States Parties shall consider all relevant information, including the report submitted by the fact-finding mission, and may request the requested State Party to take measures to address the compliance issue within a specified period of time. The requested State Party shall report on all measures taken in response to this request.

19. The Meeting of the States Parties or the Special Meeting of the States Parties may suggest to the States Parties concerned ways and means to further clarify or resolve the matter under consideration, including the initiation of appropriate procedures in conformity with international law. In circumstances where the issue at hand is determined to be due to circumstances beyond the control of the requested State Party, the Meeting of the States Parties or the Special Meeting of the States Parties may recommend appropriate measures, including the use of cooperative measures referred to in Article 6.

20. The Meeting of the States Parties or the Special Meeting of the States Parties shall make every effort to reach its decisions referred to in paragraphs 18 and 19 by consensus, otherwise by a two-thirds majority of States Parties present and voting.

### Article 9. National implementation measures

Each State Party shall take all appropriate legal, administrative and other measures, including the imposition of penal sanctions, to prevent and suppress any activity prohibited to a State Party under this Convention undertaken by persons or on territory under its jurisdiction or control.

### Article 10. Settlement of disputes

1. The States Parties shall consult and cooperate with each other to settle any dispute that may arise with regard to the application or the interpretation of this Convention. Each State Party may bring any such dispute before the Meeting of the States Parties.

2. The Meeting of the States Parties may contribute to the settlement of the dispute by whatever means it deems appropriate, including offering its good offices, calling upon the States Parties to a dispute to start the settlement procedure of their choice and recommending a time-limit for any agreed procedure.

3. This Article is without prejudice to the provisions of this Convention on facilitation and clarification of compliance.

**Article 11. Meetings of the States Parties**

1. The States Parties shall meet regularly in order to consider any matter with regard to the application or implementation of this Convention, including:

(a) The operation and status of this Convention;
(b) Matters arising from the reports submitted under the provisions of this Convention;
(c) International cooperation and assistance in accordance with Article 6;
(d) The development of technologies to clear anti-personnel mines;
(e) Submissions of States Parties under Article 8; and
(f) Decisions relating to submissions of States Parties as provided for in Article 5.

2. The First Meeting of the States Parties shall be convened by the Secretary-General of the United Nations within one year after the entry into force of this Convention. The subsequent meetings shall be convened by the Secretary-General of the United Nations annually until the first Review Conference.

3. Under the conditions set out in Article 8, the Secretary-General of the United Nations shall convene a Special Meeting of the States Parties.

4. States not parties to this Convention, as well as the United Nations, other relevant international organizations or institutions, regional organizations, the International Committee of the Red Cross and relevant non-governmental organizations may be invited to attend these meetings as observers in accordance with the agreed Rules of Procedure.

**Article 12. Review Conferences**

1. A Review Conference shall be convened by the Secretary-General of the United Nations five years after the entry into force of this Convention. Further Review Conferences shall be convened by the Secretary-General of the United Nations if so requested by one or more States Parties, provided that the interval between Review Conferences shall in no case be less than five years. All States Parties to this Convention shall be invited to each Review Conference.

2. The purpose of the Review Conference shall be:

(a) To review the operation and status of this Convention;
(b) To consider the need for and the interval between further Meetings of the States Parties referred to in paragraph 2 of Article 11;
(c) To take decisions on submissions of States Parties as provided for in Article 5; and
(d) To adopt, if necessary, in its final report conclusions related to the implementation of this Convention.

3. States not parties to this Convention, as well as the United Nations, other relevant international organizations or institutions, regional organizations, the International Committee of the Red Cross and relevant non-governmental organizations may be invited to attend each Review Conference as observers in accordance with the agreed Rules of Procedure.

## Article 13.  Amendments

1.  At any time after the entry into force of this Convention any State Party may propose amendments to this Convention. Any proposal for an amendment shall be communicated to the Depositary, who shall circulate it to all States Parties and shall seek their views on whether an Amendment Conference should be convened to consider the proposal. If a majority of the States Parties notify the Depositary no later than 30 days after its circulation that they support further consideration of the proposal, the Depositary shall convene an Amendment Conference to which all States Parties shall be invited.

2.  States not parties to this Convention, as well as the United Nations, other relevant international organizations or institutions, regional organizations, the International Committee of the Red Cross and relevant non-governmental organizations may be invited to attend each Amendment Conference as observers in accordance with the agreed Rules of Procedure.

3.  The Amendment Conference shall be held immediately following a Meeting of the States Parties or a Review Conference unless a majority of the States Parties request that it be held earlier.

4.  Any amendment to this Convention shall be adopted by a majority of two-thirds of the States Parties present and voting at the Amendment Conference. The Depositary shall communicate any amendment so adopted to the States Parties.

5.  An amendment to this Convention shall enter into force for all States Parties to this Convention which have accepted it, upon the deposit with the Depositary of instruments of acceptance by a majority of States Parties. Thereafter it shall enter into force for any remaining State Party on the date of deposit of its instrument of acceptance.

## Article 14.  Costs

1.  The costs of the Meetings of the States Parties, the Special Meetings of the States Parties, the Review Conferences and the Amendment Conferences shall be borne by the States Parties and States not parties to this Convention participating therein, in accordance with the United Nations scale of assessment adjusted appropriately.

2.  The costs incurred by the Secretary-General of the United Nations under Articles 7 and 8 and the costs of any fact-finding mission shall be borne by the States Parties in accordance with the United Nations scale of assessment adjusted appropriately.

## Article 15.  Signature

This Convention, done at Oslo, Norway, on 18 September 1997, shall be open for signature at Ottawa, Canada, by all States from 3 December 1997 until 4 December 1997, and at the United Nations Headquarters in New York from 5 December 1997 until its entry into force.

## Article 16.  Ratification, acceptance, approval or accession

1.  This Convention is subject to ratification, acceptance or approval of the Signatories.

2.  It shall be open for accession by any State which has not signed the Convention.

3. The instruments of ratification, acceptance, approval or accession shall be deposited with the Depositary.

### Article 17. Entry into force

1. This Convention shall enter into force on the first day of the sixth month after the month in which the 40th instrument of ratification, acceptance, approval or accession has been deposited.

2. For any State which deposits its instrument of ratification, acceptance, approval or accession after the date of the deposit of the 40th instrument of ratification, acceptance, approval or accession, this Convention shall enter into force on the first day of the sixth month after the date on which that State has deposited its instrument of ratification, acceptance, approval or accession.

### Article 18. Provisional application

Any State may at the time of its ratification, acceptance, approval or accession, declare that it will apply provisionally paragraph 1 of Article 1 of this Convention pending its entry into force.

### Article 19. Reservations

The Articles of this Convention shall not be subject to reservations.

### Article 20. Duration and withdrawal

1. This Convention shall be of unlimited duration.

2. Each State Party shall, in exercising its national sovereignty, have the right to withdraw from this Convention. It shall give notice of such withdrawal to all other States Parties, to the Depositary and to the United Nations Security Council. Such instrument of withdrawal shall include a full explanation of the reasons motivating this withdrawal.

3. Such withdrawal shall only take effect six months after the receipt of the instrument of withdrawal by the Depositary. If, however, on the expiry of that six-month period, the withdrawing State Party is engaged in an armed conflict, the withdrawal shall not take effect before the end of the armed conflict.

4. The withdrawal of a State Party from this Convention shall not in any way affect the duty of States to continue fulfilling the obligations assumed under any relevant rules of international law.

### Article 21. Depositary

The Secretary-General of the United Nations is hereby designated as the Depositary of this Convention.

### Article 22. Authentic texts

The original of this Convention, of which the Arabic, Chinese, English, French, Russian and Spanish texts are equally authentic, shall be deposited with the Secretary-General of the United Nations.

# Index